The YORÙBÁ

Akinwumi Ogundiran

The YORÙBÁ

A New History

INDIANA UNIVERSITY PRESS

This book is a publication of

Indiana University Press
Office of Scholarly Publishing
Herman B Wells Library 350
1320 East 10th Street
Bloomington, Indiana 47405 USA

iupress.indiana.edu

 The paper used in this publication meets the minimum requirements of the American National Standard for Information Sciences—Permanence of Paper for Printed Library Materials, ANSI Z39.48-1992.

Manufactured in the United States of America

Cataloging information is available from the Library of Congress.

ISBN 978-0-253-05148-6 (hardback)
ISBN 978-0-253-05149-3 (paperback)
ISBN 978-0-253-05150-9 (web PDF)

1 2 3 4 5 26 25 24 23 22 21

For Lea
and our boys,
Olúrẹ̀mí
and
Oyèbánjí

CONTENTS

Illustrations

Figures

Plates

Tables

Preface

The deep-time history of the Yorùbá is the subject of this book. It is an account of (1) the experiences and events that shaped the long-term history of the ancestral Yorùbá people; (2) the generative actions that they used to translate their experiences into new practices or traditions; and (3) the principles and values that made life meaningful for them between ca. 300 BC and AD 1840. Based on new questions, evidence, and conceptual frameworks, this book offers the opportunity to rethink Yorùbá history in new ways. In the following pages, I emphasize the cultural-historical approach in order to understand the "ways of being" of the Yorùbá as historical subjects (ontology); their "theories of knowledge" (epistemology); and the regimes of value and aspirational principles (axiology) that they created at different historical junctures. With these, I account for the cultural forms, practices, events, and ideas, as well as mentalities, imaginations, and meanings that constituted the Yorùbá experience for about two thousand years.

The book comprises ten chapters divided into five parts. The first chapter lays out the theoretical, conceptual, and methodological frameworks that shape the themes and contents of the volume. I make the case why it is necessary to bring empirical-, comparative-, and theoretical-minded habits to the study of Yorùbá history. In chapter 2, I provide a sketch of the historical groundwork that laid the foundation for the emergence of the Yorùbá world ca. 300 BC–AD 500. I also use a suite of archaeological, historical, and linguistic data to shed light on the four core principles that shaped the Yorùbá cultural identity in the second half of the first millennium AD. The first is the *ilé* (House), the building block of their sociopolitical organization. The second, the dyadic *ọba/ìlú-aládé* (divine kingship/urban), served as the model of political culture and ideology of governance. The third is the complementarity of gendered duality as the epistemological framework for constructing and imagining social order. And the fourth centers on the search for meaningful living through the quest for immortality. In chapter 3, I examine how these four principles and the knowledge capital associated with primary glass production and a universal cosmology/theogony were deployed to create the consciousness of a regional Yorùbá community of practice between the eleventh and the late fourteenth century.

In the next two chapters, I examine how turmoil beset the Yorùbá world between the 1420s and 1570s as a result of internal and external sources of stress that upturned the lives of several communities (chap. 4), and the processes of recovery that followed between 1570 and 1650 (chap. 5). During the age of restoration that followed the crisis, new practices of political culture and power relations developed that necessitated the revision of the community's theogony and many aspects of its epistemology. The aftermath of these processes, especially their culmination in the rise of new hegemonic states and the entanglement of the Yorùbá in the Atlantic commercial revolution, 1630–1840, is the subject of chapters 6–9. In those four chapters, I examine the interlocking threads of the political, economic, social, ideological, and intellectual innovations that wove the Yorùbá world into the web of the early modern economy, and the impact on the development of a new regime of value. My emphasis in this section of the book is on the permeation of the Atlantic merchant capital into the different domains of everyday life, both in the intimate spaces of the household and at the macro level of the state.

I explore two themes in chapter 6: (1) the inauguration of slave/merchant-capital exchange and the hegemonic power politics that sustained it; and (2) the use of the imports deriving from the Atlantic slave trade as merchant capital and their investment in the commercialization of the region's economy. In chapter 7, I focus on the regime of value—especially practices of taste, self-realization, aspiration, and social difference—created by the merchant-capital revolution. The chapter emphasizes the socialization of Atlantic imports into everyday life and the implications for the emergence of an object-centered Yorùbá world. Chapter 8 examines how the experiences of monetization, specialized production, a market economy, slave/merchant-capital exchange, and hegemonic power politics created new practices of labor relations and new avenues for highly pyramidal unequal accumulation. As a result, gender and class inequalities widened; the relationships between the individual and corporate groups were redefined; and the vertical and horizontal boundaries of social differences hardened. All of these led to a cataclysmic breakdown of social order, the subject of chapter 9. I link this breakdown to the persistent demands for African labor in the Americas and the unsustainability of the merchant-capital revolution that underwrote hegemonic power and individual accumulation. The outcome was protracted intra-elite conflict, underclass revolt, and predation. In the final chapter, I examine the implications of comparative and deep-time approaches to Yorùbá history and summarize the major trends, events, eventfulness, practices, meanings, and experiences that anchored this two-thousand-year history.

All histories are patently particular and local, including those often presented as global or world history. In this regard, this book is no different. It is a regional history of the Yorùbá before 1840. Even so, I have paid close attention to the global and regional interactions that framed the actions of local actors who created their own theory of knowledge and defined it as their universal. In so doing, I draw attention to how the ancestral Yorùbá experiences were constitutive of global, transcontinental, and subcontinental histories, and vice versa.

Acknowledgments

I have benefited from the generosity of several individuals and institutions in the course of researching and writing this book. First and foremost, I am grateful for the support of my research collaborators, assistants, and informants, as well as the various communities who hosted me in Nigeria for so many years. The list is very long, and I cannot do justice to naming everyone and every place here. The reader will come across the names of some of my informants/teachers and host communities in the reference sections of the book. My special gratitude goes to Babátúndé Agbájé-Williams, a great mentor and friend, who laid the intellectual foundations that made this book thinkable for me. My appreciation also goes to Christopher Ehret for his friendship through the years. He is the mastermind behind the historical linguistics aspects of this book. Of colleagues and friends who traveled the roads with (and without) me, tracking down sources and information, the following deserve special mention: Raphael Àlàbí, Olú Àlérù, Nurudeen Amuda-Arógundádé, Akinlolú Ìgè, Olúṣẹ́gun Moyib, Àdìsá Ògúnfọlákàn, Babájídé Ọlọ́lájùlọ, Kọ́lá Òsénì, Délé Ọdúǹbákú, Bọ́láńlé Túbọ̀sún, Arí-bidésí Usman, and Constanze Weise. Ẹ ṣé o.

I am grateful to the following agencies and institutions for funding several of my research projects that culminated in this book: Ìjẹ̀ṣà Cultural Foundation (awarded to Agbaje-Williams), M. K. O. Abiọla Postgraduate Grant (University of Ibadan), National Endowment for the Humanities, Wenner-Gren Foundation for Anthropological Research, Carnegie Foundation, American Philosophical Society, and the Garden and Landscape Studies program of Dumbarton Oaks. It was in the idyllic environment of the National Humanities Center (NHC) in North Carolina that this book began to take its current shape, thanks to the Delta Delta Delta Fellowship the center granted me during the 2015–16 academic year. I thank all the staff of the center and other fellows for making that year memorable and highly rewarding. And my appointment as a Yip Fellow of the Magdalene College (2018), University of Cambridge, gave me the much-needed time and comfortable atmosphere to bring the manuscript to completion. I thank Lord Rowan Williams (Master of the College), Jane Hughes (College President), Simon Stoddart, and other members of the college governing board for generously hosting me. My special thanks go to Pamela Smith for serving as the torchbearer of my Cambridge visit.

The University of North Carolina at Charlotte has made my itinerant academic life possible through financial and time grants. In this respect, I am particularly grateful to Dean Nancy Gutierrez of the College of Liberal Arts and Sciences for enthusiastically supporting my research endeavors. My colleagues in the Department of Africana Studies also deserve praises for enriching my interdisciplinary thinking and approaches to the study of Africa's past. Not least, the interlibrary loan staff of the J. Murrey Atkins Library at UNC Charlotte made important contributions to this book by accommodating my numerous requests.

I thank the two anonymous reviewers for taking the time out of their busy schedules to read and provide very detailed feedback. I have benefited from their insights. Even so, the usual disclaimer applies: I alone am responsible for any omission or error that may be present in this book. Finally, I am grateful to Dee Mortensen, past editorial director of Indiana University Press (IUP), for her patience and encouragement. This book is one of her last acquisitions before she retired in December 2019 after more than twenty years of supporting scholarship in African Studies and other areas. She is a rare gem, and I wish her a joyful retirement. In moving this book through the production process, her colleagues in the various IUP departments did what I have known the press for since 2006: extraordinary professionalism, timeliness, meticulousness, and care. This book is not the beginning of our wonderful relationship. May it not be the last, *Àṣẹ*.

Akinwumi Ogundiran,
Charlotte, 2020

The YORÙBÁ

Part I:
Introduction

1

Writing a New History

EVERYTHING HAS A HISTORY. THIS simple, self-evident statement is universally true, whether we are talking about social or natural life; time or tradition; an object, an idea, or an institution; a practice or a person; a community, a place, a polity, or a people.[1] When we apply this maxim to a people and their culture, we immediately face questions of origins and beginnings, the processes of their becoming, and the practices that constituted their experience across different horizons of time. However, this simple truth that "everything has a history" is not always self-evident in the scholarship on African peoples, cultures, and practices, to say nothing of policies and public commentaries about them. This situation is particularly glaring in Yorùbá studies. Although the literature on the Yorùbá is vast and represents some of the groundbreaking works of African studies,[2] the deep-time history that defines the Yorùbá experience and its process of becoming are poorly understood. There is an abundance of structural analysis of Yorùbá cultural forms, but the historical analysis is lacking or inadequate in most of those studies. As a result of this gap, we have a growing body of literature that flattens the deep-time Yorùbá history and treats culture as fossilized in a timeless past. Traditions are treated as if they have repeated themselves over several centuries without change. At worst, this void has been lately filled with unrestrained and sometimes grotesque speculations by some entrepreneurial members of the public and scholars. At best, the tendency has been to represent the period of the Christian missionaries and colonial encounters of the mid-nineteenth century as the locus and gravitational center of cultural change rather than seeing the effects of colonialism as a continuum of deep-time changes stretching back at least two millennia.

This problem, which I seek to rectify, represents both the legacy of colonial historiography and the unfinished agenda for a decolonized African historiography. The intellectual project of the British, French, and German colonial administrations that partitioned and incorporated the Yorùbá region into Nigeria, Benin Republic, and Togoland respectively was based on the principles of functionalism and structuralism. Both offer an ahistorical perspective of the colonized traditions and their precolonial past. The European colonial administrations, through their institutions of government, the law, and education, succeeded in creating a fossilized sense of the past for the so-called natives (colonized). Both colonial anthropologists and administrative officers obscured the role of colonized people and their ancestors as historical agents, bracketed off native cultures as unchanging, and constituted the colonized as an object rather than a subject of social life.[3]

In the waning years of European colonial rule in Africa and the early years of independence, the 1950s–1960s, there was a sense of urgency on the part of African intellectuals and political leaders, and their non-African allies, to account for the precolonial history of the erstwhile colonial subjects who were now citizens of independent states. The goal was to develop a new historiography that would indigenize academic history by aligning it with the critical self-awareness of Africans. A large part of this concern focused on the issue of methodology—that is, appropriate sources that would disclose Africa's deep-time historical sensibility. Another aspect of this decolonizing agenda was the quest to infuse the study of African history with African epistemologies.[4] Hence, there have been several periodic evaluations of alternative sources and theories for studying African history outside the colonial archives and beyond the limits of Western worldviews and epistemologies.[5] An early response to this decolonizing agenda in Yorùbá historiography was the eclectic methodology that Saburi Biobaku and his collaborators outlined in *Sources of Yorùbá History*, published in 1973. However, most of the novel sources discussed in that book have not moved beyond the occasional explorations and reflective critiques. No one has implemented the kind of transdisciplinary research agenda proposed in *Sources* for conceptualizing and writing a comprehensive Yorùbá history. Of the nine "nonwritten" sources that the book identifies, only archaeology has provided a sustained interest in deep-time Yorùbá history.[6] However, these archaeological interests have focused on the familiar staples of disciplinary themes such as urbanization, migration, political formation, regional interactions, technology, and trade.[7] While archaeologists have been able to divide local archaeological assemblages into stratigraphic and chronological sequences, they have not engaged a regional history that is grounded in Yorùbá theories of knowledge, ways of being, logics of value, experience of time, and history of practice.

It is not surprising, then, that the historiography of Yorùbá's deep past continues to reproduce presentist epistemologies and is unable to recover multiple layers of social temporalities (experiences of time). This historiography not only assumes a static ontology but also privileges an essentialist conceptualization of culture and tradition, even when most scholars agree in principle that all of these are "eternally in motion."[8] Moreover, most archaeologists and other scholars of history have generally deferred to Eurocentric periodization schemes that masquerade as universal.[9] Instead of using their findings to challenge and revise the structures of temporality and periodization imposed (through colonialism) on the Yorùbá experience of time, these scholars have tended to place their stratigraphies, artifact typologies, and oral traditions into European-centered chronologies that speak more to the Western experience of time and global hegemony rather than to Yorùbá social temporality.[10] One of the repercussions of this situation is that scholars of Yorùbá history have been unable to reconcile archaeological stratigraphy with social stratigraphy, events with structure, innovation with tradition, change with continuity, and ideas with practice. Likewise, theoretical reflexivity that is rooted in everyday philosophy has not been used to interrogate historical sources and questions. Oral traditions tend to be taken at face value, and myth-historical accounts are rarely placed in the context of the experiences that produced them. Hence, despite the large volume of scholarship in Yorùbá studies, and Yorùbá history in particular, we still lack an understanding of the events and eventfulness, meanings and motivations, and social actors and processes of social valuation that shaped the ancestral Yorùbá experiences in the long term. Yet this historicized understanding must be foundational to the project of Yorùbá studies. Without this, one cannot understand the local contexts that shaped Yorùbá experience in the long term and gave it its unique qualities as an integral part of global history. Neither can we engage the Yorùbá cultural forms in cross-cultural comparison, the mainstay of anthropological interest.

To begin to fill these gaps, my goal is to write a regional deep-time history of the Yorùbá that places practices and cultural forms in specific historical contexts and delineates new chronologies that are compatible with ancestral Yorùbá experience in local, regional, and global contexts. Other scholars have pursued similar goals for other regions and cultural groups in Africa, mostly in eastern, central, and southern parts of the continent. Those studies are of two types. The first is a rapidly growing body of historical studies inspired by linguistic-historical methodology, a "capacious source of evidence about history and culture."[11]

Linguistic history is an autonomous field with its own methods, theories, and assumptions. However, its Africanist practitioners' commitment to a rigorous interdisciplinary methodology that ties systematic phonological reconstruction to archaeology, historical ethnography, materiality, and oral traditions has made linguistic history an important subfield in African historical studies. As a result, it has made significant contributions to the deep-time cultural history of Africa.[12] Most of those studies have been conducted in East and Central Africa, and they have focused on a wide range of topics, from indigenous technology, agricultural innovations, and subsistence practices to regional interactions, migrations, trade, political tradition, religion and worldview, gender, health, and the environment.[13] The second group of these deep-time historical studies is primarily based on archaeological data but with additive components of oral traditions and documentary sources. These are mainly regional studies and works of synthesis that seek to write the history of cultural groups and intergroup relations rather than the history of a sociopolitical entity. They have focused on questions about everyday lives, trade, sociopolitical formation and collapse, regional interactions, and technology.[14]

The deep-time perspectives of those regional studies, especially the attentiveness of linguist historians to African epistemologies in their interpretation of cultural forms across multiple horizons of time, have inspired my efforts in this book. However, I take a different conceptual and methodological path. The story of deep-time Yorùbá experience that I tell here is grounded in archaeology, material science, everyday objects, oral traditions, everyday language, visual arts, epic poetry, and myth-history, with additional insights from linguistic (phonology) and documentary sources. It is also informed by comparative and cross-cultural analysis and by empirically tested anthropological theories. Beginning with the Later Stone Age / Iron Age transitions in West Africa, the book covers seven overlapping time periods: the Archaic (300 BC–AD 300), Early Formative (250–750), Late Formative (650–1050), Classical (1000–1420), Intermediate (1400–1570s), Restoration (1570s–1650), and Atlantic (1630–1840) periods (table 1.1). These slices of social time are not self-contained. They overlap because practices, events, cultural forms, and ideas—the focus of this book—percolated through them. The story that I will use this periodization framework to tell is one of change and continuity.[15]

Yorùbá: Ethnonym and Community of Practice

The book is genre bending in the sense that economic, cultural, environmental, political, gender, and social histories, among others, are intertwined. It is therefore important to examine the conceptual frameworks

Table 1.1. Periodization for the Yorùbá Cultural History

Periods	Approx. Years (circa)	Major Characteristics and Events
Pre-Archaic	2500–300 BC	The proto-Yoruboid evolved as a territorial language and cultural group around the Niger-Benue Confluence.
Archaic	300 BC–AD 300	Era of intense drought; southward migrations from the ancestral Yoruboid homeland; and splitting of proto-Yoruboid into three daughter language groups—proto-Igala, proto-Ìtsekírì, and proto-Yorùbá—by AD 300.
Early Formative	AD 250–750	Stable annual rainfall returned; rapid population growth and expansion; proliferation of Yorùbá dialect branching; emergence of a full-fledged House society with formalized political institutions headed by priest-chieftain.
Late Formative	AD 650–1050	Social networks and regional trade intensified; naturalistic sculptures, especially in stonework, developed, representing ancestral figures, communal ancestors, and cultural heroes; emergence of mega-House polities characterized by large village complexes and incipient towns with embankments, populated by corporate groups of diverse familial backgrounds; federation of mega-House polities headed by an elected titular leader likely proliferated; emergence of divine kingship institution and ideology toward the end of the period.
Classical	AD 1000–1420	Commercial and knowledge capital revolution; intensification of regional and interregional trade; primary glass production began in Ilé-Ifẹ̀ and intensified throughout this period; major innovations in affective technology, especially in three-dimensional art—terracotta and later brass; emergence and proliferation of sprawling urban polities; architectural features such as potsherd pavements were common regionally; royal divine-kings became the preferred model of governance throughout the region; codification of the Yorùbá community of practice as a networked regional system; major changes in worldview and cosmogony; the rise of the Ifẹ̀ Empire with a vast network of client states and colonies.
Intermediate	AD 1400–1570s	Regional instability due to hemispherical ecological crisis and subcontinental political turbulence; a period of intense dry conditions characteriṣed by recurrent multiyear droughts; collapse of regional economy; external aggression by Nupe militarists; many prominent Yorùbá polities collapsed; the end of Ifẹ̀ political empire; Benin, a former client state of Ilé-Ifẹ̀ established political autonomy and embarked on its own expansion northward. Early stages of Atlantic commercial exchanges began in the Bight of Benin with the arrival of Portuguese traders, soon followed by the Dutch and English.
Restoration	AD 1570s–1650	A period of renewal and regeneration marked by rebuilding of old kingdoms and foundation of new ones; political landscape was transformed by warrior-kings and militaristic states such as Iléṣà, Ọ̀yọ́, and Benin.
Atlantic	AD 1630–1840	Era of merchant capital revolution and the Atlantic slave trade; monetized economy took hold; Ọ̀yọ́ became the dominant political power in the region; proliferation of centralized polities and frontier towns/market centers; incorporation into the Atlantic economy with new forms of global commodity exchange and consumption practices; intensification in everyday commodity production and craft specialization (e.g., cotton cultivation, cloth making, and dye manufacture); expansion in itinerant trading; sociopolitical instability beginning in the early nineteenth century caused by the impacts of the Atlantic slave trade, inequality, elite factional conflicts, underclass rebellion, and the jihad.

and scope of the book. The most important place to start is with the term Yorùbá as an analytical category and a unit of study. Today, Yorùbá refers to a language, a culture, and a people who are self-aware of their geographical, temporal, and historical relationships, as well as their internal similarities and differences. Scholars have used the term mostly as an ethnolinguistic category to encompass people who speak a continuum of more than thirty-five mutually intelligible dialects and whose ancestral homeland stretches between present-day southwest Nigeria and Togo.[16] This emphasis on ethnolinguistic conceptualization has led to two dominant approaches in Yorùbá studies. The first is the static ethnographic construct that reduces the Yorùbá to the sum of, or differences between, the dialects that compose the Yorùbá language group. The second approach, dominant in the historiography but not less static in conception, treats the Yorùbá regional history as an aggregate of the history of several kingdoms. Each of these kingdoms is treated as representing one of the Yorùbá dialect groups so that, for example, the history of the Ifẹ̀ subgroup is reduced to the assumed spatially circumscribed political history of Ilé-Ifẹ̀; Iléṣà kingdom served the same purpose for the Ìjẹ̀sà subgroup, and Ìjẹ̀bú-Òde for the Ìjẹ̀bú. Both of these approaches imply that these dialects and kingdoms are fossilized entities and products of a "big bang" simultaneous creation. Yet historical traditions, social memory, embodied practices, material culture, and archaeological data point to the fact that neither approach is accurate. The history of a dialect group is more than the history of a kingdom, and vice versa. Therefore, I depart from these two approaches that reinforce a static and reductionist sensibility of the past.

Before I proceed to my destination from this point of departure, let me affirm that the Yorùbá whom I am referring to here did not have their origin in the mid-nineteenth century when the label was first used to define an ethnic identity for all the speakers of the dialect continuum whom we now call by that name. The project of that ethnic identity making responded to and was necessitated by the European racialization of the globe and the European empires' insistence on classifying the world populations into "nations" through the process of colonialism and industrial capitalism during the nineteenth century.[17] This process involved vacuating the knowledge system of the colonized and forcing on the latter the imperative of taking on new identities that were compatible with the colonizers' expectations and theories of knowledge. This background information is necessary to understand why I have used the ethnonym Yorùbá to refer to the ancestors who lived many centuries before the nineteenth century. This choice of the ethnonym is not anachronistic. I am using the term to refer not to an ethnic group or a nation but to a cultural group.[18] Here then is my destination: the term Yorùbá serves to restore agency, dynamism, and movement (as opposed to static and reductionist sensibility) to the substance of our subject's historical experience before the nineteenth century. The ethnonym is used throughout this book as a marker of practices, networks, self-consciousness, and interconnectedness that constitute our subject's sociological and historical reality and whose geographical boundaries can be reconstructed from about AD 500 to 1840. In the following pages, I demonstrate that individuals and social groups became Yorùbá through learning, and creating and participating in emergent knowledge production, communicative interactions, and regional social networks. For a long time, we have lacked the vocabulary and conceptual framework to make sense of this reality because of the encumbrance of the atemporal, geographically bounded, static, and tribal model of ethnicity and identity that European colonial ethnography and historiography has bequeathed to African studies. As a result, many contemporary scholars continue to privilege the Western social science's "nation" paradigm when writing about the "other"—the colonized. They thereby persist in confusing culture with ethnicity and language with biological kinship, a perspective that is incompatible with the ancestral Yorùbá historical experience.

Fortunately, the concept of "community of practice" by Etienne Wenger and Jean Lave provides the framework and vocabulary to imagine and think about the Yorùbá as a deep-time sociohistorical group and not a biological or natural entity, a perspective that is consistent with my field evidence and the subject's conceptual category.[19] The "community of practice" concept allows me to make sense of the fluidity, permeability, and networked relations that defined the experience of ancestral Yorùbá in a broad regional context. This community was a multitiered, boundary-shifting constellation. It included networks of peoples and institutions across multiple polities and speech communities who subscribed to a common set of epistemologies and ontologies—knowledge systems, myths, reservoirs of symbols, cosmologies, and ideologies of social order through deep-time learning, socialization, and interactions. The ancestral Yorùbá who created, lived, and imagined this community did so through engagement in mutually reinforcing relationships within and outside the Yorùbá language continuum. I will show in the following chapters that some of the practices that were constitutive of this community had already developed during the Archaic period, but it was during the Late Formative period that this community began to coalesce. And the practices matured during the Classical period. More changes were to come during the periods of Restoration and Atlantic merchant capital revolution. I use two terminologies to refer to the ancestors who lived in earlier times—proto-Yoruboid (mostly before AD 250) and proto-Yorùbá (ca. AD 250–750). I will discuss the historical trajectories of these terminologies and the peoples they denote in chapters 2 and 3, and I will address the provenance of the term Yorùbá itself in chapter 4.

Applying temporality-mindedness to the concept of community of practice enables us to explore how the values, knowledge, and practices that were constitutive of the Yorùbá were recalibrated at different points in time as a result of the shifting spheres of regional interactions, transformations in political economies, and environmental changes.[20] The processes of learning and knowledge production that underpinned the formation of the Yorùbá community of practice were organic and organized. Of course, there were instability and disruptions along the way. These shaped the processes of learning, which in turn affected how this community was forged and how it transformed over time. Therefore, the conceptual framework of the community of practice provides the tool necessary to explore how the ancestral Yorùbá created their historical scripts from the meanings that they negotiated at different junctures. Although none of these scripts and meanings was uniform in every place at any particular time, but all members of the community of practice understood those scripts and used them for communicative interactions. It was through these interactions that experiences developed and were negotiated, contested, and translated into meaningful practices and traditions.

The ethnolinguistic categories—that is, relationships between language and culture—have also played a role as a denominator of the Yorùbá community of practice. After all, the various language and cultural forms that are distinctive of the present-day and ancestral Yorùbá originated from a common ancestral language and epistemological community that scholars have labeled *proto-Yoruboid*, one of several linguistically distinct societies who lived around the Niger-Benue Confluence in present-day Nigeria between around 2500 and 300 BC.[21] Some members of that ancestral community began to radiate from the confluence between 300 BC and AD 300. By AD 800, some of their descendants had split into several dialects of the Yorùbá language and had become the largest integrated cultural group in West Africa south of the Niger River, in terms of population size and territorial spread. Despite their internal differences, however, the members of the Yorúbá-speaking community became increasingly interdependent by the twelfth century, subscribing to the same epistemic institutions, regimes of value, and aspirational principles. Irrespective of geography, they articulated their everyday existence within shared and overlapping spheres of belief systems, ritual fields, political institutions, material practices, and ideology of familial relationships. These spheres of interaction were not stable. Instead, they shifted, contrasted, and expanded at different periods from the Archaic period in the early first millennium to the age of hegemonic states in the 1100s–1300s, and later the 1600s–1800s. I accounted for the processes of these interaction spheres and the experiences and practices that developed from them.

However, the Yorùbá community of practice was more than the sum of its dialect groups and political entities. As we shall see in this book, there were individuals, families, and social groups who were originally outside this language group but who became part of the Yorùbá community through military, political, and economic interactions. These peoples brought with them some of their own cultural institutions, practices, lexicons, and ideas and fused them into the Yorùbá elements. For example, some segments and individuals of Ibariba, Songhay, Nupe, and Edo backgrounds became part of the Yorùbá community of practice at different periods between the twelfth and seventeenth centuries as a result of the common interests, practices of power, projects of self-realization, and opportunities that they sought or shared with their Yorùbá-speaking neighbors and hosts. The communicative interactions that brought these other individuals and groups into the intellectual, cultural, and political project of the Yorùbá community of practice were negotiated through commercial linkages, military interventions, regional alliances, migrations (forced and voluntary), and political integration. This was not a one-way process. There were also members of the Yorùbá community of practice who became part of the Edo, Songhai, Ibariba and Nupe communities through similar processes. Defining the Yorùbá as a "community of practice" rather than as a "language community" therefore allows me to address questions that are regional, transregional, and deep-time in scope and that transcend ethnolinguistic boundaries. Thus, I am able to delineate the major historical threads that linked the different parts of the Yorùbá world together as an epistemic unit and that linked them to other cultural and epistemic zones and communities of practice at the subcontinental and transcontinental levels (e.g., Western Sudan and the Atlantic world) at different junctures of time. The "community of practice" concept also provides the conceptual framework for understanding the dynamic historical processes that produced some of the polities and dialect groups that have been treated as static in Yorùbá studies. The concept opens the way to realizing that these kingdoms and dialects belonged to different layers of time, and it also enables me to uncover the practices that produced them.

I should point out from the onset, though, that this book is not a parade of kingdoms and city-states, kingdom rule, and dynastic histories, an approach that has dominated Yorùbá historiography.[22] Neither is it my goal to account for every kingdom, big or small, or the minutiae of their rise and fall. Such an agenda is impossible to achieve, as there were hundreds of such kingdoms and polities in the long history of the Yorùbá community of practice. Nevertheless, two metropolises, Ilé-Ifẹ̀ and Ọ̀yọ́-Ilé, feature prominently in this study because they were the centrifugal forces around which much of the Yorùbá community of practice oscillated at different periods between the eleventh and early nineteenth centuries. I also bring into the study other polities, places, and social units that have never before been considered as sites of historical production but that, as I will demonstrate, played a greater role in the Yorùbá historical journeys than had been acknowledged. In this regard, the roles of major and minor kingdoms, hunting camps, and way stations; provincial towns and villages; as well as other places that are often anachronistically regarded as "Yorùbá frontiers" or regional backwaters (e.g., Okun and Èkìtì) are highlighted to show how these places shaped the changes and continuity in Yorùbá's regional history.

Theory and Concept

The concept of cultural translation drives the interpretive wheel of this book. It allows me to contemplate and investigate how members of the Yorùbá community of practice managed novel experiences in the past, from the last centuries of the first millennium BC through the early nineteenth century. Cultural translation is always embedded in communicative interactions and implicated in any process and outcome of social transformation or structural change. Throughout this book, I show that eventful experience usually elevated or intensified cultural translation, whether the event related to individual actions or structural perturbations, especially those involving encounters and entanglement of different peoples, cultures, ideas, and foreign goods.[23] Translation studies, as a field, method, and theory of inquiry, has focused mainly on three types of communicative interaction. One refers to the "activity of communication between cultural groups," and the next refers to the translation of languages in cultural, social, and political contexts. The third places the ethnographer at the center of translating the outsider culture for the community or assumed audience.[24] But there is yet another type of translation, concerned with how a society or a community translated new experiences into locally meaningful practices. This study is preoccupied with this fourth form of translation. For the Yorùbá, such eventful processes that instigated translations of practice included the effects of the ecological crisis that the proto-Yoruboid ancestors faced at the end of the first millennium BC (chap. 2); the development of sacred kingship about a thousand years later (chap. 2 and 3); the invention of Yorùbá epistemic objects such as glass beads around the eleventh century (chap. 4); transregional perturbations and institutionalization of cavalry as the instrument of warfare and power during the fifteenth and sixteenth centuries (chap. 4 and 5); and the entanglement of the Yorùbá in the webs of the Atlantic merchant capital and the Ọ̀yọ́ imperial project (chap. 5–9). These experiences generated new modalities of interaction, knowledge, and experimentation that eventually led to new practices and ways of being.

The task of a cultural historian is to make sense of the meanings and meaningfulness of the practices being translated across different and overlapping experiences of time. The practices that I emphasize in this book include logics and structures of social organization; political culture, political economy, and institutions of governance; identity formation; gender forms, ideology, and relations; paths of self-realization, construction of personhood, and the quest for immortality; class and social stratification; taste and social distinction; the production-consumption nexus; and processes of social valuation. At the core of this book are also practices about the technological and intellectual projects of creating, accumulating, and dispensing knowledge capital, as well as the process of making causative explanations. By locating each of these practices in specific experiences of time and seeking to understand their translation across overlapping temporalities and in different domains of everyday life, I account for the dialogic processes that were constitutive of how several aspects of Yorùbá traditions were created, reproduced, and transformed over the long term. The dialogues or communicative interactions among the agents in different domains of everyday life are the motors of cultural production. Therefore, it is imperative that cultural history discloses the connections between people located at different social spheres.[25] It is in these spaces of interconnection and interaction that practice or tradition is negotiated, history is made, and culture is formed. In other words, no sphere of activity is a bounded space, and it is in the interconnections between these domains that the cultural historian can uncover the processes that gave birth to particular practices and shaped their character at different historical junctures.

What sets cultural history apart from other subfields such as political, economic, religious, intellectual, gender, and social history is that it encompasses all those other areas of interest and thereby makes "total history" thinkable. In pursuing this logic of historical understanding, I am not claiming that this book is a "total history" of the Yorùbá before 1840. Rather, what I seek to achieve is an account of Yorùbá cultural history that cuts across the different spheres of social life and institutions that scholars tend to put in the silos of historical specialization. To this end, I explore those interstices of communicative interactions between different agents and domains, and across multiple scales. These include the elephant hunter and the king;[26] the way-station trader and the priest; motherhood and wifehood; personhood and community; the frontier and the metropolis; the individual and the corporate; the household and the state; and the ritual field and the commercial sphere. Other communicative interactions took place between lords and their servants; the provincial governors and the market women; rich and poor; men and women; and between different agents of early global economy, among others. By focusing on these "spaces" or loci of interactions and on the experiences that mediated them, I uncover how practices were nested in different experiences of time. The cultural turn in history has demonstrated the feasibility of this approach. For example, we now realize that an empire is not only a political project but also a cultural and gendered practice (chap. 8). And the practice turn in anthropology has clarified that kinship, or any other cultural form, is not a timeless enactment of tradition but a contextual and history-dependent negotiation of power in which institutionalized hierarchies and social inequality are constant themes (chap. 2). Likewise, technological innovations and market exchanges are more than economic activities. They are also cultural and symbolic markers of community building, identity performances, and religious expressions (chap. 3). In this book, I bring these insights to my exploration of the deep-time Yorùbá history.

In order to understand the dialogues and interactions across multiple domains of everyday life, it is imperative that I turn to hermeneutics. This art of interpretation is central to my project of writing a deep-time history of the Yorùbá because it reveals the meanings and experiences through which traditions were made, unraveled, or transformed. It accounts for the consciousness and intentionality in the historical process, and for the way historical agents made sense of events that defined their lives. But the tool of hermeneutics is not enough in the hands of the cultural historian seeking to understand how past practices came into being and how they are meaningful. Practices (as generative traditions) are social capital. Not every individual in a given community or society has equal access to the same types of practice, tradition, or social capital because individuals occupy different positions in the configuration of power that assigns value to different kinds of capital. The implication is that most individuals have constrained access to the aspirational principles and knowledge by which a society is organized. In the case of the ancestral Yorùbá, there were hierarchies of knowing subjects among whom the political elite, vested elders (patriarchs and matriarchs), masters of crafts, and priests/priestesses occupied the higher ranks. On the lower rungs of the social ladder were the new or young initiates, and below them were the uninitiated, noncitizens, servile individuals, children, and outsiders.[27] For this reason, we can say that some individuals in this community of practice played a more decisive role in articulating and influencing certain visions of the past, the present, and the future than others. These were the gatekeepers who controlled the distribution of different sorts of social capital and disproportionately influenced the making of practice. They were also the ones who determined what meaning is and what is meaningful. Hence, it becomes imperative for the cultural historian to consider the power and authority differentials, as well as the diversity of perspectives that defined the forms of practice and the processes of cultural production. These power and authority differentials have always been located in what Robert Ulin calls "the material interactions of historical existence,"[28] a reference to the political economy that shaped how resources were distributed, rewards allocated, social differences institutionalized, and certain values legitimized or delegitimized. The political economy would also constrain which representations were made possible, which types of practices were enacted, and which social forms were created. For this reason, the critical interpretive objectives of hermeneutics—meaning and meaningfulness—can be achieved only with attentiveness to the material relations of everyday life and the power structure that sustained those material relations.

Conversely, to study these "material interactions of historical existence" without hermeneutical insight is to write a history that is devoid of meaning or meaningfulness, one in which people and their communities of practice lack any existential purpose. The soul, spirit, and epistemology of the historical subject are indeed often missing in much of the historiography of the Yorùbá and other African peoples. I seek to transcend this limitation by following the path of cultural history that conjoins critical hermeneutics with political economy. The former refers to the representations, conceptualization, and symbolic constitution of experience, while the latter is about the accumulation and distribution of resources at different levels of interaction and power relations, from the individual and the household to the state and beyond. The intersectionality of hermeneutics and political economy is, for example, essential to understanding the Yorùbá involvement in the merchant-capital revolution of the seventeenth and eighteenth centuries. It also helps illuminate the process that culminated in the birth of the Yorùbá community of practice during the twelfth and thirteenth centuries, when overlapping fields of political, social, economic, and ritual networks developed between River Ovia (Nigeria) in the east and River Mono (Republic of Togo) in the west, and between the Atlantic coast and River Niger. Not all the processes of eventfulness that shaped the Yorùbá experience were internal to this community of practice. Some were inspired by external events or grew out of interactions with the outside world (chap. 4 and 6). Others originated from cataclysmic climatic patterns and nonhuman agents such as microbes that caused devastating droughts and epidemics (chap. 2, 4, and 9). It is therefore imperative, as I have done in this book, to locate how this community constituted and produced its social world in the frames of subcontinental, global, and comparative history. In this regard, I am attentive to how the desert-edge aridity in the Sahel and Western Sudan during the fifteenth century affected the experiences of the Yorùbá world and how the opening of commerce on the Atlantic rim shaped local experience after the sixteenth century. I discuss these convergences of internal, external, and environmental events, and the impacts on the practice and social forms that constituted the Yorùbá cultural history.

An experience, even when perceived and received differently by diverse agents in the same community of practice, must be translated into a mutually intelligible system of meanings. This communicative interaction is central to the coherence, resilience, self-organizing, and continuity of any community. Experience is more than what happened, what is conscious, or what is in the discursive realm. It is also the anticipated, the conscious and unconscious, the discursive and nondiscursive; the feelings, fears, sentiments, concerns, and aspirations; the consideration of what is possible and impossible; the explanation and theorization of the known and unknown; the rumor, perception of reality, and intellectual disposition of the time. All of these facets of experience—mentality—make people think and act in particular and similar ways, irrespective of the differences in their material relations, and cause them to relate to the world and others in profoundly consequential ways. Experience defines imaginaries that may become codified as mythologies, ritual performances, and iconographic representations, among others. They not only make what is seemingly unreal (to the contemporary outsider) believable but also turn the thoughts of men and women toward actualizing or preventing them. This translation of experience generates what Manfred Frank calls the "semantic foundation of any consciousness"—meaning, significance, and intention.[29]

Therefore, the experience of time generates its own transcripts and historical sources, which, in the case of the Yorùbá, include myths, objects, language, performances, and iconographies. The uniqueness of these transcripts and their value in understanding the past have served as the basis of the clamor for a decolonized African historiography. Thus, Bassey Andah, in his critique of the encumbrance of Western social science on African historical study, charged the students of African cultural history to "descend into the burrows of Africa's invisible silent times, persons, peoples, places and things, the ritual ground where one can truly examine African relationships with history in all its textual manifestation[s] and strive for control of the text of our experience."[30] He insisted that the focus of such study must be about "the daily activities, . . . social life and institutions, and . . . scientific and literary explorations" of ancestral Africans. I share Bassey Andah's conviction that this is the only pathway for identifying what he variously called "an inside history," an "authentic cultural history," and an "authentic African biography" where an African can discover his or her "true historical self."[31] This book is a response to his clarion call and those of like minds. I am not preoccupied with what we *ought* to be doing to write an inside, authentic history of Africa, as many critics of African historiography have advocated. Rather, I have set out to implement this agenda for the study of Yorùbá history. I should clarify, though, that I interpret Andah's "authentic African cultural history" as a history that is compatible with the transcripts of the Yorùbá experience in all of its epistemological, ontological, and axiological ramifications.

Sources and Methods

This book is a product of methodological pluralism and transdisciplinary interests in which I mesh multi-sited archaeological and material science data sets with oral traditions, objects and iconography, mythologies, historical ethnography, festivals, and several aspects of embodied practices, including bodily movements and language sources. I have also mined a very thin layer of documentary sources from both Yorùbá and European sources. I have devoted more time and resources to collecting archaeological data than to studying any of these other sources simply because archaeological research is the most time-consuming and most expensive of all of these fields of historical inquiry. It also has unique potential for filling some of the most critical gaps in the transcripts of experience that defined the Yorùbá community of practice before the mid-nineteenth century. Bringing together diverse sources allowed me to move beyond the singularity of narratives and linear cause-effect relationships. This endeavor is about more than adding one source to the other or using one knowledge system to cross-check the other. It is about juxtaposing, blending, integrating, disaggregating, and aggregating different knowledge systems, each of which requires different skill sets. Literacy and education in the subject's language, cultural idioms, epistemology, ontology, and axiology are as important as literacy in archaeological stratigraphy, artifact interpretation, and material science.

The book reflects my primary field research journey, which began in central Yorùbá in 1986, first as a scholar apprentice in the Ìjẹ̀ṣà region and later (1990–2000) as a principal investigator focusing specifically on Ìpolé-Ìjẹ̀ṣà, Ìlàrè, and Ìbòkun under the banner of the Ẹ̀ka Ọ̀ṣun Archaeological and Historical Research Project.[32] In 2003, I launched the Upper Ọ̀ṣun Archaeological and Historical Project, expanding my study area to Ọ̀ṣogbo, Ẹdẹ, Awó, Ọ̀jo, Apòmù, Ìkirè, and Ilé-Ifẹ̀. These are all in the central Yorùbá region, an important junction of regional interactions since the twelfth century. Recently, I have begun a new phase of archaeological research in the metropolitan area of the old Ọ̀yọ́ Empire, in the Yorùbá northwest—"The Ọ̀yọ́ Empire Archaeology and Heritage Project." The technical reports and interpretative essays of the results of these archaeological projects have been published and presented to professional audiences and institutions over the years. I have drawn heavily from those published and unpublished materials to write this book. A consistent feature of my interest in these archaeological studies is the multi-scalar networks through which local communities, polities, and households were produced and people lived their lives. These networks ranged from local interactions to regional and transcontinental relationships. Some were politically circumscribed while others were economically, culturally, and socially determined. I have supplemented the Ẹ̀ka Ò̩ṣun, Upper Ọ̀ṣun, and Ọ̀yọ́ Empire research projects with short-term fieldwork, including archaeological reconnaissance and collection of oral traditions in Òkè Ògùn (northwest Yorùbá), Èkìtì (eastern Yorùbá), Oǹdó and Ìjẹ̀bú (southeast and southern Yorùbá), and the Edo-Esan areas (fig. 1.1). A small cohort of research assistants have also "taken me" to places I could not physically visit myself, from the Okun to the Lagoon-Àwórì and Yéwá (Ẹ̀gbádò) areas, conducting ethnographic and language-based fieldwork on my behalf. In addition, my visit to several repositories of heritage materials provided me with unique insights into Yorùbá cultural history. These repositories include museums and Òrìṣà temples. Their holdings of artifacts, performative resources, and related materials are important cultural archives that are invaluable to the historical inquiry of this nature.[33]

A branch of evidence that has proven very useful in my study of early Yorùbá history is linguistic data. Assisted by anthropologists Babájídé Ọlọ́lájúlọ́ and Babátúndé Agbájé-Williams in the fieldwork and historical linguist Christopher Ehret for conceptualization and data analysis, I documented a 105-word list for twenty of the major Yorùbá dialects and their close relatives—Igala and Itsekiri (Ìṣẹ̀kìrì). This provides the basis to reconstruct the spatial patterns, genealogies, and temporal sequences in the emergence of these dialects/languages whose proto ancestors innovated and diverged from the original proto-Yoruboid language ca. 300 BC–AD 250 (app. 1).

Insights from oral traditions pervaded this book, and their collection began very early in my quest to understand indigenous epistemology and representations of community history, from verbal (orality) to performative (rituals and festivals) and visual (iconography and sculpture) renditions. At the surface level, the verbal aspects of oral traditions are usually preoccupied with the origin issues, ethnogenesis, and development of political institutions. These are also the topics that have attracted the interests of most scholars. Whenever questions of origin and ethnogenesis are at stake, we must be aware that the seeming completeness, coherence, and finality of oral traditions may serve the purpose of providing

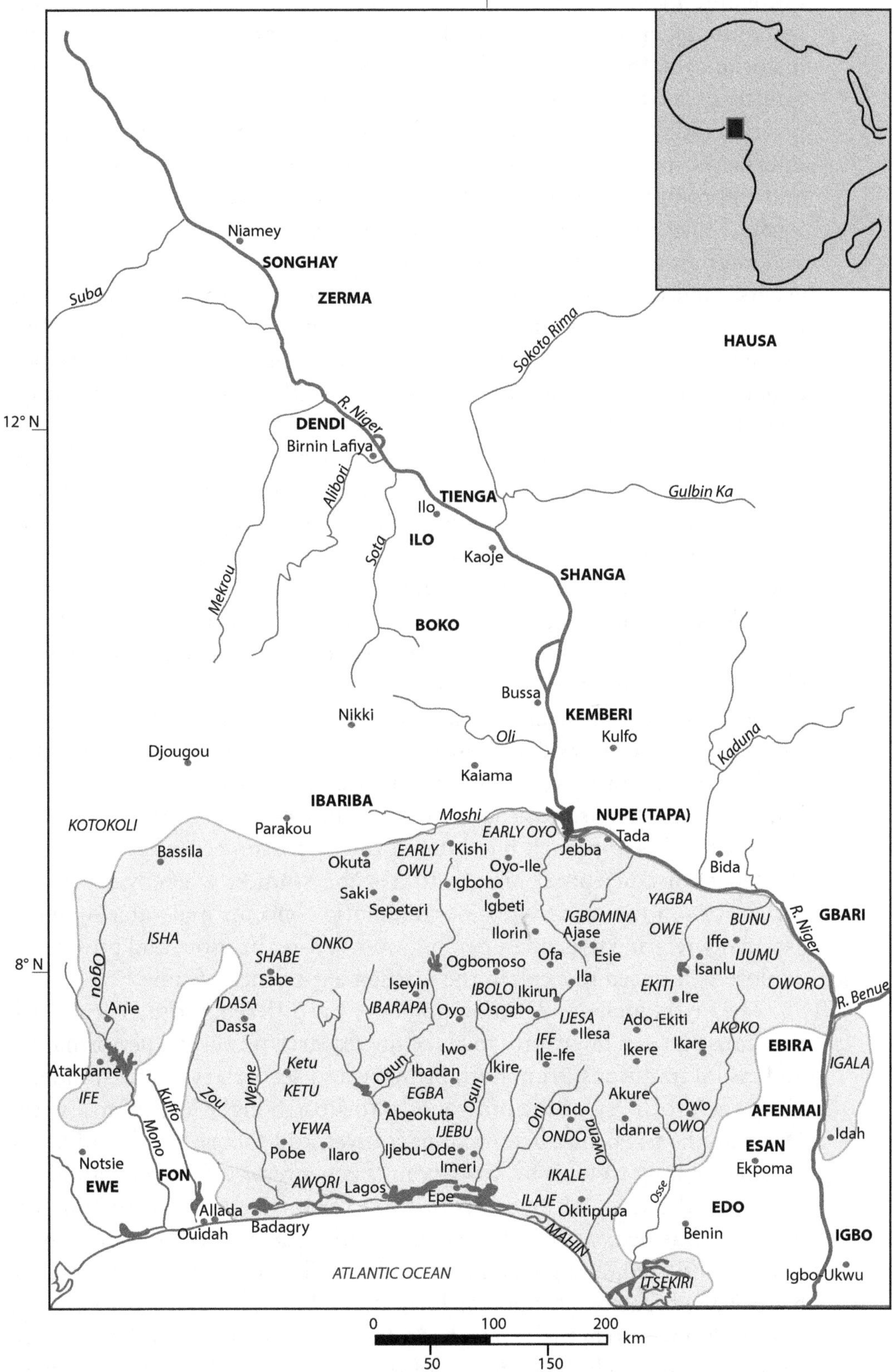

Figure 1.1. Composite map of the Yorùbá- and Yoruboid-speaking region

rationality or justification for the configurations of power relations and communal identity at the time of their telling, not unlike what academic historians do. In any oral tradition–based research, therefore, it is important to speak to as many people as possible, especially across different positionalities. To have a diversity of perspectives, I usually avoided group interviews, preferring one-on-one conversations and sometimes casual and impromptu interactions. Oral traditions, of course, are a distinct form of historical archive, and their holdings contain more than origin and migration stories. They are products of social memory about people, events, landscape, practices, and ideas. Therefore, in addition to collecting traditions of origin, information on migrations and settlement history, as well as dynastic and lineage history, I have also collected information about how people and communities interact with places and the landscape over the long term.

Likewise, I have used the process of documenting oral traditions to interrogate what the everyday language can tell us about historical memory and to explore questions about the meaning of a wide range of concepts, ideas, and worldviews that are central to the objectives of this book. This holistic approach to oral traditions made it possible to explore how ideas and meanings shaped Yorùbá history; how these changed over time and why; and how different layers of ideas and meanings influenced social memory and the creation of oral archives. This engagement with people's intellectual lives and knowledge has enabled me to place my subjects at the center of their history; use their language as the basis of disclosing their history; and use their discursive forms, metaphors, logics, and sensibility as the groundwork for understanding their past. More important, this approach has offered the opportunity to apply some of the tenets of conceptual history to Yorùbá studies, whereby the transformations in the meaning of paradigmatic concepts and value systems, especially relating to gender, personhood, self-realization, and power, are explored and used to explain the Yorùbá experience of time.[34]

The mythologies and iconographies of the different Òrìṣà (Yorùbá deities) constitute an important focus of my research on verbal, performative, and visual traditions, from both primary and secondary sources. Indeed, given the proclivity of the indigenous Yorùbá thought leaders to use the Òrìṣà myths to encode historical narratives and theorize the world, one must be willing to look for history in this genre of the Yorùbá archives. Although the value of myth-histories of various deities for studying the deep past has been acknowledged in Yorùbá studies,[35] these sources have not been utilized in any systematic and significant way to interrogate the historical processes of cultural formation. I have attempted to change that. Not only do myths and legends draw our attention "to those practical verities in which the members of the community all believe and live," but they also bear the psychological and higher metaphysical truths of historical experiences.[36] As we shall see in the following pages, the myths of the Òrìṣà reveal the composition of responses to many layers of experiences and the society's translation of those experiences into theories and ways of living.

My turn to myth-history as a historical transcript is essential to the project of discovering the epistemological frameworks that shaped the deep-time Yorùbá history and how social lives were meaningfully constituted. The Òrìṣà myth-history is also critical to understanding the ways in which ancestral Yorùbá (and their descendants) informed and shaped their perceptions of self and the world and composed a system of thought about reality.[37] The richness of these myths offers the opportunity to explore a deep understanding of the circumstances in which several gods and goddesses in the pantheon were created, renewed, and transformed as part of the historical processes that shaped the Yorùbá community of practice. Hence, I show how the myth-history of deities such as Ṣàngó, Ọ̀ṣun, and Yemọja reveals the cultural, social, economic, and political transformations in the Yorùbá world during the era of the Ọ̀yọ́ Empire and Atlantic commercial revolution (chap. 5–8). Likewise, I locate the myths of Ọbàtálá, Ọbalùfọ̀n, Ifá, Ṣàngó, and Ògún, among others, in the experiences that birthed, threatened, and sustained the Yorùbá community of practice between AD 800 and 1600 (chap. 3 and 5).

It should be clear by now that I treat all three facets of tradition—verbal, performative, and visual renditions—as historical sources rather than as anthropological representations. I am interested in what these renditions can tell us about the past. For this reason, the contemporary self-understanding of my informants as individuals, is not the final or ultimate focus of my inquiry, as they might be in an anthropological study that is devoid of historical sensibility. Instead, the informant's representation is a palimpsest that the historian must place under a magnifying glass or microscope to view or glimpse the multiple and, often, blurring layers of the deep and recent past. I interrogated and critiqued these representations for plausibility, engaged in source criticism, and subjected them to critical analysis before I accepted them as historical evidence. Therefore, my interest in indigenous epistemology does not imply that I must take anything at face value.[38] As an interpretative account of the past, history must be based on credible, plausible, inclusive, and relevant sources, though these sources are never as complete as any historian would like them to be. Their reevaluation is therefore necessary as new evidence comes to light.

Meanwhile, the quality of the oral tradition archives as a source of history depends on the kinds of people whose bodies of knowledge and indigenous epistemology one is privileged to have access. One must begin with people whose everyday living and mentality are rooted in indigenous epistemology. Not every self-identified Yorùbá native, even among those who occupy high traditional political positions today, fulfills this condition. In both its discursive and nondiscursive forms, indigenous epistemology is an idea and a practice; it is a social product that is learned, and people are socialized into it. It is a product of history, a cumulative living tradition that changes, with additions and subtractions, from time to time. Therefore, it is not an untethered invention or imaginary of a person. In the Yorùbá world today, as in the past, there are institutions and practices that safeguard and make use of this epistemology and its knowledge systems. The people (communities and individuals) who are versed in this knowledge system are embedded in these institutions. They are priests and priestesses, chieftains of Yorùbá political and social institutions, diviners, and members of the different schools of Òrìṣà thought. These are the Yorùbá intellectuals, cutting across several socioeconomic spectra and power relations, from whom I have garnered the verbal, performative, and visual representations that underpin this study. Much of the information came about through long-term relationships rather than one-off formal interviews. The digital age has also made a lot of this information easily accessible to the global public. Many masters and students of Yorùbá epistemology, especially priests and priestesses, now use several online forums to share their knowledge, teach, and debate. I have taken advantage of these rich online sources.

The last pieces of evidence that inform this book are the documentary sources. These were lacking for early Yorùbá history and did not become available, mostly in the form of European travelers' and traders' accounts, until the late fifteenth century via the Bight of Benin. Even then, these meager sources—primarily Dutch, German, Portuguese, and English, and spanning 1472 and 1850—are limited to the coastal area, between Rivers Ovia and Mono.[39] The few Portuguese, Dutch, and English traders who ventured inland left a trove of small but valuable sources for Benin City, from the late fifteenth through the eighteenth centuries, and there were at least two Portuguese visits to Ijebu-Ode between 1500 and 1553.[40] The emphasis of these sources is on commerce and the political interventions in economic activities. However, there are occasional cursory remarks about the everyday lives and spectacular observations. It was not until 1826–1832 that the first detailed accounts of mainland Yorùbá began to appear, but these were limited to only a narrow western flank of the region, the Ọyọ́ Empire, and they comprised mainly the observations of three British visitors in their travels between Badagry and Oyo-Ile—Hugh Clapperton and Richard and John Lander.[41]

The oral accounts of three Yorùbá men caught in the web of the Atlantic slave trade during the first quarter of the nineteenth century are also useful for understanding the events that unraveled in the Yorùbá region during that period. Ọ̀ṣìnfẹ̀kundé, Samuel Àjàyí Crowther, and Joseph Wright of the Ìjẹ̀bú, Ọ̀yọ́, and Ẹ̀gbá subgroups respectively gave accounts of their childhood memories, especially on the eve of their capture and the immediate aftermath of their enslavement.[42] I am mindful of the weaknesses in these sources, in terms of the effects of trauma on memory and the fact that European interlocutors, with little to no Yorùbá cultural literacy, mediated the transcription of their accounts. Nevertheless, these are the earliest sources that focused on intimate everyday lives and cultural institutions as well as the events of the early nineteenth century in Yorùbá mainland. The mid-nineteenth century witnessed an increase in the number of sources, mostly in the form of missionary accounts written by both the Yorùbá and Europeans between 1855 and 1877. They address many themes and provide insightful reference points for the last four decades covered in this study, 1800–1840.[43]

The spatial units of all of these sources are patently local, whether I am using archaeological techniques, collecting oral historical and language-based information, or documenting performative data (e.g., rituals). However, I have always been attentive to the fact that the meanings of place-specific artifacts, oral traditions, and embodied practices must be set in the contexts of regional history. After all, no archaeological site, village, town, or polity was ever an island unto itself. The comparative analysis of the materials and data from these different locations repeatedly confirms that local communities, individuals and households, and polities were products of, and were part of, far-flung regional networks. These inter-site comparative perspectives and the focus of most of my research on the frontiers of metropolitan centers have made me acutely aware of the shifting patterns of regional networks in which local communities were entangled and the fact that the regional networks and their local nodes were integral parts of larger and global processes. These had significant impacts on everyday lives and the processes of cultural formation.

I have privileged the material aspects of social relations in the stories that I tell in this book. I do so because materiality takes us to the intimate spaces and deep recesses where the experience of time and culture formation were negotiated and produced by people, communities, institutions, and polities. For example, I show that glass beads, as epistemic objects, hold the key to understanding the formation of a pan-regional Yorùbá community of practice between the eleventh and fourteenth centuries. Likewise, I argue that we cannot fully understand how the Yorùbá became entangled in the Atlantic commercial revolution of the seventeenth and eighteenth centuries without paying attention to the role of tobacco and cowrie shells. These are the linchpins for the taste, pleasure, addiction, and aspiration that facilitated the entanglement. These commodities were, therefore, constitutive of the experience of early modernity in the Yorùbá world. The everyday relationship between people and things (materiality) enables me to explore new questions and themes that link individuals and communities to one another and to broad historical processes. The attentiveness to materiality provides useful insights into the intimate processes by which culture is made, tradition is invented, and society is born.

Of all of the source materials that I have used, archaeological and documentary sources are the only ones that lend themselves to direct dating. Nonetheless, oral traditions, myth-history, rituals and festivals, language, and iconography are also social and cultural artifacts of the time. Therefore, they are amenable to chronological estimation. The hermeneutic approach has been useful to disclosing the historicity and layers of time embedded in these embodied sources. Making use of a wide range of sources in this book led me to new questions, answers, and conclusions about the deep-time Yorùbá history. In their assortment and varieties, these sources allow for cross-referencing, and their divergence from one another is as informative as their convergence. Each of these sources has different imports for various experiences of time. I depend on linguistic and archaeological sources, for example, to understand the prelude to the formation of the Yorùbá community of practice, especially between AD 250 and 800. And archaeology, material science (including petrology and geochemistry), oral traditions, myth-historical sources, and visual arts/iconography are central to my investigation of how the community of practice came into existence and thrived between AD 800 and 1840. Through close reading, I mined nuggets of history from the few documentary sources and interwove them with archaeological, oral, and myth-historical sources to illuminate the quotidian lives and the impacts on the cultural and social changes as a result of the Yorùbá entanglement in the early modern commercial revolution. Although my primary research inspired this book, I have benefited from the research findings and secondary sources generated by others in different parts of the Yorùbá region and beyond, and across many disciplines.

Summing Up

My use of eclectic methodology is consistent with the nature of cultural history as a transgressive form of historical studies.[44] With its rejection of methodological purity and de-emphasis of disciplinary loyalty, cultural history has imported and adapted ideas and methods from almost every discipline in the humanities and social sciences. This book belongs to this cast of studies. In the following pages, therefore, history meets anthropology, material science engages mythology, pottery and poetry are reconciled in their historical contexts, and everyday philosophies and language are in conversation. In this regard, this book is as much an anthropology-infused history as it is a history-infused anthropology. Or, put differently, it is an anthropological view of the past and a historical vision of how the present came to be. For reasons that will become obvious in the following chapters, this eclectic methodology and infidelity to one source are necessary for a study that makes historicity of experience, practice, and cultural forms the focus of its inquiry. Writing about the past requires some creativity in interpreting the information derived from our multifaceted sources. The imagination that we deploy is shaped by the kinds of questions we seek to answer and the story we want to tell. Whenever possible, I have used certain individuals and materials as the springboard for my narratives and structural analysis of events, actions, thoughts, and practices. The names of many historical actors are preserved in the oral traditions and documentary sources. In other sources, especially in archaeological sites, we come across the remains of individuals whose names we do not know. I have taken the liberty of giving these individuals nicknames—first, to acknowledge their personhood as social beings whose actions and thoughts contributed to the making of Yorùbá history, and second, to realize my preference for the narrative style in some sections of the book.

Altogether, the questions and themes that drive the wheel of this book, as well as its methodological plurality, lead to new answers that disrupt some of the canonical renditions in Yorùbá historiography and public performances of history. These conclusions do not always fit the familiar molds of interpretation. It, therefore, becomes necessary to develop new molds, what William Sewell calls "new vocabularies and conceptual schemas," for the building blocks of Yorùbá history.[45] All of these challenge us to imagine Yorùbá history in new ways and to rethink what we believe we know about it.

Notes

1. "Everything has a history" is a recent mantra of the American Historical Association aimed at affirming the ever-present qualities of historical understanding in everyday lives and multiple scales, from personal decisions and household budgeting to public policies. See Grossman's essay "Everything Has a History."

2. Vogel, "Foreword," 10.

3. Ulin, *Understanding Cultures*, 211.

4. The list is long and includes the following: Ajayi and Alagoa, *Black Africa*; Depelchin, *Reclaiming African History*; Jewsiewicki and Newbury, *African Historiographies*; Schmidt and Patterson, *Making Alternative Histories*; Sweet, "Reimagining the African-Atlantic Archive."

5. For example, Gabel and Bennett, *Reconstructing African Culture History*; Falola and Jennings, *Sources and Methods*; McCall, "Prehistory as a Kind of History"; Philips, *Writing African History*; Vansina, *Oral Tradition.*

6. These "nonwritten" sources are oral traditions, linguistics, archaeology, social and political structure, Ifá literary corpus, praise songs, art forms, ritual and ceremony, and weaponry.

7. Some of the major archaeological works on the Yorùbá region over the past forty years include Agbaje-Williams, *Contribution to the Archaeology of Old Oyo*; Alabi, *Environmental Archaeological Study of the Coastal Region*; Aleru, *Investigation into Aspects of Historical Archaeology*; Aremu, *Archaeology of North-East Yorubaland*; Babalola, *Archaeological Investigation of Early Glass*; Ogundiran, *Archaeology and History in Ìlàrè District*; Ogunfolakan, *Conflict, War, Displacement and Archaeology*; Oyelaran, *Archaeological and Palaeoenvironmental Investigations*; Usman, *Yoruba Frontier.* All are products of research that originated as doctoral dissertations. For a recent synthesis of the archaeology of the Yorùbá region, see Usman and Falola: *The Yoruba: From Prehistory.*

8. Haberland, *Leo Frobenius*, 3.

9. González-Ruibal, "Archaeology and the Time of Modernity."

10. These chronological types (periodization) tend to be tripartite: precolonial, colonial, and independence periods. There have been attempts to delineate a periodization scheme for the precolonial, but these also usually end up being tripartite and arbitrary. Therefore, we have such slices of time as pre-classical, classical, and post-classical (Willett, *Ife in the History of West African Sculpture*); pre-pavement, pavement, and post-pavement (Eyo, *Recent Excavations at Ife and Owo*); or pre-efflorescence, efflorescence, and post-efflorescence (Blier, *Art and Risk*). There are other versions that seek a two-level chronology, as in "pre-urban" and "urban" (Agbaje-Williams, *Archaeology and Yoruba Studies*).

11. Ehret, "Linguistic Archaeology," 125.

12. De Luna, Fleischer, and McIntosh, "Thinking across the African Past."

13. Examples include de Luna, *Collecting Food*; Ehret, *African Classical Age*; Gonzales, *Societies, Religion, and History*; Klieman, *"Pygmies Were Our Compass"*; Saidi, *Women's Authority and Society*; Schoenbrun, *A Green Place*; Stephens, *History of African Motherhood*; Vansina, *Paths in the Rainforest.*

14. See Kusimba, *Rise and Fall of Swahili States*; Pikirayi, *Zimbabwe Culture*; and Stahl, *Making History in Banda* for the Banda region in modern Ghana.

15. This periodization scheme is a revision and an expansion of the one that I first developed in 2003. See Ogundiran, "Chronology, Material Culture, and Pathways."

16. Adetugbo, "Yoruba Language."

17. For Yorùbá case studies of this process, see Peel, *Religious Encounter*; Zachernuk, *Colonial Subjects.*

18. Andrew Apter has also made this point in *Oduduwa's Chain*, 155.

19. Lave and Wenger, *Situated Learning*; Wenger, *Communities of Practice.*

20. Also see Roddick and Stahl, "Introduction," 5.

21. *Proto-Yoruboid* is a scholarly term for the ancestral ethnolinguistic group from which the present Yorùbá, Igala, and Itsekiri speech communities

derived. See Akinkugbe, *Comparative Phonology*; Armstrong, *Study of West African Languages.*

22. For a contrast, see Akintoye, *History of the Yoruba*; Smith, *Kingdoms of the Yoruba.*

23. Hühn, "Event and Eventfulness."

24. Pym, *Exploring Translation Theories.*

25. Burke, *Varieties of Cultural History*, 201.

26. In the literature, the Yorùbá word *ọba* has been translated mostly as king. However, some scholars have recently challenged the appropriateness of this equivalent, noting that whereas *ọba* is a genderless term referring to the divine head (male or female) of a territory or polity, *king* strictly refers to a male crowned head in the English language. While I acknowledge this distinction between *ọba* and king, I have treated the term *king* in this book as a genderless concept when writing about the Yorùbá. That is, a king can be a biological male or female as is the case for an *ọba*. By the same logic, a kingdom can be led by a male or female king.

27. Drewal, Pemberton, and Abiodun, *Yoruba*, 14.

28. Ulin, *Understanding Cultures*, 164.

29. Frank, *What Is Neostructuralism?*, 7.

30. Andah, "Prologue," 2.

31. Andah, "Studying African Societies," 180.

32. Between 1986 and 1990, I trained under Professor Agbaje-Williams in his archaeological, historical, and ethnographic fieldwork across the Ìjẹ̀ṣà country. Agbaje-Williams, Fieldnotes; Agbaje-Williams and Ogundiran, *Cultural Resources*; Ogundiran, *Archaeological Reconnaissance*; Ogundiran, "Archaeological Survey at Ipole-Ijesa"; and Ogundiran, *Archaeology and History.*

33. I particularly acknowledge the following: the British Museum, London; the Fowler Museum, the University of California at Los Angeles; the Metropolitan Museum of Art, New York; Mint Museum Randolph, Charlotte; National Museum, Ilé-Ifẹ̀; National Museum, Lagos; National Museum, Èsìẹ́; Obòkun Temple, Ìbòkun; Oduduwa Grove, Ilé-Ifẹ̀; Ọbàtála Temple, Ilé-Ifẹ̀; Ọ̀ṣun Lákọ́kàn Temples in Ìsàlẹ̀-Ọ̀ṣun and Ọ̀ṣun Grove, Òṣogbo; Ọ̀ṣun Temples in Ọ̀ṣun Grove and Atáọ́ja Palace, Òṣogbo; and Ọwá Àdìmúlà Palace, Iléṣà.

34. Goering, "Concepts, History"; Müller, "On Conceptual History"; Stephens and Fleisch, "Theories and Methods."

35. E.g., Akinjogbin, *Cradle of a Race*; Beier, "Before Oduduwa"; Ogunba, "Ceremonies"; Verger, "Oral Tradition in the Cult of the Orishas."

36. Mali, *Mythistory*, 4–5.

37. Drewal, Pemberton, and Abiodun, *Yoruba*, 158. Also see Isichei, *Voices of the Poor.*

38. There are, however, different approaches and assumptions relating to the use of subject epistemologies for studying the past. For example, Schmidt and Kehoe, *Archaeologies of Listening.*

39. The major ones relevant to Yorùbá studies, all published, include Barbot, *Description of the Coasts*; Bosman, *New and Accurate Description*; Dapper, *Description de l'Afrique*; Jones, *German Sources, West Africa.*

40. The first ca. 1500–1508 (Pereira, *Esmeraldo* [for English translation, see Kimble, *Esmeraldo*]), and the second in 1553 ("Relatorio de Jacome Leite a

el-Rei," August 8, 1553, in Brasio, Monumenta Missionaria, 2:292 [see Ryder, *Benin and the Europeans*, 74]. Although there were mentions of Ìjẹ̀bú-Òde in the Dutch writings of the seventeenth and eighteenth centuries, these were plagiarized copies of Pereira's writings. Law, "Early European Sources."

41. Clapperton, *Journal of a Second Expedition* (Also see Bruce-Lockhart and Lovejoy, *Hugh Clapperton*); Hallett, *Niger Journal*; Lander, *Records of Captain Clapperton's Last Expedition* (2 vols.); Lander and Lander, *Journal of an Expedition.*

42. Curtin, *Africa Remembered.*

43. For example, Hinderer, *Seventeen Years*; Crowther, *Journal of an Expedition*; Curtin, *Africa Remembered.*

44. Glickman, "*Cultural Turn.*" Also see Burke, *Varieties of Cultural History.*

45. Sewell, *Logics of History*, 5.

Part II: Birth of the Yorùbá Community of Practice, ca. 300 BC–AD 1420

2

The Emergence of a House Society

ONE DAY IN THE THIRD or second century BC, a young adult of about twenty to twenty-four years old was laid to rest in Ìtaàkpá rockshelter (Iffe-Ijumu), in southwest Niger-Benue Confluence (see fig. 1.1). Buried about fifty centimeters below the then ground surface, the individual's final resting place was dug into a layer of cultural debris that had accumulated at the site over several centuries. The debris included thousands of stone chips and flakes (debitage from microlithic tool manufacture), quartz microlithic tools, and ground stone axes. The bones of small and medium-sized animals (e.g., antelope), plant materials (especially palm kernel remains), pottery, and tubular beads made of ceramic and resin were also present in the sediment where the individual was buried.[1] By the time this person was born, the speakers of proto-Yoruboid had occupied the confluence area for about twenty-five hundred years. They were one of several proto-Benue-Kwa language groups in the Niger-Benue Confluence area during the third century BC.[2] The others included proto-Nupoid, proto-Akpa, proto-Idoma, proto-Tiv, proto-Igbira, and proto-Bassa. Each of these language communities was territorial and had adapted to specific ecological niches and geomorphological landscapes for more than two millennia. The proto-Yoruboid speakers were mainly in the southwest region of the confluence, and the individual likely spoke this language. We do not know the individual's name or sex. Given that *ọni* is the generic word for "person" or "personhood" among the contemporary speakers of about seven Yorùbá dialects in the southwest confluence area, I will refer to this individual as Ọni Ìtaàkpá (the Person of Ìtaàkpá) or simply as Ọni (table 2.1).[3]

Table 2.1. Vocabulary for *Person* in Yorùbá Dialects, Itsekiri, and Igala

Dialect (Yoruba Region)	Subdialect/Town	Person
Okun (Northeast)	Ijùmú	ọni
Okun (Northeast)	Ìsánlú (Yàgbà)	ọni
Okun (Northeast)	Owé	ọni
Èkìtì (North central)	Àkúrẹ́	ọni
Èkìtì (North central)	Ọyẹ́-Èkìtì	ọni
Èkìtì (North central)	Adó-Èkìtì	ọni
Èkìtì (North central)	Ùsẹ̀-Èkìtì	ọ̀nìyàn
Èkìtì (North central)	Ọ̀rìn-Èkìtì	ọ̀nìyàn
Èkìtì (North central)	Ìgèdè-Èkìtì	ọ̀nìyàn
Èkìtì (North central)	Ẹfọ̀n-Aláayè	ọ̀nìyàn
Ìjẹ̀ṣà (Central)	Iléṣà	ọ̀nìyàn
Ifẹ̀ (Central)	Ilé-Ifẹ̀	ọ̀nìyàn
Ọ̀wọ̀ (East)	Ọ̀wọ̀	ọnẹ
Àkókó (East)	Ìkárẹ́ Àkókó	ọnẹ
Ìkálẹ̀ (Southeast)	Ìkálẹ̀	ọnẹ
Ìlájẹ́ (Southeast)	Ìlájẹ́	ọnẹ
Yéwá (Southwest)	Ìlarò	ẹni
Rẹ́mọ (South central)	Ṣàgámù	ẹni
Ìbọ̀lọ̀ (Central)	Òkò	ẹni
Àkókó (East)	Ọ̀kà-Àkókó	eni
Ọ̀yọ́ (North central)	Ọ̀yọ́ Town	ènìyàn/èéyán
Ìgbómìnà (North central)	Ìlá	ènìyàn/èéyán
Ìjẹ̀bú (South central)	Ìjẹ̀bú-Ìlesè	ènìyàn/èéyán
Ẹ̀gbá (South central)	Abẹ́òkúta (Aké)	ènìyàn/èéyán
Òǹkò (Northwest)	Òkè-Ihò	ẹnìkẹn
Oǹdó (Southeast)	Ilẹ̀-Olújǐ	iáyé
Oǹdó (Southeast)	Oǹdó Town	iáyé
Àkókó (East)	Ùgbẹ̀-Àkókó (Àkókó)	ọnà
Itsekiri	Itsekiri	ọnẹ/ọniye
Igala	Igala	ọnẹ

The over-two-thousand-year-old accumulated deposits in Ìtaàkpá show that the rockshelter was frequented for several centuries before and after the burial. Located between two granitic hills, the Ògìdì and Oróké-Ọ̀tún, the rockshelter overlooks a narrow valley through which a seasonal stream, Apamimoya, now runs (fig. 2.1). Bare and vast granitic hills, slopes of different gradients, broad and narrow valleys, and several rockshelters define the landforms of the area. Hundreds of rivulets, streams, and rivers cut through this rugged but scenic landscape, emptying into the nearby Niger River. This area, like other parts of the Niger-Benue Confluence, was thriving with agricultural communities during the third and second centuries BC. Ọni would have belonged to one of the several hundreds of households and hamlets occupying the southwest confluence during this period. These populations lived mostly on the gentle slopes at the lower altitudes of the hills, rather than on hilltops or in the valley below. The sloping landscape offered better drainage than the valley floors, especially during the rainy seasons. It was in these foothill areas where simple homes, made of grass and clay, would have been constructed. Since the hills far outnumber the rockshelters, we can assume that the latter were accessible to only a very few families. The rock overhangs were valuable as shelters, and they were used for defense and recreation.[4] They also provided a great view of the valley below and the hilltops around. These rockshelters were part of the hill complexes highly revered in the area as embodiments of sacred power. They offered access into some of these ancient, "timeless," massive rocks. It is understandable that families or social groups with longer ties to the area—the firstcomers—would likely have laid claim to the rockshelters as a means of invoking special relationships with the landscape. Those special relationships were also the basis of claims of privilege, power, and authority. For their multiple uses and symbolic value, therefore, the rockshelters would have been coveted places where the rights of land ownership and sociopolitical authority were negotiated and contested among the different agricultural and even hunter-gatherer communities that populated the landscape. Whereas most people would have been buried along the slopes within and around the residences, burial within the rockshelters would have served as a means of claiming ownership of, and marking a special relationship with, the landscape over which the granitic hills towered. That is, such burials served to establish the privileged relationship that a family had with the dominant landforms in the area—the hills. They were a vital action of memory making and inscription of genealogy-derived authority on the landscape. This would explain why Ìtaàkpá rockshelter was used continuously for about two thousand years.[5]

In the context of the Late Stone Age history of West Africa, Ọni Ìtaàkpá's deep-time ancestry possibly belonged to the eastern branch of the

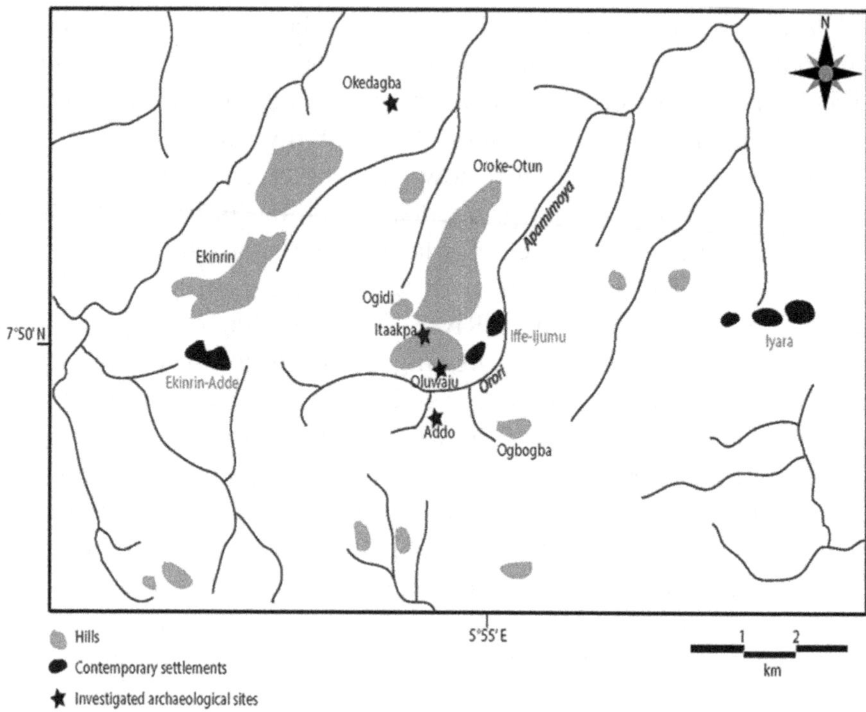

Figure 2.1. Archaeological sites in Iffe-Ijumu

Niger-Congo people known as proto-Benue-Kwa.[6] These people moved from the dry grassland into the wooded (guinea) savanna during the sixth millennium BC. Before that, their proto-Niger-Congo ancestors in what is now the Western Sudan had adapted to the warm climate and higher precipitation that kicked off the Holocene era during the twelfth millennium BC. The then vast open savanna grassland vegetation included a variety of edible wild grains that spread across the dry but more humid landscape.[7] There is archaeological-paleoecological evidence in what is now Dogon country in Mali (Ounjougou region) that the proto-Niger-Congo hunter-gatherers invented pottery and used these clay vessels to cook and store the wild grains that they collected. Chief among these grains were sorghum and fonio. Through horticultural experiments, these grains were soon domesticated. Considering that pottery making is an exclusively female activity among almost all Niger Congo peoples today, one can argue that proto-Niger-Congo women played the major role in the invention of pottery during the tenth millennium BC in Ounjougou region. They might also have played a central role in the domestication of sorghum and fonio during the same period. By 6000 BC, a branch of these proto-Niger-Congo peoples left the dry savanna area in the north and settled in the wet, guinea (woodland) savanna in the south. There, they developed a new subsistence culture that was based on a different kind of agriculture—the cultivation of yams and palm oil rather than grains.[8] Valued for their oil and wine (food) as well as fibers and wood (crafts, clothing, and house construction), the palm trees were most likely self-propagating around the settlements of these pioneer farmers, but the trees would have been jealously protected by families who laid claim to the land on which they grew. In contrast, yams had to be planted using a cutting of the tuber. Over the next one thousand years, the descendants of these migrants from the dry grassland developed a new branch of the proto-Niger-Congo language. Today, we call these pioneer farmers in the guinea savanna the proto-Benue-Kwa speakers.

Both yams and palm trees thrive in the woodland, but only in the cleared areas where they have direct access to sunlight. Hence, to effectively cultivate yams in the thick vegetation of the guinea savanna, the proto-Benue-Kwa people developed ground stone implements, especially axes and adzes, for clearing the vegetation cover.[9] These tools they added to the much older microlithic tools initially developed for hunting but also used for harvesting grains in the dry grassland. The proto-Benue-Kwa farmers were very successful in this moist and wooded landscape. Armed with stone axes and adzes, they spread across the guinea savanna and penetrated the West African rain forests. Tools were not the only innovations they brought. They also introduced new methods of farming whereby the vegetation they cut down was scattered on the ground to protect the lateritic soil from erosion and hardening as a result of torrential rainfall and the effect of the scorching sun.[10] These Late Stone Age (LSA) people did not, however, forget their past. They had the advantage of the dry savanna heritage, and they brought this into the wet and thickly vegetated woodland. Hence, not only did they cultivate yams, palm oil, and raffia palm, which were all native to the guinea savanna, but they also introduced some of the crops of the grassland, such as fonio, millet, and sorghum, into the woodland. They were able to cultivate these in open areas where the vegetation was light and the soil was suitable. Moving into the rain forest, they collected and later grew crops such as okro, aerial yams, and varieties of legumes that are native to the woodland savanna and high rainfall zones.[11] No wonder that, with this mixed agricultural economy, in addition to hunting and fishing, by 2500 BC the proto-Benue-Kwa descendants succeeded in populating a vast area of the guinea savanna and the rain forest stretching from present-day Côte d'Ivoire to Cameroon.[12] They possibly also adopted domesticated goats from their northern Sahelian neighbors by 3000 BC.[13]

The proto-Yoruboid was one of the language communities that developed from the proto-Benue-Kwa expansion between ca. 4000 and 2500 BC. The Niger-Benue Confluence had the most substantial diversity of these languages. While some of these proto-Benue-Kwa siblings in the confluence pushed southward into the rain forest belt, where proto-Igboid, proto-Bantu, and proto-Edoid took root, a large number of them, including the proto-Yoruboid, proto-Nupoid, proto-Akpa, proto-Idoma, proto-Tiv, proto-Igbira, and proto-Bassa, stayed behind in the guinea savanna of the confluence. The proto-Yoruboid group demonstrated a preference for the mountainous landscape of the southwest confluence, with its stable but diversified ecology. The intermixture of predominantly savanna and patches of the forest in this area provided the Yoruboid ancestors the opportunity to diversify their subsistence strategies. The dentition of the Ìtaàkpá adult, for example, indicates a diet that was based on the mixture of farming and hunting-gathering.[14] The presence of polished stone axes (for digging and tree felling) and microlithic tools (for hunting) in the soil layers where Ọni was buried provides additional evidence of this subsistence diversity.

Tuber cultivation defined the agricultural practice of the proto-Benue-Kwa peoples. This innovation was an adaptation to the wooded savanna, but it required an enormous amount of work in vegetation clearing. The nature of agricultural strategy in the mosaic guinea savanna and rain forest landscape may have forced the proto-Benue-Kwa men to assume more roles in farming ca. 5000 BC than their proto-Niger-Congo ancestral fathers did in the dry grassland homeland. Historical ethnography indicates that yam cultivation was associated with men's labor in most parts of ancestral Benue-Kwa communities. Among their contemporary descendants in woodland savanna and the rain forest still committed to an agrarian lifestyle, from Côte d'Ivoire to Nigeria, the yam is the preeminent symbol of male identity and manly achievement, as well as a marker of masculine "social prestige."[15] The planting and harvesting of yams also remained one of the central ways of measuring time and paying homage to the deep-time ancestors in those agrarian communities.[16] All of these indicate the primary role that yam cultivation played in the deep-time history of Benue-Kwa peoples. The association of yam cultivation with the proto-Benue-Kwa masculine attributes does not mean that the womenfolk were relieved from agricultural labor. To the contrary, they were the anchor of their sedentary agrarian society. They were responsible for cultivating most of the other crops, especially vegetables and legumes. Tending farming plots near the household likely allowed women to perform subsistence activities while caring for the aged and the children in an efficient way. They also engaged in a myriad of craft, including potting and weaving. In addition to yam cultivation, palm wine tapping, and palm tree fruit harvesting, the men also engaged in hunting, wood carving, and manufacture of stone tools. A complex gendered division of labor had, therefore, evolved over those five thousand years, before the birth of Ọni Ìtaàkpá, to support agricultural and craft innovations in the woodlands of West Africa.

Historical linguistic evidence has shown that the ancestral proto-Niger-Congo peoples were matrilineal in their social configuration.[17] However, it is likely that the proto-Yoruboid were already innovating and experimenting with the double matrilineal and patrilineal descent traditions by the time Ọni was born, as a result of the increasing gendered divisions of labor and the interdependency of both the male and female work for social sustainability.[18] Nevertheless, we should come to terms with the fact that the world in which Ọni was born did not emphasize that girls should become wives but instead socialized them to become mothers. And boys were raised to become men based on their social roles as a father rather than to become a husband. The reason is that in Ọni's deep-time proto-Benue-Kwa ancestry, family units were built around the genealogy of mothers, and cohabitation of male and female partners was matrilocal. A man lived with his female partner's family, and the children also lived and were socialized in their mother's family or household. Before the liaison between a young man and young woman could be formalized and publicly recognized, the former provided the latter's family with a myriad of services, including giving farm labor, tapping wine, hunting game, and possibly making stone and wooden tools for the woman's family. After satisfactory performance, the matriarchal household would permit the suitor to move in as the liaison of a daughter of the house. This implies that this male could be expelled by the household if it was deemed necessary, and he too could leave to return to his mother's house or enter into a new relationship. But the longer a man stayed in the household of his female companion (the mother of his children), the more his ranking and authority increased. After all, *tí ewé bá pẹ́ l'ára ọṣẹ, a má a d'ọṣẹ*: "if a leaf stays long enough on the soap, it becomes part of the soap." In this arrangement, the headship of a family or household was a shared responsibility between the oldest and assumed wisest male and female, who also served as the chief priests of the house, acting as spiritual intermediaries between the people of the multifamily household and the ancestral spirits. In these dual-gendered roles, the male and female coheads also adjudicated disputes and allocated resources. This arrangement of matrilocality benefited women more than men. It allowed women and their natal households to control their own labor and that of others. Most important, the matrifocal households dominated the redistribution of agricultural products. They were the repository of surplus. This could be why the women in Niger-Congo cultures, especially the descendants of proto-Benue-Kwa (including the Yorùbá), have dominated the market space even to this day.

At least four millennia before Ọni was born, the proto-Benue-Kwa female ancestors also seem to have figured out how to make clothing fabric from the fibers of the raffia palm's long leaves. These women, as early as ca. 4000 BC, invented an earlier version of the broadloom for weaving fabric sheets from raffia fibers, which they used to clothe the members of their households.[19] Christopher Ehret described this invention as a "major historical significance over the longer term."[20] Raffia cloth was a prestige and social-capital good among the proto-Benue-Kwa peoples, and it may have laid one of the foundations for long-distance trading in the region, moving along the same exchange routes that ground stone axes (manufactured by men) traveled across West and Central Africa. Raffia fibers were not only used for weaving cloth. They were also utilized to make basketry, rope, hats, and possibly sandals. With the varieties of soft and hard wood that the proto-Benue-Kwa encountered in their guinea savanna and rain forest environment, Ọni could also boast of an ancestral legacy that was versatile in wood carving. Some of the animals that were hunted in the diverse landscape also provided the skins for drum making. Wood carving and membrane drums (animal skin on hollowed wood), two critical contributions of Ọni's ancestry to the world heritage of visual art and music, played significant roles in the religious and aesthetic expressions of the proto-Yoruboid and other Niger-Congo peoples. Both endeavors were predominantly male spheres of craftsmanship, as were the manufacture of agricultural and hunting tools. The menfolk possibly also carved the wooden mortars and pestles used for pounding boiled yams into the thick but smooth-textured foofoo (*iyán*), the reputed king of all foods among the Yorùbá and most other woodland savanna and rain forest peoples of West Africa till today.

Ọni's deep-time proto-Benue-Kwa ancestors also practiced a version of monotheism in which the "Creator God" or "God of Beginning" sat atop a pyramid of spirits and deities. According to Christopher Ehret, we can reconstruct a specific word for the Creator God, *Nyambe*, in the proto-Benue-Kwa language to the sixth millennium BC, and he also noted that the wide distribution of the term in contemporary Niger-Congo languages indicates that it may well go back to the very beginning of Niger-Congo civilization in the twelfth millennium BC.[21] For Ọni Ìtaàkpá and the other proto-Yoruboid people, that Creator God lived on the top of and beyond the massive and ageless granitic hills of the southwest confluence. In a tradition that continues till today among many Yorùbá subgroups, the sky god is believed to reside on those hills and is associated with "the making of rain and the creation of the day."[22] The proto-Yoruboid believed that the sky god ruled over the elements of the sky—thunder, lightning, and rain—and their earthly implications—fertility of the soil, water, and agricultural productivity.[23] Those bare granite formations were the anchor of the hamlets and homesteads that dotted the lower slopes of the rugged landscape in the last quarter of the first millennium BC. They were more than the backdrop for the proto-Yoruboid communities. They were also the compasses that provided individuals and communities with a sense of direction and their location in space and time. Not surprising, as women were the pillars of the society into which Ọni was born, these massive rocky hills were also gendered feminine, as evident in the names many of them still bear and the fertility attributes they are accorded.[24] The Creator God of the proto-Yoruboid world was likely androgynous but may have been more feminine than masculine in the gender spectrum. However, the Creator God was a distant figure in the everyday religious lives of the proto-Yoruboid and other proto-Benue-Kwa groups. The focus of worship was on the territorial deities presiding over the hills, valleys, drainages, and other landscape features as well as on the ancestors—the deceased heads, priests, and priestesses of houses, families, villages, and communities. The ancestors were incorporated into the pantheon and called upon to intercede with the greater and more distant Creator God and the territorial deities during the daily devotions, seasonal festivals, and times of crisis.

The Big Dry

The proto-Yoruboid world was stable in terms of technology, ecology, social structure, and economy for more than two millennia. However, Ọni Ìtaàkpá's short life unfolded at the beginning of dramatic climatic, technological, and social transformations. This individual was born soon after the onset of the six-hundred-year climatic crisis, dubbed "the Big Dry."[25] Characterized by a new seasonal pattern that reduced the duration and predictability of rainfall and increased the length and intensity of the dry season, this crisis lasted from the fourth century BC to the third century AD across West Africa. Under this new climatic regime, the northern trade winds associated with the Northern Hemisphere's winter "brought dry air further to the south for a longer period of the year."[26] This meant prolonged dry seasons that lasted for nine months of the year became a common occurrence.

Conversely, the rainy season, if it came at all, was shortened to about three months. It arrived with violent force; it was heavy and caused damaging erosion to the land already parched by the long dry season. The cumulative consequence of these persistent episodes of low annual precipitation had a far-reaching ecological change in a matter of decades. The lake levels across West and West-Central Africa declined between 400 BC and AD 300, and the pollen counts in the profiles of these lakes show evidence of drier conditions and reduced forest vegetation.[27] The ecological crisis of the Big Dry era, lasting for about six hundred years, severely affected many areas of the guinea savanna, such as the Niger-Benue Confluence. As the water level receded drastically in the erstwhile fertile floodplains of the Middle Niger and Middle Senegal valleys, the water discharge into the Lower Niger River was also significantly reduced.[28] These ecological changes had cascading disruptive effects on the confluence peoples, including the proto-Yoruboid. The dramatic rise in oil palm pollens found in an 80 cm profile of Esa pond, in the same vicinity as Ìtaàkpá rockshelter, could be an indicator for this loss of vegetation cover, since palm trees generally thrive in direct sunlight and not in closed forest.[29]

The ecological changes that resulted from the new climatic conditions brought socioeconomic challenges, but there were also opportunities. While some cultural traditions (practices) were unable to adjust their subsistence strategies to cope with the new ecological reality, others did. For example, while the Big Dry climate change seems to have accelerated the end of the Nok culture, the Janruwa C culture in present-day Middle Nigeria emerged at the end of the first millennium BC in what appears to be a tailor-made adaptation to the era's ecological hiccups.[30] The Janruwa C people diversified their subsistence economy by taking advantage of the various ecological niches that the prolonged droughts and unpredictable rainfall had created. Likewise, the receding water level of the Inland Niger Delta (Mali) enabled iron-using agricultural communities, fishermen, and herders to move into the area for the first time ca. 300 BC and therefore laid the foundation for what later became Jenne-jeno, a major urban center in West Africa, AD 250–900.[31] Therefore, as cataclysmic as the Big Dry was across the board, there were also stories of resilience and adaptive innovations. The Big Dry era forced the proto-Yoruboid people of the confluence to adjust to the annual cycle of three-month violent and unpredictable rainfall rather than the nine months of steady rainfall to which their ancestors had been accustomed. The prolonged dry conditions meant a greater risk of famine and hunger than in the previous centuries. Animals faced the same challenges as humans, especially with the increasing thinning out of vegetation caused by multiyear droughts, increased incidences of bushfires, and acute water shortage. The returns from hunting declined severely. The involvement of men in agriculture likely intensified, far more than ever before, throughout the Big Dry period, especially with the drastic decline in the wildlife population. One challenge that was difficult to surmount was water shortage. Some of the streams that had flowed down the hills of the southwest confluence and some of the swamps in the lowlands dried up, while the discharges of many large rivers reduced remarkably during that long period of environmental cataclysm. The search for water corridors pushed many proto-Yoruboid people out of their ancestral confluence home between 300 BC and AD 200.

Another significant change coincided with the onset of the Big Dry: the adoption of iron technology. At present, the only direct evidence for iron production in the southwest confluence dates to the early first millennium AD, also in Iffe-Ijumu area (fig. 2.1). The evidence consisted of a "substantial quantity of iron slag and tuyères" found in Oluwaju rockshelter, about half a kilometer from Ìtaàkpá (see fig. 2.1).[32] The five fragments of clay nozzles found in the stratigraphic level above the one in which Ọni was buried may also have been used as tuyeres for iron production.[33] Given the ceramic stylistic continuity between the Late Stone Age and iron-bearing deposits in the Iffe-Ijumu area, it seems the same cultural groups were responsible for both the microlithic and iron technologies straddling the onset and peak of the Big Dry period. The tuyere-like nozzles in Ìtaàkpá cave also seem to belong to the same iron production complex in the nearby Oluwaju.[34] It appears, then, that Ọni was born at a time of transition from the Late Stone Age technology dominated by microliths and polished stone axes to iron technology, a long-drawn process that possibly began in the southwestern confluence by at least 300 BC. The last three centuries of the first millennium BC were, therefore, a period of mixed technology in the southwest confluence. During this period, as evident in Iffe-Ijumu, microlithic tools in Ìtaàkpá, polished stone axes in Okedagba, and a variety of utilitarian iron tools and implements in Oluwaju were all being manufactured and used simultaneously.[35] Ọni belonged to one of those proto-Yoruboid generations of the third or second century BC who were discovering the possibilities of the new iron technology. Iron had already been integrated into the technology of the nearby Nok culture by 900–700 BC,[36] and the technology likely expanded among the proto-Yoruboid in the context of the intense population reshuffling that accompanied the Big Dry. It is not clear how fast the new technology caught on, but it is certain that iron tools had become the mainstay of technological and economic life among the proto-Yoruboid populations by the end of the first millennium BC.

Farming, hunting, and domestic tools were fashioned from the bloom produced by the iron smelting furnaces being set up across the southwest area of the confluence. This new technology had a distinctive male-centered character. Given the mythology and rituality of iron among the Yorùbá and other Niger-Congo peoples, the entire chain of production associated with iron smelting and smithing was carried out only by men.[37] And the use of these tools outside the domestic space also privileged the male individual. With a broad iron hoe hafted into a long wooden stick and a machete with wooden handle, a person could bring far more land under cultivation than would have been possible with polished stone axes and digging sticks. The iron hoes were especially used to make larger heaps than what a digging stone or stick could create. This translated into more productivity in the cultivation of yams, the staple crop of the guinea savanna. The pervasiveness of iron technology gave birth to a new male. The adoption of iron tools enhanced the role of the male in agriculture. With his machete, he cleared the thickets, and with the broad-rimmed hoe, he made large heaps into which he sowed his yam tubers. Broad-bladed iron hoes and long iron machetes were the quintessential tools of the new agricultural man. The tools helped him to increase farming output and to begin to exercise more assertiveness over the landscape and over those who depended on the products of his labor. While the Big Dry era upended ecological and social stability, the adoption of iron implements in agriculture laid the groundwork for a new gender relationship. As the intensification of dry conditions prevailed for about six hundred years and forced almost all men to take on farming, these farmers also had to deal with the imperatives of finding suitable farmland in this drought-stricken landscape. This meant that the "new agrarian men" had to travel farther away from their multifamily hamlets and possibly villages to their farms. These men became the arrowheads of migration. Others followed them.

Considering all of the above, Ọni Ìtaàkpá lived at the beginning of an era of major changes that I have dubbed the Archaic period (see table 1.1).[38] It was an era of climatic change and ecological crisis, innovation in technology and social organization, and unprecedented scale of migration. More important, the period also marked the beginning of the splitting of proto-Yoruboid into new daughter languages and dialects. As men assumed an increasing role in agricultural production and led migrations into new areas in search of better environments for farming and water supply, patrilocal households likely flourished far more than ever before. This means that the households whose men were able to provide sustaining food supplies during the Big Dry period had higher chances of retaining both their men and their women. These were also the households able to bring in young women, as wives, from less-endowed families. This period was possibly the beginning of an increasing practice of virilocal residence, whereby a young woman (wife) was incorporated into the household of her male partner (husband) as a junior member. As a result, the idea and practice of wifehood (*ìyàwó*) would have gained significant ground in that era of ecological stress. These wives augmented the labor of their new homes, and their primary goal was to bear and raise children. However, Yorùbá ethnography provides clues that these women never lost membership and inheritance rights in their natal homes and could return there, especially after fulfilling the obligations of childbearing. Likewise, their children had the privilege of claiming bilateral descent.[39]

The adjustment to and consequences of the ecological crisis of the Archaic period also instigated other processes of cultural change that launched the proto-Yoruboid people on the path of sociopolitical and demographic differentiation from several of their proto-Benue-Kwa peers in the confluence area. Until the beginning of the first millennium AD, the proto-Yoruboid were undifferentiated from the other confluence language communities in group size, modes of subsistence, and technology. But as the nine-month dry season became the new normal in the guinea savanna and as several water sources dried up, it became more frequent for communities, households, and individuals to branch off from the older units in search of greener pastures. The early emigrants appeared to have stayed close to and traveled along the major rivers. Between AD 100 and 250, those proto-Yoruboid migrants birthed a new daughter language on the eastern side of the River Niger. This was the ancestor of the contemporary Igala speech community. By around 250, another wave of proto-Yoruboid migrants had reached land's end and settled on the Atlantic coast (fig. 2.2). These were the ancestors of the Itsekiri. Focusing on the exploitation of aquatic resources for their subsistence, they seem to have paddled their way downstream on the Osse River to their new destination, the estuary where the river emptied into the Atlantic Ocean. Linguistic evidence indicates that by AD 250 the proto-Yoruboid had branched into at least three daughter languages: the proto-Igala in the southeast of the confluence, the proto-Itsekiri on the estuary of River Osse and the Atlantic, and the proto-Yorùbá in the southwest of the confluence. The third was the most influential in that it gave birth to all the contemporary Yorùbá language subgroups and dialects (plate 1). Unlike the proto-Igala and proto-Itsekiri, the proto-Yorùbá radiated slowly by land in what appears to be three directions. A branch of proto-Yoruboid traveled northwest along the Moshi River. The second and larger waves of migrants spread southwest across the rugged landscape of hills, slopes, and valleys in what are now the Èkìtì and Ìgbómìnà areas. And the third group radiated southward into the Àkókó-Ọ̀wọ̀-Oǹdó-Ìlàjẹ axis. Toward the end of the Big Dry, the southward momentum of migration intensified in often overlapping directions (plate 1 and fig. 2.2). As these agricultural families, households, and communities branched off from one another and became relatively isolated in their farming villages between the years 250 and 600, they spun off several mutually intelligible dialects that laid the foundations for most of the present-day Yorùbá dialect/language continuum.

The landscape that these proto-Yoruboid ancestors were moving into, however, was not devoid of human populations. The Later Stone Age

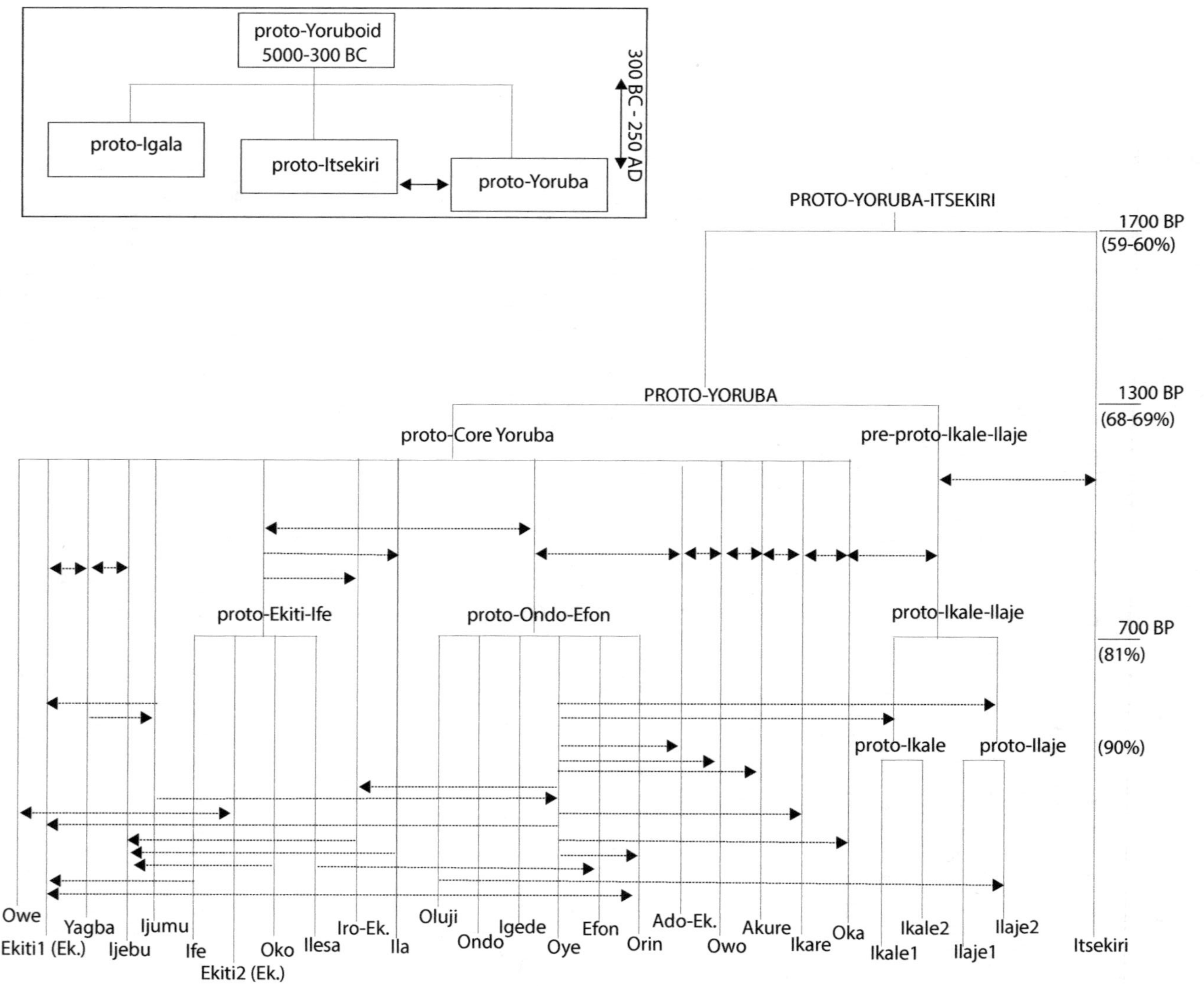

Figure 2.2. Proto-Yoruboid and Proto-Yorùbá language divergence (courtesy of Christopher Ehret)

(LSA) populations had occupied the region as early as the ninth millennium BC as shown by the findings at Iwò Elérú, near Àkúrẹ́.[40] Their numbers increased, and their populations spread across the region between the third millennium and fourth century BC, as evident at the Mèjíró rockshelter in Ọ̀yọ́-Ilé; Ìrẹ̀sì rockshelters near Ikirun; Àyànbándélé rockshelter and other sites in the environs of Ilé-Ifẹ̀; Ajíbọ́dẹ in Ibadan; Ọ̀kè-Ẹ̀rì in the Ìjẹ̀bú region; Ihò Olóko and Ìta-Ọ̀gbólú in Èkìtì; and even in the coastal areas of Badagry, among others (plate 1).[41] Nevertheless, the proto-Yorùbá migrants seem to have gained the upper hand in their southward radiation. They displaced, and also integrated, with these aboriginal LSA populations, who were already practicing a combination of agriculture, horticulture, and hunting, similar to what the proto-Yorùbá and their descendant migrants were familiar with in their Niger-Benue ancestral homeland. Two critical assets that these proto-Yorùbá migrants brought into their new homes were iron technology and a multihousehold type of sociopolitical organization.

The proto-Yorùbá ancestors seem to have followed the path of least resistance in their southward push. They avoided the territories of LSA and incipient Iron Age peoples living in the Afenmai hills, a terrain similar to that of Okun and Èkìtì. The Afenmai LSA peoples were likely the ancestors of the modern Edoid peoples—Etsako, Esan, Edo, and Urhobo, among others.[42] By the middle of the first millennium AD, these aboriginal proto-Edoid peoples were not only building large villages but also demarcating the boundaries of their communities with embankments, perhaps in competition with one another and as a defensive mechanism against the Yoruboid migrants moving into the rain forest belt. Likewise, the proto-Edoid groups were innovating their technology with the adoption of iron about the same time that the proto-Yoruboid groups were doing the same. Facing this chain of formidable communities stretching hundreds of kilometers into the rain forest, the Yoruboid migrants had no choice but to move southwesterly of River Osse where the several LSA communities living there seem to have offered the least resistance to the newcomers.

Most of the Archaic period was defined by demographic instability. The Big Dry crisis lowered the carrying capacity of most areas and prevented large population concentration. The return of a stable wet climatic regime during the fourth century AD, however, began to facilitate dependable seasonal agricultural harvests and resulted in population increase and faster localized population buildup. All of these stimulated the persistent quest for new agricultural land, especially with farming practices that depended on fallow and shifting cultivation strategies. With the increased and well-sustained precipitation, the proto-Yorùbá agricultural communities proliferated throughout the mid-first millennium, ca. 400 to 600. Although the prolonged droughts associated with the Big Dry era were the immediate cause of the original expansion and southward push of the proto-Yoruboid, the pace did not slow down with the return of the wet phase during the fourth century. Increases in population necessitated the insatiable search for suitable agricultural land, water corridors, and optimal raw materials for iron production.

There is another explanation for this expansionist drive. Before the proto-Yoruboid ancestors began to spread from their southwest confluence at the end of the first millennium BC, they seem to have shown a preference for territorialized, stratified, and institutionalized social order. Their descendants—proto-Igala, proto-Itsekiri, and proto-Yorùbá—carried this template of social organization into their new homes and immediately began to innovate it for the purpose of maximal adaptation to the diverse environments they were encountering. The success of the proto-Yorùbá demographic expansion between AD 250 and 500 likely resulted from the political culture and ideology of governance carried over from the proto-Yoruboid ancestors. During this period, the proto-Yorùbá began to split into several mutually intelligible dialects, but they retained the kernel of their sociopolitical traditions and continued to make use of the same cultural vocabulary. The evolution and splitting of proto-Yoruboid into three daughter languages—proto-Igala, proto-Itsekiri, and proto-Yorùbá—during the third century marked the beginning of what I have termed the Early Formative period (EFP).[43] This was a period characterized by large multilineage polities with institutionalized social hierarchies and political systems. There were at least two major centers for the incubation and evolution of the cultural and political practices that defined this period: the present-day Èkìtì-Ìgbómìnà (central Yorùbá) and the Oǹdó-Ọ̀wọ̀-Ìjẹ̀bú (southeast Yorùbá) axes; the latter possibly included the Itsekiri. There may have been other centers during the third quarter of the first millennium AD, especially in the present-day northwestern and western Yorùbá. However, none of these left as much impact on the later cultural development of the Yorùbá as those of the central and southeastern regions.

The migrations, encounters, and demographic growth that culminated in the Early Formative are imprinted (if only faintly) in the social memory and on the landscape of many contemporary Yorùbá-speaking communities. The language would have been an important criterion on the part of these immigrants for self-identification, interaction, and the securing of competitive advantages, especially against the aboriginal LSA communities they were meeting in their new places. Linguistic evidence indeed shows that between AD 500 and 800, there was an increased tempo in the emergence of several ancestors of present-day Yorùbá dialects—Òwè, Yàgbà, Ìjùmú, Ìjẹ̀bú, Èkìtì, Oǹdó-Ẹ̀fọ̀n, Ọ̀wọ̀, and Ìkálẹ̀-Ìlàjẹ. By the year 800, the Yorùbá dialects in what is now the central, northeastern, eastern, and southern areas of the Yorùbá world had assumed their distinctive identities (see plate 1). As these dialect variations were taking shape, however, the sociopolitical organization among them also retained a striking similarity that was the legacy of their common ancestry in the confluence.

Ilé: Sociopolitical Elaboration I

Fierce competition for territories seems to have dominated the political landscape of the mid-first millennium in the rain forest belt, especially between the Pra-Birim River in present-day south-central Ghana and River Ovia, southwestern Nigeria (see fig. 1.1).[44] Many of the village communities that emerged in that region during this time marked their territories by constructing ramparts around the perimeters of their settlements, an indication that competition for land resources accompanied the population explosion of ca. AD 500–800. The increasing precipitation that took off during the fourth century continued for the rest of the first millennium. During that period of optimum wet conditions, the imperatives for bush and forest clearing and farming accentuated the need for collaborative efforts between household units, and many of those developed into multihousehold cooperatives. A sizable population was needed to protect and maintain those cleared prime lands from potential takeover by hostile neighbors or new immigrants. Land may have been plentiful in aggregate, but not every piece of it had the same value, and with the prevailing farming strategies of leaving fields fallow and shifting cultivation, the desired parcel of land was not readily accessible to everyone. Therefore, the right to hold on to a cleared and cultivated land could be challenged by others.

As a result, a new social configuration featuring formalized association and integration of multiple households under a single leadership became necessary as a means of organizing and safeguarding land and labor. It was the beginning of a departure from the two- to three-generation households and hamlets that had been the preferred unit of social organization in the preceding centuries. The new social configuration was the House—what the Yorùbá call an *ilé* (literally, "house"), an emergent corporate group that has since formed the primary basis of the Yorùbá social organization. In its contemporary usage among the Yorùbá, *ilé* could mean a residential building, the people living in the building, or the place of origin of a community. It could also refer to a village, a town, a polity, an ancestral place, or a religious order and its members (e.g., followers of a deity). However, its most salient usage refers to a multi-sited kinship network that transcended blood and marriage ties but included and evolved from other types of interpersonal and social bonds, including patron-client relationships, friendship, and fraternities. The semantic elasticity of *ilé*, as I will show later in this chapter, illustrates the fact that this concept has been the primary and principal unit on which the Yorùbá society was organized and conceptualized for most of its history.

According to Susan Gillespie, paraphrasing Claude Lévi-Strauss, "in the absence of contractual or class-based relationships binding people to one another," the agglomeration of agrarian households and individuals into the House social formation was often the only option for creating a stable and viable social unit.[45] Lévi-Strauss called the people who operated this model of social organization *sociétés à maisons*, or "house societies." He used this concept to overcome the rigid typological limitations of kinship, lineage, and clan models, which are rarely compatible with the practices and conceptualization of social organization in societies around the world.[46] He defined the House institution thus: "A corporate body holding an estate made up of both material and immaterial wealth, which perpetuates itself through the transmission of its name, its goods, and its titles down a real or imaginary line, considered legitimate as long as this continuity can express itself in the language of kinship or of affinity and, most often, of both."[47]

I find Lévi-Strauss's concept of the House society compatible with the Yorùbá construct of the *ilé*—an estate made up of multiple households, individuals, land, skills, knowledge, history, heirlooms, deities, shrines, rituals, and certain trappings of honor, respect, fame, and even notoriety. Unburdened by the narrow kinship typologies, the House society concept is useful for theorizing and explicating the multidimensional relationships among the various Yorùbá-speaking individuals, households, and families who were forming new sociopolitical configurations in the second half of the first millennium AD.[48]

The Yorùbá House society emerged in the mid-first millennium at a time when the security of life, property, and two factors of production (land and labor) became an important social value in a competitive and sometimes hostile landscape. The quest to safeguard and multiply land and labor, in particular, heightened the need for specialized and formalized political leadership to manage social relations and organize the access of individuals and households (as members of the House) to subsistence resources, especially the land needed for rotational farming, foraging, and residence. Organized under a hierarchy of leadership, members and units of an *ilé* shared access to land and other means of production; maintained a common narrative of origin; and subscribed to the same ritual practices, deities, ancestors, taboos, and metaphysics. As a dynamic emergent and protean configuration, the concept of the *ilé* was the primary theory of knowledge that the Yorùbá of the late first millennium and the early second millennium used for conceptualizing personhood, community building, social formation, and sociopolitical organization. It was the principal foundation for anchoring people in a place as social beings, and it offered primary networks for actualizing the aspirations of individuals and households. However, this was not a one-way phenomenon. While it was through the *ilé* that an individual (descendant or ancestor) manifested personhood and sought to achieve self-realization, it was also through the individual (living or deceased) that the *ilé* could be realized. In the Yorùbá ethnographies, there are sufficient historical clues that the emergent Yorùbá House society of AD 250–750 (Early Formative period) abided by the principle of double descent—that is, an individual can belong to two or more *ilé,* on both the father's and mother's sides. Moreover, recruitment into the House and access to its resources (political, economic, and social) was by both blood and fictive kinship. And the leadership of a House was determined not only by age and genealogical seniority but also by competition. All of these gave the House the flexibility to diversify the skill sets of its members and compete for the retention and loyalty of its most valuable associates.[49]

By the end of the sixth century, fairly large clusters of multihousehold units that were contiguously located (villages) formed the preferred mode of settlement and social organization. This increasing scale of sociopolitical organization grew from the smaller prototypes that were already established by the late proto-Yoruboid in the Niger-Benue Confluence. That is, before the beginning of the "great migration" and the initial splitting of the proto-Yoruboid into daughter dialects/languages—proto-Igala, proto-Itsekiri, and proto-Yorùbá—the practice of clustering several scattered multigenerational household units (hamlets) into loose associations for reciprocity, social networking, security, and self-preservation purposes was already in place. In that system of networked households, a leader who managed conflicts and priestly functions may have been recognized. Such a leader would have been regarded as embodying the duality and complementarity of the male and female essences. If both men and women had had the opportunity of occupying the position of corporate leadership before the Archaic period, the impacts of the Big Dry crisis, the intensification of agriculture as the primary basis of subsistence, and the adoption of iron technology seem to have favored men for the leadership of these bigger sociopolitical formations during the early Intermediate period. However, one could become a House leader through patrilineal or matrilineal descent and by election, selection, or usurpation in extreme circumstances.

By the seventh century, if not earlier, such leaders bore the title of *ọba* in central and northeastern areas of the present Yorùbá region (fig. 2.3). However, in Èkìtì and Yàgbà (a subgroup of Okun), the title *ọwá* was

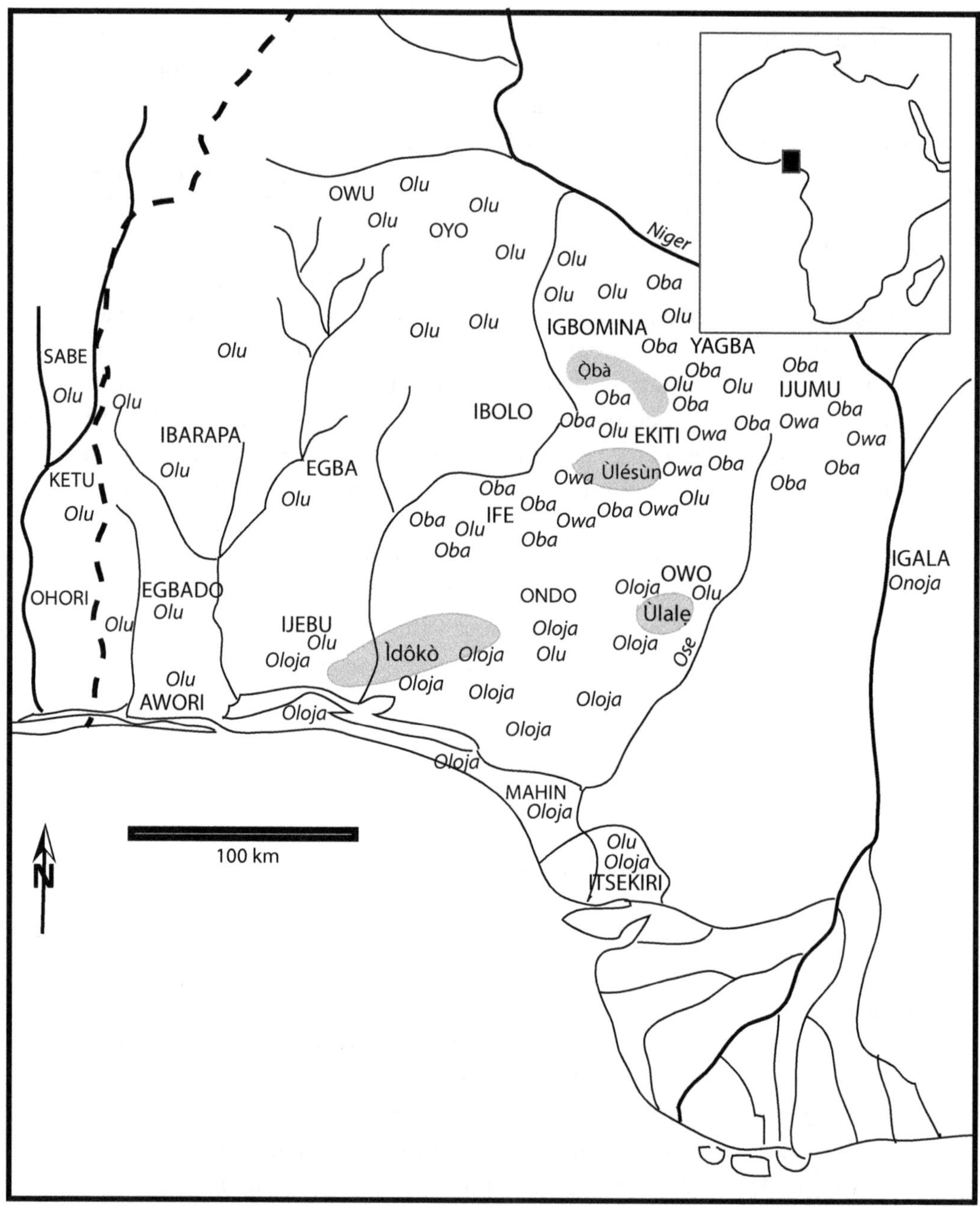

Figure 2.3. Late Formative polities (shaded) and distribution of specialized titles for leaders of *ilé*, ca. AD 500–1000

also widely used. Whereas *ọba* denotes the leader of a corporate group or House (*ilé*), *ọwá* refers to "a great house" or "Lord of the Great House."[50] Moreover, in all the descendant languages of proto-Yoruboid, the word *olú* was retained as the generic title for the ultimate leader or head of a community. This term was especially preferred in the western area of the Yorùbá region, and it served as the prefix for the title of the ultimate political leader among the Igala, the Itsekiri, and eastern and southeastern groups. However, among the Igala, the proto-Yoruboid fortis /l/ in *olú* changed to /n/: *onu*. *Ọjà* is another word that has a deep-time origin in proto-Yoruboid. Among the Igala, Itsekiri, and southeastern Yorùbá dialects (Ìjẹ̀bú, Ọ̀wọ̀, and Oǹdó, among others), the word means a settlement, village, community, or piazza. Hence, in parts of the southeastern Yorùbá area, especially in Oǹdó and Itsekiri, the title *ọlọ́jà* (a contraction of "*olú* of *ọjà*" meaning "leader of a settlement, village, or community") was predominantly used for the head of a corporate group. This is similar to the title *ọ̀nọ́jà* (*onú* of *ọjà*) used in the Igala region. In other descendant dialects of the proto-Yoruboid, in central, north-central, northwest, and southwest Yorùbá, *ọjà* became the standard term for a market or a place of congregation for business transactions, thereby retaining its proto-Yoruboid root as the term for "a shared space for public gathering."

All these titles—*ọba, ọwá, ọlọ́jà, ọ̀nọ́jà, olú*, and *onú*—originally referred to institutionalized or formal leadership designated for men. The titles were associated with the emergence and codification of *ilé* (Houses) for organizing and integrating multiple households and individuals of different origins/backgrounds into corporate groups during the Early Formative period. These corporate leaders were the conduits of social wealth and opportunities for members of their Houses, and they worked in a political economy that was based on assembling, redistributing, and managing labor, land, and skills for the benefit of the *ilé* and its members. This managerial role also allowed the *ọba* to have access to surpluses and dependents (labor). These were used to defray the cost of political power and to institutionalize social inequalities. Therefore, *ilé* was an idea and practice rooted in hierarchical social order as early as the mid-first millennium AD, if not earlier. As I will elaborate below, the households and subgroups that constituted an *ilé* were not equal, and likewise, the individuals in the *ilé* were ranked based on age, gender, heredity, life-course accomplishments, and household affiliation. Each House usually had an alpha (leading or chief) household at any given time. The surplus garnered by the alpha household enabled it to increase its numbers at a rate that was faster than that of other households in the *ilé*. And the *ọba* of a House was able to increase his household's number by attracting more women (from other Houses) as wives and therefore begetting more children. Through marriage practices, the *ọba* and other men who were close to the trappings of power were able to expand their social network much wider than the other members of the House. The *ọba* in particular had the advantage of recruiting new members into the house, including clients, captives, debtors, and immigrants who were converted into bona fide members through fictive kinship reckonings. These *ọba*, however, did not only manage people and economic resources, especially land and labor. They also managed the temples, shrines, and festivals dedicated to their Houses' deities and ancestors. Likewise, they managed conflicts, especially at the interhousehold and inter-House levels. The *ọba* were strong men, as is evident in many parts of the Yorùbá region where elaborate oral traditions exist for the exploits of such men as Àjàlọ́run Ọ̀rọ̀ of Ìlàrè, Ológò of Ògò, Ìtá of Ìlémùré, Elésùn of Ìlésùn, and Olókù of Òúkú, among others.[51] They often bore the names and titles of the founding ancestors, by which they personified the spirit of their Houses.

Hostilities, as well as cooperation and alliances, were common between contiguous Houses. Cooperation and alliances were necessary to enable the recruitment of marriage partners—the foundation for guaranteeing the sustainability of each House. Virilocal marriages no doubt helped to taper down the potentials of inter-House conflict while also ensuring interdependency and support in periods of stress.[52] Nevertheless, conflicts and outright wars occurred. As in other areas of the world, such hostilities were "part of a broader ideological agenda used in the competition for followers and typically consist[ed] of raids and skirmishes intended to weaken and delegitimize one's rivals" in the bid for land, people, and authority.[53]

True to Lévi-Strauss's proposal about House societies, the origin of the Yorùbá *ilé* was grounded in political economy. It emerged primarily to protect and to provide its members with access to "material and symbolic resources, labor, power, and legitimacy."[54] As an actor-network principle, *ilé* is semantically situational across time and place, allowing compounding and seemingly contradictory forces to be in operation at the same time—patrilineal and matrilineal descent, filiation and residence, virilocality and uxorilocality, and heredity and election, among others. Because it is a corporate body (spiritual and physical) of households, individuals, and residential groups, all members of the *ilé* are bound together ontologically by very flexible and elaborate modalities of kinship, what the Yorùbá call *ẹbí*.[55] This is an ideology of social relations and a mechanism for social bonding to make the House operational or functional; it gives the House its charter of existence and cohesion, and it helps to disguise the fundamental inequality among the members of the *ilé*. The constructivist concept of *ẹbí* (kinship—filial and fictive) enables the *ilé's* actor-network framework to operate. Together, both *ilé* and *ẹbí* constitute the instrumental, conditional, and negotiated praxis (as idea and practice) of social relations situated at "the intersection of . . . antithetical perspectives."[56] Their flexibility allows them to make rules about social formation and to break them when necessary.

From *Ilé* to *Ìlú*: Sociopolitical Elaboration II

It is at Ilé-Ifẹ̀ (also referred to as "Ifẹ̀" in this book) where the memory of the formation of House society is most elaborately preserved, although almost every part of the Yorùbá region has oral traditions that refer to this era of sociopolitical innovation.[57] For reasons that will be obvious below, the dramatic processes associated with the political history of the House complexes in Ilé-Ifẹ̀ and their later elaboration into *ìlú*—a city-state, kingdom, town, or urban space—ca. AD 900–1000 have left a stronger and more lasting imprint on the social memory of the Yorùbá region. The geography of Ilé-Ifẹ̀ played an important role in shaping this dramatic history. In the mid-first millennium, the physical landscape of Ilé-Ifẹ̀ was characterized by a seasonally flooded, swampy fourteen-kilometer-wide valley ringed by voluminous granitic hills and inselbergs with steep slopes. Geographer Lawrence K. Jeje has called this valley the Ifẹ̀ Bowl, a poorly drained but resource-rich landscape that was not attractive for settlement until about the end of the first millennium.[58] In contrast, settlements and farmlands were concentrated on the rims (edges) of the bowl (Ifẹ̀ Rims), where well-drained, fertile soils existed. It was in this area, overlooking the seasonally flooded and swampy valley below, where population buildup took place between the fifth and ninth century.

As population and settlements increased in the circumscribed rim of the Ifẹ̀ Bowl, competition for land and resources among the Houses intensified during the last centuries of the Early Formative period, perhaps as early as AD 600. The competitions spurred some of these Houses to build alliances with one another and against other Houses. The alliances resulted in the merging of two or more Houses under a wide range of arrangements. These processes resulted in the birth of the "mega-House" as a new organizational structure. This meant that some of the Houses that had acted as autonomous corporate units lost some of their autonomy in order to become members of a larger sociopolitical unit. Of course, mega-Houses were also formed through forceful incorporation of weak Houses into stronger ones. This development led to the increasing specialization and elaboration of political leadership and to a heightened territorial sensibility.[59] In Ifẹ̀ oral traditions, thirteen mega-Houses are remembered to have existed during this period of political engineering. These are Ìdó, Ìdèta, Ìlọràn, Ìlóròmú, Ìjùgbẹ̀, Ìmọjùbì, Ìráyè, Ìwìnrìn, Odin, Òkè Àwo, Òkè-Ọjà, Ọmọlógun, and Parakin (fig. 2.4).[60] Each of these mega-House polities, what Ade Obayemi called "mini-states," was a federation of contiguous Houses separated by stretches of woods that ranged in distance from a few hundred meters to about a kilometer, but a recognizable ruler from an alpha House governed each of these mega-Houses as a corporate unit.[61] The Ìjùgbẹ̀ mega-House, for example, comprised Ìjùgbẹ̀—the alpha House—and four minor Houses: Eranyiba, Igbogbe, Ipa, and Ita-Asin, each with its own leader, who was also its chief priest. All the leaders of the four corporate houses reported to Obaléjùgbè, "the Lord or Leader of Ìjùgbẹ̀." Similarly, the Ìdèta mega-House was made up of Ìdèta (the alpha House) and three other Houses: Ìlálẹ̀, Ìlésùn, and Ìlià,

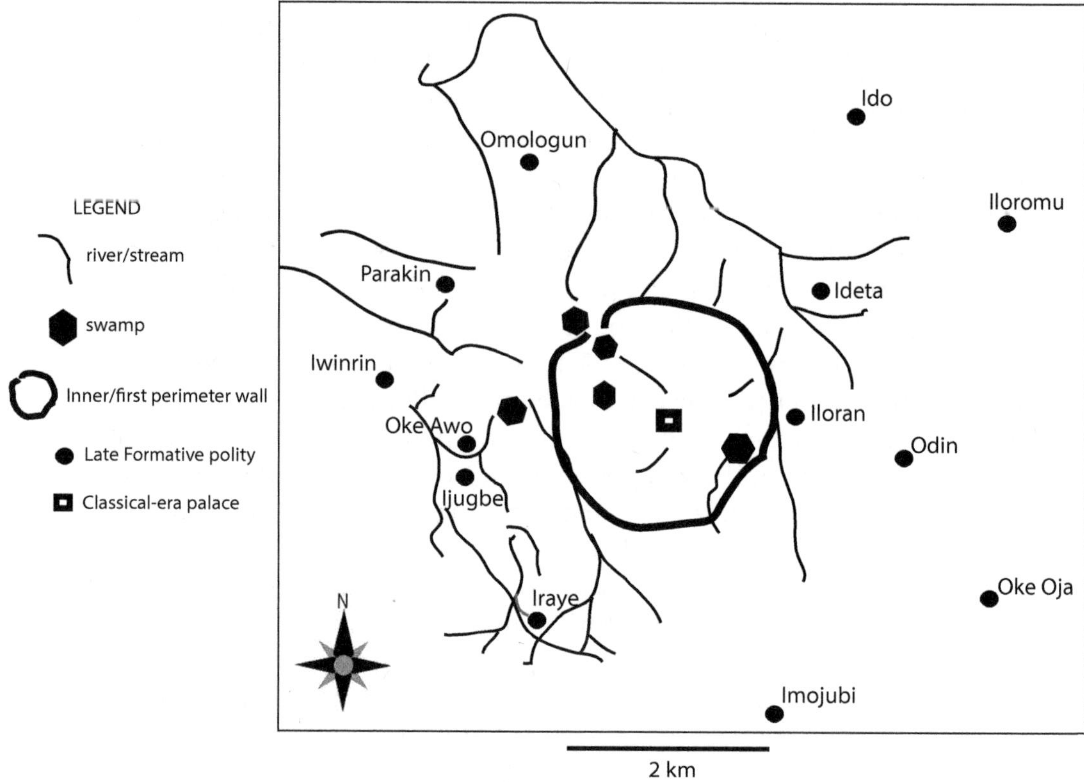

Figure 2.4. Approximate location of mega-House polities in Ilé-Ifẹ̀, ca. 800–1000

headed by Ọbalálẹ̀, Ọbalésùn, and Ọbalíá respectively. These heads of the minor Houses were in turn under the political leadership of Ọbatálá, the paramount ruler of Ìdèta.[62]

Located between the steep and rolling inselbergs above and the swampy valley below, the Ifẹ̀ Rims were the optimum areas conducive to settlement and farming between AD 500 and 900. The administration of this prime land increasingly tested the skills of the area's political leadership throughout the last two centuries of the first millennium. Managing the increasing population's access to natural and social resources, and the conflicts that ensued from the competing claims to these resources, presented opportunities for new organizational structures. As a result, several of the mega-Houses began to form themselves into confederacy-like associations. The most prominent of these was the Ifẹ̀ "confederacy," and it seems to have been formed as an alliance against other social groups in the area, especially the Ùgbò, an older group that oral traditions refer to as the aborigines of the area.[63] The Ùgbò possibly constituted a cultural and language group, one of the descendants of the Later Stone Age communities that lived in what is now Ifẹ̀-Ìjẹ̀ṣà, Ìjẹ̀bú-Òndó, and southern riverine Yorùbá regions during the first millennium BC. They did not form a united political unit. Instead, they were distributed in hamlets and small villages across the southern rain forest during the first millennium AD. Their specific relationship to the proto-Yorùbá is not clear. The Ùgbò group in Ilé-Ifẹ, also known as Olúyarè or Ìgàrè, may have consisted of several clans or subgroups. Their antiquity in the area preceded the Late Formative period, and the swampy Ifẹ̀ Bowl seems to be the preferred settlement site where they subsisted on fishing, hunting, and foraging, but with very limited farming, if at all. The ecological mosaic of the area would have encouraged interdependency and exchanges of farm and riverine products between the Ifẹ̀ of the rim and the Ùgbò of the bowl. However, as the Ifẹ̀ multiplied in number and sought a replacement for their exhausted farmland, conflicts with the Ùgbò would have been inevitable.

The Ifẹ̀ confederacy was a loose political alliance with no central political offices. Yet the head of the council (possibly chosen by his peers for his charisma, spiritual power, organizational abilities, and number or quality of followers) presided not only over secular matters affecting the confederacy as a whole but also over the rituals and ceremonies that united the confederacy in the worship of a common deity. The most notable and influential of the Ifẹ̀ confederacy leaders during the tenth or early eleventh century was an individual whom traditions remember as Ọbàtálá. Not only did he chair the Ifẹ̀ confederacy, but he was also the chief priest of the deity, Ọ̀raǹfẹ̀—literally, the Ọ̀ra of Ifẹ̀. Both the confederacy and the deity were instituted to provide a uniform identity, ideology, and organizational platform to the motley of groups who now called themselves Ifẹ̀. They needed this unified front in their struggle for self-preservation in what was becoming a very hostile situation between them and other interest groups. Oral traditions credit Ọbàtálá with promoting the adoption of Ọ̀raǹfẹ̀ as the unifying deity for the members of Ifẹ̀ confederacy and as the focus of the annual festival in which all the constituent members of the confederacy were represented. Not surprisingly, the hill (Ọ̀ra) regarded as the primal home of Ọ̀raǹfẹ̀ formed the backdrop for the ancient settlement of Ìdèta. This was where Ọbàtálá supposedly resided, and it served as the center of Ìdèta mega-House during the Late Formative period. Ọ̀raǹfẹ̀ is an avatar of the sky god that was already prevalent among the early agricultural communities in the proto-Yoruboid homeland in the confluence. Their Late Formative Yorùbá descendants in Èkìtì, Ìgbómìnà, and Ifẹ̀ areas where these granitic hill formations were also prevalent continued to associate these hills with the sky god.

The political innovations of the Late Formative period inspired the advent of representation of human figures in stone sculptures, executed in a "minimalist-realist" style (fig. 2.5). These granite sculptures are associated with the political leaders of the Late Formative period in Ilé-Ifẹ̀, such

Figure 2.5. Formative Period minimalist naturalistic figures in Èsìẹ́ (*left*, H. 82 cm) and Ilé-Ifẹ̀ (*right*, H. 103 cm)

as Ọbatálá, Orelúere, and Ìjùgbẹ̀.[64] The figures project the impression of leaders with calm and strong personalities who occupied specialized political offices that required the wearing of simple but recognizable badges of authority in the form of beaded necklaces, anklets, and waist/hip sashes. The sculptures identify these individuals as the embodiment of power, wisdom, knowledge, honor, authority, and privilege in the society. In the oral traditions, they are celebrated for their mastery of the intricacies of governance and social order.[65]

The elaborate Ifẹ̀ oral traditions on mega-House formation notwithstanding, similar political transformations and associated artistic and cultural innovations took place in multiple places across the Yorùbá region between AD 750 and 1000.[66] For example, the presence of similar minimalist-realist sculptures in nearby Èkìtì, especially at Ẹ̀ṣùrẹ́, suggests that the same sociopolitical-artistic development that prevailed in Ilé-Ifẹ̀ also thrived in the Èkìtì-Ìgbómìnà area, where this political elaboration and artistic development seems to have a deeper history.[67] In the Èkìtì-Ìgbómìnà axis, there are autochthonous traditions of origin that some of the descendant communities and polities in the area, such as Ọ̀tùn and Ọ̀bà, maintained until very recent times. For example, the Ọ̀bà people claimed that their founding ancestors did not migrate from anywhere but "emerged from the ground," and the cognomen (*oríkì*) of the Ọ̀bà describes them as *ọmọ ẹrẹ̀*, "offspring of the mud" or swamp.[68] A descendant Ọ̀bà community, six kilometers from Àkúrẹ́, claims that their ancestors did not have a pantheon of deities as in most other parts of the Yorùbá region. Rather, they worshipped the earth and a sky god "whose attributes included the making of rain and the creation of the day."[69] This community also claimed autochthonous origins and maintained that their defunct kingdom was older than that of Ilé-Ifẹ̀. In addition, there is a surviving tradition among the Ọ̀tùn (also in Èkìtì) that their founder, Òòrè, emerged from the large body of water that covered the entire earth at the time of creation.[70] A similar myth of creation is found in Ilé-Ifẹ̀. The only twist is that the founding deities/ancestors such as Ọbàtálá, Odùduwà, Ògún, and Ọ̀rúnmìlà descended from the hills of Ifẹ̀ and, working under the command of Olódùmarè (the supreme being) or Ọ̀ramfẹ̀ (the chief god of Ifẹ̀ hills), depending on the version, they magically drained the watery mass in the Ifẹ̀ Bowl and made it fit for human habitation.[71]

The slow but steady southward expansion of the various proto-Yorùbá groups in the mid-first millennium AD made the Èkìtì-Ìgbómìnà valleys the centers of incubation for the sociopolitical elaboration that later flourished in Ilé-Ifẹ̀ during the eighth or ninth century. Those accounts of origins from bodies of water refer to the swampy and poorly drained valleys in the aftermath of the return of optimal rainfall in the fourth and fifth centuries. The Èkìtì-Ìgbómìnà witnessed a large concentration of population during this period, as settlements of various sizes thrived in the fertile slopes and valleys that drained the granitic hills towering above the settled areas. In fact, between AD 500 and 800, the number of mega-House-type polities that flourished in the Èkìtì area alone, based on the oral traditions and comparative ethnography, seems to surpass that of any other contemporaneous Yorùbá subgroup.[72] Those valleys provided fertile farming grounds and secure settlement spaces, but the continuous population buildup in those narrow valleys of Èkìtì later spilled over into nearby areas, such as Ilé-Ifẹ̀.

The stone sculptures that have been found in Èsìẹ́ and its environs provide another strong indication that the Èkìtì-Ìgbómìnà area was a primary center of sociopolitical innovation in the Yorùbá region during the Late Formative period. These were executed in a more advanced and elaborate style than those of Ifẹ̀'s minimalist sculptures, and they were made of soapstone (steatite). In Èsìẹ́ alone, more than eight hundred of these figures and a handful of terracotta sculptures of men and women of very diverse social status and authority have been recorded.[73] The Èsìẹ́-type steatite figures have also been identified in the neighboring sites of Igbó Ilowe, Oko Odò, Pee, Ìjárá, and Ọ̀fàró, all within a thirty-five-kilometer radius of Èsìẹ́.[74] The radiocarbon and thermoluminescence dates of around the ninth through the early fifteenth century associated with these sculptures suggest that a sophisticated society with institutionalized full-time political leaders and diverse economic pursuits thrived in the Ìgbómìnà area contemporaneously with Ilé-Ifẹ̀. There was only a seventy-five-kilometer distance between the two. [75]

It is very likely, as Ade Obayemi has proposed, that the Èsìẹ́ figures belong to the famed Ọ̀bà cultural complex and polity, which flourished in the general area between Ìgbómìnà and northern Èkìtì beginning in the last quarter of the first millennium AD and reaching its apogee ca. 1000–1200 before its decline between 1200 and 1300 (see fig 2.3).[76] If this is the case, then the centralized sociopolitical organization and artistic tradition that defined Ọ̀bà seem far more elaborate than what prevailed in Ilé-Ifẹ̀ in the last quarter of the first millennium. The forms and styles of the soapstone figures in Èsìẹ́ give us a coarse but clear picture of the society that produced them. The diversity of hairstyles and facial marks is suggestive of a community composed of people with diverse corporate identities. Of the more than 800 sculptures, 516 depict individuals in seated poses. Ninety-nine percent of these are depicted with bead necklaces, as well as wrist and ankle beads or bracelets, even when they do not hold any other object that indicates their social status; 71 percent are male, and 29 percent are female (table 2.2). The male figures are predominantly represented as hunters, warriors, blacksmiths, diviners, medicine men, and musicians. More than one-third of the male figures hold weapons, such as a bow, quiver, shield, or dagger. On the other hand, female figures predominantly hold machetes. The stone carvers convey the impression that the male segment of the population was predominantly associated with hunting and warfare, whereas women were associated with farming. However, we should also consider that these representations were possibly meant to idealize these activities as masculine (warfare and hunting) and feminine (farming) or to invoke the essential complementarity of masculine and feminine energies in social organization. Very few of the images (representing only 1 percent of the total identified figures) show men and women in postures of servitude or as votaries. An intriguing aspect of this marginal group is their one-sided shaved heads, a hairstyle that was, and still is, associated with palace officials or with the initiates of different *òrìṣà* (deities) in many parts of the Yorùbá region.

The sculptures were executed broadly in the same style, but there are noticeable differences in the quality of craftsmanship.[77] The Èsìẹ́ sculptors focused on idealized images of adult individuals rendered mostly

Table 2.2. Tools/Implements Associated with the Èsìẹ́ Male and Female Figures*

	Male	Female
Complete/Near Complete Figures	**368**	**148**
Figures with Tools/Implements		
Dagger/bow/quiver pouch/shield	93	2
Machete	2	54
Staff	30	2
Fly whisk	5	-
Musical instrument	6	-
Total	**136**	58
Posture of Servitude or Votary Status		
Shaved-head figures	3	4
Naked figures	2	1
Kneeling/offering posture	-	4
Total	5	9

*Note: Many of the figures are broken. Only figures with at least one-third of their original form are included.

in the seated position, and in stylized naturalism. The more than eight hundred sculptures were likely made over a long period of time beyond a generation. There is evidence that the figures were sculpted with the local steatite outcrops in the vicinity where the sculptures were found.[78] The Èsìẹ́ sculptures emphasized social identity rather than individual identity. They likely served as the focus of communal memorial ceremonies to celebrate real and imagined ancestors. Here, ancestral worship seem to have served as a platform for community building rather than individual family remembrance rituals. The detailed rendition of body marks on the face and back of most of the sculptures indicates that the sculptors were concerned with depicting the House or familial affiliation and social identity of the individuals represented in the images. There are also some gender differences in clothing. Many men are depicted with conical or domed hats, whereas no woman is shown wearing a hat. However, the male figures without a hat wear the same hairstyles as women, from chevron-braided to multitiered and nodal hairstyles. Most of the images depict the male and female ancestral figures, and these may have been the initial focus of the sculptors. In time, other elements such as the votary or servant figures, musicians, and the like were added to demonstrate the completeness of the community formation that was the focus of the memorial. On the basis of the forms and styles of the soapstone figures, we can infer that the society responsible for these images had institutionalized government and social ranking in which both female and male authorities played important roles. Clothing, beaded necklaces, and wrist or ankle bracelets were markers of high status, and the variations in the number of beaded necklaces per figure may indicate the social ranking and wealth of the individuals whose essences were captured in those sculptures.

Another early center of sociopolitical intensification was the Ìjẹ̀bú area, in southcentral Yorùbá region. Radiocarbon dates secured from the profiles of the Sùngbọ́ ditch-embankment complex indicate that House and mega-House polities were flourishing in the area during the Late Formative period, if not earlier.[79] It seems that several autonomous enclosures, demarcating Houses and mega-Houses, were brought together to form one political unit during that period. As in the case of Ọ̀bà in Èkìtì-Ìgbómìnà, oral traditions faintly remember the polity of Ìdôkò as a product of this early process of synoecism with a territory that stretched from the present-day Ìdôkò in the Ìjẹ̀bú area to Ùdòko in Oǹdó.[80] This integration may have continued or renewed during the thirteenth or fourteenth century under a new political dispensation championed by the Ìjẹ̀bú-Òde kingdom and its pioneering leader, Ọbáńta.[81] By the mid-fifteenth century, at the latest, the cluster of enclosures had formed almost a single 170-kilometer-long bank and ditch that is now popularly called the Sùngbọ́ Erédò "wall" complex, encircling an area of between 1,025 and 1,400 square kilometers (fig. 2.6).[82]

The local traditions on this subject of sociopolitical development during the Late Formative period are copious across the Yorùbá world. The process was similar, with a group of House and mega-House polities uniting to form a confederacy. Strong and influential leaders from the constituent Houses were initially intended to lead these confederacies in rotation, providing ceremonial and symbolic roles rather than executive authority. However, what usually started as a ceremonial position quickly became an executive and hereditary office restricted to one House. Hence, this process of synoecism between AD 750 and 1000 also marked the beginning, across the region, of the bringing of loose associations of Houses and mega-Houses under centralized governments. By the end of the first millennium, many of them were developing a new model of political institution and settlement culture. This model involved the concentration of power in the hands of the alpha House or mega-House whose leader now had political authority (even if expressed in symbolic terms) over the other mega-Houses and Houses. These leaders were adorned with investitures of office that differed from the ones associated with the other House or mega-House leaders. The salient mark of this new leader was the headwear made with unique stone beads, of which the red jasper seems to have gained rapid popularity.

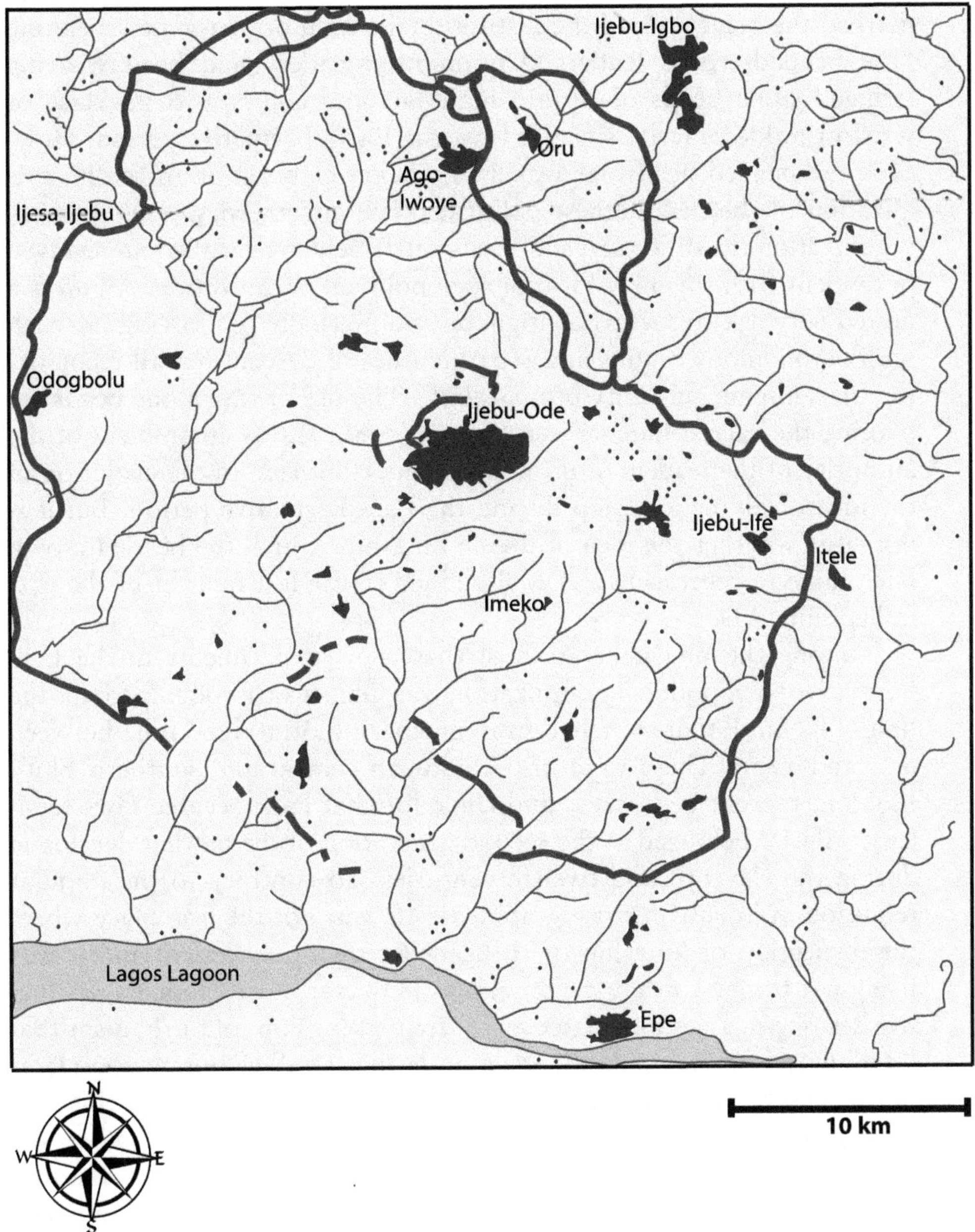

Figure 2.6. Sùngbọ̀ Erédò "wall" complex, showing major drainage and some of the extant settlements in the area (based on Darling, "Sungbo's Eredo")

The shape of the headwear recalls the type of conical hat depicted in Late Formative Èsìẹ́ and Ifẹ̀ sculptures. It appears that such conical hats were the preferred symbol of *ọba/ọwá* authority in the Ifẹ̀, Èkìtì, and Ìgbómìnà areas throughout the second half of the first millennium, but now those who had the legitimacy to wear the beaded version of these hats were recognized as *ọba-aládé*. These special hats marked the beginning of the institutionalization of *ọba-aládé*, meaning "the beaded-crown leader." Community leaders had been wearing stringed stone beads of certain materials and colors as a necklace or wrist or ankle bracelet since at least the Early Formative period. However, the beaded headwear was a significant elaboration in the materialization of the new highest political office and the new sociopolitical organization the office served. A new settlement type, called *ìlú*, evolved in tandem with this new form of sociopolitical organization. An *ìlú* is a nested network of several contiguous and mutually reinforcing *ilé*, each with autonomous origins and separate lines of descent but all recognizing the supreme authority of *ọba-aládé*. The use of rare stone beads for making the sacred hats (crowns) that now served as an emblem of the authority of the leaders of *ìlú* was an important step in the evolution of the idea of divine kingship during the Late Formative period. But it is not clear whether the idea of divine kingship, which the beaded crown later came to represent, was well defined in the last quarter of the first millennium AD.

Among the first generation of these new experiments in the Late Formative sociopolitical organization was Ọ̀bà, a vast polity, perhaps the first of its kind, that stretched from northern Èkìtì to Ìgbómìnà between 800 and 1200. There were also Ùlésùn in central and southern Èkìtì, Ìdôkò in present Ìjẹ̀bú area, and Ùlalẹ̀ in what later became Ọ̀wọ̀ territory.[83] Ilé-Ifẹ̀ belonged to the second generation of the *ìlú* that developed during the eleventh and twelfth centuries. So contrary to the popular rendition in Yorùbá historiography, Ilé-Ifẹ̀ was not the first place where the institution of kingship (with beaded crown) developed, and it was likely not the first urban center either. However, it developed a distinctive set of practices associated with divine kingship and urbanism that set it apart from its predecessors, a point that I will elaborate upon later in this and the next chapter. But for now, let us focus on how this political process unfolded in Ilé-Ifẹ̀. The history of the Ifẹ̀ area had stayed on the rim of the swampy bowl for most of the second half of the first millennium. But this was about to change. Between the tenth and eleventh century, a new consciousness of social order developed in the Ifẹ̀ Bowl that had a far-reaching impact locally. The consequences also had reverberating effect across the expansive Yorùbá-speaking world and beyond.

The Classical Period

The confederacy-like arrangement among the thirteen mega-Houses that populated the rim of the Ifẹ̀ Bowl during the Late Formative period may have minimized conflicts over access to resources, but it did not provide a lasting solution. The bowl itself seems to have been the eye of the storm. The diversity of the swamp resources and the opportunities these offered for agriculture, hunting, fishing, and water made the bowl the focus of intense population aggregation and competition during the last two centuries of the first millennium.[84] This period was the onset of a warmer hemispheric climate, when the amount of rainfall began to drop. That is, the stable optimum wet period that had begun since ca. AD 300 was now coming to an end, replaced by an unstable climate characterized by oscillation between unpredictable annual droughts and a rainfall pattern that was similar to that of today. The reduced annual rainfall started the drying-up process in the swampy Ifẹ̀ Bowl. This ecological change helped to open up the area for increased settlement and farming activities. The ensuing massive clearance of vegetation for agriculture and settlement accelerated the rate of evaporation, water runoff, and draining of the heavy clay that had characterized the swamp.[85] Those moving in were not only from the old communities on the nearby rim. Many were also migrants beyond the ring of Ifẹ̀ hills. As a result of this population increase, conflicts and the quest to define territorial boundaries accelerated. Out of this contestation emerged a group of people who succeeded in building a large perimeter wall (now known to archaeologists as the Inner Wall) in this prime ecological area during the tenth or eleventh century. Measuring about 7 kilometers in circumference with a diameter of about 2.3 kilometers, the wall was an embankment built of packed earth that enclosed what would soon become the core urban center of Ilé-Ifẹ̀. The builders used this embankment to stake their territorial claim in the bowl (see fig. 2.4).

The Inner Wall projected a strong sense of permanence and ownership, but oral traditions imply that intense conflicts characterized the events that culminated in its construction. To start, the builders of the Inner Wall were, literally and figuratively, right in the middle of at least thirteen mega-House polities that were already engaging in factional competitions among themselves (despite the confederacy) and with other groups over the control of the resources in the area. The influx of new settlers into the bowl, especially the group responsible for the building of the perimeter wall, would have affected the Ùgbò communities the most. After all, they were the ones who had lived in this area for centuries. They were therefore at the center of the conflict over the control of the bowl. Their initial nemesis were the farmers moving down from the Ifẹ̀ Rim. But the displacement of these Ùgbò settlements, caused by the construction of the Inner Wall, seems to have galvanized them to join the Ọbàtálá group against the builders of the wall. Doing so meant that they recognized the leadership of Ọbàtálá. Hence, one of the sobriquets of Ọbàtálá is *ọba Ùgbò*—that is "the leader of Ùgbò."[86] The singular objective that united the constituent members of the Ọbàtálá group was the defeat of the people responsible for the Inner Wall.

The building of the perimeter wall signaled a significant division among the Houses and mega-Houses that had constituted the Ifẹ̀ confederacy. It may even have coincided with the collapse or distress of several of the polities on the Ifẹ̀ Rim. Oral traditions have elaborate renditions of this event, claiming that there were long, drawn-out conflicts between different factions of the confederacy and between some of them and the walled settlement below.[87] Despite the attacks that were mounted against the walled settlement, the latter not only prevailed but also caused the relocation of some of the displaced population from the rims to the bowl. The Inner Wall settlement and its leaders had become the proverbial water lettuce, which always floats to the top of the pond. They had turned the Ifẹ̀ Bowl into the center of power.

Studies on social memory have shown that transformative moments or events that led to structural changes (e.g., radical changes in sociopolitical organization or worldview) often leave some of the most enduring imprints in oral traditions, even if the specificity of the original events that caused those radical changes are attenuated and mythologized in subsequent years.[88] This seems to have been the case at Ilé-Ifẹ̀, where the orature and commemorative rituals about these transformative events are very lively. The traditions unambiguously identify Odùduwà as the leader of the group responsible for building the wall. His actions reportedly destabilized the delicate balance of power among the constituent members of the confederacy and led to open confrontations. The historical narratives and analysis of the political conflicts that rocked Ilé-Ifẹ̀ between the old confederacy on one hand and the Odùduwà group on the other have received attention from a host of scholars. In both historical studies and local traditions, these conflicts tend to be reduced to the struggle between two personalities: Ọbàtálá and Odùduwà. This is a stereotypical representation of several personalities and factions involved in the conflicts that lasted several generations, in the tenth and eleventh centuries, beyond the lifetime of any of the historical actors. Nevertheless, the later phase of the conflicts coalesced into two dominant opposing camps identified with Ọbatálá (the older order) and Odùduwà (the newer order).

As the conflict raged on, many Houses and mega-Houses collapsed, and their settlement complexes were abandoned. Some of their members joined other Houses, while others moved farther away from Ilé-Ifẹ̀.[89] The annual rituals and festivals celebrating the origins of several towns, dynasties, and kingships in the central Yorùbá region often reenact these migrations.[90] Within Ilé-Ifẹ̀ itself, this conflict and its eventual resolution are the subjects of several annual commemorative festivals that have continued till today.[91] From these commemorations, we learn that the conflict between the two groups reached a stalemate for several decades, if not generations. The stalemate ended when a bout of pox epidemic, possibly a *Variola* (smallpox) outbreak, ravaged the stronghold of the Ọbàtálá House at Ìdèta. Weakened and decimated, the Ọbàtálá group was forced to arrange for a truce with its archenemy, the Odùduwà group. The annual Ìtàpá festival in Ilé-Ifẹ̀ does not only commemorate the end of that conflict, the reconciliation that followed, and the integration of the Ọbàtálá group into the political and civic life of Ilé-Ifẹ̀. It also memorializes the pox outbreak. During the festival, the imagery of smallpox lesions is painted on the bodies of Ọbàtálá priests with white chalk.

However, not every party to the conflict was happy. It is not surprising that most of the aboriginal Ùgbò elements vehemently opposed the subsequent truce between the Ọbàtálá and Odùduwà groups and the alliance that followed. The Ùgbò possibly considered the Ọbàtálá group as traitors. Several of these aboriginal communities took on guerilla-style attacks against the fledgling polity and its people. The tradition remembers one of the insurgent leaders as Kùtùkùtù Ọba Ùgbò (Kùtùkùtù, the leader of Ùgbò), though it is not clear whether the Ùgbò fought under one potentate or under several clan leaders. Nevertheless, they created enough panic and menacing disturbances to handicap free movement and economic activities. Many Ifẹ̀, irrespective of their previous loyalty or faction, were reportedly abducted by the Ùgbò mauraders.

According to a highly celebrated tradition, an Ifẹ̀ woman, Mọ́rèmí, took it upon herself to find out the source of the advantages that the Ùgbò had on the Ifẹ̀. She allowed herself to be captured in one of the incessant Ùgbò raids. Oral traditions remember Mọ́rèmí as an extraordinarily beautiful woman and state that the Ùgbò chieftain who captured her could not resist her dazzling beauty. He made her his wife, and in due course she also gained his full trust. Using her feminine power and wifely status, Mọ́rèmí soon learned the secret of her captors' indomitability. She later escaped from her captors, returned to Ilé-Ifẹ̀, and divulged the secret to the leaders of Ifẹ̀. Knowledge is power. The Ifẹ̀ eventually used this information to defeat the Ùgbò. As a result, many members of the group were expelled from surroundings of Ilé-Ifẹ̀.[92] However, a rump of the Ùgbò who professed loyalty to Ifẹ̀ authorities were integrated into the political institution of the city. The leader of this group, also known as Olúyarè or Ìgàrè, became one of the six powerful religious lords of Ifẹ̀ under the new political dispensation. The presence of these Ùgbò elements and their important politico-religious role in the affairs of Ilé-Ifẹ̀ has survived till today.[93]

The Odùduwà group won the day. However, the institutions, *ilé*, and leaders of the old confederacy that survived the conflict were accommodated within the new centralized and integrated political order championed by the Odùduwà group. The Ìrẹ́mọ area, which had by then become the center of political and civic life in Ifẹ̀ Bowl, was the nucleus of this new political order, which was based on the divine kingship institution (*ọba-aládé*) and the city-state model of organization. By the beginning of the twelfth century, Ifẹ̀ was on its way to becoming the largest city in the rain forest belt of West Africa. Two Yorùbá aphorisms—*nínú ìkòkò dúdú ni ẹ̀kọ funfun ti ń jáde* ("the whitish corn porridge comes out of the pot with black-soot stain") and *ìkòkò tí ó jẹ ata ìdí rẹ á gbóná* ("the pot that will cook the spicy soup must be ready to stay long on the hot stove")—call attention to the beauty that can come out of messy, ugly, and painful circumstances. The cloud of conflict that had hung over Ifẹ̀ for many decades had emptied its waters, and the hot embers of war that had scorched the land for a number of generations were now cooling down—hence the appellation of Ilé-Ifẹ̀ as *Ifẹ̀ oòyè* (Ifẹ̀, the survivor). So it was that the political crisis of the last century during the Late Formative period in Ilé-Ifẹ̀ gave way to political integration, consolidation, stability, cultural efflorescence, and dramatic elaboration in material life by the end of the eleventh century. The end of the conflict marked the beginning of a new era that has left overwhelming footprints in the archaeological landscape of Ilé-Ifẹ̀ and has rightly been called the Classical period.[94] The sociopolitical outcome of the instability was qualitatively different from that of the preceding era.

The hallmarks of the Classical period include the development of an urban capital with concentric embankments. There were also life-size terracotta and copper or brass sculptures with detailed, idealized naturalism that point to the existence of a class of wealthy and powerful chieftains who presided over a stratified society. The diversity of the iconography of political authority in mortuary and shrine contexts indicates the existence of an elaborate sacred and divine kingship institution and formal sociopolitical hierarchies.[95] Ilé-Ifẹ̀ also reorganized its economy at this time. Craft specialization defined the everyday economic life, in which the production of high-value crafts such as glass-bead production featured prominently. Likewise, innovations in technique brought a significant expansion of iron production. A chemical and mineralogical composition study on iron slags, ore samples, and a furnace wall sample obtained from Classical-era deposits in Ilé-Ifẹ̀ shows that the smelters used blended ore for their operations. This method involved adding ilmenitic black sand, obtained from the surface, to a goethic or ilmonite-rich ore mined from the subsoil. The result is an iron product high in titanium content. Moreover, by locating their furnaces on hillsides in the path of the wind, the smelters facilitated natural self-drafting, relieving themselves of the hard labor needed to blow air into the furnace to maintain a high temperature throughout the firing process. All of these allowed for the production of high-quality iron, which probably included steel.[96] The manufacture of primary glass and glass beads, terracotta sculptures, titanium-enriched iron products, and copper-alloy sculpture distinguished Ilé-Ifẹ̀ economically from its neighbors. Ceramic production also indicates standardization and specialization. On the political side, the ceremonial and utilitarian artifacts demonstrate an elaborate suite of iconography that highlight the idea of royalty and specialized institutions of power and authority. These were connected to a new field of public rituals that focused on both royal personalities and ancestral heroes of the great nonroyal Houses. Other archaeological indicators of this period include elaborate mortuary rituals. There is also evidence that Ilé-Ifẹ̀ promoted long-distance trade and became the dominant emporium in the region from the twelfth through the fourteenth century.

In the aftermath of the resolution of the political conflicts that had plagued Ifẹ̀ for several decades, the area of the Ifẹ̀ Bowl witnessed a rapid expansion of population beyond the Inner Wall. In response to this growth, the community built a second perimeter embankment with an outer ditch (the Outer Wall) during the thirteenth century. It appears that the settlement expansion preceded the second perimeter embankment by at least a century, as some of the walls were constructed on top of earlier cultural features, such as paved stone and ceramic tile floors.[97] With a circumference of 15 kilometers and a maximum diameter of 5.2 kilometers, the area covered by the Outer Wall doubled that of the Inner Wall (fig. 2.7).[98] The area between the Inner and Outer Walls has been the focus of several archaeological excavations, and these have yielded a rich diversity of artifacts and information on the Classical culture of Ifẹ̀. A characteristic of the new urban space was the paving of several of its major thoroughfares with potsherd tiles. Most of these were laid on edge in herringbone patterns, and their borders were sometimes lined with small ceramic disks in order to give the architectural feature an ornate finish and to prevent erosion. There is also evidence that the floors of elite houses and religious sites at Ifẹ̀ were paved with potsherds and cobblestones, as is evident at Ìta Yemòó, Láfógido, Odò Ògbè, Ọbalára, Woyè Àṣírí, and Ọ̀run Ọba Adó, as well as in the areas around the Odùduwà Grove.[99] Most of the potsherd tiles were arranged linearly in herringbone patterns; and black and red sherds were arranged in geometric mosaics. In some instances, such as in the area of Odùduwà Grove, the potsherd pavement was laid in concentric patterns and bordered by cobblestones. Likewise, the walls and columns of religious and elite buildings were decorated with ceramic disks (fig. 2.8). The ceramic tile and cobblestone pavements provided an aesthetically pleasing landscape and also made the movement of people easier, especially during the rainy season, when

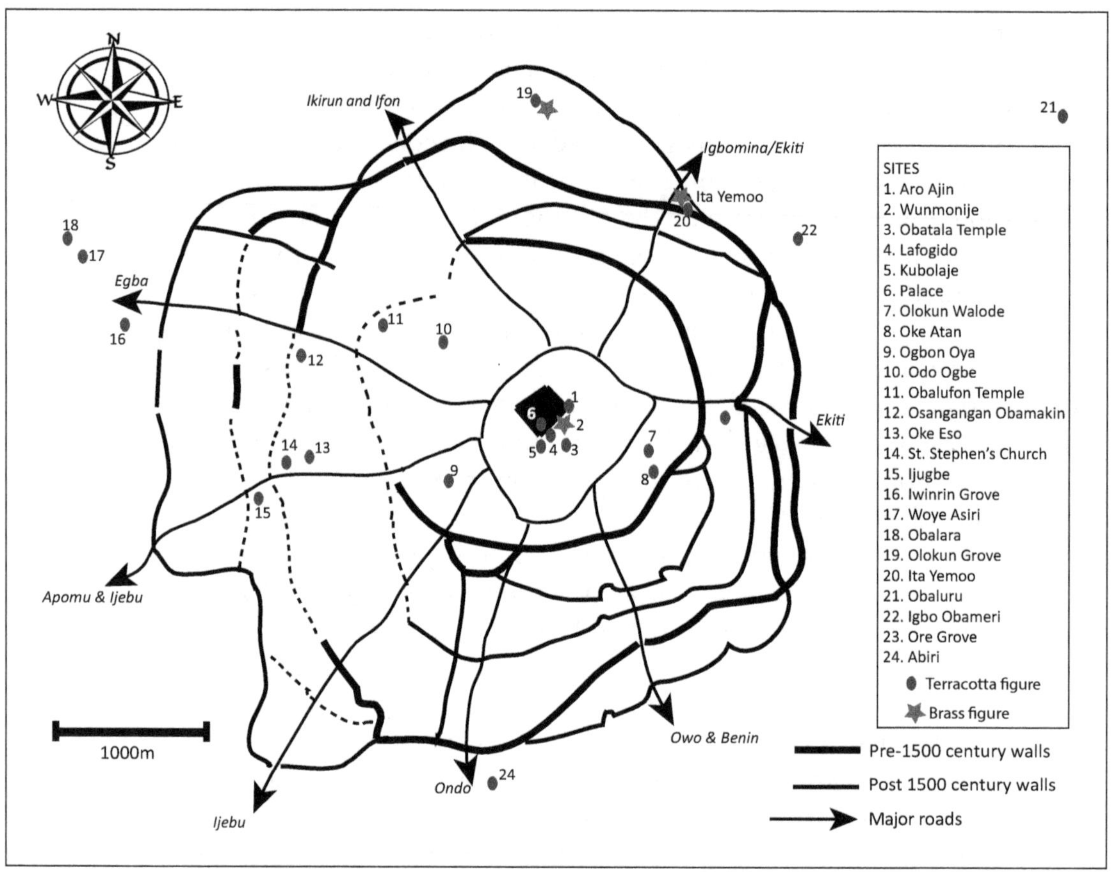

Figure 2.7. Inner and Outer Walls, Ilé-Ifẹ̀

the heavy clayey soils of Ifẹ̀ were slippery and hazardous for travelers. The paved thoroughfares tremendously improved the urban landscape of Ilé-Ifẹ̀, but some of these citywide potsherd pavements were likely products of public works that required massive extraction of labor from citizens and other residents, including conscription and obligatory service.[100] The occurrence of potsherd pavements in virtually every part of the area within the Inner and Outer Walls and beyond indicate that the city was densely populated. One estimate put the population in the range of 70,000–105,000 during the mid-fourteenth century.[101]

In Classical Ifẹ̀, the social, political, and economic lives anchored on a new spatial model of settlement, which the ancestral Yorùbá called *ìlú*. In its essence, *ìlú* is an integrated network of several *ilé* governed by a central authority, but the word has multiple meanings in Yorùbá usage. It could mean a town, a city, or a kingdom. It also refers to the people who are citizens of this politically charged and sociological space. The idea and practice of *ìlú* predated Ilé-Ifẹ̀, as the oral traditions of Ọ̀bà, among others, have indicated. However, this phenomenon achieved its utmost

Figure 2.8. Ceramic disks (Ìlàrè) and potsherd pavement (Ilé-Ifẹ̀)

elaboration in Ilé-Ifẹ̀. The processes that culminated in the formation of an *ìlú* are also best known here. With the triumph of the Odùduwà group, several settlements and Houses were relocated to the bowl and were positioned in a closer contiguity to create the largest settlement density ever seen in the area. This spatial dislocation and relocation indicates that the leadership of the older Houses now recognized the authority of the central government established at Ìrẹ́mọ. This was the beginning of *ìlú* as a new organizational structure for Ilé-Ifẹ̀. The very same title that had been reserved for the head of a House or mega-House, *ọba*, now became the generic designation for the head of this *ìlú*, but the paraphernalia of his office was more elaborate than that of the *ọba* of an *ilé*. Of such paraphernalia, the *adé* was the most important. This was a unique kind of beaded tall conical hat, sometimes with a veil, used to distinguish this new centralizing figure from the other *ọba* of the *ilé*, who were now under him. As previously mentioned, the *adé* was an elaboration of the tall conical hats that the Late Formative leaders of Houses and mega-Houses in Ifẹ̀, Èkìtì, and Ìgbómìnà had worn as the symbol of their power and authority.

This material symbol of power and authority represented a significant change in political ideology. Unlike in the pre-Classical period, when the *ọba* of an *ilé* was regarded as a manifestation of the ancestors and representative of the Òrìṣà (the deities), the leader of *ìlú* in Classical Ifẹ̀ was a deity, and both his personality and office were divine. In other words, the human body of the king was more than the vessel in which the Òrìṣà and the ancestors were manifested, which it had been during the Late Formative period. Instead, the *ọba* of an *ìlú* was an Òrìṣà, a god or divine being in his own right. He did not have to wait to be deified after his death, as in the case of the pre-Classical *ọba* of an *ilé* (e.g., Ọbàtálá). Rather, he was deified upon assuming the office and putting on an *adé*. From that moment, he is believed to have attained immortality and joined the ranks of the Òrìṣà.[102] This idea of a living god in human form sitting atop the political organization of the *ìlú* was a profound shift in Yorùbá political ideology. While this idea may have already started developing in earlier polities, such as Ọ̀bà and Ùlésùn, it appears it was in Ilé-Ifẹ̀ that this concept of divine kingship became most elaborate and its institutional forms first fully theorized and implemented, as we shall see in chapter 3. In view of this innovation, the title of *ọba* ceased to be used to refer to the leader of an *ilé* during the Classical period. Instead, it was reserved strictly for the leader of an *ìlú*.[103]

The political resolution that followed the Odùduwà-Ọbàtálá conflict, and the conflict with other factions such as the Ùgbò, was one of collaboration and negotiated peace between the victor and the vanquished. Power was not concentrated in the hands of the divine *ọba*; it was shared by a vast network of chieftains, of whom there were two main categories. The first was an elaborate hierarchy of palace officials whose primary role was to serve the *ọba-aládé*, and the second group comprised the leaders of several *ilé*, the formerly autonomous Houses and mega-Houses who were now incorporated into the central administration of the larger estate (*ìlú*). The House chieftains represented the interest of their *ilé* in the central administration, but their responsibility transcended the boundaries of their *ilé* because as a group of councilors to the divine *ọba*, they were responsible for governing the entire *ìlú* as an organic unit. In that spirit of integration and community building, many sociocultural repertoires and political titles of the Late Formative period were incorporated into the central political institution, rituals, and cosmogony of classical Ifẹ̀ and the other parts of the Yorùbá world where this model of governance took root. In fact, many of the kings of Ifẹ̀ who ruled in the aftermath of the consolidation of the eleventh century were the descendants of groups that had opposed the Odùduwà faction. In this sense, the vision of Odùduwà to unite all Houses and mega-Houses under one central administration won the day, but the subsequent managers of the vision came from the Houses and families whose ancestors had originally opposed that vision.[104]

Nevertheless, the creation of *ìlú* out of the amalgamation of the Late Formative period Houses did not eradicate the importance of *ilé*. Instead, they gained more relevance as the primary building blocks of the *ìlú*. That is, the chieftains of the House system lost their political autonomy, but the development of *ìlú* at Ilé-Ifẹ̀ and in other parts of the Yorùbá-speaking region was not a break with the *ilé* model. Rather, the rights of an individual as a citizen or a civic member of an *ìlú* derived from his or her membership in one or more *ilé* (House), on both the patrilineal and matrilineal sides. Membership in an *ilé* was needed not only for residential purposes but, more importantly, for administration (e.g., for public work and taxation) and political representation (e.g., access to the political office). The *ilé* was also the conduit for enjoying the benefits of citizenship (e.g., protection), performing religious and ritual obligations, and gaining access to land and other resources. Hence, the rights and potentiality of an individual and his or her citizenship in the *ìlú* were rooted in the *ilé*.

The resilience and strength of an *ìlú* were not defined only by the power at the center (the palace) but also by the diversity and unique assets of the several *ilé* that constituted the *ìlú*, since the former served as the investment portfolio of the latter. These various *ilé* must collaborate and be interdependent in order to make the *ìlú* functional, but mutual differentiation and social distance between the Houses were also important features of *ìlú*. The groups in an *ilé* defined their external boundaries and internal homogeneity in relation to the other *ilé* through different but complementary social, ritual, political, and economic practices. Social differentiation among these corporate groups (Houses) manifested in their distinctive economic and craft specializations, patron deities and the associated rituals and taboos, and the roles that each *ilé* played in the division of labor for public works. The inter-House differentiation also manifested in the number and importance of hereditary chieftaincy titles that each *ilé* had access to in the central government, and in the types of land resources that an *ilé* controlled. Each *ilé* was supposed to provide unique services to its *ìlú* in the areas of knowledge and skills, public works, and defense. Not all *ilé* were equal in the political configuration of the *ilu*. They were usually ranked based on their relative longevity, whereby the older Houses had more and better access to power, decision-making, and economic opportunities than the newly formed Houses did. However, the fortunes of a House might change because of political displacement or demotion arising from conflicts with other Houses and the palace, lack of effective leadership, or depletion of the population of an *ilé* because of war, disease, or internal conflict. And the converse is also the case: a junior *ilé* could rise to attain a senior position in *ìlú* in the course of time.

The Yorùbá *ìlú* was, therefore, by its constitution, a heterogeneous entity composed of complementary and competing *ilé*. One of the primary duties of the divine *ọba* was to serve as the binding and enabling force for this competitive and complementary corporate diversity. The annual cycle of rituals that focused on the king, the weekly market fairs, public works (e.g., road maintenance and construction of city or town walls), defense, and intermarriages between the Houses were some of the ways that the divergent interests of the urban populace were harmonized. Although *ilé* was the pathway or gateway to the emergence of *ìlú*, the latter was more than the sum of the *ilé* that constituted it. There are two reasons for this. First, the emergent qualities of *ìlú* as a complex system are different from those of *ilé*, even with the grafting of the principles of *ilé* on *ìlú* for organizational purposes. Second, although *ilé* was the building block of *ìlú*, it was by no means the only category of units that constituted *ìlú*. There was also the "extra-House," a networked institution that transcended the corporate identities of the Houses, blood ties (real or fictive), and privileges of birth. The extra-House mediated the relationship between *ìlú* and *ilé*—that is, between the palace and the Houses. The extra-House was potentially accessible to different individuals irrespective of their background. While the corporate goals of *ilé* could restrict the ambitions of a person, the extra-House provided such individuals with the opportunity to pursue their ambitions and talents without the restriction of age, circumstance of birth, hierarchy, and other limitations that *ilé* might unwittingly impose on its members.

There were two categories of extra-House: (1) the palace-affiliated institution; and (2) the professional, civic, and religious institutions. The former consisted of individuals and households who were appendages of the palace (and lived close to it) and from whom palace officials—the king's spokespersons, bodyguards, pages, police, and messengers—were recruited. In Ilé-Ifẹ̀, and in many other parts of central Yorùbá region, these individuals and their households formed a group known today as *mọdéwá* ("children or dependents of the king"). There are indications that in the past, members of the *mọdéwá* could be recruited from among the war captives, migrants, or free citizens of any of the Houses in the *ìlú*.[105] Those joining the *mọdéwá* from any of the *ilé* must, however, renounce their House membership, as well as the privileges and rights they may have in any of their previous Houses.[106] This process usually involved an elaborate ceremony and the payment of fees. The individuals and households in *mọdéwá* were members of neither the royal House nor the nonroyal Houses. They served the palace and the institution of kingship only, and they were expected to be loyal to only the reigning king, the embodiment of the state. In turn, they were exempted from the responsibilities that members of *ilé* had to the state, including taxation and provision of corvée for public projects.[107] This palace-affiliated extra-House served as the buffer between the king and the House chieftains who represented the interest of the *ilé* in the palace and also constituted a major priestly class. Because of the ambivalent status of the *mọdéwá*, whose members belonged neither to the royal House nor to any of the nonroyal Houses but yet were the closest to the palace, this institution played a major role in negotiating the balance of power between the palace and the town (the nonroyal Houses). The tension between these palace officials and the town chiefs (the *ilé*) was therefore always palpable.[108]

The second type of extra-House stood apart from the palace and the nonroyal *ilé* but enjoyed the patronage of both. In this group were associations of age grades, guilds of traders, and professional groups, as well as schools or cults of the prominent regional deities. The members of this second group did not have to relinquish their membership, rights, and privileges in any of the Houses; and those affiliated with either the royal or the nonroyal Houses or with the palace extra-House could belong to any of these professional, civic, or religious extra-Houses. One of the most important and influential extra-Houses in this second category was the *Ògbóni*, a civic association of religious and political chieftains, social elites, and respected elders that cut across virtually all the Houses—royal and nonroyal—and any other social groups. The *Ògbóni* may have initially evolved as an underground body devoted to promoting the ethos of indigeneity and protecting the collective rights of those considered to be the indigenous majority (the nonroyal *ilé*), especially following the political reorganization that culminated in the Classical period. Over time, however, as the ideas of indigeneity changed, this extra-House evolved into the most important binding and moderating force for the diverse interest groups that constituted *ìlú*. In this regard, it began to perform a wide range of civic and delicate judicial functions that simultaneously catered to the interests of citizenship, indigeneity, state (*ìlú*), and the corporate groups (*ilé*). The membership of *Ògbóni* was by invitation only and included only men and women of substance selectively drawn from the different segments of *ìlú*. But the affairs of the *Ògbóni* were not subject to public view. If the goal of *mọdéwá* was to enlarge and empower the palace at the expense of the nonroyal Houses, that of the *Ògbóni* was to harmonize the diversity of the interest groups that constituted *ìlú* and to create a common ground of dialogue for many of the leaders of these diverse interest groups—craft guilds, traders, Òrìṣà cults, Houses, and the palace.[109]

As an extra-House within the *ilú* configuration, *Ògbóni* embodied the two primary strands of ancestral Yorùbá theory of social order: (1) gendered duality; and (2) the inevitability of tension and conflict in the constitution of social life. The institution of *Ògbóni* evolved to uphold the first and to prevent the latter from leading to social breakdown. To accomplish this mission, the *Ògbóni* operated on the theory of knowledge that reduced all the modalities of social life into competing interests and relationships between the patricentric and matricentric fields (gendered duality, both in literal and metaphoric terms). However, it insisted that these two fields are complementary, coequal, and interdependent, although they have competing and sometimes conflicting interests. Therefore, to prevent this duality from disintegrating into a binary ontology, it set up practices that emphasized complementarity, collaboration, and reconciliation between these two fields of social life. These practices are the basis of *Ògbóni's* attributes as an extrajudicial and extra-political institution in Yorùbá governance. The institution was a field of power dedicated to fostering complementarity between the civic/earth/*ilé* (feminine) and royal/hegemonic/palace (masculine) authorities. Indeed, the *Ògbóni* institution was needed as an arbiter between the two, considering the ontology of *ìlú* as a product of conflict and an amalgamation of several and diverse self-interested *ilé* each jealously guarding its unique corporate identity.

The principles of gendered duality and conflict resolution, embodied in the *Ògbóni,* are most evident in the conjoined male-female brass figure excavated at Ìta Yemòó in Ilé-Ifẹ̀ (plate 2). The elaborate insignia of office the pair is adorned with—beaded necklaces, beaded crowns, bead-decorated cloth, beads on the wrists and ankles—suggest that this sculpture was associated in some way with royalty or the wealth and privileges that usually came from royal authority. This intriguing and exquisite brass sculpture represents an early prototype of the large, freestanding paired sculptures (stylized rather than naturalistic) that are found in the innermost sanctuaries of *ògbóni* temples still today, and the smaller version that *ògbóni* members wear on their neck.[110] The sculptural male and female pair in plate 2 lock their forefingers in a gesture of oneness, and their legs are intertwined so that only three "legs" are touching the ground. True to the ethos of *ògbóni,* this male-female paired composition articulates the idea of shared power and corulership between two complementary, interdependent, but potentially mutually opposed forces. These are the matricentric and patricentric fields, which roughly correlate to the female and the male spheres. The intertwined fingers and legs of this sculptural composition affirm "the interdependency and recognition of the male and female powers," the idealism of the "equality of the gender" in the Classical Yorùbá thought, and the indispensability of both the male and female essence (*ìwà*) for maintaining social order.[111] So, this paired sculpture connotes the unification of two opposing forces and the resolution of the potential and real conflict that might threaten the social order. As is the practice in the *Ògbóni* chambers today, this Ìta Yemòó sculpture would have been placed in the inner recess of the meeting chamber to remind members of the importance of transcending difference, harmonizing the opposing forces of duality, and committing to conflict resolution.

The extra-Houses, such as the *mọdéwá* and *Ògbóni* institutions, were glues that bound the Houses (royal and nonroyal) together as the primary constituents of an *ìlú*. They helped to sharpen the difference and purpose of both *ilé* and *ìlú* while also extolling the virtues of complementarity between the self-interested goals and uniqueness of the Houses on one hand and the community-building and social wellness of the *ìlú* on the other. The extra-Houses enabled the *ìlú* to develop its identity in contradistinction to that of *ilé* and vice versa. For example, since the raison d'être of *ilé* was to accumulate and redistribute resources among their members, it was imperative for the members of *ilé* to emphasize homogeneity and sectional corporate interests. To the contrary, the *ìlú* stressed the heterogeneity of its primary constituent parts—the *ilé*, while also extolling the virtues of unification among these units. The *ìlú* was not the primal unit of accumulation, but it was the dominant extractor of resources from members of the *ilé* through taxes, tolls, corvée, and other levies. With these resources, the *ìlú* was able to put on the grandest rituals and ceremonies, finance public projects, and maintain a large cadre of administrators. The institution of *ọba-aládé* was the conduit for the accumulation and disposal of these resources, but the chieftains of the Houses also participated in these processes; they transferred some of the wealth from their Houses to the *ọba-aládé*, and they also shared in some of the proceeds. The *ọba-aládé* as a divine power was the chief priest of his *ìlú*, and "all the high priests of all the cults were, in principle, his assistants."[112] And through the elaborate extra-House officials of the palace, the largest dependent workforce in the *ìlú*, the *ọba* came to control a large body of labor and loyal citizens that could also be mobilized for war, internally against a recalcitrant House or externally against the outside foe.

Ancestor and Immortality

Despite these qualitative differences between *ìlú* and *ilé*, the former was thinkable only in the symbolic and archetypical structures of *ilé*. The range of naturalistic and personalized terracotta and copper-alloy (mostly brass) figurines in classical Ifẹ̀ reveals the importance of the

House ancestors to the well-being of both the *ilé* and the *ìlú*. Between the twelfth and fifteenth centuries, ancestral figures were represented in two primary media: terracotta and copper alloys (mostly brass). Unlike the minimalist naturalism of the Late Formative ancestors' stone sculptures in the Ifẹ̀, Ìgbómìnà, and Èkìtì areas, the Classical period's ancestral sculptures in Ifẹ̀ and Ọ̀wọ̀, among others, have a more evolved naturalism.[113] The latter emphasize each ancestor's individuality and a preference for idealized prime adulthood (plate 3). The terracotta figures suggest portrait-like representations. Sporting different hairstyles, clothing styles, paraphernalia of office, and facial marks that served as signifiers of individual and group identities, these are portraits of the ancestors of different Houses. The diversity of the terracotta figures is an excellent testament to the cosmopolitanism of Ifẹ̀ populations during the Classical period. For this, the city captures the metaphor of a salad-bowl diversity where the character and essence (*ìwà*) of each ingredient (personality) stood out, confidently calling attention to self and, by extension, to the uniqueness of the individual's House.

More than two hundred Classical period terracotta figures of ancestors have been found in Ilé-Ifẹ̀. Women are represented in this medium, but the portraits of men are in the majority. Some of these sculptures bear the insignia of royalty. However, the majority belong to nonroyal personalities. With the exception of those made for healing purposes, as protective sculptures to ward off evil forces, or as representations of human sacrifice, most of the terracotta figures were originally part of mortuary assemblages and ancestral shrines. That is, they served the purpose of ancestral veneration. The sculptors of Classical Ifẹ̀, more than in any other other part of Yorùbá world, before or after them, paid careful attention to the *ìwà* of these individuals in order to capture the distinctive likeness and character of the ancestor being depicted. Through the attentive representation of body scarification and attire in these sculptures, the artists made faithful efforts to showcase the social attributes of the *ilé* that each ancestor represented. However, the sculptors generally ignored the emotional aspects and physical blemishes of these ancestors, "idealizing only those features that facilitate identity" and conveying a sense of perfection so that the whole composition lies between the states of "absolute abstraction and absolute likeness."[114] These sculptures are works of uncommon beauty, proficiency, mastery, confidence, and certainty that made the ancestors the focal point for the conceptualization of time. They were the fodders for thinking about historical trajectories and the continuity of the House and its members. These ancestral sculptures were also a mnemonic subject that linked the past, the present, and the future.

No doubt, the use of sculpture in ancestral veneration during the Classical period in Ilé-Ifẹ̀ and other parts of the Yorùbá world was a continuation of a much older practice that dated to the inauguration of the Early Formative House society in the region. However, there was a significant difference. In the Late Formative Èsìẹ́ and Ifẹ̀, ancestral figures were conceptual portraits whereby the sculptors were "concerned with the essence of the subject or the metaphysical self" (see fig. 2.5).[115] In the case of Èsìẹ́ in particular, the sculptures of ancestors from different Houses were placed in a public or communal place, not in the private House/household shrines. The corpus therefore did not emphasize individuality but rather focused on social identity in order to represent the aggregates of different segments of the society. These multi-House ancestors were then venerated collectively as part of the process of community building.[116] In contrast, the ancestral figures depicted in the sculptures of Classical Ifẹ̀, also found in Ọ̀wọ̀, Ìkìrun, Ìré, and Òṣogbo, were individualized (see plate 3d), limited to elite or distinguished men and women, and associated with particular Houses/households where their shrines were located. The Classical period elite burials in Ilé-Ifẹ̀ were, therefore, shrines elaborately furnished with highly prized mortuary goods. The naturalistic busts in these shrines indicate that the elite ancestors were the focus of multigenerational veneration. They were also part of both private and public displays that usually commenced with the grand burial ceremonies, known as *àko*.[117] In subsequent years, the bust became part of the periodic ancestral commemorative ceremonies during which the identity and history of the House were also celebrated. However, there were ancestral terracotta heads that were small in size (sometimes less than a quarter of life-size) and schematized in form (see plate 3f). Babatunde Lawal may be right that such miniatures were not intended for public display but were "designed to fit into private . . . indoor spaces . . . restricted to a handful of people" as a focus of "periodic prayers and sacrifices to the . . . ancestral dead."[118] Perhaps such figurative ancestral heads were used by households with little means. After all, as a Yorùbá proverb puts it, the size of the mouse determines the size of its nest.

During the thirteenth and fourteenth centuries, ancestral remains were interred in the common area within the residence (e.g., a courtyard) or in the reception or sleeping room of the deceased.[119] These burial practices highlight the importance of ancestors to the continuity of the House, in matters of legitimacy for political power, authority, inheritance, and group identity. Some of these burial spaces evolved into specialized shrines or temples as the focus of periodic commemoration and worship, as assembly places for House members to celebrate or honor any aspect of the life cycle: birth, puberty, marriage, death, or the annual founder's festival. Such ancestral loci were also preferred for settling disputes among the members of the House. These ancestral shrines anchored members of the *ilé* in place and reaffirmed the cohesion and permanence of the House.

These shrines were not marked only by sculptures but also by the physical remains of the deceased. The disarticulated bones and incomplete skeletal remains of burials at the Ọbalára site in Ilé-Ifẹ̀, Ìloyì in the Ìlàrè district, and Igbó'Làjà in Ọ̀wọ̀, all dating to the Classical period (app. 2), are indicative of the curation of ancestral bones.

These remains were treated in ways similar to those of the sculptures of ancestors.[120] They were shrines (*ojúbọ*) and the focus of periodic veneration. The postmortem disarticulation of skeletal remains was the product of periodic exhumation and reburial as part of the process of transforming the deceased person into an ancestor. Such treatment of the remains of the deceased affirmed the legitimacy and continuity of the House and served to legitimize the claims of some of the survivors to the material and nonmaterial assets of the *ilé* over which the ancestor had presided before death. In this light, the burial of a deceased person, especially an ancestor who was the conduit of inheritance and identity for the living household members, did "not always terminate in the placement of a full skeleton at the final burial site" within the residential premises.[121] Parts of the remains of the deceased could also be buried in different locations. On such occasions that the Yorùbá call "second burial ceremony," the skeleton may be exhumed from the original burial site and different parts of the individual's remains may be buried in multiple sites of the House's real estate. These include locations that the House members might consider to be part of their inalienable material and spiritual property, including farmlands, the ancestral courtyard, the former living premises of the deceased, and so on.[122] The burial and commemorative ceremony often involved "the retention of certain skeletal elements (particularly crania and long bones)" as heirlooms used by the living descendants "as potent symbols of inherited power."[123] Some of the disarticulated skeletal remains found in Ọbalára site in Ilé-Ifẹ̀ may belong to this category of curated ancestral heirlooms. This may also explain the missing skeletal parts of a human burial in Ilòyì (Ìlàrè).[124] The terracotta figures that have been found all over the city of Classical Ifẹ̀, however, show the prolific use of sculptures as proxies for the remains of the revered ancestors. These sculptures, placed on the ancestor's altar, were important for laying claim to the descendants' rootedness in the *ilé* and *ìlú* and to the privileges and resources that such rootedness offered.[125]

True to the nature of the *ilé* as an engine of social inequality, not every deceased adult could become an ancestor of the House. The deceased adults with children or relatives who were not members of the core, alpha, or major ancestral line of the House would be buried within their respective household structures. In those instances, these non-elite remained ancestors of the minor branches of the House but not of the House itself, and their names could not be invoked in the periodic rituals dedicated to the House as a whole. In contrast, only those who were part of the elite family of the House (the alpha household) and recognized as descendants of the founding ancestors could be buried in the central courtyard—the seat of power of the House and also its major religious center. The ancestors of the House were, therefore, a select subgroup whose names were called out during the invocation of the House's genealogy or prayers for the House's well-being. Only the direct descendants of these elite ancestors (fictive or real) could inherit the special honors, privileges, resource rights, titles, and obligations associated with the House. Of course, a member of the minor families in the House could be buried in the central House's courtyard or other designated mausoleum as a result of the special accomplishments of that individual or his or her emerging influence within the House. That feat could make the erstwhile minor household become part of the alpha household. And, in circumstances in which an individual from the minor household rose to become the head of the entire House, his household could become the alpha household or a branch of it. In other words, the ancestral history of the House was always being revised.

I have so far offered a materialist interpretation of ancestral veneration, consistent with the purpose of the House as the primary unit of accumulation, redistribution of wealth and privileges, and self-realization. There is more to this. First, the ancestral Yorùbá believed in the immortality of the soul and reincarnation of the deceased ancestors.[126] Second, the ancestral Yorùbá House was a composition of "the ancestors, the living, and the unborn children."[127] The ancestors and the unborn children were regarded as different manifestations of the same being, in that the ancestors were believed to be reborn as the children of the House.[128] The generations of the House, therefore, had "a cyclical and endless character."[129] For these reasons, the curation of ancestral remains and the ancestor's sculpture as the focus of veneration was a way of keeping the nonmaterial property of the ancestor within the physical structure of the House. The retention of these ancestral remains within the confines of the residence also served to secure the soul (the nonmaterial essence) of the ancestor firmly within the House. Failure to do this would make the soul of the ancestor restless, in a permanent roaming state. This dangerous state of affairs would cause the unhappy deceased to return and cause misfortune for the descendants who had neglected him or her.[130] This "soulful" interpretation is not exclusive of the materialist version offered above but complementary to it. Ancestral veneration was a means of both making claims to resources of the *ilé* and also anchoring the presence of the ancestral souls in the residential space of the descendants.[131] The burial rituals transformed the physical mortal into a spiritual immortal and an omnipresent being. For the resource claim of the descendants to be viable and realized, the soul and spirit of the ancestor had to be healthy, happy, and at peace. It was this state of peace and happiness of the ancestors that guaranteed the well-being of the descendants. Anchoring the souls of the ancestors in place (at home) guaranteed the reincarnation of the ancestors through the arrival of newborn babies, the next generation. Hence, the life goal of becoming an ancestor was tied to the quest for immortality and divinity as well as the reproduction and perpetuity of the *ilé*.

These principles and practices of ancestral veneration were highly elaborated in the royal mortuary rituals of Ifẹ̀. Since the royal house was just one of many Houses in the *ìlú*, it also needed to protect its patrimony, estate, ancestral spirits, and privileges. Just like the other *ilé*, the members of the royal house also used terracotta to represent their ancestors, as is evident in the diadems and insignia represented on some of these sculptures (plate 3). It seems that sometime in the late thirteenth or early fourteenth century, the Ifẹ̀ royal ancestors were also being represented in copper-alloy sculptures using a combination of the lost-wax technique, hammering, and soldering. In contrast to the terracotta, the copper-alloy sculptures have very little diversity in their appearance and paraphernalia.[132] Thermoluminescence dating of the clay core samples in the interior of the sculptures reveals the early through the mid-fourteenth century as the general period when the Ifẹ̀ copper-alloy sculptures were made.[133] These dates belong to the climax of Ifẹ̀'s Classical period. The entire corpus of twenty-five copper-alloy sculptures, found at only three sites, was likely executed within a relatively short period of time by the same school of casters. The number of Ifẹ̀ kings who commissioned these copper-alloy figures may have been as small as two. Unlike the terracotta, many of the copper-alloy images were likely intended for use in the royal ceremony and rituals, and they may be a retrospective portrayal of several past kings.[134] The monarchs who commissioned these copper-alloy sculptures for their mortuary cults likely asked their artists to make the idealized and generic representations of the preceding kings, the ancestors from whom these late Classical kings claimed legitimacy to the throne. In this regard, these sculptures (like other ancestral figures) were used for recording time and presenting stories about the past. The individuals represented in these images were cited as the cause and effect of past events and the link between the past and the present. The stories of their exploits provided contexts for imagining the future.

All the human figures in Ilé-Ifẹ̀, irrespective of media—including the ones found at other sites in the Yorùbá region during the Classical period—represent adult men and women. They do not depict the coming of age of adolescents or the children of the elite family or alpha household. Rather, the sculptures served to celebrate the final success of individuals at the end of their life's journey, although the images show them in their idealized prime age. For these men and women, the Yorùbá would say *àtubọ̀tán wọn dàra*, an acknowledgment of a "successful life journey." The measure of this success was to become an ancestor. This was the ultimate and primary goal of living, and it explains the lavishness of ancestral veneration and the retention of several sculptors to support this mortuary economy during the Classical period. Becoming an ancestor was the basis of a full self-realization and the stepping-stone to achieve immortality. Hence the saying *K'á kú ní kékeré, ó sàn ju k'á dàgbà lâì l'ádìye ìrànà*: "It is better to die young (and be forgotten) than to die in old age without having people (progeny and followers) who will give one a befitting burial." Such a burial would be possible only if one were to die and leave behind a healthy and active household. The corpus of sculptures in the Yorùbá region, from the ninth through the fourteenth century, is revealing not only in what is represented but also in what is not represented—childhood and adolescence. When this is examined in relation to the ethnography of the nineteenth and first half of the twentieth century, one realizes that children and adolescents from highly ranked households and Houses were not assigned high-ranking status in death.[135] Reaching adulthood and accomplishing the expectations of adulthood—marriage and children—were essential to the process of becoming an ancestor, the ultimate goal of self-realization.

Summing Up

The long-term process through which the Yorùbá created the House society is central to understanding the principles and practices that shaped their history. This story began in their ancestral homeland, southwest of the Niger-Benue Confluence. The proto-Yoruboid as a linguistic group did not just survive the Big Dry; they prospered, drastically expanded their territorial unit, and were significantly transformed as a result of it. In the course of about a thousand years after Ọni Ìtaàkpá was laid to rest, the descendants of the proto-Yoruboid fanned out from their ancestral home to become the largest language-cultural group, by territory, in West Africa south of the River Niger. It was in the course of this expansion that the distinctive mutually intelligible Yorùbá dialects developed. There were two hot spots for the development of these dialects between AD 250 and 800—the Èkìtì-Ìgbómìnà (central) and the Oǹdó-Ọ̀wọ̀-Ìjẹ̀bú-Ìkálẹ̀ (southeastern) in present-day Nigeria. This process of dialect splitting continued between the ninth and fourteenth century when the Àjàṣẹ́-Ṣábẹ́-Àtàpamẹ̀ (western), in the present-day Benin Republic and Togo, and the Òwu-Ọ̀yọ́-Òǹkò-Ẹ̀gbá dialect group (northwestern) developed. Their ability to utilize diverse ecologies, establish far-flung social networks, and manage the relationships with the aboriginal groups they encountered accounted for this expansionist success. Social organization played a far greater role than technology in the success of their southern thrust between 300 BC and AD 500.

More than any other social attribute, the *ilé* (House) was the primary basis of Yorùbá social organization and the fulcrum of its social reproduction. The Yorùbá became a full-fledged House society during the mid-first millennium, but this system grew out of the existing multigenerational households that their proto-Yoruboid ancestors had already developed. The corporate and corporeal properties of *ilé* shaped the ideas of personhood, community, and ancestors. Through the *ilé*, the ancestral Yorùbá defined what it meant to be a person and a member of a community. The Yorùbá also defined the meaningfulness of being in terms of becoming an ancestor. As their push into different environments accelerated in the second half of the first millennium, strong men created communities that were founded on both collaboration and conflict, especially as each House (and later, mega-House) struggled to gain competitive advantages in the recruitment of members. The men who founded and led these Houses and mega-Houses became ancestors upon their death, but the minor households within the House also maintained their ancestral figures, who included both men and women. The primary purpose of living, for the Yorùbá of the Formative and Classical periods, was to become an ancestor, and therefore to live eternally through reincarnation. Becoming an ancestor also meant becoming a deity whose three-dimensional figure was represented on the family or House altar. All these aspirations were possible only when a House (descendants) existed, and the House could not exist without the ancestors.

Social hierarchy was the fabric of the Yorùbá House society. Stratification was based not only on privileges of age and birth but also on the individual's talents, skills, potentials, and achievements (or lack thereof). However, social stratification did not deny any member of the House access to the means of subsistence. One of the fundamental privileges of being a member of a House was the guaranteed access to land and the social networks that supported the means of production. The House was also the fundamental guarantor of protection of life, property, and dignity. These responsibilities of the House did not change even with the emergence of the *ìlú*. The inability of a House to meet any of these goals meant that individuals and households could vote with their feet, or change their House affiliation. For this reason, Houses were always in competition with one another and even with extra-Houses such as the *mọdéwá* in the central Yorùbá area. Astute and competent leaders were therefore needed to manage the affairs of the House, to recruit and retain diverse members, and to maintain and multiply the resources of the House. Hence, an appointment to the leadership of *ilé* was not strictly hereditary or based on primogeniture but was open to competition and consideration of the most worthy promising member of the House, even if some of the competitors had a humble origin within the House. Those who lost out in the competition for leadership could break away by moving their households and other clients out of the House.[136]

This blueprint of *ilé* guided the framework for the development of *ìlú* sometime in the last quarter of the first millennium. An *ìlú* was an amalgamation and integration of several *ilé* led by a centralizing figure known as *ọba-aládé* (divine king). The process of this integration often involved conflict and collaboration. Unlike the *ọba* of the Houses and mega-Houses of the Early and Late Formative periods in Ilé-Ifẹ̀, the *ọba-aládé* of *ìlú* of the Classical period did not have to wait till death to become ancestors and deities. They were living gods who could not die. This new model of political tradition, the *ìlú/ọba-aládé* dyad, was defined by unique formal, aesthetic, philosophical, and ceremonial properties, and it spread across the Yorùbá region in the first three centuries of the second millennium. We have drawn most of our Late Formative (mega-House) and Classical period (*ìlú/ọba-aládé* dyad) examples from Ilé-Ifẹ̀ because this is where the bulk of the archaeological evidence and detailed oral historical traditions about these two developments come from. But there were multiple centers that laid the groundwork for these political traditions between 800 and 1000. The Èkìtì-Ìgbómìnà axis was an important nucleus for the evolution of this tradition. In fact, Ilé-Ifẹ̀ was a product of this Èkìtì-Ìgbómìnà version, not its originator. Nevertheless, as we shall see in the next chapter, it was in Ilé-Ifẹ̀ that this tradition reached full maturity. The political entrepreneurs and intellectuals of Ilé-Ifẹ̀ succeeded in transforming this hotchpotch of local innovations into a coherent regional ideology of governance and social order. And, beginning in the twelfth century, they used this ideology to create and define the charter for what I have called the Yorùbá community of practice. What did this community of practice look like between the early twelfth and the early fifteenth century, and how was it created? I will answer these questions in the following chapter.

Notes

1. Only fragmentary facial bones of the individual survived, comprising the right half of the mandible (with five teeth attached), partial right maxilla containing seven teeth, root of the lower first premolar, tooth crowns from a lower left third molar and the lower right first premolar, and nine other isolated teeth, all belonging to one individual (Allsworth-Jones et al., "Itaakpa," 168).

2. Obayemi, "States and Peoples of the Niger-Benue," 148.

3. These dialects—Ọ̀wè, Ìyàgbà, Ìjùmú, Gbede, Bùnú, Ikiri and Ọ̀wọ̀rọ̀—collectively known as Okun, are likely the oldest branch of the proto-Yorùbá

language, which in turn was one of the three most direct descendants of the proto-Yoruboid language community who lived in the region at the end of the first millennium BC. The other two are proto-Igala and proto-Itsekiri. More will be said about the process of language splitting later in the chapter. Obayemi, "States and peoples of the Niger-Benue confluence."

4. Bakinde, "Oral Narrations on the Origin and Settlement Patterns," 54.

5. Oyelaran, "Early Settlement."

6. Ehret, "Agricultural Origins," 73.

7. Huysecom et al., "Emergence of Pottery in Africa," 8.

8. Alabi, "Late Stone Age."

9. Casey, "Stone to Metal Age."

10. Fourshey, Gonzales, and Saidi, *Bantu Africa*, 15.

11. These legumes include *Brachystegia eurycoma*, *Sphenostylis stenocarpa*, *Parkia biglobosa*, *Canavalia* species, and *Mucuna* species. See Bhat and Karim, "Exploring the Nutritional Potential."

12. Casey, "Stone to Metal Age."

13. Alabi, "Late Stone Age," 99.

14. Allsworth-Jones et al., "Itaakpa," 173.

15. Obidiegwu and Akpabio, "Geography of Yam Cultivation," 29. Among the Igbo, Ibibio, and Efik, for example, all activities associated with yam cultivation, including "bush clearing, tillage operation, preparation of yam setts and tubers, staking and trailing the yam vine, harvesting, preparation of yam barns, tying the tubers on the barn are traditionally reserved for men, whereas women are restricted to weeding, carting yam tubers from the farm site to homestead yam barns, cooking, and food processing." See Obidiegwu and Akpabio, 33. Similar gendered division of labor in yam cultivation can be seen among all the other peoples of the Benue-Kwa branch of the Niger-Congo language family.

16. Coursey and Coursey, "New Yam."

17. Ehret, *Civilizations of Africa*, 63.

18. For comparative insight in other parts of the Niger-Congo language family, see Fourshey, Gonzales, and Saidi, *Bantu Africa*; Saidi, *Women's Authority and Society*; Stephens, *History of African Motherhood*.

19. The survival till today of the vertical broadloom as the characteristic female equipment for cloth weaving throughout the Niger-Congo world is a testimony to the deep-time antiquity of the relationship of women with the craft of cloth weaving.

20. Ehret, *Civilizations of Africa*, 62.

21. Ehret, 68.

22. Agiri, "Early Oyo," 7.

23. The moisture draining from these hills was an important source of water. It came from the year-round condensation due to "radiation fogs and hill-top clouds" (see Ozanne, "New Archaeological Survey," 32). For those living on the slopes and valleys below, the massiveness of the inselbergs and their near-constant emission of fogs would have been a spectacular and reverent sight to behold, and the people were certainly aware of the gift of water percolating down from these hills to hydrate them, their livestock, and the plants.

24. The pantheon of the southwest Niger-Benue Confluence, now known as the Okun area, is still predominantly populated by female deities. See Pemberton and Afọlayan, *Yoruba Sacred Kingship*, 45. In Ìgbẹ́tì, a town located in

the valley of a chain of massive igneous hills in northwest Yorùbá (a continuation of the hills from the northeast), the largest of these rocky hill formations is called Ìyámàpó, meaning "Mother's Pillar."

25. McIntosh, "Social Memory."

26. Höhn and Neumann, "Palaeovegetation of Janruwa," 349.

27. These lakes include Bosumtwi in Ghana and Nyabessan, Ossa, and Barombi Mbo in southern Cameroon. See Shanahan et al., "Atlantic Forcing"; Ngomanda et al., "Seasonality Change."

28. McIntosh, "Social Memory," 155. During the same Big Dry period (300 BC–AD 300), the Nile discharge was also drastically reduced; see Hassan and Stucki, "Nile Floods," 45.

29. Oyelaran, *Archaeological and Palaeoenvironmental Investigations.*

30. Breunig and Rupp, "Outline of Recent Studies"; Höhn and Neumann, "Palaeovegetation of Janruwa." The Nok people lived within 100–200 km, north and east of the proto-Yoruboid people. Their almost two-thousand-year-old civilization disappeared from the archaeological record by AD 200.

31. McIntosh, "Social Memory"; McIntosh and McIntosh, *Prehistoric Investigations.*

32. A radiocarbon date of 1840 BP±125 obtained from a charcoal sample found at a depth of 35 cm in Oluwaju rockshelter was reported by Ade Obayemi from his 1972 excavations. The calibrated average age of this date at 2-sigma is AD 134–209 (see Ogundiran, "Chronology, Material Culture, and Pathways," 52). A follow-up excavation carried out by Philip Oyelaran at the site in 1988 yielded iron slag and tuyere at 83 cm deep in an undisturbed primary context, but this level-unit has not been radiocarbon dated. Given the stratigraphic relationships between the two excavated units, it is most likely that iron manufacture in Oluwaju started much earlier than the second century AD (Oyelaran, "Early Settlement," 72). Iron production in the southwest confluence was likely already in operation by the last quarter of the first millennium BC.

33. Allsworth-Jones et al., "Itaakpa," 171–72.

34. Oyelaran, "Early Settlement," 72–73.

35. For details, see Oyelaran, *Archaeological and Palaeoenvironmental Investigations.*

36. Breunig and Rupp, "Outline of Recent Studies."

37. For comparative examples, see Adeniji, *Iṣẹ́ irin wíwa àti sísun*; Goucher, *Iron Industry of Bassar*; Schmidt, *Iron Technology in East Africa.*

38. Ogundiran, "Chronology, Material Culture, and Pathways," 38.

39. Lloyd, "Agnatic and Cognatic Descent."

40. Shaw and Daniels, *Excavations at Iwo Eleru.*

41. Many of the youngest LSA sites have pottery and stone axes, evidence of food production or intensive gathering. See Alabi, "Environment and Subsistence"; Eyo, "Recent Excavations"; Lasisi, "Excavations at Sungbo's Eredo"; Lasisi and Aremu, "New Lights"; and recent unpublished finds at Ìrẹ̀sì by Dr. Olúṣẹ́gun Ọpádèjì (University of Ibadan), according to an email sent to Nigerian Archaeologist Listserv, April 22, 2019 (https://groups.google.com/forum/#!forum/nigerian-archaeologist). Undated LSA sites, with microliths only, have also been reported at Ọ̀yọ́-Ilé (Willett, "Investigations at Old Oyo"). Another LSA occurrence with microliths and ground stone axes was reported at Ifẹ̀tẹ̀dó (Fatunsin, "Ifetedo"). Olusegun Moyib (Department of

Archaeology and Anthropology, University of Ibadan) also reported finding a ground stone axe in the Ajíbọ́de area of Ìbàdàn, near the main campus of the University of Ibadan (personal communication, May 30, 2017).

42. Darling, *Archaeology and History in Southern Nigeria.*

43. Ogundiran, "Chronology, Material Culture, and Pathways."

44. Ogundiran, "Towns and States," 861.

45. Gillespie, "When Is a House?," 41.

46. Lévi-Strauss, *Anthropology and Myth.*

47. Lévi-Strauss, *Way of the Masks*, 174.

48. Also see Beck, *Durable House*; Joyce and Gillespie, *Beyond Kinship.* In this sense, the House concept is broader than the framework of a polygynous household led by a big man, which Jan Vansina applied to the discussion of the historical process of sociopolitical formations in central Africa (Vansina, *Paths in the Rainforest*).

49. Bascom, *Yoruba*; Schwab, "Kinship and Lineage."

50. Olomola, *Thousands Year's*, 44.

51. Agbaje-Williams and Ogundiran, *Cultural Resources*; Beier, "Palace of the Ogogas"; Ogundiran, "Factional Competition"; Oguntuyi, *Short History.*

52. Gillespie, "When Is a House?," 37.

53. Beck, *Chiefdoms, Collapse, and Coalescence*, 31. A good example of such intergroup conflicts is the narrative of competition between Léigun of Ìgigun House and Àjàlọ́run Ọ̀rọ̀ of Ìlàrè House; another is the moietal conflict between Ìtá of Ìlémùré and Àjàlọ́run Ọ̀rọ̀ of Ìlàrè in the Upper Osun region. A primary goal of such conflicts and warfare was for the victorious House to incorporate as many members of the vanquished House as possible into its rank. See Ogundiran, "Factional Competition."

54. Gillespie, "When Is a House?," 41.

55. Barber, *I Could Speak until Tomorrow*, 158; Lloyd, "Agnatic and Cognatic Descent"; Schwab, "Kinship and Lineage."

56. Lévi-Strauss, *Way of the Masks*, 186.

57. Akintoye, *History of the Yoruba*; Obayemi, "The Yoruba and Edo-speaking peoples."

58. Jeje, "Ife Division," 24.

59. These two scenarios were the norm in the adjacent areas, such as the Edoid region, where more than forty walled enclosures (mega-Houses), each covering areas of 1–5 km in diameter, developed in an 80 km^2 area during the second half of the first millennium AD. Darling, *Archaeology and History in Southern Nigeria.*

60. Eluyemi, "Role of Oral Traditions," 121.

61. Obayemi, "Yoruba and Edo-Speaking Peoples."

62. Adediran, "Early Beginnings," 80.

63. Chief Ọlájídé Fárótìmí Fálọ́ba, Ọbadio and Chief Priest of Odùdùwà (oral interview, Ilé-Ifẹ̀, July 2, 2015). For elaboration on the aboriginal status of the Ùgbò, see Ademakinwa, *Ife, Cradle of the Yoruba*; Aremu et al., "Significance of Igbarubi-edi in Edi festival"; Olupona, *City of 201 Gods*, chap. 7.

64. Ọbàtálá, the most prominent of these Late Formative rulers in Ilé-Ifẹ̀, is credited in oral traditions with this early trend of humanism in artistic representation. Now regarded as the father of the Yorùbá pantheon and patron deity of artists, Ọbàtálá personifies visual art creativity in the Yorùbá

worldview and philosophy. Willett, *Ife in the History*, 122–23. Also see Lawuyi, "Obatala Factor."

65. Adediran, "Early Beginnings."

66. Olomola, "Ife before Oduduwa"; Obayemi, "Yoruba and Edo-Speaking Peoples."

67. Willett and Dempster, "Stone Carvings."

68. Afọlayan, "Towards a History of Eastern Yorubaland," 76; Usman, *Yoruba Frontier*, 59.

69. Agiri, "Early Oyo History," 7; Beier, "Before Oduduwa," 30; Esan, "Correspondence."

70. Atolagbe, *Itan Oore, Otun ati Moba.*

71. Chief Ọláolú Ọládọ̀tun Ôkánlàwọ́n Dàda, Ọbalésùn of Ifẹ̀ and Chief Priest of Ọbàtálá (oral interview, Ilé-Ifẹ̀, June 22, 2015). Also see Idowu, *Olódùmarè*, 19–20.

72. Among the other mega-House polities of deep antiquity in this region for which we have oral historical reference and surviving descendant communities are Ọ̀gọ̀tún, Erijiyan, Ìjerò, Ùlésùn, Osi, Ẹwọ, and Asin, near Ìkọ̀lé. For these insights, oral interviews were conducted with Ọba Ọládìran Agúnbíadé, the Olósi of Osi-Èkìtì (Osi-Èkìtì, June 6, 2016); Chief Àrọ̀wá of Ìrè-Èkìtì (Ìrè-Èkìtì, June 7, 2016). The tendency in the historiography and local traditions is to refer to the sixteen primary Èkìtì kingdoms (for a recent iteration of this, see Olufemi, "Alaafin of Oyo Writes Fayemi"). The idea that the Èkìtì had sixteen primary kings is a stereotypical standardization, consistent with the numerological symbolism in Yorùbá culture. This idea was particularly promoted under the British rule. Samuel Rowe, the British governor of the Gold Coast colony, captured the sense (but not the accuracy) of the vast number of polities in this area when he stated, referring to Èkìtì region, "There are said to be 132 kings among them." Samuel Rowe, "Further Notes on the Island of Lagos," May 29, 1883 (cited in Atolagbe, *Itan Oore, Otun Ati Moba*).

73. Most of these finds are accidental discoveries, and their sites have been the focus of several archaeological excavations. More than ten trenches have been excavated in the primary concentration area of the Èsìẹ́ figures. These have revealed the living floors of houses and activity areas of the communities that produced the sculptures. The recovered artifacts include many fragmentary and complete stone sculptures, fragments of terracotta figures, potsherds, stone tools (including LSA axes), iron slag, bone remains, and ashes. See Akinade, *Archaeological Perspective on the Esie*, Adekola, "Spatio-Temporal Inferences."

74. Akinade, *Archaeological Perspective on the Esie*, 8, 71; Usman, *Yoruba Frontier*, 64.

75. A radiocarbon date of AD 1016±13 (Cal AD 998–1024, Cal AD 993–1027, 2-sigma) has come from Oko-Òdò, a Late Formative community 4.5 km south of Èsìẹ́, where an Èsìẹ́-style sculpture as well as fragments of tuyere, iron slag, iron ore, and iron furnace wall have been found (Akinade, "Archaeological Perspective on the Esie," 71). Likewise, two thermoluminescence dates from Èsìẹ́ terracotta yielded 890±75 years (± 10 error) and 770 ± 70 (± 10 error) respectively. Statistically, these two dates indicate that the terracotta figures were made no later than AD 1100 (Stevens, *Stone Images*, 83). Kola Adekola's excavations of Èsìẹ́-period sites also have produced two latter

radiocarbon dates of Cal AD 1280–1390—Beta-314876, 2-sigma and Cal AD 1320–1450 AD (510+_50 BP)—Beta-299369, 2-sigma (Adekola, Spatio-Temporal Inferences, 130). These dates, from the ninth through the early fifteenth century, place Èsìẹ́ within the Late Formative and Classical periods as Ilé-Ifẹ̀. That is, the two were contemporaneous centers of artistic and sociopolitical innovations.

76. Obayemi, "Yoruba and Edo-Speaking Peoples," 291.

77. Pogoson, "Stylistic Possibilities in Esie."

78. Archaeologists have found unfinished sculptures in Èsìẹ́ and the surrounding areas. Likewise, mineralogical similarities between the sculptures and the natural steatite deposits at Òkè Òsu Ọlọ and Ìjan villages near Èsìẹ́ lend weight to the local origins of the sculptures. Ige and Swanson, "Provenance Studies of Esie"; Onabajo and Ige, "Mineralogy and Raw Material Characterization"; Usman, "Report on Newly Discovered Soapstone Figurines."

79. The two radiocarbon dates reported by Patrick Darling from excavations and exposed sections of Sungbo's embankment in Ketu and Oke-Eri (AD 870 and AD 670–1050) indicate that the construction of this monument began at least during the eighth or ninth century; while the recent work by Gerard Chouin and others in the Ìlárá-Ẹ̀pẹ́ sections of the embankment has yielded eight radiocarbon dates that suggest that the construction of the wall continued or resumed during the fifteenth century. Darling, "Sungbo's Eredo"; Darling, "Sungbo's Eredo, Southern Nigeria"; Lasisi and Aremu, "New Lights"; Chouin, "Ife-Sungbo."

80. Ọba Adeyemi Samuel Akinmusire, the Olúdòko of Ùdòko (oral interview, Ùdòko, May 28–29, 2016).

81. Oduwobi, "Oral Traditions"; Okùbọ́tẹ̀, *Ìwé Ìtàn Ìjẹ̀bú.*

82. Darling, "Sungbo's Eredo."

83. Ùlésùn was one of the largest polities in central Yorubaland supposedly preceding the Classical period. Isola Olomola describes it as an ancient kingdom of unknown antiquity. The oral tradition suggests that, at its height, Ùlésùn covered most of Ekitiland, including the entire central Èkìtì and "parts of Èkìtì East, Èkìtì south, Èkìtì southeast, and Ero," Olomola, *Thousands Year's*, 3. An archaeological reconnaissance survey in Èkìtì region conducted by this author and Professor Raphael Alabi (University of Ibadan) in 2016 also uncovered large ancient towns (now abandoned) often exceeding 1 km in diameter. There are many more of these archaeological sites waiting to be identified and investigated in the region. The archaeological investigation of these sites promises to establish the central role that Èkìtì played in the early Yorùbá history.

84. This is evident at Ọ̀run Ọba Adó, where occupation levels dating to the eighth and ninth centuries have been found. Willett, "Archaeology," 130.

85. Ozanne, "New Archaeological Survey," 32–33.

86. Obayemi, "Ancient Ile-Ife," 164.

87. Adediran, "Early Beginnings"; Akinjogbin, "Growth of Ife." The accounts of these conflicts are also recorded by Ọmọ́tọ̀ṣọ́ Elúyẹmí during his oral history field research in Ilé-Ifẹ̀ during the 1970s, Field Notes (private collection, courtesy of Nurudeen Amuda-Arogundade, Obafemi Awolowo University. Accessed July 10, 2014).

88. E.g., Connerton, *How Societies Remember*; Mali, *Mythistory.*

89. Eluyemi, "Role of Oral Traditions," 122.

90. The Ìrẹ̀lẹ̀ festival in Ìlàrè and Ikirun is one of such commemorative rituals. In the 1990s, when I was conducting oral historical research in the Ìjẹ̀ṣà region, many of the descendants of these ancient communities referred to their founding ancestors—such as Àjàlọ́run, Ol.ógò, and Ìtá—as the senior brothers of Odùduwà. This goes against the standard narratives in most parts of Yorubaland, where Odùduwà is regarded as the "father of the Yorùbá nation." These informants insisted that their own eponymous ancestors were already in Ilé-Ifẹ̀ before Odùduwà arrived, and when there was not enough space to accommodate them and Odùduwà's followers, their ancestors vacated the place to come to their current locations. Ọba Adéjọrọ̀ Ọ̀tẹ̀bọlákù, Ògìdán III, the Ọwálàrè of Ìlàrè (oral interview, Ìlàrè-Ìjẹ̀ṣà, January 11, 1997). Also see Ogundiran, "Filling a Gap"; Ogungbemi, "Igbo Baba Ilare"; and Oyelade, "Ọdún Ìrẹ̀lẹ̀," regarding this tradition in Ìlàrè; and Beier, "Before Oduduwa"; Olomola, "Ife before Oduduwa" for related narratives in Èkìtì area.

91. Olupona, *City of 201 Gods.*

92. Today, the Ùgbò communities are restricted to the 80 km stretch of Màhin coastal area, where about two hundred small fishing communities exist under the paramount leadership of Olúgbò of Ùgbò. The Ùgbò preference for settling near water and their traditional fishing occupation may be a retention of their pre-Classic subsistence in Ilé-Ifẹ̀, where they seem to have lived as fishers and foragers along the rivers and around the lakes in the Ifẹ̀ Bowl. In recent years, it appears the feud that happened more than a thousand years ago between the Ifẹ̀ and Ùgbò has been resuscitated by the Olúgbò of Ùgbò, Ọba Ọbátẹ́rù Akínrùntán, over his claims of seniority in the comity of Yorùbá kings. See Bello, "Ugbò-Ìlàjẹ́'s Place in Yorùbá History." Also see the response by the Ọ̀ọ̀ni of Ifẹ̀ in Makinde, "Olugbo's Outburst."

93. Before embarking on her dangerous spying mission, Mọ́rèmí reportedly made a vow to the goddess of Ẹ̀sínmírìn River that if the goddess protected her and she returned to Ilé-Ifẹ̀ safely, she will give the goddess whatever she demanded. Following the Ifẹ̀ victory and commencement of stability, Mọ́rèmí returned to Ẹ̀sínmírìn River goddess to ask the price of her success. To her surprise, the goddess asked for the sacrifice of Olúorogbo, the only son of Mọ́rèmí. With sadness but with appreciation for what the goddess has done for her city, she delivered Olúorogbo as the sacrifice for her success. Generations of Ifẹ̀ children (and indeed children of the Yorùbá community of practice) would have been regaled with this story as the best virtue of citizenship, honor, bravery, and self-sacrifice in which the need and well-being of the city was greater than the desire of the individual. These stories are still being told today in different literary and performative genres of popular culture (e.g., Ladipo, *Moremi*; Ogunremi, *Moremi Ajasoro*). And the events that culminated in the sacrifice of Olúorogbo are celebrated and commemorated in Ẹ̀di festival, an important event on the contemporary ritual calendar of Ilé-Ifẹ̀ (Olúpọ̀nà, *City of 201 Gods,* 203–223).

94. Willett, *Ife*; see also Ogundiran, "Chronology, Material Culture, and Pathways"; and Usman, *Yoruba Frontier.*

95. Blier, *Art and Risk*; Willett, *Ife.*

96. See Ige and Rehren, "Black Sand and Iron Stone." It was not only in Ilé-Ifẹ̀ that this strategy of iron production was used; evidence for this self-drafting smelting process abounds, especially in the Igbomina area.

97. There is an ongoing program of archaeological excavations that focuses on the Outer Wall, especially in the Ìta Yemòó and Òkè Àtàn areas of Ilé-Ifẹ̀, and this may shed more light on the long-term chronology of embankment construction in Ilé-Ifẹ̀. Chouin and Ogunfolakan, "Ife–Sungbo Archaeological Project."

98. Ozanne, "New Archaeological Survey."

99. For distribution of potsherd pavements in Ile-Ife, see Garlake, "Excavations at Obalara's Land"; Garlake, "Excavations on the Woye Asiri Family Land"; Ogunfolakan, "Archaeological survey of North-East"; and Eyo, "Odo Ogbe Street and Lafogido"; Willett, *Ife*.

100. Oral traditions credit Lúwò Gbágìdá, listed on the Ifẹ̀ regnal list as a female king, with the draining of many ravines in Ilé-Ifẹ̀ and with the paving of the major thoroughfares of the city with potsherds. She has been judged harshly in the oral traditions for the human tolls that resulted from the exacting forced labor involved in the building project. One tradition claimed that many laborers died in the ravines in the course of carrying out the public project. See Akinjogbin, "Growth of Ife," 104; Willett, *Ife*, 104. This contemporary memory may have been a post-Classical fabrication that is far from the experience of the Classical period. To start, the construction of the pavement, like most other aspects of Classical-era material life, was unlikely restricted to the reign of one king. Rather, the building project most likely took place throughout the Classical period, lasting at least three hundred years. Second, the position of Lúwò on the king list put her in the post-seventeenth-century period, when the construction of these pavements had already ended. So the popular association of Lúwò with potsherd pavement in Ifẹ̀ traditions has no historical credibility. As I will show in chap. 4, Lúwò is a stock character in Ifẹ̀ oral traditions for whatever post-sixteenth-century historians of Ifẹ̀ considered to be an embodiment of bad leadership.

101. Kusimba, Barut-Kusimba, and Agbaje-Williams, "Precolonial African Cities," 157.

102. I use the pronouns *he* and *him* here because these early *ọba* of *ìlú* and almost all of their descendants in different parts of the Yorùbá world were men. Occasionally, we have women assuming the roles of *ọba-aládé*.

103. In contemporary Ilé-Ifẹ̀, "*ọba*" has survived till today as prefix in the titles of the House and mega-House leaders whose ancestry predated the Classical period. Examples include Ọbatálá, Ọbalálẹ̀, Ọbalésùn, Ọbalíá, Ọbalọ́ràn, and Obaléjùgbè.

104. A notable example is Ọbalùfọ̀n Aláyémọrẹ́, a king of Ifẹ̀ during the mid to late fourteenth century. Aláyémọrẹ́ is claimed to be a son of Ọ̀sángangan Ọbamakin, a staunch opponent of Odùduwà and devotee of Ọ̀ramfẹ̀. Ọbamakin had deep ancestral roots in the Late Formative period. See Adediran, "Early Beginnings"; Akinjogbin, "Growth of Ife," 90. Also, Akintoye, *History of the Yoruba*; Blier, *Art and Risk*.

105. Bascom, *Yoruba*, 34–35.

106. Chief Ọlájídé Fárótìmí Fálọ́ba, Obadio of Ifẹ̀ and Chief Priest of Odùduwà (oral interview, Ilé-Ifẹ̀, July 2, 2015).

107. This status was reversible for those who had been members of an *ilé* before joining the *mọdéwá*. Those could at any time return to become a member of a House, but the individual had to renounce any appointment within the palace that arose from his status as a *mọdéwá*.

108. This situation is not restricted to Ifẹ̀ but exists across the Yorùbá region where the divine king institution became the primary basis of governance toward the close of the first millennium AD. Local traditions in Ilé-Ifẹ̀ recall that the elite *mọdéwá* sometimes took advantage of the levers of power they controlled in the palace to attempt a power grab at the expense of the nonroyal chieftains. There are also references in the oral traditions of Ifẹ̀ to instances when some *mọdéwá* chieftains usurped the throne and ruled as kings. One such usurper was Lájùwà, a chamberlain said to have killed the reigning Ọ̀ọ̀ni and used disguises to rule in the name of the murdered king until the plot was uncovered. The frequent reference to usurpation of the throne by different palace officials demonstrates the power that these extra-House officials wielded in the administration of *ìlú*, their coveted position as confidants of the king, and the anxieties over the balance of power between the palace officials and the town (House) chiefs. See Akinjogbin, "Growth of Ife," 99; Idowu, *Olódùmarè*, 224–25.
109. I owe this discussion on the *Ògbóni* to several conversations that I had with Chief Edward Fádípẹ̀, the Ṣàjúkú of Ìpolé Ìjẹ̀ṣà, especially in July 5–10, 1990. I thank the elders of Ìpolé Ìjẹ̀ṣà for giving me the opportunity to observe.
110. Lawal, "À Yà Gbó, À Yà Tó," 37.
111. Abiodun, *Yorùbá Art and Language*, 159–60. As I have shown in the preceding pages, this idealism has a deep root in the Archaic period of Yorùbá history and, in fact, goes further back to the proto-Niger-Congo history.
112. Akintoye, *History of the Yoruba*, 131. This explains why the installation of a new king in Yorubaland usually involved initiation of the king-elect to the schools of the major deities in the metropolis and the required visit of the king-elect to the temples of these deities during the course of the coronation rituals. For example, see Eluyemi, *Selecting an Ooni.*
113. Eyo, *Recent Excavations at Ife and Owo.*
114. Lawal, "Àwòrán," 503. There are very few exceptions to this rule. One is the bust of an elderly priest with a contorted and swollen face and an open mouth suggesting an act of invocation. The figure wears a bead on the upper forehead and a simian- or human-skull pendant. Another example of realist-naturalism is a terracotta head from Ọ̀wọ̀ labeled "Bearded Head." See Drewal, Pemberton, and Abiodun, *Yoruba*, 64, 95, figs. 69 and 96.
115. Lawal, "Àwòrán," 511.
116. Ogundiran, "Towns and States," 870.
117. Abiodun, "Reconsideration"; Willett, "On the Funeral Effigies of Owo and Benin."
118. Lawal, "Àwòrán," 517.
119. Garlake, "Excavations at Ọbalara's Land"; Ogundiran, *Archaeology and History in Ìlàrè District.*
120. Garlake, "Excavations at Obalara's Land"; Ogundiran, "Filling a Gap"; Eyo, "Igbo'Laja."
121. McAnany, *Living with the Ancestors*, 60. Also see Freedman, *Chinese Lineage and Society*; Fortes, *Religion, Morality, and the Person.*
122. Chief Ọ̀dọlé Fágbilé (oral interview, Ìlàrè-Ìjẹ̀ṣà, April 19, 1997) and Chief J. A. Ajé (oral interview, Ìlàrè-Ìjẹ̀ṣà, March 15, 1997) offered this explanation with reference to a thirteenth-century burial with fragmented remains that I excavated at Igbó Ìloyì in Ìlàrè district.

123. McAnany, *Living with the Ancestors*, 61.
124. Ogundiran, "Filling a Gap," 47.
125. The multiple disarticulated skeletal remains from Ọbalára site are the best example we have so far of ancestral veneration in Classical Ifẹ̀. Found in a matrix of six potsherd pavements, the burial deposits were in different concentrations. Relevant to our discussion here is a concentration of eight complete human crania, thirty-one fragmented calvaria, and two fragments of long bone (Concentration B). About two meters from this concentration is a mass of human long bones associated with animal mandibles, an intermix of sheep/goat and human teeth, and a single human skull (Concentration F). No other skeletal part—especially ribs, scapulae, or vertebrae—was present in these concentrations. The following artifacts were also part of these two deposits: iron nails, rods, and staffs; glass beads; complete and broken vessels; polished stone axes; mullers; stone slabs; and a wide range of fragmented human terracotta figures. Eight other concentrations of artifacts were found at the excavated site, all pointing to several ritual activities involving not only the primary burial of certain individuals but also the periodic exhumation and reburial of their skeletal remains in a process that lasted for several years, if not generations. The locus where these activities took place had elaborate potsherd/stone pavement. This multigenerational ancestral shrine would have been the focal point of several sacrificial events, festivities, and prayer sessions that invoked the spirits of the ancestors.
126. Schwab, "Kinship and Lineage."
127. Adegoke, *Study of the Role of Women*, 95.
128. Idowu, *Olódùmarè*, 194.
129. Bascom, *Ifa Divination*, 115.
130. Bascom, *Yoruba*, 68.
131. Gillespie, "Body and Soul," 73.
132. The Ifẹ̀ copper-alloy works are mainly brass (copper and zinc), and they generally have high lead and arsenic contents with low antinomy. Willett, "Bronze Figures"; Werner and Willett, "Composition of brasses from Ife."
133. Willett, "Radiocarbon Dates."
134. Willett, "Bronze Figures," 308.
135. William Bascom wrote that no funeral rites were performed for deceased children. Such individuals were "buried immediately in the back yard or the forest without being bathed, shaved, or dressed . . . (and) childless persons were treated in this fashion." *Yoruba*, 65. Also see Abimbola, "Yoruba Concept of Human Personality."
136. Lloyd, "Conflict Theory."

3

Knowledge Capital and Referentiality

BETWEEN MARCH AND MAY 1830, Richard Lander (accompanied by his brother John) led a British expedition across the Yorùbá country to determine the course and termination of the River Niger. The explorers spent nine days in Ọ̀yọ́-Ilé, capital of the Ọ̀yọ́ Empire. Richard Lander was not new to the city. The visit was his third over a period of four years.[1] On May 15, he visited the city's largest daytime market, Ọjà Ayaba, where he came across an object that arrested his attention. He described this object as a "curious and singular kind of stone. . . . It consists of a variety of little transparent stones, white, green, and every shade of blue, all embedded in a species of clayey earth, resembling rough mosaic work."[2] What Richard Lander mistook for a rare piece of stone was *ajé ìlẹ̀kẹ̀* (plate 4), a remnant product from glass manufacture, described eighty-three years later by a German explorer in Ilé-Ifẹ̀ as a fragment of the glass-bead crucible with "a mass of fused bits of glass" on the interior surface.[3] Lander not only bought the "stone" but also asked the seller questions about its origins. He summed up the response to his inquiry thus: "The natives informed us that it was dug from the earth, in a country called Iffie [Ifẹ̀] which is stated to be 'four moons' [*sic*] journey from Katunga [Ọ̀yọ́-Ilé], where, according to their tradition, their first parents were created, and from whence all Africa was peopled."[4]

In this encounter, we see how the origin of the people of Ọ̀yọ́-Ilé was revealed to Lander through an object. Lander's informants located the origins of their forebears in a place about 150 kilometers away. This is the same Ilé-Ifẹ̀ that we came across in the previous chapter, a place with an unusual *oríkì* (a panegyric or poetic appellation): *Ifẹ̀ oòyè, Ifẹ̀ oòdáyé, ibi tí ojúmọ tí n mọ́ wá, Ifẹ̀ olórí ayé gbogbo*—"Ilé-Ifẹ̀, the place of survivors, the birthplace of the world, the source of daybreak, the leader of the entire world."[5]

It was not only in Ọ̀yọ́-Ilé that the importance of Ilé-Ifẹ̀ was conveyed to the early European visitors in the region. And it was not the first time. During his four visits to Benin kingdom in the 1490s, Portuguese explorer Duarte Pacheco Pereira was informed of another state farther inland whose king was called Hooguanee. He noted that the people of Benin described this inland king with a palpable reverence, prompting him to liken the status of Hooguanee in Benin to what "the Pope is among us [Portuguese]."[6] This great reverence for Hooguanee was also expressed by an ambassador of Benin who visited Portugal in 1540. In his synthesis of the reports of early Portuguese visitors to Benin and the accounts given by the Benin ambassador, the foremost Portuguese historian of his generation, João de Barros, wrote:

> Among the many things which the King D. João learnt from the ambassador of the king of Beny [Benin] . . . was that to the east of Beny at twenty moons' journey—which . . . would be about two hundred and fifty of our leagues—there lived the most powerful monarch of these parts, who was called Ogané. . . . He was held in as great veneration as is the Supreme Pontif with us. In accordance with a very ancient custom, the king of Beny, on ascending the throne, sends ambassadors to him with rich gifts to announce that by the decease of his predecessor he has succeeded to the kingdom of Beny, and to request confirmation. To signify his assent, the prince Ogané sends the king a staff and a headpiece of shining brass, fashioned like a Spanish helmet, in place of a crown and sceptre. He also sends a cross, likewise of brass, to be worn round the neck, a holy and religious emblem similar to that worn by the Knights of the Order of Saint John. Without these emblems the people do not recognize him as lawful ruler, nor can he call himself truly king.[7]

Who was this lord of an inland kingdom responsible for legitimizing the authority of the king of Benin? This question has been a subject of historical debate. Scholars who privilege oral traditions and other spheres of African cultural production, such as visual arts, have identified Ilé-Ifẹ̀ as the inland kingdom. A few others who take the Portuguese sources literally have argued that the area of the Niger-Benue valley lies to the east of Benin and that this must have been the location of this revered kingdom.[8] As I will show below, the evidence is incontrovertibly in support of the former, that Ilé-Ifẹ̀ is the point of reference in those fifteenth- and sixteenth-century Benin and Portuguese accounts.

Let us begin with the transliteration of Benin oral sources into Portuguese documentary accounts. Ilé-Ifẹ̀ lies to the west of Benin, whereas the Portuguese sources claimed that Hooguanee's kingdom was located "east" of Benin. This has been a source of confusion to some of the contemporary academic historians who took this geographical rendition of the "east" in Portuguese sources literally and have therefore questioned the validity of the claim that Ilé-Ifẹ̀ was the place referred to in these Portuguese sources. The confusion arose from the inattentiveness of these historians to the importance of metaphor in African oratures. First, the Benin oral traditions describing Ogané and his land as "the source of the daybreak" or "rising sun" were mistranslated by both Pereira and Barros as the "east."[9] However, the metaphor of "the source of the rising sun" in both Benin (Edo-speaking) and Yorùbá oral traditions does not mean "the east." It means "the source of vitality" and "place of origin." This is Ilé-Ifẹ̀, the founding source of Benin *ọba*'s dynasty, and a place of reference for Benin's royal identity. This identity is rooted in Ifẹ̀-Benin cultural historical relationships, so well evident in both archaeological and visual arts sources.[10]

Moreover, De Barros's Ogané is the same as Pereira's Hooguanee. Both are Portuguese phonetic transcriptions of *oghene*, the Benin/Edo word for "mighty or great lord." The phonetic similarity of *oghene* and *ọ̀ọ̀ni*, the Yorùbá title of the king of Ilé-Ifẹ̀, is also obvious. Etymologically, *ọ̀ọ̀ni* is a contraction of three syllables: *ọ̀-wọ̀-ni* (or *ọ-ghọ-ni* in southeastern Yorùbá dialect).[11] It means "a mighty lord." In Benin's Edo language, the king of Ilé-Ifẹ̀ is referred to as *Oghene ne Uhe*—"Mighty Lord of Ifẹ̀."[12] Therefore, these Portuguese accounts are the earliest textual sources that we have on the historical relationship between Ilé-Ifẹ̀ and Benin, especially the role that the former played in legitimizing the ascension of any king-elect to Benin's throne. Archaeological evidence has corroborated the historical sources indicating that the relationships between the two polities date to at least the thirteenth century.[13] As I show in this chapter, the evidence is overwhelming that the Ogané and Hooguanee in the Portuguese sources refer to the king of Ilé-Ifẹ̀.

Benin and Ọ̀yọ́-Ilé are 350 kilometers apart, with Ilé-Ifẹ̀ being approximately equidistant from both of them (see fig. 1.1). And, the encounters between Africa and Europe cited above, in Ọ̀yọ́ and Benin, were separated by almost 340 years. But in both cities, those encounters point to the importance of Ilé-Ifẹ̀ in the consciousness of the Yorùbá and Edo peoples as a place of reverence and reference. Richard Lander's encounter in the Queen's Market at Ọ̀yọ́-Ilé; Duarte Pacheco Pereira's recounting of the stories he heard in Benin; and João de Barros's synthesis evoke Ilé-Ifẹ̀ as the reference point for social order, temporality, regional identity, memory, and meaning. These representations were not random or episodic but part of the system of thought among the Yoruba- and Edo-speaking people. They were products of an integrated regional identity, the Yorùbá community of practice, that Ilé-Ifẹ̀ championed between 1100 and 1400. This community was a political, economic, intellectual, and sociological universe with a uniform cosmology and theogony. It was predicated on the ideology of divine kingship. The universe of this community revolved around Ilé-Ifẹ̀ as its point of reference, and Benin and Ọ̀yọ́ were two of its anchors. Before the mid-twentieth century, when Christian and Islamic cosmologies became pervasive in the region's mentality, Ilé-Ifẹ̀ was universally regarded in this Yorùbá community of practice as the ultimate place of origin, located between the earth and heaven. It was believed across the Yorùbá-Edo world that the souls of the deceased individuals returned to Ilé-Ifẹ̀, where they reincarnated in preparation for a new life.[14]

To understand the historical processes that produced this community and its integrated consciousness, I seek to answer these three overlapping questions:

1. What were the characteristics of the Yorùbá community of practice, and how was it created?
2. What roles did Ilé-Ifẹ̀ play in the crafting, dissemination, and consolidation of a consciousness for this community?
3. How did Ilé-Ifẹ̀ emerge as the place of reference for the community's ideas about kingship institution, cosmology, and regional identity? What actions, events, and people enabled Ilé-Ifẹ̀ to attain this status of referentiality so that in the late fifteenth-century Benin and early nineteenth-century Ọ̀yọ́-Ilé, local identities and institutions were thinkable only with reference to Ilé-Ifẹ̀?

The key to answering these questions lies in understanding how "knowledge capital" (KC) is created and used to generate value. KC is an asset of people, skills, infrastructure, technical know-how, information, and organizational processes mobilized to create replicating value for a wide interaction sphere. This sphere of interaction could be regional, continental, or global.[15] KC is a product of rigorous experimentation, discovery, learning, and mastery of intellectual property at the local level. The ownership and effective coordination of these assets distinguishes a corporate unit (e.g., an *ilé* or *ìlú*) from its peers and potentially gives it strategic advantages in a competitive field of interactions. The referential status of Ilé-Ifẹ̀, as we shall soon see, developed from the knowledge capital that it created and through which far-flung polities and peoples across the Yorùbá-speaking region and beyond began to translate their worldview and historical experiences during the twelfth century. There are three components of Ifẹ̀'s knowledge capital:

1. High-stakes intellectual property in the manufacture of glass and glass beads, and other crafts, especially copper-alloy sculptures.
2. A legitimizing ideology of kingship through a large corpus of discursive, performative, and material representations.
3. A compendium of well-integrated intellectual products, including cosmogony, theogony, rituals, mytho-history, and metaphysics (*ifá* divination) that made universal claims and served as a source of systematic study, reflection, and interpretation for problem solving.

None of these three categories of knowledge capital was autonomous from the others. They were interrelated. It was the simultaneous mobilization of all of them that enabled Ilé-Ifẹ̀ to champion the integration of several polities and principalities into a network of hierarchical peer-polities between the twelfth and fourteenth centuries, and to become the reference point for that network. However, these facets of Ifẹ̀'s knowledge capital and their use in creating the Yorùbá community of practice can only be understood in the context of the *ìlú/ọba-aládé* dyad, a sociopolitical innovation that developed and intensified between ca. AD 800 and 1000 in different parts of the Yorùbá region. As we have seen in the previous chapter, Ilé-Ifẹ̀ was not the primary instigator of this innovation but was its beneficiary. However, Ilé-Ifẹ̀ served as the most ardent propagator of a version of this dyadic system of governance and made it the epistemological basis of a regional social order.

Glass Bead: Technological and Economic Basis of the Yorùbá Community of Practice

How did this all happen? To answer this question, we must start with the role that beads played in Yoruboid/Yorùbá political tradition. As early as the Archaic period, the beads made of certain gem crystals were the sine qua non legitimating index for chiefly authority as well as a symbol of political office and spiritual power.[16] In the Late Formative sites of Èsìẹ́, Èsùré, and Ilé-Ifẹ̀, all the stone sculptures of chiefly figures were depicted with the representation of beads on the neck, ankle, and wrist. These beads convey the honor, prestige, power, and authority associated with the wearers and call attention to the good fortune of men and women who attained the heights of their divine potentiality or self-realization. As political authority became increasingly specialized during the Early Formative period, so did the categories of beads that represented this power. Jasper was the preferred material for the beads of power. There were also carnelian and other red and brown chalcedonic varieties. The social valuation and metaphysical importance of jasper beads (*àkún*) as the badges with which power and authority were vested in individuals continued with the advent of the *ìlú/ọba-aládé* model of governance, around the ninth or tenth century. Several varieties of these cryptocrystalline silica beads have been found in Ọ̀yọ́-Ilé, Ìgbómìnà, Ilé-Ifẹ̀, Iléṣà, and Benin, in archaeological contexts ranging from the ninth through the early nineteenth century.[17]

The geology of northern and central Yorùbá contains some deposits of cryptocrystalline silica rocks (chalcedony).[18] But jasper was more abundant farther up the Niger River, especially in the areas of Karey Gorou, Litingo, and Kirtashi that now adjoin Songhai, Dendi, and Tienga territories (see fig. 1.1).[19] These rocks were transported down the Niger and funneled through the Moshi-Niger area into the Yorùbá country, where they were used for bead manufacture. The large concentrations of complete stone beads and their fragments, as well as stone bead polishers in Ọ̀bà-Ìgbómìnà (presumed capital of the famed Ọ̀bà kingdom), are indicative of large-scale production or reworking of stone beads.[20] In the Ọ̀yọ́-Ilé area, where the manufacture of jasper beads may be as old as AD 900–1000, beadworkers fashioned these "rocks into highly polished reddish brown beads in a variety of shapes and sizes," including cylindrical and barrel-shaped, triangular pendants, as well as elongated hexagons.[21] Although of a much later date, ca. 1780–1830, two partially worked triangular-shaped jasper pendant along with two polishing stones that were likely used for bead-working have turned up in the recent excavations at Ọ̀yọ́-Ilé (see plate 4).

The production of jasper-carnelian beads was a laborious and lengthy process, requiring "skill, strength, and considerable patience."[22] Ethnographic sources indicate that it could take four to seven days of full-time work for one professional beadworker to produce a necklace of eighteen beads.[23] The high cost of production, in terms of material, labor, and skill—from quarrying, transporting, or importing appropriate rocks, to shaping, grinding, boring, polishing, and stringing—perennially kept small quantities in circulation. This helped to maintain the high social and economic valuation of *àkún,* the Yorùbá name for these red stones. The limited volume in circulation also facilitated the implementation of the sumptuary laws that were put in place to control the distribution and acquisition of these beads as legitimizing objects of power.[24] The temporal and spiritual powers of a chieftain, including the Late Formative House *ọba*, ultimately depended on the wearing of these beads, for they embodied the *àṣẹ* that was associated with their authority to cause any utterance of blessing, vow, or curse to come to pass.[25] The raging fire of specialized leadership that was spreading across the region after AD 500 necessitated the standardization of the emblem of authority. These precious reddish stones served that role and of legitimizing the authority of those who occupied the highest leadership positions. Hence, whenever the succession to any of these Formative-era offices was in dispute, the contestant who possessed the *àkún* beads had the upper hand in making a claim of legitimacy to the office.[26] This symbolism of authority was carried over to the era of *ọba-aládé* (divine kingship). The demand for beaded attire, made of chalcedony rocks, significantly increased ca. AD 800–1000 as a result of the proliferation of centralized political systems and the dyadic *ìlú/ọba-aládé* institution. The demand expanded long-distance commerce and also gave rise to manufacturing depots in the northern Yorùbá-speaking area, especially near the Moshi-Niger River system, the major entry point for these valuable materials into the Yorùbá world. As a result, the control of the distribution of these objects of power and authority became a strategic political goal for those polities on the distribution networks.

However, the monopoly that jasper/carnelian and other variants of red chalcedony beads held as the emblem of divine and political power was challenged by Ilé-Ifẹ̀ during the eleventh century, soon after its political consolidation. This challenge came in the form of locally manufactured glass beads, which Ilé-Ifẹ̀ added to its repertoire of elite paraphernalia. It was once thought that the glass-bead production in Ilé-Ifẹ̀ was based on the remelting and refurbishing of imported glass and glass beads from Medieval Europe, Mediterranean, and Asia.[27] Recent archaeological excavations in Ilé-Ifẹ̀ and Òṣogbo, as well as geochemical analyses of the excavated glass beads, glass manufacture debris, and raw materials from these and other sites across the Yorùbá region, have produced stunning results that lead to the following conclusions:

1. The majority of glass materials from Ilé-Ifẹ̀ dating to the Classical period (in Olókun Grove, Ìta Yemọ̀ọ́, and Ọ̀run Ọba Adó) are of unusually high lime, high alumina content (HLHA). These glassy objects have proportions of alumina and lime that are unusually higher than those found in ancient Islamic, European, and Asian glasses. This indicates that these glass beads were produced with recipes different from those of other glass-manufacturing centers in the ancient world.
2. For raw materials, the Ifẹ̀ glassmakers and their later offshoots in other parts of Yorùbá region used feldspathic pegmatite (granites) as their silica base (bulk material or formers). They added potash to the recipe to lower the melting point for the formers, and powdered snail shells were used as the source of calcium to stabilize and harden the glass and to improve the mechanical properties and physical appearance of the final product. In addition, the glassmakers used locally available mineral deposits of cobalt, nickel, and iron oxides, as well as imported copper alloys, to produce beads in a variety of colors.[28]

3. Radiocarbon dates show that glass-bead production began in Ilé-Ifẹ̀ during the eleventh century. The production was operated on an industrial scale, and it reached apogee during the fourteenth century.
4. These high lime, high alumina (HLHA) glasses from Ifẹ̀ and other parts of West Africa have been called "Yorùbá glass" on account of their unique chemical signatures, raw materials, and recipes. The glasses were granite-based, different from the plant-ash-based glass of the Islamic world (including India), late Bronze Age Egypt, and Mesopotamia; the mineral natron glass of the Greek, Roman, and Byzantine Empires; the lead and lead-barium glass of Han China; or the wood-ash and ash-lime glass of medieval Europe.[29]

Ilé-Ifẹ̀ was not the first to develop the *ìlú/ọba-aládé* dyad, but it appears to be the first to succeed in using its own locally produced material, glass beads, to validate the institution of divine kingship (*ọba-aládé*). Ilé-Ifẹ̀ used its glass beads to challenge the monopoly that the red jasper beads had enjoyed as the preferred emblems of power and authority, at least during the Late Formative period. As we shall see below, the beginning of glass production in Ilé-Ifẹ̀ significantly liberated the Yorùbá *ìlú/ọba-aládé* polities from dependency on external sources as the means of validating their locally crafted ideology of power, the idealism of social order, and the legitimacy of those who held the levers of power and authority. Ilé-Ifẹ̀ used its glass-technology know-how to destabilize the supply chain of the jasper beads coming from the Moshi-Niger area. It did this by marketing two of its prime glass products—the blue (*ṣẹ̀gi*) and red (*iyùn*) dichroic glass beads—to the surrounding region as the primary identifiers of royal and elite status. Soon, these beads became synonymous with the *ìlú/ọba-aládé* dyad, and they served as prestige goods that sustained the elaborate rank system and chiefly authorities that accompanied the proliferation of this dyad across the Yorùbá-speaking world.

To be sure, the Ifẹ̀ glass did not totally replace Moshi-Niger rock. The latter continued to be relevant. In fact, both were combined as markers of grandeur, wealth, honor, and power. However, Ilé-Ifẹ̀ promoted its glass beads as the spiritual essence of royal authority. This was possible because the Ifẹ̀ glass-bead industry had the following advantages over the Moshi-Niger's jasper beads. Whereas the latter produced only one category of power-vested beads, *àkún*, Ilé-Ifẹ̀ produced different varieties (in colors and materials) of power-vested glass beads, of which *ṣẹ̀gi*, the bluish dichroic glass beads, and *iyùn*, the reddish dichroic glass beads, were preponderant (see plate 4). These multiple categories of beads catered to different segments of social hierarchies and allowed for differentiated taste and accumulation beyond the royal and noble classes. Moreover, because of the renewable nature of the raw materials needed for glass production, and the ability to mass-produce them, Ilé-Ifẹ̀ was able to make its glass-bead products far more accessible to a larger area than *àkún* makers were able to manage. Within a few decades of its nascent glass industry during the eleventh century, Ilé-Ifẹ̀ would have succeeded in outstripping the quantities of jasper/carnelian beads that the Moshi-Niger area and all other areas combined were able to supply into the Yorùbá region. Likewise, the complex production process of glass, the high level of skills involved, and the dichroic qualities of the final product gave these beads the "magical" effect. Soon, they became objects of desire across and beyond the Yorùbá region.[30]

The Ifẹ̀ glass beads appeared to have quickly risen to the highest chart on the material index of social valuation, and they played a significant role in the evolution of the integrated regional network that developed in the Yorùbá-speaking world and beyond between 1100 and 1400. The story of glass beads in the Yorùbá world represents an early example of technological nationalism in West Africa, whereby Ilé-Ifẹ̀ moved the instrument of political validation away from external sources and used its own products to promote a new vision of integrated regional social order.[31] In other words, Ilé-Ifẹ̀ used its technological know-how in glass production to forge regional connectedness and to foster the dependency of other polities on its own locally produced objects of power. It did this by creating an idea of regional identity that made glass beads indispensable to conceptualizing social order and to legitimizing the power, authority, and institutions needed for realizing that order. With the rising demands for Ifẹ̀ glass beads by the growing number of elites and other segments of society across the region, commerce significantly expanded within and beyond the Yorùbá-speaking world. It was this glass technology and its products that defined the Yorùbá Classical period as an era of prosperity. With its glass industry, Ilé-Ifẹ̀ became the dominant emporium of that era.

For most of its history, the Ifẹ̀ glass production was concentrated in Olókun Grove, in the northernmost part of the walled city (see fig. 2.8).[32] It was an industrial site that occupied about 268 hectares during its apogee.[33] The production center was under the patronage of the *ọ̀ọ̀ni* of Ifẹ̀, who appointed an official, *wàlódè*, to supervise the production center. The portfolio of this powerful official during the Classical period included the supervision of market affairs. He was also in charge of the annual Olókun festival, to honor the patron deity of commerce, glass production, and prosperity.[34] Many years of archaeological research in Olókun Grove have yielded thousands of crucible fragments. These crucibles were the very thick pots in which the grinded recipes of pegmatite, snail shell, and colorants were melted under very high temperatures to produce glass.[35] The scale of glass production was enormous. In a 16-square-meter area excavated by archaeologist Babatunde Babalola, 812 crucible fragments, over 13,000 complete beads, almost 3 kilograms of glass waste and cullet, in addition to several production tools, which included 403 fragments of ceramic cylinders, were found.[36] The range of artifacts from the site demonstrates that all the various stages of glass production were present in Olókun Grove, and the volume of glass-production-related finds shows that the industry was a large-scale operation. Billions of glass beads would have been manufactured there in the course of about four hundred years.[37] Most of these beads were exported to various destinations across and beyond the Yorùbá world. This glass industry financed the city's imports.

The elaborate and complicated *chaîne opératoire* and skills involved in glass and glass-bead production accentuated the value of the final products. The process of mining and crushing pegmatite rocks, blending these with snail shells and colorants, and turning the mixture into glass products in a highly controlled temperature was the most complicated craft that developed in the Yorùbá world during this era. The glassmakers demonstrated an advanced mastery of the chemistry and mineral properties of their raw materials; experimented with different recipes; and produced beads of various physical properties, in terms of hardness, texture, color, and durability. All of these advances had emotional and magical effects on consumers and raised the social valuation of glass beads as objects of power and desire. These beads served multiple roles in the different social fields, including such cycles of life as marriage, conception, motherhood, childhood, puberty, adulthood, and other milestones on the ladders of social hierarchies and self-realization. At the peak of their game, the glassmakers of Ifẹ̀ produced not only for kings and chiefs but also for members of religious orders and for the common people. Hence, while the red stone *àkún* was locked up in the sphere of political power circulation, the Ifẹ̀ glass beads had more permeating roles in multiple social fields. What is striking in the production of this knowledge capital is that the raw materials needed for glass production were not only abundant but also renewable and inexhaustible within Ilé-Ifẹ̀ and its immediate environs. What might have been scarce were the skill sets required to produce different categories of beads for a diverse market and the labor needed to source and process the raw materials in order to meet the demands of consumers near and far. The political elite of Ilé-Ifẹ̀ seem to have jealously guarded the knowledge of this labor-intensive and sophisticated skill-dependent craft. It was the secret of their competitive advantage in the region. Mythical stories about the origins of glass beads therefore gained ground and spread farther afield. These stories served to entrench the idea of a mystical and spiritual relationship between Ilé-Ifẹ̀ and its glass beads.[38]

The communicative interactions across multiple but overlapping spheres of knowledge communities, involving the political chieftains, priests of religious orders, and master glassmakers in Ilé-Ifẹ̀ on one hand and the wider region they served on the other, turned glass beads into conceptual objects for thinking about and contemplating a wide range of social, political, and religious issues. For example, glass beads of diverse physical attributes—material composition, hardness, luster, and color—were associated with different *àṣẹ* (transformative power and energy). And these attributes and their *àṣẹ* were associated with particular deities and institutional powers. Hence, the political and religious chieftains wore beads that were compatible with the *ìwà* (essence), *àṣẹ*, and purpose of their respective offices and *òrìṣà*.[39] In fact, the diversity of the colors of the glass beads produced in Ifẹ̀'s furnaces—"pale transparent greenish blue, brilliant peacock-blue, rich dark red, olive-brown, dark green, turquoise,"[40] as well as milky white and yellow—may have been used during the Classical period to develop a standardized chromatic system. These colors were used for coding the temperament and essence (*ìwà*) of the several deities who were populating the region's pantheon, and for marking the multiplicity of titles, offices, and authorities that formed the core of the *ìlú/ọba-aládé* government.[41]

The Ifẹ̀ glass beads were both knowledge capital and epistemic objects. As epistemic objects, glass beads were more than things. They were deployed to legitimize the institutions of divine kingship and the individuals who were the leaders and officers of those institutions, including the king and palace officials, the House chieftains, and priests and priestesses, among others. These glass beads were also representations of things and ideas. They had universal appeal and desire because they enjoyed ready acceptance by members of the community of practice for what they represented—social order, wealth, power, legitimacy, honor, aspiration, self-realization, and knowledge. As objects of knowledge capital, they had the quality of not being inordinately scarce; neither were they common. Rather, they were accessible but could not be replicated outside their home of production. As a result of these qualities, Ilé-Ifẹ̀ succeeded in converting its most labor- and skill-intensive manufactured product into an indispensable representation of social order and wellness, and therefore into an object and a subject of ultimate desire. It vigorously marketed these products to other peoples and places through a wide range of exchange practices, of which two predominated. On the one hand, the distribution of the beads was embedded in Ifẹ̀'s political and cosmogonic-intellectual networks. On the other hand, the distribution operated as a market activity independent of these networks. In other words, glass beads circulated in the spectrum of gift and prestige goods, linked to political relationships, but they also circulated as traded commodities along market-driven exchange registers guided by motivations for profit and personal gain, and by supply-and-demand imperatives.

However, these two spheres of exchange intimately overlapped, allowing Ilé-Ifẹ̀ to package its technological know-how (glass-bead production) as knowledge capital that stood for power, authority, social order, wealth, and wellness. With its monopoly on primary glass production in the Yorùbá-speaking world and the adjacent other speech communities, Ilé-Ifẹ̀ was able to dominate the distribution of materials and symbols that naturalized and legitimized political (*ọba-aládé*) and spiritual (*òrìṣà*) authorities in many parts of the region. This enabled Ilé-Ifẹ̀ to promote its brand of kingship institution as the natural order of existence. The materiality of this brand was crucial to the transformation of Ilé-Ifẹ̀ into the primal center of the Yorùbá world system after 1100. This process of materialization is akin to what Timothy Earle has succinctly described for another world area: "The transformation of ideas, values, stories, myths, and the like into physical reality . . . can take the form of ceremonial events, symbolic objects, monuments, and writing. It is the process by which culture is created, codified, and contained. Ideas and objects unite and are inseparable; ideas, unconnected to the objects of the world, have no means of being communicated, experienced, used, and owned. Ideas must be materialized to become social, to become cultural things."[42]

Herein lies the root of Ilé-Ifẹ̀'s success: the ability to encode ideas in material, myth, and ritual terms and to package and export this as universal knowledge. The massive production of glass and glass beads in Ilé-Ifẹ̀ and the distribution of these across the Yorùbá and the other West African regions enabled enterprising and prosperous potentates elsewhere to access the glass beads needed to make their beaded crowns—the symbol of divine royalty—and to attract and retain followers. Ilé-Ifẹ̀, therefore, succeeded in controlling the idea of divine kingship through the monopoly of the production of objects that legitimized this idea, without which any claim to the office of kingship would not be valid. However, in view of the circulation of glass beads through the market networks, Ilé-Ifẹ̀ was not able to prevent the use of the beaded crowns and other beaded paraphernalia that legitimized kingship, especially if a potentate was able to back up this possession with military power against a protesting and aggressive neighbor. Nevertheless, such a potentate might look to Ilé-Ifẹ̀ to sanctify his right to wear the beaded crown. For three major reasons, it would have been a good investment of political capital for Ilé-Ifẹ̀ to grant such requests: to gain access to a new market for its glass beads and other products, to secure a new client and political ally who would also be a new source of gifts to the treasury of Ilé-Ifẹ̀, and to expand and further burnish the prestige of Ilé-Ifẹ̀ as the guarantor of social order. Hence, many potentates and princes aspiring to the divinity status of *ọba-aládé* visited and allied with Ilé-Ifẹ̀—the ultimate source of the paraphernalia and symbols that validated the divinity of kingship and the *àṣẹ* of the political and religious elite. And successions of well-established *ọba-aládé* dynasties in various *ìlú* also sought to strengthen their relationship with the "city of abundance." These political clients needed Ilé-Ifẹ̀ not only to (re)validate and renew the spiritual basis of their political power but also to take advantage of the economic opportunities that Ilé-Ifẹ̀ offered as the largest emporium in the region.

The new techniques for studying the geochemistry of glass have now made it possible to understand, on a very fine scale, the distribution of Ifẹ̀ glass across the Yorùbá region and beyond.[43] The presence of HLHA blue dichroic beads in different parts of the region in thirteenth- through eighteenth-century contexts, especially at Òṣogbo, Ẹdẹ-Ilé, Ìdànrè, Iléṣà, Ìlàrè, Ọ̀wọ̀, Ọ̀yọ́-Ilé, and Benin, demonstrates that the Ifẹ̀ glass beads were traded widely (table 3.1; fig. 3.1). Although the initial production of glass beads in the eleventh and twelfth centuries would have served only the elite prestige-goods exchange system, the scale of production quickly outstripped these narrow elite demands. By the thirteenth century, the production of glass beads was already linked to a more open market network. Benin, Ọ̀wọ̀, Òwu, Ifọ́n, and possibly Ìjẹ̀bú-Ode, were among the early political centers within the trading orbit of Ilé-Ifẹ̀ serving as redistribution nodes for HLHA beads. During the fourteenth century, the distribution networks for these glass beads extended to the littorals of the Bight of Benin, from Òde-Ìtsekiri to Popo, and as far as the coastal modern Ghana, where the Ifẹ̀ dichroic beads were later called "blue Popo beads."[44] These beads also reached Ṣábé (Savé), one of the westernmost areas in the Yorùbá-speaking world during the later phase of the Classical period.[45]

The dichroic bluish, greenish, and yellowish beads of the same HLHA chemical properties as those of Ilé-Ifẹ̀ have been identified farther afield, from Igbo-Ukwu in southeastern Nigeria and Birnin Lafiya in northeast Benin Republic to Kissi in Burkina Faso, Diouboye in Senegal, Gao Ancien and Essouk in Mali, and Koumbi Saleh in Mauritania, all in twelfth- to fourteenth-century contexts.[46] Ilé-Ifẹ̀, the only known industrial center for HLHA glass production, was the supplier of these beads to several locations in West Africa. As these exquisite imports permeated the subcontinental market and social lives, so did the fame of the city spread far and wide. Ibn Battuta, the fourteenth-century globetrotting Moroccan scholar, was informed during his visit to Mali (February 1352–December 1353) about a powerful kingdom to the south. The name of the kingdom is rendered in Ibn Battuta's travel account as Yūfī, which his informants described as "one of the biggest countries of the Sudan, and their sultan

Table 3.1. Major and Minor Elemental Composition of HLHA Beads from a Selection of Sites in Central Yorùbá Region (AD 1000–1837)

		Ilé-Ifẹ̀ 1000–1400		**Ìloyì 1200–1500**		**Early Òṣogbo 1590–1750**		**Òjé-Ilé 1600–1837**	**Ẹdẹ-Ilé 1600–1837**		**Ìlọ́jà 1700–1830**
Sample No. →		IFE-G48	IFE-G21	ILY-G1	ILY-G2	OSG-G1	OSG-G2	OJE-G1	EDI-G2	EDI-G1	ILJ-G1
	SiO_2	58.96%	61.24%	64.35%	56.29%	61.05%	59.48%	61.41%	64.58%	62.04%	59.72%
	Na_2O	1.50%	3.33%	4.90%	3.75%	2.17%	3.22%	2.54%	1.84%	4.36%	2.89%
	MgO	0.93%	0.12%	0.09%	0.06%	0.05%	0.04%	0.03%	0.03%	0.15%	0.43%
Alumina	Al_2O_3	14.13%	14.03%	12.49%	15.91%	13.72%	13.36%	14.09%	13.19%	13.96%	13.44%
	P_2O_3	0.27%	0.09%	0.19%	0.13%	0.08%	0.06%	0.10%	0.11%	0.28%	0.19%
	K_2O	7.03%	3.39%	1.09%	3.72%	7.12%	4.11%	7.86%	7.63%	3.74%	5.35%
Lime	CaO	15.92%	15.80%	15.53%	18.94%	14.62%	17.36%	13.18%	11.65%	14.37%	14.65%
	MnO	0.43%	0.10%	0.20%	0.23%	0.51%	1.47%	0.38%	0.63%	0.58%	0.25%
	Fe_2O_3	0.79%	1.87%	1.09%	0.94%	0.51%	0.58%	0.33%	0.27%	0.47%	3.05%
	CuO	0.00%	0.00%	0.00%	0.00%	0.01%	0.03%	0.01%	0.01%	0.01%	0.01%
	SnO_2	0.00%	0.00%	0.00%	0.00%	0.00%	0.00%	0.00%	0.00%	0.00%	0.00%
	PbO_2	0.00%	0.00%	0.00%	0.01%	0.01%	0.01%	0.01%	0.01%	0.01%	0.01%

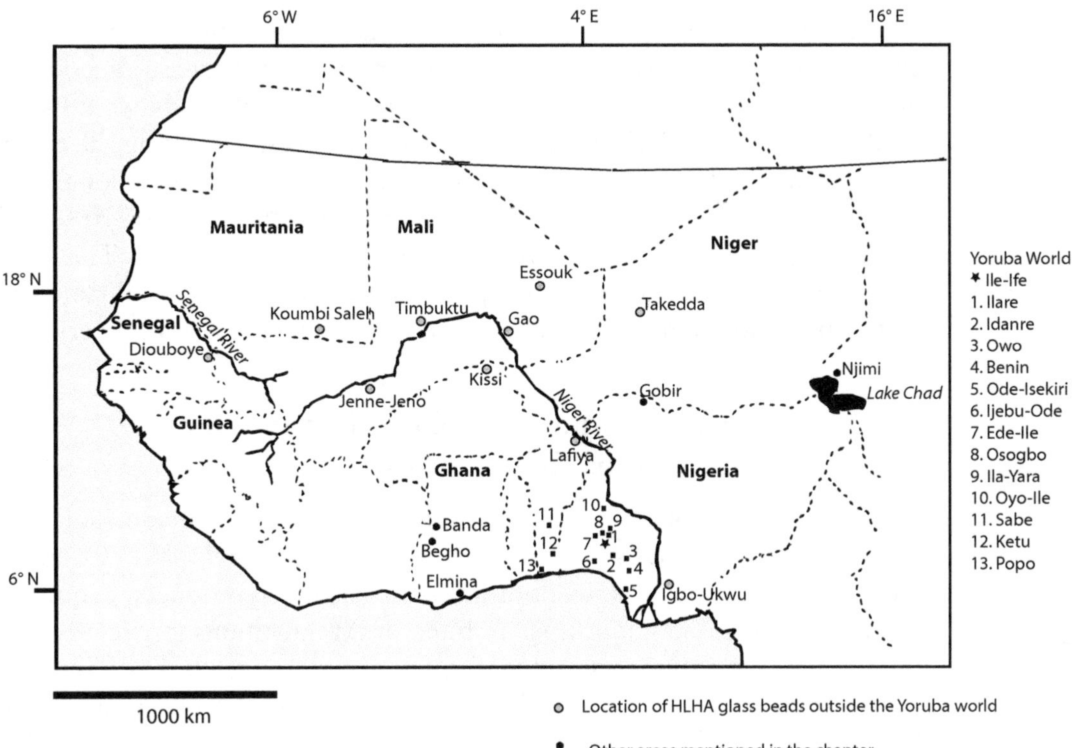

Figure 3.1. Distribution of HLHA dichroic beads in West Africa

one of their [*sic*] greatest sultans."[47] Ilé-Ifẹ̀ was the largest urban center, the biggest emporium, and the wealthiest polity in West Africa's rain forest belt south of the Niger River during the mid-fourteenth century, with more than two centuries of trading contact with the Western Sudan. On account of these facts alone, it is the best match for Ibn Battuta's Yūfī. Moreover, on linguistic grounds, Yūfī is a Mandé or an Arabic transliteration of "Ufẹ̀," the proper name for "Ifẹ̀" in central Yorùbá dialect.[48] And, as late as 1908, the people of the Niger Bend (present-day Mali) recognized Ilé-Ifẹ̀ as the source of the dichroic beads that Leo Frobenius found there. For example, it was in Timbuktu that Frobenius first heard about the bead treasures of Olókun Grove. He used that information to locate and visit Ilé-Ifẹ̀ in 1910.[49]

Given their quality as a high-value and low-bulk commodity, long-distance travelers likely carried Ifẹ̀ glass beads across the Yorùbá world and the adjacent areas as a means of payment for provisions on their journeys.[50] The durability and affective qualities of these dichroic beads, especially the most common *ṣẹ̀gi*, and the guarantee of their supply and demand encouraged people to use them as a means of high-value exchange and for storing wealth. We are short of evidence on whether glass beads evolved to serve as a standard currency, especially as a means of pricing. However, strings and other standard measurements of beads were likely used for purchasing high-value products and services. Protecting the trade routes on which these valuables traveled was an important concern for all the trading partners along the "Bead Road," which stretched from Ilé-Ifẹ̀ to the Moshi-Niger area and as far as the Niger Bend in present-day Mali. This concern, as we shall see later in this chapter, shaped the dynamics of diplomacy and conflict, and of regional alliance and war during the Classical period.

"*Ẹbí* Fraternity": Ideological Basis of the Yorùbá Community of Practice

The diverse genres of arts and crafts in Ilé-Ifẹ̀ demonstrate an unusual concentration of skills and specialization in the "city of daybreak." Copper-alloy sculptures and artifacts, titanium-enriched iron products, exquisite terracotta and stone sculptures, architectural innovations (especially the use of potsherd pavements and wall tiles), and primary glass production all attest to these multiple skill sets. The diversity of facial marks and headgear, evidence of group and cultural identities, represented on the terracotta figures of Classical Ifẹ̀ demonstrate that the city's residents originated from different backgrounds and that the city was a magnet for visitors from different parts of the surrounding region (see plate 3). In fact, Ilé-Ifẹ̀ gained its name from this cosmopolitan status as the hub of wealth, knowledge, and population diversity. Literally, the name of Ilé-Ifẹ̀ means a house of abundance, expansiveness, or merriment. Its name evokes "a society that was not only . . . prosperous and progressive but also stable and welcoming to indigenes and non-indigenes alike," a place of "economic prosperity; political, religious, artistic, and intellectual richness; and sophistication."[51]

Scholars have traditionally treated Ilé-Ifẹ̀ as a place of departure for waves of migrations that peopled the Yorùbá region or as a place from which all the founders of beaded-crown dynasties originated. As we learned in chapter 2, the former did not happen. Neither did the overwhelming majority of the beaded-crown dynasties (*ọba-aládé*) in the Yorùbá world originate from Ilé-Ifẹ̀ through princely migrations. The "house of abundance" or the "source of daybreak," as Ilé-Ifẹ̀ was called, no doubt influenced the concept of divine kingship and brought many prominent kingdoms in Èkìtì and other parts of the Yorùbá and Edo regions under its influence at different times between 1200 and 1400, but it was not the source or origin of most of these kingdoms or their kingship institutions.[52] With the economic and political expansion as well as cultural efflorescence that followed the political consolidation of the eleventh century, Ilé-Ifẹ̀ would have needed almost all its capable citizens at home as managers and workers of its prosperous economy. And it would have had to recruit new talents and labor from outside in order for the city to maintain the unprecedented scale of craft production and construction projects that are the hallmarks of Ife's Classical age. Of course, there were migrations out of the city, including colonists, traders, soldiers, and priests, but all in all, Ilé-Ifẹ̀ would have been a net receiver of migrants between 1100 and 1400. Its cosmopolitanism, wealth, fecundity of ideas, high taste for the finest art, and commitment to excellence gave it an unparalleled advantage to recruit and retain the finest thinkers, talents, and workers from near and far. The diversity of people who rose to become ancestors, as evident in the terracotta figures, shows that the city was a land of opportunity for natives and foreigners. The city's openness to diversity was therefore one of the secrets of its success. The lore and lure of the glass-bead wealth made all roads lead to Ilé-Ifẹ̀ for those searching for the abundance that Olókun—the goddess of glass beads—had given to the city. Hence, people flocked to the "house of abundance" in search of better prospects. In fact, between 1100 and 1400, no metropolis in West Africa south of the Niger River held as much promise for wealth and self-realization as Ilé-Ifẹ̀. Its glass industry exerted a strong gravitational pull for migrants. And, as a result, it may have impoverished many areas in the region of talents, ideas, and labor.

Ilé-Ifẹ̀ was the emporium of the Yorùbá community of practice during the Classical period. This status was maintained not only by traders but also by political emissaries, soldiers, priests, fortune seekers, and pilgrims. The multiple and overlapping directions of these different groups of people ensured that ideas, information, practices, and styles spread quickly across the region. The relationships between Ilé-Ifẹ̀ and the other parts of the Yorùbá community of practice are usually described and interpreted with kinship idioms, both in the local traditions and in the historiography. These idioms of filial relationship, *ẹbí*, had their roots in the ideology of the House society that had defined the Yorùbá political evolution since the Early Formative period. And this same *ẹbí* metaphor provided the framework for conceptualizing and codifying the regional integration as well as inter-polity hierarchies that defined the Yorùbá community of practice during the Classical period. Thus, Adéagbo Akínjọ́gbìn coined the term *ẹbí commonwealth* to explain the operational framework by which this community evolved.[53]

According to the oral traditions that provided the basis for this concept, a commonwealth of city-states was founded by royal brothers, cousins, and nephews at a conference held at Ìta Ìjerò in Ilé-Ifẹ̀ following the triumph of the Odùduwà group in the epic Ọbatálá-Odùduwà conflict. At the end of the conference, each prince went away to establish his kingdom, with the promise that they would all keep in touch as brothers and support one another in times of trouble. Perhaps, perceiving the pervasiveness of kinship idioms in Yorùbá sociopolitical thought, Akínjọ́gbìn was led to conclude that the regional peer-polity hierarchy was an orderly formulation produced by a specific historical event in which the bond of kinship shaped the purpose and outcome. His *ẹbí commonwealth* therefore served to validate the "Ìta Ìjerò legend," the oral traditions that princes dispersed in waves from Ilé-Ifẹ̀ to other parts of the Yorùbá-Edo region.[54] In this regard, Akínjọ́gbìn erred in taking this legend literally as a historical event rather than seeing it as an Ifẹ̀-centric ideological invention that sought to legitimize Ilé-Ifẹ̀ as the source of divine kingship and the beaded crown, and the centrifugal force for the Yorùbá community of practice.[55] Akínjọ́gbìn's *ẹbí commonwealth*, especially in its later iterations, is nevertheless useful for understanding the Yorùbá political philosophy as well as the ideology of interstate relations and regional integration that developed by the twelfth century.[56] However, the regional polities that this ideology sought to integrate were far from a commonwealth.

The kingdoms and city-states that populated the Yorùbá community of practice were not a loose formation of polities with a shared loyalty, nor were they brought under a single government in one historical event. Although Ilé-Ifẹ̀ instigated the development of this community, the process was drawn out, cumulative, and contingent. The community of practice was a system of social networks and hierarchically linked polities. Its composition was shaped by diplomacy and conflict, and the relationships among the polities within this system were transactional, ideological, and political (tributary and patron-client); and driven by economic, security, and spiritual interests. Not all of these relationships were formed from consent and self-interest. Wars and conquest also brought many of these polities into overlapping spheres of interaction. As I shall discuss below, the term *ẹbí fraternity* is better suited (than *ẹbí commonwealth*) to understanding and conceptualizing the historical processes that produced the Yorùbá community of practice during the Classical period. The same way that "fictive kinship" ideology was used to legitimize *ilé* and *ìlú*, so it was used to forge the consciousness of *ẹbí* fraternity for the members of this interaction sphere. Centered on the spiritual, commercial, military, and political might, as well as knowledge capital, of Ilé-Ifẹ̀, the self-awareness of this fraternity was created and embellished by stories of kinship relationships among the peer kingdoms in the region. Of course, as part of its hegemonic project, Ilé-Ifẹ̀ masterminded this consciousness and created the Ìta Ìjerò legend to give it a coherent framework. This consciousness seems to have gained region-wide recognition by the thirteenth century.

The Ìta Ìjerò legend served the purpose of masking the expansionist policy that Ilé-Ifẹ̀ pursued, through military and diplomatic strategies, in reorganizing the regional political landscape and making it spin around the emporium's axis. It is, however, not the only tradition that was used as glue to bind the Yorùbá community of practice together as a "family." There is another legend that speaks to the creation of the *ẹbí* fraternity via strategic political maneuvering. This is known as the Ọ̀rànmíyàn legend, a stock narrative that legitimized Ifẹ̀'s expansionist agenda, especially its bid to bring other polities into its commercial network, political sphere, beaded-crown kingship ideology, and ritual field via conquest and alliance building. The legend is the historical charter for Ilé-Ifẹ̀'s expansionist ambition and success during the twelfth through the fourteenth centuries. In it, several generations and scores of military leaders and diplomats who spearheaded Ifẹ̀'s political expansion were stereotyped into the career of one person, Ọ̀rànmíyàn. If indeed Ọ̀rànmíyàn was a commander of the army at some point, he must have been the most celebrated military leader that the city ever produced.

There are many versions of the Ọ̀rànmíyàn legend. Here is a composite account. In Ilé-Ifẹ̀, Benin, and Ọ̀yọ́ traditions, Ọ̀rànmíyàn is often presented as either a son or a grandson of Odùduwà.[57] Far more than the other sons and grandsons of Odùduwà, he is credited with spreading the Ifẹ̀ model of kingship to different parts of the Yorùbá world—notably for establishing the two most important Ifẹ̀-centric dynasties, one in Benin and the other in Ọ̀yọ́. In Benin, Ọ̀rànmíyàn fathered Eweka, the first *ọba* of Benin.[58] In Ọ̀yọ́, he sired Ṣàngó, the first *aláàfin*. Whereas Eweka's mother was the daughter of a Benin noble, the mother of Ṣàngó was a Nupe princess. Many other Yorùbá kingdoms—Adó-Èkìtì, Àkúrẹ́, and Òkò (Ẹ̀gbá)—also associate their Ilé-Ifẹ̀ origins with the Ọ̀rànmíyàn legend.[59] While some of these traditions emphasize Ọ̀rànmíyàn's princely roles in fathering princes and founding dynasties, others highlight his military prowess and present him as the most important agent of Ifẹ̀'s "imperial age."[60] The legend served as a means for the "city of daybreak" to cement its political and economic relationships with diverse polities, languages, and cultures and to legitimize Ifẹ̀'s conquests and diplomatic arrangements across the region. Hence, in many traditions at Ilé-Ifẹ̀, Ọ̀rànmíyàn is stereotypically associated with almost all aspects of the city's wars of expansion and serves as a composite of many military personalities and war-related events throughout the Classical period.[61] Following his military and expansionist achievements, Ọ̀rànmíyàn supposedly returned to Ilé-Ifẹ̀ to claim the throne of his father. He fought the incumbent king, Ọbalùfọ̀n (some would say Ọbalùfọ̀n II, otherwise known as Ọbalùfọ̀n Aláyémorẹ́), and sent him into exile. Ọ̀rànmíyàn then ruled Ilé-Ifẹ̀, but only for a brief period before he joined his ancestors.[62]

Archaeological Geography of Ifẹ̀-Centric Regional Networks

Both the Ìta Ìjerò and Ọ̀rànmíyàn legends explain the hierarchical peer-polity relationships that defined the Yorùbá community of practice and the legitimating authority of Ilé-Ifẹ̀ at the apex of that hierarchical regional system. They also reveal that Ilé-Ifẹ̀ was more than a city-state or a regal-ritual polity, as almost all studies in Yorùbá historiography have characterized the polity. The city was a religious center, a commercial hub, and a powerful military force. And it used these three resources to build the first empire in the Yorùbá world, a massive political formation covering about half of the region (fig. 3.2). Apart from the oral traditions, there is abundant archaeological evidence that an Ifẹ̀-centric regional network was indeed in full operation during the Classical period. In addition to the glass beads mentioned above, special objects such as terracotta and copper-alloy figures of unmistakable Ifẹ̀ craftsmanship have been found across the Yorùbá region, giving additional weight to the referentiality of Ilé-Ifẹ̀ in religion, worldview, and governance. Ekpo Eyo has shown that at least eleven terracotta heads found at the Igbó-Làjà site in Ọ̀wọ̀ "were executed in Ilé-Ifẹ̀ classical style" and were deposited between the late fourteenth and early fifteenth century.[63] There are also Ifẹ̀ naturalistic terracotta figures in Òṣogbo, Ìré, and Ìkìrun to the north and Ìdànrè to the east.[64] A miniature copper-alloy figure, wearing a veil and bearing facial striations, a garment, and beaded paraphernalia that are characteristic of Ifẹ̀ sculptures, was also found in the palace ground of Benin during a renovation project in the early 1960s (see plate 3d–f).[65] This regional distribution of Ifẹ̀-style sculptures illustrates the influence that the "city of daybreak" maintained through the ties of ritual interdependency and elite-goods transactions, as well as the networks of "trade, tribute, patronage, clientship, and migration" across the Yorùbá-Edo region.[66]

The similar ceramic styles found along the Ifẹ̀-Ìjẹ̀ṣà-Ọ̀wọ̀-Oǹdó-Benin axis and the Ifẹ̀-Upper Ọ̀ṣun-Ìgbómìnà corridor from the thirteenth through the fifteenth century further demonstrate the cultural unity that encompasses at least the northcentral, central, and eastern wings of the Yorùbá community of practice. Named the "Ifẹ̀ ceramic sphere," this ceramic geography covered a distance of about 250 kilometers between Benin in the south and Ìgbómìnà in the north; and about 150 kilometers between Ọ̀wọ̀ in the east and Òṣogbo in the west (see plate 4).[67] The motifs that unite this ceramic sphere include applied bosses, cordons, keloid forms, cowrieform motifs, hyphenated crosshatched incisions, stamped geometric impressions, circular stylus motifs, reliefs of guilloché and rosette designs, rustication, and red slip on vessel rims or lips. The diagnostic value of these decorations, as indices of cultural historical relationship, is illustrated by their presence in other categories

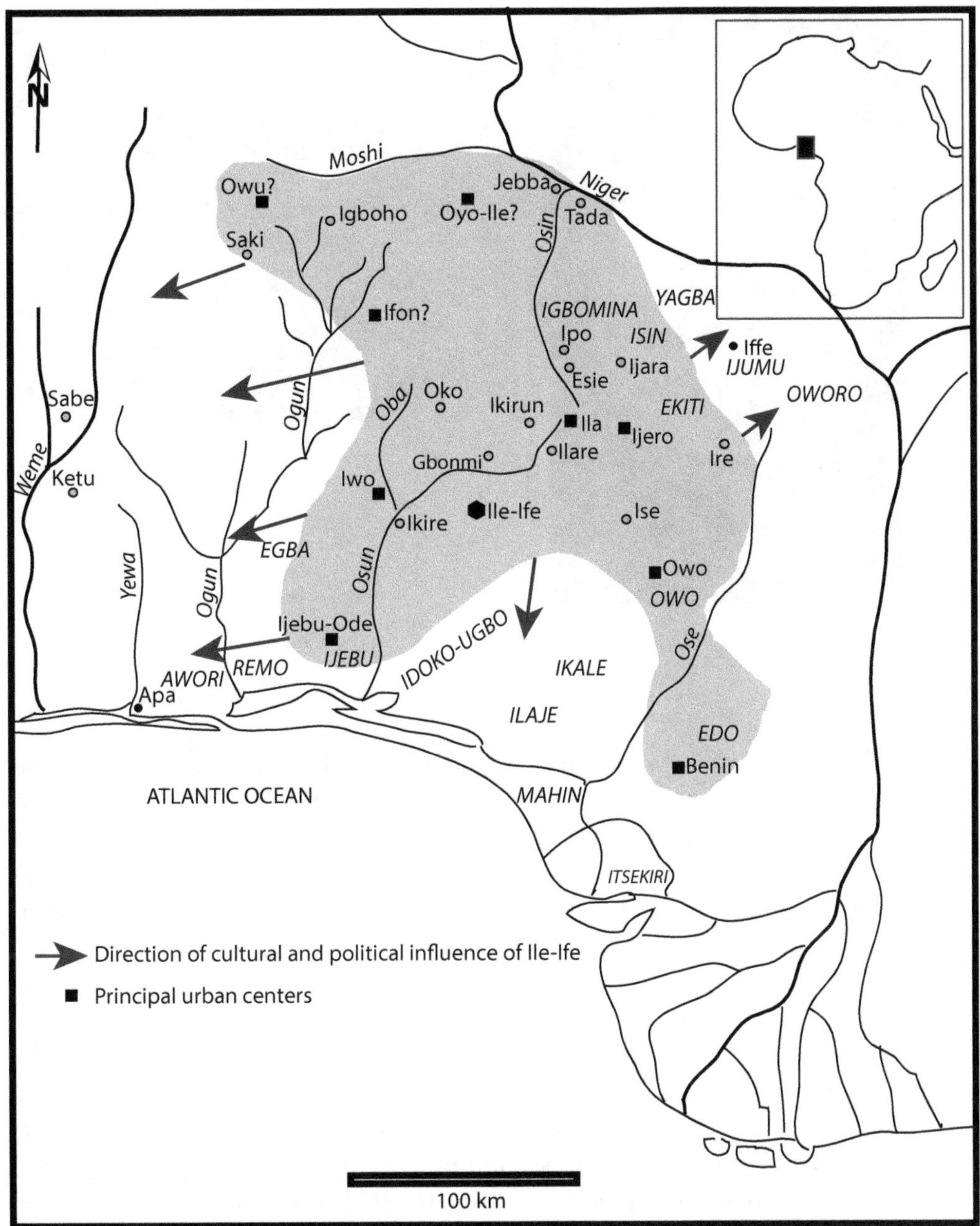

Figure 3.2. Ifẹ̀ Empire, mid-fourteenth century

of artifacts, especially the Classical terracotta sculptures. For example, rustication and crosshatched motifs, as well as applied motifs of cowrie-form, bosses, keloids, and cordons, are present on both ceramic vessels and terracottas. The rectangular cordons that are applied and etched on the shoulders of flanged-shoulder bowls, simple hemispherical bowls, and flared-rim bowls in Iloyi, Ilé-Ifẹ̀, Ọ̀wọ̀, and Benin are also represented

Figure 3.3. Crosshatched motifs on a bowl and terracotta figure

as beads on the crowns, ankles, and wrists of the terracotta figures in Ilé-Ifẹ̀ and Ọ̀wọ̀. Likewise, herringbone and hyphenated crosshatched incised motifs were used at Ilé-Ifẹ̀, Ọ̀wọ̀, and Benin during the same period to decorate ceramic vessels as well as human and animal terracotta sculptures (fig. 3.3). All of these are evidence of an Ife-centered regional integration.

The creation of a regional community of practice, which Ilé-Ifẹ̀ vigorously pursued during the Classical period, was not without some resistance. One source of opposition to this Ifẹ̀-centric hegemony was found in the Òwẹ̀nà frontier, an area between the southern parts of the Ọ̀ṣun and Ose Rivers that stretched to the lagoons. This frontier was a crossroad important to the regional interaction, communication linkages, and commercial networks across the southern region of the Ifẹ̀ Empire. Several trade routes wound through Òwẹ̀nà, linking the rain forest/savanna transitional zones with the coast. Safe paths through the thickly forested and hilly landscape of this area were needed for the sustenance of the political, cultural, and economic networks between Benin-Ọ̀wọ̀ axis in the east and Ilé-Ifẹ̀ in the west. But this intermediate zone was a hotbed of anti-Ifẹ̀-centric sentiments, led by the vast Ìdôkò polity (encompassing most of the current Oǹdó-, Ìlàjẹ-, Ìkálẹ̀- and parts of Ìjẹ̀bú-speaking areas) and the Ùgbò . The populations of the latter were decimated in Ilé-Ifẹ̀, and most of the remnant groups were pushed farther south into the Ìdôkò territory between the hills of Òkìtìpupa and coastal Màhin during the eleventh century (see chap. 2).

Throughout the Classical period, both the Ìdôkò and Ùgbò resisted, with some success, the effort to bring the Òwẹ̀nà frontier under any of the large polities in the region—Ọ̀wọ̀, Benin, or Ifẹ̀. Despite their resistance to Ifẹ̀-centric political control and ritual influences, however, the Ìdôkò-Ùgbò duo was likely part of the Ifẹ̀-centered commercial networks. Their strategic location gave them the advantage to hold on to their political autonomy while also controlling the commercial traffic passing through their territories. In spite of their political holdout though, the Ìdôkò and Ùgbò were not impervious to the Classical-era Ifẹ̀-centric elite culture and political organization.

Of the various axes of Ifẹ̀'s interaction sphere, none was as important as the northern axis. This strategic area linked Ilé-Ifẹ̀ with the trade termini on the River Niger and gave the Yorùbá world access to the commercial traffic between the Western Sudan and the Mediterranean. Saharan copper and salt, as well as Mediterranean and Chinese silk and other clothing materials, were entering the Yorùbá region from across the Niger by the eleventh or twelfth century in exchange for sundry rain forest goods, of which Ifẹ̀ glass beads and ivory were the most highly prized.[68] Therefore, early in its development, Ilé-Ifẹ̀ employed military and diplomatic strategies to open up and protect the trade routes to the River Niger, especially between Moshi and Ọsin tributaries. These efforts are encapsulated in the oral traditions regarding the activities of Ọ̀rànmíyàn, who is said to have launched military campaigns in the River Niger area.[69] The stories of this legendary figure reveal Ilé-Ifẹ̀'s efforts to secure the safe passage of its exports and imports across the river. Indeed, Ifẹ̀ trading stations were located in this zone of trading termini, in addition to several Yorùbá-speaking communities that occupied a 310-kilometer stretch of land on both banks of River Niger for most of the Classical period. This was a zone of transition in which trading stations, and port towns and villages received exports from Ilé-Ifẹ̀ and other parts of the Yorùbá world and imports from the Sudan. The Ifẹ̀-style copper-alloy figures found in the Tada and Jebba areas call attention to the connections between Ilé-Ifẹ̀ and these River Niger communities (fig. 3.4; also see fig. 3.2). Those figures were most likely stationed in these commercial frontier ports for juridical and metaphysical purposes to protect the commercial and political interests of Ilé-Ifẹ̀.[70] The River Niger was the last frontier of the Yorùbá homeland where the northbound Ifẹ̀ and other Yorùbá traders were received and protected. A chain of colonies, tributary polities, and peer polities linked Ilé-Ifẹ̀ to these port towns on River Niger. It is, therefore, not surprising that some of the dramatic events of contestation, conflict, and collaboration that shaped Ifẹ̀ hegemony took place in this northern axis of commerce, especially between Ìgbómìnà and the Moshi-Niger area.

Figure 3.4. Ifẹ̀-style copper figure from Tada (H. 54 cm). National Commission for Museums and Monuments, Nigeria

Ifẹ̀ Empire and Its Hegemony: Allies and Critics, Compradors and Rebels

Far from being acquiescing frontiers or members of a peaceful *ẹbí* fraternity reverentially kowtowing to the spiritual majesty of Ilé-Ifẹ̀, some of the frontier communities on this northern axis challenged the ritual, intellectual, and political hegemony of Ilé-Ifẹ̀. These included those polities who were in fact closely plugged into and were beneficiaries of Ifẹ̀'s commercial networks. Some engaged Ilé-Ifẹ̀ in proxy wars in the quest to gain more control over the same trade routes that were the backbones of Ifẹ̀'s commercial power. Others were contented with the economic relationship that they had with Ilé-Ifẹ̀ but were dissatisfied with the latter's political ideology, and they therefore offered a cultural critique of the "city of sunrise." Included in the latter were the Ifẹ̀ colonies who enthusiastically protected the commercial and political interests of the empire in the frontiers but aligned themselves with political factions different from that of the reigning dynasty at home. The rhetoric and tactics employed by these critics give us a deep insight into the internal political dynamics of Ilé-Ifẹ̀, especially the ideological factionalism between the palace and the nonroyal Houses, and between the loyalists of Ọbatálá heritage and those of Odùduwà heritage. These two groups dominated the factional politics in Ilé-Ifẹ̀ throughout the Classical period, and this factionalism had effects far beyond the walls of the city. I will use two case studies to illustrate these different modalities of resistance. One was an ideological critique of the Ife-centric political ideology, and the other was an outright rebellion. Both examples originated from the frontier colonies and clients of the empire. One came from Òwu, an early Ifẹ̀-centric client polity in the northern extremity of the Ifẹ̀ Empire (see Early Owu in fig. 1.1). The other originated from Ifọ̀n, a colony of Ifẹ̀ and the empire's provincial capital in the upper reaches of Ògùn River (fig. 3.2).[71] The oral traditions reveal a complicated and dynamic relationship between Ilé-Ifẹ̀ and each of these polities.

We shall start with the critics of Ife-centric political ideology at Ifọ̀n and then consider the proxy war that Òwu launched against its patron, Ilé-Ifẹ̀. It is striking that the extensive *oríkì orílẹ̀* (deep-time panegyric) of Ifọ̀n and its founding ancestor, Ọláòṣà, identifies Ọbàtálá as the founding ancestor and Ilé-Ifẹ̀ as their ancestral land. Interestingly, Ifọ̀n's *oríkì orílẹ̀* explicitly rejects any genealogical relationship with Odùduwà:[72]

Odùduwà ni baba Ọbalùfọ̀n
Ọbatálá ló bí Ọláòṣà
Mo ni ń ó rèé dọ́dọ̀ Ọbamakin
Nílé yánbí n lólú
Ọmọ ojú rábẹsá
Ọmọ à-pè-wáá-joyè
Tó tún'fọ̀n ṣe
Àbú Olúfẹ̀ Ọ̀ọ̀ni
Ní'fẹ̀ Oòdáyé, Ifẹ̀ Oòyè
Níbí ojúmọ́ gbé mọ́ wá
L'orírun baba àwa n'ílé wa
Kí Aládìkún Ọláòṣà
Tí í ṣ'ọmọ Ọbatálá tó lọ̀ọ́ tẹ'fọ̀n àkọ̀kọ̀ dó
Nífọ̀n Òrólú
Ọmọ aládé ṣẹ́ṣẹ́ ẹfun.

Translation:

Odùduwà is the father of Ọbalùfọ̀n[73]
Ọbatálá is the father of Ọláòṣà
I say I will visit Ọbamakin[74]
In the house of the great one
The child of those who refused facial marks

He who was called into royalty
To improve Ifọn
Àbú, the king of Ifẹ̀
Ifẹ̀, the creator of the world, the land of survivors
The source of daybreak
That is our fathers' ancestral origin
Before Aládìkún Ọláòṣà
The son of Ọbàtálá came to establish Ifọn
The Ifọn of Òrólú
The child of the white beads.

This *oríkì* presents a counter-hegemonic discourse that identifies Ọláòṣà, also known as Aládìkún, Òrólú, and Olúfọn, as a pro-Ọbàtálá and anti-Odùduwà frontier leader. It seems that he was one of the leaders who left Ilé-Ifẹ̀ in the aftermath of the long-drawn conflict between the Odùduwà and Ọbàtálá factions. There were many episodes of this conflict. Although the first major one ended sometime during the eleventh century, others reared their heads periodically, in the form of succession disputes to the throne and opposition of the nonroyal Houses to some of the reigning kings. It is not clear which of these conflicts propelled Ọláòṣà to leave Ilé-Ifẹ̀ to establish Ifọn-Ẹ̀gà, the first and oldest Ifọn kingdom (henceforth, Ifọn). The exact location of this ancient polity is not currently known, but oral informants generally point to the area between the present-day Ògbómọ̀ṣọ́ and Sẹ̀pẹ̀tẹ̀rí as the original site (see fig. 1.1).[75] The antiquity of Ifọn is also indicated by its prominent mention in the *ifá* literary corpus as one of the ancient Yorùbá kingdoms.[76] The founders of Ifọn were surely not pacifists. They were individuals who combined military prowess with esoteric ritual knowledge. One of the cognomens of Aládìkún Ọláòṣà is *Akọgun ẹrùjẹ̀jẹ̀ àdúgbò*: "The brave warrior, the terror of the neighborhood." This cognomen indicates that Ifọn was founded through military conquest and that its rulers maintained a military reputation.[77] Hence, the next verse tells us about the military and esoteric powers of the people of Ifọn:

Ọmọ àgbàrá òjò
Tí ń báwọn ọ́ń jà
Tí ń gbòde baba wọ́n lọ
Ènìyàn tó mú wọn l'ájẹ̀ẹ́ kò parọ́
N'ílé Olúfọn Adé
Igbá orí ni wọ́n fi ń mu'mi
Ẹ̀jẹ̀ ènìyàn ni wọ́n fi ń ro'kà l'Árè
Bẹ́ẹ̀ni, eegun ènìyàn lẹ fi ń t'ẹ̀pá òṣoòrò.

Translation:

The child of the flooding rain
The attacker of the enemy

Destroyer of their father's courtyard
Those who called them witches and wizards are not lying
In the House of Olúfọ̀n Adé
They drink water from a human skull
They use human blood to make sorghum foofoo
Yes, they use human bones as walking sticks during ritual events.

However, while the identity of Ifọ̀n embodied the Ọbàtálá-Odùduwà polarity, the polity was integrated into the commercial and ritual networks of Ilé-Ifẹ̀. Ifọ̀n is described in the oral traditions as an important market center where Ifẹ̀ glass beads, especially *ṣẹ̀gi*, were sold. It was also a redistribution center for the acquisition of *ṣẹ̀gi*-beaded crowns—the hallmark of the Ifẹ̀-centric political system. Likewise, the city-state was an important ritual center for the worship of Ọbàtálá, for ritual works related to healing and wellness, and as a desired destination for the pursuit of learning on the esoteric *òrìṣà* knowledge. Ifọ̀n was therefore an outpost of Ifẹ̀'s commercial-ritual networks even if this outpost was explicitly anti-Odùduwà in its rhetoric.[78] The status of Ifọ̀n as a frontier market center serving a wider region and connected to other famous market towns, such as Èjìgbòmẹkùn, is illustrated thus:

Òòṣà Ọlọ́jà ló dá'léé Ifọ̀n
Ọjà mẹ́rin l'Ọbàtálá dá n'ílé Olúfọ̀n
Òní mo báwọn n'ájà ṣẹ̀gi
Ọ̀la mo báwọn n'ájà iyùn n'ílé Olúfọ̀n
Ọ̀tunla òní mo báwọn n'ájà ṣẹ̀ṣẹ̀ ẹfun
Taa ní ńlọ ilé Olúfọ̀n?
Kó bá mi kí Ọbàtálá Ọbatáàsà
Taa ni ń r'òde Èjìgbòmẹkùn?
Kó bá mi kí Òòṣàtàlàbí
Ọmọ Èjìgbòmẹkùn
Kó bá mi kí Ọlọ́pọ̀ndá
Ọmọ Alágbàá[79] n'ílé Ifọ̀n.

Translation:

It is the patron deity of commerce that established Ifọ̀n
There are four markets that Ọbàtálá founded in Ifọ̀n
Today, I attend the *ṣẹ̀gi* market
Tomorrow, I will go to the *iyùn* market
In two days, I will visit the white-bead market
Who is going to the House of Olúfọ̀n?
Greet Ọbàtálá for me
Who is going to Èjìgbòmẹkùn?
Greet Òòṣàtàlàbí for me
The child of Èjìgbòmẹkùn[80]
Greet Ọlọ́pọ̀ndá
The child of Alágbàá in Ifọ̀n.

The above verse represents a layer in the history of Ifọ̀n, showing that the town became a prominent and prosperous trading colony of Ilé-Ifẹ̀. It was a busy market town where a diversity of glass beads could be bought and sold. Ifọ̀n was also plugged into the network of other market towns in the region. In that kind of thriving commercial center, one would expect to find a wide range of craftspeople, at least those associated with using beads to make a sundry of products. The role of Ifọ̀n as a frontier market hub for redistributing Ifẹ̀ glass beads and other merchandise explains why it claimed to have a large repository of beaded crowns and why many people were drawn to its gate to acquire these crowns. For example, the potentate of Ọ̀yọ́ is said to have lacked a beaded crown in the early years of the polity, and it was from Ifọ̀n that the *aláàfin*, the paramount ruler of Ọ̀yọ́, secured his crowns.

Kín ni mo wá r'òde Àdìkún
Mo ní mo w'órí adé lọ
Orí adé kò yọ ṣẹ̀gi
Òrólú, Ọmọ l'ádé l'ádé l'ádé
Aláàfin ò l'ádé
Adé Òrólú la gbà f'Áláàfin
Mo ṣubú lu'fọ̀n
Mo wá da'yùn mọ́ ṣẹ̀gi

Translation:

What did I go to Àdìkún[81] to find?
I went to search for the crown
The head of crown cannot do without *ṣẹ̀gi*
Òrólú, the child of many crowns
Aláàfin did not originally have a crown
It was the crown of Òrólú that was given to Aláàfin
I fell on Ifọ̀n
I joyfully mixed up *iyùn* and *ṣẹ̀gi*

We may therefore see in Ifọ̀n a secondary center and a prominent Ifẹ̀ colony that introduced a new form of royal symbol and prestige, as well as the new concept that those objects represented, to the Upper Ògùn area. Writing about the relationship between Ọ̀yọ́ and Ifọ̀n, Òrìsàtóyìnbó surmised: "In the evolution of the Ọ̀yọ́ monarchical system, the Aláàfin benefited immensely from the concept of divine kingship already established in Ifọ̀n-Òrólú."[82] Yet the expression that "Aláàfin did not originally have a crown, it was the crown of Òrólú that was given to Aláàfin" is also suggestive that at some point, Òrólú lost its privileged position as a secondary regional market center to Ọ̀yọ́. I will have more to say about this later.

In the meantime, it was not only the genealogy of Odùduwà that Ifọ́n rejected. Despite serving as a redistribution center for Ifẹ̀ glass beads and as a thriving manufacturing center for the beaded crowns so desired across the Yorùbá world during the Classical period, Ifọ́n also rejected the material symbols of power and prestige that were associated with the Odùduwà ascendancy and the Ifẹ̀-centric *ìlú/ọba-aládé* dyad. Hence, Ifọ́n's king did not use brass or copper, and Ifọ́n's royalty considered *ṣẹ̀gi* to be an unclean object. Instead, the lord of Ifọ́n (Olúfọ́n) wore only the white beads (*ṣẹ́ṣẹ́ ẹfun*) and crowns made of those beads, although beads and crowns of *ṣẹ̀gi* and *iyùn* as well as copper-alloy were available for purchase in Ifọ́n.

Ọwọ́ ọ̀tún mi yẹ'dẹ
N kò gbọdọ̀ l'odẹ
Ẹsẹ̀ mi sì yẹ bàbà
N kò gbọdọ̀ lo bàbà
Àtọ̀tún àtòsì
Ni ńmú b'òjé f'Ólúfọ̀n
Ẹ ní ṣẹ̀gi nìlẹ̀kẹ̀ ọ̀bùn
Olúfọ̀n Adé
Ọmọ aládé ṣẹ́ṣẹ́ ẹfun.

Translation:

My right wrist is good for brass
But I must not wear brass
My ankle is appropriate for copper
I must not use copper
On both the right and left sides of my body
I will wear lead ornaments in honor of Olúfọ̀n (avatar of Ọbàtálá)
You say *ṣẹ̀gi* is the bead of the unclean people
Olúfọ̀n Adé
The child of the pure white beads.

The counter-hegemonic discourses taking place in Ifọ́n proclaimed an unalloyed loyalty to the Ọbàtálá institution, whose symbolic color was (and still is) white, and objects of adornments were made of lead (òjé) and white beads (*ṣẹ́ṣẹ́ ẹfun*). The panegyric celebrated the Ifẹ̀ ancestry of Ifọ́n but rejected the two primary objects that Classical Ifẹ̀ used as its hegemonic capital to construct a regional identity that centered on the divine kingship. The Ifọ́n political elite rejected the idea that *ṣẹ̀gi*, *iyùn*, and *àkún* were the only material symbols for realizing kingship and divinity. In their place, they extolled the virtues of *ṣẹ́ṣẹ́ ẹfun* for purity, wellness, and social order. Although the economic well-being of Ifọ́n depended on marketing the Ifẹ̀ glass beads, the kings of Ifọ́n found the use of these products anathema to their spiritual well-being. Therefore, from this case of Ifọ́n-Ifẹ̀ relationship, it is obvious that not every polity or emporium that operated within the commercial realm of Ifẹ̀ accepted the latter's ideology and brand of divine kingship. Ifọ̀n's defiant and confident resistance to Ifẹ̀'s hegemonic construct would have been a source of consternation and embarrassment to the political chieftains of the "city of abundance." They needed Ifọ̀n's cooperation as an outlet for Ifẹ̀ exports. Ifọ̀n's anti-Odùduwà rhetoric and distaste for Ifẹ̀'s material symbol of royalty and kingship institution, however, placed the frontier kingdom and commercial center at odds with the metropolis's imperial ambitions and political philosophy. Those in the capital would have seen Ifọ̀n as a colony of Ifẹ̀. If so, the colony was in an ambiguous political relationship with the metropole. Nevertheless, the people of Ifọ̀n regarded their kingdom as an extension of Ifẹ̀'s commercial and ritual fields, especially as a major cult center of Ọbatálá and as a major market outlet for Ifẹ̀'s most precious product (glass beads).

Ifọ̀n's anathema toward the material basis of Ifẹ̀'s *ọba-aládé* institution seems to have grown out of the internal political dynamics in Ilé-Ifẹ̀ itself—the historical struggle between the Ọbàtálá and Odùduwà factions. And the trouble between the "city of sunrise" and its frontier colony and trading agent appears to be more about philosophical disputation than political. After all, the latter was not trying to displace the former from its position at the apex of the regional political and commercial hierarchy. For this reason, Ilé-Ifẹ̀ might have found it expedient to tolerate Ifọ̀n's philosophical rhetoric in order to maintain the full cooperation of one of its major colonies and allies. As we turn to examine Òwu and the relationship that it developed with Ilé-Ifẹ̀ in the high noon of the Classical period, we shall see that indeed Ilé-Ifẹ̀ had a bigger fish to fry than Ifọ̀n's counter-hegemonic "ideological war."

Of all the northern Yorùbá polities of the middle Classical period, Òwu was the most prominent and the largest. Located in the wooded savanna, between the present-day Ṣakí and Kísì (see fig. 3.2), it was one of the earliest colonies or client states of Ifẹ̀.[83] This ancient kingdom was strategically located to protect and control the trade routes linking the Yorùbá world to the Western Sudan through the Ìbàrìbá country. Òwu's domestic economy was based on the production and export of iron products and cotton cloth. Traces of its importance as a center for iron production and large-scale cultivation of cotton are still found in the local memory of the northwest Yorùbá people today.[84] But more important, the city-state derived phenomenal wealth from its control of the trade routes that linked the Western Sudan with the Yorùbá region and through which the Ifẹ̀ glass beads passed into the Middle Niger valley. It appears that in the early fourteenth century, Òwu began to use the profits from these commercial opportunities to buy horses from their northern Wasangari, Mossi, Mandé, and Songhai neighbors and soon became the first cavalry state in the Yorùbá world.[85] The polity might have initially needed these horses for protection against the Wasangari military leaders who held sway over the nearby Ìbàrìbá territories. However, as its wealth grew on account of its control of the shortest trade routes that linked the Western Sudan to the rain forest, Òwu embarked on an ambitious expansionist agenda. At the peak of its power during the mid-fourteenth century, its territory encompassed Ṣakí in the west and the early Ìlá kingdom (Ìlá-Yàrà) in the east.[86] The Ọ̀yọ́ kingdom was also one of its prized vassal states. And Òwu controlled some of the Ìbàràpá polities to the south.[87] The use of cavalry made this vast territorial gain across the woodland savanna possible.

Like many other Yorùbá polities during the Classical period, Òwu was within the Ifẹ̀ ritual field. Its patron deity, Áńlugbùà, was (and still is) an avatar of Ọbatálá. However, emboldened by its wealth, military strength, and strategic commercial location, Òwu began to undermine the commercial and political interests of Ifẹ̀, militarily and ideologically. With its invasion of Ifẹ̀'s spheres of influence as far as Ìgbómìnà, Òwu declared open war on the political and economic interests of Ifẹ̀. The Òwu leaders did not stop there. They also began to make strong ideological claims that theirs was the first kingdom in the Yorùbá world's *ẹbí* fraternity. Hence the saying *Òwu l'akọ́dá*: "Òwu is the oldest kingdom." This primus inter pares ideology directly challenged the apical status of Ifẹ̀ in the Yorùbá community of practice. By taking these steps, Òwu left no doubt that it was not only seeking to remove itself from under the eaves of Ifẹ̀'s commercial tent and political clientage. It was also determined to control Ifẹ̀'s territories in Ìgbómìnà and monopolize the trade routes that linked Ilé-Ifẹ̀ to the trading termini on the Niger River. And in the quest to achieve these goals, Òwu was ready to rewrite history (by creating a new legend) and invent a new ideology of legitimation.[88]

Òwu's expansionist agenda, hegemonic ambitions, and military forays into Ìgbómìnà posed a serious threat to the northern thrust of Ifẹ̀'s commercial empire. Containing this threat was the centerpiece of Ọbalùfọ̀n Aláyémorẹ̀'s political agenda when he ascended the throne of Ifẹ̀ during the mid-fourteenth century. Also known as Ọbalùfọ̀n II in the historiography, he is reputed to have pursued vigorous military campaigns and political diplomacy in order to reinstate Ifẹ̀'s influence and control of commercial networks along the northern axis. Ọbalùfọ̀n II resuscitated the expansionist programs that his earlier predecessors had put in place during the twelfth and thirteenth centuries. Those efforts had already built the Ifẹ̀ Empire by adding Òwu, Ọ̀wọ̀, and Edo, as well as most of the Èkìtì and Ìgbómìnà territories, to the sphere of Ilé-Ifẹ̀'s influence. By the time Ọbalùfọ̀n II came to power, most of the northern frontiers of the empire were under Òwu. In order to turn the tide, the king focused his attention on the Ìgbómìnà area. This was necessary to halt the advance of Òwu into Ilé-Ifẹ̀ itself.

There is a version of the tradition suggesting that by the time Ọbalùfọ̀n II came to the throne, Òwu had planted several of its colonies in the Ìgbómìnà area and was already collecting tribute from the Ìlá kingdom, the dominant polity in the area.[89] This would mean that by the mid-fourteenth century, Òwu was controlling about half of the four-hundred-kilometer span of the northern Yorùbá world and was blocking Ifẹ̀'s direct access to most of the commercial entrepôts on the Niger. The battle for the soul and soil of Ìgbómìnà was an epic one between Òwu and Ilé-Ifẹ̀ because of what it meant for the grand ambitions of the former and the very existence of the latter. The battle preoccupied the political agenda of Ọbalùfọ̀n II, who came to power after a bitter civil war in Ilé-Ifẹ̀.[90] Òwu's success at encroaching on the northern frontiers and trade routes of Ifẹ̀ may have resulted from the political instability in the "the city of daybreak." The domestic crisis in Ilé-Ifẹ̀ possibly drew the attention of its leaders away from the northern axis of commerce, thereby forcing Òwu to seek to fill the void. It is also likely that Ifẹ̀'s political crisis drew in the outlying territories and provinces in the empire, with each taking sides with the different factions in the metropolitan conflict.

Whatever the motivations for Òwu's expansionist program, the outcome of the struggle between the frontier kingdom and Ilé-Ifẹ̀ proved that Ọbalùfọ̀n II was the right man for the occasion. The oral traditions of Ifẹ̀ credit him with military vigor, expansionist drive, and political sagacity, and the traditions in Ìgbómìnà celebrate him for downgrading Òwu's influence and taking over Òwu's colonies and outposts in the area.[91] Ọbalùfọ̀n II reclaimed lost territories and established new Ifẹ colonies in Ìgbómìnà. His success was credited to frontiersmen, who tended to be hunters, warriors, and ironworkers rather than princes.[92] At the peak of Ọbalùfọ̀n II's reign, Ilé-Ifẹ̀ controlled a vast network of towns and villages along the trade routes that linked central Yorùbáland with the Niger River. For example, a chain of settlements whose repertoire of material culture is similar to those of Ilé-Ifẹ̀ (especially in terms of ceramic styles and architectural materials—potsherd pavements and wall tiles) has been found stretching from Ilé-Ifẹ̀ through Upper Ọ̀ṣun (Èjìgbò, Gbọ́nmi [Òṣogbo], and Ìkìrun); Ìgbómìnà (Aùń, Òró, Àjàbà, Ọ̀bà-Ìsin, Òkègì, Ìlá-Ọ̀ràngún, Ìlá-Yàrà, Èsìẹ́, Òbágbó, Olúpẹfọ̀n, and Gbàgede); and Èkìtì (Ìmẹ̀sí Lásígidi, Ìfàkì, and Ìtajì).[93] These settlements developed or were reinforced to secure Ilé-Ifẹ̀'s access to the River Niger.

The "city of abundance" recorded the height of its Classical age during the reign of Ọbalùfọ̀n II. There was overall peace and prosperity across the land, and his name became synonymous with wealth, innovation, security, and stability across the region. The importation of copper alloys to Ilé-Ifẹ̀, for example, increased dramatically during his reign, and he is widely credited in the oral traditions with having the images of the royal ancestors cast in brass. Many of the brass casters from Ilé-Ifẹ̀ who carried their craft to many parts of the Yorùbá world possibly did so during his reign, as oral traditions in Ilé-Ifẹ̀, Ìjẹ̀bú-Òde, and Benin indicate. As a result, Ọbalùfọ̀n II is widely recognized in many parts of the Yorùbá world, including Benin, as the patron deity of copper-alloy crafts.[94]

Ọbalùfọ̀n II's success in breaking off Òwu's control of Ìgbómìnà did not immediately remove Òwu's threat to Ifẹ̀'s commercial interest in the Moshi-Niger area. Neither did it guarantee that the ambitious leaders of other polities with closer proximity to River Niger valley would not disrupt the flow of Ifẹ̀'s commercial traffic in that area. One of these potential trouble spots was Ọ̀yọ́. Although the Ọ̀yọ́ were brought under the control of Òwu in the first half of the fourteenth century, the former continued to resist this vassalage. Ọbalùfọ̀n and his frontiersmen therefore saw an opportunity. In order to resecure the vast northern frontiers of Ifẹ̀'s commercial empire, they turned to Ọ̀yọ́ for an alliance against Òwu. As the largest polity located in the Moshi-Niger area, Ọ̀yọ́ was well placed to control the riverside trading entrepôts if they could get Òwu off their back. After all, Ifẹ̀'s trading colonies in the nearby Jebba-Tada area and in Ìgbómìnà were closer to Ọ̀yọ́ than Òwu. The potentials of Ifẹ̀'s alliance with Ọ̀yọ́ therefore offered a promising solution to the Òwu problem. We do not know whether Ilé-Ifẹ̀ gave any direct military support to Ọ̀yọ́ against Òwu. However, the evidence suggests that Ilé-Ifẹ̀ pursued a strategy of alliance that manipulated the Ifẹ̀-centric ritual field to prop up the political status of Ọ̀yọ́ in the comity of peer polities. It did this in two converging ways. First, Ilé-Ifẹ̀ made Ọ̀yọ́ its privileged trading partner by funneling its trading goods through Ọ̀yọ́, a critical step that possibly cut off Òwu from Ife's commercial network. Second, it extended the ideology of beaded-crown legitimacy to Ọ̀yọ́ through the legend of Ọ̀rànmíyàn. This means Ọ̀rànmíyàn, the intrepid warrior-prince in Ifẹ̀'s stock narratives, was touted as the founder of the royal dynasty at Ọ̀yọ́. This would have countered the ideology of primus inter pares that Òwu had fabricated.

According to the legend, Ọ̀rànmíyàn was the father of Ṣàngó, the mythical founder of Ọ̀yọ́—whose mother was a Nupe princess. From this point, the legend is silent on the supposed immediate successors of Ṣàngó—Ajaka and Àgànjù—but instead focuses on Kórì, the Ọ̀yọ́ king whose rule took place sometime in the last quarter of the fourteenth century. The Ọ̀rànmíyàn legend alludes to the relationship between Kórì and Ilé-Ifẹ̀. Kórì's father was Àgànjù, but his mother was a princess from Ọ̀gbọ̀rọ̀ in the early Òwu territory.[95] The name of Kórì's mother, Ìyáayùn ("mother of *iyùn*"), is derived from Ifẹ̀'s red glass bead—*iyùn*. Ìyáayùn is said to have introduced *ifá* divination—an important element of the Ifẹ̀ ritual field—to Ọ̀yọ́. All of these suggest that Ilé-Ifẹ̀ and Ọ̀yọ́ did not only develop diplomatic and commercial relationships in the late fourteenth century. The relationships also involved the incorporation of Ọ̀yọ́ into the Ifẹ̀ ritual field, through the cult of *ifá*. Kórì's reign appears to mark a pivotal moment when Ọ̀yọ́ became the last major kingdom to be incorporated into the *ẹbí* fraternity. This was close to the end of the Classical period, and it explains why Ọ̀yọ́ is regarded in Yorùbá traditional history as the last of the children of Odùduwà.

The integration of Ọ̀yọ́ into the Ifẹ̀-centric *ẹbí* fraternity (political sphere) and ritual field cemented the alliance between the upstart polity and the old, revered metropolis. It guaranteed the flow of Ifẹ̀'s commerce, especially its two chief products, *ṣẹ̀gi* and *iyùn*, into Ọ̀yọ́'s spheres of control. And this was a powerful incentive for Ọ̀yọ́ to protect Ifẹ̀'s interest in the Moshi-Niger area. The go-between in this new Ifẹ̀-Ọ̀yọ́ alliance was Ifọ̀n, the famed market town previously discussed. Ifọ̀n's ideological differences with Ilé-Ifẹ̀ and its counter-hegemonic rhetoric may have subsided under the heavy hand of Ọbalùfọ̀n II's reign and in response to the threat that Òwu posed to regional stability. There are indications that it was from Ifọ̀n that the sacred beaded crown secured for the king of Ọ̀yọ́-Ilé was sanctified by the Ọbatálá priests. Hence the saying *Aláàfin ò l'ádé, Adé Òrólú la gbà f'Áláàfin*: "The Aláàfin [king of Ọ̀yọ́-Ilé] originally had no crown, it was the crown of Òrólú [king of Ifọ̀n] that was given to Aláàfin." This cryptic saying may also allude to the fact that Ọ̀yọ́'s entry into the alliance with Ilé-Ifẹ̀ displaced Ifọ̀n's commercial and political influence. The Ifẹ̀-Ọ̀yọ́ alliance stabilized the regional trade for Ilé-Ifẹ̀ and its allies, and wealth accrued to Ọ̀yọ́ as a result of its status as a privileged trading partner of Ilé-Ifẹ̀.

The Ifẹ̀-Ọ̀yọ́ alliance was a significant milestone in the unfolding history of the Yorùbá community of practice. The process vividly shows how the ideology of the *ẹbí* fraternity was used to consolidate and glue diplomatic relations and foreign affairs. The process by which Ọ̀yọ́ entered the fraternity in the late fourteenth century reveals the dynamic intellectual works that were mobilized to sustain and legitimize regional integration within the orbit of Ifẹ̀ cultural- and knowledge-capital hegemony. It shows the brilliance with which Ifẹ̀'s political intellectuals used stories to build a community of consciousness across a vast region. However, the Ọ̀rànmíyàn legend was not only Ifẹ̀'s invention. Kórì and his court participated in cocreating it in order to cope with and solve a myriad of political and economic problems that they were also confronting. Indeed, for the sake of Ọ̀yọ́'s sociopolitical stability and economic well-being, Kórì and his predecessor needed this Ifẹ̀-centric genealogy in order to cement the integration of their kingdom into the Yorùbá community of practice.

The Moshi-Niger area had always been a hotbed of cultural bricolage. The Yorùbá population lived side by side with several other cultural groups, including the Nupe, Ìbàrìbá, and various Songhai elements, especially the Djerma (see fig. 1.1). They were all drawn to the area because of its opportunities as a commercial entrepôt and its abundant resources for agriculture and fishing.[96] This area was a patchwork of language groups whose diverse cultural and religious lives intersected in admirably cosmopolitan ways. For example, the name Ṣàngó, what later became the royal cult of Ọ̀yọ́, seems to have originated from the Djerma, where this deity of thunder and lightning was called Donko. However, as Babátúndé Agírí has noted, the deity of thunder and lightning in the Yorùbá world did not begin with Ṣàngó. The deity was originally known as Jàkúta in Ọ̀yọ́-Ilé. The deity of thunder and lightning was also known as Ọramfẹ̀ in Ilé-Ifẹ̀ and as Sogba in Yàgbà. Jàkúta, Ọramfẹ̀, and Sogba are different names for the same sky-god complex in the deep-time Yorùbá cosmology.[97] The Djerma must have exercised a good measure of influence in Ọ̀yọ́ and the Moshi-Niger area for Ṣàngó to have been substituted for Jàkúta. This influence was political, economic, cultural, and religious. The Djerma were major trading partners of Ọ̀yọ́ and other Yorùbá groups. They appear to be the preeminent carriers of Yorùbá exports into the Niger Bend and of imports from the Mediterranean-Sahara and Western Sudan into the Yorùbá world via the Moshi-Niger trading stations during the Classical period. As a result, there would have been tremendous cultural and population flow between the Djerma and the Yorùbá groups. Considering the destabilization effect of Òwu expansion on commerce in the area, it is possible that some of the Djerma merchants were part of the negotiation with Ilé-Ifẹ̀. Identifying Ṣàngó as a son of Ọ̀rànmíyàn was an obvious attempt to carry along the Djerma community in the diplomacy being worked out between Ọ̀yọ́ and Ilé-Ifẹ̀. This could also reflect the fact that the Djerma priests of Ṣàngó had become prominent in the political affairs and spiritual life of Ọ̀yọ́ during the late fourteenth century. The reference to the Nupe origin of Ṣàngó's mother in the oral traditions also indicates the prominence of the Nupe elements in the political affairs of Ọ̀yọ́, and it may allude to the integration of some of the Nupe elements into the Ọ̀yọ́ royal households through marriage.[98]

However, during this very same period (late fourteenth century), the emerging process of political centralization in the Nupe heartland was already displacing the Yorùbá settlements along the Niger (what is now southern Nupe).[99] Ọ̀yọ́ would have received a large proportion of the Yorùbá being displaced from the troubled zone. The Moshi-Niger area was the economic hub of Ọ̀yọ́ kingdom, and the latter also had territorial claims over some of the Yorùbá and other communities that populated the area. The Òwu expansionist project in the west, the turbulence of political centralization among the Nupe in the east, and the effects of all of these on the Moshi-Niger communities would have been a major concern for Ọ̀yọ́. Kórì and his immediate predecessor, Àgànjú, must have looked up to Ilé-Ifẹ̀ as the source of their cultural capital, regional alliance, and legitimacy—as well as of economic partnership and military support. After all, Ilé-Ifẹ̀ was still the largest and most prominent political formation in the region. Kórì completed what Àgànjú possibly started in forming an alliance with Ilé-Ifẹ̀ during the reign of Ọbalùfọ̀n II. Therefore, Kórì's court would have been an enthusiastic cocreator of the Ọ̀rànmíyàn legend. The legend used the *ẹbí* fraternity charter to create an Ifẹ̀-centric (Yorùbá) identity for Ọ̀yọ́, especially its royal House, and to transform the evolving political and commercial partnership between Ilé-Ifẹ̀ and Ọ̀yọ́ into an ideological one. It was an alliance of patron-client relationship and a brilliant diplomatic effort to secure their mutual interests in this strategic but contentious frontier. We shall see in the next chapter how the winds of change blowing southward across the Moshi-Niger area would affect this relationship. For now, let us turn our attention to the other aspects of the intellectual tradition that Ilé-Ifẹ̀ invented, borrowed, embellished, and mobilized to cement its referential status as the center of the Yorùbá world.

Òrìṣà: Theogonic and Intellectual Basis of the Yorùbá Community of Practice

Ilé-Ifẹ̀ did more than leverage its knowledge capital in glass-bead production and develop a coherent ideology for the *ìlú/ọba-aládé* dyad and *ẹbí* fraternity to craft the idea of the Yorùbá community of practice and promote itself as the head of that community. It also attained referential status through a grand program of theogonic invention and revision. This involved the integration of deities from different backgrounds and ritual fields across the region into a standardized and universalized pantheon, and the cultivation of learning and intellectual pursuit that was associated with the several schools (cults) of these deities. During the Archaic through the Late Formative periods, the proto-Yoruboid and proto-Yorùbá in different localities had accumulated elaborate mythologies, ritualized ceremonies, and epistemological frameworks that formed the templates for their worldviews. Each local pantheon was a hierarchy of deities, with overlapping relationships in which each deity ruled over one or more spheres of the human condition.[100] However, several of those deities (*òrìṣà*) that were conceptual in nature, rather than ancestral, had regional appeal because they addressed broad human conditions and derived from common origins and deep-time experiences. Òrìṣà Òkè or Òrìṣà Ńlá (the supreme sky god associated with the hills), Ògún (the patron deity of iron technology and justice), and Òrúnmìlà or Ifá (deity of divination and knowledge) are a few of those deities. Their origins had a deep history, and they spread with the waves of proto-Yorùbá expansions throughout the first millennium AD. Building on the legacy of this deep-time cosmological and theogonic thought, Ilé-Ifẹ̀ led the charge, beginning in the eleventh century, to reconceptualize the community of *òrìṣà* in the image of the *ìlú/ọba-aládé* dyad and *ẹbí* fraternity. This process evolved throughout the Classical period. It included translating those deities that had regional appeal into a system of filial relationships (*ẹbí*) and using them as parallel mirrors for viewing and reflecting on the everyday social lives. The light bouncing from these everyday lives, to borrow the lingo of optical physics, created the infinity effect on these parallel mirrors—the *òrìṣà* pantheon. The *òrìṣà* offered the multiple angles to view everyday lives in a series of reflections that receded into an infinite distance. It would take deep learning, knowledge, and expertise to observe, read, and interpret these reflections. And, inasmuch as the everyday life is not static, the pantheon could not be static. New deities (new parallel mirrors) were therefore created from time to time to capture and account for these new everyday experiences.

It was therefore in Ilé-Ifẹ̀ that a new charter of integrated theogony and worldview was developed to support the evolving regional integration that the "city of daybreak" was championing with its invented glass technology and institutionalization of the *ìlú/ọba-aládé* dyad. The city's cosmopolitan and metropolitan profile meant that it was a recipient of a diversity of people and ideas from across the region jostling for prominence and competitive advantages. This was a fertile ground for organizing, experimenting, revising, and standardizing the diverse pantheons from across the region into a coherent (but not singular) system of thought. Hence, just as Ilé-Ifẹ̀ standardized the materiality and philosophy of the *ìlú/ọba-aládé* dyad and created an ideological charter for the *ẹbí* fraternity for the purpose of regional integration, it also developed a reputation as the center of knowledge and learning about "the ways of the *òrìṣà*." Although Ilé-Ifẹ̀ was not by any means the sole inventor of the *òrìṣà* pantheon, it played a dominant role in standardizing and promoting a version of it. It was the place where the ancestral deities that had evolved out of Ifẹ̀'s own local political experience were integrated into the existing pan-regional deities. The city's intellectuals also gave most of those existing pan-regional deities their own flavor by domesticating them as local deities. One of those methods of domestication was the insistence that those deities had their origins in Ilé-Ifẹ̀. The Ifẹ̀ intellectuals worked with the same cosmogony that was widely known to their neighbors, but they filled it with Ifẹ̀-centric dramatis personae. As a result, a new ritual field that was an amalgamation of the regional and local elements was created, and the intellectuals of the city promoted it as a universal experience. In other words, Ilé-Ifẹ̀ was the place of coalescence where "the ways of the *òrìṣà*" from different parts of the Yorùbá region, before and during the Classical period, were integrated, repackaged, and standardized. This was the birth of the Ifẹ̀-centric *òrìṣà* ritual field, which expanded along the overlapping political, economic, and social networks that the city unquestionably created and dominated from the twelfth century through the beginning of the fifteenth century. And, as other kingdoms and dynasties began to write their histories on the basis of the Ifẹ̀-centric template, they also developed genealogies that connected their local deities to the theogony and theology being promoted by the intellectuals of Ilé-Ifẹ̀ as the universal system of thought and practice. This system became an epistemology and a compass for navigating life's journey and memory, managing both social order and turbulence, exploring the relationships between the earthly and the spiritual worlds, and seeking meanings.

I will use the cultural biography of Ọ̀rúnmìlà (also known as Ifá), the patron deity of divination and the intellectual anchor of the Yorùbá pantheon, to illustrate this process of revision, appropriation, domestication, and coalescence. At the very core of the Classical Yoruba world was the metaphysics of *ifá*, a systematic divination method and hermeneutical science for seeking solutions and explaining meaning.[101] *Ifá* is the elite and superior form of divination in the Yorùbá world today, and in the Ifẹ̀-centric myth-history, Ọ̀rúnmìlà is considered as its founder.[102] Here, I show that although the Èkìtì and Okun areas played important roles in the development of *ifá*, Ilé-Ifẹ̀ appropriated and redefined this method of knowing and domesticated it as a unique Ifẹ̀ invention before then promoting it as a universal system of knowledge for the Yorùbá community of practice.

To understand *ifá* evolution, one should begin with its primary instruments of divination, two of which have survived to the present: *ọ̀pẹ̀lẹ̀*, eight flat seed pods joined together by a chain or cord, and *ikin*, sixteen palm nuts with four indentations (eyes) produced by a rare mutated form of oil palm tree.[103] There were many other divination types and methods, but *Ifá* is distinguished from those by its thousands of elaborate verses (*ẹsẹ̀ ifá*), which are divided into sixteen principal *odù*—"books," or branches of knowledge. Each book is, in turn, subdivided into 16 chapters (minor *odù*).[104] In total, then, there are 256 chapters in *ifá*. William Bascom noted that these texts are of greater importance than *ifá*'s instruments: "The verses form an important corpus of verbal art, including myths, folktales, praise names, incantations, songs, proverbs, and even riddles; but to the Yorùbá their 'literary' or aesthetic merit is secondary to their religious significance. In effect, these verses constitute their unwritten scriptures. The verses embody myths recounting the activities of the deities and justifying details of ritual, and they are often cited to settle a disputed point of theology or ritual."[105]

The arrangement of the *ikin/ọpẹ̀lẹ̀* on each casting dictates what texts the diviner will use to identify, analyze, and explain the problems facing the client in order to prescribe the appropriate solutions. In other words, there are 256 possible signs the divination instrument can produce, and each has a unique body of texts (a chapter) dealing with specific aspects of human situations. According to mathematician Adeniran Adeboye, the *ifá* divination system is based on the philosophical precept of logical realism as well as the principle of probability.[106] Its goal is to bridge the ontological gap between reality and the limits of human cognition through the probability algorithms provided by the divination wand (*ikin* or *ọpẹ̀lẹ̀*). Noting the binary structure of each divination sign and the hierarchical structure of each *odù*, computer scientist Tunde Adegbola and others have noted that this science of geomancy is based on the same logic as simulation techniques in operations research—a branch of study that uses computation and mathematical algorithms for identifying optimal or near-optimal solutions to complex problems.[107] Taken altogether, the *ifá* divination techniques and the signs and texts of *odù* provide the procedural rules, schemata, precedents, and metaphysical concepts for solving existential problems dealing with experience and sense impressions. There is virtually no aspect of the human condition that the *ifá* corpus does not cover or for which it does not provide an opening for further exploration and inquiry.[108]

The master *ifá* diviner, the *babaláwo*, was the fountain of knowledge in the Yorùbá community of practice.[109] The *babaláwo* was (and still is) a learned man who sought to solve material, social, spiritual, and ailing problems through processes of diagnosis and prescription that came out of learning and knowledge. An authority on metaphysics, everyday riddles, and religion, he was required to have an in-depth understanding of the history, sociology, and philosophy associated with each of the deities and the other forces that inhabited the Yorùbá world. Through his divination, he prescribed the sacrifices that were appropriate for the *òrìṣà*, the *ajogun* (malevolent forces), and the ancestors in order to solve his clients' problems. His position required many years of training and a lifelong search for knowledge. He transacted exclusively in the life of the mind, not only to seek causal relationships but also to understand the deep meanings of those relationships. The *babaláwo* was the focal point of civic and religious life and was accessible to everyone in private or public spaces for consultation "on every undertaking" or whenever there was any doubt about the future.[110] Hence, the *babaláwo* helped his clients to navigate the maze of life, in their search for healing, self-realization, knowledge, and meaning.

No indigenous African divination system has enjoyed as extensive a geographical influence as *ifá*.[111] However, the regional variations of the Yorùbá divination systems give some clues (but not certainty) to the origins of *ifá* and the role that Ilé-Ifẹ̀ played in the process. To start, a version of divination called *ifá* is found among the Igala of the Niger-Benue Confluence, but its method is more similar to the *agbigba* type common among the Yàgbà (Okun) subgroup of the Yorùbá near the confluence.[112] The *agbigba* method of divination consisted of four strands of four seed pods each (totaling sixteen pods). It seems that *ọ̀pẹ̀lẹ̀*'s one strand of eight seed pods is a consolidation and simplification of the *agbigba* method. However, unlike the latter, which is poor in the literary corpus, the *ọ̀pẹ̀lẹ̀-ifá* has a rich and expanding corpus. It should be noted that the *agbigba* version was, until the recent century, much more widespread across central and southeast Nigeria, including among the Edo, where it is called *iha ominigbon* and practiced side by side with the *ọ̀pẹ̀lẹ̀-ifá*.

Considering the sequence of Yoruboid migrations from the confluence area, discussed in chapter 2, these regional similarities suggest that *agbigba* was likely the prototype and much older form of divination that developed in the Niger-Benue Confluence. It may have already become widespread among some of the descendants of the proto-Benue-Kwa groups before the proto-Yoruboid dispersal began in earnest at the end of the first millennium BC.[113] In other words, the *ọ̀pẹ̀lẹ̀-ifá* divination was an innovation of an existing and widespread divination system of which *agbigba* was the prototype. It is not clear at what point or where the *ọ̀pẹ̀lẹ̀-ifá* innovation took place. Neither do we have any indication as to when the *ikin* method began. But both may also have a deep antiquity. The literary corpora of *both* ikin and *ọ̀pẹ̀lẹ̀* are the same and have prominent references to the Èkìtì area. Therefore, it is likely that the early phase of the innovations of both the *ọ̀pẹ̀lẹ̀* and the *ikin* methods of *ifá* divination, in terms of the techniques and texts, took place in the Èkìtì heartland during the Early and Late Formative periods (ca. AD 500–1000), and these later spread to Ilé-Ifẹ̀.[114]

Although both variants of *ifá* possibly coexisted in various Yorùbá-speaking communities, the *ọ̀pẹ̀lẹ̀* version may have enjoyed preeminence in Èkìtì and Ilé-Ifẹ̀ area during the Late Formative period. However, at some point during the Classical period, the Ifẹ̀ political elites and intellectuals declared their preference for the *ikin* method over *ọ̀pẹ̀lẹ̀*. This was part of their revisionist agenda to domestic *ifá* in the new social order they were creating. Their domestication efforts included restructuring the books of *ifá* (the *odù*) and rearranging the texts of each *odù* and its chapters in ways that made them Ifẹ̀-centric. Despite these efforts, however, the corpus retained its deep Èkìtì imprints. In the myth-historical narratives that evolved to explain the elevation of *ikin* and demotion of *ọ̀pẹ̀lẹ̀*, the latter is depicted as a foreigner (the "other") and an ungrateful servant of the deity of divination, Ọ̀rúnmìlà, whose preferred divination method was the *ikin*. That is, *ọ̀pẹ̀lẹ̀* was portrayed as an illegitimate form of *ifá*, and *ikin* was promoted as the authentic. As we shall see below, this blatant revisionist strategy to minimize the influence of the much older *agbigba* divination method and its *ọ̀pẹ̀lẹ̀* derivative was tied to the agenda of displacing them in the official political affairs of Ilé-Ifẹ̀. It was a contentious process that required the Classical Ifẹ̀ intellectuals to provide a rationale for their action. A verse in Èjìogbè, the heraldic or first book of Ifá, describes the situation thus:

> It was divined for Ọ̀rúnmìlà, on the day he was going to the market.
> He was told to first put money on what he did not want to buy.
> When Ọ̀rúnmìlà arrived in the market, he looked around for the items he wanted to buy.
> Then he remembered what his diviner told him.
> He saw Ọ̀pẹ̀lẹ̀, a . . . slave with a limp.
> Ọ̀rúnmìlà bought Ọ̀pẹ̀lẹ̀, and took him home.
> Ọ̀rúnmìlà was using Ọ̀pẹ̀lẹ̀ as a housekeeper and for other menial tasks.
> One day, clients came to visit Ọ̀rúnmìlà.
> They met Ọ̀pẹ̀lẹ̀ in front of the house.
> Ọ̀pẹ̀lẹ̀ divined for them.
> He solved their problems before they reached Ọ̀rúnmìlà.
> Ọ̀rúnmìlà discovered that Ọ̀pẹ̀lẹ̀ had knowledge of divination, and he began to treat him well.
> Ọ̀pẹ̀lẹ̀ became Ọ̀rúnmìlà's assistant and he was allowed to divine for Ọ̀rúnmìlà's clients.
> Ọ̀pẹ̀lẹ̀ gained fame and respect but he began to speak ill of Ọ̀rúnmìlà.
> He became an ingrate; he spread rumors that Ọ̀rúnmìlà did not have true power or deep knowledge of divination,
> That he Ọ̀pẹ̀lẹ̀ had more power than Ọ̀rúnmìlà.
> One day when Ọ̀rúnmìlà was traveling, Ọ̀pẹ̀lẹ̀ was called to Ọlọ́fin's [the king of Ilé-Ifẹ̀] palace to divine.
> Ọ̀pẹ̀lẹ̀ committed a major offense during the divination and he was expelled from the palace.
> When Ọ̀rúnmìlà returned to the town, he was informed of Ọ̀pẹ̀lẹ̀'s transgressions.
> Ọ̀rúnmìlà begged Ọlọ́fin for forgiveness, a request that Ọlọ́fin granted.
> Ọ̀rúnmìlà performed another divination for Ọlọ́fin, who rewarded him handsomely with gifts.
> Ọ̀rúnmìlà returned home to ask Ọ̀pẹ̀lẹ̀ about his transgressions but Ọ̀pẹ̀lẹ̀ started to insult Ọ̀rúnmìlà.
> Ọ̀rúnmìlà had had enough.
> He smacked Ọ̀pẹ̀lẹ̀ with his sacred tapping wand, *ìrọ́kẹ́*, and Ọ̀pẹ̀lẹ̀ broke into pieces.

Ọ̀pẹ̀lẹ̀ broke into five elements: bones, cowries, stone, broken dishes, and snail buttons.
Òrúnmìlà did not want to throw Ọ̀pẹ̀lẹ̀'s remains away.
He realized that, even in death, Ọ̀pẹ̀lẹ̀ is still powerful and useful.
So he joined the pieces together with a rope and gave them to his other assistants to use for divination.
This is what has become *ifá-ọ̀pẹ̀lẹ̀* today.[115]

The preceding story indicates that different schools of diviners were competing for the minds and souls of the political class and populace of Ilé-Ifẹ̀ (and possibly other areas) during the Classical period. It is possible that *ọ̀pẹ̀lẹ̀* was far more popular than *ikin* at the time this revisionism was taking place. Hence the need to go to the extent of delegitimizing *ọ̀pẹ̀lẹ̀* in the hierarchy of divination. Just as the political struggle in Ilé-Ifẹ̀ was stereotyped to the Ọbàtálá-Odùduwà conflict, the struggle among the gatekeepers of knowledge was also reduced to that between two competing schools of *ifá* divination. The above Èjìogbè verse suggests that the turf war between the *ikin* and *ọ̀pẹ̀lẹ̀* diviners was aligned along the cleavages of the insider-outsider debate, between those who supported the agents of change and those who opposed it, and between the contested notions of the native/indigene and the foreigner/migrant. In this struggle over recrafting the idea of citizenship and belonging, the *ikin* was considered the authentic native, superior, and most accurate means of accessing the knowledge of divination, while *ọ̀pẹ̀lẹ̀* represented the outsider and inferior, non-trustworthy means of seeking deep knowledge.

The quest for political unity and the struggle for influence by different factions at the end of the conflicts that heralded the Classical period possibly shaped this turf war in which two dominant groups of divination experts were involved. However, the *ikin* diviners won the political struggle. From their ranks, a cadre of sixteen elite diviners would be selected as spiritual advisers of the *ọọ̀ni*, the king of Ifẹ̀.[116] Known as *awo ọọ̀ni* (*ọọ̀ni*'s diviners), this committee was composed of the highest-ranking diviners in the land, appointed or elected by their peers within the council of the master *ifá* diviners. As the official diviners of the state, obligated to perform divination for the *ọọ̀ni* at regular intervals or whenever he called on them, these elite diviners had to be indigenes of Ilé-Ifẹ̀ and must use *ikin* in their practice of *ifá*.[117] The triumph of the *ikin* faction was a political victory just as the competition itself was political rather than philosophical or theological. And the outcome pushed the practitioners of *ọ̀pẹ̀lẹ̀* and other forms of divination out of the political sphere. Their exclusion from the palace and official state divination meant that these and other methods of divination were downgraded in the official hierarchy of knowledge. To legitimize this new power arrangement, *ọ̀pẹ̀lẹ̀*, the main antagonist in the divination war, was placed in an a priori servile status in relation to *ikin*, the master, state-sanctioned divination method. This change began the process of divination standardization, like other homogenizing programs that Ilé-Ifẹ̀ embarked on throughout the Classical period.

Benefiting from state patronage and Ifẹ̀-centric identity affirmation, the *ikin*-based *ifá* divination enlarged in prestige, and it became the focus of rigorous learning and selective membership. Henceforth, diviners of Ilé-Ifẹ̀ would do far more than any other polity to systematically enlarge the contents of the *ifá* literary corpus and to disseminate its brand of divination along the trails of its commercial and political networks throughout the Yorùbá community of practice and the outlying areas. The efforts by Ilé-Ifẹ̀ to standardize and control the intellectual capital of *ifá* divination bore fruit. The city gained fame as the prime center for *ifá* study. The prestigious school of *ifá*, reportedly headquartered at Òkè-Ìtasẹ̀, atop the highest hill in the Ifẹ̀ Bowl, attracted students, apprentices, master diviners, and pilgrims from far and near in search of knowledge and prestige.[118] However, despite their political demotion, *ọ̀pẹ̀lẹ̀* divination methods continued to flourish in the broader society, and they were in fact the most practiced divination methods serving the larger populace. In contrast, *agbigba*, the likely ancestral source of Yorùbá divination, declined in importance in Ilé-Ifẹ̀ and other parts of the Yorùbá-speaking region, but it has survived till today in Yàgbà and other parts of Okun, its primary geography of origin.

Ilé-Ifẹ̀ became the reference point for the cosmogonic and intellectual resources that sustained the Yorùbá community of practice in part because it was a coalescence of multiple theogonic traditions that originated elsewhere. The vast "army" of priest-intellectuals and statesmen in Ilé-Ifẹ̀ was confronted by two challenges during the Classical period. One was to create an ideology of unity for the political factions at home. The other was to create an ideology that would raise the profile of Ilé-Ifẹ̀ and supplant the older centers of power, some of which were resisting the ascendancy of Ilé-Ifẹ̀. These priest-intellectuals and statesmen achieved both. First, they harmonized the pre-Classical ancestors of the different Houses and factions in Ilé-Ifẹ̀ into a network of interacting and intersecting pantheons from whom the *ọ̀ọ̀ni* received his divine power to rule. Second, they created and standardized the template of *òrìṣà* myths and universalized them for the broader region. In other words, the various local myths of origin and relationships circulating in the region were reworked into accommodative and integrationist narratives; the pre-Classical deities were redefined to fit into the new sociopolitical agenda; and new deities were created to manage new experiences. Many of the deities and myths in these traditions were actually part of regional archetypes that could not easily be traced to one place of origin.

A good example is the myth of creation, in which the founding ancestors descended from the sky, landed on the water, and created land out of it. This myth had deep roots among the proto-Yoruba people, and it was carried on by many Formative-era Yorùbá polities, such as the Ọ̀bà in the Ìgbómìnà-Èkìtì area and other communities in the eastern Yorùbá area (chap. 2). The local events that gave birth to the Classical Ifẹ̀ (e.g., the struggle for supremacy between the Ọbàtálá and Odùduwà groups) were, however, inserted into this story of primeval origins and repackaged as the story of origin, not just of Ilé-Ifẹ̀, but of the entire Yorùbá community of practice. In this Ifẹ̀-centric myth of origin, Ọbàtálá became central to imagining, theorizing, and explicating the pre-Odùduwà past and the birth of the Classical era, during which Ilé-Ifẹ̀ began its journey as *olórí ayé gbogbo*, "the leader of the whole world." That imagining promoted Ọbàtálá to the peak of Ifẹ̀'s cosmogony and pantheon, as both the archetypal leader of Late Formative Ifẹ̀ and the cocreator of the orderly universal world of the Classical period. This myth-history was about the defeat, resilience, and eventual triumph of Ọbàtálá, a process that required and called attention to the virtues of patience as the quintessential quality of leadership. Ọbàtálá was set up as the opposite of the warrior-king Odùduwà. And the virtues of peace, moderation, self-denial, service for the common good, and moral order that characterized Ọbàtálá's leadership and authority were (and still are) extolled.[119] Therefore, the intellectual process of Ilé-Ifẹ̀'s knowledge capital involved blending the local experience with widely held regional ideas and repackaging these as universals. The result was the development of a more complete model of theogony in Ilé-Ifẹ̀ whereby the origins and genealogies of its deities and ancestors, as well as the interactions among them, were used as a template for the Yorùbá community of practice.

By turning its peculiar history and experience into universal history, Ilé-Ifẹ̀ was using the strategy that had been well practiced by many empires in world history for many millennia. It redefined the experience of time for members of the Yorùbá community of practice—including those who voluntarily subscribed to the Ifẹ̀-centric *ìlú/ọba-aládé* dyad and those who were forcefully brought under its political authority. Ilé-Ifẹ̀, therefore, became the beginning and the end of time for a wide region. It was believed that every member of the Yorùbá community of practice originated from Ifẹ̀ and that their soul would return there after death.[120] In this act of creating and facilitating a new experience of time, the Ifẹ̀ intellectuals and state-builders also fashioned their city into a place of memory making and pilgrimage. Several sacred sites and commemorative cenotaphs dedicated to numerous deities were set up across the core of the city. Some of these sites, especially the religious groves, were also centers of learning and sanctuaries for healing. Many of the groves were reached by roads paved with potsherd tiles and were the focus of spectacular ceremonies and rituals dedicated to numerous gods, goddesses, deified heroes, and ancestors, and to the splendor of the kingship institution. The news of such a splendid place no doubt traveled far and drew pilgrims, ambassadors, and political emissaries, as well as ambitious young people, fortune seekers, and entrepreneurs to Ilé-Ifẹ̀. Many of these visitors would have returned home to implement or imitate some of the novel things they saw in the "city of abundance." Some of the pilgrims were initiated into different orders of the Ifẹ̀ pantheon, and they returned home better fortified with the necessary paraphernalia and knowledge that not only enhanced their own status at home but helped integrate their communities into the Ifẹ̀ cultural universe. The preponderance of cults of Ifẹ̀ origin, especially those of Ọbalùfọ̀n, Ọbatálá, Odùduwà, and Ọ̀rañfẹ̀, in other major Yorùbá and non-Yorùbá polities and towns (even when these towns and kingdoms maintained their own local deities) is a testimony to the regional dissemination of Ifẹ̀'s religious traditions.[121]

Summing Up

An unprecedented wealth that was based on proprietary glass-bead production, the ideology of divine kingship (*ìlú/ọba-aládé* dyad), and the theogonic universalism and metaphysical intellectualism represented by *ifá* (*ikin*) divination created and sustained the referential status of Ilé-Ifẹ̀ during the Classical period. In their quest to build an empire and a cultural hegemony, the political and intellectual elite of Ifẹ̀ used the *ṣẹ̀gi-iyùn* power object to forge a homogeneous regional political culture and integrated regional identity. They also transformed their city into a huge bank of knowledge capital that had far-reaching influence beyond the Yorùbá-speaking world. This was the genesis of the Yorùbá community of practice, nurtured by a standardized theogony, commercial networks, and the *ẹbí* fraternity of the *ìlú/ọba-aládé* dyad. The House society of the Early and Late Formative periods laid the groundwork for this development. As political hierarchies became institutionalized during the middle of the first millennium AD, the material means for communicating those hierarchies also became restricted to an easily recognizable set of prestige goods that circulated through channels of exchanges dominated by the political elites. These were initially jasper/carnelian beads. Locally manufactured glass beads were added around the eleventh century. The ability of Ilé-Ifẹ̀ to produce unprecedented large quantities of glass beads from abundant raw materials gave it an edge in the struggle for control of prestige goods associated with validating elite authorities, especially the divine king institution. The linkage of these power objects and their technology to the creation of an integrated Yorùbá community of practice is akin to the process of technological nationalism that has defined nation building and global hegemony in the modern world. It is not surprising, therefore, that within a very short time of dominating the production and distribution of these glass beads, Ilé-Ifẹ̀ also came to dominate the ideology of the social relations, hierarchies, and political traditions that these glass beads symbolized. And, by using its bead products to control the region's commercial networks, the city succeeded in attracting the best talents to its gates and building a vast network of client polities that constituted the Yorùbá community of practice.

Hence, knowledge capital was the source of Ifẹ̀'s hegemony and the basis of its referential status. It was a form of soft power, although we know that Ilé-Ifẹ̀ backed it up with military intervention in strategic areas throughout the Classical period.[122] With this soft power, neither Ifẹ̀'s referentiality nor the idea of the Yorùbá integrated world was a one-way or top-down stream. No doubt, Ilé-Ifẹ̀ took the lead, but the process involved feedback from the outlying territories through discursive and nondiscursive practices. Some of the feedback was adversarial (e.g., Òwu). The other forms of feedback were mere ideological criticisms debating with Ilé-Ifẹ̀ the very meaning and purpose of social order and the material basis for supporting it (e.g., the Ifọ́n counter-hegemonic discourse). The majority in this expanding field of Ifẹ̀-dominated Yorùbá world were overwhelmed by the opportunities that the "city of daybreak" offered, and they sought to bask in the glory of its sunshine. But in doing so, they had broad latitude to mold the ideological and historical templates of this Ifẹ̀-centric world, as their own experience and contingent circumstances allowed. However, this community of practice was not an ethnic nation. In fact, it was multilingual, encompassing several dialects of the Yorùbá language and the Bini (Edo) language, and it succeeded in absorbing the individuals and families from other cultural groups, such as the Nupe and Djerma, into its fold during the Classical period. The community was fabricated with things and ideas, objects and stories. At the close of the fourteenth century, the sphere of influence of this Ifẹ̀-centric fraternity of interdependent, hierarchized polities extended from the River Niger to the shores of the Atlantic Ocean, and it recruited members from a vast area that stretched from River Mono in the west (present-day Togo Republic) to River Ovia (Benin Kingdom, Nigeria) in the east. Even some of those polities and peoples who rejected the Ifẹ̀-centric ideology of the *ìlú/ọba-aládé* dyad and its *òrìṣà* pantheon were integrated into the commercial networks dominated by Ilé-Ifẹ̀. At its peak, the military power and diplomatic mission of this first empire in the Yorùbá world stretched across about three hundred kilometers, from Early Owu in the northwest to Benin in the southeast. Its commercial prowess and fame ranged far into the Mandé world, and both its political ideology and hegemonic ritual field united an unprecedented number of polities and peoples in the history of West Africa.

Notes

1. He first visited Ọ̀yọ́-Ilé as a member of Hugh Clapperton's exploration mission of 1826 on the way to the Central Sudan. He passed through Ọ̀yọ́-Ilé again in 1827 on the return journey to the Atlantic Coast. See Lander, *Records of Captain Clapperton's Last Expedition*, vols. 1 and 2.

2. Hallett, *Niger Journal*, 88–89.

3. Frobenius, *Voice of Africa*, 1: 309. *Ajé ìlẹ̀kẹ̀* is fused glass on a crucible fragment or fused waste materials from glass production. Till today, they are rare objects that are highly valued—regarded as the "mother lode of beads," treated as family heirlooms, and often placed on altars of ancestors and other deities. Symbolizing abundance and fecundity, *ajé ìlẹ̀kẹ̀* occasionally featured as bridal gifts. See Ige, "Ancient Glass Making," for more on the symbolism of *ajé ìlẹ̀kẹ̀*.

4. Hallett, *Niger Journal*, 88–89. With a distance of approximately 150 km between Ọ̀yọ́-Ilé and Ilé-Ifẹ̀, one would expect a one-way journey between the two cities to take about ten to fifteen days. This would make it a half-moon journey.

5. Ọbadio Ọlájídé Fárótìmí Fálọba, July 16, 2015. For variants of the appellation, also see Ademakinwa, *Ife*, 12.

6. Pereira, *Esmeraldo*, 126 (The *Esmeraldo* manuscript was originally written in 1506. It was edited by Da Silva Dias and published in Portuguese in 1905, and translated into English by George H. T. Kimble and published in 1937). The English version is used here.

7. This extract is translated from João de Barros's original work, *Decadas de Asia* (Lisbon, 1552), by G. R. Crone, *Voyages of Cadamosto*, 126–27.

8. For the former, see Ben-Amos, *Art of Benin*; Egharevba, *Short History of Benin*. For the latter, Ryder, *Benin and the Europeans*; Thornton, "Traditions, Documents."

9. This mistranslation suited the preconception and sensibility of the Portuguese who were seeking to reach the mythic King Prester John. According to the fertile imagination of medieval Europe, this king was believed to rule over a Christian kingdom in the Orient, somewhere in India. However, by the early sixteenth century, the Portuguese had convinced themselves that Preston John's kingdom was in Ethiopia. The Benin story about *oghene* was fitted into the Portuguese mental geography, and it was for some time thought that it would be possible to reach this Christian king via Benin.

10. For examples, Ben-Amos, *Art of Benin*; Ben-Amos, *Art, Innovation, and Politics*; Egharevba, *Short History of Benin*; Fagg, *Nigerian Images*; Ogundiran, "Filling a Gap"; Willett, *Ife*.

11. The velar fricative sound, */gh/* in eastern Yorùbá dialects and Edoid languages, especially Edo and Urhobo, is the equivalent of */w/*—labio-velar approximant—in central and western Yorùbá dialects, and vice versa. However, in the Portuguese transcription of sounds in the Bight of Benin languages, the sound */gh/* was often represented as */g/* (a voiced velar stop sound). Hence, Oghene becomes Ogané.

12. This translates in Ifẹ̀ (central Yorùbá) dialect to "Ọ̀ọ̀ni Ufẹ̀."

13. Connah, *Archaeology of Benin*; Eyo, "Recent Excavations"; Ogundiran, *Archaeology and History*; Ogundiran, "Filling a Gap."

14. Abiodun, *Yorùbá Art and Language*, 223. Isaac A. Akinjogbin reported that when he was conducting research in Ìlá Ọ̀ràngún in 1959, "an old woman being interviewed was awestruck when I declared that I had come from Ifẹ̀ that day. It sounded to her as if someone had come from heaven" (*Cradle*, 121). And for many centuries before the twentieth century, parts of the remains of the deceased kings of Benin were interred in Ilé-Ifẹ̀ at a place called Ọ̀run Ọba Adó, which translates to "the burial ground of the king of Edo."

15. Chatzkel, *Knowledge Capital.*

16. The social valuation of gem rocks is as old as human origins. Their rarity as well as "attractive colours and pleasing, uniform shapes" stimulated ideas in their special magical attributes for healing and protection (Walters, *Power of Gemstones*, 9). And, as societies became complex in social organization, these special rocks became associated with political and ritual authorities. In the Niger-Benue area, jasper/carnelian may have been the most magical and valued of such gem rocks. We know that by 900 BC, the northern neighbors of the Yoruboid, the Nok people, used the red jasper/carnelian and other red chalcedony beads as index of rank, and possibly wealth and healing; see Breunig, "Nok."

17. Aleru, *Old Oyo and the Hinterland*; Garlake, "Excavations at Obalara's Land"; Connah, *Archaeology of Benin*; Garlake, "Excavations on the Woye Asiri Family Land"; Willett, "Investigations at Old Oyo"; Willett, "A Survey of Recent Results in the Radiocarbon Chronology"; Willett, "Archaeology."

18. Adetunji, "Industrial Mineral Exploitation." Some of these were exploited as early as the Later Stone Age, dating to 3000–9000 BC, for the manufacture of tools and possibly ornaments.

19. Haour et al., "Settlement Mound," 700; Magnavita, "Sahelian Crossroads," 91.

20. Aleru, *Old Oyo and the Hinterland*; Obayemi, "Evolution of the Culture"; Obayemi, "Cultural Evolution of Northern Yoruba."

21. O'Hear, "Ilorin Lantana Beads," 36.

22. O'Hear, 36.

23. Clarke, "Ilorin Stone Bead Making," 156–57; Nadel, *Black Byzantium*, 283.

24. As late as the mid-seventeenth century, for example, the distribution of the red *akun* (coral) was the prerogative of the Ọba of Benin. Described as "royal goods," the jasper/carnelian bead merchandise could be purchased only by the king. A nonroyal procurer of these power goods did so at the risk of his life, if discovered. The awarding of these beads to individuals was part of the process of investment of chiefly offices, but these strings of beads (and the title they connoted) could be taken away from those chieftains who fell out of favor with the king. See Jones, *West Africa in the Mid-Seventeenth Century*, 53–54.

25. Abiodun, "Understanding Yorùbá Art."

26. Ben-Amos, *Art, Innovation, and Politics*, 124.

27. For example, Davison, "Glass Beads"; Euba, "Of Blue and Red"; Willett, *Baubles, Bangles and Beads*. I partook in this erroneous conclusion in some of my earlier publications, such as Ogundiran, "Of Small Things Remembered." However, I have corrected this in later publications as a

result of the new evidence, e.g., Ogundiran and Ige, "'Our Ancestors Were Material Scientists.'" It is important to note that Omotoso Eluyemi and Robin Horton had much earlier argued for indigenous primary glass production in Ilé-Ifẹ̀ (Eluyemi, "Technology of the Ife Glass Beads"; Horton, "Ancient Ife").

28. See Babalola, "Archaeological Investigation"; Babalola et al., "Ile-Ife and Igbo Olokun"; Ige, "Ancient Glass Making"; Lankton, "Early Primary Glass Production"; Ogundiran and Ige, "'Our Ancestors Were Material Scientists.'"

29. Ogundiran and Ige, "'Our Ancestors Were Material Scientists'"; Rehren and Freestone, "Ancient Glass."

30. The dichroic quality of the beads means that they show different colors in different light exposures, ranging, for example, from blue-green to blue-yellow for the blue glass beads (*ṣẹ̀gi*).

31. *Technological nationalism* refers to how certain nations have used particular technologies to forge national identity, competitive advantages in global economy, national economic growth, and global connectedness. For example, the British cotton textiles of the Industrial Revolution and Japanese consumer electronics come to mind (see Charland, "Technological Nationalism"; Edgerton, "Contradictions of Techno-Nationalism"). Ilé-Ifẹ̀ used glass technology to forge a pan-regional identity that transcended ethnonationalism. This also helped to strengthen the political economy of the city-state and its regional political tentacles.

32. Although there are indications that glass working took place in other parts of the city (especially at Ayélabówó), Olókun Grove was the dominant center of glass and glass bead production throughout the Classical period. See Babalola, "Archaeological Investigation"; Adeduntan, Early Glass Bead Technology"; Eluyemi, "Technology of the Ife Glass Beads"; Willett, *Baubles, Bangles and Beads.*

33. This inference is based on Babatunde Babalola's estimate, "Archaeological Investigation," 24. The debris of glass beads of different varieties, including blue, green, red, olive-brown, and turquoise, and of glass wastes, as well as materials used in glass-bead manufacture, such as ceramic crucibles, fragments of tuyères and furnaces, conical/tubular clay objects, dimpled stones for grinding, and polishing beads, have been found in this area.

34. The holder of the title *wàlódè* was neither one of the great House chiefs (the *ìsorò*) nor one of the palace chiefs (*mọdéwá*). He belonged to the specialist chieftaincy group. But he was the only one among the various crafts-guild chieftaincies that played a role (and still does) in the coronation of a new king of Ifẹ̀. See Adediran, "Early Beginnings"; Horton, "Ancient Ife." Till today, the *ọ̣̀ọ̀ni*-elect must meet with the *wàlódè* for certain rites during his coronation rituals. Those rites symbolize the confidential briefing the new king would have received from the manager of the state-controlled industry about aspects of the political economy of Ilé-Ifẹ̀, glass-bead production, and the organization of the distribution system.

35. These crucibles were formed using kaolinitic clay with high alumina content and quartz grains inclusions. This material gave the crucible the refractory strength to "withstand the temperatures of 900–1150°C needed to melt glass." Babalola, et al., "The Glass Making Crucibles," 15.

36. Babalola et al., "Ile-Ife and Igbo Olokun," 736.

37. In Olókun Grove, two types of crucibles have been identified: the ovoid and barrel-shaped vessels with narrow opening. The ovoid crucibles tend to be bigger, 25–35 cm in height with average useable capacity of 3–7 liters. The barrel-shaped crucibles, on the other hand, are generally smaller, 16–22 cm in height and usable volume capacity of 0.5–3 liters. Whereas the large crucible has the capacity to produce up to 65,000 small beads per smelting operation, the smaller crucible could produce 25,000 small beads. It is estimated that if the thirty-six crucibles reconstructed from Olókun Grove were used in only one glass-making operation, they would have produced between 1.08 and 6.1 million small glass beads, of the type that is commonly found in Ilé-Ifẹ̀. Considering that several hundreds if not thousands of these crucibles would have been used more than once to produce glass and glass beads over a period of about four hundred years, the number of beads that were produced in Olókun Grove would have been in the billions. Babalola et al., "Glass Making Crucibles."

38. One such myth describes glass beads as *imí Ọ̀ṣùmàrè*—excrement of the rainbow. Ọ̀ṣùmàrè (rainbow) is a deity believed to reside in Olókun Grove. The boa constrictor is the physical manifestation of the deity, whose multicolored excrement (glass beads) is believed to accumulate as the gifts of the deity to Ilé-Ifẹ̀ (Lijadu, *Orunmila*, 73–74). German explorer Leo Frobenius was also told by informants in Ilé-Ifẹ̀ and other parts of West Africa that glass beads were the gift of the goddess Olókun to the people of Ilé-Ifẹ̀ so that "they might grow richer than the rest of all mankind" (Frobenius, *Voice of Africa*, 1:307).

39. Ige, "Classification and Preservation," 66.

40. Willett, *Ife*, 24.

41. In this regard, historical ethnography and oral traditions give the clue that these beads may have been classified into two temperament groups: hot (*gbígbóná*) and cool (*tútù*). Red and yellow are regarded as hot colors, whereas white, blue, black, and green represent coolness. Those who wielded the power and authority of divine kingship could not afford to be monochromatic. By virtue of their mandate to establish balance between the hot and cool forces that constitute social lives, the *ọba-aládé* embodied both the hot and cool essence (wrath and benevolence, respectively). Hence, the royal regalia are generally multicolor, dominated by the blue (cool) *ṣẹ̀gi* and red (hot) *iyùn*. The twentieth-century ethnography indicates that each secular/spiritual office was represented by a particular color of bead. Such colors indicate the character of a political office or Òrìṣà. For example, Ọbatálá is a cool Òrìṣà and is represented by white beads. Yemọja, also a cool Òrìṣà, is represented by indigo beads. Ogun and Ṣàngó are hot Òrìṣà, and their priests wear reddish beads. Drewal and Mason, *Beads, Body, and Soul*, 110. These chromatic practices have a deep history in Yorùbá thought.

42. Earle, *How Chiefs Come to Power*, 151.

43. Laser ablation inductively coupled plasma mass spectrometry (LA-ICP) is the most advanced of these techniques and has been used to study the glass and glass beads from Ilé-Ifẹ̀ and from many other sites in the Yorùbá region and West Africa. For examples, Babalola, "Archaeological Investigation"; Ogundiran and Ige, "'Our Ancestors Were Material Scientists.'" LA-ICP enables elemental and isotopic analysis to be carried out directly on solid samples with minimal preparation and without destroying the samples. It provides

high resolution information on the physical and chemical properties of the object in four categories: major, minor, trace, and rare earth elements.

44. Fage, "Some Remarks on Beads," 345.

45. In Ṣábẹ́, for example, archaeologist Andrew Gurstelle and his collaborators found a cylindrical, semitransparent dichroic light-blue bead "at a depth of 140cm, 20cm below a fragment of wood charcoal dated to cal.AD 1311–1434 (550±30BP; OS-109259)," Gurstelle, Labiyi, and Agani, "Settlement History," 237. This is most likely a product of the Ifẹ̀ glass industry.

46. Babalola et al., "Ile-Ife and Igbo Olokun," 746; Davison, "Glass Beads," 272; Haour et al., "Settlement Mound," 700; Insoll, *Urbanism, Archaeology and Trade*, 4; Magnavita, "Some Aspects on the Iron Age," 91.

47. Levtzion and Hopkins, *Corpus*, 287. Ibn Battuta dictated his travel accounts to Ibn Juzayy, a scribe in the court of Sultan Abu 'Inan, between 1354 and 1355.

48. John Thornton's speculation that Yufi refers to Nupe is inaccurate ("Traditions, Documents"). The transliteration of Nupe would not have come out as Yufi in any of the speech patterns of the Mandé languages. In Ifẹ̀ and other central Yorùbá dialects, Ifẹ̀ is pronounced as Ufẹ. It is only in the standardized Yorùbá language (written form) that Ufẹ̀ is written as Ifẹ̀ or Ulé-Ufẹ̀ as Ilé-Ifẹ̀, as I have done in this book. See Adetugbo, "Yorùbá Language."

49. Frobenius, *Voice of Africa*, 1:32.

50. According to Ibn Battuta, across the Sahara and Western Sudan trade routes, travelers carried "only pieces of salt and the glass trinkets . . . and a few spicy commodities," which they used to buy supplies during their journey (Levtzion and Hopkins, *Corpus*, 287).

51. Abiodun, *Yorùbá Art and Language*, 222.

52. The data collected for the Yorùbá Dialect Project indeed shows that the Ifẹ̀ dialect, though it belongs to the central Yorùbá group, bears marks of influence from the southeast (Ondo), north central (Ìgbómìnà), and northeast (especially Yagba) dialects during the early second millennium AD (see table 2.2). This would suggest that Ilé-Ifẹ̀ received large populations from those areas in a period that possibly ranged between 1200 and 1500 (Ehret and Ogundiran, "Archaeological and Linguistic Overviews"; Christopher Ehret, email correspondence, October 22, 2015).

53. Akinjogbin, *Dahomey.*

54. For example, Akinrinade, "Akinjogbin."

55. For a critique of the *ẹbí* thesis, see Law, "Book Review of *Dahomey.*"

56. Akinjogbin, *Dahomey*; Akinjogbin, "Ebi System"; Akinjogbin, *Milestones and Concepts.*

57. Egharevba, *Short History of Benin*; Johnson, *History of the Yorubas*; Ogumefu, *Staff of Oranyan.*

58. According to the historical charter that explains the dynastic relationship between Benin and Ilé-Ifẹ̀, there was a period of political turmoil in Benin during which the leaders of several House polities could not agree on a leader. They sent a delegation to the king of Ilé-Ifẹ̀ to ask him to send a prince to Benin to rule them. Ọ̀rànmíyàn was the prince selected for the task. Ọ̀rànmíyàn married a daughter of one of the leaders of the Great Houses of Benin, who bore him a son called Eweka. After some time, the warlike and restless Ọ̀rànmíyàn was tired of ruling over a people whose language he did not understand. He also preferred the adventures of military life to the slow-paced

art of governance. So he left Eweka and his wife in the care of his father-in-law and decreed that Eweka should serve as the king of Benin once he was of age. Several members of his retinue from Ilé-Ifẹ̀ were also left behind to assist the young king in statecraft (Egharevba, *Short History of Benin*). One may argue that this story masks the conquest of Benin by Ilé-Ifẹ̀. However, such an invitation of a professed guarantor of social order to assist in troubling times was not far-fetched. Ilé-Ifẹ̀ possibly played the role of an arbiter in several factional conflicts in the region on account of its referential status as a place of moral authority, a home of the gods, and a land of wealth.

59. For example, the Adó Èkìtì palace traditions identified its founder, Awamaro (the restless one) as an "older brother" of Ọ̀rànmíyàn. He followed Ọ̀rànmíyàn to Benin, where he helped him to accomplish his mission—establish an Ifẹ̀ dynasty. Afterward, Awamaro set out to establish his own kingdom in Adó-Èkìtì. Likewise, a version of the Àkúrẹ́ palace traditions identifies the founder of the kingdom as Asọdẹbóyèdé. An Ifẹ̀ prince, he left Ilé-Ifẹ̀ with Òrànmíyàn on one of the latter's military expeditions, but he parted with Òrànmíyàn to establish the Àkúrẹ́ kingdom (Akintoye, *History of the Yoruba People*, 99–101). There is also a little-known tradition claiming that Ọ̀rànmíyàn was the founder of the Ẹ̀gbá kingdom of Òkò, now Òkè-Ọnà Ẹ̀gbá (Tejuoso, *Ọ̀rànmíyàn*).

60. Babayemi, *Myths of Oranyan.*

61. Akinjogbin, "Growth of Ife," 110.

62. A carved monolith of granite gneiss, about 5.2 m in height, is one of the most spectacular monuments in Ilé-Ifẹ̀. In the city's myth-history, the monolith is regarded as the sword (and sometimes as the walking stick) of Ọ̀rànmíyàn. This serves to indicate the warrior's extraordinary personality (see Drewal, Pemberton, and Abiodun, *Yoruba*, 48). The monolith is an enigma. The traditions that are more attuned to realistic interpretation identify it as a public commemorative stela to denote Òrànmíyàn's burial ground. There are engravings at the top of the monolith, and almost its entire length is studded with spiral-headed iron nails. Other monoliths (with bored holes and inserted spiral-headed nails), though not as elaborate as Òrànmíyàn's, have been found in other parts of Ilé-Ifẹ̀, at Ọrẹ̀ Grove, Ògún Ládìn, Ògún Éésà, and Ìjùgbẹ̀. Suzanne Blier and Frank Willett have also suggested that the Ọ̀rànmíyàn stela and other stelae might have something to do with record keeping or management of time, cardinal direction, and cosmology. See Blier, "Cosmic References"; Willett, *Art of Ife.*

63. Eyo, "Recent Excavations," 321.

64. Allison, "Terra-Cotta Head"; Ogundiran, "Making of an Internal Frontier"; Willett, *Ife.*

65. Frank Willett (*Ife*, 186) argued, convincingly I believe, that this figure represented an *ọ̀ọ̀ni* of Ilé-Ifẹ̀. He speculated that the figurine was brought from Ilé-Ifẹ̀ to Benin as part of the gift-exchange relationship between the two cities. Local historian Jacob Egharevba, however, suggested that the piece was the work of Iguegha e, the master bronzecaster whom Ilé-Ifẹ̀ sent to Benin to teach bronze casting to the craftsmen in the royal court (*Short History of Benin*).

66. Mabogunje and Richards, "Land and People," 9.

67. For summary, see Ogundiran, "Ceramic Spheres." For details of the ceramic complexes from a number of sites in the region, see Connah,

Archaeology of Benin; Eyo, "Recent Excavations"; Garlake, "Excavations on the Woye Asiri Family Land"; Ogundiran, *Archaeology and History*; Usman, *Yoruba Frontier.*

68. The copper deposits in the Benue Trough (see fig. 3.2) may have been one of the sources of Ifẹ̀'s copper imports (for the exploitation of the copper deposits in the trough, see Chikwendu and Umeji, "Local Sources of Raw Material"; Craddock et al., "Metal Sources"). However, Takkeda in modern Mali and other Saharan mining sites appear to be the major sources of supply for Ifẹ̀'s copper-alloy sculptures. Mansa Musa, the King of Mali between 1312 and 1337, reportedly told his hosts in Cairo during his pilgrimage to Mecca (1324) that the copper mined at Takkeda was traded to "the lands of the black pagans where we sell one mithkäl of it for two-thirds of its weight in gold" (Niane, "Mali," 150). Those bars of copper were sold to the southernmost termini of the trans-Saharan trade routes, including Timbuktu, Gao, Gobir, and Njimi, as indicated by Ibn Battuta in the accounts of his travels to Western Sudan fourteen years after Mansa Musa's death (Dunn, *Adventures*). From there, the copper moved farther south into another transitional ecological zone: the northern edges of the rain forest, such as Begho and Banda (central Ghana), where archaeological evidence has revealed Saharan copper dating to the thirteenth and fourteenth centuries (Posnansky, "Aspects of Early West African Trade"; Stahl, *Making History in Banda*). Ilé-Ifẹ̀ is also located on this northern edge of the rain forest. Unlike Begho, which paid for its copper and other trans-Saharan products with gold, Ilé-Ifẹ̀ would have paid for those copper bars with glass beads, and other export items might have included ivory and locally produced silk.

69. Babayemi, *Myths of Oranyan.*

70. There are two propositions regarding the Ifẹ̀ ritual field to which these sculptures belong. Susan Blier argues that the copper-alloy sculptures would have served in roles similar to the juridical functions of the Ògbóni institution, mentioned in chap. 2 (*Art and Risk*, 243). On the other hand, Abiodun (*Yorùbá Art and Language*, 229–35) suggests that at least one of the figures, the famous Tada seated figure, represents an Ifá divination priest. It is possible that these sculptures in fact belonged to multiple and different segments of the Ifẹ̀ ritual fields, including the Ògbóni, Ifá, and Èsù (keeper of the road and heraldic deity in the Yorùbá pantheon), among others. In this sense, some of these sculptures might have been placed in toll-collecting stations to mark the limits of the Ifẹ̀ territory. They could also have served juridical and divination purposes as well as serving in commemorative ceremonies honoring the Ifẹ̀ royalty or the trading class.

71. The exact location of this ancient commercial center is not yet known, but it seems to be in the area between Ògbómọ̀ṣọ́ and Ìgbẹ́tì (see fig. 1.1).

72. All the panegyric texts about Ifọ̀n cited here are culled (and rearranged for clarity) from the magisterial master's thesis written by Olawale Hakeem (*Ìtúpalẹ̀ Aláwòmọ́ Lítíreṣọ̀*, 2011) at Obafemi Awolowo University. The texts are supplemented by my oral interviews with Baálẹ̀ Ògúnlékè Ògúndípẹ̀ of Arárọ̀mí-Ṣẹ̀pẹ̀tẹ̀rí (June 9, 2016, Arárọ̀mí-Ṣẹ̀pẹ̀tẹ̀rí) and Ọládọjà Ọlátúnbọ̀sún, Ìgbẹ́tì, October 4, 1992.

73. There were two kings by name of Ọbalùfọ̀n who reigned in Ilé-Ifẹ̀ (Adediran, "Early Beginnings," 89–92). The second Ọbalùfọ̀n (known as

Ọbalùfọ̀n Aláyémọrẹ̀ or Ọbalùfọ̀n II) reigned in the late fourteenth century. For more discussion on Ọbalùfọ̀n, see Blier's *Art and Risk*.

74. Both Ọbàtálá and Ọbamakin are pre-Classical leaders in Ilé-Ifẹ̀.

75. Báálẹ̀ Ògúnlékè Ògúndípẹ̀, Arárọ̀mí Ṣẹ̀pẹ̀tẹ̀rí, June 9, 2016; Ọládọjà Ọlátúnbọ̀sún, Ìgbẹ́tì, October 4, 1992. Also, Hakeem, *Ìtúpalẹ̀ Aláwọ̀mọ́ Lítíreṣọ̀*; Orisatoyinbo, *History and Traditions of Ancient Ifon*.

76. Abimbola, *Ìjìnlè: Apá Kìn-ín-ní*; Abimbola, *Ìjìnlẹ̀: Apá Kejì*.

77. Hakeem, *Ìtúpalẹ̀ Aláwọ̀mọ́ Lítíreṣọ̀*, 87.

78. This is not a contradiction since Ilé-Ifẹ̀ itself witnessed the decline in the political influence of the descendant Odùduwà group and the ascension of the members of Ọbatálá and other descendants of the Late Formative groups to the throne during the thirteenth century. The latter however continued to maintain the *ìlú/ọba-aládé* vision usually associated with the Odùduwà political revolution. For example, Ọbalùfọ̀n Aláyémọré (Ọbalùfọ̀n II), the most prominent of the Ifẹ̀ classical kings, is claimed to belong to the Ọbatálá group. See Adediran, "Early Beginnings," 90–91.

79. The chief priest of Égúngún cult.

80. It appears that there were many market towns with the name of Èjìgbòmẹ̀kùn during the Classical period, and all served as Ifẹ̀'s trading outposts. There was a major market town by this name in Èkìtì, and there was another one in the outskirts of Ilé-Ifẹ̀, in the present-day area of Obafemi Awolowo University, near the University Guest House.

81. Another name of Ifọ́n.

82. Orisatoyinbo, *History and Traditions*, 35.

83. Ọba S. A. Adékólúrẹ̀jọ, the Olówu of Òwu-Epé, Epe-Ìjẹ̀ṣà, September 9, 1991.

84. The elders in Ìgbẹ́tì, Ìgbòho, and Ṣakí areas (especially those over sixty years old) usually refer to the iron slag they encounter on their farms as *ìdàrọ́ Olówu*, meaning Olówu's slag (the slag of the king of Owú). Alhaji Babatúndé Ògúndìran, Ògúndìran village, Ìgbẹ́tì district, May 24, 2017); Adémọ́lá Lawal, Ògúndìran village, Ìgbẹ́tì district, May 26, 2017. For Òwu's cotton production and weaving, see Mabogunje and Omer-Cooper, *Owu in Yoruba History*, 34.

85. Adewusi, "Owu Communities," 46; Atanda, *Comprehensive History*, 42.

86. Adewusi, "Owu Communities," 45; Pemberton and Afọlayan, *Yoruba Sacred Kingship*, 38.

87. The fact that a river that passes through Ṣakí and terminates in what is now Ọ̀kẹ̀rẹ̀ gorge is called River Owú further supports the conclusion of several authors and informants that the area between Ṣakí and Ọ̀yọ́-Ilé was the nucleus of the former Òwu Kingdom. For examples, Adewusi, "Òwu Communities"; Johnson, *History of the Yorubas*, 149; Mabogunje and Omer-Cooper, *Owu in Yoruba History*. Alhaji Babatúndé Ògúndìran, oral interview, Ògúndìran village, Ìgbẹ́tì, May 24, 2017.

88. For some of these traditions about the early history of Òwu, see Adewusi, "Owu Communities"; Mabogunje and Omer-Cooper, *Owu in Yoruba History*.

89. Pemberton and Afọlayan, *Yoruba Sacred Kingship*, 38. The Òwu towns that have survived till the present time in Ìgbómìnà include Owú-Isin, Owú-Òkeyá-Ìpo, Owú-Ọbalôyán, and Igbó-Òwu (Adewusi, "Owu Communities,"

37). However, it is possible that some of these were established in the fifteenth or sixteenth century following the collapse of the first Òwu kingdom.

90. Adediran, "Early Beginnings," 90–91; Akinjogbin, "Growth of Ife," 98–99.

91. Ọmọtọ́ṣọ̀ Elúyẹmí, "Field Notes" (courtesy of Nurudeen Amuda-Arógundádé, Obafemi Awolowo University, July 10, 2014); Usman, *Yoruba Frontier*, 26.

92. According to historical traditions, they were armed with *ògbo* (cutlasses) granted to them by Odùduwà at Ifẹ̀, and these enabled them not only to cut through the dense wooded landscape but also to conquer the existing populations. Usman, *Yoruba Frontier.*

93. Aleru, *Old Oyo and the Hinterland*; Obayemi, "States and Peoples of the Niger-Benue Confluence"; Ogunfolakan, *Archaeological Survey of North-East Osun State*; Usman, *Yoruba Frontier.*

94. Blier, *Art and Risk*; Egharevba, *Short History of Benin*; Fagg, *Nigerian Images.* However, there seems to be a tradition of copper casting (though on a much smaller scale, using minimalist humanist style) in the Okun-Yorùbá area that may be older than that of Ilé-Ifẹ̀. The Okun copper-alloy craftsmanship was part of the broader Niger-Benue Confluence metal-casting tradition and was also based on the lost wax technique. It is possible that Ilé-Ifẹ̀ benefited from that much older copper-alloy technology in the Niger-Benue. Obayemi, "Yorùbá and Edo-Speaking Peoples," 293. Also see Aremu, "Archaeology of North-East Yorubaland."

95. The town that bears this name and claims to be the descendant of the ancient site is now located between the present-day Ṣakí and Ìgbòho.

96. See Agiri, "Early Oyo History," 8–10; Frobenius, *Voice of Africa*, 1:177, 219–23; Obayemi, "History, Culture, Yoruba," 82–83.

97. Agiri, "Early Oyo History," 9.

98. Agiri, 8.

99. Babayemi, *Myths of Oranyan*, 19–21, 31–32. Also see Nadel, *Black Byzantium.* Nineteenth-century explorers, especially Hugh Clapperton and Samuel Ajayi Crowther, reported the Yorùbá cultural elements in art, language, and religion along the Niger and north of it. Crowther (*Gospel on the Banks of the Niger*, 117), for example, recorded in 1857 that the priest who invoked Ketsa, the deity that inhabits a rock in the middle of River Niger near Jebba, used an archaic Yorùbá language although a dialect of Nupe was predominantly spoken in the area. Also, Lander, *Records of Captain Clapperton's Last Expedition*, vols. 1 and 2.

100. Idowu, *Olódùmarè*; Olupona, *City of 201 Gods.*

101. Olupona and Abiodun, *Ifa Divination.*

102. The other divination methods include the sixteen-cowrie (*ẹ́ẹ́ríndìnlógún*), kola nut casting, sand casting, and water gazing.

103. These flat pieces of *ọ̀pẹ̀lẹ̀* wand are made of the pear-shaped seed pods of the *ọ̀pẹ̀lẹ̀* tree (*Schrebera golungensis*), from which this instrument derives its name. Other materials for making the wand are the *egbére* seed from the *epu* tree and the shells of *àpọ̀n* seed, obtained from the wild mango tree (*Irvingia gabonensis*) (Bascom, *Ifa Divination*, 30–31). In contrast, the *ikin* palm nuts come from a species of oil palm tree that J. M. Dalziel (*Useful Plants*) calls *Elaeis guineensis idolatrica.* In contrast to the regular oil palm trees (*Elaeis guineensis*), the *idolatrica* palm trees have darker, half-furled leaves and

droop less (Bascom, *Ifa Divination*, 26). The indentations on the seeds are taken for two eyes, a nose, and a mouth (Eason, *Ifa*, 49).
104. Although a*gbigba* and *ẹ̀ẹ́rìndínlógún* have sixteen major *odu* like *ifá* (though of different names), the verses associated with their *odù* and chapters are very short and lack the details of history and myth that *ifá* usually has. See Olúnládé, "Divinatory Systems," 103.
105. Bascom, *Ifa Divination*, 11–12.
106. Adeniran Adeboye, email correspondences, January 17–25, 2016.
107. Adegbola, "Transmission of Scientific Knowledge."
108. E.g., Abimbola, *Ifá: An Exposition*; Bascom, *Ifa Divination.*
109. The professsional practitioners of *ifá* are (and have been) mostly men. Hence, the title *babaláwo* and the use of the gender-specific pronoun in the text. However, it seems there were women in the past who learned the knowledge of *Ifá,* usually as daughters or wives of babaláwo. It is not clear whether such women were able to practice the *ifá* divination in the public and to clients. However, there are now women, though in very small number and mostly in the diaspora, involved in *ifá* divination. They are called Iyanifa. Brandon, *Hierarchy without a Head.*
110. Bascom, *Ifa Divination*, 13.
111. Herskovits, *Dahomey*, 201–30; Talbot, *Peoples of Southern Nigeria*, 2:186. There have been unsubstantiated claims that placed Yorùbá *ifá*'s origins in Islamic divination traditions (e.g., Obayemi, "History, Culture, Yoruba"; Peel, *Religious Encounter*). These claims are based on the perceived similarities in the geomantic numerology between Yorùbá *ifá* and Islamic divination systems. But this assumption disregards this common occurrence in many cultures in Europe, Middle East, and Asia, as well as in Africa (e.g., Peek, *African Divination Systems*). Whatever similarities may exist in the geomantic numerology of *ifá* and Islamic divination systems, the philosophical and intellectual contents of *ifá* significantly set it apart from the Islamic divination system or the Greek influence.
112. Boston, "Ifa Divination in Igala."
113. *Agbigba* is also found throughout the area east of the Yorùbá region, even though these methods of divination have names that have the *ifá* root. Hence, among the Igbo, the *agbigba* form of divination is called *afa*, *aha*, or *efa*; among the Ekoi it is known as *efa*; while the Idoma and the Isoko call it *eba* and *eva* respectively. Among the Edo, however, *agbigba* is called *Ogwega.* The phonetic similarities between the two are unmistakable, showing that they derived from a common origin (Bascom, *Ifa Divination*, 7; also see Manfredi, *Before Wazobia*). While the Igala likely played a central role in the dissemination of *agbigba* southeast of the Niger, the Yorùbá (especially the Ifẹ̀) were responsible for the expansion of the Ifá westward as far as modern Ghana. Known as Fa among the Fon and Ewe peoples in present-day Benin, Togo, and Ghana, these groups acknowledge the Yorùbá city of Ifẹ̀ as the place of Ifá origin (Bascom, *Ifá Divination*, 3).
114. See Abimbola, *Ìjìnlè: Apá Kìn-ín-ní*; Abimbola, *Ìjìnlẹ̀: Apá Kejì.* Considering the other lines of evidence discussed in chap. 2–5, I take this to confirm that Ilé-Ifẹ̀ itself is a product of the Èkìtì political culture and that it was more closely connected to Èkìtì than the other areas in all aspects of interaction, a point that Ade Obayemi ("The Political Culture of the Ekiti") also alluded to, prompting him to argue for more research on the Ifẹ̀-Èkìtì historical origins.

115. Culled and rearranged from http://orishada.com/wordpress/?tag=ikin, accessed November 24, 2015. I also obtained a short version of this story from Professor Wándé Abímbọ̀lá, personal communication, Boston University, Boston, MA, October 1998; and Priestess Osunfunke Lakokan, interview, August 2, 2011, Osogbo.

116. Hence, the palace was always associated with a hierarchy of Ifá priests led by Àràbà—the head of the elite council of *ifá* priests. This was one of the innovations that many polities adopted across Yorùbáland during the Classical period as part of the institutionalization of the dyadic *ìlú/ọba-aládé* sociopolitical structure.

117. Eason, *Ifa*, 58.

118. This does not, however, mean that homogeneity has ever been achieved in Ifá divination, whether in the method of casting (*ikin* or *ọ̀pẹ̀lẹ̀*) or in the organization and contents of the *odù*. See Amherd, *Reciting Ifa*, for insights into some of these regional variations.

119. Adewuyi, *Obatala*.

120. See Abiodun, *Yorùbá Art and Language*, 223; Akinjogbin, *Cradle*, 121.

121. For a glimpse of these deities in various Yorùbá towns, see Adediran, *Frontier States*; Apter, *Black Critics and Kings*; Barber, *I Could Speak until Tomorrow*; Drewal, *Yoruba Ritual*; Olupona, *Kingship, Religion, and Rituals*; Peel, *Ijeshas and Nigerians*.

122. For a conceptualization of the meaning and processes of soft power, see Nye, *Soft Power*.

Part III:
Atrophy and Regeneration, ca. 1400–1650

4

Atrophy

YORÙBÁ INTELLECTUALS HAVE DESCRIBED THEIR civilization as "the river that never rests." They conceptualize the experience of time as a highly modulated continuous change that often shifts between swift- and slow-moving currents and that can be either deep and quiet or turbulent and overpowering.[1] By the end of the fourteenth century, there were signs that the discharge and velocity of the river of the Yorùbá community of practice were becoming slower and more unpredictable. Over the next 150 years, there were eruptions and other disturbances, metaphorically speaking, in the riverbeds and watersheds of the Yorùbá civilization that significantly changed the direction and currents of the region's history. These aquatic and geological analogies refer to the political, economic, and security upheavals that destroyed several dynasties; led to the collapse, displacement, and truncation of many polities between the early fifteenth and the mid-sixteenth century. The crisis also forced the migration of individuals, families, and households across the region. The river never ceased moving, but the perturbations changed the course of Yorùbá history. The account of the causes and sources of these problems is the focus of this chapter.

Internal and external sources provoked the instability that engulfed this region early in the fifteenth century. The major internal sources of instability were the collapse of Ilé-Ifẹ̀'s economy and what appears to be domestic political crisis in the "city of daybreak." Both had a stormy effect on many members of the Yorùbá community of practice, especially those that were integrated into Ifẹ̀'s commercial and political orbits. The events that had distant and atmospheric origins, however, also shaped and escalated some of the local crises. These external factors included episodes of severe drought at the subcontinental level; outbursts of epidemic diseases at the regional level; political conflicts across the Sudan between ca. 1375 and 1600; relentless attacks from Nupe cavalrymen from ca. 1450 through 1560; and the opening up of the Yorùbá coastland for intercontinental trade in the last quarter of the fifteenth century. It is impossible to disaggregate these sources of perturbation from one another. They were all linked together.

Depression, Drought, and Disease

Ilé-Ifẹ̀ was the center of gravity of the Yorùbá world system, in political, economic, and cultural terms, through the end of the fourteenth century. The story of stress and atrophy that descended on the region in the following century must therefore start with Ilé-Ifẹ̀. There were already signs of trouble during the late fourteenth century, but they became more noticeable in the early fifteenth century following the death of Ọbalùfọ̀n II. The declining political and economic fortunes of the region's largest emporium, Ilé-Ifẹ̀, significantly contributed to the instability across the Yorùbá world in the first half of the fifteenth century. Ọbalùfọ̀n Aláyémọrẹ́ (Ọbalùfọ̀n II) was the last great king of Classical Ifẹ̀. He came to the throne after a debilitating civil war that no doubt exhausted the treasury of the city and fueled rebellion in the northern axis of Ifẹ̀'s commercial network. Nevertheless, as we saw in chapter 3, Ọbalùfọ̀n II regained the lost ground, and his reign marked the pinnacle of the Yorùbá Classical-age cultural efflorescence and economic glory.

We may ask, how did Ọbalùfọ̀n II finance his wars, diplomacy, and external commerce, especially in the northern axis? How did he keep the other city-states aligned in Ifẹ̀'s galactic orbit? He seems to have used the most significant asset that Ilé-Ifẹ̀ had: he produced more glass beads, perhaps more efficiently and in unprecedented quantity. Initially, more glass beads meant success in recruiting more valuable clients like Ọ̀yọ́ into the Ifẹ̀'s sphere of regional influence. With glass beads, Ọbalùfọ̀n II also increased the buying power of Ilé-Ifẹ̀ in the regional and continental markets. Unlike the wares of all other known great emporia in West Africa, the exports of Ilé-Ifẹ̀—glass beads—were not extractive or agricultural products like gold, copper, salt, ivory, and kola nut, five of the major trade goods in the subcontinent. Rather, they were products of proprietary knowledge. With cheap, abundant, and almost inexhaustible raw materials for glass production, the Ifẹ̀ chief export was not based on the principles of scarcity. Its production operated on the principles of abundance and mass production of desire. And its distribution was rationalized through wide-ranging exchange networks and strategies.[2] These qualities of abundance, however, eventually led to overproduction. There does not seem to have been any measure in place to control the volume of beads in circulation. Therefore, the increased and continuous production would have saturated the market, and their price index value, wealth storage value, and potency as elite goods would have gradually diminished. These are all recipes for an economic recession. *Ṣẹ̀gi* and *iyùn* might have lost some of their awe factor for the political class in the Yorùbá community of practice during this time. This would explain the reason that by the mid-fifteenth century, the king and the major chieftains of Benin had abandoned the use of *ṣẹ̀gi* and *iyùn* beads as markers of power and authority. Instead, they were using the jasper/carnelian beads imported via Ọ̀yọ́ and other places across the River Niger as their badges of office.[3] Nevertheless, the demand for Ifẹ̀ glass beads was not waning in the larger society, because of what they represented in the everyday social fields and spheres of interaction—spirituality, healing, wellness, aesthetics, and cultural valuation (e.g., identity).[4]

Hence, although Ọbalùfọ̀n II was credited with political and commercial expansion, defeat of insurgences far and near, and consolidation of the Ifẹ̀-centric hegemony over the Yorùbá community of practice, the downturn in the political and economic fortunes of Ilé-Ifẹ̀ seems to have also started toward the end of his long reign.[5] This would be consistent with the cycles of bubble and burst that tend to characterize the period of phenomenal economic growth and organizational maturity of hegemonic polities.[6] It seems that in the course of expanding the city's commercial boundaries and broadening its fields of economic and diplomatic relations, the regime of Ọbalùfọ̀n II inadvertently also laid the groundwork for the decline of Ifẹ̀'s economy. Hence, the "city of abundance" may have suffered economically from overproduction and politically from overextension. It may also have suffered from complacency and lack of vigor during Ọbalùfọ̀n II's old age, with the court living more on reputation and old glory than on sound economic policy and real wealth. This would be the bubble phase. Even if the collapse of the economy was not yet discernible to most observers during the last years of Ọbalùfọ̀n II's reign, the process of decline accelerated immediately after his demise, especially in the early fifteenth century.[7] His successors were hardly the causes of the decline. They were men of privilege thrust into a sinking ship, and they lacked the wherewithal to save themselves or the ship.

At the close of the fourteenth century, the frequent episodes of drought in Ilé-Ifẹ̀ and other parts of the central Yorùbá region worsened the effects of economic crisis. The oral traditions of Ifẹ̀ indeed recall the debilitating episodes of drought and famine that began sometime in the late fourteenth and the early fifteenth century, and these sources mention the effects on mass migrations from the city.[8] These traditions are consistent with paleoecological evidence and historical sources showing that intense cyclical multiyear droughts began across West Africa ca. 1380 and did not subside until the middle of the sixteenth century.[9] These episodes of drought were the worst in the region's history since that of the Big Dry in 300 BC–AD 300 (see chap. 2). The impact of the diminishing precipitation is more remembered in the traditions than the drought itself. Hence, Isaac Akinjogbin recorded narratives about the frequent occurrences of famine in the latter years of the Classical period.[10] Those narratives blame rapid population increase in Ilé-Ifẹ̀ for food shortages and state that these, in turn, led to waves of emigration to decongest the overpopulated city. We see in these traditions references to the effect that the once prosperous emporium and "house of abundance" became a "house of scarcity" and a shell of its old self in the early fifteenth century.

There are also indications that the city suffered from one or more incidents of pox epidemic during at least the early phase of the drought. Indeed, Ọbalùfọ̀n II appears to have died of an infectious disease that ravaged the city during the last years of his reign.[11] This infection was likely smallpox (*Variola major*), a recurrent epidemic in Ifẹ̀ history, usually associated with periods of drought or more intense dry seasons.[12] This is not the first time we encounter the story of epidemic as a major causal event in the history of Ilé-Ifẹ̀. The better known and widely cited epidemic in Ifẹ̀ oral traditions was the pox outbreak that brought an end to the Ọbàtálá-Odùduwà conflict, discussed in chapter 2. Although the association of Ọbalùfọ̀n's death with infectious disease tends to be suppressed in Ifẹ̀ traditions, those same traditions give us enough clues that Ọbalùfọ̀n II was afflicted by a contagion. The original palace and temple of Ọbalùfọ̀n II was located near the current Odùduwà temple in the center of the city (fig. 4.1).[13] An exquisite mosaic of potsherd-cobble pavement flooring is associated with this site (fig. 4.2).[14] The king is said to have taken ill in his old age. As a result, he was removed from the palace and relocated to the Mọ̀rẹ̀ area, where his temple is now located, more than one kilometer from the city center and close to the edge of the Inner Wall (see figs. 2.7 and 4.1). The location of this temple makes it an outlier compared to the other temples of the classical kings and chieftains, all located at the center of the city. The Mọ̀rẹ̀ temple is said to have served as the king's last residence. The contraction of a contagious disease such as smallpox was the only cause that would have led to the removal of Ọbalùfọ̀n II from the palace in the center of the city and his transfer to the city's edge. After all, as the saying goes in Ilé-Ifẹ̀, *igbó nà ń gbẹ́lẹ́fọ̀n rè*, "the forest/bush is the home of a pox-afflicted person," a reference to the use of isolation methods for separating those with a highly contagious disease, such as smallpox, from people who are not sick.[15] It was in the

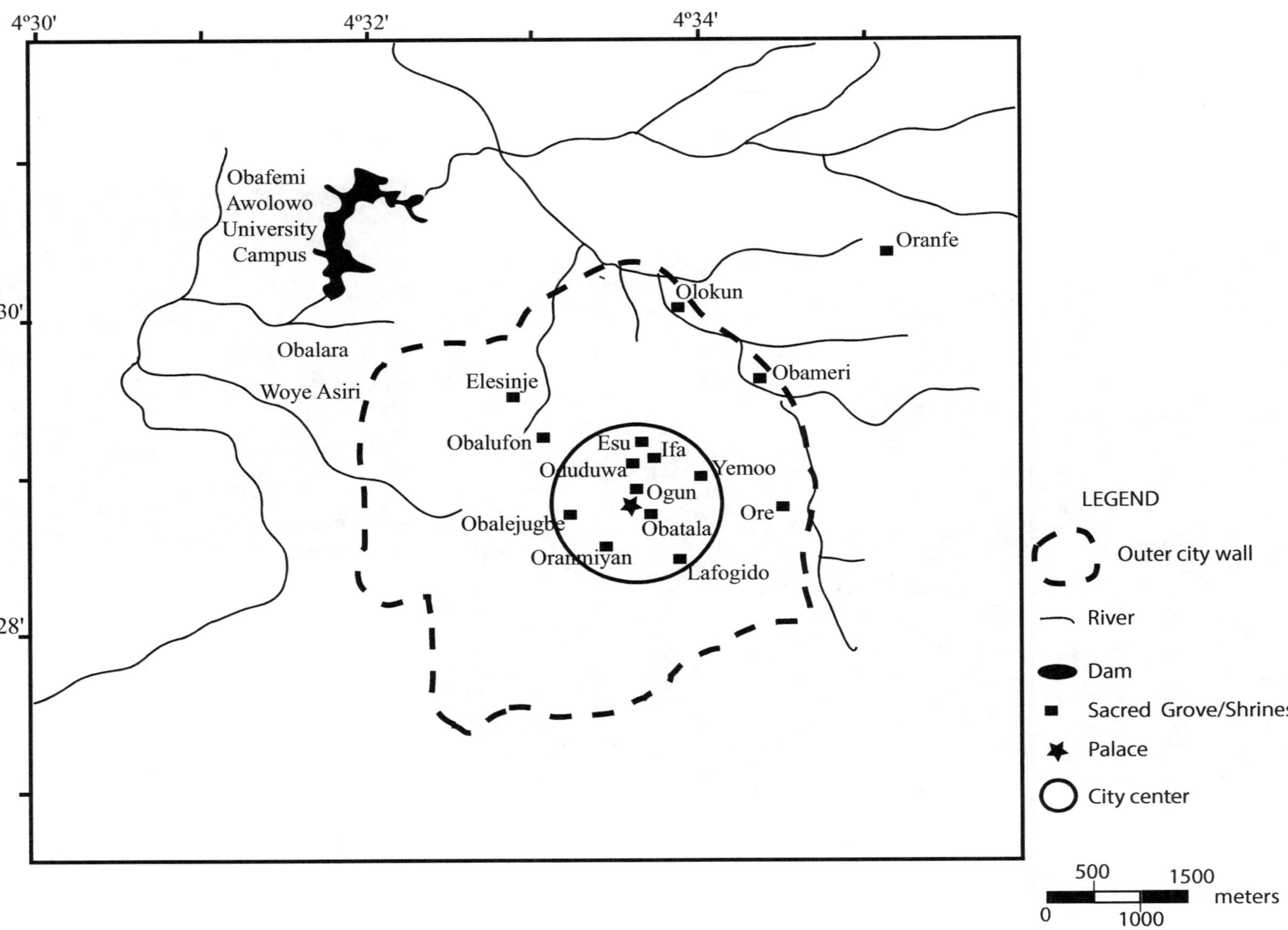

Figure 4.1. Location of major sacred groves in Ilé-Ifẹ̀

Figure 4.2. Aerial view of Odùduwà grove (courtesy of Gérard Chouin), showing the abandoned Ọbalùfọ̀n II's temple and associated potsherd pavement

bush (e.g., a sacred grove) where the sick who had the support of family networks would be cared for, until recovery or death.[16] It is apparent that the great king passed away in the Mọ̀rẹ̀ area, on the edge of the old city, where his temple is now located. So the great diplomat, military strategist, innovator, renowned patron of art, and empire builder who took the city of Ifẹ̀ to the pinnacle of its glory seemed to have lived the last days of his life in an isolated place outside the palace. He survived the intrigues at home and abroad but succumbed to the wrath of an infectious disease in a sacred grove.[17]

An infectious disease such as pox epidemic would have been a disease of equal opportunity, especially in a densely populated city like Classical Ifẹ̀. This was the kind of place that smallpox tended to strike with more frequency and intensity. What affected one, affected all. Many people other than Ọbalùfọ̀n II would have died from this infection. The impact on Ilé-Ifẹ̀ must have been debilitating for a city that was already experiencing social fragility due to economic depression and was facing political uncertainty in the last years of the aging king's reign and in the aftermath of his transition. It is not clear how intensive and widespread the epidemic outbreak was in Ilé-Ifẹ̀ and across the region. The outbreak and its effects may have been very localized. But, considering the vast integrated landscape of villages, towns, and cities across the region, the epidemic could have also spread rapidly on the highways of commercial, ritual, social, and political networks. In that case, the continuous flow of population from neighboring areas would have raised the propensity for new outbreaks, and this possibly prolonged the life span of the epidemic.[18]

The infectious disease that claimed the life of Ọbalùfọ̀n II and possibly hundreds of others, and the drought and famine that preceded the outbreak seemed to have accelerated the end of the Classical period. Archaeological evidence shows that the occupation of several Classical-era sites such as Woyè Àsírí and Ọbalára ended within the first quarter of the fifteenth century, not long after Ọbalùfọ̀n II's death.[19] It was also during this period that those distinctive naturalistic ancestral figures that defined the plastic art of the Classical age disappeared altogether in the archaeological profiles. Without descendants to carry out proper veneration rituals, and without the wealth, pomp, and circumstance of the Classical period, the surviving great sculptors of Ifẹ̀ naturalism lost patronage. Some of the naturalistic figures that had adorned ancestral altars were buried under the rubble of collapsed shrines and abandoned houses, as evident at the Ọbalára site. As a sign of the times, defined by disconnection from the past, some of those sculptures were taken to the edges of the city to be buried in mass graves, as happened at Igbó'Làjà in Ọ̀wọ̀. The production of glass beads also ended in the course of the fifteenth century. Overall, the Classical period effectively came to an end during the first quarter of the century, succeeded by a new era that I have called the Intermediate period, lasting through 1570.[20] It is instructive that while one smallpox outbreak reportedly brought an end to the Late Formative era and ushered in the Classical period, another epidemic outbreak contributed to the demise of the great period of economic prosperity, high cultural attainment, and artistic efflorescence for Ifẹ̀ and most parts of the Yorùbá world.

The crisis in the region's emporium meant trouble for its most dependent allies and provinces, especially Upper Ọ̀ṣun, Ìbòlò, Èkìtì, Ìgbómìnà, and the areas between Upper Ògùn and River Niger. They were all in disarray by the early 1400s. The people of Ìgbómìnà and many other areas vividly recall this period of instability in their oral traditions.[21] Meanwhile, unsettling developments around the Niger-Benue Confluence and the Moshi-Niger area early in the fifteenth century exacerbated the domestic crisis in other parts of the Yorùbá region. Although there were already signs of trouble in the late fourteenth century (chap. 3), these came to a head in the early fifteenth century as the Yorùbá communities, such as the Gbèdègì in Jebba and Mokwa, Kyede around Tada, the Okun-related groups in the Koton Karifi area, and the Koyi of Kakanda came under the intense attack of the Nupe militarists. As a result, many of the Yorùbá-speaking peoples living along the Niger, especially in the port towns and villages, began to flee their homes and migrate southward. With the center of the Yorùbá community of practice in turmoil and its major port towns in flames, the old social order broke down. Peer-polity conflicts, brigandage, and succession disputes appear to have intensified throughout the region during the first half of the fifteenth century. This period, according to two students of Yorùbá history, was "a turbulent time in the history of towns and kingdoms throughout the area."[22] Waves of migration crisscrossed the landscape in flight from drought and famine, brigandage, political instability, and epidemic outbreaks, searching for new homes and opportunities. Likewise, bitter civil wars and invasions ensued in many parts of the region during the early fifteenth century, leading, for example, to the turbulent dynastic change in Benin ca. 1440. This had far-reaching consequences for the entire eastern flank of the Yorùbá world.

From Client States to Political Autonomy: The Benin Example

It is important to say more about what happened in Benin ca. 1440, and its consequences, to better understand the devastating effects of the collapse of Ifẹ̀ Empire and the regional turbulence that followed. Benin was one of the prominent secondary centers in the Ifẹ̀-centric *ẹbí* fraternity during the Classical period. It did not escape the crisis that engulfed its patron city, Ilé-Ifẹ̀, but the crisis was short-lived for the Edo kingdom. At the very same time that Ilé-Ifẹ̀ was reeling from post-Ọbalùfọ̀n political blues; the Yorùbá frontier communities along the Niger River were being displaced; and Ìgbómìnà, Èkìtì, and even Ọ̀wọ̀ were in disarray, Benin was also experiencing a civil war that arose from succession disputes. The political and economic instability in Ilé-Ifẹ̀ likely contributed to the political division in Benin, as different leaders made conflicting claims about a better future for the kingdom. With the referential city for the Yorùbá community of practice in crisis, a protracted and biting civil war ensued in Benin. The outcome was a violent dynastic change in the mid-fifteenth century, bringing Ewuare the Great (r. ca. 1440–73) to the throne. Renowned as a strategic warrior-king and perceptive state builder, the appellation *the Great* was added to his name by later Benin historians in recognition of the transformative impacts of his rule.[23] Ewuare, also nicknamed Ògún (after the Yorùbá deity of iron and warfare), appears to have been a prominent military figure before he ascended the throne. It is not clear whether he instigated a military takeover out of duty to his people to reestablish stability, or whether he was an opportunist soldier who took advantage of the royal intrigues to seize power. Whatever his motive, he was a usurper of the Benin throne, but he proved to be a great leader. He ended the internal succession squabble and civil war and set about restoring order.[24]

At the time Ewuare came to power, Ilé-Ifẹ̀ was already a shell of its old self; it was living on reputation rather than on substance. The bottom of Ifẹ̀'s economy had fallen out, its domination of the long-distance trade based on glass-bead production had practically ceased, and it had lost its prescriptive voice in the political affairs of the community of practice that it had helped to create. With most of the core members of the Yorùbá community of practice in disarray, Ewuare saw a golden opportunity, and he seized it. He launched Benin on the path of territorial expansion and made internal political and administrative changes that laid the foundation for the ambition and reputation of Benin as a warring state. He invaded the Èkìtì, Afenmai, and western Igbo areas and took up battle with nearby Ọ̀wọ̀—also a major state in the *ẹbí* fraternity.[25] The warring king was also active in resolving several domestic issues relating to power-sharing. He did this by creating new arms of government such as the chamber of town chiefs (*Eghaevbo n'Ore*), which he integrated into the central administration alongside the preexisting palace chiefs (*Eghaevbo n'Ogbe*). This facilitated the participation of more segments of the city in the administration of the kingdom. He also attempted to change, though unsuccessfully, the name of the kingdom from Ubini (a Yorùbá-derived name) to Edo (an older, locally derived name). It was a move aimed at emphasizing local identities and cultural pride. In addition, he sought to institutionalize the principle of primogeniture in the succession to the throne by creating the title of *edaiken* (crown prince). He is also credited with constructing the inner wall-ditch complex in Benin.[26] And he is remembered as a great patron of art.[27]

In Ewuare, Benin finally had a king who for the first time stepped outside the umbrella of Ifẹ̀'s political patronage. Ewuare made his own umbrella, but he and the Benin kings who followed him were careful not to sever links with Ilé-Ifẹ̀, if only for the potent legitimacy that their affiliation with the ancient city accorded their rule (see chap. 3). With the collapse of Ifẹ̀'s emporium status, Ewuare brought an end to the dependency of his kingdom on the glass beads of the "city of abundance." One of the key decisions he made was to elevate jasper beads and other chalcedony varieties as the badge of office. This means that Ifẹ̀'s *iyùn* ceased to be the currency of power. Ewuare's expansionist adventures and foreign policy were therefore aimed at creating pathways for Benin to open a direct communication channel with the trading stations on the Niger River and the Niger-Benue Confluence, controlling trade routes, and securing safety and favorable bargaining opportunities for Benin (royal) traders. His forays into Èkìtì filled the vacuum that Ifẹ̀'s waning fortunes had left in eastern and central Yorùbá, allowing him to secure the region for the safe passage of Benin trading missions to the River Niger trading posts, which were now controlled by the Ọ̀yọ́, Nupe, and other groups. His combative measures in Àkókó were geared toward keeping the increasingly aggressive Igala kingdom and the audacious Nupe principalities from establishing influence in Benin's northern frontiers. This northward expansion was also an effort to establish direct commercial relations with Ọ̀yọ́, the strongest Yorùbá polity near the Niger River, where large imports of chalcedony beads (*àkòrì*) and other Sudanese and savanna products, including natron, salt, and copper, were arriving to be exchanged for rain forest products, especially ivory.

Nupe Militarists, Regional Instability, and Transregional Alliances: The Ọ̀yọ́ Example

The causality of Ifẹ̀'s economic decline and the resultant crisis in the Yorùbá community of practice also had an external component, mostly from the northern axis of Ifẹ̀'s commercial realm. Although Ọbalùfọ̀n II subdued some of the troubles in that realm, he did not fully eradicate them, as we shall soon discover. Ọbalùfọ̀n's successors certainly lacked his political sagacity, and they seem to have been overwhelmed by the regional crisis that Ọbalùfọ̀n had fought so hard to contain, especially in the Moshi-Niger area. About the same time that Benin was establishing a decidedly northward policy of expansion and Benin and Ọ̀yọ́ were forging new commercial relations in the mid-fifteenth century, the Nupe were also embarking on the process of political centralization. By then, several fragmented Nupe villages and principalities were consolidating into confederacies. The largest of these was the Beni confederacy.[28] However, the incipient political centralization taking place among the Nupe came at the expense of the several culturally hybrid, but Yorùbá-dominant, communities along the Niger.[29] Many of these communities north of the Niger were already being displaced in the last decades of the fourteenth century. More of them, south of the river and mostly Yorùbá-speaking, fell under Nupe's control in the first half of the fifteenth century. With the loss of the Ifẹ̀-centric and predominantly Yorùbá-speaking frontier ports in Jebba and Tada to Nupe's political consolidation and hostilities, the alternative trade routes from the heartland of the Yorùbá world to the Sudanic belt shifted westward. Ọ̀yọ́ temporarily benefited from this development. Most especially, the central and eastern areas of the Yorùbá community of practice, including Benin, increasingly relied on Ọ̀yọ́ in order to gain access to the Sudanese market and products. If extending the genealogy of Ọ̀rànmíyàn to Ọ̀yọ́ was an attempt to avert a collapse of Ifẹ̀'s external commerce and cut the stem of troubles in the northern Yorùbá frontiers, the effort did not succeed beyond the reign of Ọbalùfọ̀n II. The Ọ̀yọ́, under Aláàfin Kórì and Olúasó, stood their ground against the Nupe incursion. Nevertheless, things were about to get worse.

Of all the sources of perturbation previously mentioned, none threatened the existential future of the Yorùbá world with as much devastating and transformational effect as the Nupe's military adventures. At about the same time that Ewuare came to the throne of Benin, the newly created Nupe polities were militarily penetrating deeper into the Yorùbá country beyond the Niger valley. But their art and motive of war seem to be different from the ones the region had known. The Nupe chieftains and their militarists were not interested in the preciosity that had animated commercial life in the Yorùbá community of practice. Their wars were in the form of brigandage, and their goal was to take human captives. This modus operandi was in full swing by the middle of the fifteenth century, and it lasted for about a century. Not all Nupe groups bought into this militarist agenda, and many were in fact victims of its activities and goals, as we shall see below.

Equipped with horses—their newly found military hardware—Nupe militarists engaged in activities that affected the northern frontiers of the Yorùbá world, and they penetrated over one hundred kilometers deep into the region, ransacking the Yàgbà and other Okun areas (see fig. 1.1). Westward, the militarists were involved in conflicts against their Ìbàrìbá neighbors in the Niger-Moshi area. And, toward the end of the century, the Nupe invaded and sacked Ọ̀yọ́, laying waste the core of the kingdom.[30] The displaced Ọ̀yọ́ population set up new homes in Ṣakí, Kìṣí,

Ìgbẹ̀tì, and Ìgbòho, as well as in Ìbàrìbá country. A section of the Ọ̀yọ́ royal House managed to keep the idea of the kingdom alive by relocating the seat of power to Ìgbòho, where four *aláàfins* (kings of Ọ̀yọ́) ruled in the sixteenth century.[31] Tasting the sweetness of victory in the north, the Nupe militarists penetrated deep into Ìgbómìnà, Èkìtì, and Ìbòlò—all Ifẹ̀-centric areas. Massive abandonment of towns and villages preceded and followed those attacks.

The Nupe militarist crisis was not an isolated local event. It was directly connected to the political and economic troubles in Central and Western Sudan and to the subcontinental ecological crisis in the Sahel. These developments had started in the late fourteenth century, but they intensified in the middle of the fifteenth century. The story of these Sudanese troubles must begin with the succession disputes that rocked the Keita dynasty following the death of Mansa Suleyman of Mali Empire in 1360 (fig. 4.3).[32] The palace intrigues laid the groundwork for political instability in Western Sudan. Mali's vassal states took advantage of the metropolis's weakness, and the Songhai and Wolof tributary states began to peel away from the empire. Hence, by the second quarter of the fourteenth century, Mali had begun its slow but steady downfall. This political situation was compounded by the declining and unpredictable rainfall across West Africa, beginning around the end of the fourteenth century, the very same hemispheric climate change that was destabilizing Ilé-Ifẹ̀ and other parts of the Yorùbá region farther south. The severity of low precipitation would have been particularly hard on the desert edge and the Sudanic grassland. The severe droughts that accompanied the onset of low and unpredictable rainfall caused significant changes in the economy and demography of the affected areas, and unleashed instability and political problems across Western Sudan. The droughts pushed the boundaries of the desert southward, while the Sahel boundaries moved into the erstwhile savanna, and some of the northern fringes of the rain forest turned into savanna.[33] These ecological shifts led to population movements, bringing people from different vegetation bands practicing different economies into closer contact. These processes were the perfect storm for conflicts, as those migrants competed for the scarce water and land resources with the local communities. For example, the ecologically displaced nomads and pastoralists from different directions, including the Tuareg from the Sahara edge and the Fulbe from Upper Senegal, made brazen attacks on Mali's emporia in the Niger Bend throughout the late fourteenth and early fifteenth century.[34] The ecological crises sped up the disintegration of the Mali Empire. In its place arose the Songhai Empire in 1468. Its heroic leader, Sonni Ali, restored stability in the eastern arc of the Niger Bend, from Timbuktu to Gao. He also embarked on an expansionist program that incorporated most of the old Mali Empire's

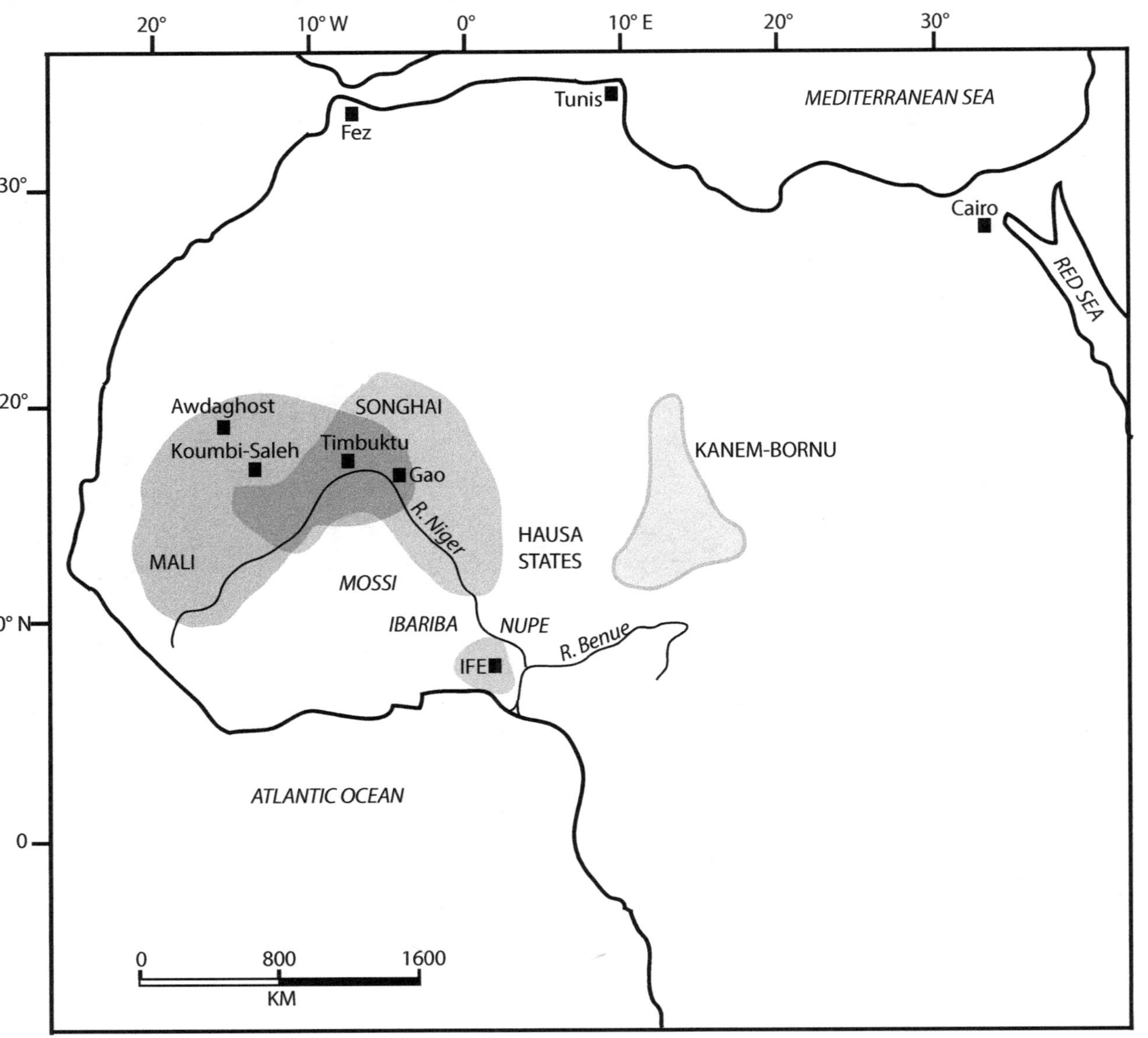

Figure 4.3. Composite major West African states, 1300–1570

territories into Songhai. Eastward, this very same ecological crisis may have been the proximate cause of the internal political intrigues that culminated in the collapse of the Kanem Empire between 1380 and 1460.

The cumulative effects of the droughts in the Sahel caused massive migrations toward the more ecologically stable Central Sudan, especially the Hausa region. The need to manage the political-economic implications of droughts informed the southeast expansion of the Songhai toward the Hausa territories and southward on the Niger River. Some of the displaced people from the old Kanem Empire also saw in the Hausa region the opportunities to restart their lives. Merchants, artisans, and farmers from Western Sudan and the Lake Chad area therefore flocked into this area. As a result, some of the trans-Saharan trade termini were relocated southward from the Niger Bend and Kanem. Several Hausa walled villages and towns had existed before the fifteenth century, but they benefited as sites of population aggregation, expanded agricultural production, and favored commercial entrepôts during the midcentury. As agricultural lands were being lost to drought in the Sahel, Central Sudan became the food basket for both the Sahel and the Saharan peoples, a development that unleashed intense competition for farmland and labor. From these struggles for land, labor, and security, five Hausa city-states became dominant by the end of the fifteenth century. "Kano, Katsina, Gobir, Kebbi and Zazzau," according to Paul Lovejoy, "grew larger with military conquest, commercial expansion, and immigration" and became the hub of commercial and agricultural production from ca. 1475.[35] Muhammad Rumfa, the King of Kano (ca. 1463–1499), and Queen Amina of Zazzau (late fifteenth or early sixteenth century) are associated with some of the economic expansion, military conquests, and political consolidation that defined this era of transformation in Central Sudan. The success of these Hausa city-states lies in the use of cavalry in their wars of expansion for land and labor. With their war captives, they established slave colonies to work the land. In this regard, the old economic system of Western Sudan and Kanem, whereby colonies of slaves were established to work the royal farmlands, mines, and crafts centers, became entrenched in the Hausa region. All of this grew out of the local commercial expansion, linked to the trans-Saharan trade.[36]

About the same time that the expansionist program of Songhai Empire began, Mai Ali Dunamami of Kanem-Bornu gained political power and launched his military expansion westward to control the salt-mining sites and trade links with Hausaland. According to Kano Chronicles, several Hausa city-states were already acquiring horses from Kanem-Bornu by the early fifteenth century.[37] These states intensified the process of building up their cavalry war machine in the second half of the century as a result of the political developments and demographic changes taking place around them. They relied on Kanem-Bornu for their equine supply.[38] The use of cavalry helped secure the conquest of territories. However, the intensive agricultural plantations that were developing in the last quarter of the fifteenth century required more labor than the conquered population could supply. Therefore, the Hausa city-states looked farther south, outside their political sphere, for slave labor. The most important exports that the Hausa traders had in exchange for slaves were horses. Located south of the Hausa region, the political entrepreneurs in many of the Nupe principalities took advantage of the "horse-slave exchange," and they were soon trading captives from the neighboring regions—including Kemberi, the northern Yorùbá, and parts of Ìbàrìbá—for the Hausa horses. Some of the captives were used domestically in the Sudan (especially for agricultural production), while others were sold to other parts of the Sudan and across the Sahara.

With horses, the Nupe principalities gained the upper hand over their more numerous Yorùbá neighbors. Since horse breeding was not effective in the Nupe homeland because of trypanosomiasis infections, the Nupe militarist leaders had to use the imported horses to acquire more captives to replenish their equine supply from Central Sudan. It was a dilemma and a vicious cycle: the Nupe political and brigand leaders had to repeatedly raid their neighbors for more captives to maintain their cavalry power advantages. Here lies the genesis of Nupe forays into the Yorùbá region. The goal was geared toward neither establishing political dominions nor controlling trade routes. Their sole purpose was to plunder, capture, and enslave. Given that the Nupe were divided into several political principalities in the late fifteenth century, several independent units of horsemen-led warlords planned and initiated invasions into the Yorùbá region. This explains why the crisis lasted for such a long time and spread across a vast territory within a short period. However, access to Central Sudanese horses also hastened the process of political centralization among the Nupe, as several fragmented Nupe principalities used the horse advantage to consolidate their political holdings. This process reached its peak sometime between 1525 and 1535 when Tsoede supposedly completed the task of political centralization in Nupe.[39] This development provided a more centrally coordinated military program for some of the later invasions. Nupe oral traditions tend to suggest that Tsoede ruled the north central and northeastern areas of the Yorùbá region—parts of Ìgbómìnà and most of Okun. In contrast, the Yorùbá oral traditions claim that Nupe militarists repeatedly raided those areas for captives between the mid-fifteenth and mid-sixteenth century.[40]

The droughts of those centuries aided the Nupe incursions into the Yorùbá world; those dry conditions extended the boundaries of the savanna southward, thinning out the rain forest and creating a more open landscape. As a result, the Nupe horsemen were able to reach areas that would have been impenetrable for cavalry in the preceding centuries. The drastically thinned vegetation in the erstwhile wooded savanna enabled the swift attack-and-withdraw tactics needed for these raiding operations, especially during the prolonged dry seasons. In the hilly areas of Okun and Èkìtì, the marauders would have employed surprise attacks on the entire village or town, or laid ambush on the narrow paths that crisscrossed the region.[41] The Nupe intrusion during the second half of the fifteenth century took advantage of, and exacerbated, the already weak sociopolitical situation in the Yorùbá world, which was reeling from the collapse of the Ifẹ̀-centric commercial network and from severe multiyear episodes of drought and epidemic outbreaks.

The method, purpose, and scale of Nupe incursions were unprecedented in the history of the Yorùbá world. The size of cavalry that the Òwu and, later, the Ọ̀yọ́ had used in their warfare paled in comparison to the number of horses that the Nupe militarists employed. It was also the first time that massive enslavement had been the purpose of those horse-mounted attacks. Never before had a group of attackers ravaged such a vast landscape as the Nupe militarists did in the northern and central Yorùbá areas, lasting for at least four generations (ca. 1440–1550). These attacks marked the first regional offensive against the Yorùbá community of practice as a group. Their devastating impacts on the Ọ̀yọ́, Ìgbómìnà, Okun, and Èkìtì areas created the longest unrest that the region had ever faced, and they tested the political efficacy of its *ẹbí* fraternity ideology. These attacks are etched deeply into the historical memory of those areas and beyond, yet they have received surprisingly perfunctory attention in the historiography.[42] However, as we shall see below, the Nupe incursions and the aftermath changed the dynamics of regional power; created a new roadmap for regional cooperation; and unleashed the processes for a different kind of political and economic formation in the Yorùbá world.

For many decades, there was no effective coordinated response in the Yorùbá region to curtail the Nupe militarists' attacks. The Okun, Ìgbómìnà, and Èkìtì were too fragmented and weak to put up any serious resistance, although they did not give up. Benin certainly clashed with the Nupe cavalry on and off in the Èkìtì areas between ca. 1440 and 1550 as part of the strategy of protecting its commercial interests.[43] But it was Nupe's military assaults on Ọ̀yọ́, and the subsequent evacuation of the latter's capital sometime in the last decade of the fifteenth century, that laid the groundwork for a coordinated effort to put an end to Nupe's menace.[44] According to a Yorùbá maxim on the art of war, *mọ̀'jà mọ̀'sá là ń m'akínkanjú l'ógun, akínkanjú tó m'ọ̀jà tí kò mọ̀'sá á b'ógun lọ*: "Retreat and offensive strategies are the hallmark of bravery, a valiant warrior who does not know when to retreat or attack will die prematurely on the battlefield." The Ọ̀yọ́ followed this axiom. They realized that they lacked the military hardware to successfully confront the mounted forces of the Nupe. Humiliated but defiant, the *aláàfin* and his chieftains retreated and began planning the Ọ̀yọ́ comeback in exile. In the wake of the evacuation of Ọ̀yọ́, Aláàfin Onigbogí sought refuge in the Ìbàrìbá country. However, his successor Òfinràn founded a temporary capital farther south in Ìgbòho, in the Yorùbá country (see fig. 1.1). Here, he and his chieftains began to rebuild the manpower and resources needed to defeat the Nupe. Fired by the spirit of nationalism, the urgent drive to avenge the humiliation of the ancestors, and an unalloyed commitment to a more secure future, the efforts to repel the Nupe from the northern Yorùbá territory preoccupied the reign of the five *aláàfin* in Ìgbòho—Òfinràn, Egungunojú, Ọrọ̀m̀pọ̀tọ̀, Ajíbóyèdé, and Abípa.

From their base in Ìgbòho, Ọ̀yọ́ monarchs built one of the largest regional and intercultural military coalitions that West Africa has ever witnessed. The coalition included the Ìbàrìbá, Wasangari, Wangarawa, Djerma, and Mossi. To start, the initial sojourn of the Ọ̀yọ́ court in Ìbàrìbá country was not in vain. In the Ìbàrìbá, the Ọ̀yọ́ found a ready, trusted, and committed ally. Both the Ọ̀yọ́ and Ìbàrìbá had a common interest. At the time that the Ọ̀yọ́ were displaced from their ancestral home, the Ìbàrìbá were being squeezed between the imperialist Songhai expansionists from the north and the Nupe marauders from the east. Hence, the Ìbàrìbá had the same concern as the Ọ̀yọ́: to remove the Nupe thorn from their flesh. Laying aside narrow interests, Ọ̀yọ́ and Ìbàrìbá leaders began to pool their military resources, in men, weaponry, and tactics. With Ìgbòho as their base, the Ọ̀yọ́ recruited several Ìbàrìbá itinerant hunters and militia to join their cause.[45] The two groups embarked on the slow but steady process of counterattack. This was not simply a war of numbers of soldiers; it was a war of horses. In the savanna landscape where the Ọ̀yọ́-Ìbàrìbá coalition was planning their showdown with the Nupe, a cavalry force had immense advantages over infantry. Hence the Yorùbá adage *A kì í bá òmùwẹ̀ jagun odò, kò s'ẹ́lẹ́ṣẹ̀ tí í bá ẹlẹ́ṣin jagun pápá*: "A non-swimmer must avoid fighting a swimmer in the middle of the river; no infantry is a match for the cavalry in the plains."

This is where the Wasangari, Djerma, and Mossi came in. Ọ̀yọ́ needed their cooperation in order to procure the horses required to match up against the Nupe on the battlefield. The Wasangari, the ruling elite of Ìbàrìbá country, built their power on cavalry warfare.[46] They were reputed horse fighters, but the breed of horses they used and needed for warfare had to be purchased from their northern neighbors—the Djerma, southern Mossi, Malinke (Mali), and Wangarawa (Soninke). These were the African Barbary horses highly sought after for their great hardiness, stamina, and fiery temperament. It was obvious to the exiled political leaders of Ọ̀yọ́ that their hope of returning to and securing their homeland depended on acquiring the horses of this breed and becoming adept at using them for military purposes. The resolve to end the insecurity posed by the Nupe militarists pushed the Ọ̀yọ́ to develop their own cavalry with the help of their Ìbàrìbá comrades.

Ọ̀yọ́'s environment was conducive to maintaining large herds of horses but difficult for breeding them. Therefore, like the Nupe and Wasangari, the Ọ̀yọ́ had to import their horses and many of the warhorse accessories. The Ọ̀yọ́ tapped into their old alliances to accomplish this. In the Djerma, the Ọ̀yọ́ found a reliable ally who believed in their cause. A subgroup of the Songhai who had traded and lived with the Ọ̀yọ́ in the Moshi-Niger area since the fourteenth century, if not earlier, the Djerma (also known as Zarma), along with their southern Mossi neighbors, were proficient horse breeders. From them, the Ọ̀yọ́ began to acquire and build their stables.[47] And the Wasangari rulers of Ìbàrìbá cooperated. They allowed the transportation of these horses through their territories. The Djerma, Mossi, and Wasangari were also excellent horsemen, and their elite mounted lancers had a reputation for deadly swiftness and precision.[48] These groups not only provided the Ọ̀yọ́ with their equine supplies but also trained the latter's soldiers in cavalry warfare. The Ọ̀yọ́ may also have recruited mercenaries from the ranks of Wasangari, Djerma, and Mossi. In order to pay for the horses that it was importing from the Djerma and Mossi, the Ọ̀yọ́ would have had to raid and take captives wherever they could find them. In other words, the strategy that the Nupe used to finance their horse imports from the Hausa and Kanuri peoples in the Central Sudan was the same one the Ọ̀yọ́ used to underwrite their equestrian imports from the Djerma (Songhai), Mossi, Malinke, and possibly Wangarawa traders, all in the Western Sudan. The linguistic evidence indeed shows that whereas the Ọ̀yọ́ obtained their horses, horsemen, and stable hands from the Western Sudan, the Nupe procured theirs from the Hausa-Kanuri axis. *Ẹsin*, the word for horse in both the Yorùbá and Ìbàrìbá languages, is derived from the Arabic word *esin* or *asi*, which would have filtered through the Western Sudanese people who originally imported the Barbary horses from the Maghreb (North Africa, excluding Egypt). This contrasts with *doko*, Nupe's word for horse, which is derived from Hausa and Kanuri's *doki*.

Common interest made the regional coalition that supported Ọ̀yọ́'s cause possible. The Ọ̀yọ́ and Ìbàrìbá were not the only ones who were gored by Nupe's rising military power and political centralization. Their other neighbors to the west also felt apprehension about the development in Nupe. In particular, the Wasangari and the Djerma viewed the Nupe militarists as potential enemies since the later were the allies of the Hausa and Kanuri, the people against whom the Songhai expanded westward and with whom they shared boundaries and occasionally clashed. The Nupe political consolidation and the impacts of horse imports from the Kanuri-Hausa axis were unsettling for those neighbors. It was therefore in the best interests of the Djerma and Wasangari to support the Ọ̀yọ́-Ìbàrìbá coalition against the Nupe, whose military project was not focused on protecting trade routes and establishing political stability but was preoccupied with enslavement and the creation of political disorder. Hence, the military and security crisis that unfolded in the Yorùbá region between the mid-fifteenth and most of the sixteenth century had a wider subcontinental implication, between the Yorùbá-Ìbàrìbá-Songhai-Mossi axis in the west and the Nupe-Hausa-Kanuri axis in the east.

The Ọ̀yọ́ were not the only Yorùbá elements seeking to expel the Nupe militarists from their homeland. Farther south, in the upper reaches of the rain forest, several Èkìtì polities fought the Nupe under the banner of Benin. Ilé-Ifẹ̀ is also said to have been engaged in a protracted and costly war at Ará (in Èkìtì country) during the sixteenth century. This was in alliance with several Èkìtì polities against the Nupe brigands, a topic that I will return to in the next chapter.[49] However, while the Ọ̀yọ́ in exile were able to mount a resistance against the Nupe militarists, many other Yorùbá polities and communities in the Moshi-Niger frontier did not survive the Nupe scourge and the military maneuver that followed. For example, the savanna metropolis of Òwu, west of River Ògùn, was liquidated either by Nupe militarists or by the combined forces of the Ọ̀yọ́ and their allies. For the latter, it would have been a revenge attack on Ọ̀yọ́'s former overlord. Whatever the case, the turbulence in the Moshi-Niger area pushed the Òwu southward into the rain forest, where they rebuilt their polities in the area between the Ifẹ̀ and Ẹ̀gbá territories in the late sixteenth century.

After about a hundred years of brigandage and instability, Nupe's military might was finally downgraded in many fronts, especially in the Moshi-Niger area and in the north central, northwestern, and central Yorùbá regions. The militants were expelled from the Èkìtì-Ìgbómìnà-Okun area during the third quarter of the sixteenth century, and in the 1570s the Ọ̀yọ́ were able to reoccupy the area of their old core kingdom but not likely the old capital itself.[50] Both the course and the end of the Nupe militarist crisis had far-reaching impacts on the Yorùbá world, as we shall see in chapter 5. The war was costly in terms of the time it took to bring it to a close, the large-scale displacement, the human toll (number killed or displaced), the concomitant social breakdown, and the reliance on captives and enslavement to procure the military hardware—the Barbary horses—needed to prosecute the war.

The Nupe brigandage was the first crisis that provoked the mobilization and coordination of multiple polities in the Yorùbá community of practice against a common enemy, with several alliances fighting on different fronts. This coordination made sense, for the Nupe brigands did not discriminate about which groups among the Yorùbá they attacked or enslaved, and they used a common name for all the Yorùbá-speaking peoples—Eyagi or Yarbanci. Neither did the recipients of the enslaved Yorùbá in Western or Central Sudan distinguish among the various Yorùbá dialect groups—Ọ̀yọ́, Yàgbà, Ijùmú, Bunu, Èkìtì, or Ìgbómìnà—from whom captives were obtained. In fact, the Yorùbá captives formed a recognizable critical mass of the enslaved in the Sudan, to the extent that their Mandé, Berber, and Hausa hosts and masters identified them by a common name: Yorùbá. This name must have been used in the course of the sixteenth century, if not much earlier, although the earliest known written rendition dates to the early seventeenth century, when Berber-Songhai scholar Ahmad Baba al-Massufi (1556–1627) used the term in his book *Mizra* in 1615. There he classified the Yorùbá as among the West African sociolinguistic groups that could be legitimately enslaved because they were nonbelievers (non-Muslim).[51]

We can, therefore, trace the ethnonym Yorùbá to this gloomy Intermediate period. Phonetically, Yorùbá is a transliterated Songhai/Mandé adaption (in Arabic text) of Yàgbà, one of the largest and oldest Yorùbá subgroups, whose territory is contiguous to that of the Nupe and in whose territory the Nupe had the longest brigandage activities.[52] The spoken version in Songhai (and Mandé) languages may have been slightly different, but this ethnonym ultimately originated from the Nupe, whose name for the Yorùbá is Yarbanci. This is clearly an adaption of Yàgbà because in Nupe language there is the grammatical rule of adding the suffix *-ci* at the end of a noun to describe who a person or a group is. The suffix is an adjective. Hence, *-ci* means "the one who is," so that Yarbanci means "a person who is Yarba" or "a Yarba person." (The plural "Yarbanzi" means "Yarba people.")[53] The ethnonym Yorùbá is therefore not an autonomous Arabic, Songhai, Hausa, or Nupe word, whether written as Yariba, Uraba, Euroba, or Yarbanci, as some scholars have proposed.[54] Rather, both Songhai's Yorùbá and Nupe's Yarbanci derived from the ethnonym of the largest northeastern Yorùbá subgroup, the Yàgbà, with whom the Nupe had several centuries of interactions before the sixteenth century.[55] Given their small-scale segmentary sociopolitical system (House and mega-House polities), as well as their proximity to the centers of the Niger-Moshi and Niger-Benue Confluence troubles, the Yàgbà had been susceptible to military overruns from their northern neighbors since the fifteenth century. The largest of the five Okun-Yorùbá groups, they likely accounted for the majority of Yorùbá captives taken to the Sudan during the late fifteenth and sixteenth century. Their prominence in number and deep history in the confluence explains how they gave their name (in an adapted form) to the Yorùbá-speaking peoples.[56]

Prelude to the Atlantic Age

The Sudan was not the only magnetic pull for the Yorùbá during the fifteenth and sixteenth centuries. The second gravitational force during this period came in the opposite direction, in the form of the nascent Atlantic trade. At the very time that the cocktail of events that led to Nupe brigandage was being mixed, the trenches for the foundations of the Atlantic commerce were also being dug by the Portuguese, the pioneers of the European trading activities in Africa. The Portuguese made exploratory visits to the coastlands of the Bight of Benin in 1472, about the last year of Ewuare's reign, but they did not venture inland to visit the great king. It was not until 1480 that they began regular trading missions to the coastal communities of Itsekiri and Ijọ. Their primary purpose was to purchase captives in addition to a sundry of items—pepper, ivory, and tropical curios. The African gold traders at Costa de Mina (Elmina in modern Ghana), where the Portuguese had just established a lucrative trading post, preferred slaves as payment for their gold exports. Those slaves were used as sources of labor in the Akan gold fields. Meanwhile, the agricultural plantations being set up in the newly acquired Portuguese colony of Fernando Po also needed labor.

The Portuguese arrived in the Western delta at a time when the teeming villages and House polities occupying the creeks and swampy forests of the area were engaged in moietal conflict and competition over fishing and land rights.[57] The Portuguese interest in slaves and the handsome profits awaiting the sellers turned fishers and salt makers into kidnappers, raiding their neighboring communities for captives. On the first Portuguese trading mission to the Benin and Forcados Rivers in January 1480, "more than four hundred slaves" were reportedly purchased from Itsekiri and Ijọ traders, "most of whom were subsequently bartered for gold" in Costa de Mina.[58] Although the Itsekiri were the first Yoruboid group to have participated in the Atlantic trade, the effect of Portuguese presence was not felt on the mainland until the early seventeenth century. The militarist Nupe invasions preoccupied the attention of the core Yorùbá region, especially in the central and northern areas.

It was from the Ijọ and Itsekiri that the Portuguese heard about the city of Benin, eighty miles inland, but it was not until 1486 that the first Portuguese emissaries, led by João Afonso d'Aveiros, arrived in the city to explore trading opportunities with its monarch. He met Ọba Ozolua, who was well-disposed to establishing commercial relations with the Iberian traders. Hence, between 1487 and 1507, the Portuguese ran a trading post at Ughoton, one of Benin kingdom's coastal villages. By and large, this early Atlantic trade was marginal to the economic interests of Benin. The commerce was mainly between the king of Benin and the king of Portugal through their agents. It was estimated that fewer than 250 slaves were sold by the king of Benin annually to the Portuguese between 1487 and 1507. Benin exports also included *ṣẹ̀gi*, cotton cloth, ivory, and melegueta pepper. Of these, melegueta pepper was the chief export and the main source of profit for both the Benin and Portuguese crowns. During those early years, Benin-Portugal trade saw an unprecedented import of manillas into Benin. The other imports included Indian silk and Mediterranean glass beads. All these imports were elite goods trapped in the restricted sphere of personal adornment and chiefly distinctions. However, the profitability of the commerce was soon undercut by the larger supplies of pepper from the Indian subcontinent to the Portuguese market in the first decade of the sixteenth century. This development led to the official proscription of Benin pepper trade in Portugal in 1506. A year later, the king of Portugal shut down his Ughoton trading port. This decision, however, did not end the Benin-Portugal trade; it only transferred the king of Portugal's trading interests to private hands.[59]

The commercial relations between the two kingdoms grew following the lease of the Portuguese crown's trading rights in the Bight of Benin to privateers. A significant component of this growth was the massive export of cowries (the *Monetaria moneta* species) and manillas to Benin in the 1520s. Neither item was new to Benin. Copper alloy had been introduced to Benin, first through Ilé-Ifẹ̀ and later through the Moshi-Niger and Niger-Benue Confluence entrepôts. Cowries, imported from across the Sahara, were already reaching Benin through the Niger-Benue trading networks by the mid-fifteenth century, if not earlier.[60] Indeed, before the Portuguese import of cowries began in the 1490s, there was already a sufficient accumulation of them in Benin, to the extent that they were being used in market transactions to "buy everything," according to Duarte Pacheco Pereira, a contemporary Portuguese observer. He also noted that those who owned large stores of cowries were the richest.[61] Ewuare's opening of direct commercial channels with the River Niger entrepôts was most likely responsible for the infusion of Benin's market with these Indian Ocean shells. While the imported cowries were pushed into the market sphere, the use of copper alloys remained a strictly royal prerogative. This continued to be the case following the commencement of trade with the Portuguese, leading to a significant increase in the volume of copper-alloy import to Benin between 1487 and 1553. But it was the importation of cowrie shells that had an immediate impact on everyday lives. In 1526 alone, about 1.15 million cowrie shells were imported from the Maldives, compared to about 200,000 shells imported in 1522.[62]

Despite these lucrative commercial relations, Benin-Portugal trade had a checkered history. The unbearable length of time it often took the king's agents to obtain and gather the required export merchandise posed a challenge to Portuguese merchants. The delays cut back on profits and increased the Portuguese mortality rate due to prolonged exposure to both sea-induced sickness and tropical ailments. On top of these, the successive kings of Benin in the sixteenth century were unwilling to meet the rising Portuguese demand for slaves. It must have been a frustrating experience for Portuguese traders when in the early 1520s the Benin monarch embargoed the sale of men but allowed the sale of women.[63] However, it was male labor that the Portuguese needed on their São Tomé plantation and at their Elmina trading post for gold exchange. Hence, as late as 1526, Benin's supply of enslaved captives remained at the same level as it had been in the 1490s, despite the rising Portuguese demand. Throughout the first half of the sixteenth century, therefore, Benin-Portugal trade faltered, partly because of Benin's inability to meet the Portuguese demand for slaves and partly because of the long time it took to load Benin's supplies. Therefore, in 1553, the Portuguese traders decided to end commercial relations with the kingdom.[64] Before this decision, however, the Portuguese were already exploring and engaging with alternative trading partners in the Bight of Benin. They first established direct trading contacts with the king of Ìjẹ̀bú-Òde sometime between 1500 and 1508 via the Ọ̀nà River.[65] On that first visit, the Portuguese traded copper and brass bracelets for slaves and elephant tusks.[66] The trade with the Ìjẹ̀bú continued afterward on the lagoon rather than on the mainland, and more trading agents other than the king were involved. By 1519, the cotton cloth of Ìjẹ̀bú manufacture had become a major export in the Bight of Benin. There is evidence that by 1530, if not before, Màhin also served as a Portuguese trading port where much Ìjẹ̀bú cloth was sold. There is no evidence of a direct trading link with the city of Ìjẹ̀bú-Òde or its king after 1508, but the breakdown of Portugal-Benin trade temporarily revived direct commercial contacts with Ìjẹ̀bú-Òde in 1553.

The proliferation of Portuguese commercial activities on the coast gave the Benin monarchs the impetus to embark on coastal expansion, first to secure their boundaries and second to control the trade. With their war canoes following in the wake of Portuguese ships, successive Benin monarchs made it clear that the refusal of the Iberian merchants to anchor in Ughoton would not deter them from dictating the terms of commerce on the coast.[67] After all, control of trade routes was generally more lucrative and profitable, through tolls, taxes, and other levies, than supplying the merchandise for those routes. Between 1575 and 1590, therefore, Benin established its littoral control as far as Lagos, where it set up a military base, and it may have maintained some control over Allada at the end of the century (see fig. 1.1).[68] Its camp in Lagos was placed strategically so its army could supervise all trading activities taking place on the lagoon and block the Europeans from having direct relations with Ìjẹ̀bú-Òde and other polities in the area. Thus, by 1603, Benin's military camp in Lagos had become a trading entrepôt, with many people coming to it "by water and land, with their wares," as recounted by Andreas Josua Ulsheimer, a German surgeon aboard a Dutch merchant ship. Chief among these wares were "beautiful cotton cloths woven in all kinds of colours and patterns." These would have come from the Ìjẹ̀bú area and other Yorùbá groups nearby, especially the Ẹ̀gbá, Àwórì, and Kétu. Elephant tusks and tails, as well as peppers, were among the commodities that also entered the Lagos commercial entrepot. Ulsheimer recognized that the people of Lagos and the surrounding areas, including the Benin and Ìjẹ̀bú kingdoms, did not care for gold or silver but wanted copper alloys. Of greater value were cowries, what he calls the "little snail-shells," which were used as money for buying "anything [that] one wants."[69] Because of the openness of Lagos to all traders and the security it offered, as well as the presence of the Portuguese and Dutch trading ships, a large volume of the southern Yorùbá commercial traffic was diverted to the entrepôt between 1590 and 1610.

In Lagos, as in Ughoton, the Portuguese did not secure the merchandise they needed the most: slaves. Therefore, they pushed farther west in their search for human cargo. They struck it lucky in the small kingdom of Allada. Starting in the 1590s, Allada was able to deliver far more slaves to the Portuguese ships than the much bigger Benin or Ìjẹ̀bú kingdoms could. Unlike in Ughoton, Màhin, Ìjẹ̀bú-Òde, and Lagos, whose exports were composed mainly of commodities, the principal export of Allada was slaves. As a result, the Portuguese trade with Allada was reckoned in 1607 "to be more valuable than that with Benin."[70] Nevertheless, the Allada commerce was partly sustained by the flow of cloth, ivory, and other commodities from the Yorùbá-speaking areas, ferried by canoes from across the lagoons and brought by porters across overland routes.

Summing Up

The economic collapse of Ilé-Ifẹ̀ and the associated political crisis set the stage for the atrophy of the Yorùbá community of practice during the early fifteenth century. The 150-year intense drought also began about that time. The episodes of famine, as well as the epidemic outbreaks associated with the multiyear drought episodes, compounded the political and economic problems. Conflict, displacement, and insecurity intensified, and these dragged on as a result of the external crises that also beset the region from ca. 1450 through 1570. The clouds of Nupe brigandage, which had its provenance in a wider regional instability that originated from the Sahel and the Sudan, hung over the Yorùbá region during that period. In other words, the Nupe militarists served as a conduit for bringing the political unrest of the Sahel-Sudan corridors to the doorsteps of the Yorùbá community of practice. The Nupe brigandage, and the horse-slave exchange between them and Hausaland, exacerbated the internal problems in the Yorùbá region. These external factors disrupted the ancient commercial routes that linked the Yorùbá hinterland with the Sudan, and they caused political collapse and population displacement in the northern and central parts of the Yorùbá world. With the sinking economic ship of Ilé-Ifẹ̀, the emporium's two chief clients and provinces—Ọ̀yọ́ and Benin—explored new alliances for their own economic survival, and this brought the two kingdoms closer together in commercial relations. However, the disruptive economy of slave raiding spearheaded by the mounted Nupe brigands gained the upper hand, halted the rising economic and political profile of Ọ̀yọ́ in the early sixteenth century, and culminated in the abandonment of the capital of the old Ọ̀yọ́ kingdom, somewhere near the River Niger. The Nupe brigandage also penetrated deep into Yorùbá country, and this led to the collapse of many population centers in Yàgbà, Ìgbómìnà, Ìbòlò, and Èkìtì. It would take wide-ranging strategies of regional alliances, by the Ọ̀yọ́ in northwest Yorùbá and the Benin-Èkìtì-Ifẹ̀ in central Yorùbá, to push the Nupe back, to the other side of the River Niger. But the nearly one hundred years of Nupe brigandage had a long-lasting effect on the region.

The number of Yorùbá entering the Sudan as agricultural, mining, manufacturing, and domestic laborers or being shipped across the Sahara to North Africa must have steadily risen between 1450 and 1550. By the turn of the sixteenth century, if not much earlier, the ethnonym Yorùbá, a name that was adapted from Yàgbà, had gained currency across the Western and Central Sudan. It appears that while the other parts of the Yorùbá world were in turmoil, the southern parts of the region, especially the band of rain forest that stretched from Ọ̀wọ and Benin in the east to Ìjẹ̀bú and Ẹ̀gbá in the west were stable and prospering. During this period, Benin became the most powerful kingdom in the rain forest belt. Ọ̀wọ̀ also recovered much earlier than many other kingdoms. It clashed with Benin on a number of occasions, but the two later worked out a truce in which Ọ̀wọ̀ recognized Benin's suzerainty. The region of Ìjẹ̀bú was blossoming, while its immediate neighbors to the north faced uncertainty. The oral traditions suggest that the Ìjẹ̀bú area received large influxes of migrants from the area of Ilé-Ifẹ̀ and other parts of central Yorùbá during the peak of the crisis in the fifteenth century.[71] Such migrations originated from the hot spots of disturbances, as demonstrated in the names that some of their descendants bear today, such as Ìjẹ̀bú-Ifẹ̀ and Ìjẹ̀bú-Òwu. Archaeological findings have shown that the economy of the Ìjẹ̀bú area had a strong foothold in iron production during this period. More than five hundred iron-smelting furnaces have been reported in the Ìmẹ̀rí area, east of Ìjẹ̀bú-Ode, all within a three-kilometer radius (see fig. 1.1).[72] This is the largest concentration of iron production so far known in the Yorùbá region. A radiocarbon date of ca. 1435–1610, obtained from one of the excavated furnaces, shows that massive ironworking was going on in this area at the peak of the regional crisis that engulfed the other parts of the Yorùbá world. The Ìjẹ̀bú area was also famous for its cotton cloth production. It was a major export commodity during the early phase of the Atlantic trade in the Bight of Benin, but it must have also played an important role in the regional and inter-lagoon trade before the arrival of European traders.

Shortly after the Nupe horsemen started dashing across the River Niger for slave raiding in the Yorùbá world, the Portuguese also began to cruise the lapping waves of the Yorùbá coastland. Hence, at the very time that the northern, central, and eastern parts of the Yorùbá community of practice were fighting to repel the Nupe militants and contain other sources of instability, the southern areas of the region were becoming entangled in the web of early modern commerce. Of these two developments, the Nupe militarists were far more demanding of the attention of the region than the presence of the Portuguese, and of the Dutch and English who followed them. However, both the Nupe crisis and European commerce were connected to the external demands for slave labor. Whereas the Nupe sought to enslave via pillaging, the Portuguese made efforts to procure slaves through the existing sociopolitical and commercial channels. However, what the Yorùbá world, including Benin, was willing to supply was far below what the Portuguese desired. The coastal communities and their immediate neighbors on the mainland were more interested in the exports of local manufactures and products—cotton cloth, dyestuff, and ivory—than in slave trading. It was through Benin and later Ìjẹ̀bú-Òde that the Yorùbá community of practice would slowly become involved in the Atlantic trade in the early sixteenth century. Of the two, only Benin was preoccupied with the northern (Nupe and Igala) military affairs. Yet Benin played the most significant and dominant role in shaping the evolution of the Atlantic experience for the Yorùbá community of practice. Its actions, including what it did and refused to do, narrowed the choices available to the pioneering European trading nations—Portugal, England, and the Netherlands. The choices made by Benin also defined the pace and extent of the southern Yorùbá involvement in the new commercial opportunities that opened up on the coast.

Over the next hundred years, the Yorùbá world was gradually pulled into the orbit of the Atlantic trade through four major trading centers—Ughoton (Benin), Màhin, Èkó (Lagos), and Allada—unevenly distributed along the four-hundred-kilometer coastline (see fig. 1.1). Through these outlets, not only did the Yorùbá region in the rain forest belt sell their ivory, woven cloth, pepper, and indigo directly and indirectly to European merchants, but a number of them also entered the trade as commodities, mainly as prisoners of war, as convicts, and as tributes to states such as Benin and Ìjẹ̀bú-Òde.[73]

It would not be until the end of the Nupe wars, however, that the northern and central Yorùbá mainland began to take a more active interest in the coastal trade. What was once a cultural backwater, and a cul-de-sac, was now becoming a great emporium and an outlet to the wider world. Before the Yorùbá mainland could take advantage of this new frontier of commerce, however, it first had to recover from the atrophy of the Intermediate period and put its house in order. The strategies and processes of that recovery and the impacts on political and cultural transformations of the region will be examined in the next chapter.

Notes

1. Drewal, Pemberton, and Abiodun, *Yoruba*, 234. The Yorùbá intellectuals here are those who use indigenous epistemology as their reference points.

2. Styhre, "Knowledge-Intensive Company," 232.

3. Egharevba, *Twelve Works*, 37.

4. The large volume of Ifẹ̀ glass beads in circulation across West Africa between 1480 and 1500, after their production had declined or ended in Ilé-Ifẹ̀, indicates the massive amount that was produced between 1100 and 1400 (see chap. 2). For example, European accounts of the late fifteenth and early sixteenth century testify to the high demand for Ifẹ̀ blue glass beads throughout the Atlantic littorals as far as the Gold Coast and Central Africa, where they were valued for spiritual, healing, and aesthetic reasons (Euba, "Of Blue and Red," 120; Ryder, *Benin and the Europeans*, 37). And this demand continued into the late seventeenth century on the Gold Coast, where Willem Bosman traded for fourteen years. Of these beads he wrote: "A sort of blew [*sic*] coral, which we call *Agrie*, and the Negroes *Accorri*, which . . . is so much valued, that 'tis generally weighed against Gold." (*New and Accurate Description*, 119). Here, the Dutch merchant was referring to *ṣẹ̀gi*.

5. Ọbalùfọ̀n II is said to have lived very long—hence his nickname, *ògbóg-bódinrin* ("as old as iron"). Chief Ọláolú Ọládọ̀tun Ôkánlàwọ̀n Dàda, June 22, 2015; Chief Ọlájídé Fárótìmí Fálọ̀ba, Ọbadio of Ifẹ̀, July 15, 2015. Also see Olaniyan and Akinjogbin, "Sources," 40.

6. Glubb, *Fate of Empires*; Higgins, *Economic Growth and Sustainability*

7. Horton, "Economy of Ife," 135.

8. Horton, 135.

9. Geomorphologic, isotopic, and geochemical study of the sediments of Lake Bosumtwi, Ghana (Shanahan et al., "Atlantic Forcing of Persistent

Drought") shows the long patterns of precipitation fluctuations in West Africa over the past three thousand years, including the three-century-long (1450–1750) spike in severe and persistent droughts. Paleobotanical studies in central Ghana have also confirmed these intense drought activities during the fifteenth and sixteenth centuries (Logan and Stahl, "Genealogies of Practice"). Oral traditions in Ọ̀ṣogbo and Ìgbómìnà make references to these episodes of drought. See Horton, "Economy of Ife," 135; Ogundiran, "Making of an Internal Frontier," 1; Pemberton and Afọlayan, *Yoruba Sacred Kingship*, 50. For other historical sources in West Africa about this period of intense drought, see Brooks, *Landlords and Strangers*.

10. Akinjogbin, "Towards a Political Geography."

11. Chief Ọlájídé Fárótìmí Fálọba, July 16, 2015.

12. Until its eradication in the twentieth century, smallpox was endemic all over the world. Before then, no disease was as dreadful as smallpox among the Yorùbá. Once it "arrived in a virgin community," according to Donald R. Hopkins (*Greatest Killer*, 8), "the virus never disappeared entirely . . . going from one susceptible person to another and erupting into epidemics every five to fifteen years or so, when enough susceptible persons had accumulated." Hence, of all the contagious diseases, it was the one that reoccurred most regularly but with unpredictable suddenness. Its high rate of infection and propensity to spread and kill swiftly made it the most disruptive of all contagions. The seasonality of its prevalence, the height of the dry season (January–February) in the tropics, also made it an opportunistic killer, because it attacked its victims at the time they were most vulnerable—when they had low food and low water supplies. Because of its indiscriminate attack, killing both the rich and the poor, the powerful and the weak, the Yoruba created a patron deity for the disease and regarded the deity as the "king of kings." Hence the name Ọbalúayé, "the king who is lord of the world," or Babalúayé, "the father who is the lord of the earth" (Idowu, *Olódùmarè*, 99–101). Also called Ṣọ̀npọ̀ná, this deity of many names was believed to unleash smallpox outbreaks when offended and displeased, and retreat after he had been assuaged with sacrifices. The priests of Ọbalúayé/Ṣọ̀npọ̀ná presided over the management of the disease. They immunized people through inoculation, provided medical care for the afflicted, and conducted burial for those who died from the disease. These priests were also feared for their ability and know-how to unleash infection.

13. I am grateful to Chief Ọlájídé Fárótìmí Fálọba, July 16, 2015, for showing me and Prof. Àdìsá Ògúnfọlákàn this location.

14. The general area where the original palace and temple of Ọbalùfọ̀n II once stood, near Odùduwà grove, is now devoid of any ritual activity, and the original *ojúbọ* (shrine) is overgrown with brush.

15. I am grateful to Nurudeen Amuda-Arógundádé, graduate student, Department of History, Obafemi Awolowo University, Ilé-Ifẹ̀, July 3, 2014, for this aphorism. This practice of isolation demonstrates a sound knowledge about the contagious nature of the disease, the dynamics of its infection processes, and strategies for minimizing its human-to-human spread (inhalation of contaminated air through face-to-face contact with the afflicted person).

16. Unfortunately, the afflicted individuals without family support were also abandoned in the sacred grove to expire.

17. If this infection was indeed *Variola*, this would place Ọbalùfọ̀n II in the ranks of other great monarchs and nobles who succumbed to the disease over a period of about three thousand years: King Ramesses V of Egypt (d. 1145 BC), King Louis I of Spain (d. 1724), Tsar Peter II of Russia (d. 1730), King Louis XV of France (d. 1774), and Maximilian III Joseph, Elector of Bavaria (d. 1777), as well as several monarchs of the East, including two Qing emperors of China, Shunzhi (d. 1661) and Tongzhi (d. 1875), and two Japanese monarchs, Empress Kōken (d. 770) and Emperor Higashiyama of Japan (d. 1710). Wikipedia, "Deaths from Smallpox."

18. Some have speculated that several areas of West Africa, in different ecological zones, experienced population contraction in the fourteenth and fifteenth centuries because of the bubonic plague that spread from the Mediterranean world. Chouin, "Forests of Power and Memory," 641; Dueppen, "Archaeology of West Africa," 252. It is surprising that such a calamitous event has no resonance in either documentary or oral tradition sources in the Sahel, Sudan, and rain forest belt of West Africa. This is a topic that only systematic paleopathological and biomolecular studies of well-preserved skeletal remains can shed light on.

19. Garlake, "Excavations at Obalara's Land."

20. Ogundiran, "Chronology, Material Culture, and Pathways."

21. Ogundiran, "Factional Competition"; Pemberton and Afọlayan, *Yoruba Sacred Kingship*. Archaeological findings in northern Ijesa and Ìgbómìnà sites have corroborated some of these traditions. See Ogundiran, *Archaeology and History in Ìlàrè District*; Ogunfolakan, "Conflict, War, Displacement"; Usman, Aleru, and Alabi, "Sociopolitical Formation on the Yoruba Northern Frontier."

22. Pemberton and Afọlayan, *Yoruba Sacred Kingship*, 50.

23. Bradbury, "Chronological Problems," 284; Egharevba, *Short History*, 22–23; Ryder, *Benin and the Europeans*, 8–9.

24. This subject has been treated by R. E. Bradbury and A. F. C. Ryder, cited above. The suggestion that Ewuare usurped the throne is unpopular in recent Benin historiography, although no one denies his military background. For one of the latest sympathetic treatments of Ewuare in Benin history, see Aisien, *Ewuare*.

25. Olugbadehan, *Owo Kingdom*.

26. See Egharevba, *Short History*; Ryder, *Benin and the Europeans*.

27. For example, Ewuare "introduced the casting of commemorative heads and other large objects" made of the brass that he imported from across the River Niger (Ben-Amos, *Art of Benin*, 28).

28. This comprised at least five mega-Houses: Beni (the alpha House), Ebe, Ebagi, Batci, and Dibo. Adamu, "The Hausa and Their Neighbours," 283.

29. This cultural hybridity has persisted until the present day, and Ade Obayemi has noted its origins in pre-sixteenth-century migrations and interactions; see Obayemi, "History, Culture, Yoruba."

30. Some scholars have suggested that the capital of the Ọ̀yọ́ Kingdom during the mid-fifteenth century was closer to the Niger-Moshi area than the later imperial capital of Ọ̀yọ́-Ile (Law, *Oyo Empire*; Smith, *Kingdoms of the Yoruba*). My ongoing study in the metropolitan area of the empire supports this proposition.

31. Adekunle, *Politics and Society*.

32. Mansa Suleyman was an older brother of Mansa Musa. He reigned from 1341 to 1360, following the rule of Musa's son, Mansa Maghan (1337–41). Mansa Musa reigned between ca. 1312 and 1337.

33. Webb, "Desert Frontier."

34. Oliver and Atmore, *Medieval Africa*, 66–67. Some of the disturbances that unfolded in the Yorùbá world in the late fourteenth century, especially in the northern axis of Ifẹ̀ commercial networks, were a product of the political instability in the Western Sudan.

35. Lovejoy, "Role of the Wangara," 186.

36. Lovejoy, *Transformations in Slavery.*

37. Palmer, *Sudanese Memoirs*, vol. 3.

38. The people of Kanem-Bornu (elites) are in turn said to have started purchasing "large numbers of horses from Egypt during the fourteenth century," and they may have started breeding their own horses soon after that. Law, "Horses, Firearms, and Political Power," 119.

39. Nadel, *Black Byzantium*, 74.

40. Usman, "Crisis and Catastrophe."

41. For details on the strategies of cavalry warfare and brigandage, see Law, *Horse in West African History*; Fisher, "'He Swalloweth the Ground,'" parts 1 and 2.

42. For brief mentioning, see Akintoye, *History*, 143; Eyo, "Recent Excavations," 308; Oguntuyi, *Short History*; Usman, *Yoruba Frontier*, 102. The late fifteenth- and early sixteenth-century Nupe invasions in the north central and central Yoruba region tend to be confused with the late eighteenth- and early nineteenth-century Nupe attacks. This has led to historical telescoping in the oral traditions (e.g., Abiọla, Babafẹmi, and Ataiyero, *Iwe Itan Ijẹṣa*, 44–48; Olunlade, *Ede*, 2–3), which has been repeated in the academic history of Iléṣà and Ọ̀yọ́ (see Peel, "Kings, Titles, and Quarters," 141; Law, *Oyo Empire*, 38.

43. Ryder, *Benin and the Europeans*, 8–15.

44. Smith, "Alafin in Exile."

45. The descendants of some of these sixteenth-century Ìbàrìbá settlers in Ìgbòho, especially those who played important roles in the counterattacks against the Nupe, still hold chieftaincy titles in the town (Adekunle, *Politics and Society*, 43).

46. Kuba and Akinwumi, "Precolonial Borgu," 322.

47. Oliver and Atmore, *Medieval Africa*, 67.

48. It is most likely that Òwu as a cavalry state had relied on the Wasangari rulers for their own horse supply in previous centuries.

49. Akinjogbin, "Growth of Ifẹ̀," 112.

50. The 1570s date is based on the comparison of related contemporary events in Benin, Èkìtì, Nupe, Iléṣà, Ilé-Ifẹ̀, and the Ìlàrè district (see Akintoye, *History*; Egharevba, *Short History*; Ogundiran, *Archaeology and History in Ìlàrè District*; Peel, "Kings, Titles, and Quarters," I). Robin Law suggested ca. 1610 for the reoccupation of Old Ọ̀yọ́, on the basis of Robert Smith's arbitrary "method of calculating an average regnal length for the later Aláàfin and extrapolating this average back into the earlier period" (Law, *Oyo Empire*, 56; Smith, "Alafin in Exile," 72–74). This method of establishing regnal years is creative, but it is grossly misleading (for a critique, see Agiri, "Early Ọ̀yọ́ History,"16).

51. Law, "Ethnicity and the Slave Trade," 206. As Paul Lovejoy has effectively argued, the ethnonym in its origin did not originally refer to the Ọ̀yọ́ subgroup only but to all Yorùbá-speaking peoples. See Lovejoy, "Ethnic Designations"; Lovejoy, "Yoruba Factor."

52. Here, the /gb/ sound, a voiced labial-velar stop, in Yagba is replaced with the voiced bilabial stop of /b/ so that Ya-gba becomes Ya-ba.

53. Compare the two syllables Ya-gba with those of Ya-ban. By the same token, the Nupe refer to themselves in the singular as a Nupeci and collectively as Nupezi.

54. Law, "Ethnicity and the Slave Trade," 206.

55. For the effects of Nupe-Yoruba interactions on their respective cultures, see Nadel, *Black Byzantium*, 82, 211–13; also Obayemi, "Cultural Evolution, II."

56. It is also important to note that about half a century before Ahmad Baba Massufi wrote the term "Yoruba" in the early seventeenth century, Europeans were referring to the Yoruba phonetically as Lukumi. The first known trace of the term in written documents is dated to 1547, when two slaves on an estate in Hispaniola (Santo Domingo) were referred to as Lucume (Thornton, *Africa and Africans*, 112, 198). This term would become the dominant ethnonym for the Yoruba in the New World, especially in Cuba. Lucumi, Lukumi, Ulkami, and Ulkuma, among others, appear profusely in the European records of the seventeenth and eighteenth centuries (Law, "Ethnicity and the Slave Trade," 209). All of these terms are transliterations of *o-lù-kú-mi*, the term that peoples of north central (Yàgbà, Bunu, Ijùmú, Oworo) and central eastern Yorùbá (especially Èkìtì), among other groups, used for greetings. This term is usually translated as "my companion" or "my friend" but it could also mean a "wish for long life." Not only would this mean that Yàgbà lent its name (at least phonetically) to the coinage of the Yorùbá or Yarbanci ethnonym, but the cultural universe of Yàgbà and Èkìtì, two dominant groups in the north central and central eastern axis of the Yorùbá-speaking world, also lent the vocabulary of their greeting to the coinage of the Yorùbá ethnonym via the coast. A derivative and shorter version of *o-lù-kú-mi* prevailed among the northwestern Yoruba (Ọ̀yọ́) form of greeting as *ẹ kú* (meaning "may you live long"). And the ethnonym for the liberated Yorùbá-speaking population in Sierra Leone during the nineteenth century, Aku, also derived from this greeting (*ẹ kú*) because the majority of the dislocated Yorùbá there were of Ọ̀yọ́ subgroup (see chap. 9).

57. Alagoa, *History of the Niger Delta*; Moore, *History of Itsekiri.*

58. Ryder, *Benin and the Europeans*, 26.

59. For details, see Ryder, *Benin and the Europeans.*

60. Mansa Musa, during his pilgrimage to Mecca (AD 1324–25), reportedly told his hosts in Egypt that cowries were the chief currency of the Western Sudan and that "the merchants, whose principal import these are, make big profits on them" (Levtzion and Hopkins, *Corpus*, 269). Several baskets of cowries and two thousand copper and brass rods were included in the cache of merchandise that French archaeologist Théodore Monod excavated in the Sahara in the 1960s. The merchandise, neatly buried in the hot sand of Maʿdin Ijāfin in present-day northern Mauritania, was destined for the Western Sudan market and may have been abandoned because of death or loss of the caravan to sandstorm, robbery, or other calamity. It was estimated

that the merchandise was five to six camel loads, each weighing 180–200 kg (Lydon, *On Trans-Saharan Trails*, 74).

61. Pereira, *Esmeraldo*, 145.

62. Ryder, *Benin and the Europeans*, 63. This calculation is based on Jan Hogendorn's estimate of 20,000 cowries per head load ("Slaves as Money," 58).Throughout the 1520s, cowries and manillas were the chief means of payment for Benin's exports. In 1526, the pilots of São Miguel paid as much as 6,500 cowries for a slave, while an average of 19.5 manillas were used to purchase one elephant tusk (Ryder, *Benin and the Europeans*, 21).

63. The sale of men was allowed by the special permission of the king, but this was rarely granted. The decision to embargo the sale of men must have resulted from the competing needs for male labor domestically, as well as the reality that females accounted for the majority of war captives from Benin's military campaigns.

64. Following the departure of the Portuguese, the English and Dutch established trading posts in Ughoton, attracted by the profits that could be made from Benin's export of pepper and ivory. The Benin-English trade, however, was sporadic between 1553 and 1591. The last of these trading missions during the sixteenth century took place in 1591, midway into the reign of Ehengbuda, the hero of Benin's victory over the Nupe and the annexing of several Èkìtì territories. Between January 10 and April 27, 1591, the English ship *Richard of Arundell* acquired "589 serons of pepper, 150 tusks and 32 barrels of palm oil," in addition to sundry manufactured curios (Ryder, *Benin and the Europeans*, 84). The Dutch would take the position of the English in 1593, bringing with them "brass and copper manillas, beads, Silesian cloth, red, yellow, and blue Kerseys, brandy and wine" in exchange for Benin's pepper, cotton cloths, glass beads, and ivory (Ryder, *Benin and the Europeans*, 86).

65. Law, "Early European Sources," 246.

66. Pereira, *Esmeraldo*, 124.

67. Law, "Trade and Politics," 348.

68. The Benin oral traditions claim that Ehengbuda shifted the attention of his expansionist agenda to the littorals, and he personally led military operations as far as Lagos. He had an accident during one of those military operations and drowned in the lagoon. This development led to a change in policy whereby Benin kings were forbidden to lead wars, thus ending about 150 years of Benin's warrior-king tradition (Egharevba, *Short History*, 34).

69. Jones, *German Sources*, 41.

70. Law, "Trade and Politics," 335.

71. Okùbọ̀tẹ̀, *Ìwé Ìtàn Ìjẹ̀bú.*

72. Dr. Olúṣẹ́gun Ọ̀pádèjì, Ibadan, June 5, 2016. I visited a number of these iron-smelting sites at Ìmẹ̀rí and Odò Olóko, with the assistance of Olúṣẹ́gun Moyib, on May 28–29, 2016.

73. For details, see Law, *Slave Coast*; Ryder, *Benin and the Europeans.*

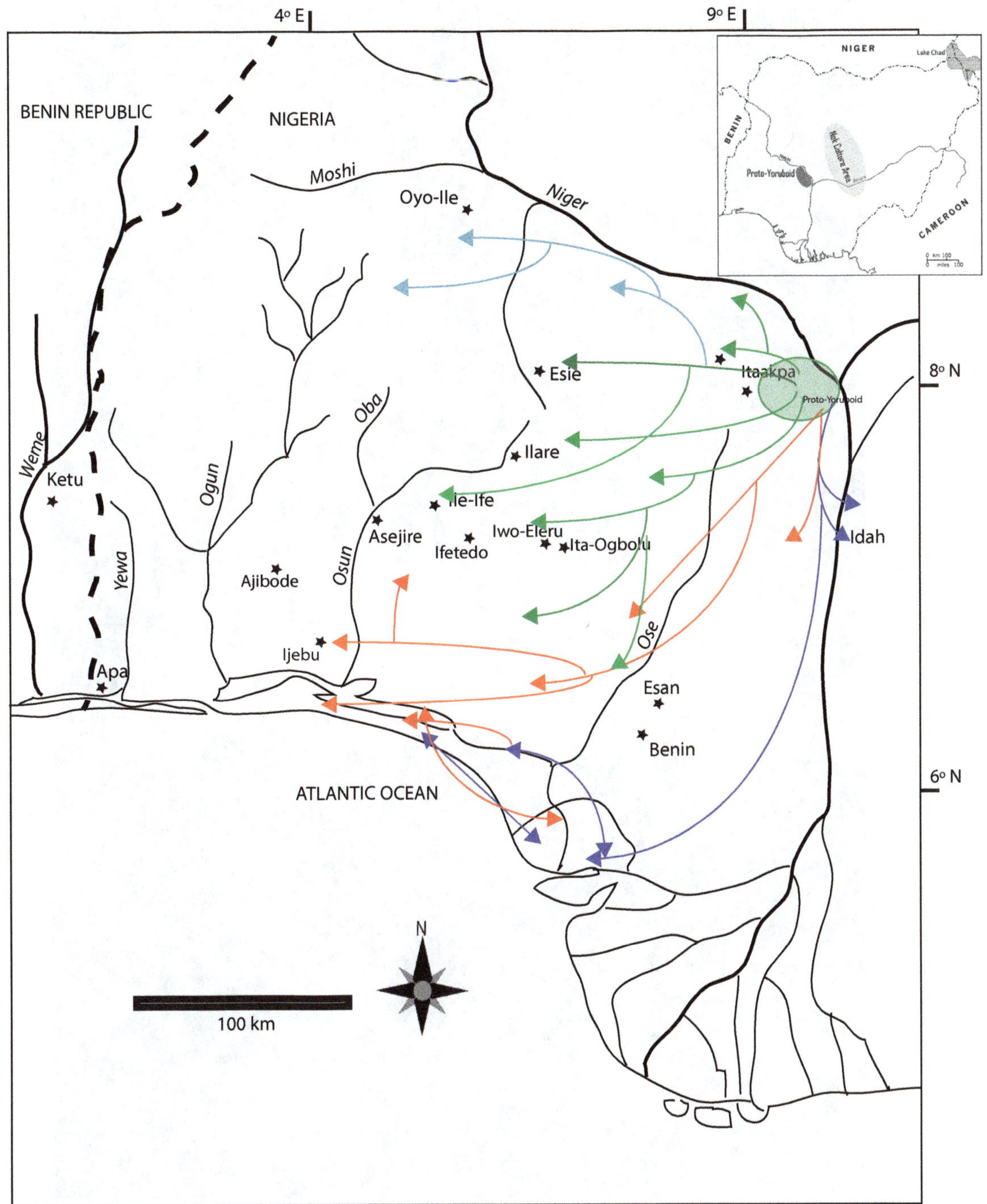

Plate 1. Late Stone Age sites (*) and schematic model of proto-Yoruboid/Yorùbá expansion, ca. 100 BC–500 AD

Plate 2. Brass male-female figure at Ìta Yemòo (14th century, H. 19 cm), National Museum, Ilé-Ifẹ̀

Plate 3. Classical-period figures: terracotta, Ilé-Ifẹ̀ [a–d]; brass, Ilé-Ifẹ̀ [e–g]; terracotta fragment, Early Òṣogbo [h]

a. Aje ileke [Ile-Ife]

b. carnelian/jasper beads

c. partially-worked jasper (two sides) [Oyo-Ile]

e. segi [Ile-Ife]

g. fragment of glass-making crucible [Early Osogbo]

f. iyun [Ile-Ife]

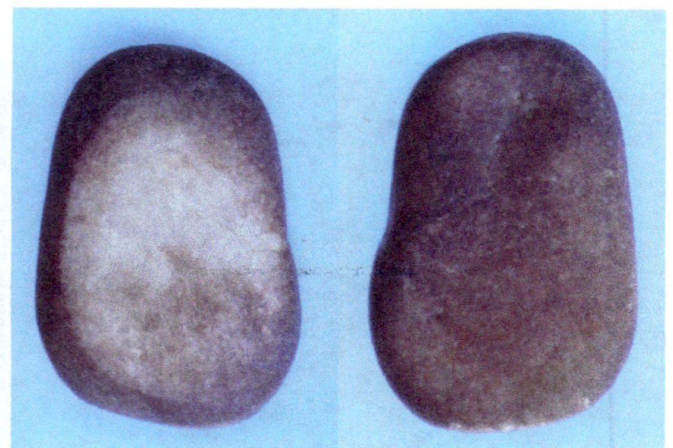

d. bead polishing stone (two sides) [Oyo-Ile]

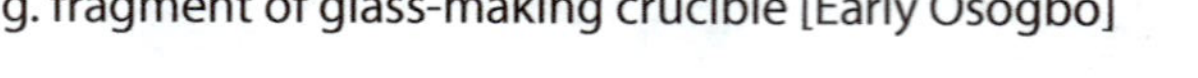

Plate 4. Bead-related artifacts *(The carnelian/jasper beads were excavated from the site of Birnin Lafiya, northern Benin Republic, courtesy of Dr. Anne Haour. The ṣẹgi and iyùn beads came from Ilé-Ifẹ̀, courtesy of Dr. Akinlolu Ige.)*

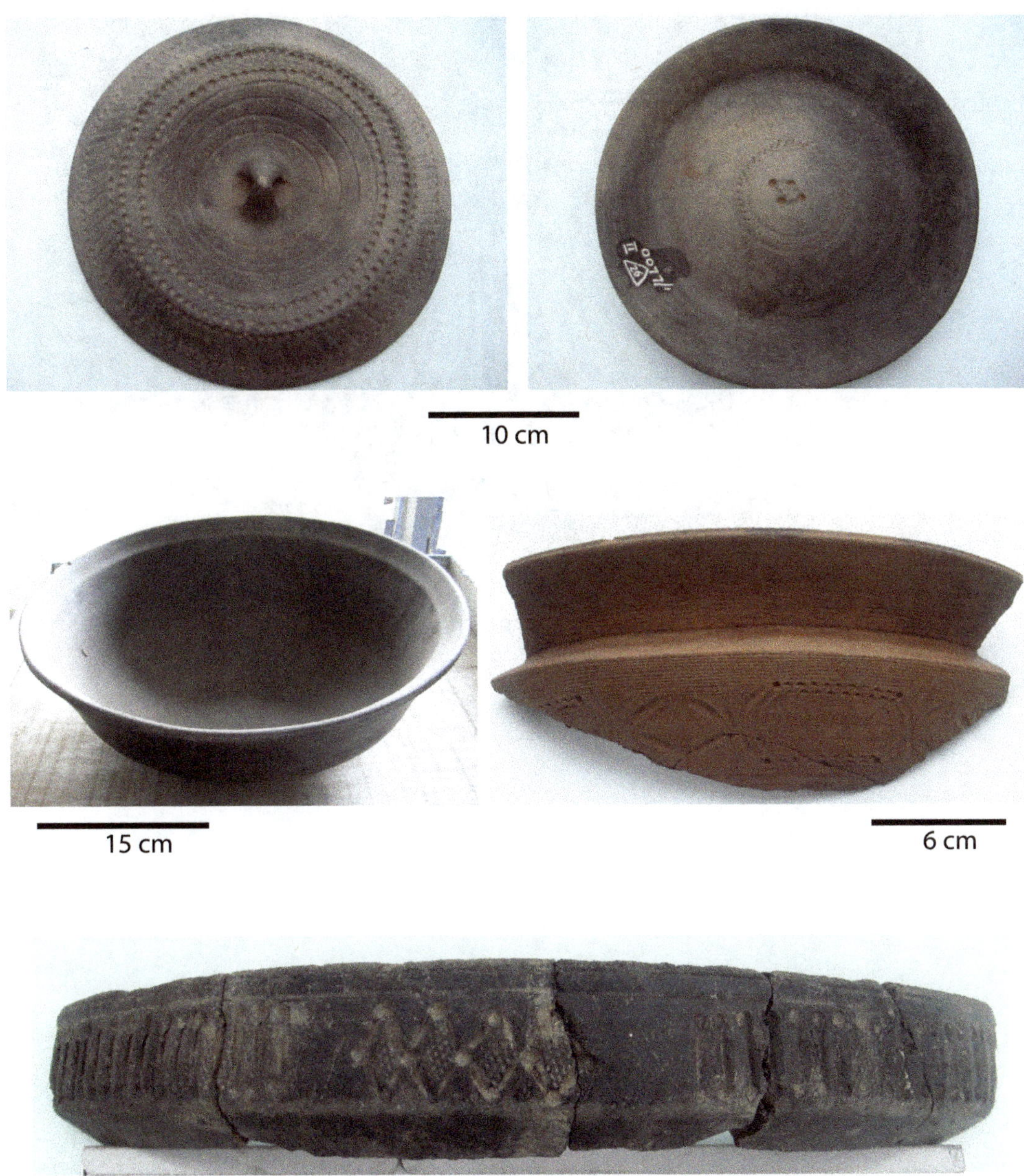

Plate 5. Varieties of Ọ̀yọ́ earthenware

Plate 6. Gbárìyẹ̀-onígba-awẹ́ garment (reproduced with the permission of Professor Rowland Abiodun)

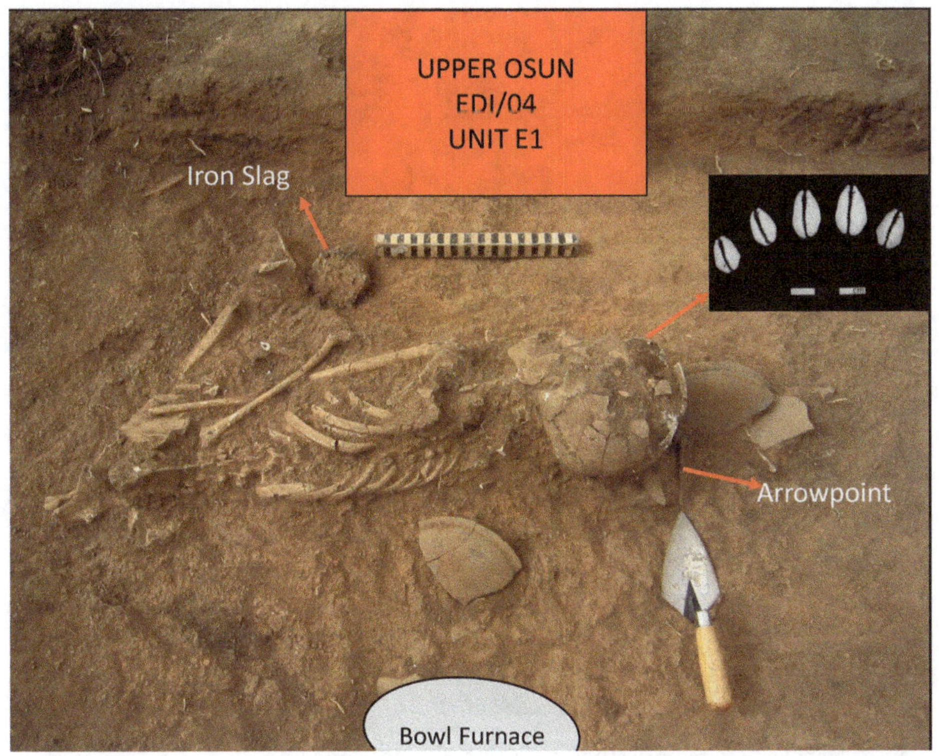

Plate 7. Skeletal remains of Alágbẹ̀dẹ, Ẹdẹ-Ilé, ca. 1650–1830

Plate 8. Female-centered priesthood of Ọ̀ṣun, Òṣogbo, 2004

5

Regeneration and Restoration

THE SCOURGE OF NUPE BRIGANDAGE declined after 1550 and seemed to have ended by 1560–70, but the crisis that the brigands had taken advantage of was still there. The vast political vacuum created by the collapse of Ifẹ̀ Empire in the early fifteenth century was yet to be filled, especially in the central and northern areas of the Yorùbá region. Therefore, the immediate task confronting the forces who downgraded and eventually expelled the Nupe brigands was to fill this vacuum. The individuals who set about this task were of three kinds. Some were committed to returning to and repairing the homes from which they or their ancestors had been displaced; others were interested in building new homes elsewhere; and then there were individuals whose reputation as war heroes gave them the confidence and aspiration to create and rule large polities from the fragmented communities that had survived the century-and-a-half-long crisis. Lasting from about 1570 through 1650, this era of regeneration and restoration resulted in the creation of a new society.

With the removal of the threat of the Nupe militarists, there were vast territories to stabilize, new trade routes and interregional market centers to access or control, and new political boundaries to establish, especially in the northern and central areas of the Yorùbá world. The instability had lasted for more than four generations, as a result of which several thousands of people were displaced, hundreds of polities collapsed, and the Classical-era political geography was destroyed. Rebuilding the old battered polities or creating new ones required the recruitment of people and diversification of the strength, skill sets, and specializations of their population groups. The challenges of regeneration ahead would require dagger and diplomacy in the competitive struggle to redraw the region's political map. Those who rose up to the challenges were some of the most daring warrior-kings and sagacious political entrepreneurs in Yorùbá history. They were usually men of charisma who wielded both swords and wits. They were also skillful intellectuals who created new mythologies and rituals to mask the scars of conquest they were inflicting on others and to legitimize the new regional hierarchies they were creating. Those years of regeneration and restoration were therefore defined not by peace but by a new wave of military actions tied to territorial power politics and the creation of a new social order. The end of the Nupe crisis brought a new wave of hardship for the western Èkìtì, southern Ìgbómìnà, and Upper Ọ̀ṣun areas far more than any other areas of the Yorùbá community of practice (fig. 5.1). These areas used to be part of the vast northern suburb and provinces of Ifẹ̀ metropolitan area, comprising hundreds of small towns, villages, and kingdoms whose economy, culture, and politics were intimately tied to those of the Classical city. The instability created by Ifẹ̀'s collapse was acutely felt in this area more than in any other part of the Yorùbá region. Many communities and polities in the area had mobilized soldiers to the battlefronts in the Èkìtì heartland, where the decisive defeat of the Nupe militarists took place during the third quarter of the sixteenth century. At the end of the wars against the Nupe, the strongmen of the victorious coalitions treated the beleaguered Ifẹ̀ suburbs as a spoil of war in the fierce struggle among themselves to establish political stability, for self-preservation, and sometimes for opportunistic power grabbing.

Although warrior-kings were the major actors during this period, others with less dramatic powers also mobilized their agentive resources from below and made indelible marks on the Yorùbá political topography. Traders, hunters, and frontier migrants were among these latter agents of change. Most sought to take advantage of the commercial opportunities on the coast, as the expanding commercial networks across the Atlantic Ocean increased the volume of trade in the Bight of Benin.[1] The coastal economic opportunities shaped the domestic policies and territorial ambitions of most of those political scions of the Restoration era. By the time the process of regeneration was completed in 1650, the region's political map had been redrawn and the building blocks for a new economic regime were in place. The new institutions, practices, and worldviews that evolved from the militarist and hegemonic power politics of the period were also maturing. By then, the regional political economy and regime of value were no longer revolving around Ilé-Ifẹ̀, and the Classical age had now receded into the dim memory. It was remarkable that the Yorùbá community of practice that was on the brink of falling apart in the

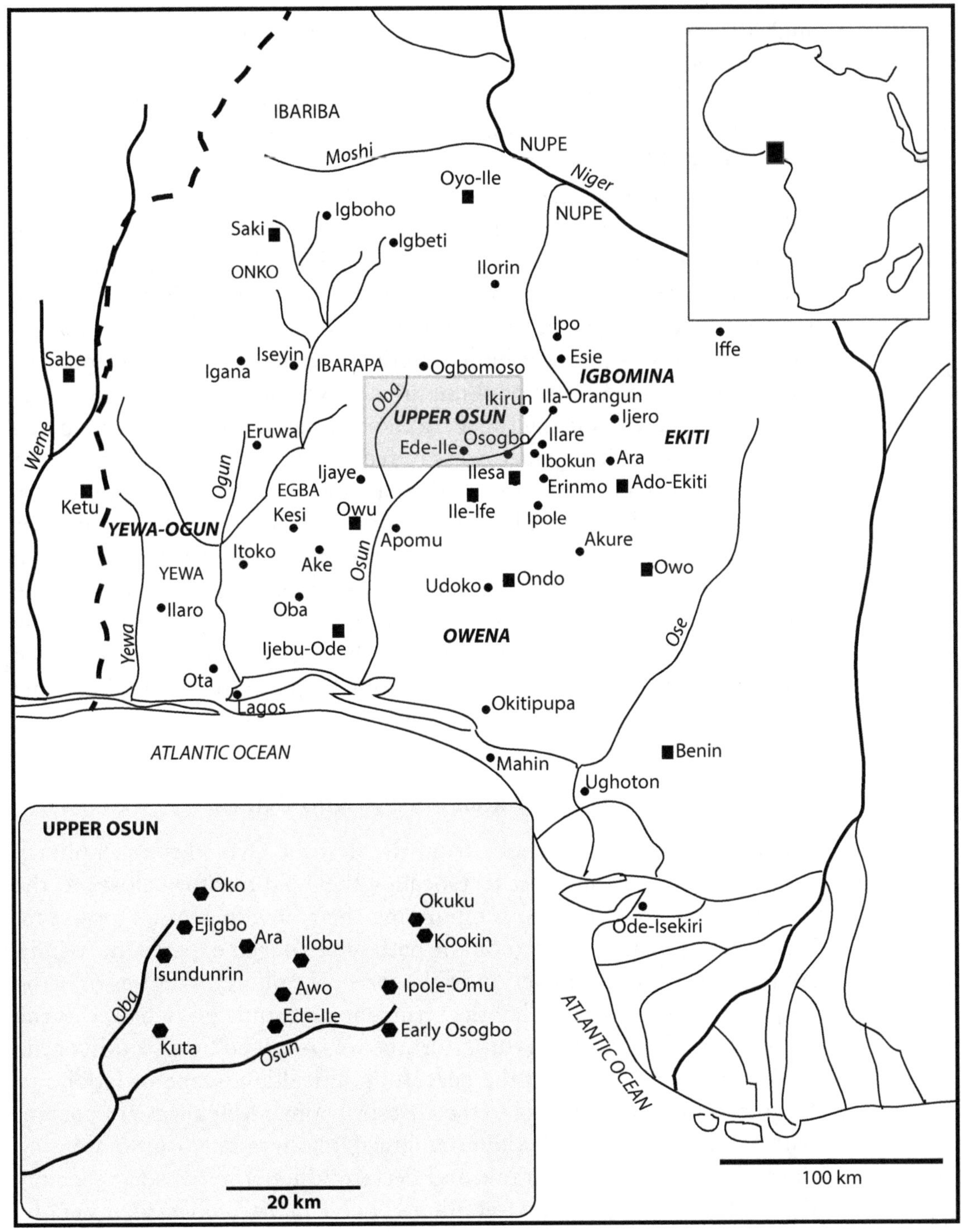

Figure 5.1. Major political units and three frontier zones in Yorùbá region, ca. 1630

mid-fifteenth century was on the path of regeneration in the 1570s. By the second quarter of the seventeenth century, it was far more integrated and even larger in size than ever before. The processes of this regeneration, the reasons for its success, and its political and cultural consequences are the focus of this chapter.

Two political juggernauts—Ọ̀yọ́ and Benin—feature prominently in this story of rejuvenation, although the latter entered political hibernation during the second half of the Restoration period. These two did not, however, rearrange the political landscape all by themselves. There were other significant actors. The most prominent of them was in fact a brand-new kingdom—Ilésà—that was built directly on what used to be the northern suburb of Ifẹ̀ greater metropolitan area. It was one of several new kingdoms that emerged during this period of regeneration, but it contributed more than any of its upstart peers in redrawing the political map of the region between 1570 and 1650. We shall start with what the post-Nupe militarism and the political vacuum created by the collapse of Ifẹ̀ Empire meant for Ọ̀yọ́ and Benin; then turn to the aftermath of these troubles in the Ifẹ̀-Èkìtì axis where Iléṣà kingdom was established. We will also take a look at the frontier politics that evolved during this period, especially the role of frontiersmen and women in shaping the political map of the Yorùbá world. We will conclude with some of the cultural and theogonic transformations that defined this period of recovery.

State Builders I: Ọ̀yọ́ and Benin

The removal of Nupe's thorn from the flesh of Ọ̀yọ́ (through military victories) allowed the latter to reoccupy their old territory closer to the Moshi-Niger area and begin rebuilding their kingdom, ca. 1570–1590. Those victories also set Ọ̀yọ́ on the path of territorial expansion. Aláàfin Abípa achieved the completion of the series of military victories over the Nupe. He also vigorously led the return-home campaign, which was the centerpiece of his reign. In this effort, he was opposed by a section of the Ọ̀yọ́ nobles who preferred the peaceful political landscape of Ìgbòho to the uncertainty of returning to the ancestral home. Abípa was not content with merely degrading the Nupe militarily; he was bent on dominating them. The only way to do this and declare full victory was to reoccupy the land of his ancestors. After all, *a kì í gba àkàtà lọ́wọ́ akítì, a kì í gba ilé baba ẹni lọ̀wọ́ ẹni*: "one cannot deprive the monkey of its agility, no one should be deprived of his or her inheritance." Abípa possibly reasoned that if the core area of the old Ọ̀yọ́ kingdom was left unoccupied, Ìgbòho itself would not be safe in the long run. Against the advice of some of his chieftains, Abípa sought military assistance from the leading Ọ̀yọ́ and Ìbàrìbá warriors resident in Ìgbòho who had fought with him for the liberation of the Moshi-Niger area. Traditions remember Alépatà, Boni, Igiisubu, Loko, Gbandan, and Alomo as among the brave men of Ìbàrìbá extraction who joined Abípa and other Ọ̀yọ́ pro-returnists in accomplishing the feat of reoccupying the territory of the old kingdom.[2] The *aláàfin* selected the southernmost part of the old kingdom as his new capital. There is archaeological evidence that a network of small farming (and possibly pastoralist) communities, belonging to what I have called Atòkúta culture, existed in this area between the thirteenth and mid-sixteenth century, if not earlier. But it is not yet clear what relationships these pre-empire communities had with the late sixteenth-century Ọ̀yọ́ settlers, if any.[3] Ancestral links to the land may have been a consideration, but security and good soil appear to be the overriding factors in the choice of this area as the capital of the reconstituted Ọ̀yọ́ polity. The towering inselbergs of this area, what became the metropolis of Ọ̀yọ́-Ilé, provided a natural defense. The vast landscape of sandy, ferruginous clay and decomposed migmatite soils provided opportunities for diversified agriculture and animal grazing. And the runoffs and streams rolling down the hills would have reassured the founders of the new capital of a dependable water supply. Wells and reservoirs were also dug to supplement the water supply during the dry season. Abípa's determination to relocate the seat of his government closer to the old capital was part of the grand objective to secure Ọ̀yọ́'s boundaries against any future Nupe intrusion; recapture the trading routes linking the Moshi-Niger to the Central Sudanese and Western Sudanese market, important sources for Ọ̀yọ́'s horses; and launch an expansionist military agenda that would bring a vast tributary area under Ọ̀yọ́'s control.

With the defeat of the Nupe brigands, Ọ̀yọ́ emerged as the dominant state in the Yorùbá savanna. Abípa and his chieftains immediately began using their newly acquired military hardware—horses—to launch a swift expansion across the entire northern Yorùbá region. His successor, Ọbalókun, maintained the momentum. One of the most celebrated warrior-kings in Ọ̀yọ́ history, Ọbalókun used the restless spirit of his soldiers to accelerate Ọ̀yọ́'s expansionist campaigns during the 1590s and the first decade of the seventeenth century, fighting wars in many directions: in Ìgbómìnà, east central Èkìtì, Upper Ọ̀ṣun, Ẹ̀gbá, and the Yéwá-Ògùn area. He also engaged in skirmishes in Òwẹ̀nà (see fig. 5.1). He completed the process of transforming Ọ̀yọ́'s cavalry from defensive to offensive force and laid a comprehensive framework for Ọ̀yọ́'s imperial ambitions, even if his equestrian forays sometimes had to deal with many detours, as well as trial and error. His forays farther afield from the Ọ̀yọ́ metropolis were daring and unprecedented, given the different ecological zones his men traveled, ranging from the open savanna to the thick rain forest. His expansionist drive earned him the sobriquet *aágànná erin*, "the plundering elephant."[4] His name, Ọbalókun ("King of the Ocean"), reveals the central place the Atlantic coastal market occupied in his expansionist agenda. He penetrated the rain forest in his march toward the coast, but he had mixed results. Because of his relentless ambition, however, the limitations and possibilities of Ọ̀yọ́'s cavalry were tested under his rule. These provided his successors with better insights into the effective military and diplomatic strategies to use for their expansionist drive. Ọbalókun's military projects recorded both success and failure, but overall his reign witnessed a significant increase in Ọ̀yọ́-controlled territory.

Ọbalókun and his successors, especially Àjàgbó, did not look only southward for new territories. The collapse of the Songhai Empire following the Moroccan invasion of 1591 also offered prospects for Ọ̀yọ́'s northward expansion. They took advantage of the instability that followed the withdrawal of Songhai. The former apprentice in cavalry warfare had now become a master. The Ọ̀yọ́ forces penetrated deep into the Ìbàrìbá country toward Bussa and reduced many principalities and polities along the way to tributary status. This move helped to secure Ọ̀yọ́ northern boundaries against Dendi, one of the numerous Songhai successor kingdoms. It also allowed them to gain control of important trade routes, especially the same old commercial routes that Òwu and Ọ̀yọ́ traders and their Wasangari, Wangara, and Djerma trading partners had used during the Yorùbá Classical period. In addition, Ọ̀yọ́'s northern policy provided some measure of stability and security that had eluded several Ìbàrìbá principalities because of attacks from the Songhai and Nupe from ca. 1450 through 1570. Not only that, the Ọ̀yọ́ pursued military expansion westward, establishing suzerainty over Ṣábẹ. Eastward, they captured the vital port towns of Ògòdò and Jebba from the Nupe and effectively reduced the Nupe kingdom to tributary status. By 1650, almost all of Ìgbómìnà was under the political control of Ọ̀yọ́. These stampeding horsemen of the savanna also pressed southward, deep into what used to be the greater metropolitan area of Ilé-Ifẹ̀. To secure their territorial gains, the Ọ̀yọ́ used the same colony outpost model that Òwu and Ilé-Ifẹ̀ had used during the Classical period (chap. 3).

The new Ọ̀yọ́ polity that emerged from the turbulence of the fifteenth and sixteenth centuries retained the ethnic diversity that must have characterized the earlier Ọ̀yọ́ kingdom, but more so now than ever before. The Yorùbá elements remained the dominant population in the reconstituted polity. Next to them in influence were the Ìbàrìbá, and joining this multiethnic polity were elements of Nupe and Songhai-Mossi. The presence of Ìbàrìbá, Songhai, and Mossi facial marks such as *gọ̀m̀bọ́*, *bààmú*, *máǹdè*, *túrè*, and *jáǹgbadì* among the Ọ̀yọ́ population provides the direct evidence for this multiethnic and multicultural integration in

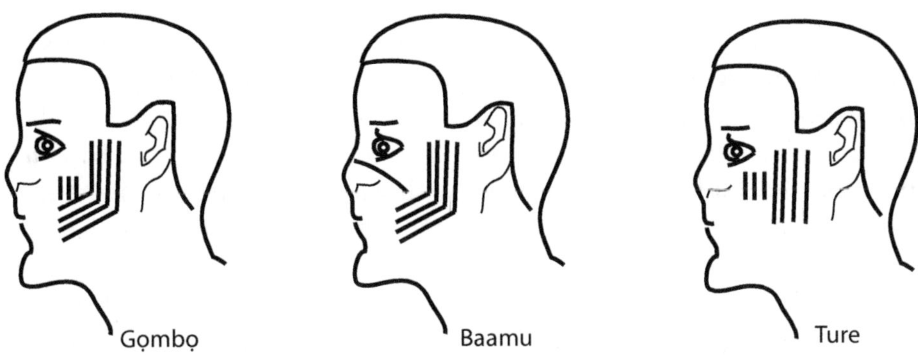

Figure 5.2. Ọ̀yọ́ facial marks of northern provenance (adapted from Johnson, *History*, 104)

the formation of the Ọ̀yọ́ identity after 1570 (fig. 5.2).[5] The *bààmú* facial mark, for example, is of Ìbàrìbá origin, and the royal House of Ògbómọ̀ṣọ́ has historically used this mark to associate with the Ìbàrìbá origins of its founding ancestor, Ogunlọlá.[6] The Ìbàrìbá were the most populous allies in the coalition that the Ọ̀yọ́ built to ward off the menace of Nupe militarists. Hence, the political arrangement that emerged in the revitalized Ọ̀yọ́ polity after 1570 bore the strong marks of power sharing between the two.

The new Ọ̀yọ́ polity had multicultural composition, a continuation of the cosmopolitan spirit of Yorùbá urbanism during the Classical period. The non-Yorùbá elements within it—the Ìbàrìbá, Nupe, Songhai, Mossi, and others—adopted the Ọ̀yọ́ political identity and by extension became members of the Yorùbá community of practice. The Yorùbá branch of the coalition retained the office of the *aláàfin*, the king of Ọ̀yọ́, whereas the Ìbàrìbá families controlled the office of *baṣọ̀run*, an office likened to that of "the Prime Minister and Chancellor of the Kingdom."[7] The *baṣọ̀run* was the head of the seven highest-ranking nonroyal lords of the state, collectively called the *ọ̀yọ́mèsì*. This was the council of nobility. Each noble or lord (*iba*) represented a mega-House in the metropolis, and the council advised the king on state affairs. Together, these lords represented the interests of the nonroyal majority in the central government headed by the *aláàfin*. They were the voice of the people, and they also served as kingmakers. In turn, although the titles of these nonroyal lords were hereditary and exclusive to the alpha family of each mega-House, the *aláàfin* made the final decision on the appointment of an *ọ̀yọ́mèsì*.

The power and influence of the *baṣọ̀run* were, however, far greater than those of the other six noblemen, and he played a far more decisive role in the selection of the new king. It is instructive that from about 1570 through 1750, the names of several *baṣọ̀run* resonate with Ìbàrìbá or non-Yorùbá origins. Magaji, Woruda, Biri, Yamba, Jambu, and Gáà are some of these names.[8] With the position of *baṣọ̀run*, the Ìbàrìbá elements in Ọ̀yọ́ were rewarded with the highest political office, second only to that of the *aláàfin*. This must have played a major role in integrating the families of Ìbàrìbá backgrounds into the new Ọ̀yọ́ polity. The post-1570 *baṣọ̀run* line was, understandably, associated with warfare and militarism, and it bore the totem name of Ògún (the Yorùbá deity associated with warfare during the sixteenth century). Therefore, it appears that the primary duty of the earlier *baṣọ̀run* was to lead military campaigns on behalf of the state. All members of the *ọ̀yọ́mèsì* and the *aláàfin* were expected to contribute people, weapons, and other logistics to the war effort, just as they expected to share in the war booty. It is not surprising that the Ìbàrìbá elements were entrusted with the leadership of the Ọ̀yọ́ army in the aftermath of the Nupe crisis. After all, they introduced Ọ̀yọ́ to cavalry, fought side by side with the exiled Ọ̀yọ́ against their foes, and helped to rebuild the broken city-state into an expanding military machine during the last quarter of the sixteenth century. The Ìbàrìbá were not the only non-Yorùbá elements who rose to prominence in Ọ̀yọ́ after 1570. The Nupe elements who fought on the side of the Ọ̀yọ́ were also rewarded with the important title of *alápinnì*, head of the *égúngún* cult (cult of the ancestors) and minister of religious affairs in the *ọ̀yọ́mèsì* council.[9]

The Ọ̀yọ́ political leaders of this period of rejuvenation also used the advantages of their ethnolinguistic and cultural diversity to manage the spoils of war and their growing territory. They took caution to make sure that distinguished soldiers were sent out as governors, resident commissioners, and turnpike managers to areas where they did not have any cultural or familial affiliation. Hence, Ìbàrìbá soldiers were sent to lead the provinces like Ògbómọ̀ṣọ́, Ṣakí, and Ìgànná (in the Yorùbá area). In turn, Yorùbá war captains were posted to head the Ọ̀yọ́ colonies and provinces in Ìbàrìbá country.[10] By 1650, for example, most of what is now southern Ìbàrìbá as far as River Ọpara held several Ọ̀yọ́ colonies, such as Okuta and Iléṣà (see fig. 1.1).[11] This appointment strategy minimized the risk of the provincial leaders rebelling against the metropolis. Instead, it had the effect of strengthening the loyalty of the appointed governors and resident commissioners to the metropolis.

At the time the Ọ̀yọ́ and central Yorùbá peoples were beginning to rebuild their political structure, Benin had become the most powerful militaristic state and the largest emporium in the Yorùbá world. And it significantly contributed to the expulsion of Nupe brigands from the eastern Èkìtì territory in the mid-sixteenth century. Therefore, securing the latter for its own security, political, and economic interests became Benin's priority in the second half of the century, not against the Nupe but against the expansionist ambitions of Ọ̀yọ́. Under Ehengbuda, Benin moved quickly to achieve this mission. Sometime in the 1580s, Benin established its northern frontier military base in Adó-Èkìtì. The provincial governor of Adó-Èkìtì (*ewì*) was charged with the responsibility of protecting Benin's general interests in Èkìtì, including managing trade, political affairs, and collection of tributes. With this political backing, Benin traders (private and state) and political agents fanned out across eastern and central Yorùbá, mopping up pepper, elephant tusks, woven cloth, and even dyestuff through commerce and tributes and redirecting these to the coastal markets through the capital.[12] Dominant in the Atlantic trade and well plugged to the commercial activities on the River Niger, Benin was the wealthiest kingdom in the region during the sixteenth and early seventeenth centuries. As a consequence, the splendor of its royal court was significantly elaborated, and this attracted the best and finest of craftsmen from within Edo as well as from the surrounding Yorùbá cultural areas, especially from Ilé-Ifẹ̀, Èkìtì, and Ọ̀wọ̀.[13]

State Builders II: Regional Power Politics and the Rise of Iléṣà

Ọ̀yọ́ and Benin established themselves as the two dominant powers in the Yorùbá world in the aftermath of the Nupe militarist crisis, but their stories do not tell us everything about the regional political reorganization that took place between 1570 and 1650. They were not the only ones seeking to fill the lingering vacuum that the collapse of Ifẹ̀ Empire had created in the central Yorùbá region, composed mostly of Èkìtì in the east, Upper Ọ̀ṣun in the west, and southern Ìgbómìnà in the north (see fig. 5.1). The spate of military activities and political maneuvering that took place in this area between 1570 and 1590 was the most important and dramatic development on the political landscape of the Yorùbá region during the Restoration period. The power politics associated with these events led to the creation of a new kingdom, Iléṣà, in the 1580s, just twenty kilometers northeast of Ilé-Ifẹ̀. Over a period of three decades (1580–1610), this young kingdom was instrumental in redrawing the political geography of the central Yorùbá region. Located almost equidistant between the capitals of Ọ̀yọ́ and Benin, Iléṣà influenced the external policies of those two regional powers far more than any other polity during the decades of regeneration. The trajectory of its rise from the ashes of Ifẹ̀ Empire's implosion and Nupe militarist conflagration deserves close examination because it gives us deep insights into the political, economic, and cultural processes that shaped Yorùbá regional history during the period under review.

Like their peers in Ọ̀yọ́ and Benin, the warriors from the Ifẹ̀ and Èkìtì areas who were involved in the final expulsion of the Nupe horsemen were restless and ambitious. This was especially the case for many of the Ifẹ̀-Èkìtì fighters in the Ará War, named after the kingdom where the last major assault on the Nupe militarists was executed. With the retreat of the Nupe, these liberators turned their attention to the northern suburbs of the old Ifẹ̀ greater metropolis. The suzerainty of Ilé-Ifẹ̀ over this area had slipped early in the fifteenth century, and the surviving polities in the area had shrunk in size. The Ará War veterans were mostly of Ifẹ̀-Èkìtì extraction. It was therefore to these northern Ifẹ̀ suburbs that the war veterans returned. Many were going home; others were seeking to build a new home. The ambitious among them were not seeking to lay down their weapons and turn to farming, crafts, and trading. They wanted to carve out new political territories from the old decimated ones. They wanted the power to lead, dominate, and control.

Oral traditions vividly portray the ruthless actions of these men of war in Upper Ọ̀ṣun, especially in what is now northern Ìjẹ̀ṣà, where they attacked several surviving polities; killed, displaced, or demoted their leaders; imposed themselves as new rulers; established new dynasties; and even renamed several of the conquered towns and villages. Ọ̀bàràbarà Olókùnẹ̀ṣin (hence Ọ̀bàrà) was the most renowned of these men. He and his squad of roving warriors succeeded in overrunning a large swath of ancient polities in the Ìlàrè-Ìbòkun area. At the time of Ọ̀bàrà's arrival, the dominant polity in the area was Ẹ̀ka Ọ̀ṣun, with Ìlàrè as its chief town (see fig. 5.1).[14] Ẹ̀ka Ọ̀ṣun had exercised suzerainty over parts of northern Ìjẹ̀ṣà between the thirteenth and sixteenth centuries. In the epic confrontation between the forces of Alàrè, the defender of the old order, and Ọ̀bàràbarà Olókùnẹ̀ṣin, the leader of the new order, Ẹ̀ka Ọ̀ṣun was vanquished. Ìlàrè and several of its satellite villages and towns—Ìgigun, Ìkètèwí, Ìpèpèjí, Ìlọ̀jà, and Ìgún—were abandoned, bringing an end to Ìlàrè's three-hundred-year dominance in the area.[15] Some of the House and mega-House polities that were under the control of Ìlàrè (Ẹ̀ka Ọ̀ṣun)—Ìlémùré, Ùlógò, Ìpásẹ̀, Iporo, Òbóó, Ìnikùn, Ìmẹ̀sí, Òyè, and Asé—survived, but this seems to have been the result of their cooperation with Ọ̀bàrà in the battle against Alàrè. Nevertheless, the leaders of these surviving polities lost their political power and came under the control of Ọ̀bàrà or one of his lieutenants. Many of them were reduced to serving in religious and ritual roles, especially as earth priests.[16] In their place, military personalities loyal to Ọ̀bàrà were appointed to govern the conquered territory. In the process, some of these old polities were renamed. Hence, Ìlémùré became Ìbòkun, and Ùlógò was renamed Ìlọ̀wá.[17] These new warrior-leaders are represented in the oral traditions and visual arts as horsemen. The second part of the commander's dual name, "Olókùnẹ̀ṣin," in fact means "owner of the horse bridle," thereby showing his equestrian identity. There is no doubt that the person who owns or holds the bridle of the horse also controls the horse's direction and action. It is unlikely that horses played any significant role in the wars of conquest pursued by Ọ̀bàràbarà Olókùnẹ̀ṣin, given the expensive nature of such an investment in the rain forest. He may have owned one or more horses to display and emphasize his grandeur and indomitability, or he may have acquired this moniker for what it implies about his power and ability to command, lead, execute, and provide direction.

From Ẹ̀ka Ọ̀ṣun, these Ifẹ̀-Èkìtì militarists pushed southward in the direction of Ilé-Ifẹ̀. By the 1580s, an area about forty kilometers long and thirty kilometers wide was under their control. Ọ̀bàrà died soon afterward, and Ọwálúṣẹ́ is credited with completing this decade-long spate of conquests, making Iléṣà the seat of government of a new kingdom, and creating the political institutions that integrated all the conquered territories under Iléṣà's control.[18] All of this took place shortly after the Ọ̀yọ́ had driven the Nupe to the other side of the Niger River and established Ọ̀yọ́-Ilé as their capital—and about the same time that Benin began to secure its northern frontiers in the Èkìtì and Àkókó areas under Orhogbua and Ehengbuda. Ọwálúṣẹ́'s rule was contemporaneous with at least the first decade of Ehengbuda's reign in Benin (ca. 1578–1606), and it probably overlapped with the last years of Abípa's reign and the early years of Ọbalókun's rule in Ọ̀yọ́. However, before Ọwálúṣẹ́ could establish the seat of government in Iléṣà and build a stable state, he first had to defeat a powerful rival, Ọwárì, a fearsome war hero who had overrun the nearby ancient town of Ìlájé (about 10 km south of Ilesa), established his base there, and renamed it Ipole (see fig. 5.1).[19]

Like Ọ̀bàrà, Ọwárì is referred to in the oral traditions as an intruder and conqueror. Local historians described him as *àlejò gòdògbò tí ńgbilé mọ́ onílé*: "the overwhelming stranger who displaced the indigenes from their ancestral land." His sobriquets include *àkànle òkúta* (hard stone) and *ọká* (puff adder, a venomous viper species); and his *oríkì* (panegyric) mentions that he fought in Ará, Ìgèdè-Àpà, and Ẹ̀rìnmọ̀ (all in Èkìtì):

> Ọwárì, the hard rock
> He ordered that palm-wine should be brought for him
> Yet, he was holding an iron sword
> The invincible man who killed the people of Ará and spared only twenty
> He killed the people of Ìgèdè-Àpà and spared only thirty
> He killed all, but three, in Ẹ̀rìnmọ̀
> Ọwárì, the dangerous roadside cobra
> That chased men helter-skelter
> Fear! the hard rock.[20]

The above panegyric suggests that Ọwárì was one of the veterans of the Ará War in Èkìtì. He was one of those warriors, like Ọ̀bàrà and Ọwálúṣẹ́, seeking to create their political fortunes out of the rubble of instability that had plagued the Ifẹ̀-Èkìtì area for about four generations.

However, Ọwálúṣẹ́'s decision to build a new capital only ten kilometers south of Ìlájé collided with Ọwárì's interests.

Their struggle centered on the control of a significant old suburb of Ifẹ̀ metropolis, especially around Iléṣà, about twenty kilometers from the walls of the ancient city. From his base in Ìlájé (Ìpolé), Ọwárì was already laying claim to the very area where Ọwálúṣẹ́ was planning to build his future capital. Neither was willing to back away from his ambition and claim, but two rams cannot drink from the same bowl. The hostility between the two men soon led into open confrontations. Ọwárì gained the upper hand in the initial battles and forced Ọwálúṣẹ́ to run off into exile. Ọwálúṣẹ́ did not go far. He sought refuge in nearby southern Ìgbómìnà, where the Ọ̀yọ́ forces were already active.[21] In exile, he gained the support of Ọ̀yọ́'s commanding officers, and it was with them that he returned to confront Ọwárì at Ìlájé. With Ọ̀yọ́'s military backing, Ọwálúṣẹ́ was able to defeat Ọwárì. Ọ̀yọ́ then provided some of the personnel and political logistics that enabled Ọwálúṣẹ́ to set up Ilẹ́ṣà as the capital of his new kingdom.[22] The Ọ̀yọ́'s involvement in the Ilẹ́ṣà affair was part of their strategy of having a strong foothold in the central Yorùbá region. At the time that Ọ̀bàrà and other militants were actively taking control of the polities in the old provinces of Ilé-Ifẹ̀ (the 1580s and 1590s), the Ọ̀yọ́ were also busy establishing order in the nearby Ìgbómìnà and Upper Ọ̀ṣun areas. Investing military and administrative resources in Ọwálúṣẹ́'s ambition, the Ọ̀yọ́ strategists saw the potential in using Iléṣà as a stepping-stone to advance their interests deep in the rain forest belt. This was part of Ọ̀yọ́'s goal (under Ọbalókun): to create secured access routes to the commercial centers that were sprouting up along the coast, from Ughoton to Lagos.

The assistance provided by Ọ̀yọ́ in the establishment of Iléṣà illustrates the kinds of regional collaboration and strategic diplomacy taking place among the triumphant state-building warriors of the late sixteenth century. The inclusion of the Èkìtì title for a lord—Ọwá—in the prefix of Ọwálúṣẹ́'s and Ọwárì's names clearly illustrates the cultural affinity of the two men with the Èkìtì cultural sphere. It is likely that the reference in the oral traditions to Ọwálúṣẹ́ as the son of an Ọ̀yọ́ princess was an attempt to naturalize and legitimize the political relationships between Ọ̀yọ́ and the emerging new kingdom of Iléṣà in *ẹbí* fraternity terms. Not only that, but to demonstrate the importance of Ọ̀yọ́ in the foundation of Iléṣà, traditional historians even go to the extent of explaining that the palace that Ọwálúṣẹ́ built faced the direction of Ọ̀yọ́. In contrast, the back of the palace turned toward the Òkèṣà community, an aboriginal group that was forcefully incorporated to form the bulk of the new city's population.[23] This allegory implies that Ọwálúṣẹ́ depended on the protection of Ọ̀yọ́ military and political figures in order to defeat his detractors and establish his grip on the levers of power during the early years of Iléṣà's existence. It also shows the tension that pervaded the relationship between Ọwálúṣẹ́'s government and the aborigines on whose land the new city was being built.

Òkèṣà was the largest of the several polities that were thriving in the area before the Ọ̀yọ́-backed Ọwálúṣẹ́'s force appeared. The others were Ìrorò, Ìjòfì, Ìgbógì, Ìrère, Ìsọ́rọ̀, Ìtajì, Ìmíkàn, and Ìmọ̀.[24] Most of these old settlements were relocated to form the core of the new town of Iléṣà. The impression that one gets from the oral traditions is that these aboriginal communities were the northern rural suburbs of Ifẹ̀, some of which served as the city's food basket during the Classical period. It is obvious that Ilé-Ifẹ̀ was too weak politically to prevent Ọwálúṣẹ́ and his Ọ̀yọ́ patrons from setting up the capital of this new kingdom in its backyard. Ọwálúṣẹ́'s success launched the process of creating a new ethnocultural identity and political community, which we now call Ìjẹ̀ṣà. Therefore, what became Ìjẹ̀ṣà as a sub-Yorùbá ethnonym was a creation of Iléṣà during the period of regeneration that began in the 1570s. In other words, some of the Ifẹ̀-Èkìtì warlords who were veterans of the Ará War (against the Nupe) created both Iléṣà kingdom and Ìjẹ̀ṣà identity in one of the suburbs of the old Ifẹ̀ metropolis.

There is another clue that the founders of Iléṣà were products of the Ará War. The first minister of war in Iléṣà, Arápatẹ́, not only carried the name Ará as a prefix but is also said to have arrived in Iléṣà as the leader of a contingent of soldiers from Ará (now known as Arámọkọ), the ancient town that was the theater of the final battles against the Nupe militarists. His name was later codified in the chiefly hierarchy as the title of Iléṣà's minister of war. It is also interesting that the holders of the title have historically served as the fief lord of the kingdom's northern province, which included Ìlàrè, Ìbòkun, and Ìláṣẹ̀. This was where the power politics and the wave of territorial conquests that created the Iléṣà kingdom began.[25] In this regard, Arápatẹ́ must have played a leading role in the final years of the war that routed the Nupe militarists from Ará, and he was also one of several warriors who turned their attention to the project of conquest and state-building at the end of Ará War under the leadership of Ọ̀bàrà and Ọwálúṣẹ́, respectively.[26]

Ilé-Ifẹ̀ was not the only one in severe political contraction during the late sixteenth century. Many of the old political stars in Ìgbómìnà and Èkìtì (e.g., Ìlá-Ọ̀ràngún, Ìlàrè, and Ará) either lost their luster or disappeared altogether. In their place, new stars were being born and a new political galaxy was emerging. These new stars had to renegotiate their circumstellar borders, legitimize their intrusion into the old political landscape, and institutionalize the new relationships they were forging with others. The new social order that was being established, however, made use of the existing principles that had given shape to the Yorùbá community of practice. In fact, those that were new to the political landscape, such as Iléṣà, sought to write themselves, even if forcefully, into the preexisting regional structure of the Ifẹ̀-centric *ẹbí* fraternity.[27] This is the origin of Iléṣà's Ajíbógun Obòkun legend, a legitimating charter for the origins of Iléṣà's kingship and its Ọwá Obòkun dynasty.

According to this legend, Ajíbógun Obòkun was the last son of Odùduwà and the only one left at home after his brothers had departed the city to establish their respective kingdoms in the aftermath of the Ìta Ìjerò conference mentioned in chapter 3.[28] When Odùduwà grew old, he lost his eyesight, and his medicine men prescribed seawater as the remedy for him to regain his sight. Finding this remedy would require traveling to the Atlantic Ocean. Ajíbógun (meaning "the one who wakes up into conflict/war") volunteered to go to the ocean to fetch the seawater. He was gone for many years, and many thought he had died in the course of the mission. However, he succeeded in fetching the seawater and returned to Ilé-Ifẹ̀. Once it was used as prescribed, Odùduwà regained his sight. For achieving this feat, Ajíbógun acquired the nickname Obòkun ("he who fetched the seawater"). By the time he returned, all his older brothers had already divided the royal inheritance, including all the crowns, among themselves. With no inheritance left, Odùduwà blessed Ajíbógun Obòkun and gave him a magic sword. He then commanded him to go forth and use the sword to conquer some of the territories that his senior brothers had already acquired. According to the legend, it was this mission of conquest that brought Ajíbógun Obòkun to Ẹ̀ka Ọ̀ṣun (a province of Ifẹ̀ during the Classical period). Soon after conquering several polities in the area, Ajíbógun Obòkun died, and his son, Ọ̀bàrà, took over the mantle of leadership. The latter settled in Ìlémùré and renamed it Ìbòkun (after his father). From there, Ọ̀bàràbarà continued the process of military conquest until his son, Ọwálúṣẹ́, established a permanent seat of government in Iléṣà. Ajíbógun Obòkun is therefore regarded as the founding ancestor of the Ọwá Obòkun dynasty of Iléṣà.[29]

The Ajíbógun Obòkun legend serves, first and foremost, to make a case for Iléṣà's membership in the Ifẹ̀-centric *ẹbí* fraternity, similar to what the Ọ̀rànmíyàn legend did for Benin and Ọ̀yọ́ in the previous two to three hundred years. The Obòkun legend justifies Iléṣà's appropriation of what used to be Ifẹ̀'s territory, legitimizes Iléṣà as a hegemonic *ọba-aládé* state, and recognizes the importance of the Atlantic coast to the state-building program of Iléṣà's founding heroes, a point that I will later expatiate on. The creation of an Ifẹ̀-centric legend of origin by Iléṣà, possibly in the first half of the seventeenth century, as a way of legitimizing the new but ambitious kingdom, demonstrates the adaptability and open-endedness of the principle of the Yorùbá community of practice that Ifẹ̀ had created almost five hundred years earlier. It shows that this principle was still relevant in the seventeenth century although Ifẹ̀ had lost its political and economic power in the regional affairs by that time.

With his defeat of Ọwárì and other competitors and foes, and with his successful establishment of Iléṣà as the capital of the new kingdom, Ọwálúṣẹ́ laid the foundation for what would soon become the most powerful kingdom in the central Yorùbá region, east of River Ọ̀ṣun. His successor, Àtàkúnmọ̀sà, continued this momentum by consolidating the power of Iléṣà through military conquests and creating a template for the kingdom's external relations. He proved to be a perceptive leader who understood the importance of regional network building through diplomacy and military operations. Àtàkúnmọ̀sà accurately calculated that the viability of his fledgling kingdom could not be sustained by relying on Ọ̀yọ́ as its sole patron. He realized that Ọ̀yọ́'s interest in Iléṣà was to use the new kingdom as a stepping-stone to gain access to the new port towns on the Atlantic coast. Although his predecessor had made himself a client of Ọ̀yọ́ and Àtàkúnmọ̀sà was expected to follow suit, the young king had a different plan. He was not going to be the minion of the *aláàfin*. His ambition was political independence and territorial expansion. He likely saw it coming that Ọ̀yọ́ and Iléṣà interests would soon collide and that Iléṣà would need a powerful patron against Ọ̀yọ́'s future hostilities. The subsequent events showed that he read the signs accurately.

Àtàkúnmọ̀sà faced some immediate challenges: to populate his capital by attracting a diverse population with different skill sets from other *ìlú*, big and small; to turn Iléṣà into an emporium; to make it attractive for traders; to provide security; and to incorporate more communities and polities into Iléṣà's political sphere. Iléṣà and Benin oral traditions record Àtàkúnmọ̀sà as having embarked on a long diplomatic mission to Benin, where he spent some time in the court of Ehengbuda.[30] Àtàkúnmọ̀sà's visit to Benin would have taken place before he ascended the throne. In this case, Ọwálúṣẹ́ likely arranged for his son to be trained in the court of the most powerful and richest kingdom in the region as a strategy to secure Benin's diplomatic support for the young city-state. This singular act would have made Ọwálúṣẹ́ a shrewd Janus-faced diplomat, dealing amicably with the two most powerful states in the region—Ọ̀yọ́ and Benin—simultaneously. While Ọwálúṣẹ́ was looking up to Ọ̀yọ́'s patronage, he was preparing his son and successor to look away from it. Security, commerce, knowledge of statecraft and the art of war, and populating Iléṣà with people who have skills in a diverse range of crafts and knowledge were among the issues that would have preoccupied Àtàkúnmọ̀sà's mission to Ehengbuda's court.[31] The prince would have witnessed one or more of the European trading missions to Benin, and he might have followed Ehengbuda to some of his military operations on the

Lagos lagoon. Àtàkúnmọ̀sà's sojourn in Benin paid off for Iléṣà's expansionist project. He used his mission to Ehengbuda to negotiate a favorable boundary between Benin and Iléṣà, which was set at Àkúrẹ́.[32] He did not stop there. On his return home, he pushed his forces into Ọ̀gọ̀tún, Ẹ̀fọ̀n, and Ará, placing these Èkìtì polities and their adjoining areas under Iléṣà and using them as boundary towns with the eastern Èkìtì towns under Benin's control. And it seems that Àtàkúnmọ̀sà and his successors played influential political roles in several of the northeastern Èkìtì polities, such as Òmùò and Ìkọ̀lé. When Benin's grip on those territories relaxed following the death of Ehengbuda around 1608, Iléṣà took them over. Several Èkìtì polities are also said to have contributed labor to the construction of Iléṣà's defensive walls during the seventeenth century, a further indication that Iléṣà held a number of Èkìtì polities in tributary status.[33]

Judging by his depiction in the oral traditions of Iléṣà, Benin, Àkúrẹ́, and Èkìtì as a roving diplomat and warrior, it is certain that Àtàkúnmọ̀sà was a warrior-king like his contemporaries in other kingdoms. He was also a well-traveled prince and king. The etymology of his name embodies a cosmopolitan experience, and his external policies demonstrate a keen and superior understanding of the dynamics of power politics in the region. His name has two possible meanings: "He who knows the Atlantic Ocean and the lagoon," and "One who threaded and treaded on a rope to reach the lagoon."[34] Both meanings direct our attention to the success of Àtàkúnmọ̀sà in setting the eyes of Iléṣà toward the coast for commercial opportunities and building regional political alliances.[35] On political, security, and economic grounds, the alliance that he forged with Benin, almost on equal terms, was a major achievement for this very young and ambitious kingdom. It should be noted, however, that this was possible because Benin also needed Iléṣà in order to gain access to the commerce of central Yorùbá region. By courting Iléṣà's loyalty and by opening its market to the young kingdom, Benin helped to prop up Iléṣà as an independent polity. This was also a way for both Benin and Iléṣà to undermine Ọ̀yọ́'s influence in the central Yorùbá region.

The Portuguese, English, and Dutch quests for pepper, elephant tusks, dyestuff, cotton cloth, gum, and enslaved captives had stimulated the expansion of Benin's trading networks and proliferation of its long-distance traders, many of whom were working for the king. By attracting Benin traders to his city, Àtàkúnmọ̀sà helped direct a large volume of central Yorùbá's commercial flows through Iléṣà. This inspired the development of several frontier markets on the northern edges of the rain forest in the early decades of the seventeenth century. Àtàkúnmọ̀sà's political shrewdness was a major headache for Ọ̀yọ́ because he had become a stumbling block to the latter's eastward expansion.[36] By splitting Iléṣà's alliance between Ọ̀yọ́ and Benin, Àtàkúnmọ̀sà left no one in doubt that

Iléṣà was preparing to call its own shots and was not ready to be the puppet of either of the two big and older brothers in the *ẹbí* fraternity.

Recovery in Ilé-Ifẹ̀

While all of this was going on, what became of Ilé-Ifẹ̀? In the 1570s, the ancient city would have been a skeleton of its Classical-age size. By the 1620s, Ilé-Ifẹ̀ had lost its far-flung and nearby territories to the new powers—Iléṣà, Benin, Ọ̀yọ́, and Ìjẹ̀bú-Òde. Its recovery was slower compared to the other polities mentioned above. Nevertheless, Ifẹ̀ was still held in awe as a sacred city and as the revered home of the gods and goddesses on whose shoulders the social order of the region rested. Even with their galloping horses, new commercial wealth, and audacious militarism, none of the new regional powers sought to replace Ifẹ̀'s spiritual aura. Hence, while the militaristic men of the late sixteenth and early seventeenth century were fighting over some of the provinces in the defunct Ifẹ̀ Empire—Èkìtì, Upper Ọ̀ṣun, and Ìgbómìnà—the old city escaped their rapacious appetites for territorial accumulation. Ilé-Ifẹ̀ looked on as its new neighbors and former clients constructed their future on the very same territories that had once either belonged to it or had been within its sphere of patronage. Without the military wherewithal to challenge the intruders, all Ifẹ̀ could do was focus on sorting out its own internal political problems. Ilé-Ifẹ̀ experienced a delayed recovery, but it was not left out of the political rejuvenation that began in the last quarter of the sixteenth century. Its time of rebirth eventually came during the second quarter of the seventeenth century.

Lájamìsán was the king of Ilé-Ifẹ̀ who managed to secure the full recovery of the ancient city. He is remembered in the oral traditions as the founder of post-Classical Ifẹ̀ dynasty and is nicknamed Óṣẹ̀gànderùkù: "He who turned the forest into dust." This appellation indicates that Lájamìsán facilitated the growth of population and urban expansion. One of his accomplishments was the rebuilding of some of the outer walls of the city, which had fallen into disrepair during the Intermediate period. His sons, Lájódogun and Láfogído, who reigned in turn after him, may have actually completed the walls. By the time Lájamìsán took over the reins of power in Ilé-Ifẹ̀, three aspects of material life that defined the Classical period—potsherd pavement, naturalistic terracotta and copper-alloy sculptures, and glass production—had ceased. Considering this discontinuity in the material life and inferences from the oral traditions, Paul Ozanne has noted that Lájamìsán represented a clean break from the Classical-era kings and that he was the founder not only of a new dynasty but also of the "modern" city of Ifẹ̀.[37] The tradition is indeed fuzzy and mostly silent on the relationships of Lájamìsán with the Classical-era kings.[38] From the end of the fourteenth century through the beginning of the seventeenth century, Ifẹ̀ went through about two hundred years of undistinguished leadership. The imploded city may not even have had any *ọ̀ọ̀ni* at the peak of the Nupe militarist crisis during the early sixteenth century, but instead it was governed by the leaders of the mega-Houses and the religious orders, including the Ògbóni.[39] We should therefore expect such a long period of instability to have produced a new line of rulers whose legitimacy was based more on the ability to get things done than on the purity of genetic relationship with one of the founding ancestors—Odùduwà, Ọbàtálá, or Ọbalùfọ̀n. Lájamìsán and his immediate successors are powerful figures in Ifẹ̀ traditions, the like of which had eluded Ifẹ̀ since the reign of Ọbalùfọ̀n Aláyémọrẹ́ in the fourteenth century. With militarist kingdoms nearby—especially Iléṣà, Òwu, and Ìjẹ̀bú-Òde—and the generally heightened militarization of the region's political landscape, the people of Ifẹ̀ needed a strong leader. Lájamìsán emerged in response to these new imperatives, and his two sons who reigned after him—Lájódogun and Láfogído—carried on with the implementation of his political agenda.[40]

Hunters and Ivory

The militaristic state-builders were not the only ones making history in the last quarter of the sixteenth century. The evolving Atlantic trade also introduced a new dimension of social formation that privileged hunters as historymakers. The most lucrative product that the Yorùbá world could offer the Atlantic market in the sixteenth and early seventeenth centuries was ivory. The insatiable appetite of European traders for elephant tusks stimulated hunters—perhaps former warriors—to fan out into the frontier woods to track and kill elephants for their valuable incisors. In the 1590s through 1630s, several hunting camps arose in the northern and central Yorùbá region at the interstices of kingdoms, towns, and villages that were being rebuilt or newly founded. The oral traditions of many polities that emerged in the Restorative period, therefore, have a strong hunter character. Ọ̀yán, for example, attributed its early seventeenth-century origin to two hunters—Odù from Ilé-Ifẹ̀ and Epé from Ìlá-Ọ̀ràngún. The town of Ìrágbìjí also grew out of the fusion of two hunting camps. Likewise, the savanna woodlands in the upper reaches of the Ọbà River were swarming with hunting camps in the early seventeenth century, of which four—Ìdí Ajágbọn, Aálẹ̀, Oń̄ṣílé, and Òrìṣàtólú—became prominent.[41] The leaders of the hunting camps were of Ìbàrìbá and Yorùbá extraction, and they formed a mutual-aid association known as *àlòńgò*. They used the association as a cooperative for group hunting, for which elephant tusks were the main target. It was also a cooperative for sharing the profits that accrued from selling elephant tusks and other animal products. Likewise, the *àlòńgò* association served as the bulwark of defense against brigandage. These hunting camps, located on a busy highway linking Ọ̀yọ́-Ilé with the rain forest, soon became important way stations where travelers stopped to rest, take refreshment, or pass the night. It was from these hunting camps that the town of Ògbómọ̀ṣọ́ developed, with each camp forming the seed that eventually grew into a House. Hence, Ìsapa House developed from Òrìṣàtólú camp, Ìjẹru House from Ońṣílé camp, and Òkè-Elérin (Elephant Hill) from Áálẹ̀ camp.[42]

The increasing demands by European traders for elephant ivory accelerated the scale of elephant hunting in the southern areas of the Yorùbá region (the rain forest zone) faster than in the northern areas during the period of Restoration. The five original *ilé* that constituted Ìjẹ̀bú-Igbó town, for example, originated from hunting camps—Òkè-Sopin, Ojowo, Òkè-Ago, Atikori, and Japara. Oral traditions recall that one of these, Atikori, developed specifically as an elephant-kill site early in the seventeenth century.[43] The western Yorùbá region was also teeming with camps established by professional hunters. Some of them are named as founders of several towns in the area, including Àfọ̀n, Ìmẹ̀kọ, Ìdòfà, Ìpàyà, Ìmálà, and Ẹ̀wọn in the present-day Yéwá (Ẹ̀gbádò) area. Látóyọ̀ Akínsòkun, an itinerant hunter from Ọ̀yọ́, founded Àfọ̀n as his major hunting camp, and he was reportedly associated with other satellite camps, including Okokòkó, Àgẹsinwọ̀ Ọ̀tapẹ̀lẹ́, Igbó-Ẹ̀wọn, Iporo-Aya, Iko, Gbigbo Bebe, and Tofi.[44] An important dimension of these hunting stations was that they were created by guilds of elephant hunters who rapidly mushroomed across the rain forest belt of the Yorùbá world during the sixteenth and early seventeenth century in tandem with the expanding market for ivory on the coast.[45]

Hence, at the very time that the state-builders of the 1570s through 1640s were carving out new political territories, other kinds of social formation were being created in the region outside the metropolises. These were small-scale farming communities and hunting camps. Elephant tusks were not the only reason that hunters fanned out into the woods. Such hunters also pioneered the creation of new settlements as a result of the periodic outbursts of drought across Western Africa throughout the seventeenth century, from Senegambia to the Congo, although not as intense as those of the 1380s–1550s.[46] With the unpredictable rainfall patterns, several communities sought out new settlements that were closer to the fewer dependable water corridors in the region. Dispersed hamlets and small villages offered a better and more flexible adaptive strategy than densely populated towns for coping with the hardships of drought. Hunting helped to diversify economic activities in this ecological landscape chapped by the low precipitation. Those episodes of drought were a source of stress for both humans and animals. The droughts made the animals an easy target, and they were exploited to augment food resources and commercial opportunities, especially in the case of the elephants hunted for their tusks. Professional hunters also helped to decimate the population of wild animals in some areas before full-scale agricultural settlements could develop. This role of hunters as vanguards of farming settlements is captured in the panegyric of Látóyọ̀ Akínsòkun, one of the most celebrated hunters and frontier migrants of the western Yorùbá region, who later ruled as a king: *Ọba ọ̀pẹ̀kùn perè, ọba tí kò jẹ́ k'ẹ́fọ̀n lè j'oko àbàtà*: "The king who killed leopard and python, and prevented buffalo from destroying farms in the swamps."[47] Hence, warlords and military tacticians were not the only state-builders in the age of regeneration and restoration; hunters were also agents of state formation.

Contested New Frontiers: Òwẹ̀nà, Upper Ọ̀ṣun, and Yéwá-Ògùn

The growing importance of the Atlantic coast as the premier terminus of the regional commerce did not end the commercial traffic across the River Niger. But, for the Yorùbá region, the volume of trade on its littorals had surpassed the trade volume on the banks of the River Niger by the end of the sixteenth century. In this regard, the northern and central Yorùbá groups were latecomers to what the southern areas, especially Ìjẹ̀bú, Àwórì, Màhin, Itsekiri, and Benin, had been part of since the early sixteenth century. By 1610, the coastal commercial activities were being deeply felt in the mainland, especially with the increase in the European demand for African products—cloth on the Benin River and slaves in Allada and Ouidah. New trade routes connecting the mainland to the coast developed. The high volume, value, and variety of commodities being carried along these routes created envy, anxiety, and a sense of urgency for the mainland's new metropolitan centers. It was imperative that they control these trade routes and market centers. If Ìgbómìnà and Èkìtì were the contested internal frontiers of the Classical period, three new frontier hot spots were discernible during the first quarter of the seventeenth century: the Òwẹ̀nà, Upper Ọ̀ṣun, and Yéwá-Ògùn (see fig. 5.1). Located at the interstices of the major metropolises and kingdoms, these frontiers were the territories of desire, as pathways to the coast and as places of exploitation of labor and natural resources for the Atlantic market and the metropolises.

As a result, colonies, way stations, market towns, and turnpike stations began to multiply in these new frontiers during the early seventeenth century. These played significant roles in accelerating the pace of regional integration. By linking the Yorùbá mainland to the coastal ports, and moving new categories of goods and people in a volume and frequency that the region had never experienced, these frontiers were crucial to the rejuvenation of the Yorùbá community of practice during the seventeenth century. Given their indispensability to the movement of goods and people, these frontiers became sites of intense contestation among the major metropolises, and between them and the local communities who called the frontiers home. These frontier hot spots were also spaces of disruption. They were occupied not only by farmers and hunters but also by social outcasts, rebels, and opportunistic brigands. Some of these preyed on the native communities and travelers through extortion and kidnapping, and they also frustrated the efforts of the nearby states to foster social order in these frontiers.[48] Containing these anti-order and opportunistic individuals became a primary concern for many polities, small and big. They needed to establish safe and secure trading routes to attain their goal of economic well-being. Let us take a closer look at how these three frontier hot spots emerged between 1570 and 1650.

The Òwẹ̀nà area was an old frontier when viewed through Ifẹ̀-centric lenses (chap. 3). It connected Ilé-Ifẹ̀ and its client states of Ọ̀wọ̀ and Benin throughout the Classical period. However, this area between the Rivers Ọ̀ṣun and Ọ̀wẹ̀nà was the home of the vast kingdom of Ìdôkò, whose antiquity dated to the Late Formative period. Although Ilé-Ifẹ̀ and its allies degraded the power of Ìdôkò during the Classical period, the remnants of this group and others, such as the Ùgbò (Màhin area), exercised a good measure of autonomy in the Òwẹ̀nà frontier through the late sixteenth century. The contestation for the control of Òwẹ̀nà among the neighboring powers—Ọ̀wọ̀, Benin, Ìjẹ̀bú-Òde, and even Ọ̀yọ́—was revived in the last quarter of the century as a result of the rising tide of the Atlantic trade and the gushing wind of political consolidation that was sweeping across the region. The strategic importance of the Òwẹ̀nà frontier was accentuated by its large herds of elephants, whose ivory commanded high profits on the coast. Hence, this area became a magnet for hunters, traders, and soldiers from Ìjẹ̀bú, Màhin, Benin, Ọ̀wọ̀, and later Ọ̀yọ́. These men and women of the frontiers jostled for the exploitation of the large elephant populations in Ọ̀wẹ̀nà and for the use of the area as a passage to the coast.[49]

Apart from the rivalry that the exploitation of the herds of elephants created, Òwẹ̀nà was also a place of conflict between immigrants and aboriginal groups over the control of trade routes and management of political boundaries and new settlements emerging in the area. The thwarted attempt by Ọ̀yọ́ to establish control over Òwẹ̀nà during the late sixteenth century shows how important the area was to the struggle to connect to the new commercial opportunities on the coast. The far-distant Ọ̀yọ́ metropolis was not the only one that took a keen interest in the area.

A diverse range of people from nearby Ọwọ̀, Èkìtì, Benin, and Ìjẹ̀bú also flooded into the area during the late sixteenth and early seventeenth century. The Oǹdó kingdom emerged sometime between 1580 and 1620, for example, as a coalition of these migrants—hunters, soldiers, mercenaries, outlaws, farmers, and traders—and some of the aboriginal communities in the area.[50] The new kingdom eventually supplanted the power of the older polities of Ùdòko, Ìfọ̀rẹ́, and Ọ̀kà, which had held sway over this northern part of the Òwẹ̀nà frontier for several centuries.[51] The Ondo traditions of origin, dynastic history, royal court culture, and public rituals embodied the variegated character of the kingdom's beginning as an internal frontier community. These traditions reflect the fact that many of the initial settlers who populated the kingdom came from Ọ̀yọ́, Ìjẹ̀bú, Ifẹ̀, Ọ̀wọ̀, and Benin backgrounds.[52] With the emergence of Oǹdó as the dominant political force in the northern Òwẹ̀nà frontier, some stability and order were put in place, which benefited the flow of commercial traffic. In order to enable traders and political emissaries to enjoy unmolested passage across this vast rain forest belt, it was in the best interest of many of the metropolises in the region to maintain peaceful relationships with Oǹdó. The result was that the *ẹbí* fraternity was extended to include the Oǹdó monarchy—the "new kid on the block." This was done by ranking the Òṣemàwé dynasty of Oǹdó as a junior brother of the older dynasties of Ọ̀yọ́, Ọ̀wọ̀, Benin, Ìjẹ̀bú-Òde, and Ifẹ̀. With this, the Òṣemàwé was written into the Ifẹ̀-centric charter of royal kinship.

Likewise, the Upper Òṣun frontier (the area between the Ọ̀bà and Òṣun Rivers), which used to be within the orbit of Classical Ifẹ̀ cultural influence and political patronage, became a locus of contestation between Ọ̀yọ́ and Iléṣà during the first quarter of the seventeenth century. The area gained more attention as the booming market on the coast made traders from the southern region penetrate deeper into the mainland in search of the supplies of gum, pepper, textiles, ivory, and captives much needed by the European traders. While Ọ̀yọ́ was plotting to establish colonies in Upper Òṣun and use them as conduits to establish a direct trading network with the coast, Iléṣà and other rain forest metropolises, especially Ìjẹ̀bú-Òde, were already making demands on the area for supplies needed for the same coastal market. The most peculiar of these supplies were human captives. The political atrophy of Ilé-Ifẹ̀ had created a leadership vacuum for the small-scale polities that dotted the landscape of this area. As a result, several polities, such as Gbọ́nmi (now a neighborhood in Òṣogbo), had either died out or drastically shrunk in size in the wake of the collapse of Ifẹ̀ Empire and the subsequent Nupe militarist crisis. The whole area remained in a state of disarray during the last quarter of the sixteenth century. The surge in abduction and raiding of the area for captives during the early seventeenth century is deeply imprinted in the historical memory of the local communities. The traditions in Òjo, Awó, and Arà, three of the ancient communities in Upper Òṣun, especially recall how, during the reign of Uyìarère (an *ọba* of Iléṣà), brigands ravaged their communities for captives and disrupted social lives. They "kidnapped women, children, and men; farmers could not go to their farms, and women could not go to the market for fear of their lives," as the paramount ruler of Òjo feelingly put it.[53]

Local informants refer to these brigands as Ìjẹ̀ṣà Aràra, an abbreviation of "the Ìjẹ̀ṣà of Uyì-a-rère," the king of Iléṣà who embarked on a vigorous expansionist program in Èkìtì and Upper Ọ̀ṣun from the 1630s to the 1650s.[54] These brigands may have included groups other than the Ìjẹ̀ṣà, but the traditions suggest that the reign of Uyìarère marked the high point of disturbance in the area. If, by supporting Ọwálúṣẹ́ in the 1580s, Ọ̀yọ́ had intended to use Iléṣà as a stepping-stone to reach the coast, the investment was not yielding the desired dividends for Ọ̀yọ́. Àtàkúnmọ̀sà's astute diplomacy kept the Ọ̀yọ́ at arm's length. Now under his successor, Uyìarère, the situation was getting worse. Uyìarère is credited with taking control of a fledgling frontier trading center, Early Òṣogbo, which a group of hunters and frontier migrants had established near River Òṣun during the last decade of the sixteenth century.[55] This takeover meant that Iléṣà was now able to control a strategic area of the commercial traffic in Upper Òṣun. This audacious act alarmed Ọ̀yọ́, whose leaders realized that Iléṣà might acquire the strength to effectively block Ọ̀yọ́'s access to the coast. The Iléṣà problem preoccupied Ọbalókun, and it also engaged the attention of his immediate successors, Olúodò and Àjàgbó respectively.

With its intimidating cavalry, Ọ̀yọ́ moved against Iléṣà on more than one occasion, especially during the reigns of both Ọbalókun and Àjàgbó. The early attacks seem to have ended in a stalemate.[56] While Iléṣà sources claimed that Ọ̀yọ́'s hostility was aimed at turning Iléṣà into a vassal state, Ọ̀yọ́ sources claimed that their goal was to punish Iléṣà for brigandage activities in Upper Òṣun. There is no doubt, however, that both saw Upper Òṣun as a strategic frontier. Ọ̀yọ́'s quest to establish a political foothold in the area was incompatible with the territorial aspirations of Iléṣà. Likewise, Iléṣà's emerging political influence in Upper Òṣun was unfavorable to the future of Ọ̀yọ́'s economic and political interests. This conflict of goals was resolved both militarily and diplomatically, with the following outcomes: (1) Iléṣà maintained its autonomy and continued to recognize Ọ̀yọ́ as its senior brother in the *ẹbí* fratenity, basically affirming its ceremonial client status to Ọ̀yọ́; (2) Ọ̀yọ́ halted Iléṣà's further expansion into Upper Òṣun and significantly curtailed brigand activities in the area; (3) the cavalry state established a frontier colony in Upper Òṣun (at Ẹdẹ-Ilé), a process that launched Ọ̀yọ́ on the path of becoming an imperial formation by the second quarter of the seventeenth century; and (4)

Ọ̀yọ́ recognized Early Òṣogbo as Iléṣà's frontier market town, a step that also opened the market to Ọ̀yọ́ traders.

Ọ̀yọ́'s political ascendancy in Upper Òṣun was a product of the efforts of relentless metropolitan leaders, as well as capable war captains who were also astute diplomats. To secure the area, Ọ̀yọ́ established a military outpost that eventually grew into the colony Ẹdẹ-Ilé, through a population resettlement program from the metropolitan area to the frontier. An enterprising warrior and brilliant archer, Tìmì Àgbàlé (nicknamed *Ọlọ́fà Iná*—"Owner of the flaming arrows"), was placed as the governor of this outpost to protect trade routes, rout out marauders, provide safe passage for Ọ̀yọ́ traders, set up turnpikes along the trading routes, and collect customs from those turnpike stations.[57] For this service, according to local historians, the frontier governor levied a toll of five cowries on every trader, with which he supported his family, "and as a good and loyal subject, he paid the surplus into the royal treasury" of Ọ̀yọ́.[58] The supposed amount of tolls levied on each trader is merely a cliché. The purpose of the story is to affirm that tributes and customs were funneled to the coffers of the metropolis through the colony. The colonization strategy that Ọ̀yọ́ pursued in Upper Òṣun would provide the template for the future Ọ̀yọ́ expansionist program.[59] The establishment of Ẹdẹ-Ilé as a colony of Ọ̀yọ́ is widely acclaimed to have brought security, peace, and stability to Upper Òṣun. Virtually all the communities in Upper Òṣun, except Òṣogbo, came under the governor of Ẹdẹ-Ilé.[60] The pacification of Upper Òṣun was therefore a major accomplishment in Ọ̀yọ́'s foreign policy. This decisive step allowed Ọ̀yọ́ to extend its territory into the central Yorùbá heartland and to begin to burnish its image as an agent of regional integration. By the time Àjàgbó resolved the Iléṣà question, the former savanna polity of Òwu had begun to thrive in the rain forest belt, between the Ifẹ̀ and Ẹ̀gbá territories. They did not escape the attention of Àjàgbó and his men. In order to secure their territorial holdings in Upper Ọ̀ṣun, the Ọ̀yọ́ used both carrot and stick to bring Òwu under Ọ̀yọ́'s political control, as both a client and a vassal state. Three hundred years after their first encounters, there was now a clear reverse of fortune between the two old foes.

At the time that Ọ̀yọ́ was vigorously pursuing its Upper Òṣun policy, especially during the 1620s and 1630s, its intended destinations on the coast—Ughoton, Màhin, and Lagos—were already losing their market shares to the Aja port towns on the western side of the Bight of Benin (present-day Benin Republic and Togo). For example, by 1630, Whydah and Allada had become the most lucrative centers of European commercial interest in the Bight of Benin.[61] Unlike at other ports in the Bight, human captives were the primary exports from these two ports, in response to the rising demand for labor in Europe's American colonies.

Though spearheaded by the Portuguese, several other European nations—the Spanish, Swedish, English, French, and Danish—soon joined to set up trading stations in the Aja coastland between 1640 and 1650. They were all in search of human cargo to load onto their America-bound ships. Ivory, cotton cloth, and dyestuff were also being exported via Mahi, but these commodities were secondary in value to human cargo.[62] With the expansion of commercial opportunities in Ouidah and Allada, Ọ̀yọ́ accelerated the mobilization of its military, political, and demographic resources toward gaining access to the coast via the Yéwá-Ògùn frontier. This area lies between the Rivers Weme and Ògùn in the south, and it includes the Ìbàrápá-Yorùba subgroup in the middle and the Òǹkò-Yorùbá in the north.

Bordering the vast, variegated landscape of hills, massive inselbergs, rivers, and lowlands on the west side of the frontier were two formidable ancient kingdoms, Ṣábẹ̀ and Kétu. Through political maneuvering and military threats, these two became allies rather than antagonists of Ọ̀yọ́ in its southward drive. And by 1625, several Ẹ̀gbá principalities were fully within the orbit of Ọ̀yọ́'s political control. Hence, at the very time that Ọ̀yọ́ was consolidating its hold on Upper Ọ̀ṣun through Ẹdẹ-Ilé, different detachments of its soldiers and administrators were also redrawing the political map of the Yéwá-Ògùn frontier. In the upper reaches of this area, Ọ̀yọ́ set up client towns and colonies at Ìgànná, Èrúwà, and Tápà by the mid-seventeenth century. Other Ọ̀yọ́ colonists pressed farther south. Among them were men such as Òrónà, Asakanran, Obaseru, and Ọbálajú, who established Ọ̀yọ́ colonies in Ìlarò, Ìbèsè, Ìṣàgá, and Jìga respectively.[63] Of these colonists, Òrónà, the pioneer governor of Ìlarò, was the most successful. He brought several communities in the area under his control, created political stability for this increasingly important frontier, and provided security for the pursuit of commerce. The Yéwá-Ògùn frontier was the jewel on the crown of the Ọ̀yọ́ imperial project. Of all the territorial possessions of the empire, none would be as profitable as this corridor of commerce. It gave Ọ̀yọ́ access to the coastal markets on the western side of the Bight of Benin and to several tributary and client states for almost two hundred years. I will return to this in chapter 6.

The Òrìṣà Pantheon Revised

The new military and hegemonic culture that took hold of the Yorùbá region in the Restoration period, as well as the demographic reshuffling, the burst of political consolidation and territorial expansion, and the new economic opportunities that defined this era of recovery, unleashed new ideas, intellectual reflections, and practices. Most important, between

1570 and 1650 the Yorùbá *òrìṣà* pantheon was reorganized and reinterpreted to create a cosmology compatible with the ongoing political and economic transformations, as well as with the new social order and hegemonic geography. New *òrìṣà* mythologies evolved to legitimize the emerging hegemonic states, rationalize and contest the power relations that configured this new differentiated political landscape, and articulate the anxieties that developed as a result. These mythoi constituted the means of communicative interactions between the different regions being integrated through territorial expansion and the new commercial networks. In chapter 3, I likened the Yorùbá *òrìṣà* pantheon to the parallel mirrors that produce the infinite reflections of the objects situated between them. In this case, the objects are the historical experience and everyday life. It is, therefore, not surprising that the infinite images projected on these mirrors are as unstable as the objects that they reflect. Hence, a longtime student of Yorùbá art, culture, and religion pertinently observes that "Whatever else it was, Yorùbá religion was a dynamic system, ever sensitive to the ongoing experience of an individual, a household, a town, or a region, ever changing and shaping anew the perception of self and [the] world."[64]

It is therefore to the *òrìṣà* myth-history and cultural biographies that we must again turn to understand some of the cultural transformations that accompanied the political and economic changes of this era of regeneration. These sources enable us to examine how the Yorùbá intellectuals of the early seventeenth century understood and explained the historical changes they were going through. I will use three case studies to illustrate this development. One is the symbolism of horses and its deployment in the Èkìtì region to articulate the experiences and memory of the atrophy of 1400–1570 and the restoration of 1570–1650. The second examines the expansion of the portfolio of Ògún from the folk deity of iron and hunting to the patron deity of the new warrior-kings and their hegemonic states. The third example highlights how the *òrìṣà* pantheon was reorganized, expanded, and reinterpreted to legitimize the new hegemonic states and their geographies of power.

The Horse Culture

Although during the Classical period the horse was used as a representation of prestige and honor, and also employed for warfare by Òwu, the actions of the Nupe militarists for more than a century finally made the Yorùbá world grapple with the reality of the horse as the quintessential hardware of warfare. The horse became synonymous with the ultimate symbol of indomitable military power. While Òwu was the first Yorùbá state to use cavalry during the fourteenth century, the Ọ̀yọ́ significantly expanded the use of horses in their wars of liberation and aggression during the sixteenth century. The endemic trypanosomiasis disease and the prohibitive cost of purchasing and maintaining horses, however, prevented the development of cavalry in the rain forest, especially in major political centers such as Iléṣà, Ilé-Ifẹ̀, Ọ̀wọ̀, and Benin.[65] Nevertheless, the experience of 1450 through 1550 made equestrian images to permeate many nexuses of social life in the Yorùbá world, so that equine representations became associated with the virtues of honor, "strength, bravery, physical courage, prowess," domination, virility, and militarism.[66] Likewise, the horse imagery became associated with speed, the overcoming of distance barriers, and the collapse of time and space.[67]

Across the Yorùbá world, there are differences in the raisons d'être for these invocations of horse imagery. The hegemonic states of Ọ̀yọ́ and Benin, for example, used the horse as a symbol of royalty and conquest in the elite visual arts and state performative arts. However, while horses were instruments of both war and royal ceremony in Ọ̀yọ́, horses were not mounted in Benin but were reserved only for the pomp and pageantry of its royalty. In contrast, the pervasive use of horse imagery among the Èkìtì had nothing to do with kingship. Instead, it was associated with the Ẹpa festivals, annual religious events and communal ceremonies that originally served to commemorate ancestors and invoke prayers for fertility. This was (and still is) a masked tradition involving the wearing of "hoodlike headpieces . . . surmounted by animal and human figures" in annual public ceremonies.[68] Armies were not mounted in Èkìtì, and for the most part, their political elite did not own horses. The incorporation of horse images into Ẹpa masks would have begun in the aftermath of the brigandage activities by Nupe horsemen, as J. R. O. Ojo noted in this excellent exposition: "These echoes of war [equestrian motifs] in Ẹpa-type masquerade and other rituals in Èkìtì (and Ìgbómìnà) can be regarded as reflections of the wars waged against the people of the area by various armies from as early as the sixteenth century to the closing years of the nineteenth century."[69]

The equestrian/warrior motifs constitute only one of three types of Ẹpa mask (fig. 5.3). The other two originated in the pre-sixteenth century masking tradition and focused on two concerns: (1) fertility and abundance (agriculture and reproduction), and (2) healing and wellness, especially against the pox viruses that periodically flared into epidemic outbreaks. The iconography of the former is usually mother and children, while the latter is represented by the imagery of the deity of medicine (Ọ̀sanyìn). The equestrian imagery was added in the aftermath of the Nupe crisis, not to celebrate royalty and conquest but to commemorate that crisis, honor ancestral memory, and invoke equestrian power for communal protection. Hence, the Èkìtì's equestrian experience was

Figure 5.3. Ẹpa mask (*left*, H. 78 cm) and Ọ̀bàràbarà Olókùnẹṣin mask (*right*, H. 81 cm)

integrated into the existing Ẹpa tradition, becoming a new yarn of time woven into the much older two yarns. The fertility and healing motifs in Ẹpa masks most likely dated to the Early Formative period, and they may have deep roots in the proto-Yoruboid cultural substratum.[70] In their contemporary performances, the equestrian images in Ẹpa masks are not generally directed at any named war hero. Rather, they are called *ológun* (warrior) masks and could be owned by the *ilé* (House) or *ìlú* (kingdom).[71] They invoked generalized war agents instead of commemorating particular war heroes or being associated with a warrior-king. This contrasts with the case of Ọ̀yọ́, where the horse-military imagery was an integral part of the iconography of Ṣàngó, the mythic warrior-king founder and patron deity of the state.[72]

The Èkìtì and their Okun neighbors in the north—the Yàgbà, Ijùmú, and Bùnú—bore the brunt of the cycle of invasions that began with the brigandage of Nupe militarists. And it was Èkìtì that served as the theater of the final battles that eventually dislodged the Nupe militarists from the central Yorùbá region. However, in the aftermath of the Nupe invasions, Èkìtì was treated as a spoil of war by the hegemonic states of Ọ̀yọ́ and Benin and their junior brother city-state, Ilẹ́ṣà. Through all of this, the

Èkìtì did not have the wherewithal to develop cavalry, and their rain forest environment was not conducive to horse keeping. So, one may ask, what were the non-cavalry, politically marginalized Èkìtì of the late sixteenth and early seventeenth century doing in their annual communal festivals with the object of their oppression—equestrian imagery? The answer is not far-fetched. Through the horse imagery, the Èkìtì remember the many layers of external aggressions against them dating back to the late fifteenth and sixteenth century, and they have used this imagery to commemorate and celebrate their resistance and survival. Hence, the imagery of Ẹpa horsemen, "shown in traditional military uniform, brandishing weapons of war, ready for battle . . . engaging in [an] actual war on the battlefield, capturing slaves, and bringing home plunder," has been a performative counter-narrative and a subversive representation directed against the mounted foreign attackers who once ravaged the Èkìtì region.[73]

J. R. O. Ojo, following Victor Turner, has called this stock representation a "ritual role reversal."[74] That is, the various Èkìtì communities appropriated and sought to domesticate the powers of the various foreign cavalries who disrupted their lives and livelihood at different periods since the mid-fifteenth century. In other words, the equestrian images in Ẹpa served to contain and dissipate the horror, disruption, and dislocation introduced to the Èkìtì region by Nupe horsemen and later by other hegemonic states, especially Benin and Ọ̀yọ́. The Ẹpa maskers appropriated the foreign power of cavalry so that their ancient deities could be better attuned to the new instruments of war and be able to prevent or overcome such attacks in the future. The annual festivals in which these masks were danced or performed offered a subtle but potent critique of the hegemonic powers that had tormented the Èkìtì.[75] The Ẹpa equestrian masks did not only serve as a way of experiencing multiple layers of time relating to mounted invasions; they have also served to commemorate those who were lost to these external aggressions, either through death or enslavement. Hence, men of warrior age played prominent roles in the Ẹpa *ológun* masking. With war songs and martial styles of dance, they would carry the masks "round the town, with the masquerade stopping at all entries to the town, all shrine houses and compounds," to offer prayers and sacrifices.[76]

Masks with horseman imagery are not limited to the Èkìtì and Okun areas. Nearby, in the old Ẹ̀ka Ọ̀ṣun territory (in Ìbòkun), the Ẹpa-like masking tradition is also performed during the annual festival of Obòkun-Ọ̀bàrà to honor the father-son complex for their military exploits and to commemorate their role as the founding ancestors of the Iléṣà kingdom.[77] We have already noted the strong Èkìtì affinities of Ọ̀bàrà and other men who began the spate of conquests that gave birth to Iléṣà during the final quarter of the sixteenth century. Surmounted by a large figure depicting the man, his horse, and his weapons (see fig. 5.3), the warrior's equestrian mask is unmistakably Ẹpa-like. This further lends support to my previous submission that what we now know as Ìjẹ̀ṣà is an Ifẹ̀-Èkìtì cultural continuum and that many of the warriors who were responsible for the waves of conquests in Ẹ̀ka Ọ̀ṣun (now northern Ìjẹ̀ṣàland) during the late sixteenth century were of Ifẹ̀-Èkìtì cultural background and were veterans of the war that ended the Nupe brigandage in the area. The equestrian figures of Obòkun-Ọ̀bàrà complex and of Ẹpa in various Èkìtì communities are, therefore, all related to their common sixteenth-century experiences. However, this is where the similarity ends. The equestrian motifs in the Obòkun-Ọ̀bàrà festival celebrated the power of domination and commemorated the role of the mythical Obòkun (the father) and the historical Ọ̀bàrà (the son) as war heroes and founders of the Iléṣà kingdom. The festival and the equestrian mask also sought the help of these deified heroes against the enemies of the state and its citizens (Iléṣà).[78] In contrast, the Èkìtì's Ẹpa equestrian motifs articulated a rejection of those hegemonic powers, wishing them to remain outside the walls of their towns.

Ògún: Hero Deity of the Age of Restoration

The Restoration period did not only give us a new generation of warrior-kings and war heroes such as Abípa, Ọbalókun, and Àjàgbó of Ọ̀yọ́; Orhogbua and Ehengbuda of Benin; and Ọ̀bàrà, Ọwálúṣẹ́, and Àtàkúnmọ̀sà of Ifẹ̀-Èkìtì and Iléṣà kingdom. It also transformed a folk *òrìṣà* into the patron deity of these warrior-kings. Ògún was the deity of this new age of regeneration. Virtually all the new kingdoms and dynasties established in the Upper Ọ̀ṣun-Ìgbómìnà-Ìjẹ̀ṣà-Èkìtì axis between the late sixteenth and early seventeenth century adopted Ògún as their patron deity.[79] Even the Ìbàrìbá warriors who started the line of *baṣọ̀run* nobility in Ọ̀yọ́-Ilé in the late sixteenth century adopted Ògún as their patron deity. The Restoration period therefore marked the beginning of the age of Ògún.

Ògún is one of the oldest concept deities in the Yorùbá pantheon. Linguistic and cultural historical trails suggest that the Ògún complex originated in the Later Stone Age proto-Yoruboid communities of the confluence, where Ògún was associated with the iconic tool of the period—the polished stone axe.[80] The Ògún concept was then transposed to the iron-related activities and technology that began to emerge during the second half of the first millennium BC. The Ògún complex would have been well established before the proto-Yoruboid populations began their southward expansion at the end of the first millennium BC. It is therefore instructive that the myth of origins in Ilé-Ifẹ̀ recognized Ògún as one of the primordial deities, whose iron implements cleared the path in the cosmic journey of Odùduwà, Ọbàtálá, and other political ancestors to create the Earth at Ilé-Ifẹ̀. The role of Ògún in these narratives was one of path clearer, blacksmith, and iron smelter. He was a facilitator of the political will of two leaders—Odùduwà and Ọbàtálá, not a warrior-king. Unlike most other major deities in Ilé-Ifẹ̀ with Classical-era provenance, especially those whose origins were associated with political power and ancestors, Ògún did not begin his career in the Yorùbá pantheon as a deity of the state, royal authority, and war. Rather, as I will argue below, Ògún was originally associated with iron production and dispensation of impartial justice.[81]

Again, the Èkìtì area seems to have played a significant role in the development and maturity of Ògún's iron production–justice administration complex before the fifteenth century. It was in that same area that Ògún's spheres of influence also included hunting, farming, and heraldic activities. In contrast, in the northwestern, southern, and western parts of the Yorùbá region, hunting was separated from Ògún and instead had its own deity, commonly known as Erinlẹ̀ or Ọsọ́ọ̀sì. Moreover, prior to the Intermediate period, Ògún was not the focus of royal festivals, and neither was warfare emphasized in his worship. Rather, he was a folk deity, the all-permeating deity whose iron implements and tools were essential to everyday life. This all changed during the sixteenth century, when the portfolio and cultural biography of Ògún were enlarged to include not only iron production, the everyday use of iron, and hunting but also statecraft and empire-building. This expansion was a product of the sociopolitical turmoil and prevailing warfare of the fifteenth and sixteenth centuries, as well as the emergence of militaristic states between 1570 and 1650.

For those *ìlú* whose foundation or rebuilding was shaped by the warring activities that prevailed during the Restorative period, Ògún became intimately associated with kingship institution, warfare, urbanization, and state formation.[82] The politicization of Ògún and the preference for warrior kings were two characteristics common to the new polities and dynasties that emerged in Ifẹ̀, Èkìtì, Ìgbómìnà, Oǹdó, Ìjẹ̀ṣà, and Ọ̀yọ́ areas from the last quarter of the sixteenth to the mid-seventeenth century.[83] In contrast, those areas that lost out in this new geography of power (e.g., Ìlàrè, Ìkìrun, Awó, and Òjo) shunned Ògún in their royal festivals. Ògún accumulated new attributes during that period, and these were merged with the old ones. The weapons that came out of the iron forges enabled the Yorùbá-speaking areas to remain armed throughout the period of instability. Hunters must have provided the initial leadership for the war, serving as the standard-bearers on whose shoulders it fell to train recruits and lead them to war. The rise of Ògún in popularity across the Yorùbá world during the Intermediate and Restoration periods was a celebration and an acknowledgment of the collaborative roles that iron smelters, blacksmiths, hunters, and warriors played in the defeat of the Nupe militarists, and the same collaboration enabled some of the military leaders to embark immediately on state-building activities.[84] Thus, the association of Ògún with governance and statecraft in the late sixteenth century was a bricolage of different layers of time and experience, as well as of different though related elements that signified one another—iron technology, war, conquest, state-building, and new royal dynasties.

In other words, the popularity of Ògún as the deity of war arose during the fifteenth- and sixteenth-century instability. And, in the aftermath of the crisis, the Ògún complex provided the political charter and epistemology for the warrior-kings and their lieutenants, who were the champions of the new age. The association of Ògún with state formation expanded after 1570, when militarism rather than traditional inheritance or patrimony was the dominant pathway to political power. Ògún was celebrated as the mentor of these new warrior-kings and patron of their royal dynasties. The ways and manners in which Ògún is celebrated today as the center of the civic religion of many Yorùbá cities and towns reveal the war spirit that defined his transformations during the sixteenth century:

> Ǹjẹ́ níbo l'a ti pàdé Ògún?
> A pàdé Ògún níbi ìjà
> A pàdé Ògún níbi ìta
> A pàdé rẹ̀ níbi àgbàrá ẹ̀jẹ̀ ńsàn
> Àgbàrà ẹ̀jẹ̀ tí dé ni lọ̀rùn bí omi àgò

Translation:

> Where did we meet Ògún?
> We met Ògún in the conflict zone
> We met Ògún in the open space (war zone)
> We met him where the flood of blood is flowing
> In the drowning flood of blood[85]

Ògún's rituals and ceremonies show that the *òrìṣà* was regarded as the path to the new political authority and the agent for "the imposition of a new order." For the soldiers and mercenaries, as well as their political patrons, maintaining a continuous relationship with Ògún was essential for the sustenance of their "aggressive militarism" and the survival of their polities.[86] Hence, in Iléṣà and Èkìtì, as well as in the frontier town of Oǹdó, Ògún became the center of royal festivals.[87]

The likelihood that Èkìtì was the provenance of Ògún's war motif is compellingly suggested in the following version of the most popular panegyric (*oríkì*) of the deity.

Ògún méje l'Ògún mi
Ògún Alárá n'ígba ajá
Ògún Onírè a gba àgbò
Ògún Ìkọ̀lé á gba ìgbín
Ògún Ẹlẹ́mọnà n'ígba ẹ̀sún iṣu
Ògún Àkìrun á gba ìwo àgbò
Ògún gbẹ́nàgbẹ́nà ẹran ahun ní jẹ
Ògún mákindé ti d'Ògún lẹ́hìn odi
Bí kò bá gba Tápà, a gba Àbókí,
A gba Uku-Uku, a gba Kemberi

Translation:

My Ògún is of seven types
The Ògún of Alárá (king of Ará) takes the dog for sacrifice
The Ògún of Onírè (king of Ìrè) takes the ram
The Ògún of Ìkọ̀lé town takes the snail
The Ògún of the king of Ìmọ̀nà takes roasted yam
The Ògún of the king of Ìkìrun takes the ram's horn
The Ògún of woodcarvers eats tortoise
The Ògún sacrifice performed for war victories and in honor of warriors
takes place outside the city walls
If it does not accept Tápà (Nupe) for sacrifice,
It will take Àbókí (Hausa), or Uku-uku, or Kemberi

The kingdoms of Ará, Ìrè, Ìkọ̀lé, and Ìmọ̀nà, mentioned above, are all in Èkìtì, whereas Ìkìrun is in the Upper Ọ̀ṣun area (see fig. 5.1). The panegyric indicates that the cultural biography of Ògún is an assemblage of many elements from different places and multiple spheres of activities, with most of them centering on Èkìtì. The composition of the *oríkì* suggests the shared experience and history of the Èkìtì kingdoms. It also reveals whom they regarded as outsiders and emphasizes who deserved to be sacrificed to Ògún or killed on the battle field outside the city walls. Here, the Tápà (the Yorùbá name for the Nupe), two other confluence people (Uku-uku and Kemberi), and Àbókí (Hausa) are the stereotypical outsiders and enemies deemed appropriate for such sacrifice in honor of Ògún, the victorious warrior. The Kemberi and Uku-uku were among the allies (and sometimes victims) of the Nupe militarists. And not only did the Àbókí (Hausa) supply the Nupe with the horses that drove the latter's brigandage operations, but many of the captives that Nupe brigands carted away from the Yorùbá-speaking region were sold to the Hausa during the fifteenth and sixteenth centuries. In addition, the above panegyric demonstrates that in contrast to the beheading of enemies (warfare) to propitiate Ògún outside the city walls, sacrifices of dogs, rams, snails, roasted yam, and tortoises were only used to honor Ògún within the city walls. Hence, the trophy heads and other human skeletal parts tempered into the city walls of Iléṣà and the wall of Obòkun-Ọ̀bàrà temple in Ìbòkun are mentioned in the oral traditions as those of the named enemies, among whom the Nupe brigands featured prominently.[88]

Gendered Hegemonic and Counter-Hegemonic Discourses in the Frontiers

The frontiers of Upper Ọ̀ṣun and Yéwá-Ògùn also provided fertile ground for expanding the myth-history of the *òrìṣà* pantheon during this period of regeneration. It was in Upper Ọ̀ṣun that Iléṣà and Ọ̀yọ́ competed fiercely for territorial annexation and, as a result, three theogonic revisions took place. One sought to rationalize the relationships between the two foes. The second focused on the relationships between them and the old Ifẹ̀-centric authority they were replacing. And the third explained the unequal power relations that developed between the Upper Ọ̀ṣun frontier communities and the Ọ̀yọ́ metropolis. The rise of the savanna kingdom of Ọ̀yọ́ as the overlord of most of Upper Ọ̀ṣun in the rain forest belt necessitated the revision and reorganization of the intellectual and structural template of the *òrìṣà* pantheon so as to institutionalize and rationalize the new geography of regional hierarchies. The military encounters between Ọ̀yọ́ and Iléṣà, for example, were framed in the myth-history as conflicts between Ṣàngó and Ògún, respectively. The competitive and antagonistic nature of the two deities has been recited and described in several genres of Yorùbá literature and orature.[89] Although both Ọ̀yọ́ and Iléṣà eventually found a diplomatic truce to their competing interests in Upper Ọ̀ṣun, with Ọ̀yọ́ securing the larger share of the territory, they still had to contend with the fact that the territory they were annexing was not a tabula rasa. It was once a thriving province of Ilé-Ifẹ̀ under the spiritual patronage of the two most venerated Ifẹ̀-centric *òrìṣà*—Ọbàtálá and Ọ̀rúnmìlà. It became necessary for the Ọ̀yọ́ horsemen and their sword-wielding Iléṣà antagonists to legitimize their shared political domination of this erstwhile Ifẹ̀ territory. It is a testimony to the elasticity of the Ifẹ̀-centric soft power that both Ọ̀yọ́ and Iléṣà find it compelling to write themselves into the Ifẹ̀-centric pantheon and mythos in the quest to achieve this legitimacy.

To explain the encounters between the intruding militaristic states of Ọ̀yọ́ and Iléṣà on one hand and the Ifẹ̀-centric Upper Ọ̀ṣun frontier on the other, seventeenth-century Yorùbá intellectuals turned to the ancestral principles of complementary gender duality (chap. 2). The militaristic states were represented as masculine, *akọ*, and the territory they were annexing was feminized as *abo*. That is, the intrusive metropolises and their representatives constituted the field of patricentric authority, while the provincial frontier was the field of matricentric authority. The masculine deities of the metropolises—Ṣàngó in Ọ̀yọ́ and Ògún in Iléṣà—were contrasted with the feminine deities of the Upper Ọ̀ṣun frontier—Ọ̀ṣun and Ọbà goddesses. The latter were manifested in the two rivers that defined the boundaries of this frontier zone and that bear those names (see fig. 5.1). Before the intrusion of Ògún's sword and Ṣàngó's horses into the area, these river goddesses were local deities who had been the focus of identity formation and religious worship for the local communities on their banks, such as Ìwó near Ọbà River and Gbọ̀nmi and Early Ọ̀ṣogbo on the banks of River Ọ̀ṣun. New narratives were invented within the framework of the existing *òrìṣà* theogony to give ideological backing and legitimacy to the stability, power sharing, and territorial annexation that were taking place during this period of regeneration and restoration. These narratives sought to reconcile the patricentric deities of the new metropolises with the matricentric ones of the old provinces, and the patricentric deities of the new centers of power (Ọ̀yọ́ and Iléṣà) with the patricentric ones of Ifẹ̀ ritual field (Ọbàtálá, Ọ̀rúnmìlà, and Ògún). The result is a vast transcript of *òrìṣà* stories, symbols, and rituals that articulates the new changes in territorial power relations and the hegemonic and counter-hegemonic discourses taking place in Upper Ọ̀ṣun during the early seventeenth century.

The idiom of marriage was specifically used to explain the dominance of Ọ̀yọ́ in Upper Ọ̀ṣun. Hence, Ọ̀ṣun is said to have first married Ọ̀rúnmìlà (deity of wisdom, knowledge, and divination) and later Ògún. Because of her inability to conceive and have children, she divorced Ọ̀rúnmìlà and Ògún in turn and became the wife of Ṣàngó.[90] This mythos provides the precise temporal sequence of how Upper Ọ̀ṣun passed on as a province of Ilé-Ifẹ̀ (represented by Ọ̀rúnmìlà) to Iléṣà (Ògún) and then to Ọ̀yọ́ (Ṣàngó). The mythos employs the metaphor of virility, the quintessential virtue of Ṣàngó; the clichéd feminine seduction, epitomized in Ọ̀ṣun; and the sociocultural dynamics of co-wife rivalry, embodied in Ọ̀ṣun and Ọbà's hostile relationship, a common stereotypical theme in Yorùbá polygynous households. According to the narrative, Ṣàngó was attracted to Upper Ọ̀ṣun territory by the beauty of two river goddesses—Ọ̀ṣun and Ọbà (the largest rivers in the area).[91] The intrepid, hypermasculine, and charming Ṣàngó married both. Afterward, the two women were locked in bitter co-wife rivalry in order to retain Ṣàngó's affection. One version of the mythos recounts how Ọbà went to the extent of cutting off one of her ears and using it to make a love potion for Ṣàngó. Apparently, Ọbà's desperation did not work. In fact, her magical quest for Ṣàngó's attention backfired. Ṣàngó found out this trickery and banished her from the palace. This was the beginning of the fortune of Ọ̀ṣun. Regarded as the epitome of feminine sensuality, flirtation, fecundity, and industriousness,

Ọ̀ṣun became the cynosure of Ṣàngó's attention, and he "built her a glorious brass palace where she bore him the blessing of twins."[92]

The Ọ̀ṣun-Ọ̀bà co-wife rivalry is a mythic representation of the competitions that took place among the various communities in Upper Ọ̀ṣun for political and commercial advantages. The intervention of Iléṣà and Ọ̀yọ́ enabled Early Ọ̀ṣogbo, for which Ọ̀ṣun served as the patron deity (and the river, the basis of its communal identity), to emerge out of that struggle as the premier market town of Upper Ọ̀ṣun. Traders from across the region—Ọ̀yọ́, Iléṣà, Ìjẹ̀bú, Ọ̀wu, Ifẹ̀, Èkìtì, and Ìgbómìnà, among others—met there to exchange their goods and services.[93] The Upper Ọ̀ṣun area in general was the object and subject of Ọ̀yọ́'s political desire. And Early Ọ̀ṣogbo in particular was important to the nascent empire's economic project. With such a thriving market center open to Ọ̀yọ́ traders (though under Iléṣà's political control), it is not surprising that Ọ̀ṣun, the patron deity of the area, became the favorite wife of Ṣàngó. Our indigenous intellectuals encoded the unfolding transformations in power relations taking place in Upper Ọ̀ṣun at that time in the accentuated metaphors of male virility, female seduction, husbandhood, and wifehood. Ọ̀ṣun, a former wife of Ọ̀rúnmìlà and then Ògún, had gone through two marriages without any children. But Ṣàngó lured her away, and she bore him twins. The moral of the story is that Ọ̀ṣun (the province of Upper Ọ̀ṣun) would have remained barren (poor) if not for the virility (protection and power) of Ṣàngó (the metropolis, Ọ̀yọ́-Ilé). "Power," according to Wade Nobles, "is the ability to define reality and to convince other people that it is their definition."[94] Ọ̀yọ́ did not use its overwhelming military power alone to carve out a territory in Upper Ọ̀ṣun. It also used the power of stories and performance to legitimize this conquest and create a new reality. Of all the myth-historical inventions that developed after 1570, none was as successful as this mythos in writing Ṣàngó and Ọ̀ṣun into the Ifẹ̀-centric *òrìṣà* transcripts. It makes a strong case for Ọ̀yọ́'s legitimacy as the premier inheritor of Ilé-Ifẹ̀ and dispossessor of Iléṣà. This legitimacy was attributed, genderly, to the advantages of Ṣàngó's virility—sexual strength and potency. The opposite was the implied impotence and manly weakness of his archrival and brother—Ògún.[95]

Yemọja is to the Yéwá-Ògùn frontier what the goddess Ọ̀ṣun is to Upper Ọ̀ṣun. Like Ọ̀ṣun, Yemọja represents the matricentric energy.[96] Her provenance of origin lies in the upper reaches of the Ogun River, covering the Ọ̀ǹkò and Ìbàràpá areas, a region over which Ọ̀yọ́ established suzerainty and trading routes in the late sixteenth and early seventeenth century, respectively. In contrast to the accommodative and flirtatious mythos of Ọ̀ṣun toward Ṣàngó, the mythos of Yemọja expresses uncommon confidence and assertiveness. Here is the reason. As Ọ̀yọ́ embarked on territorial expansion in the Yéwá-Ògùn frontier in the last quarter of the sixteenth century, many provincial women were brought into Ọ̀yọ́-Ilé as wives.[97] The Yéwá-Ògùn women being incorporated into the metropolis of Ọ̀yọ́ as wives and mothers brought their natal deity, Yemọja, into Ọ̀yọ́ households and used this to forge solidarity among themselves, especially as their number grew in the capital. With Yéwá-Ògùn becoming important to the economic well-being of Ọ̀yọ́ in the early seventeenth century, as a passage to the coast and source of vital human and material resources needed in the capital (wives and labor), emphasis was placed on Yemọja as a wife in the house of Ṣàngó (Ọ̀yọ́-Ilé and the Alaafin's palace) and as the mother of Ṣàngó's sons, the *aláàfin*. In as much as every living *aláàfin* was (and still is) the manifestation and personification of Ṣàngó (the ancestral father), it follows that Yemọja was not just the wife of Ṣàngó but also the mother of Ṣàngó-incarnate, the reigning *aláàfin*. The Yemọja mythos therefore represented a new chapter in the history of Ọ̀yọ́ and Yéwá-Ògùn.[98] Hence, in the ritual history of the areas into which Ọ̀yọ́ expanded in the seventeenth century, the references to Yemọja as the wife of Ṣàngó are often juxtaposed with the traditions claiming that Yemọja was also his mother.[99] Therefore, the devotees of Yemọja (wife of Ṣàngó, mother of the *aláàfin*), often asserted a critical stance toward Ṣàngó, emphasizing her nurturing, diametrical, and complementary relationship with the fiery warrior-kings. For example, the following panegyric of Yemọja, collected by J. Lorand Matory, emphasizes Yemọja's nurturing, motherly role in general, the commercial importance of her home (Yéwá-Ògùn frontier) to Ọ̀yọ́, and the mother-son relationship between the provincial goddess and the metropolitan god/king.

> Yemọja who has the back to carry Sango.
> The baby sling of that youngster [Sango] is like a shining baby sling . . .
> Owner of breasts of honey, there is no hill as nice as Ìgbàdì Hill . . .
> Mighty water of endless expanse is the home of Yemọja,
> Who eats two rams in the river . . .
> The center of the house is the river.
> The great collector, our mother with breasts that go all over her chest . . .
> My spectacularly fierce mother, who eats people in the manner of the stinging caterpillar . . .
> I met Yemọja enthroned . . .
> Owner of white teeth,[100] who is a trader,
> The center of the house is the river[101]

Summing Up

The regeneration, reterritorializing, and rebuilding that began in the last quarter of the sixteenth century were fully accomplished during the second quarter of the seventeenth century. A few hegemonic states—Ọ̀yọ́, Iléṣà, Benin, and Ìjẹ̀bú-Òde—consolidated territorial power. The first would dominate the political landscape of the Yorùbá community of practice for the next two hundred years, linking the older axes of commerce via the Niger River to the new trading stations on the Atlantic littorals. By 1580, Ọ̀yọ́ was creating minions and clients from the very territory where Classical Ilé-Ifẹ̀ once collected tolls and tributes, two hundred years earlier. Iléṣà nearly outfoxed Ọ̀yọ́'s territorial ambitions in the central Yorùbá region, but the young and determined state was no match for Ọ̀yọ́'s equestrian might in the woodlands between the Ọ̀ṣun and Ọ̀bà Rivers. Although the children of Ṣàngó suffered setbacks in Èkìtì and Ọ̀wẹ̀nà, their galloping horses and flaming arrows were unstoppable in Ìgbómìnà, Moshi-Niger area, Upper Ọ̀ṣun, and Yéwá-Ògùn. In Abípa, Ọbalókun, and Àjàgbó, all *aláàfin* of Ọ̀yọ́, and their frontier agents, such as Ogunlọlá of Ògbómọ̀ṣọ́, Tìmì Àgbàlé of Ẹdẹ-Ilé, and Òrónà of Ìlarò, we see the emergence of new men who were the architects of what would soon become the largest empire south of the River Niger during the Atlantic age. These men were ambitious warriors, but they combined military tactics with shrewd diplomacy and administrative acuity. They negotiated new political boundaries and created a new social order. With their expanding territorial gains, they brought the ways of the savanna into the rain forest belt and began to use their Ọ̀yọ́-centric mythoi to define new realities and stimulate new contemplations for the region. Of course, Ọ̀yọ́ was not the only winner in that period of regeneration. Iléṣà and Benin; Ìjẹ̀bú, Oǹdó and Ọ̀wọ̀; among others, renegotiated their political topography and the hierarchies of power in the region. The careers of Ọ̀bàràbarà Olókùnẹṣin, Ọwárì, Ọwálúṣẹ́, Arápatẹ́, and Àtàkúnmọ̀sà in one of the old suburbs of Ifẹ̀ metropolis exemplify the new opportunities for social mobility that emerged at the end of the long period of instability. Ọwálúṣẹ́ and Àtàkúnmọ̀sà proved to be astute diplomats and state-builders, and their careers exemplified the high level of political sophistication that characterized the process of regenerating the Yorùbá community of practice ca. 1580–1630.

Ilé-Ifẹ̀ itself was the last of the surviving Classical-era polities to recover. Many in the Èkìtì area were not that lucky. In the turmoil that followed the collapse of Ifẹ̀ Empire, a great number of the *ìlú/ọba-aládé* in Èkìtì permanently lost their old glory, while others were obliterated from the political landscape. The frequent mention of the names of these polities in the Ifá divination orature and in the panegyrics associated with many of the *òrìṣà* recall their old fame and once important position, but often these invocations are frozen in an arcane and mythologized past.[102] Ilé-Ifẹ̀'s instrumental political power fell apart in the early fifteenth century, but the work of restoration that took place between 1570 and 1650 was still based on the *ìlú/ọba-aládé* dyadic social order, the ideology of the *ẹbí* fraternity, and the intellectual framework of an integrated *òrìṣà* pantheon, which the "city of sunrise" had championed during the Classical period. By 1650, the scale of the fraternity and the pantheon was expanding, and there were new political actors and metropolises who outshone Ilé-Ifẹ̀. Nevertheless, they all depended on the Ifẹ̀-centric template for legitimizing their political gains. The ideologies of the *ẹbí* fraternity and the *òrìṣà* pantheon provided a flexible and permeable template as well as a resilient orthodoxy that allowed the incorporation of new members (dynasties, kingdoms, provinces, and deities) into the Yorùbá community of practice. The *òrìṣà* theogony was therefore revised and expanded in order to capture the new experiences of the fifteenth through the mid-seventeenth century. Although the *ẹbí* fraternity was no longer supported by the regime of prestige goods dominated by Ilé-Ifẹ̀, the transcendental authority that those goods symbolized was strong enough to keep the expanding Yorùbá community of practice within the orbit of Ifẹ̀'s spiritual and sacred referentiality.

The surging waves of Atlantic commerce also provided the region with an economic boost for recovery. The evolving Atlantic world, of which pockets of the Yorùbá region had been a part since the sixteenth century, ended its first phase in the first quarter of the seventeenth century. The second phase of the Atlantic commercial system that took off afterward was the starting point for the atlantization of the Yorùbá world. The Atlantic Ocean (rather than the River Niger) became the reference point for commercial wealth and economic prosperity. Therefore, all roads led to the coast during the seventeenth and eighteenth centuries. The model of multicultural, cosmopolitan, and networked urban emporia of the previous centuries would serve as the blueprint for building the Yorùbá economy around this new commercial life pressing in from the coast. The entanglement with the Atlantic trade would soon exponentially expand the scale of the region's market capacity. However, unlike in the Classical period, the Yorùbá world would not control the registers of value that financed the market and the wealth that accrued from it. This new economic regime brought about a sea change in the social, intellectual, and cultural lives of the region. The unfolding of this process and its impacts between ca. 1630 and 1840 is the subject of the four chapters that follow.

Notes

1. Inikori, "Africa and the Globalization Process."
2. Adekunle, *Politics and Society*, 214.
3. A suite of three AMS dates of fourteenth through early sixteenth centuries that I obtained in 2019 from Bàrà, 2 km from Ọ̀yọ́-Ilé, in stratified deposits is casting a new light on the settlement history of what became the Ọ̀yọ́ metropolitan area during the late sixteenth century (app. 2). Though at preliminary stages of analysis, the evidence indicates that these pre-empire

communities lived in dispersed hamlets and homesteads and constructed stone markers that possibly served as the focus of community gathering and rituals. Their domestic material culture was very minimal, comprising only of small portable ceramic vessels (dominated by incised and cord-rouletted decorations), household iron implements (especially knives), and flatly laid potsherd pavement. In contrast, the late sixteenth-century Ọ̀yọ́ settlers built towns, cities, and large villages of craft specialists, especially iron smelters, and had broad and varied suites of artifacts. The ceramics of the Atòkúta and Ọ̀yọ́ occupation phases are also different in form and decoration. It appears that the Atòkúta settlements came to a sudden end ca. 1570–1580, when the Ọ̀yọ́ arrived and embarked on the process of building their capital in the area. For a report of the excavations in Bara, see Ogundiran, Mangut, and Moyib, "Archaeological Landscape of Bara." The details of these dates are available in app. 2 under Ọ̀YỌ́. The Atòkúta culture may be the same as or related to the thirteenth- and fourteenth-century occupation level that Robert Soper has called Díògún in Ọ̀yọ́-Ilé. There are even older radiocarbon dates of ninth through thirteenth centuries at Ọ̀yọ́-Ilé, reported by Agbaje-Williams, but the material culture associated with those dates is not yet well defined. See Agbaje-Williams, "Contribution"; Agbaje-Williams, Diogun and Mejiro Wares; Folorunso et al., "Revisiting Old Oyo"; Soper, "Archaeological Work"; Sowunmi et al., "Revisit."

4. Johnson, *History*, 168.

5. Johnson, 107.

6. Ogunlọlá is an unmistakable Yorùbá name, meaning "honor is derived from warfare," yet this individual is identified as a man of Ìbàrìbá descent. Kalilu, "Between Tradition and Record," 55. This shows the fluidity in the cultural works of identity in the making of Ọ̀yọ́ citizenship, and a continuation of more than five hundred years of experience of cosmopolitanism in the region.

7. Johnson, *History*, 70.

8. Johnson, *History*, 170–176.

9. The seven *ọ̀yọ́mèsì* titles are Àgbaakin, Akinniku, *Alápinnì,* Asípa, Baṣọ̀run, Lágùnà, and Ṣàmú. Each of these lords of the major nonroyal Houses performed important political and religious functions that complemented the duties of the *aláàfin* (Johnson, *History*, 72–73).

10. Law, *Oyo Empire*, 85.

11. Kuba and Akinwumi, "Precolonial Borgu," 342.

12. Ogbomo, *When Men and Women Mattered*, 124.

13. Abiodun, "Kingdom of Owo"; Ben-Amos, *Art, Innovation, and Politics*; Usuanlele, "Precolonial Benin."

14. Ẹ̀ka Ọ̀ṣun was a collective of mega-House or House polities brought together by Ìlàrè through both diplomacy and conquest. Hence Ìlàrè's cognomen, *Ọmọ olórí elú yè ó tètè yàn, ọmọ olórí elú Ẹ̀kaỌ̀ṣun*: "Descendants of the first among the other potentates, descendants of the supreme head of Ẹ̀ka Ọ̀ṣun" (Oyelade, "Odun Irele," 91).

15. Archaeological data, including radiocarbon dates, demonstrate that the chief town of Ìlàrè, located in what is now called Igbó-Ùloyì, was abandoned during this period—the late sixteenth century. Oral traditions claim that a large section of the population, especially the political class, sought refuge in Ìkìrun, an Ifẹ̀-centric polity in the Upper Ọ̀ṣun area. See Ogundiran,

"Factional Competition"; Ogundiran, "Filling a Gap"; Ogungbemi, "Igbo Baba Ilare"; Oyelade, "Odun Irele."

16. This was the case of Ìtá, the potentate of Ìlémùré. He lost his political authority to Ọ̀bàràbarà Olókùnẹ̀ṣin but retained his ritual duties.

17. Agbaje-Williams and Ogundiran, *Cultural Resources*, 16–19.

18. Abiọla, Babafẹmi, and Ataiyero, *Iwe Itan Ijẹṣa*; Atayero, *Short History*. The various versions of the Ilésà king list generally show a succession of five or six kings (supposedly in lineal genealogical order) to have been involved in that orgy of territorial conquest before Iléṣà was established as capital of the new kingdom. But these versions and the supposed paths of the conquests are convoluted and overlapping. The king list is no more than an effort in Iléṣà traditions to establish a legitimate genealogy for Ọwálúṣẹ́. The sequence of conquests and the consolidation that started with Ọ̀bàràbarà Olókùnẹṣin (who is also identified as either a son of, or the same person as, Ajíbógun Obòkun) took place sometime in the last quarter of the sixteenth century. So the burst of territorial conquests that produced Ilésà lasted for only about ten or twenty years rather than through five generations or five kings, as oral traditions tend to imply. Some of those supposed early kings, between Ọ̀bàràbarà Olókùnẹṣin and Ọwálúṣẹ́, were either contemporaries (co-warriors) or later fabrications. The likely scenario is that several warlords returning from the Ará War dislodged the old dynasties and set up independent polities across the northeastern suburbs of Ilé-Ifẹ̀ between 1570 and 1590. Ọwálúṣẹ́ in turn annexed these principalities and consolidated them into one polity between 1590 and 1600.

19. This information is based on unpublished private papers/essays and oral interviews that formed the basis of my previous discussion of this topic (Ogundiran, "Archaeological Reconnaissance," 23–25). Examples of the written sources are Popoola, "History of Ìpolé-Ìjẹ̀ṣà," and Oteyola, "History and Development of Ìpolé." Oral interviewees include Ọbà Adélẹ́gàn Pópóọlá, Ìpolé-Ìjẹ̀ṣà, July 8, 1990; Chief Edward Fádípẹ̀, Ìpolé Ìjẹ̀ṣà, July 5, 1990; Mr. O. Ajétọmọbí, Ilé-Ifẹ̀, July 8, 1990; and Madam Ọwárìtóókẹ́ Àyọlo, Ìpolé-Ìjẹ̀ṣà, October 10, 1990.

20. Madam Ọwárìtóókẹ́ Àyọlo, Ìpolé-Ìjẹ̀ṣà, October 10, 1990.

21. Ìgbómìnà featured prominently in the efforts by Ọ̀yọ́ and its allies to expel the Nupe militarists from the Yorùbá region, and after this feat was accomplished, Ọ̀yọ́ maintained various military detachments in the area, especially in the decades of political rebuilding. Among the Ìgbómìnà kingdoms that were brought under the patronage of Ọ̀yọ́ in the last quarter of the sixteenth century were Olúpẹfọ̀n, Gbàgede, Ìlá-Ọ̀ràngún, and Ọbalọ́yàn. These polities had existed by the thirteenth and fourteenth centuries, but the establishment of Ọ̀yọ́'s suzerainty over them did not predate 1570. For discussions on the political, military, and diplomatic relationships between the Ọ̀yọ́ and the Ìgbómìnà, see Aleru, *Old Oyo and the Hinterland*; Usman, *State-Periphery Relations*; Usman, *Yoruba Frontier*.

22. Peel, *Ijeshas and Nigerians*, 20. The founder of the Báṣemi lineage in Ilésà is claimed to have been one of the Ọ̀yọ́ leaders who assisted Ọwálúṣẹ́ in his triumph over Ọwárì. Oral interviews: Chief Adéfióyè Adédèjì, Iléṣà, June 6, 1986; Chief J. O. Lọ̀tùn, Iléṣà, February 9, 1991.

23. Peel, *Ijeshas and Nigerians*, 20.

24. The following are the titles of the leaders, with the names of their aboriginal community in parenthesis: Ọbańlá (Òkè̩ṣà), Àrojò (Ìrojò), Eninutan (Ìjòfì), Onírère (Ìrère) Síndilè (Ìgbógì), Alásorò (Ìṣorò), Onítajì (Ìtajì), Onímíkàn (Ìmíkàn), and Onímọ̀ (Ìmọ̀). See Agbaje-Williams and Ogundiran, *Cultural Resources*, 24.

25. Peel, "Kings, Titles, and Quarters," 140–41.

26. The oral traditions tend to conflate the sixteenth- and late eighteenth-century Nupe attacks, as well as the Yorùbá wars of the mid-nineteenth century, into one event, thereby presenting a cobweb of confusion for historians. Hence, J. D. Y. Peel ("Kings, Titles, and Quarters," 141) misleadingly proposed that the office of Arápatẹ́ was created in the aftermath of the Nupe wars of the eighteenth century. His reliance on only the oral traditions from Ilésà caused this error. Likewise, Samuel Johnson (*History*, 317) confused the Ará War of the sixteenth century with the Èkìtì and Ìjẹ̀ṣà rebellion of 1878–86 against Ibadan imperialism. For the same problem, see Awe, "Ajele System." The comparison of the Iléṣà traditions with those of Ifẹ̀, Èkìtì, and other Ìjẹ̀ṣà areas removes this confusion caused by historical telescoping.

27. There have been oral traditions in Ilésà dating back to the 1940s claiming that the boundaries between Ilésà and Ilé-Ifẹ̀ lie in the front yard of *ọ̀ọ̀ni*'s palace at Ẹnuwá, in Ilé-Ifẹ̀. Such exaggerated claims by the Iléṣà royal court should be read in the context of the fierce rivalry and old conflicts between the two adjacent city-states (e.g., Atayero, *Short History*). This rivalry certainly dates to the sixteenth century when Ilésà was being set up on what was once an Ifẹ̀ territory. The rivalry between the two neighbors still manifests itself in the contemporary politics of Nigeria. For example, see a 2015 news report on the leadership tussle between the king of Ilésà and the king of Ilé-Ifẹ̀: Adeseri, Olarinoye, and Akinrefon, "Osun State Traditional Council."

28. This is similar to the claim that originated in the late fourteenth century that the Aláàfin of Ọ̀yọ́ was the last child of Odùduwà.

29. See Abiọla, Babafẹmi, and Ataiyero, *Iwe Itan Ijẹṣa*; Atayero, *Short History*.

30. In the Benin traditions, Àtàkúnmọ̀sà is remembered as Atakumarha (Egharevba, *Short History*, 3).

31. According to the oral traditions collected by J. D. Y. Peel ("Kings, Titles, and Quarters," 121), the titled lineages (Houses) founded by some of the leaders who followed Àtàkúnmọ̀sà from Benin to Ilésà are Ògbóni (one of the six nonroyal lords of Ilésà), Oṣòdì (a titled priesthood), Eejigbo, and Bakinna (responsible for taking messages from the king of Ilésà to Benin and entertaining Benin messengers on their visit to Ilésà, a duty that would have required proficiency in both Edo and Yorùbá languages).

32. Àtàkúnmọ̀sà is identified in Àkúrẹ́ traditions as the founder of the kingdom's royal dynasty (Akintoye, *Revolution and Power Politics*, 226; also see Arifalo, *Analysis and Comparison*).

33. Abiọla, Babafẹmi, and Ataiyero, *Iwe Itan Ijẹṣa*.

34. Chief Adéfióyè Adédèjì, Iléṣà, July 10, 1997; Chief Edward Fádípẹ̀, Ìpolé Ìjẹ̀ṣà, July 5, 1990.

35. This is the reason the legend of Obòkun is strongly associated with the Atlantic coast.

36. Ọ̀yọ́'s southeastern ambitions are demonstrated in the wars that it fought in Oǹdó sometime in the 1590s. Ìdànrè may also have been attacked around this time. These wars were no doubt part of the Ọ̀yọ́ military engagements in the eastern Yorùbá region, and they fit the broad objective of controlling movement of the commodities that were needed in the trading networks with Benin, especially ivory and pepper. Ọ̀yọ́'s ambition to control those areas, however, failed, although Oǹdó and Ilésà recognized Ọ̀yọ́ as senior brother within the *ẹbí* fraternity and they entered into gift-giving relations with the cavalry state. For more details on Ọ̀yọ́'s military engagements in Oǹdó and Ìdànrè, see Leigh, *History of Ondo*. For a historiographic assessment of these oral traditions, see Law, *Oyo Empire*, 130–32.

37. Ozanne, "New Archaeological Survey," 39–41.

38. One such tradition claims "that Lájamìsán was the son of Ayétise, who was in Ifẹ̀ before the coming of Odùduwà." Ayétise himself was never a king, and there is no doubt that this genealogical invention was an attempt to establish legitimacy for Lájamìsán's claim to the throne of Ifẹ̀. Akinjogbin, "Growth of Ife," 100.

39. There is reference to a female leader or *ọ̀ọ̀ni* of Ilé-Ifẹ̀ named Léèdé, whose grave site is reportedly kept in the Odùduwà Grove. She is said to have provided leadership in the distant past when men were scarce or mostly unavailable to perform the duties of king or priest. She was referred to specifically as the priest of Odùduwà (Ọbadio Ọlájídé Fárótìmí Fálọba, Ilé-Ifẹ̀, July 16, 2015). The female personalities such as Léèdé and Lúwò in Ifẹ̀ traditions may refer to the early Intermediate period, when women had to take leadership roles in Ilé-Ifẹ̀ on account of the tolls of war and famine that ravaged the region.

40. All four branches of the royal House from whom the kings of Ifẹ̀ are selected today trace their ancestry to Lájamìsán (Akinjogbin, "Growth of Ife," 105).

41. Adewuyi, "Agba Festival in Oyan"; Taiwo, "History of Iragbiji."

42. Oyerinde, *Iwe Itan Ogbomọṣọ*.

43. Orefejo, "History of Ijebu-Igbo," 8–11.

44. Adegbite, "Afon and its Neighbours," 15. Although the oral traditions claim that Látóyọ̀ Akínsòkun established these hunting camps, it is more likely that he consolidated many camps independently founded by other hunting guilds under his political and administrative control, either through delegated authority by the hunters in those camps, by coercion, or both.

45. The king of Benin in fact organized a guild of elephant hunters for which a village was established at Oregbeni on the outskirts of Benin City. According to Joseph Osagie and Frank Ikponmwosa, "Craft Guilds," 7: "The Ọba received the tusks of every elephant killed in Benin forest from the elephant hunters of Oregbeni," which he traded for European imports. They continue, "Through the trade in tusk, the Ọba's economic fortune . . . was greatly enhanced." There is no evidence of such centrally controlled elephant-tusk hunting in the other parts of the Yorùbá community of practice.

46. E.g., Brooks, *Eurafricans in Western Africa*; Miller, "Significance of Drought"; Ogundiran, "Making of an Internal Frontier."

47. Adegbite, "Afon and Its Neighbours," 7.

48. A well-known example in Yorùbá history is Ẹlẹ́mọ̀ṣọ́, a notorious brigand in the Ògbómọ̀ṣọ́ area during the seventeenth century. His name suggests that he was a former high-ranking soldier in the Ọ̀yọ́ army before taking to brigandage. This story is the subject of a popular play and a film released in the 1980s titled *Ògbórí Ẹlẹ́mọ̀ṣọ́* (accessed July 21, 2017, https://www.youtube.com/watch?v=1Q5PPIVvLUg).

49. Much of the ivory used in the sculptures of Ọ̀wọ̀ and Benin, and sold by Benin, Ìjẹ̀bú, and other traders on the coast, came from the exploitation of these Òwẹ̀nà herds (Drewal, "Image and Indeterminacy," 189). The buried skull of an African forest elephant (*Loxodonta africana cyclotis*) at Ìdànrè provides independent archaeological evidence of elephant hunting in the area (Ogunfolakan and Olayemi, "Preliminary Report," 37). A moneta cowrie (*Monetaria moneta*)—a category of artifacts that became abundant in the southern Yorùbá region as a result of European contact—was found with the buried elephant skull.

50. The tendency in recent historiography of Oǹdó is to arbitrarily assign dates to the king list without providing an explanation for how these dates are derived (for example, Ajayi, *Evolution of Ondo Kingdom*, 4). Hence, the first ruler of Oǹdó—a female—is dated to 1510–1530, and the fourth king, Okuta, is dated to 1590–1614. Okuta appears to be the first historical figure on the king list, while those preceding him were likely mythical, created to provide legitimacy for the historical figures who ruled from the last decade of the sixteenth century.

51. Olupona, "Where a Woman Was King," 8.

52. See Adeyemi and Aluko-Olokun, *Ondo Kingdom*; Ajayi, *Evolution of Ondo Kingdom*; Bada, *Iwe Itan Ondo*; Egharevba, *Short History*.

53. This information was obtained from the private papers of Ọba Musa Ọlátúnbọ̀sún-Adébáyọ̀, Akínṣílọ II, the Aláwó of Awó, accessed May 6, 2004, and from oral interviews with Ọba Ọláyinká Gbọ́lágade Tiamiyu II, Òjo, July 22, 2009.

54. Law, *Oyo Empire*, 129.

55. Ogundiran, "Making of an Internal Frontier."

56. In one of those early attacks, the Ọ̀yọ́ military expedition was ambushed and defeated by Iléṣà forces. "So great was the loss of life in this expedition that the *Ologbo* was sent out as a town crier to inform the bereaved of their losses in this war," according to Samuel Johnson's nineteenth-century Ọ̀yọ́ informants, who also rationalized this defeat by saying that the Ọ̀yọ́'s cavalry was "then unaccustomed to bush (rainforest) fighting." Indeed, engaging Ọ̀yọ́'s cavalry in a rain forest battle was an error of strategy (Johnson, *History*, 168).

57. Ọbà Tijani Oyèdòkun Àgbọ́nrán II, the late Timi of Ẹdẹ (oral interview, January 21, 2004); Ọba Musa Ọlátúnbọ̀sún-Adébáyọ̀, Akínṣílọ II, the Aláwó of Awó (oral interview, May 6, 2004).

58. Johnson, *History*, 156.

59. The archaeological evidence from Ẹdẹ-Ilé indeed shows that the town was an implantation of the Ọ̀yọ́ metropolis in a faraway territory, and the colonists made every effort to replicate the ways of life of their homeland. First, they introduced baobab trees to Ẹdẹ-Ilé, thereby animating the rain forest environment with the visual landscape of their savanna homeland. Second, the large number of horse remains found in the governor's compound at

Ẹdẹ-Ilé demonstrates the huge investment that Ọ̀yọ́ made in military hardware and means of communication to secure its frontier territory. Third, the prevalence of Ọ̀yọ́ ceramics in Ẹdẹ-Ilé (more than 97% of all ceramic forms) also affirmed Ọ̀yọ́ aesthetics in cuisine, cooking, and food culture. See Ogundiran, "Material Life and Domestic Economy"; Ogundiran, "Formation of an Oyo Imperial Colony"; Ogundiran and Saunders, "Potters' Marks."

60. This statement is based on the oral traditions collected in Òjo, Arà, and Awó, three prominent Ifẹ̀-centric polities in Upper Ọ̀ṣun. These communities seem to have been established during the Classical period. In their traditions, they generally frame Ọ̀yọ́'s intervention as a protection against their powerful neighbor, Iléṣà, rather than as a loss of their autonomy.

61. Law, *Slave Coast*; Strickrodt, *Afro-European Trade.*

62. In Arbo, on the Benin River, where the Dutch set up a trading post in 1644, nonhuman commodities were the chief exports. For example, it was estimated that the Dutch bought at least sixteen thousand pieces of cloth in Arbo between 1644 and 1646, and the English may have bought even more in Arbo during the same period (Ryder, *Benin and the Europeans*, 233).

63. Fọlayan, "Egbado to 1832," 16.

64. Pemberton, "Descriptive Catalog," 52.

65. It is therefore the case that the very few instances of horse imagery in Classical Ifẹ̀ art were symbolic expressions of what horses represent rather than evidence of the use of horses in warfare. For discussion of horses in Classical Ifẹ̀, see Blier, *Art and Risk*, 329–30.

66. Iliffe, *Honour*, 1.

67. Abiodun, *Yoruba Art*, 125–41.

68. Ojo, "Symbolism," 455.

69. Ojo, 462.

70. Given the centrality of Ẹpa to the ritual and festival calendar of almost all Èkìtì communities till today and the association of Ẹpa ceremonies with primeval Mother Earth worship, the masking tradition is most likely as ancient as the formation of House polities in Èkìtì during the Early Formative period. As shown in the work of Famule, *Art and Spirituality*, similar mask traditions are pervasive among Èkìtì's northern neighbors—the Okun (see chap. 2). All of these point to the proto-Yoruboid origins of Ẹpa.

71. In both cases, they are "kept by the lineage heads and town chiefs either on behalf of the lineage or the town" (Ojo, "Symbolism," 456).

72. Lawal, "Yoruba Sango Sculpture."

73. Abiodun, *Yoruba Art*, 130.

74. Ojo, "Symbolism," 463; Turner, *Ritual Process*, 172–74.

75. Antonio Gramsci's elaboration on the cerebral workings of hegemony, counter-hegemony, and anti-hegemony offers rich insights for reinterpreting the political and emancipatory project of the Ẹpa masking tradition beyond the preoccupation with forms and rituals that has dominated its analysis as a visual and performative art. See Gramsci, *Antonio Gramsci*; Morton, *Unravelling Gramsci Hegemony.*

76. Ojo, "Symbolism," 457.

77. More popularly called Obòkun festival, this annual commemorative event is primarily associated with Ajíbógun Obòkun, the reputed founder of the Ọwá Obòkun dynasty in Iléṣà. However, the name is often used interchangeably with Ọ̀bàràbarà Olókùnẹṣin, and it is sometimes suggested that

the two names belong to one person or to a father-son complex—Ajíbógun Obòkun the father, and Ọ̀bàràbarà Olókùnẹ̀ṣin the son. Oral interviews: Chief Samuel Fákúlújọ, Ìbòkun, April 2, 1986; Ọba J. O. Fásọ̀yìn, Ìlọ̀wá, June 6, 1986; Chief Emmanuel Ọ̀rìṣàsùnmi, Ìbòkun, September 11, 1991.

78. Oral interview, Chief Emmanuel Ọ̀rìṣàsùnmí, Ìbòkun, July 12, 1997.

79. Hence, T. M. Ilesanmi described Ògún as the national god of Ilésà (cited in Lawuyi, "Ogun," 131); and Jacob Olupona (*Kingship, Religion, and Rituals*, 112) refers to Ògún as "the religion of the masses *par excellence*."

80. Armstrong, "Etymology," 34. For example, the same Ògún complex is known as Ogwu in the Igala and Idoma, both on the eastern side of the Niger-Benue Confluence.

81. In Ilé-Ifẹ̀, there is an Ògún shrine (Ògún Láádìn) within the *ọ̀ọ̀ni's* palace that focused on the administration of justice, including oath swearing. However, there is a public Ògún shrine outside the palace, at Òkemògún, where those deemed to be the enemies of the state and social order (especially convicted criminals) were executed. This temple is also the focus of the annual Ọlọ́jọ́ festival that continues today, during which the *ọ̀ọ̀ni* visits Òkèmògún to renew his oath of office and his chiefs and diviners congregate there to perform divination for the king. This is the occasion, and the only time in the year, that the *ọ̀ọ̀ni* wears the sacred *àrè* crown in public. In popular and scholarly literature, Ọlọ́jọ́ has been erroneously regarded as a royal festival dedicated only to Ògún. However, as Jacob Olupona has observed, Ọlọ́jọ́ is dedicated to three principal deities: "Ògún, god of war and iron; Ajé, goddess of wealth and prosperity; and Ọ̀rànmíyàn, warlord and culture hero" (Olupona, *City of 201 Gods*, 138). The festival is also dedicated, secondarily, to all royal ancestors and the ancestral princes who left Ilé-Ifẹ̀ to establish their own kingdoms, according to local traditions. In essence, all the ancestors of *ìlúlọba-aládé* in Yorùbáland are also the focus of Ọlọ́jọ́. Unlike in Èkìtì and Ìjẹ̀ṣà territories, where Ògún enjoys the singular focus of the royal festival, Ògún does not enjoy the status of first position, not even primus inter pares status, in the sacred triumvirate that constitutes the royal Ọlọ́jọ́ festival in Ilé-Ifẹ̀.

82. Adepegba, "Associated Place-Names"; Barnes, *Africa's Ogun*.

83. According to Roy Abraham, (*Dictionary*, 164, 482), the early kings of Ọ̀yọ́ worshipped Erinlẹ̀, the deity of hunters. His informants told him that it was Aláàfin Abìọ̀dún (ca. 1760–89) who adopted Ògún and made it into a royal deity. This is consistent with the information that Samuel Johnson (*History*, 43–45) also collected in the late nineteenth century stating that the Ògún shrine is the last of several shrines that the king-elect must visit and the place where he must make sacrifices before he is considered to be fully invested as a divine king. It is after the king-elect's visit to the Ògún shrine, on the fifteenth day of the coronation ritual, that he enters the palace for the first time. However, Ògún was the patron deity of Baṣọ̀run, the Ọ̀yọ́ chieftaincy that was most associated with warfare in the aftermath of the Nupe crisis and the beginning of the Ọ̀yọ́ imperial period.

84. Williams, *Icon and Image*, 83.

85. For different versions of this rendition, see Idowu, *Olódùmarè*; Olupona, *Kingship, Religion, and Rituals*; Peel, *Ijeshas and Nigerians*; Pemberton, "Dreadful God."

86. Barnes and Ben-Amos, "Ogun," 39.

87. See, Olupona, *Kingship, Religion, and Rituals*; Peel, *Ijeshas and Nigerians*. In Ilésà, the Ògún festival is at the center of the annual festivals in honor of the monarchy, past and present. The annual festival marks the beginning of the New Year. Ògún is the most publicized deity on Ilésà's ritual calendar and the first deity that is worshipped in the three-month annual ritual cycle held in honor of the royal ancestors of Ilésà, including Ajíbógun Obòkun/Ọ̀bàràbarà Olókùnẹṣin, Ọwálúṣẹ́, Àtàkúnmọ̀sà, Bíládù, Bílágbayọ̀, Uyìarère, and Wáyeró (Agbaje-Williams and Ogundiran, *Cultural Resources*, 31).

88. Chief Emmanuel Òrìṣàsùnmí, Ìbòkun, July 12, 1997. The frontal wall of the temple of Obokun/Ọ̀bàràbarà Olokuesin, which is still standing today, bears the remains of those enemies supposedly from the early wars of conquest. I counted more than forty-two human skulls and several disarticulated arm and hand bones (radius, ulna, humerus, carpal, and phalanges) in the wall when I conducted research there in the 1990s (Ogundiran, *Archaeology and History*, 114; also see Agbaje-Williams and Ogundiran, *Cultural Resources*, 16–17). However, this wall of human skeletons pales in comparison to the one that Iléṣà constructed as part of its defensive wall system in the seventeenth and eighteenth centuries. The mid-nineteenth-century observers estimated the outer ditch of the city's defensive complex to be about twenty feet deep and ten feet wide, and the walls (embankments) about eighteen feet high and six feet thick (Clarke, *Travels and Explorations*, 130). In addition, David Hinderer reported in 1857 that he had observed hundreds of human skulls that were inserted into these walls, all of which, according to his informants, were of war captives. David Hinderer, report of his tour to Ilésà, 1857, CMS, CAO/049.

89. For example, see Tishken, Akínyemí, and Falola, *Sàngó in Africa*; Matory, *Sex and the Empire*; Peel, "Comparative Analysis of Ogun."

90. E.g., Adepegba, "Osun and Brass," 107.

91. Whereas the center of Ọ̀ṣun worship is at Òṣogbo, that of Ọbà is at the Igbọ́n-Ògbómọ̀ṣọ́ area. See Bascom, *African Folktales*, 1–17; Badejo, *Osun Seegesi*.

92. Neimark, *Way of the Orisa*, 142.

93. Ceramics in the Ọ̀yọ́- and Ifẹ̀-centric traditions, as well as trade goods from the coast and across the region, have been found at the site, showing the accessibility of the market town to various communities and trading networks in the region. See Ogundiran, "Multiplex Landscape"; Ogundiran, "Making of an Internal Frontier."

94. Nobles, "Critical Ideas and Concepts."

95. It should be noted that the virility of these two deities is celebrated in other myths. See Barnes, *Africa's Ogun*; Olupona and Abiodun, *Ifa Divination*.

96. Apter, *Black Critics*, 64; Matory, *Sex and the Empire*, 126.

97. There are traditions that the mothers of some of the early kings of Ọ̀yọ́ originated from the Yéwá-Ògùn frontier. This pattern of intermarriage increased following the incorporation of the Yéwá-Ògùn into the political field of Ọ̀yọ́ (see chap. 8 for details).

98. The earlier rendition of Elempe's daughter as the mother of Ṣàngó did not go away in the traditions (chap. 3), and neither did this new mythos contradict the former. The Elempe connection belonged to the middle to late fourteenth century and was useful in dealing with the competitions with the Nupe

to control the Moshi-Niger trading entrepôts during the Classical period. However, the Yemọja mythoi was created in the early seventeenth century to legitimize Ọ̀yọ́'s political agenda in the newly acquired Yéwá-Ògùn frontier, a critical route to the coastal markets.

99. Drewal, Pemberton, and Abiodun, *Yorùbá*, 159.

100. This is a reference to ivory hunting in Yéwá-Ògùn and to the importance of the frontier to commerce.

101. Matory, *Sex and the Empire*, 231–32.

102. For example, Ará, Ọ̀tùn, Akégi, Eléré, Ìsòdè, Ẹlẹ́jẹ̀lú, Èju, Ìlalà, Ìjegúje. See Abimbola, *Ìjìnlẹ̀ Ohùn Ẹnu Ifá, Apá Kìíní,* 47, 55, and 133.

Part IV: Atlantic Entanglements, 1630–1840

6

Merchant Capital Revolution

ỌBALÓKUN, THE CULTURAL HERO AND architect of Ọ̀yọ́'s Atlantic policy, accumulated many successes in his expansionist agenda, although there were also some setbacks, as we saw in chapter 5. According to the late nineteenth-century oral traditions, the king not only established trading contacts with the Atlantic coast but also opened diplomatic relations with a European king. However, what happened afterward poured cold water on the fire of Ọbalókun's alleged accomplishments in transatlantic relations: "It was said that the King [Ọbalókun] sent 800 messengers with presents to . . . [a] European sovereign, but that they were never heard of again. Tradition says that the sounds of bells ringing in the skies was [*sic*] plainly heard in the Akẹsan (King's) market [in Ọ̀yọ́-Ilé], and it was conjectured that it was the voices of the unfortunates speaking to them from the other world to tell their fate."[1]

It is conceivable that Ọbalókun indeed tried to establish direct relations with one or more of the European trading missions (Portuguese, Dutch, or English) on the coast during his reign ca. the 1590s–1620s, and he may have lost some of his men (e.g., through abduction) to that endeavor. However, considering that the Ọ̀yọ́ involvement in the coastal trade lasted for more than two hundred years, the above story is a compression of time and actors into a single event, a stock representation of the multiple experiences of loss to the Atlantic exchange.[2] The story is a work of memory and a critique of the state regarding the Atlantic policy of Ọbalókun and that of his successors, and a critique of the European traders who transformed the Bight of Benin into a chain of slave trade emporia at the beginning of the early seventeenth century. It is also a critical commentary on the social consequences of the entanglement of Ọ̀yọ́ in the Atlantic slave trade. The story alludes to the strategies and risks that the Ọ̀yọ́ political elite undertook to create political linkages with the new emporia on the coast, about 320 kilometers from their capital, and the sacrifices that the empire's cavalrymen, archers, emissaries, and common people made toward achieving that goal. Unfolding this scroll of political strategies, risks, gains, losses, and contradictions is the subject of this chapter. It will emphasize three themes: (1) the ways the Yorùbá mainland became entangled in the Atlantic slave trade; (2) the roles that subcontinental and transcontinental labor redistribution, power politics, and regional or global political economies played in that entanglement; and (3) the impacts of a new regime of value—merchant capital—on the Yorùbá domestic economy.

Ọbalókun and his immediate successors, Olúodò and Àjàgbó, cleared the paths that brought Ọ̀yọ́'s Atlantic dream into reality. In the decades that followed the reigns of these three warrior-monarchs, Ọ̀yọ́ became the largest Yorùbá state. It also controlled the largest share of the trade with the coastal ports, by volume of exports and imports, despite the fact that it was the farthest Yorùbá metropolis from the Bight of Benin's shoreline. The economic opportunities offered by the European commercial presence played an important role in the expansionist programs and external relations policies that Ọ̀yọ́ and other Yorùbá states pursued after 1570. As a result, the involvement of the region in the coastal trade accelerated during the second quarter of the seventeenth century. This marked the beginning of the Yorùbá Atlantic period, which lasted until ca. 1840. It was a period defined by the integration of the Yorùbá domestic economies into the global transatlantic commercial networks. Through the Bight of Benin, the Yorùbá mainland was linked with the European oceanic trade and plantation economies in the Americas. These networks and exchanges, however, thrived on human trafficking—by volume, the largest slave trade in world history.

The Atlantic Slave Trade

The second quarter of the seventeenth century was a period of momentous change in the patterns, directions, and contents of Atlantic commerce. It was during this period that the dynamics of the trade in the Bight of Benin shifted from the export of primary and manufactured commodities—ivory, dyestuff, and cotton cloth—to predominantly human cargo exports. The Ọ̀yọ́ narrative that attributes the loss of the kingdom's eight hundred men to an imaginary friendship between Ọbalókun and a European king is a sedimented and condensed memory of that change. Prior to 1650,

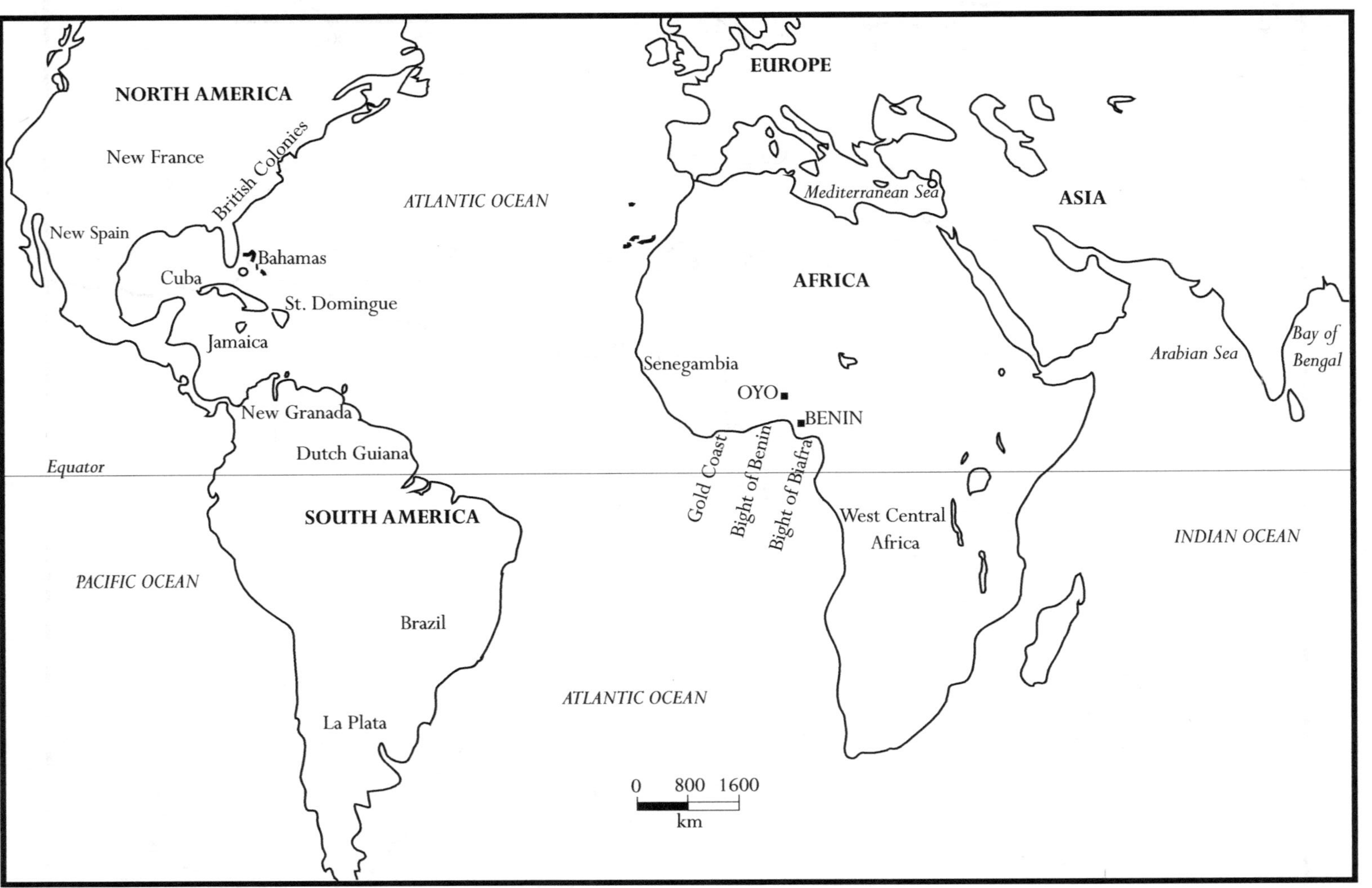

Figure 6.1. Atlantic world

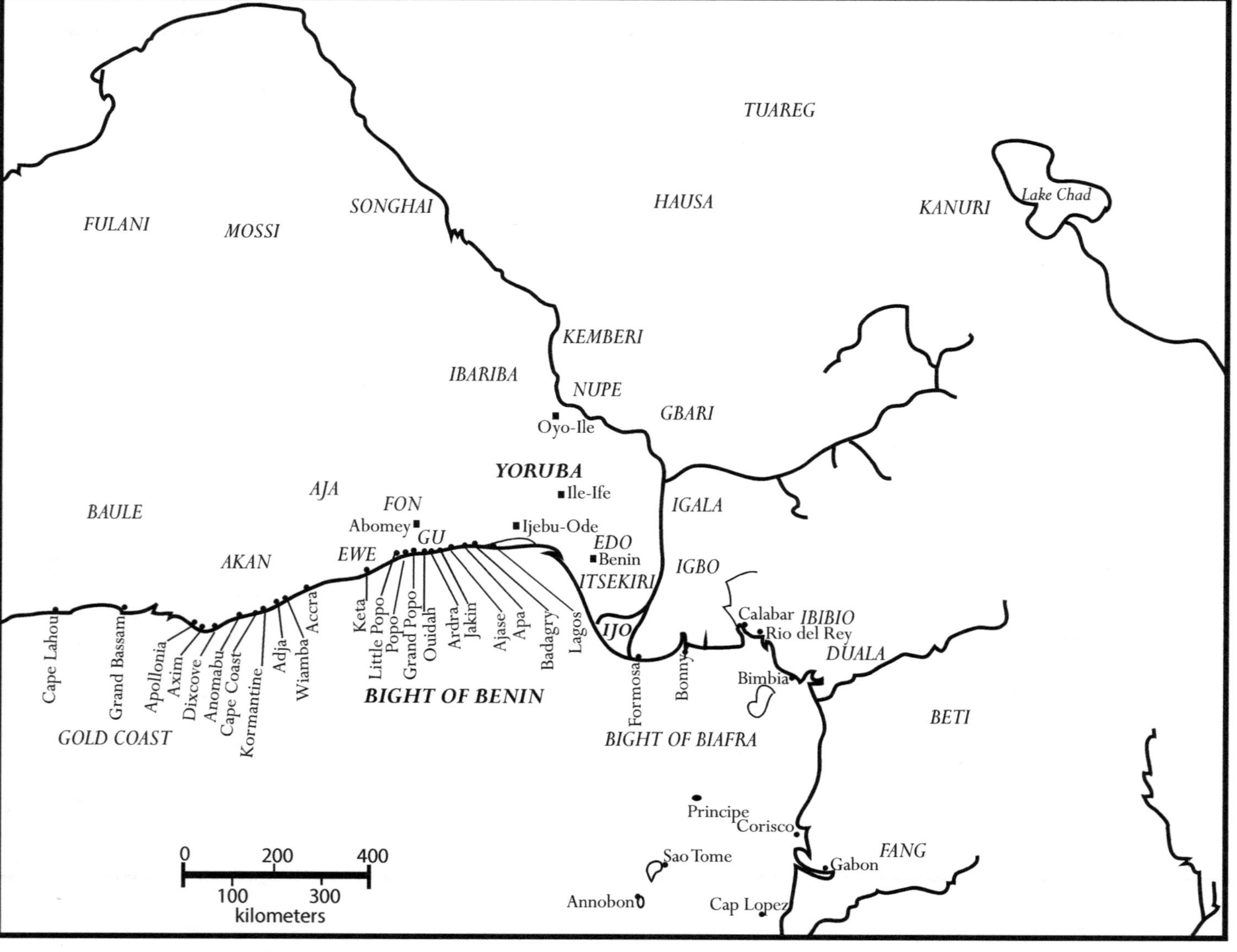

Figure 6.2. The Yorùbá-speaking world in relation to the other cultural groups in West Africa and the Bight of Benin ports

the commercial relations between Africans and Europeans facilitated an increase in the value of the Bight of Benin's manufactures in the Atlantic basin. Between 1550 and 1650 especially, manufactured cotton cloth was the king export. It was the dominant manufacture leaving the shores of the Yorùbá world, from the Benin River to Lagos Lagoon (see chap. 5). The Portuguese and the Dutch shipped these textiles to different parts of the Atlantic basin, from Luanda (in West Central Africa) to Olinda (Brazil), and from Curaçao (Caribbean) to New Netherland (New York), where they sold at a good profit. Although this intercontinental trade in textiles in the Bight of Benin was still going on as late as 1641–42, according to Dutchman Cornelis Hendrickx Ouman, the European demand for them had declined precipitously at that time.[3] So, at the very juncture when the Yorùbá mainland was fully ready to join the train of Atlantic commerce via commodity exchange, the European traders had had enough of their manufactured cotton cloth. The voracious appetites of European merchants for human cargo were expanding, and by the first decade of the seventeenth century, the African warrior-merchants and warrior-kings on the western side of the Bight of Benin had become eager suppliers (chap. 4).

What caused this change? Following in the footsteps of the sixteenth-century Portuguese, Spanish, and Dutch conquistadors and settlers in the Americas, the English and the French accelerated the process of their colonization efforts in the New World after 1610. The demand for labor in the Americas therefore mounted in the second quarter of the seventeenth century because of the increase in European settlements and the quest to exploit the vast agricultural and mineral resources of the "new" continents, from the eastern seaboards of North America and the Caribbean to Central and South America (fig. 6.1). About the same time, the Portuguese persistence in the Bight of Benin for a reliable supply of slave labor paid off when between 1590 and 1610 they found the kingdom of Allada to be a willing and reliable supplier. Other coastal kingdoms soon joined this business of human trafficking, so that between 1630 and 1680, several trading ports, including Offra, Jakin, and Glehue (Ouidah) emerged along the coast, stretching from the eastern edge of present-day Ghana to the western corner of present-day Nigeria (fig. 6.2).[4] Known in the contemporary European sources variously as Bight of Benin, Costa da Mina (Mina Coast), and the Slave Coast, this was the outlet for the entanglement of the Yorùbá in the Atlantic commerce.

Enslaved Africans had been arriving in the Americas since the second half of the sixteenth century, but for about a hundred years, the Bight of Benin had lagged behind Senegambia/Sierra Leone, the Bight of Biafra, and West Central Africa as a source of the captives sent across the ocean. This was about to change. The number of enslaved men and women leaving the Bight of Benin sharply rose between 1651 and 1675, tripling the combined figures for the first half of the seventeenth century. From 1676 onward, the number steadily increased through the second half of the eighteenth century (table 6.1). The Mina polities of the seventeenth and early eighteenth century—Allada, Hucda, and Popo (Hula), among others—were comparatively small kingdoms.[5] Although they were able to obtain captives through militarized operations in the territories around them, especially in the Gbe region,[6] the number they could gather was limited compared to the volume desired by European traders.[7] The merchant-potentates of these polities near the coast were, however, able to use European imports to finance slave trading with the much larger states farther inland. The largest of these was Ọ̀yọ́, which became a steady supplier of slaves to these coastal kingdoms during the reign of Ọbalókun. And it would become the largest mainland supplier to the coastal slave marts by 1650. The enslaved individuals that Ọ̀yọ́ marched to the coast between 1650 and 1750 came primarily from three sources, in ascending order of importance: (1) tributes from the provinces; (2) captives from the wars waged by Ọ̀yọ́ purposely to achieve two goals—directly conscript bodies for the Atlantic slave trade and expand their political boundaries so that the conquered territory might serve as a source of future tributes; and (3) slaves bought from the Nupe, Ìbàrìbá, Bornu, and Hausa traders. The third accounted for the largest percentage of the slaves that Ọ̀yọ́ sold on the coast until the 1750s.

In the late seventeenth century, the trading centers in the Moshi-Niger area—Kaiama and Nikki (Ìbàrìbá), Kulfo (Nupe), and Ògòdò (Yorùbá)—were famous as great market centers, offering a diverse range of commodities and captives from different backgrounds.[8] The Ọ̀yọ́ Empire dominated these trading centers, which were major crossroads between the Hausa-Kanuri and Yorùbá trading routes. Captives from the Central Sudan and the northern Niger-Benue Confluence dominated the number of people offered for sale in these markets between 1630 and 1730. This was a reversal of the experience of the previous mid-fifteenth through the mid-sixteenth century, when the Yorùbá were swelling the enslaved population in Central Sudan. Now, enslaved Hausa, Kanuri, and several other ethnolinguistic groups were entering the Yorùbá region in an unprecedented number. Two converging events were responsible for this. The first was the collapse of the Songhai Empire in 1591 following the defeat of its army by Moroccan forces seeking to control the salt and gold trade across the Sahara. Moroccan superiority on the battlefield did not, however, lead to effective administration. The result was political instability, especially as the former provinces of the defunct Songhai Empire began to declare their independence. Confusion ensued as warring peer-polities proliferated across the Western Sudan. This development had reverberating

Table 6.1. Number of Captives Embarked for the Middle Passage from Major Ports in Atlantic Africa

Year Range	Senegambia	Sierra Leone	Windward Coast	Gold Coast	Bight of Benin	Bight of Biafra	West Central Africa	Southeast Africa	Other Regions Africa	Total
1501–1525	324	0	0	0	0	359	624	0	0	1,307
1526–1550	28,673	0	0	0	0	2,154	359	0	1,092	32,278
1551–1575	37,737	1,408	0	0	0	2,980	0	0	2,995	45,120
1576–1600	86,589	0	0	0	0	6,290	32,614	0	94,669	220,162
1601–1625	37,456	0	0	0	4,709	9,579	144,523	0	50,562	246,829
1626–1650	20,141	90	0	1,061	5,550	15,691	112,667	0	14,769	169,969
1651–1675	13,661	793	316	15,557	31,544	29,434	40,141	940	43,780	176,166
1676–1700	32,815	1,997	180	41,891	143,441	41,819	89,076	10,424	109,058	470,701
1701–1725	29,116	3,217	5,156	124,090	280,164	43,123	127,321	7,035	239,013	858,235
1726–1750	50,912	7,305	14,979	134,389	290,807	93,109	369,048	1,887	382,419	1,344,855
1751–1775	111,944	72,453	113,257	184,615	248,053	266,920	479,520	4,167	250,405	1,731,334
1776–1800	72,723	70,022	44,746	182,826	242,382	302,415	603,285	45,508	206,804	1,770,711
1801–1825	63,594	47,381	17,438	54,501	162,501	188,042	789,582	158,939	344,125	1,826,103
1826–1850	10,132	36,220	3,779	2,983	105,904	101,163	592,738	160,889	400,930	1,414,738
1851–1875	0	1,640	0	0	13,184	675	70,408	12,126	129,196	227,229
Total	595,817	242,526	199,851	741,913	1,528,239	1,103,753	3,451,906	401,915	2,270,307	10,535,737

Source: Slave Voyages, accessed April 29, 2019, https://www.slavevoyages.org/voyage/database.

effects on Central Sudan, where many of the displaced Songhai, Fulani, and Tuareg populations sought refuge. These new immigrants from the Sahel and Western Sudan strained the resources and stability of the Hausa polities. Second, after the relatively improved precipitation of ca. 1550–1610, drought episodes intensified across West Africa in the early seventeenth century and continued through the first half of the eighteenth century. At its peak, the drought pushed the Sahelian belt southward by about 150 kilometers, creating familiar conflicts over resource use and worsening the political instability in Central Sudan.[9] Both population increase and intense drought exhausted the soil and diminished agricultural productivity. These weakened the Hausa city-states at the onset of the seventeenth century. The profitability of the external commerce of the various Hausa city-states was also drastically reduced by Songhai's political crisis. This was a difficult time across the Sudan. Between the early seventeenth and mid-eighteenth century, the Hausa city-states were at each other's throats, and brigandage intensified throughout the region. Those who were displaced from their villages by drought, famine, and war became vulnerable to predatory warlords and slavers. This instability yielded bounty harvests of captives for the Atlantic slave trade, from Senegambia to the Bight of Benin.

Ọ̀yọ́ was a beneficiary of the instability in the Central Sudan, as thousands of Central Sudanese victims of the ecological crisis and political conflict entered Ọ̀yọ́ as slaves between 1630 and 1750. This situation facilitated the redistribution of labor in favor of the expanding cavalry state, and also in favor of the European plantations in the Americas. The onset of the Sudanese crisis was the very time that Ọ̀yọ́ was consolidating its power. It needed manpower to maintain its military edge over its neighbors and to expand its metropolitan economy in agriculture and manufacturing. It was also the time that several European colonists in the Americas escalated their demands for slaves from the Bight of Benin. Of all the Yorùbá polities of the seventeenth and early eighteenth centuries, only the Ọ̀yọ́ had the wherewithal to buy and transport the enslaved to the coast in the unprecedented numbers desired by European traders. On the River Niger, Ọ̀yọ́ traders paid for slaves and horses in European imports (merchant capital), especially cowries, beads, and Asian cloth. Cowrie shells were highly desired in the Central Sudan, where they had been used as currency probably since the late fifteenth century via the trans-Saharan shipment. It was from the late seventeenth century, however, that the region began to receive a steady supply of cowries from the coast via Ọ̀yọ́.[10] The quest of the Central Sudan for this commodity currency strengthened the middleman position of Ọ̀yọ́ between the Sudan and the coast. Ọ̀yọ́ was also the conduit for a high volume of local products between the Yorùbá and the Hausa-Kanuri regions. Hence, the Central

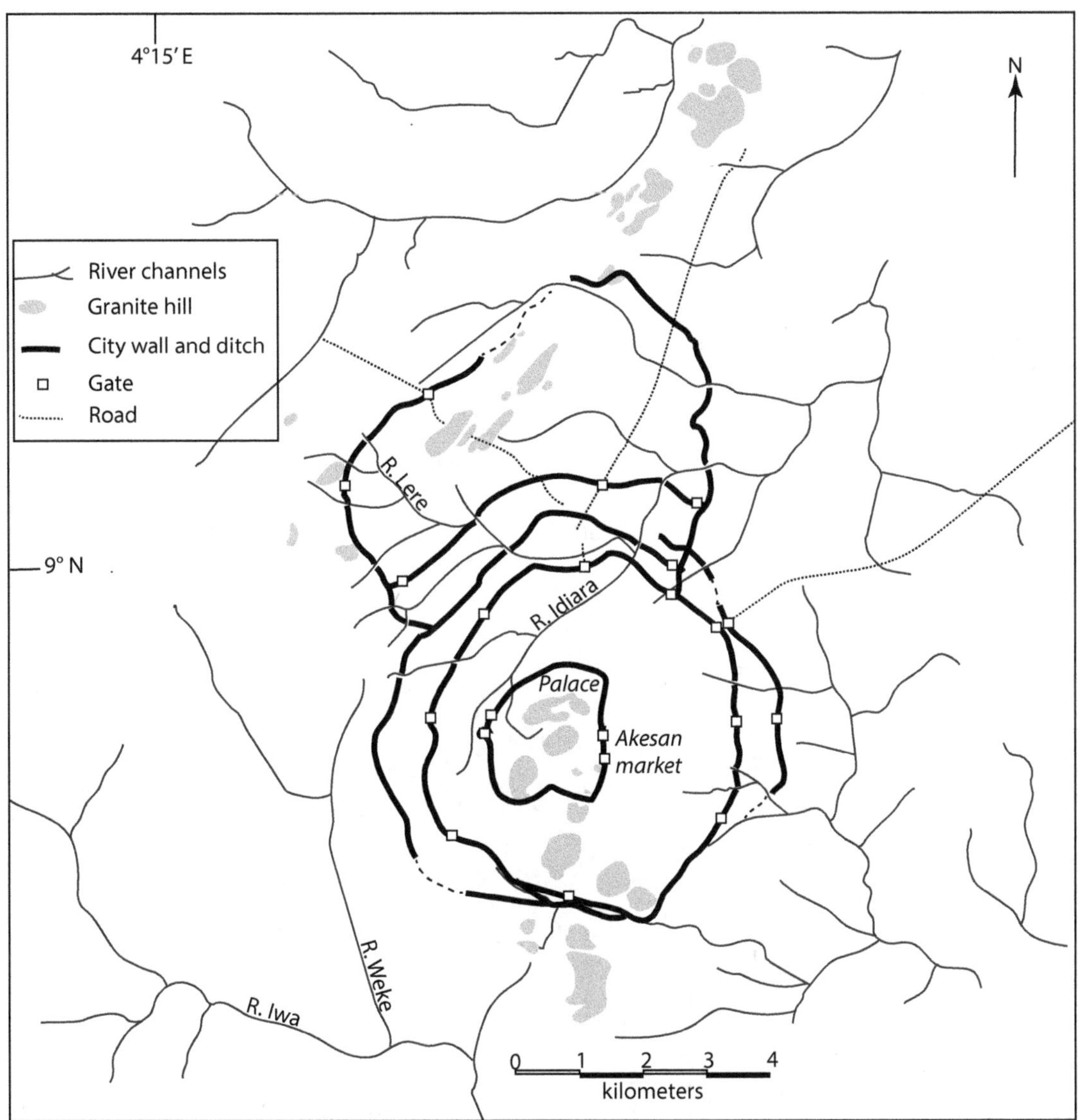

Figure 6.3. Perimeter walls of Ọ̀yọ́-Ilé

Sudanese local manufactures (e.g., leatherworks and clothing), as well as mined, agricultural, and semi-processed products (e.g., natron, grains, and cotton), entered the Yorùbá world through Ọ̀yọ́; and a large volume of Yorùbá products (e.g., cloth, kola nut, pepper) passed through the Ọ̀yọ́ metropolis (Ọ̀yọ́-Ilé) and its northern satellite towns to the Sudan. Between 1650 and 1750, Ọ̀yọ́-Ilé grew in leaps and bounds to become the largest Yorùbá emporium. During the same period, the political entrepreneurs in the capital presided over a vigorous expansionist policy that brought a vast network of towns, villages, colonies, and kingdoms under their control. By 1675, the sons of Ṣàngó were comfortably presiding over

Figure 6.4. Ọ̀yọ́ Empire, ca. 1776

the second empire in the history of the Yorùbá community of practice, and by 1770, they had created the biggest city and the largest political formation in West Africa south of the River Niger (figs. 6.3 and 6.4). The unfolding events on the coast shaped the formation of the Ọ̀yọ́ Empire.

Power Politics in the Bight of Benin

During most of the seventeenth century, Ọ̀yọ́ used the Ṣábẹ́-Kétu-Mahi-Allada (Yéwá-Ògùn frontier) routes to march its captives and other products to the coast and to send European merchandise to the metropolis. Ọ̀yọ́'s access to this route was made possible by the transformation of Ṣábẹ́, Kétu, and Allada into client states. The Ọ̀yọ́ were content to use the king and merchants of Allada as brokers rather than dealing directly with the European slave merchants.[11] Allada was the largest kingdom and overlord of the entire Mina Coast from about 1610 through 1710. Although bringing it under direct Ọ̀yọ́ suzerainty did not seem to have involved much military action, Ọ̀yọ́ reportedly disciplined the kingdom in 1694 when the latter appeared to be developing policies that were against Ọ̀yọ́'s interests.[12] As the economic and political strength of Ọ̀yọ́ increasingly depended on the coastal market, it became necessary for Ọ̀yọ́ to invest more military presence in the southern Yéwá-Ògùn frontier, if only as a deterrence to potential troublemakers in the area. The meteoric rise of Dahomey and its expansionist policies in the early eighteenth century further compelled Ọ̀yọ́ to increase its military activities and develop a hands-on political strategy in this frontier.

Dahomey was an inland principality between the Wẹ̀mẹ̀ and Mono Rivers and seems to have become a client or vassal of Allada kingdom in mid-seventeenth century. Dahomey, however, embarked on military expansion in the last decade of the seventeenth century. Between the 1690s and 1720s, it annexed several Gbe and Yorùbá communities in the area.[13] The Ọ̀yọ́ political chieftains recognized the implications of Dahomey's menace for Ọ̀yọ́'s coastal agenda. Hence, they attacked the rising power of Mina in the dry season of 1719–20, but this did not seem to have any effect. Undeterred, Dahomey conquered its former overlord, Allada, and destroyed the latter's trading port at Jakin in 1724. Its determined soldiers pushed farther south in 1727, defeated Hueda kingdom, destroyed its capital at Savi, and annexed its port town Ouidah. Allada and Hueda were the two dominant kingdoms in the Mina area of the Bight of Benin, and they had controlled the two most important slave ports in the region for more than a hundred years (1607–1727). Following these victories, the chieftains of Dahomey were not interested in pursuing the same laissez-faire policy that Allada had developed with Ọyọ́ and the European trading partners. Rather, it sought to dictate the terms of commerce to both African and European merchants on the coast.

With this development, Dahomey posed an existential threat to Ọyọ́. Apart from its goal to monopolize the coastal trade, the new kingdom was bent on pursuing territorial expansion toward the Yéwá-Ògùn frontier, and therefore to block Ọyọ́'s untaxed, direct access to the coastal market. Dahomey had become the proverbial "crooked firewood" (*igi wọ́rọ́kọ́*) in Ọyọ́'s stove (*àdògán*). As far as the metropolitan Òyó chieftains were concerned, it was a misfit that could put out the burning fire of their political ambitions and economic well-being. Removing this crooked firewood from their stove became the preoccupation of the *aláàfin*, the *ọ̀yọ́mèsì*, and their military commanders. It was an urgent priority for Ọyọ́ to contain Dahomey's expansionist agenda in order to protect its direct access to the coastal markets via the Yéwá-Ògùn frontier. There was also a moral pressure on Ọyọ́ to punish Dahomey for invading Allada, a loyal client state of Ọyọ́, and for disrupting commerce on the coast. Hence, Aláàfin Òjìgí's army confronted and defeated Dahomey's forces in 1726, but it took several more attacks, which continued until 1730, for King Agaja to seek a truce, through the intervention of European negotiators and the potentate of Cana, one of the Yorùbá towns that Dahomey had previously annexed. In the negotiation that followed, Agaja reportedly gave six hundred men and women and rich imported goods, including coral beads, to the *aláàfin*.

But Ọyọ́ was not the only source of Agaja's headache. There were two other constituencies angered by Dahomey's territorial expansion. First, a number of Gbe-speaking princes who hailed from several of the principalities and kingdoms (including Allada, Mahi, Wẹ̀mẹ̀, and Hueda), defeated by Dahomey, mounted gallant guerilla-style attacks on the coastal holdings of their tormentor.[14] The second opposition came from European traders, who objected to the high customs duties imposed on them by Agaja, and resisted his economic policy aimed at keeping the price of slaves high. The traders grumbled that the king was seeking to monopolize slave trading in Mina by concentrating trade in the Dahomey-controlled port of Ouidah. The monarch possibly countered that he was only trying to protect his market share and prevent prices from falling. After all, the demands for African labor in the Americas were also rising, so why should the price remain low? The European slave traders were concerned that Dahomey's trade policy was eating deep into the high profit margins they were accustomed to under the relaxed rules of Allada and Hueda. They therefore took steps to sabotage Dahomey's trading interests. The consequence was the escalation of hostilities between the African monarch and European merchants throughout the

1730s and continuing through the reign of Agaja's successor, Tegbesu (r. 1740–74).[15]

The hostilities and political instability on Mina Coast made several European slaving merchants to begin to look for alternative ports, outside the reach of Dahomey, to dock their ship and load human cargo. In doing so, they also wanted to reduce the cost of slave procurement, blunt the sharp edges of Dahomey's monopolistic impulse, increase the supply of slaves to the Middle Passage, and boost or stabilize the profit margins for themselves and their investors. Hence, Dutch trader Hendrik Hertogh seized the opportunity provided by anti-Dahomey sentiment on Mina Coast and followed a group of Ogu princes rebelling against Dahomey to Àpá village (a Yorùbá community in present-day Nigeria), where they established a trading port, Badagry, in 1736. A year later, he built another trading port at Ẹ̀pẹ́.[16] Badagry was the first full-fledged slave-trading port on the coast of the Yorùbá-speaking region.[17] It immediately drew the attention of Portuguese/Brazilian, Spanish/Cuban, British, and French slavers, who began to anchor their ships there. The success of the Badagry port encouraged other European traders to explore alternative trading stations in the Bight of Benin for human trafficking. Over the next thirty years, other ports were established on the Yorùbá coastland. Àjàṣẹ́ (Porto Novo) was one of those second wave of ports established as a result of the political instability created by Dahomey's rising power in the Bight of Benin.[18] Following the conquest of Allada by Dahomey, a faction of the Allada royal house took refuge in Àjàṣẹ́ and placed themselves under the protection of Ọ̀yọ́. A group of Brazilian-Portuguese traders, worried by the uncertainties that followed Dahomey's takeover of Ouidah port, also relocated to Àjàṣẹ́. Another port that developed in the aftermath of Dahomey's conquest of Allada was located in Lagos (1760s). It was established by João de Oliveira, a liberated African slave who had lived in northeast Brazil. The Lagos port did not, however, become a viable commercial center until the 1790s.[19]

The opening of Badagry for slave trading brought the Atlantic market closer to the Ẹ̀gbá, Àwórì, and Ìjẹ̀bú territories in the southern Yoruba region. As a result, the Ìjẹ̀bú and Rẹ́mọ (henceforth, Ìjẹ̀bú-Rẹ́mọ) used their closeness to the coast and access to European imports to open up the Ọ̀ṣun and Ọ̀wẹ̀na frontiers to the Atlantic slave trade. As the chief carriers of European imports, especially cowries, tobacco, and textiles (damask and silk), into those areas, the Ìjẹ̀bú-Rẹ́mọ traders were the arrowhead for the penetration of the slave/merchant-capital exchange into the central and eastern Yorùbá territories. The Benin kingdom had resisted this type of exchange in the previous centuries, but it also jumped on this bandwagon in the eighteenth century.[20] The new opportunities for coastal commerce accelerated the southward migration of the Ẹ̀gbá from the northern fringes of the rain forest; caused major demographic changes in the Ẹ̀gbá forest, between the Ògùn and Ọnà Rivers; and put pressure on the restructuring of the hierarchies of power among several Ẹ̀gbá peer-polities. Prior to the mid-eighteenth century, the Ẹ̀gbá had been dominated by three kings—Agùrá of Ìdó (capital of the Gbágùrá), Òṣìlẹ̀ of Òkò (capital of Òkè-Ọnà), and Òjòko of Késì (capital of Àgbèyìn). However, the opening of Badagry trade significantly increased commercial traffic in the southern Ẹ̀gbá forest. Hence, Aké, Ọbà, and Ìkèrèkú, located "within the reach of the coast" and on the trade routes connecting the coast and the mainland, used their geographical advantage to challenge the authority of the older and more prominent Ẹ̀gbá metropolises farther north.[21] The new commercial wealth particularly gave Aké the resources to finance political expansion and bring several outlying towns and villages under its control. Hence, sometime in the third quarter of the eighteenth century, Aké displaced Késì as the chief town in the southwest Ẹ̀gbá territory (see fig. 6.4).

However, of all the polities in the Yorùbá-speaking region, Ọ̀yọ́ was the greatest beneficiary of the eastward expansion and increase in the number of the slave trade ports in the Bight of Benin. The newly opened Badagry, Àpá, and Àjàṣẹ́ ports turned the southern parts of Yéwá-Ògùn into the crown jewel of the Ọ̀yọ́ Empire. This frontier became the most economically lucrative of all the trading networks that connected the Yorùbá mainland to the coast. The volume of trade passing through the area increased exponentially after 1736, quickly followed by a significant surge in the population of the area due to migration. It became far more urgent than ever before for Ọ̀yọ́ to secure the southern area of this trading corridor, between Wẹmẹ and Ògùn Rivers. In order to achieve this objective, Ọ̀yọ́ established colonies and military outposts along the trading routes. These also served as turnpikes and way stations for traders and other travelers moving between the Ọ̀yọ́ metropolitan area and the coast.

The truce of 1730, between Aláàfin Òjìgí's and Agaja's representatives included the stipulation that Dahomey must pay annual tributes to Ọ̀yọ́. This arrangement worked until 1738, when Agaja became uncooperative and refused to send the tribute. There was a valid reason for this. Dahomey was incensed that Ọ̀yọ́ was supporting and patronizing rival trading ports that were also hotbeds of anti-Dahomey opposition. Faced with declining revenue, the Dahomey monarch refused to meet its obligation as a vassal of Ọ̀yọ́. The latter therefore resumed attacks on this hardy kingdom, but Ọ̀yọ́'s behemoth calvary met its match in the nimble and resolute forces of Dahomey. The confrontations between the two forces continued on and off under Tegbesu, who ascended Dahomey's throne in 1740 following Agaja's death. However, Dahomey had become the proverbial chicken perching on a tightrope. Neither the rope nor the chicken would have any comfort. It was clear to Ọ̀yọ́ that eliminating Dahomey was no longer an option. Therefore, they pursued the tactics of reducing the latter to a tributary state—that is, bringing Dahomey under the rule of Ọ̀yọ́ and laying the ground rules that would end Dahomey's incursion into the areas of Ọ̀yọ́'s territorial and economic interests. Both Dahomey and Ọ̀yọ́ underestimated each other, but after almost ten years of repeated Ọ̀yọ́ attacks, Tegbesu finally succumbed to Ọ̀yọ́'s military pressure in 1748, agreeing to provide Ọ̀yọ́ with an extensive amount of annual tribute.[22] According to one Dahomean source, this consisted of forty-one men, forty-one women, forty-one boys, forty-one girls, forty-one bales each of forty-one pieces of cloth, forty-one baskets each of forty-one beads (including coral), forty-one rams, forty-one goats, forty-one cocks, forty-one hens, and four hundred bags of cowries (with twenty thousand cowries per bag).[23] Although the protracted belligerence of the small but militarized state was a source of headaches for Ọ̀yọ́'s cavalry, the latter's persistence had paid off. The tributary status of Dahomey to Ọ̀yọ́ stabilized from 1748 to 1827, and this helped to secure the Yéwá-Ògùn frontier under Ọ̀yọ́'s control.[24]

Nineteenth-century Ọ̀yọ́ palace historians recalled the enormous wealth that the opening of the coastal trade brought to Ọ̀yọ́-Ilé through the Yéwá-Ògùn frontier. Oníṣílé was the reigning *aláàfin* (ca. 1746 to 1754) during those years of the final push by Ọ̀yọ́ to gain total control of the commercial corridor. It was during his reign that Dahomey accepted the suzerainty of Ọ̀yọ́. Reputed for his great wealth and military accomplishments, he was also revered for his patronage of the arts and fine taste in architecture. Oníṣílé is "said to have made seven silver doors to the seven entrances of his sleeping apartment." And it was during his reign that the calabash musical instrument, *ṣẹ̀kẹ̀rẹ̀*, "was ornamented, not only with cowries, but also with costly beads," such as *ṣẹ̀gi*, *iyùn*, *ẹrinla* (striped yellow tubular beads), and *àkún* or *àkòrì*. Even the thread for stringing the beads, according to local historians, was made of imported silk.[25] All of these details are metaphors to underline the enormous wealth that Aláàfin Oníṣílé derived from the new commercial opportunities that came through the Yéwá-Ògùn corridor. The *aláàfin* were by this time no longer leading military expeditions. Instead, an ambitious Ọ̀yọ́ military commander named Gáà led the charge to ensure that the authority of Ọ̀yọ́ prevailed in the southern Yéwá-Ògùn area. He supervised large migrations of Ọ̀yọ́ colonists into the area and presided over the development of several colonies, such as Ẹ̀wọn, Idofoyi, Tibo, Ìmálà, and Aibo, among others, between the late 1730s and mid-1750s.[26] A great military tactician and shrewd administrator, Gáà and his lieutenants deserve the credit for widening the Ọ̀yọ́ Empire's trade routes, deepening the roots of its trading entrepôts, and planting colonies and turnpikes along the southern

Yéwá-Ògùn corridor. Perhaps it was in appreciation of Gáà's accomplishments that Onísílé decided to reward him with the title of *baṣọ̀run*—the second highest-ranking position in the empire, next to that of the *aláàfin*.

The imperial staff in each of those tributary states and kingdoms often comprised a resident commissioner and his military attachés. Larger detachments of Ọ̀yọ́ soldiers were, however, present in the colonies, such as Ìlarò and Ìjànà. The governors of these colonies and the resident commissioners in the tributary states kept a close watch on the political and economic activities in the frontier, prevented and took care of trouble spots, coordinated the flow of information between the coast and the metropolis, and assisted with the passage of Ọ̀yọ́ traders. Through these frontier agents, Ọ̀yọ́ inserted itself into the politics of the coastal region and closely monitored the actions of Dahomey, preventing the small but powerful state from dominating the coastal market. Ọ̀yọ́ did not establish any trading port on the coast, but it transformed a number of these ports into client and tributary states and maintained an administrative presence and cells of spies in each of them. Ọ̀yọ́'s frontier administrators also used the carrot-and-stick tactics to prevent any of the newly emerged trading ports from becoming too powerful for Ọ̀yọ́'s interest. A good example was the relationship that Ọ̀yọ́ established with the Badagry and Àjàṣẹ́ ports. Badagry's Ogu refugees/settlers (a Gbe subgroup) and their European collaborators recognized the overlordship of Ọ̀yọ́ but maintained a fairly independent status in the control of their internal affairs. In contrast, the port of Àjàṣẹ́ established by Allada princes was firmly under the protection of Ọ̀yọ́ as a province of the empire. This offered Àjàṣẹ́ the much-needed Ọ̀yọ́ protection against its powerful neighbor, Dahomey, who rightfully saw the emergence of Àjàṣẹ́, Badagry, and Ẹ̀pẹ́ as a threat to its own trading port in Ouidah.

Although the Portuguese were the first to set up their slaving shop in Àjàṣẹ́, the better-capitalized French slave merchants soon dominated Àjàṣẹ́'s commerce. There were no fewer than "seven or eight large French ships" at any time in Àjàṣẹ́, and "the richest European commodities were continually passing from thence, to be presented to the King of Eyeo [Ọ̀yọ́]."[27] Àjàṣẹ́ was therefore a far more profitable trading outlet for Ọ̀yọ́ than Badagry. Since Ọ̀yọ́ did not have the same political leverage on Badagry that it had on Àjàṣẹ́, the rising commercial profile of Badagry as a destination for the anchorage of European ships threatened Àjàṣẹ́'s market share. It was therefore in the best interest of Ọ̀yọ́ to weaken the commerce of Badagry and that of other nearby ports in order to minimize the competition with Àjàṣẹ́. But it would not be honorable for the proverbial elephant of the savanna to attack the mouse on the lagoon. The *aláàfin* and his advisers were aware that Dahomey was itching to dislodge all the competing trading ports that had emerged in Mina, especially east of Ouidah. But Ọyọ́ held the string on Dahomey, dictating the terms of external relations and military engagement to its restless vassal state.

It was during Aláàfin Abíọ́dún's reign that Ọ̀yọ́ finally gave Dahomey (under Kpengla, r. May 17, 1774–April 17, 1789) the approval to attack Badagry. In 1784, Dahomey (with the secret logistical support of Ọ̀yọ́) destroyed the port town and took captive a large number of its residents.[28] What Ọ̀yọ́ primarily gained from this event was the diversion of more trade to Àjàṣẹ́, and this meant more taxes, tributes, and gifts to the coffers of the *aláàfin* and his agents. Two years later, Ọ̀yọ́ also gave Dahomey the nod to destroy Wẹ̀mẹ̀, a principality that was posing a threat to both Àjàṣẹ́ (Ọ̀yọ́) and Ouidah (Dahomey). Again, Kpengla achieved this task, but he misinterpreted Ọ̀yọ́'s nod and readied himself to attack Ardra (the coastal offshoot of Allada kingdom). Ọ̀yọ́, however, reined him in. Abíọ́dún supposedly told Kpengla in certain terms that "Ardra was Eyeo's calabash out of which nobody should be permitted to eat but himself."[29] It became obvious to Kpengla that Abíọ́dún had only used him as his hatchet man to destroy the two threats—Badagry and Wẹ̀mẹ̀—to Ọ̀yọ́'s interests, but Abíọ́dún was not ready to allow Dahomey to annihilate Ardra, the Ọ̀yọ́ client state in charge of Àjàṣẹ́ port that was taking a huge market share away from Ouidah. A contemporary observer, Archibald Dalzel, was clinically precise in comparing Kpengla's poor political sensibilities with the political sagacity of Abíọ́dún: "Although Adahoonzou (Kpengla) possessed a great share of personal courage . . . his bravery, and enterprising spirit served only to point him out as the fit engine for accomplishing the wishes of his more politic and formidable neighbour and master, the King of Eyeo [Ọ̀yọ́]."[30]

Hence, Dahomey's interests were subverted by Ọ̀yọ́ for about seventy years, during which Ọ̀yọ́'s power politics significantly shaped the dynamics of trading policies on the coast. Ọ̀yọ́ used a combination of whip and wits to curtail the ambitions of Dahomey and other port kingdoms on the western side of the Bight of Benin while also regulating the number and power of the slave ports in the region. Ọ̀yọ́ did not own or establish any of these ports. The empire was nevertheless the rudder for stabilizing the ship of commerce on the turbulent political waters of the Bight of Benin during the eighteenth century.

Genesis of Dependency I: Cowrie and Monetization

The entanglement of the political and economic lives of the Yorùbá community of practice in the web of Atlantic circulation of people and goods in the seventeenth and eighteenth centuries was not only facilitated by power politics and reorganization of labor at regional, subcontinental, and global levels. Far more than anything else, the investment of the imported merchant capital in the commercialization of the region's economy also made this entanglement possible. The imported commodities were used to monetize domestic economy, fund economic specialization, and create political dependency. The result was a commercial revolution that significantly expanded the market economy in the Yorùbá region. However, this entire enterprise was based on the increase in the volume of the slave trade, and it aborted the process of integration of the Yorùbá world, and Atlantic Africa in general, into the global commodity production system. That is, the commodity production (e.g., cotton cloth) in the Yorùbá community of practice was not integrated into the Atlantic market at the very time that the value and volume of commerce between the region and other parts of the Atlantic world were increasing.[31] Early in the seventeenth century, human cargo became the primary export of the region rather than cotton cloth, dyestuff, ivory, and glass beads of the previous centuries. Cowries accounted for a large share of the means of payment for the enslaved men and women who left the Bight of Benin during the Atlantic period, but it was Brazilian tobacco that primarily bankrolled the African-European trade in the Bight. These two commodities constituted the dominant merchant capital that financed the exportation of human cargo from the region. The other imports—European and Asian cloth merchandise, as well as coral and glass beads, and later alcohol—floated in the sphere of elite and aspirational consumption and were not as readily accessible to the general populace as cowries and tobacco. These two commodities were objects of desire, and they quickly accrued both use- and exchange-values for facilitating social, political, and economic transactions; storing wealth; and purchasing the means of production: labor, land, and tools.

Cowries, especially *Monetaria moneta*, became an important item in the Portuguese exports to the Bight of Benin in 1515, and they were immediately integrated into the local economies on the coast and in the immediate mainland. As mentioned in chapter 4, these Indian Ocean shells had already been serving as the standardized medium of exchange fifty years before the arrival of the Portuguese in the Benin kingdom and adjacent areas. However, the Portuguese and other European traders helped expand the cowrie currency network in West Africa during the sixteenth century by importing an unprecedented quantity of the shells from the Maldives. The cowries that came with this early phase of African-European trade, dominated by African commodity exports, reinforced and expanded the preexisting interregional trade. However, the absence of cowries in the sixteenth-century archaeological deposits of most of the Yorùbá mainland confirms that the central and northern parts of the region were latecomers to the Atlantic trade, as mentioned in chapters 4 and 5.[32] This began to change during the second quarter of the seventeenth century. The volume of cowrie importation into the Bight of Benin increased phenomenally between 1630 and 1650, at the very time that the only African export the European traders were interested in was human captives.[33] The opening of Mina ports for the shipment of human cargo into other parts of the Atlantic basin became the funnel for the torrential supply of moneta cowries into the Yorùbá region—a turning point in the economic life of the Bight of Benin and its mainland. As we shall soon see, the cowrie imports fueled "the growth and geographical spread of the market economy" across most of the West African region.[34]

By the mid-seventeenth century, cowries topped the list of merchandise proposed by the Dutch and English for the purchase of slaves in the Bight of Benin. A Dutch agent particularly noted that the more cowries his countrymen included in their "merchandise the better for trade." Silk damasks were also listed to be in high demand, in addition to an assortment of other imported textile products and beads of "good quality."[35] Hence, between 1662 and 1703, 44 percent of the value of over £718,000 worth of goods brought to the Bight by the English companies was in cowrie shells (table 6.2).[36] These shell imports increased astronomically throughout the eighteenth century because of the global upsurge in the volume of trade and price revolution.[37] The Bight of Benin was therefore awash with cowries during the eighteenth century, with the Dutch and the British alone shipping about 10.5 billion shells to West Africa. This import represented a 65 percent increase over the cowrie imports in the previous century. The French and the Danish, among other smaller importers, also carried an estimated 3 billion shells to the region during the eighteenth century. In the nineteenth century, the British dominated cowrie imports to West Africa. Between 1800 and 1850 alone, they brought in between 2.2 trillion and 5.6 trillion shells, causing unprecedented price inflation across all the zones of cowrie currency.[38]

At least 70 percent of all the cowries entering West Africa between 1650 and 1850 were off-loaded in the Bight of Benin. This flood of cowrie shells served as the basis for complete monetization of the Yorùbá economy after 1630. The other notable components of that revolution were the adoption of cowrie shells as the basis of a standard price index for commercial transactions, and the integration of the economy of the Yorùbá world into the other cowrie currency zones in West Africa, stretching from the Bight of Biafra to as far as the Senegambian valley. The Yorùbá world, Central Sudan, and the Volta Basin were the core regions of this cowrie-based monetary geography. The integration of the Yorùbá mainland to a single currency system (cowrie currency) in the subcontinent was complete by the last quarter of the seventeenth century, and it significantly transformed the Yorùbá domestic economy.

Table 6.2. Distribution of European Imports in Different Regions of Atlantic Africa, 1662–1703 (in thousands of constant pound sterling, base year = 1697)

Merchandise	Upper Guinea		Gold Coast		Bight of Benin		Bight of Biafra		West-Central		Total	
	£	%	£	%	£	%	£	%	£	%	£	%
Textiles	5.8	12	331.2	77	23.4	27	1.8	1	33.6	54	395.8	55.3
Metals	12.6	27	27.2	6	7.3	8	72.2	80	7.7	12	127	17.8
Cowries	0.4	1	3.9	1	38.3	44	0.8	1	0	0	43.4	6.1
Personal Decorator	12.7	27	4.6	1	6.7	8	13	14	0.9	1	37.9	5.3
Containers	2.5	5	10	2	3.6	4	1.3	1	10.5	17	28.1	3.9
Guns/Gunpowder Supplies	1.4	3	20	5	1.2	1	0.2	1	3.4	6	26.2	3.7
Spirits/Alcohol	3.8	8	8.9	2	1.2	1	0	0	0.6	1	14.5	2
Miscellaneous	8.2	17	22.4	4	6.1	8	0.7	1	5.1	9	42.5	5.9
Total	**47.4**	**100**	**428.2**	**100**	**87.8**	**100**	**90**	**100**	**61.8**	**100**	**715.4**	**100**

Source: Eltis, *The Rise of African Slavery*, 300.

The monetization of the cowrie in West Africa was, however, a political act, not the effect of overwhelming merchant capitalism over the local barter system. With the government of the dominant states in the region (e.g., Benin, Ọ̀yọ́, Allada, Whydah, Nupe, Hausa, Asante, and later Dahomey) collecting taxes and tolls in cowries, entrepreneurs were assured of the political security of the shells for storing wealth, pricing value, and redeeming credit-debt obligations. Confidence in cowries as the medium of exchange and the unit for calculating prices therefore soared throughout the seventeenth and most of the eighteenth centuries. The cowrie-based monetization of the region's economy served four purposes:

1. It standardized the pricing for the local economic exchange system. Although cowries were exchanged in the local markets mostly in the transactions of low-value and small-scale goods and services, they also provided the pricing and accounting unit for barter exchange in wholesale or high-value commodities, such as horses and captives.
2. The cowrie currency allowed for a more efficient control of the terms of external trade, especially with Europeans.
3. It permitted efficient management and exchange of the "ever increasing volume and variety of (imported) trade goods" across multiple currency registers.[39]
4. It also enabled the state to effectively collect revenue through a single value register that could not be counterfeited. Moreover, by promoting and facilitating the conduct of economic and social exchanges in cowries, the state was assured that cowries, by the nature of their size, would be difficult to conceal and would, therefore, make the evasion of taxes and other levies difficult.[40]

The increasing supply of cowries was utilized as much in the political acts of patronage, tributes, tolls, and taxation as in the domains of economic activities—payment for goods and services. It was the intersection of these two spheres of transactions that made cowries a sustainable medium of exchange. The Ọ̀yọ́ Empire sped up the monetization process in the Yorùbá mainland after 1630. Turnpike tolls, market levies, and taxes were collected in cowries, and these accounted for a significant portion of the state revenue. To this list may be added judicial levies and fines. The provinces also paid a large portion of their tributes in the form of cowries. Richard Lander noted during his 1826–27 visits to Ọ̀yọ́-Ilé that "The King of Yariba [Ọ̀yọ́] levies a tax on every one that enters the gates of Katunga [Ọ̀yọ́-Ilé] with a load, of whatever it may consist, and also appoints persons to collect a tribute from every person attending the market with any saleable commodity. The amount of duty is always governed by the value of the beast or article sold, which is decided by accredited agents: for example, a handsome horse imported from Borghoo [Borgu], or any other country, is liable in the market to a tax of two thousand cowries."[41]

A more extensive revenue base than the metropolis's gate tolls and market levies came from the vast number of turnpikes across the empire, especially in the high commercial traffic area of southern Yéwá-Ògùn during the eighteenth century. The twenty-five-kilometer Ọ́wọ̀-Ìpókíá-Ìbèṣè road was teeming with traders and other travelers, and some of the most lucrative tollgates were located there between 1740 and 1830.[42] It was there that the Yéwá-Ògùn frontier trade routes branched off in different directions toward several port towns in the Bight of Benin.

Turnpikes like these, as well as tributary polities and Ọ̀yọ́ colonies, funneled cowries to the metropolis; and special rooms and buildings were set aside to store these cowrie revenues. Ebo, the minister of political affairs in Ọ̀yọ́-Ilé, maintained one such "apartment in his house filled with cowries."[43] Therefore, the monetization of cowries was not simply the result of a happenstance introduction of a monetary standard of value. Rather, as in all cases of commodity-currency, such as gold, silver, or even glass beads, moneta currency represented the institutionalization of a political standard of value by the dominant regional powers, who were also the largest traders on the coast—the political elite and their intermediaries.[44] By making cowries the primary means of making the everyday political payments, such as tolls and levies, the political elite succeeded in co-opting the populace as participants in the reinforcement of commodity-currency importation via the Atlantic slave trade. It was therefore through cowries that the market and political institutions intersected, making it desirable for coastal entrepreneurs to seek the small Maldives shells as the preferred form of payment for slave exports.[45] The ubiquity of moneta cowries in the archaeological deposits of seventeenth- and eighteenth-century sites across the Yorùbá world, and West Africa in general—in residential, burial, midden, market, and manufacturing contexts—shows that these Indian Ocean shells integrated the region into intercontinental markets and tied household production to the Atlantic merchant capital.[46]

The monetization of the region's economy with cowries was an integral part of the Atlantic-age commercial revolution and a distinctive experience of West Africa's Atlantic modernity.[47] However, the use of cowries as a versatile unit of price measurement and a physical instrument of accounting, exchange, payment, and trade came at a huge cost with tremendous deficits in social and political capital. During the Yorùbá Classical period (chap. 3), power and the capital (wealth) for financing it were local. In contrast, power remained local during the Atlantic period, but the capital for financing it was external. Cowries were a necessity for

Table 6.3. Generalized Price (in Cowries) per Enslaved Prime Adolescent and Adult Male in the Bight of Benin†

Year	Number of Cowries
1515	6,370[a]
1680	10,000–31,000[a]
1710	40,000–50,000[a]
1760	80,000[a]
1770	160,000–176,000[a]
1850	100,000–140,000[c]

Sources: [a]Hogendorn and Johnson, *Shell Money*, 111; [c]Crowther, *Grammar*, 9.

†The coastal prices for prime slaves between 1780 and 1850 were generally 200–600% higher than the prices in the interior markets, with the markup especially more pronounced for healthy-looking young adult males (Lovejoy and Richardson, "Competing Markets for Male").

social and political payment, but they were not locally sourced. The shells could only be obtained in market-based exchanges associated with the transatlantic trade. The political elite appropriated this external merchant capital to develop the largest market economy that the Yorùbá, up to that time, had ever experienced. As a result, cowries affected the populations of the Bight and its mainland more profoundly than any other Atlantic import. This was especially the case "at the low end of the income distribution where people who never owned another [Atlantic] import would frequently have used the cowrie . . . in local markets for . . . purchases of food and other necessities."[48] The dependency of the domestic economy on the Atlantic trade as the source of its currency commodity meant that no effective domestic fiscal policy could evolve to control or adjust the valuation of cowries. The reason is that cowries were not convertible to other currencies in the Atlantic world, especially once the cowrie/slave exchange was made on the coast of Africa.[49] Thus, since all the cowries entering West Africa had to be retained there, inflation became inevitable, even with the expansion in the market economy driven by the specialization of production. Table 6.3 illustrates one example of this inflationary trend in terms of the average price of prime adult male slaves (priced in cowries) between 1515 and 1850.

While cowrie currency began to lose its global value right from the time it arrived on the shores of the Bight of Benin as payment, the enslaved (the primary "object" of exchange for cowries after 1630) generally increased in value in the Americas, in terms of their labor and their productive and reproductive ability. The entry of the Yorùbá into the Atlantic economy, therefore, brought them into the zone of soft currency as opposed to hard currency. The former was a zone of asymmetrical exchange in which the African merchants had very little control over the valuation of the imported currency. On the one hand, the Bight of Benin's exports were mostly restricted to only one category: enslaved people, who were departing to one region of destination:—American plantations. On the other hand, these enslaved people powered the Euro-American commodity production that financed the imports brought to the Bight of Benin in exchange for more slaves.[50] And, whereas the enslaved formed an appreciative value in the network of the Atlantic economic system (production, distribution, and consumption), the cowrie currency (payment for the slaves) formed a depreciative value in the global currency linkage system. Unlike hard currencies such as gold and silver, which generally retained their value over a long time and in different spaces and across distances, soft currencies like cowries depreciated in their relative global values, over a relatively short time and usually with one destination from the point of origin.

Therefore, the merchant capital-driven economies of the Bight of Benin were disadvantaged in the Atlantic exchange, and this led to two results.[51] First, the global value of local commodity product and the overall quality of commodity imports in the Yorùbá world (and Atlantic Africa in general) declined. Second, the only way the Bight of Benin merchants could convert the imported cowries and other forms of merchant capital into the Atlantic register of value was to invest them in the accumulation of people, usually as captive labor. These captives were the primary commodified African "products" that had increasing demand and value in the African-European commercial relations, and they were also the driving force of the entire Atlantic economy. A significant consequence of Atlantic modernity's value chain—linking monetized economy, the Atlantic slave trade, the American plantation economy, and the slave/merchant-capital exchange—was that the idea of "wealth in people" became synonymous with "commodification of people." This scenario was not limited to the Yorùbá world and other parts of Atlantic Africa penetrated by the merchant capital. Even in colonial America, the basis of wealth was not the land that the Europeans conquered but the enslaved Africans whom they purchased to work the land. Governor Luis Vahia Monteiro of Rio de Janeiro (1725–32) unambiguously articulated this version of the "European wealth in people" in South America in 1729: "The most solid properties in Brazil are slaves and a man's wealth is measured by having more or fewer . . . for there are lands enough, but only he who has slaves can be master of them."[52]

The commodities produced with enslaved African labor on those plentiful (but forcefully taken) New World lands financed the early modern commercial revolution globally, including in the Bight of Benin and its mainland. Therefore, the monetization of the cowrie was not the only story of that age of merchant capital in the Yorùbá world. Neither was the cowrie the dominant import in the slave/merchant-capital exchange. Indeed, if all that the European traders had to offer were cowries, the slave trade would not have lasted that long. Overall, European traders only used cowries as partial payment for their slave cargo.[53] The remainder of the value was paid in other goods. Of the latter, Brazilian tobacco was the leading commodity that financed most European trade in the Bight of Benin between 1650 and 1860. Hence, although the emphasis has been placed on cowries as slave money, tobacco was the primary merchant capital that drove the Atlantic slave trade in the Bight of Benin. Of all the staples of merchant capital produced in the Americas, tobacco was "the most widely and rapidly distributed item."[54] We must start with the Dutch-Portuguese hostilities in the waters of Atlantic Africa to understand how this American cultigen became entangled in the business of human trafficking.

Genesis of Dependency II: Tobacco and Addictive Consumption

The Dutch dealt a heavy blow to the Iberian trading operations in West Africa in 1637 when they captured the Portuguese castle of São Jorge da Mina on the Gold Coast. At that time, the Dutch were primarily interested in the gold trade, not slaves. But by then, the explosion in the slave market was already under way in the Bight of Benin. The capture of São Jorge da Mina's castle (present-day Ghana) gave the Dutch the upper hand in controlling the commercial traffics on the Gold Coast and the Bight of Benin. It also gave them the advantage of setting the terms of trade for the Portuguese in the region.[55] Although the Dutch granted Portugal (and by extension its Brazil colony) the right to trade in the ports of Grand Popo, Ouidah, and Jakin (see fig. 6.2), they limited the Portuguese trade to the purchase of slaves (as opposed to gold and ivory). Also, the Portuguese were not allowed to "bring any goods from Europe" for trade. Instead, they were restricted to bringing only tobacco rolls from their colony, Brazil (Bahia, to be specific). Adding insult to the injury of defeat, the Dutch imposed a duty of 10 percent for each ship of Bahian tobacco arriving in the Bight of Benin.[56] This Dutch-Portuguese face-off on the waters of West Africa bore three consequences:

1. Direct trade from Portugal to the Bight of Benin ended. This forced the Portuguese crown to issue a law allowing direct trade between Brazil and Africa, a departure from the mercantilism practiced by all European metropolises that had permitted only direct trade between the colonies and their mother country and between the mother country and Africa.

2. Portuguese trade in the Bight of Benin was now at the mercy of Bahian (Brazil) tobacco production, for which, along with sugar, there was an insatiable demand for African labor.
3. Trade relationships expanded among European slavers on the coast of West Africa, where the Portuguese traders sold a portion of their tobacco cargo to other European trading factories in exchange for goods from Asia and Europe. This allowed slave ships from different European nations and Brazil to diversify their portfolio of merchant capital needed to transact business with African slave traders. For example, the Portuguese obtained cowries, Asian and European cloth, and beads, among other merchandise, from the Dutch, English, and French slavers, in exchange for the highly desired Brazilian tobacco.

If the Dutch had intended to bankrupt Portugal and Brazil with these trading restrictions, the strategy did not work; instead, tobacco became the king of merchant capital in the Bight. There was a high demand for these nicotine-bearing leaves—*Nicotiana tabacum*. However, the tobacco that Bahian slavers loaded on their ships was neither first- nor second-grade but third-grade quality, known in Brazil as *refugado*. The first two grades were reserved for Portugal and were prohibited for export to Africa. This arrangement helped keep the metropolitan merchants in business and preserved the profitability of tobacco trade between Brazil and Portugal. The African market was left with small, broken tobacco leaves forbidden by law to be imported to Portugal. What was rejected in the North Atlantic, however, became the desired product exchangeable for human life in the Bight of Benin. It was "a strange paradox," according to Pierre Verger, that the poor quality of this third-grade tobacco was the basis of its success in West Africa.[57]

Here is what happened. In order to prevent these reject leaves from excessive molding or drying out, Bahian tobacco farmers rolled them into a thick rope like the leaves of the higher grades. They then brushed the leaves with a liberal amount of molasses, more than what they normally applied to the leaves of the higher grades. The aroma of this low-grade, molasses-enriched tobacco, together with the nicotine content, was an instant success in the Bight of Benin.[58] Generations of men and women developed an acquired and addictive taste for this brand of Bahian tobacco, making it an "indispensable article of the slave trade in the area" for close to two hundred years.[59] The business was so profitable that many Brazilian planters opted to focus on cultivating these lower-grade tobacco products for the African market. With such a widespread addictive demand for tobacco, the Bahian traders even reduced the weight of tobacco rolls exported to the Bight of Benin in the 1770s to further

Table 6.4. Number of Tobacco-Laden Ships from Bahia to the Bight of Benin and Angola, 1681–1710

Year	Bight of Benin	Angola
1681–1685	11	5
1686–1690	32	3
1691–1696	49	6
1697–1700	60	2
1701–1705	102	1
1706–1710	114	0
TOTAL	**368**	**17**

Source: Verger, *Bahia and the West African Trade.*

increase their margins of profit.[60] Although some of these Bahian tobacco imports went to West Central Africa, the overwhelming majority were unloaded in the Bight of Benin. This region received 96 percent of the 385 tobacco-laden ships dispatched from Bahia to Africa over a twenty-five-year period, with the number of these vessels increasing from 16 in 1681–85 to 385 in 1706–10 (table 6.4). The near-exclusive commodity that those ships took back to Bahia were slaves. It is estimated that 164,209 of these slaves disembarked in Bahia between 1681 and 1710.[61] There were somewhere between 8,000 and 10,000 Yorùbá among them.[62]

The impact of addictive tobacco in the Bight of Benin and its mainland was clear by the mid-eighteenth century, when two French trading factors based in Ouidah, Messieurs Pruneau de Pommegorge and Guestard, sent a report to their superiors in Paris on March 18, 1750. They commented: "The negroes prefer the Brazilian tobacco to gold. . . . The negroes use so much of it that whenever the Brazilian vessels are late in arriving, the vessels in [the] harbor can get a choice prisoner for six rolls" instead of eight rolls.[63] The Portuguese-Brazilian tobacco and slave merchants, as well as plantation owners, derived unprecedented profits from this single merchant capital throughout the Atlantic age. According to Stuart B. Schwartz: "In 1752 . . . a Mina slave could be bought at Whydah [Ouidah] for eight rolls of tobacco or 28$800 réis,[64] transported for another 26$420 réis, and sold in Bahia for 100$000 réis, yielding a profit of almost 45 per cent" to the slave trader.[65] The momentum of the tobacco-slave exchange was just reaching its climax in 1799 when Portugal's minister of colonies instructed the newly appointed Governor of Bahia, Marquis of Valença, with all seriousness: "Brazilian tobacco is as necessary for the trade in negroes, as these negroes are for the existence of Portuguese America. The other colonial nations are in the same condition; none of them can do without slaves and all need our tobacco for the slave trade."[66] The minister was not exaggerating. The survival of his empire and Lusophone Atlantic civilization rested on the tobacco/slave exchange in the Bight of Benin. As late as 1819, British merchant G. A. Robertson, who had traveled extensively on the West African coast, observed that Brazilian tobacco was the "staple commodity" with which the Portuguese purchased most of the slaves in Lagos. However, the imported tobacco rolls coming through the Bight of Benin were not all consumed in the Yorùbá and Aja-Fon areas near the coast. Like cowries, they were means of payment in the multiple chains of long-distance trade that reached as far as the Sudan and the Sahel, where tobacco usage was mainly in the form of chewing and snuffing rather than smoking. The Brazilian tobacco arriving on the shores of the Bight of Benin was, therefore, a major capital, which the Yorùbá traders used to finance the purchase of Sudanese salt, leather goods, and textiles. It was also used to purchase the captives brought to the Niger River by Hausa-Kanuri merchants.[67]

Market Production and Economic Specialization

A monetized economy (based on cowrie currency), the demands of the states for political payments, and the evolving taste for aspirational (e.g., Asian textiles and cowries) and addictive (e.g., tobacco) commodities pulled the majority of subsistence producers in the Bight of Benin and its mainland into the market economy. That is, economic specialization and diversification of production became necessary for the majority to fulfill state obligations (taxes and levies), finance social responsibility (e.g., marriage), satisfy desire, and pursue goals of self-realization. If the institutionalization of the cowrie as currency marked one end of the spectrum of the merchant capital revolution, the other end was economic specialization. Specialized production was not new, as we have seen in chapters 2 and 3, but its scale was larger in the seventeenth century than in the preceding centuries. The economic specialization of the Atlantic age was supported by a fully developed market system driven by currency, credit, the abstraction of value, and pricing indexes. The unification of the currency of multiple political entities from the coast to the Sudan and across several political boundaries significantly expanded the market sphere of the Yorùbá region. These expanding commercial networks intimately connected the increasingly specialized producers from different households and at several geographical scales: within and between villages, towns, kingdoms, and regions. By 1650, the presence of the following aspects of economic life indicate that the Yorùbá world was fully operating within the sphere of a truly market system:

1. Specialization was the driving force of all three axes of economic life—production, consumption, and distribution. That is, the majority of the consumers of a product were not the producers or redistributors of the product.[68] This affected not only prestige and high-skill utilitarian goods but also low- to middle-skill commodities, including activities that had been in the subsistence and domestic spheres, such as primary agricultural production, cooked food vending, and provisioning for household clothing.
2. The organization of exchange and distribution of commodities (trading) became a full-time activity for people from different social hierarchies, so the scale of the market expanded exponentially, spreading the delivery of both utilitarian and prestige goods across great distances. All of these helped to increase the revenue of the state through collection of customs and market levies.
3. As in other parts of the world that were within the orbit of the Atlantic merchant capital revolution, wealth financing was tied to market production of both primary and nonessential commodities rather than attached to the production of elite goods. Accordingly, there was no centralized organization of production and distribution. The wide latitude that the populace had to produce and distribute their wares offered a diverse and abundant circulation of basic and special goods. These not only reinforced and elaborated specialization but also intensified competition and facilitated the production of high-quality products.

In his remarks on the specialist economy that defined the Yorùbá world during the seventeenth and eighteenth centuries, with emphasis on the Ọ̀yọ́ Empire, Robin Law has this to say:

> Craft production was normally carried on on a specialized basis by a few households in each community, so that the majority of households had to obtain their manufactured goods by purchase. Many of the inhabitants of the urban centres also obtained their food by purchase, often in already cooked form. Households engaged in craft production seem to have purchased not only their food, but also their raw materials: weaving households, for example, did not produce their own cotton thread, but purchased it from others. In consequence, all towns of any importance had flourishing markets, dealing in foodstuffs, raw materials, and manufacture.[69]

As a result, subregional specialization was the dominant element of production and commercial life as different areas used their competitive advantages in raw materials, ecology, and concentration of skills to maximum benefit in the regional market. Hence, for example, the Upper

Ọ̀ṣun became noted for its high-quality dyestuff; the Àwórì-Ẹ̀gbá-Upper Ọ̀ṣun arc for iron smelting; Ọ̀yọ́ metropolitan area for cotton, textiles, iron smelting, and leather goods; Ìjẹ̀ṣà for the best mats and kola nut; Ọ̀wọ̀ for the finest crafts in ivory; Ìjẹ̀bú for textiles and brass casting; and Èkìtì for wood carving and pottery. Cloth weaving and dyeing were widely practiced across the region, but each area brought its unique style of cloth products to the marketplace, with Ìjẹ̀bú's famous *aṣọ-ọlọ́nà* and Ọ̀yọ́'s *aṣọ-òkè* and indigo cloth being among the textiles widely traded in the Yorùbá world and beyond.

Cloth-related manufactures were by far the largest industry, and they were the driving engine of the regional economy. Different segments of the population across class and gender lines were involved in the production of cotton cloth. Before the Atlantic period, cloth weaving was the customary preserve of women, and they wove primarily to clothe their family members. Mothers, wives, sisters, and daughters were responsible for harvesting and collecting cotton, spinning it into thread, weaving it, and dyeing the white cotton cloth in desired colors (blue, yellow, red, black, and green), of which blue was the most common.[70] The increased value of clothing in the market economy not only fostered specialization and innovations but also attracted more participants, especially men who specialized in more ceremonial and expensive *aṣọ-ọlọ́nà* among the Ìjẹ̀bú and *aṣọ-òkè* among the Ọ̀yọ́. The participation of men in weaving increased during the seventeenth century because of the rising commodification of clothing. However, women continued to play the dominant role in the textile industry, from processing of raw cotton into thread (ginning, carding, combing, and spinning) to weaving, dye making, and cloth dyeing.[71]

Several towns along the busiest trading corridor of the eighteenth century, Yéwá-Ògùn, boasted large-scale clothing-related manufactories. In modestly sized households of specialist weavers, there might be as many as eight to ten looms, if not more. In Ìjànà, a town of about eight thousand to ten thousand people, Hugh Clapperton in 1826 "visited several manufactories of cloth." He also saw "three dyehouses, with upwards of twenty vats or large earthen pots in each," all busy producing excellent indigo and "durable dye," which formed an important capital in local trade.[72] In the chain of cloth-manufacture processes, cloth dyeing was the largest manufacturing enterprise, in the sense that dyeing centers tend to be concentrated in only a few places in a town and owned by only a few people, whereas weaving and other aspects of cloth production (e.g., thread spinning) were distributed among several households. Known as *ìdí-aró*, dyeing centers were capital-intensive manufactories, "very expensive to establish," and were generally "owned by the richest women in the community."[73] There were other cloth-related specialized crafts. One of these was garment embroidery. Àjàyí (later known as Samuel Àjàyí

Crowther, the first African bishop of the Anglican Church, 1864–89), was born ca. 1807–09 in Òṣoògùn, in one of the core provinces of the Ọ̀yọ́ Empire. His father, Aíyẹmí, was an embroiderer, and all his male relations—siblings and cousins—were also of that trade. The extended family specialized in making a distinctive elephant pictograph embroidery, called *aṣọ-elérin* (elephant's cloth). Àjàyí was introduced to embroidery before his twelfth birthday, showing that in his preteen years he was already being groomed to enter the trade.[74] Different lineages and families were known for specific crafts, and members of the households were generally recruited to these specialized industries, with sons taking after the father and daughters after the mother. However, nonfamilial apprentices were also recruited and groomed into several of these specialized crafts as the expansive market forces and potentials of profitability became the determining factor of profession, production, and specialization.

With economic specialization and a monetized exchange system, the value of household products expanded far beyond the immediate area of production. The more of the desired products a household produced, the more income it expected to take in. A consequence of this was that the production of many utilitarian products became not only specialized but also standardized. For example, the Ọ̀yọ́ serving and cooking earthenware reveal standardized formal, petrological, and chemical properties. They bore potters' marks and were widely distributed within and beyond the empire, allowing one to identify particular forms of Ọ̀yọ́ earthenware with particular workshop or group of potters across the Yorùbá region (plate 5). Not only do the attributes that are characteristic of the Ọ̀yọ́ ceramics predominate in the core metropolitan area of the empire—Ọ̀yọ́-Ilé, Ìgbòho, Ìpàpó, and Kòso—but they are also found in the empire's colonies, such as Ẹdẹ-Ilé and Òjé-Ilé.[75] Likewise, they are present in the provinces of the empire, at Orílè-Kéésì in Ẹ̀gbá division, Ìpo in Ìgbómìnà, and Savi and Abomey in the Aja-Fon area. These distinctive Ọ̀yọ́ bowls—especially the gray and black cooking (*ìṣaàsùn*) and serving bowls (*àwo*)—were also traded to areas that were not directly under the jurisdiction of the empire, as is evident at Òṣogbo, Iléṣà, and Benin, to mention but a few.[76] All of these show that mundane everyday objects, such as earthenware, were produced and consumed within the regional sphere of a specialized and interdependent market economy.

The textile industry was the second largest economic activity, after agriculture, in Yorùbá's domestic economy during the Atlantic period. It was, therefore, imperative to establish a stable and steady supply of indigo and cotton to support this market-driven production. These raw materials were cultivated extensively and distributed through the market channels. The savanna ecology of the Ọ̀yọ́ metropolitan area and its Ìgbómìnà provinces was conducive to the cultivation of cotton on a large scale, unlike in the rain forest environment. This enabled the metropolitan area of Ọ̀yọ́ Empire to become the hotbed of cotton cloth manufacture. The ubiquity of Yorùbá cotton cloth along the coast and in the Atlantic trade is evident in several European accounts between the seventeenth and early nineteenth centuries. Cotton cultivation is also a constant presence in these accounts.[77] Richard Lander poetically wrote of the "pleasant . . . fragrant odour" that "exhaled from the cotton plant . . . in full blossom" between the towns of Engwa (Egua) and Afoora (Afura) in the northern Yéwá-Ògùn frontier during the late dry season of 1826 (January 3). He observed several "plantations of cotton" (in addition to numerous fields of Indian corn) between this area and Ọ̀yọ́-Ilé, in well-managed farmlands "cultivated in the highest degree."[78] What Lander missed was the fact that intensive production of cotton was difficult to sustain over the long term on the same parcel of land because of the propensity of cotton to quickly deplete soil nutrients and water resources.[79] Moreover, increasing the production of cotton to meet the rising demands for cloth manufacture would have increased the amount of labor needed for the management of soil and plants, from seeding to harvest.[80] The labor investment in cotton production as a cash crop would also have increased the value of the cotton farmland, and of land that was favorable for cotton cultivation. The Ọ̀yọ́ metropolitan area (including the entire northwest Yorùbá) would have therefore belonged to what Gareth Austin called "'islands' of intensive agriculture" economies because of the pressures of the market economy and high population density.[81]

The same picture held for the second primary raw material in textile production—the indigo plant (*Indigofera spp.*). The cultivation of this perennial plant also required the intensive use of farmland on a large scale. Indigo provided the highly desired blue color variants for which the Ọ̀yọ́ cotton cloth was justly famous and highly sought after across West Africa throughout the Atlantic age. Again, in 1826 Richard Lander observed large plantations of indigo, estimated at five to six hundred acres, in the vicinity of the Ọ̀yọ́ metropolis and its satellite towns.[82] Some of these towns and cities had populations in excess of twenty thousand, located within five to ten miles of one another. The processing of these plants into indigo cakes was a large-scale operation, and they were a highly valued commodity across the Yorùbá region. Numerous women were employed as dyers in the Ọ̀yọ́ Empire during the eighteenth and early nineteenth centuries as British explorers, Hugh Clapperton and the Lander brothers, noted in their travel accounts. And every town had a few dyers on hand to serve the needs of their community and regional market. These dyers did not own indigo farms, the same way that cotton weavers did not produce cotton. Rather, they bought their indigo cakes from the market. The cultivation of indigo plants was a large-scale endeavor, and the extraction of dyestuff from these plants was a capital-intensive process. As a cash crop, indigo farms would have been highly coveted.

There were other needs for land in the Ọ̀yọ́ metropolitan area besides cotton, dyestuff, and food production. Cavalry was the backbone of Ọ̀yọ́'s army, and maintaining a high population of horses was an important consideration for land management in the metropolis. The water resources and land needed for cotton production would have competed with the needs for food-crop farming, as well as with water and fodder provisions for horses, in a densely populated urban landscape such as Ọ̀yọ́ metropolis. European visitors to Ọ̀yọ́-Ilé between 1826 and 1830 noted that the area within an eighty-kilometer radius of the imperial capital was studded with several cities and towns. In a journey of five hours between the towns of Adja and Layboo in 1826, Hugh Clapperton and his fellow travelers came across five large towns, "two or three of which were walled." The explorer was astonished and impressed by this scale of urbanism: "The further we penetrated . . . the country, the *more dense* we found the population to be, and civilization became at every step more strikingly apparent. Large towns at the distance of only a few miles from each other, we were informed lay on all sides of us."[83] He also noted that many of the towns were surrounded by cultivated fields of food and cotton as far as the eye could see.

The production of cotton and dyestuff on a large scale, provisioning for the horses that supported the extensive cavalry of the empire, and the cultivation of food for the teeming population in the metropolitan area would have been taxing on land and water resources. These competing needs for land would have led to a reconfiguration of the land tenure system in the Ọ̀yọ́ metropolitan area in order to meet the demands of market-based specialized production and the security needs of the empire. The commercialization of cotton production is one example where it was inevitable to move the needle of land tenure practices toward the capitalization of land. In fact, the pressure on agricultural land and food security in the core metropolitan area of the empire may have been one of the major reasons for the active resettlement of the Ọ̀yọ́ population in the newly conquered frontiers of the empire, especially in the southwest Yéwá-Ògùn (Ẹ̀gbádò) and Upper Ọ̀ṣun areas between 1630 and 1780. Increased population, depletion of land resources due to intensive use, and periodic episodes of drought intensified this pressure.

The monetized economy and specialization of production made daily and weekly market fairs an elaborate feature of social life during the Atlantic age. Contemporary observers noticed that the weekly market fairs especially attracted "buyers and sellers . . . many miles around," with women being "the chief, if not the only traders."[84] At its peak, the city of

Ọ̀yọ́ had several such marketplaces that opened every day, in the morning and in the evening, just before sunset. However, once every four days, the city's major market, Àkẹ̀sán, hosted two major fairs, one in the day and the other in the evening. The daytime one was called the Queen's Market, and the King's Market was held later in the evening. On Friday, May 15, 1830, one or both of the Lander brothers (Richard and John) recorded the range of commodities that were displayed in the Queen's Market. In abundance were several raw and cooked food items, including corn, peas, beans, macadamia butter, groundnuts, varieties of vegetables and pepper, beef, mutton, varieties of game and fowl, cheese, and butter. Salt and tobacco from the coast, trona from the Sudan, and imported beads from everywhere were also available for sale. Other manufactures, local and imported, included cotton cloth, indigo, jasper beads, iron knives, barbs, and hooks, as well as needles, finger rings, bracelets, and armlets (made of tin, copper, bronze, brass, iron, ivory, and bone). Old shells and animal bones for medicinal and ritual purposes were also on display in the market. Likewise, the Landers spotted a common European blue plate for sale.[85] Recent archaeological excavations in the capital, near Méjìró, have uncovered fragments of imported glassware and stoneware. These included a cobalt-blue-rimmed glass bowl made sometime between 1780 and 1810 in France or Northern Europe. The glass bowl possibly traveled inland from the Àjàṣẹ́ port, where the French traders were very active in the late eighteenth and early nineteenth centuries.

The markets in the provincial towns were no less active. An early evening market in Ìjànà on Friday, December 16, 1825, was described as one where the crowd rolled on like a sea, with women busily calling on customers to visit their stalls. The marketplace was well supplied with cooked food, such as boiled yam and *àkàsù* (corn meal), in addition to a variety of fresh vegetables and fruits, as well as supplies of country cloth and raw cotton. The fair was so packed with people and goods that it was difficult to find a passage, and men resorted to "jumping over the provision baskets" to make their way.[86] About seven miles (or half a day's journey) southwest of Ọ̀yọ́ was also a "large weekly market" in the town of Eetcho (Ẹ̀ṣọ́) that commenced at midday and attracted thousands of people "in a large open space in the heart of the town." Eetcho was a suburb of the Ọ̀yọ́ metropolis, and it would have been a place for wholesalers to sell products to retailers from Ọ̀yọ́-Ilé and other nearby towns. The dominant items at Eetcho were country cloth, indigo, and agricultural produce.[87]

The Yorùbá region was a vast network of hundreds of market towns and fairs during the seventeenth and eighteenth centuries. Linking these centers of exchange were long trains of caravansaries, as well as way stations and turnpikes. These also connected the metropolises and linked the coast and the mainland. The caravansaries were the conduits for credit-debt networks and the arteries for circulating goods, ideas, skills, and people within the region. Family- and state-organized trading corporations, as well as trading associations, thrived along these commercial routes to take advantage of economic opportunity at different locations. Because of its expansive political boundaries and its status as the Yorùbá world's largest economy, Ọ̀yọ́ played the most important role in integrating the market system of the Bight of Benin's mainland. It dominated the coastal-mainland circulation of goods and services in central and western Yorùbá region via its colonies and client states; and through its hegemonic presence in Ìgbómìnà, Upper Osun, and on the River Niger, it controlled a significant portion of the traffic of goods exported from the rain forest to the Sudan. These included red camwood from Benin, kola nut from Ifẹ̀-Ekiti-Ìjẹ̀ṣà, and textiles from everywhere.

Like other preceding West African political behemoths (e.g., Ifẹ̀, Ghana, Mali, and Songhai)—Ọ̀yọ́ was a trading empire. Its political elite, from the king and princes to the *ọ̀yọ́mèsì*, controlled a vast network of trading corporations along the commercial routes that its military conquests opened up. These chieftains were not only political leaders but also leaders of great merchant houses. They were the dominant traders, sending their agents (usually referred to as "sons" in the oral traditions) to different frontier market towns. One of these towns was at Ògòdò, where the Nupe, Hausa, and Yorùbá met for trade. According to Samuel Johnson, "nearly all the children of influential Ọ̀yọ́ chiefs resided there permanently for the purpose of trade."[88] The Atlantic imports, as well as tributes and other levies pouring into Ọ̀yọ́-Ilé, financed large trading expeditions to these market towns on the Niger. These imports and tributes were exchanged mainly for slaves and horses, the two resources of power at the core of Ọ̀yọ́'s political economy. Dealing in these resources required more than trading skills. The trading agents worked for the state, comprising the seven noble Houses (*ọ̀yọ́mèsì*) and the royal House (*aláàfin*) in the capital. Therefore, the directors (*atọ́kùn*) of these trading corporations had the authority to use the violent power of the state, whenever needed, in order to manage the business transactions, products, and profits associated with trading in slaves and horses.[89] Under these trade directors were professional horse riders, horse veterinarians, slave drivers, and soldiers and mercenaries, among others. Men were the visible figures involved in these two high-capital resources. They were the "sons"—blood, adopted, fictive, and dependent—of the chieftains who financed these trading missions. It is not surprising, therefore, that many of the princes who later became kings of Ọ̀yọ́ during the seventeenth through the early nineteenth century were in fact great traders. Ódárawu (r. ca. 1620s–1630s), Abíọ́dún (r. 1770–1789), and Aólẹ̀ (r. 1789–1796), for example, traded in the empire's frontier towns before they ascended the throne.[90] However, there were other commodities that were less power charged and whose carriers often joined these state-sponsored caravans. These included local cotton cloth, indigo, and beads, as well as imported goods. Women were the main carriers of these products, and they were also organized into caravans independent of the ones controlled by the state and powerful men.[91] Long-distance trading was therefore an important component of economic activities pursued by all and sundry, including the elite and non-elite traders.

The intensely mobile landscape of caravansaries stimulated the establishment of several towns and villages along these highways of commerce. The communities through which the trade routes passed also saw dramatic growth in their population. These towns and villages served as way stations for the mobile traders and therefore pulled in some of the wealth circulating across the region.[92] Way stations provided many services for the caravans. Food sellers sold hot meals and other refreshments, and a wide array of craftspeople came out with their wares to attend to the needs of the caravansaries. However, the large villages and towns on the caravan routes did more than provide refreshing services. They were also places where the traders could sell some of their wares and stock goods needed at the next destination. In these way station towns and villages, the caravans were usually hosted by a family member or friend, or a chieftain who might serve as a broker (*aláróbọ̀*). These brokers would also sell "to caravan traders those goods which they had collected . . . well in advance."[93] This interdependent relationship between brokers and members of caravansary helped to drastically reduce the waiting time for caravan members.

Just as the Ọ̀yọ́ Empire dominated the overland routes during the Atlantic period, the Ìjẹ̀bú traders dominated the coastal routes, as well as the south central and southeastern flanks of the inland trading networks (see fig. 6.2). The Ìjẹ̀bú took advantage of their nearness to the lagoon, and used it for conveying goods and people across the central Bight of Benin and to other major trading centers on the coast. The establishment of Badagry and Lagos ports in the eighteenth century especially favored Ìjẹ̀bú traders who served as the primary conduits for funneling European merchant capital to the south central and southeastern mainland, just as the captives and "manufactures of the interior" from those areas also passed through them to the coast.[94] Groomed from childhood for commerce, several Ìjẹ̀bú traders formed caravans that traveled inland as far as Òde-Oǹdó, Apòmù, and Kétu, and on waterways as far as Ouidah in the west and Ughoton, Warri, and Ìjọ́ villages in the east.

Ọṣìnfẹ́kundé (Osifekunde, in earlier works) was, for example, only about twelve years old when he and his brothers began to accompany their father, Adésùlú (spelled as Adde Sounlou in previous works), on his trading voyages along the coast and to the mainland.[95] Ọṣìnfẹ́kundé belonged to the third generation of a successful merchant family in the lagoon town of Ẹ̀pẹ́. The family originally hailed from Màkun, an inland town of the Rẹ́mọ subgroup. It was from there that Ọṣìnfẹ́kundé's grandfather, Ọ̀ṣínwọ̀ (Ochi-Wo), had come to Ẹ̀pẹ́, a province of the Ìjẹ̀bú-Òde kingdom.[96] Ẹ̀pẹ́ was a backwater fishing village before it became a thriving commercial town in the eighteenth century (see figs. 1.1 and 6.2). Ọ̀ṣínwọ̀'s migration was driven by the quest to take advantage of the new commercial opportunities on the lagoon. As a merchant, Ọ̀ṣínwọ̀ was very successful in his new home. He went on to marry fifteen wives, and he rose to the important office of treasurer in the town.[97] His son (Ọṣìnfẹ́kundé's father), Adésùlú, maintained the family tradition and even expanded it. He was a war captain and also a successful merchant. This combination of war with trade indicates that Adésùlú was a slave trader. He would have supplied some of the captives from his military expeditions to the Lagos-Badagry slavers in exchange for merchant capital, which he would then use to finance commercial endeavors on the mainland.[98] In other words, he acquired slaves from both war and commerce. Operating from their home base at Ẹ̀pẹ́, Ọṣìnfẹ́kundé's family traded on the lagoon as far as Ughoton and Warri in the east and as far as Lagos in the west. Ọṣìnfẹ́kundé and his father also traded in the mainland, on the northern frontiers of the Ìjẹ̀bú kingdom and within the Ọ̀wẹna frontier going as far as Benin City. It is not clear at what age Ọṣìnfẹ́kundé started trading by himself, but he certainly did not know any other occupation until his career as a merchant abruptly ended at the age of twenty-two. On an early morning in June 1820, while traveling between Lagos and Màhin in his canoe laden with "a rich assortment of European merchandise," as he later recalled, "he fell into an ambush of Ìjọ́ pirates." They took him to Warri, where he was sold into slavery and transported to Brazil. Ọṣìnfẹ́kundé's story illustrates the risks and ironies involved in plying the highways of commerce, whether on the lagoon or on land, during the age of merchant capital revolution.

Commercial life on the lagoons boomed throughout the seventeenth and eighteenth centuries, but not all the trading canoes carried human cargo. Instead, most of them sold the riverine produce (fish) and local manufactures, especially cotton cloth and salt.[99] However, the increasing activities of European slaver-traders made brigands, robbers, and human traffickers to proliferate on the waterways of the lagoon and these made intra-lagoon trade unsafe from the mid-seventeenth to mid-nineteenth century. Dutch trader David Van Nyendael mentioned in a letter to his superiors in 1702 that he had "seen several men that came from Ardra, Calbary and several other places" who had come to the Benin River to trade (an eleven-day journey from Allada by canoe) but who were captured by pirates and sold to European slavers. These pirates, he continues, "live only on robbery; they sail hence to all parts of this river, and seize all that lights in their way, whether men, beasts, or goods; all which they sell to the first that come hither."[100] Pirates were active on the lagoon, and bandits prowled the mainland woods, but the chances of profits overshadowed the potential risks. Thousands of men and women took to the road and the waters each day to pursue profit and wealth. Some never returned home. They became the ware of the Atlantic trade, as Ọ̀ṣìnfẹ́kundé would discover, and ended up in South America and the Caribbean.

Regional Integration and Networked Landscape

The distribution networks that supported the monetized economy, economic specialization, and the supply and demand forces of the market galvanized mobility and integration of people from multiple origins into new frontier communities. The Yéwá (formerly Ẹ̀gbádò) subgroup of the Yorùbá, for example, developed during the seventeenth century as a result of the integration of several Yorùbá subgroups brought together by Ọ̀yọ́'s political expansion and new economic opportunities. Comprising mainly the Ẹ̀gbá, Àwórì, Kétu, and Ọ̀yọ́, the members of these old ethnolinguistic subgroups mixed and developed the new Yéwá identity between ca. 1650 and 1750.[101] The increased mobility and political expansion also made it possible for households to spread out widely across the region. This process played out more prominently within the Ọ̀yọ́ Empire, where many households and Houses in the metropolitan area distributed themselves along the networks of colonies, market towns, way stations, and mining enclaves that Ọ̀yọ́ brought under its control. The governor of Ìlarò, for example, told English explorer Hugh Clapperton in 1825 that "he had a house at Eyeo [Ọ̀yọ́-Ilé], and that half [of] his wives were there."[102] Each branch of the "family" on these networks served as a node of supplies, information, and hospitality for the other branches, and they provided one another with access to the local markets. These networked relationships helped shorten the distances between the coast and the mainland and enabled fast dissemination of information, as thousands of individuals developed a sense of themselves as multi-sited, belonging at once to the metropolis and to the frontier. The system of multi-sited *ilé* that was prevalent in Ọ̀yọ́ Empire helped families to effectively distribute their products and people over long distances and diversify their risks while also increasing opportunities for their members. This was a society in motion. Citizenship continued to be accessed through membership in an *ilé*, but the *ilé* was no longer rooted in a place. Rather, it was widely dispersed along the contours of territorial expansion and trade routes.

Another innovation brought about by the merchant capital revolution was the elaboration of credit-debit relationships. To a considerable extent, the Atlantic slave trade was financed with credit facilities advanced to African slave dealers by their European counterparts. The volume of credit goods advanced "grew in tandem with the magnitude of the trade and the opening of new slaving frontiers, both inland and along the coast."[103] These credits linked the port towns of the Atlantic basin intimately with one another. For the Bight of Benin, those credits originated from both the South and North Atlantic, especially Bahia, Liverpool, and Bristol.[104] On the nature of this credit network in the Bight of Benin, Dutch slaver Willem Bosman recalled: "If there happen to be no stock of slaves, the [European trading] factor must then resolve to run the risk of trusting the inhabitants with goods to the value of one or two hundred slaves; which commodities they send into the inland country, in order to buy with them slaves at all markets . . . sometimes two hundred miles deep in the country."[105] Bosman was right on point about the distance that merchant capital traveled on the basis of credit-debt relationships. What he missed was the carnage that accompanied the penetration of these merchant capital credits "deep in the country," as he put it. The captives procured with those goods were not purchased from their owners (family members) but from those who had forcefully taken them from their families through predatory activities that included kidnapping and war. The merchant capital advanced on credit to the African slave merchants on the coast (such as Ọ̀ṣínwọ̀ and Adésùlú) provided the incentive for the violence associated with these captures.

The merchant capital, therefore, played a significant role in developing a chain of overlapping creditor-debtor relationships along the trading and slaving routes. This risky social arrangement of delayed economic reciprocity underpinned the expansion of the pernicious Atlantic slave trade, not only in the Bight of Benin but across the whole of Atlantic Africa.[106] It began in the second quarter of the seventeenth century as a way of reducing the waiting time for European traders on the coast. As the volume of the slave trade expanded in the Bight of Benin a hundred years later, with the establishment of Badagry, Àjàṣẹ́, and Lagos ports, these vines of credit-debt relationships spread rapidly across the creeks and lagoons, extending deep into the mainland. They penetrated the forests of the central and eastern Yorùbá regions and stretched as far as the Niger Confluence and Central Sudan.

Monetized economy and the Atlantic nexus of the credit-debt relationship also facilitated the development of indigenous financial institutions and savings, as well as domestic credit and lending facilities.[107] It was the monetized economy of the seventeenth and eighteenth centuries, for example, that led to the creation of *èsúsú*, a Yorùbá rotating credit system by which individuals formed a savings club and each contributed the same amount at fixed intervals, weekly or monthly. Each member collected the contributed sum in rotation at those intervals. The savings club might disband after all members had received their contribution, or the club might reconstitute and start all over again.[108] Another savings mechanism was *àjọ*, a system in which a group of people participated in savings and met at specific intervals in the leader's house. Each member contributed whatever he or she could afford during those meetings over a period agreed to by the members. The length of time could be as long as one year. At the end of the period, the collector of the savings deducted a mutually agreed-upon amount as his or her service fees and returned the balance to each contributor.

Summing Up

The revolutionary quality of the merchant capital during the seventeenth and eighteenth centuries stemmed from the pervasiveness of a monetized economy, the permeation of every domain of production by economic specialization, and the slavery/merchant capital exchange. The redistributive economy of the Classical period, powered by the production and circulation of locally produced prestige and epistemic objects (glass beads) and dominated by the political elite, was replaced by a market economy in which almost everything, including people, became a commodity. With domestic production now integrally linked to regional and global commerce and underwritten by imported merchant capital, economic specialization intensified, and the scale of exchange networks and long-distance trade expanded exponentially. Nestled in the web of a highly capitalized early global economy, the Yorùbá community of practice was fully incorporated into the subcontinental cowrie-currency continuum that stretched from Senegambia to the Bight of Biafra and as far north as the Western and Central Sudan. The consequences of this integration were as profound as the causes and mechanism of the revolution. The Yorùbá region experienced a monumental commercial expansion and remarkable increase in productivity, as most households sought to take advantage of market-driven production. As a result, the mobility of individuals, families, and *ilé* intensified, concomitant with the increasingly mobile merchant capital.

Four factors drove the increase in domestic production. First, a monetized economy led to economic specialization at every level and sphere of production, and it stimulated innovations in credit and finance institutions. Second, cotton textile production became the chief employer of manufacturing labor. This turned cotton and indigo into cash crops and would have heightened the value of land in the core Ọ̀yọ́ metropolitan areas while also transforming the land into capital and private property in affected areas. Third, the elaborate bureaucracy of the Ọ̀yọ́ Empire—the region's dominant political entity and largest economy—retained a massive number of state officials who worked in administrative, military, and production endeavors. The majority of this staff of the state were drafted as enslaved labor. Fourth, the intensely mobile and integrated regional landscape dominated by several urban emporia provided the networks needed to redistribute local and household products into the wider regional markets. The urban centers, and the markets that they nurtured within them and in their hinterlands, offered the dynamic space for economic specialization, as producers and consumers were brought closer to the capital, credit, and products that they desired. The Yorùbá region of the Atlantic age was therefore transformed into a vast network of market districts with caravans, peddlers, political emissaries, and military engagements. All of these kept the circulation of people, credit, capital, ideas, information, taste, and goods in constant motion. The caravans that expanded the market networks in the region were not a new mechanism of economic exchange and distribution. What distinguished the Atlantic age caravansary from the old form was that it served as the mechanism for expanding the geography of monetization. It created a web of specialized consumption-production threads and interpersonal credit-debit relationships that integrated the Yorùbá mainland into the broader Atlantic commercial world. Yet, even as the scale of the market economy reached stratospheric proportions, the market value of Yorùbá commodity production declined in the global market. In its place, the value of the enslaved Yorùbá and other people from the Bight of Benin and its mainland increased in the Atlantic market.

The commodified people (slaves) and merchant capital were the ropes that tightened the entanglement of the Bight of Benin and the Yorùbá world with western Europe and the Americas, especially the Caribbean and Brazil, between 1630 and 1860. This entanglement was revolutionary for what it meant in the structures of everyday life, political economic spheres, and the domains of religion and worldview. New practices of social status and consumption, and new cosmological and intellectual ideas, organically developed as individuals and social groups pursued their goals of self-realization in the context of the new economic and political order. The slave/merchant capital exchange contradictions, so well encapsulated in the nineteenth-century Ọ̀yọ́ palace historians' memory about Ọbalókun, also brought forth questions about what it meant to be a person in an era when personhood was convertible into a commodity through predation and purchase. The dramatic expansion in domestic slavery due to the rising tides in the Atlantic slave trade and the penetration of merchant capital into the mainland, therefore, had a significant impact on the ideas, processes, possibilities, and limitations of self-realization. Likewise, these developments transformed the institutions and practices of class, gender, kinship, and labor relations. In the process, the Yorùbá "system of the world," to borrow from Marshall Sahlins, did not remain the same.[109] It created what I call the "Yorùbá Atlantic modernity" between ca. 1630 and 1860. The cultural dimension of this modernity, especially the way the Yorùbá culturally translated and domesticated their Atlantic experience, is the subject of the next chapter.

Notes

1. Johnson, *History*, 168.
2. The Ọ̀yọ́ historians identified this royal personality as the king of France, but Samuel Johnson suggested this must have been the king of Portugal. Indeed, it was the Portuguese and not the French traders who were active in the Bight of Benin during Ọbalókun's reign, in the early seventeenth century. The French relationship with Ọ̀yọ́, through the port of Àjàṣẹ́ (Porto Novo), began in the early eighteenth century.
3. Gehring, Schiltkamp, and Stuyvesant, *Curacao Papers*, 79; Green, "Africa and the Price Revolution," 10.
4. Law and Strickrodt, *Ports of the Slave Trade*.
5. Law, *Slave Coast*.
6. The Gbe is a group of several speakers of related languages—especially Ewe, Aja, Fon, and Mina—in present-day southeast Ghana, southern Togo, and southern Benin.
7. Nevertheless, Patrick Manning (*Slavery, Colonialism*) estimated that 217,000 and 873,00 Aja peoples entered the Middle Passage between 1641–1700 and 1701–1800 respectively. This led to a drastic depopulation throughout the Aja-speaking region.
8. Johnson, *History*, 217.
9. Collins and Burns, *History of Sub-Saharan Africa*, 235.
10. At the height of the cowrie flow between the coast and Central Sudan in the last two decades of the eighteenth century, Gobir—a Hausa city-state—reportedly imported five hundred donkey loads of cowries (about twenty-five million cowries) via Nupe. Lovejoy, "Interregional Monetary Flows," 567.
11. William Snelgrave inferred that the Ọ̀yọ́ were forbidden by their spiritual taboos to look at the sea (*New Account*, 59).
12. Bosman, *New and Accurate Description*, 396–98.
13. Monroe, "In the Belly of Dan," 784.
14. Strickrodt, *Afro-European Trade*; Law, *Ouidah*.
15. One the manifestations of this hostility was the destruction of the Portuguese fort at Ouidah (Whydah) and the arrest and imprisonment of João Bazilio, director of that fort, by Tegbesu. Bazilio was accused of "being in league with the enemies" of the king. See Verger, *Bahia and the West African Trade*, 19–20.
16. Law, *Slave Coast*, 309–14.
17. Sorensen-Gilmour, "Slave-Trading along the Lagoons."

18. The Yorùbá call the port Ajàṣẹ́. It is known to Europeans as Porto Novo (Portuguese for "New Port"), and as Hogbonu to Gbe-speakers. Law, *Slave Coast*, 17. It is also referred to as Allada or Ardra in some of the eighteenth-century European accounts. See Dalzel, *History of Dahomy.*

19. Mann, *Slavery.*

20. Ben-Amos, *Art, Innovation, and Politics*; Ryder, *Benin.*

21. Biobaku, *Egba and Their Neighbours*, 3.

22. Law, *Oyo Empire*, 165.

23. French colonial administrator Gavoy noted in 1913 that forty and forty-one are the numbers that Dahomeans "associated both with royalty and with ideas of perfection or completeness" (Bay, *Wives of the Leopard*, 59).

24. Akinjogbin, *Dahomey*; Law, *Ouidah.*

25. Johnson, *History*, 176.

26. Fọlayan, "Egbado to 1832," 17. These dates are an approximation. What is certain is that Gáà died in 1774. According to the nineteenth-century palace historians of the Ọ̀yọ́, Gáà "lived to a good old age" (Johnson, *History*, 178). I am conservatively placing his birth somewhere between 1700 and 1710. Gáà's exploits on the Yéwá-Ògùn frontier were not the beginning of Ọ̀yọ́'s colonization project in the area but the second wave of it, which can be securely placed in the second quarter of the eighteenth century (especially the late 1730s through early 1750s), a period when Gáà would have been in his prime adulthood. He became *baṣọ̀run* sometime between 1753 and 1755. The accession of Aláàfin Lábísí, who reigned about the same time that Gáà became *baṣọ̀run*, is dated by Robert Smith and Robin Law to 1754 on the basis of cross dating with contemporary events on the coast. Gáà held the office of *baṣọ̀run* for about twenty years before he was killed in the civil war of 1774 (Law, *Oyo Empire*; Smith, "Alafin in Exile").

27. Dalzel, *History of Dahomy*, 207.

28. Badagry was rebuilt soon after it was destroyed by Dahomey, but it did not attract much commerce after the attack. The commercial fortune of the port town was restored in 1821 when King Àdèlé of Lagos relocated his court to Badagry following an outbreak of civil war that pitted him against his older brother, Ọṣìnlókùn. The latter had successfully seized the throne of Lagos from Adélé earlier in the year. Mann, *Slavery*, 46.

29. Dalzel, *History of Dahomy*, 196.

30. Dalzel, 206.

31. See Eltis and Jennings, "Trade between Western Africa and the Atlantic World"; Inikori, "Africa and the Globalization Process."

32. Ogundiran, "Of Small Things Remembered."

33. Law, *Oyo Empire*, 219.

34. Inikori, "Africa and the Globalization Process," 73.

35. Jones, *West Africa in the Mid-Seventeenth Century*, 233.

36. This is equivalent to almost £104 million in the 2016 commodity real price, judging by calculations at the website MeasuringWorth, "Purchasing Power of British Pounds."

37. *Price revolution* refers to the inflationary trends that continued until the nineteenth century in Atlantic Africa and arguably laid the foundation for the contemporary and postcolonial price instability in most of Africa, especially those areas that were formerly within the slave/merchant capital exchange

(see Green, "Africa and the Price Revolution"; Law, "Cowries, Gold, and Dollars").

38. Hogendorn and Johnson, *Shell Money*, 43–70. This calculation is based on the estimate that there are 45,000–48,000 *C. moneta* shells per cwt and 18,000–20,000 *C. annulus* shells per cwt.

39. Belasco, *Entrepreneur*, 82.

40. Law, "Cowries, Gold, and Dollars," 65.

41. Lander, *Records of Captain Clapperton's Last Expedition*, 2:222–23.

42. Clapperton, *Journal of a Second Expedition*, 26; Hallett, *Niger Journal*, 59. Also see Morton-Williams, "Oyo Yoruba," 35.

43. Lander, *Records of Captain Clapperton's Last Expedition*, 2:203–4. The accurate orthography of this official's nickname is "Iba," but I will keep "Ebo," the rendition provided by Hugh Clapperton and the Lander brothers, because it gives this important individual a unique identity from other high-ranking people in Ọ̀yọ́ with this honorific title. Ebo will appear later in other sections of the book. In Ọ̀yọ́, *iba* is a general honorific title for each member of the *ọ̀yọ́mèsì* and the three highest-ranking officials in the palace bureaucracy—*òsì ẹ̀fà* (minister of political affairs), *ọ̀tún ẹ̀fà* (governor of Kòso, the country royal town, 18 km north of Ọ̀yọ́-Ilé), and *ọ̀nà ẹ̀fà* (minister of legal affairs). The descriptions of the duties and persona of Ebo provided by Clapperton and the Lander brothers strongly indicate that this person was the *òsì ẹ̀fà* during the reign of Májǒtú. See Clapperton, *Journal of a Second Expedition*; Hallett, *Niger Journal*; Lander, *Records of Captain Clapperton's Last Expedition*, vols. 1 and 2. The office of *òsì ẹ̀fà* was the most honored and powerful of the three highest-ranking titles held by eunuchs. He was the closest eunuch to the king, and he had to be by his side at all times. The occupant of the office "represents the king on all occasions and in all matters civil as well as military . . . he is allowed to use the crown, the state umbrellas . . . and to have royal honors paid to him." Johnson, *History*, 59.

44. Gregory, "Cowries and Conquest," 210. Considering the multidirectional flow of cowries (in tributes, taxes, and other levies) to the metropolis at the zenith of the empire, 1750–89, it is conceivable that there would have been many such apartments or houses dedicated to storing cowries and held by nobles and royal agents. In the nineteenth century, the King of Dahomey maintained a two-story building called the "cowrie house" (*akuehue*), which "served as a storehouse for the king's wealth in cowries and goods." Law, "Finance and Credit," 30.

45. Bosman, *New and Accurate Description*, 364.

46. E.g., Monroe, "Dynamics of State Formation"; Norman, "Archaeology of West African Atlanticization"; Odunbaku, "Aspects of Settlement History"; Ogundiran, *Archaeology and History*; Omokhodion, "Northwest Benin Sites"; Usman, *State-Periphery Relations*. And in Early Osogbo and Ede-Ilé (Upper Osun), archaeological excavations have shown that cowries were stored away in jars and sacks and buried underneath the house floor with the intention of future retrieval (Ogundiran, "Material Life and Domestic Economy"; Ogundiran, "Making of an Internal Frontier Settlement").

47. For explicit use of the term, see Doyle, *Freedom's Empire*. Atlantic modernity was a global phenomenon, a product of the merchant capital revolution of the seventeenth and eighteenth centuries.

48. Hogendorn and Johnson, *Shell Money*, 2.

49. A case can be made that no merchant capital imported to Atlantic Africa was convertible. The exception was the contraband gold that was brought from Bahia to Dahomey and used as exchange for slaves, but the amount of such contraband gold was miniscule and insignificant to the operations of the slave trade. Schwartz, *Sugar Plantations*, 340.

50. The centrality of the Atlantic slave trade and enslaved African labor to the advent of the early modern global commercial revolution, merchant capitalism, and the Industrial Revolution has been widely discussed. For a sample, Inikori, "Africa and the Globalization Process"; Williams, *Capitalism and Slavery.*

51. Green, "Africa and the Price Revolution," 8. Also see Guyer, *Marginal Gains.*

52. Schwartz, "Plantations and Peripheries," 81. For a sample of Africanist perspectives on the idea of "wealth in people," see Guyer, "Wealth in People and Self-Realization"; Eltis, *Rise of African Slavery*; Miller, *Way of Death*; Thornton, *Cultural History.*

53. Bosman, *New and Accurate Description*, 364.

54. Trubowitz, "Smoking Pipes," 143.

55. Schwartz, "Plantations and Peripheries," 102. The Portuguese also lost control of Luanda (Central Africa) to the Netherlands in 1641 but regained control of it in 1648.

56. Verger, *Bahia and the West African Trade*, 5.

57. Verger, 7.

58. *Refugado* was also marketed to West Central Africa, and it was a major export to the Native Americans in the Canadian fur trade. Schwartz, "Plantations and Peripheries," 103.

59. Verger, *Bahia and the West African Trade*, 7.

60. This helped pay for the loss that accrued to the Portuguese crown because of the tax imposed on it by England in the asymmetrical North Atlantic power relations between the two countries. This imbalance of power in the North was passed on to the South Atlantic. Portugal taxed the Brazilian colonists, and they passed on the cost to African consumers in the Bight of Benin and West Central Africa. At least one of their trading partners there, King Agonglo of Dahomey, protested this unfair trading practice by the Bahians (see Alencastro, "Brazil in the South Atlantic," 144).

61. Ribeiro, "Transatlantic Slave Trade," 141.

62. This is an estimate based on David Eltis's figures for 13,900 Yorùbá disembarkments in Bahia between 1676 and 1725. Eltis, "Diaspora of Yorùbá Speakers," 31.

63. These enterprising factors even suggested to their superiors that "some Brazilian rolls could be sent as samples to San Domingo [Haiti] and Martinique so as to have similar ones produced." Verger, *Bahia and the West African Trade*, 9.

64. This price held steady in the first decade of the nineteenth century. In Lagos, a healthy-looking young adult was selling for eight to ten rolls of tobacco in 1807. Robertson, *Notes on Africa*, 288–90.

65. Schwartz, "Plantations and Peripheries," 103.

66. Verger, *Bahia and the West African Trade*, 8.

67. Lovejoy, *Salt*, 27–32.

68. Costin, "Craft Economies," 209.

69. Law, *Oyo Empire*, 207.
70. Lloyd, "Osifekunde," 263.
71. Van Nyendael, "Description of Rio Formosa."
72. Clapperton, *Journal of a Second Expedition*, 15.
73. Akintoye, *History*, 158.
74. Ajayi, "Samuel Ajayi Crowther," 292–93.
75. These attributes include twenty-three potters' marks and the following surface patterns: brush marking, shell edges, scallop-shaped impressions, dot punctation, and incised and rouletted geometric symbols (crosses, triangles, squares, and perpendicular motifs). About thirteen vessel forms (serving and cooking bowls) and three lids that are characteristic of the Ọ̀yọ́ ceramic complex bear these surface patterns. Agbaje-Williams, "Contribution"; Agbaje-Williams, "Archaeological Reconnaissance"; Agbaje-Williams, "Discovery of Koso"; Ogundiran, *Archaeology and History*; Ogundiran and Saunders, "Potters' Marks"; Ogunfolakan, Tubosun, and Aleru, "Archaeological Survey of Igbo Oje."
76. Connah, *Archaeology of Benin*; Monroe, "Dynamics of State Formation"; Norman, "Archaeology of West African Atlanticization"; Odunbaku, "Aspects of Settlement History"; Ogundiran, "Making of an Internal Frontier Settlement"; Willett, "Recent Archaeological Discoveries"; Usman, *State-Periphery Relations.*
77. E.g., Adams, *Remarks on the Country*; Barbot, *Description of the Coasts*; Clapperton, *Journal of a Second Expedition*; Hallett, *Niger Journal*; Jones, *West Africa in the Mid-Seventeenth Century*; Norris, *Memoirs.*
78. Lander, *Records of Captain Clapperton's Last Expedition*, 1:84, 89. This area is located in the southernmost part of woodland savanna, near River Ọyán, a tributary of River Ògùn.
79. Consider the comparative fact that on the American southern plains, "cotton production went from boom to bust in a mere twenty years (1920–1940) due to the impacts on soil degradation" and moisture stress (Vitale, Ouattarra, and Vognan, "Enhancing Sustainability of Cotton Production," 1161). For the same reasons, cotton production has stagnated in West Africa since the 1980s. It is estimated that the production of 1 kg of cotton (an equivalent of a male's full outer garment) could take as much as twenty thousand liters of water. These are useful comparisons for understanding the enormous stress that cloth production would have had on the land and water resources of the Ọ̀yọ́ metropolis in a fragile woodland savanna ecology.
80. Moseley and Gray, *Hanging by a Thread*, 12–14.
81. Austin, "Resources, Techniques," 592.
82. Lander, *Records of Captain Clapperton's Last Expedition*, 2:211.
83. Lander, *Records of Captain Clapperton's Last Expedition*, 1:95.
84. Hallett, *Niger Journal*, 71.
85. Hallett, 88.
86. Clapperton, *Journal of a Second Expedition*, 12.
87. Hallett, *Niger Journal*, 82.
88. Johnson, *History*, 217.
89. This is similar to the European trading corporations in the Pacific, Atlantic, and Indian Ocean regions, such as the English India Company, the Dutch United East India Company, and the Portugal's Estado da India. All "were endowed with many of the characteristics of a state, including the

capacity to wage war in furtherance of their [commercial] interests" (Tracy, *Rise of Merchant Empires*, 2).

90. Johnson, *History*, 169, 187, 189.

91. Falola, "Yoruba Caravan System."

92. Ogundiran, "Living in the Shadow."

93. Falola, "Yoruba Caravan System," 131. The *aláróbọ̀* performed the function of wholesalers. This class of merchants gathered local products from producers, either for wholesale distribution to retailers in the local markets or for itinerant traders (caravansaries), *alájàpá* (Akintoye, *History*, 167).

94. Robertson, *Notes on Africa*, 302.

95. Lloyd, "Osifekunde," 236.

96. The closest in modern Yorùbá orthography is Ọ̀ṣínwọ̀, an abbreviation of Ọ̀ṣìnọ́wọ̀, which means "The chief deity embodies the ultimate honor."

97. As a merchant, he would have been a member of *ìpàm̀pá*, the powerful association of merchants who controlled trading activities in most towns in Ìjẹ̀bú-Rẹ́mọ, performing roles similar to that of a chamber of commerce or a trading guild. Similar merchant associations are known as *pàràkòyí* in other Yorùbá towns. Both *ìpàm̀pá* and *pàràkòyí* tend to thrive in polities and market sites where the central political authority was weak or had little control over commerce. The *ìpàm̀pá* in particular set the terms of trade and managed commerce-related affairs. They also monopolized the trade in imported goods and became very influential in government affairs, all over Ìjẹ̀bú-Rẹ́mọ area, especially after 1740.

98. The compatibility of war and commerce has been elaborately discussed by Toyin Falola in the context of the political economy and power politics of Ibadan (1830–1900). His analysis is applicable to the seventeenth and eighteenth centuries. Falola, *Political Economy*, chap. 5.

99. Law, "Trade and Politics," 337.

100. Van Nyendael, "Description of Rio Formosa," 427–28.

101. Fọlayan, "Egbado to 1832."

102. Clapperton, *Journal of a Second Expedition*, 10.

103. Lovejoy and Richardson, "Trust, Pawnship, and Atlantic History," 334.

104. Haggerty, "Risk and Risk Management"; Ojo, "Organization of the Atlantic Slave Trade"; Price, "Credit in the Slave Trade."

105. Bosman, *New and Accurate Description*, 363.

106. For theoretical insights on debt as a social relationship of delayed reciprocity, see Graeber, *Debt*; Millhauser, "Debt as a Double-Edged Risk."

107. Falola and Adebayo, *Culture, Politics & Money.*

108. *Èsúsú* no doubt began before the British abolition of the Atlantic slave trade in 1807, because Yorùbá communities across the Caribbean, South America, and Western Africa (Sierra Leone) were in fact practicing this rotating savings/credit system as soon as they landed in their new destinations (Bascom, "Esusu"; Fyle, "Yoruba Diaspora"; Reis and Mamigonian, "Nagô and Mina").

109. Sahlins, "Cosmologies of Capitalism." 4.

7

Sociality of Merchant Capital

THE VALUE CHAIN THAT SUPPORTED the merchant capital revolution of the seventeenth and eighteenth centuries created "a commodity-focused economic life" in the Yorùbá world, as it did in other parts of the Atlantic basin.[1] It also led to significant changes in social relationships and in the ideologies and cosmologies that justified and sustained those relationships.[2] The economic, political, cultural, social, and racial ramifications of this revolution, as a global phenomenon, constitute what has been termed Atlantic modernity (chap. 6). The social and cultural aspects of the Yorùbá experience of that modernity is the subject of this chapter, focusing on five related topics:

1. The socialization of Atlantic merchant capital into everyday practices to create new consumption, taste, and social valuation practices.
2. The transformations that this socialization wrought on systems of thought and cosmology.
3. The assignment of new meanings and new social values to merchant capital.
4. The blending of merchant capital and local material life for making and marking both social differences and social distinctions.
5. The ways in which the slave/merchant capital exchange and its regime of value were critiqued, contested, and normalized in everyday life.

The integration of merchant capital into the everyday lives—that is, the transformation of imported commodities into social objects—in the

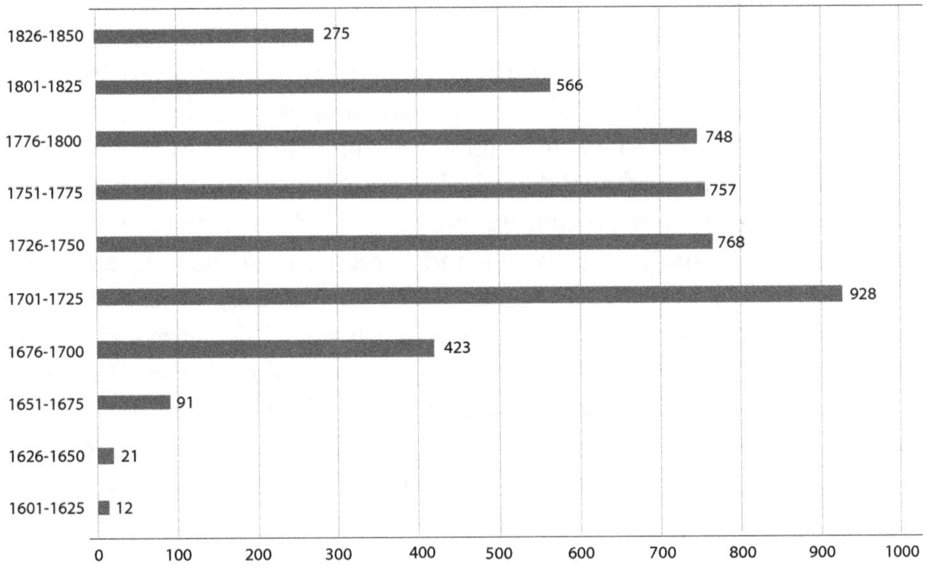

Source: Slave Voyages, https://www.slavevoyages.org/voyage/database [accessed April 30, 2019]

Figure 7.1. Minimum number of slave ships that departed the Bight of Benin, 1601–1850

Bight of Benin and its mainland made the region a desired destination for European traders. Between 1601 and 1850, more than 4,589 ships visited the Bight and exchanged merchant capital goods for human cargo (fig. 7.1). As objects of desire, merchant capital served as threads for weaving social networks, and such capital gave shape, meaning, and purpose to social relations. The result, as in most other places in the early modern period, was that the Yorùbá society developed a regime of value that thrived on an increasingly object-centered sociality. There was a hierarchy in that object-focused regime of value, in terms of desirability and accessibility. These imports also had the ability to bind individuals and communities to one another in ways that local products could not.[3] As we have seen in the previous chapter, most of the commodity imports that arrived on the shores of the Bight during that period were exchanged for people—the most expensive objectified being and the desire of others in the early modern world. Of the imported commodities implicated in the revolution, textiles, alcohol, tobacco, and cowries were the ones that affected the Yorùbá the most. Beads, crockery, metal jewelry (silver and copper alloys), and iron bars came in the second order of importance.[4]

An Encounter

The Yorùbá cultural stratigraphy clearly shows that the generations that lived through the Atlantic period had relationships with the object world in ways that their forebears did not. They had access to far more foreign and globally circulated objects than their ancestors and lived in what Karin Knorr Cetina called "object-centered environments."[5] That is, they used objects of mostly foreign origin to situate themselves in time and place; define status and social rank; imagine self-realization; construct relationships with others, including foreigners; and contemplate the world far outside their immediate reach and direct knowledge. As a result, merchant capital served as building blocks for "creating object-centered traditions" and for forging new knowledge systems.[6] This is evident in an encounter that happened on the morning of December 8, 1825, between the resident commissioner (*ajẹ́lẹ̀*) of the Ọ̀yọ́ Empire in the town of Ìpókíá and Captain Hugh Clapperton. The latter was a Scottish officer leading a contingent of explorers sent by the British government to follow "the Niger River to its delta on the Guinea Coast" and to document the geographical features of the mainland.[7] This task required the explorers to travel through the Ọ̀yọ́ Empire. Once word spread that these foreigners had entered the town, the resident commissioner galloped with fanfare to meet them. The encounter between the commissioner, Prince Adémọ́lá [Adamoli],[8] and Clapperton was the first well-documented official meeting between the representatives of these two Atlantic-world empires. The eventful meeting literally raised some dust not only from the galloping horses but also from the teeming crowd, most of whom were seeing white men for the first time. The colorful pomp and circumstance of the occasion lightened up the dull "thick and hazy" overhang of that late morning's harmattan weather in Ìpókíá.[9]

Adémọ́lá used the spectacle of horses and clothing to make his guests aware of his status, to impress and warmly welcome the European visitors who were on their way to see the *aláàfin*, about a month's journey away. A good account of his conduct by these august guests, Adémọ́lá possibly reasoned, would serve him well in the imperial capital. He arrived with fanfare on a horse, accompanied by two subordinates also on horses. A train of attendants trailed him on foot. Adémọ́lá informed Clapperton that he was meeting a "white man" for the first time, and he was quick to tell his European audience that "the various parts of his dress [outfit]" were not manufactured in his country. This "cap is of white man's velvet, these trowsers are of white man's nankeen,[10] this is a white man's shawl; we get all good things from white man, and we must therefore be glad when [a] white man come[s] to visit our country," the prince gaily announced.[11] To further burnish this imagery of long-distance connections between his empire and the European material world, the youngest member of Adémọ́lá's entourage, a five- or six-year-old boy, was dressed up in an oversized red European coat with a tail that dragged on the ground. The boy was wearing no trousers, but he sported a military cap, with an imprint of the Portuguese crown on the front. With visual, material, and rhetorical spectacle, the prince informed Clapperton that the Atlantic material world connected the two of them. Indeed, Adémọlá and about nine generations before him had received the European-imported velvet on the mainland before they met the velvet's peddler from across the ocean.

The Adémọlá-Clapperton encounter was a brief moment of coalescence, out of many, in the long encounters between the Ọ̀yọ́ Empire (and the Yorùbá world) and the Euro-American world. It may have been the first time that a European had ventured that deep into the Yéwá-Ògùn axis of Ọ̀yọ́ territory, but the empire had been interacting with European agents on the coast for at least two hundred years through its coastal subjects and allies (chap. 6). In fact, it was the empire's interest in the coastal trade that Adémọlá represented in Ìpókíá. The mandate of this Ọ̀yọ́ imperial agent was to promote trade, protect trade routes, maintain peace, collect tributes and turnpike levies, and foster the loyalty and subordination of Ìpókíá's political elite to the metropolis. It is striking but not surprising that the Adémọlá-Clapperton encounter was mediated by visual metaphors that drew from the symbols of the empire's power and the Atlantic commercial life—the horses represented the imperial power of Ọ̀yọ́,[12] and the "white man's goods" (nankeen, Portuguese cap, and velvet) embodied the material experience of the Atlantic commercial revolution.

Taste and Social Difference I: Sartorial Splendor

The integration of imported merchant capital—especially cowries, imported textiles, and Brazilian tobacco and aguardientes—into the practices of proprietary, aspirational, social, and addictive consumptions created new experiences of taste and desire. This also brought about new ideas and practices of social difference and self-realization. These imports defined the experience of early modernity for the Yorùbá. They were meaningful in the Yorùbá cultural universe precisely because they were integrated into the people's everyday material life. The imported cloth and related accessories constituted one category of a merchant capital that was used to articulate and negotiate the meaning and meaningfulness of Atlantic modernity in the Yorùbá world. The role of cloth and clothing accessories as the most pervasive markers of status and social class, and their use in negotiating aspirations of self-realization, has a long history in all cultures.[13] As the foremost material for bodily presentation, clothing was more important than any other class of objects or goods for communicating and negotiating ideas about identity, self-realization, status, wealth, authority, and power. In fact, until the mass-production and mass-consumption culture of the Industrial Revolution fully kicked in during the nineteenth century, no category of objects outstripped clothing as a source of anxiety for maintaining social order and for reinforcing conventions of social difference. It is therefore not surprising that, of all the goods that constituted the Atlantic merchant capital, clothing and its accessories were the most expressive. Their acquisition was the object of ultimate desire because clothing not only defined socioeconomic divisions (class) and hierarchies of power (rank) but also marked exclusion and inclusion (identity/social formation). This is the context in which we should understand Prince Adémọlá's enchanting introductory statement regarding the universe of imported clothing and his ability to contemplate the affinities between himself and Clapperton in terms of the clothing forms that they shared. The white man's velvet, the white man's nankeen, the white man's shawl, and even the white man's coat that Adémọlá eloquently spoke about and displayed to Clapperton represented Adémọlá's Atlantic worldliness. They also placed Adémọlá's Ọ̀yọ́ Empire and Clapperton's British Empire as coequals on the same platform of human civilization.

It was with the imported fabric that the Yorùbá elite of the Atlantic age displayed their cosmopolitanism and versatility. Imported textiles were used, as in other contemporary places, as "glorious artificial extensions" of the body, linking the individual to others beyond the immediate environment where the body is located.[14] The rich and the powerful also blended the local and foreign fabrics to present and represent their worldly and spiritual selves to the public. The cultural valuation of imported textiles was evident in the clothing that Adémọlá's entourage wore to meet their august guests. This materiality of clothing was also in full display eleven days after the spectacle of Adémọlá's and Clapperton's meeting. At the farewell reception that Onísàrẹ́, the powerful governor of Ìjànà,[15] organized for Clapperton and his entourage on December 19, 1825, the governor started the ceremony wearing an imported "rich crimson damask robe . . . and the same red velvet cap." But "to display his grandeur" to his foreign guests and his native audience, he changed his attire three times during the reception, each ensemble being richer than the previous one.[16] About four years later, on March 13, 1830, Ọmọ́-sọlá Májǒtú,[17] the *aláàfin* of Ọ̀yọ́ (1802–30), received the Lander brothers (Richard and John) in a colorful large gown made of "green silk, crimson silk damask, and green silk velvet which were all sown together like pieces of patchwork."[18] These fabrics were all imported but repurposed for a culturally acceptable style (e.g., a large gown). Aláàfin Májǒtú did not stop there. He was also wearing cotton stockings of European manufacture. However, both his beaded crown and the sandals were locally made. His throne was set on a carpet made of a "large piece of superfine light blue cloth." This was the very same kind, if not the same cloth, that Hugh Clapperton presented to the king in 1826.[19]

The red jasper-chalcedony beads (*àkún* or *àkòrì*), and their red and blue glass counterparts (*iyùn* and *ṣẹ̀gi* respectively), remained the ultimate signifiers of wealth, status, and authority during the Atlantic period (see chap. 3). The local production of jasper beads was in fact thriving in Ọ̀yọ́-Ilé at this time, as evident in the semifinished jasper rock and bead-polishing stones excavated in one of the buildings near the palace complex in the city (see plate 4). The ancient Ifẹ̀ glass beads also continued to circulate across the Yorùbá region, judging by the recycling of heirlooms and mining of manufactured glass at Olókun Grove in Ilé-Ifẹ̀. The imported European and Asian glass beads, however, filled the gaps left by the discontinuity of Ifẹ̀ glass production. Stringed objects, local and ancient, imported and new, remained the cynosure of the region's sartorial grandeur and chiefly status. Of these beads, Ọṣìnfẹ́kundé (b. ca. 1795) noted that "coral [European generic name for *iyùn*, *ṣẹ̀gi*, and *àkòrì*] is one of the most sought after adornments. The size and quality of the beads are a sign of rank and wealth. . . . The important people wear up to four strings of coral beads, hanging down to the navel, and the king wear[s] a great number."[20] No person of means and authority failed to don a few strings of these beads on the neck, ankle, and wrist during the seventeenth through the mid-nineteenth century—no different from what was already prevailing during the Late Formative and Classical periods. The difference during the Atlantic period was that there were more of such persons of importance and far more beads in circulation, both in number and variety. Men of means also sewed "coral" beads into their clothing, and women adorned their woven and plaited hair with stringed beads.[21] The European travelers passing through the Yorùbá region during the 1820s variously commented that the kings and nobles found "large handsome coral beads" the most agreeable gift. One such gift of beads, Richard Lander told us, threw Aláàfin Májŏtú "into a transport of joy."[22] This was not new. In fact, Hugh Clapperton was only repeating in 1826 what thirteen generations of European visitors before him had said when he wrote, with an interesting choice of simile, that a string of coral was as highly esteemed by the Yorùbá as diamonds were regarded by the Jews in England.[23]

The use of clothing and its accessories for social and cultural aspirations as well as for negotiation of social difference and status did not begin with the Atlantic period. The elites who were connected to the networks of long-distance commerce from across the Sahara and who controlled the social capital for trade also used different varieties of silk and other exotic textiles to define and exhibit their status during the Classical period.[24] What changed from the seventeenth century onward was that the scale of importation of these textile products increased from across the oceans, but access to foreign textiles was still limited to the expanded network of political elites and merchants who controlled the circuits of trade. These goods were outside the reach of the common people. Hence, the imported textiles remained objects of desire and aspiration, as they were used to define status and self-realization. In general, the elite incorporated Atlantic imports into the existing material signification of power and used those imports to communicate their worldly connections to the coastal emporia and the global networks of merchant capital. In the mainland, where there were intimate connections between objects of value and the authorities they represent, and between the past and present traditions, imports were not used to replace the local objects of value but to supplement them. Therefore, Aláàfin Májǒtú and many other kings and chieftains in the mainland incorporated the foreign into the familiar, embedding the exotic into the indigenous value system. In such scenarios, their clothing style embodied a type of transformative hybridity of the local and the foreign, as exemplified by the use imported velvet and silk to make a voluminous gown (*agbádá*).

However, the case was different on the coast, where some of the potentates were more disposed to appropriate and emulate European sartorial practices. A good example was Àdèlé Ajósùn, a former king of Lagos who was exiled in Badagry. Between 1821 and 1835, he ruled the port town as its de facto king. On his first meeting with Clapperton on December 2, 1827, Àdèlé wore an "immense broad brimmed hat . . . trim[m]ed with gold and ostrich feathers," a satin small coat trimmed with blue silk, and a military sash tied in front of his waist into which he inserted "a silver mounted dagger," all emulative of European dressing codes. The king rode to the meeting on "a small horse dressed in [a] red coat richly embroidered with gold lace."[25] Four boys served as his standard-bearers, each carrying a large musket. Two of those boys wore red coats and hats like Àdèlé's. It is not surprising that some of the coastal elite adopted European clothing etiquette. The institution and polity over which they were presiding were products of the Atlantic commercial world (see chap. 5 and 6). Located on the frontline of the slave/merchant capital exchange, and awash with an assortment of imports from around the globe, these political and merchant elite financed their power, prestige, and status with a wealth made possible by the direct commercial networks they established with their European counterparts. It was therefore in these coastal towns that the Atlantic merchant capital was most visibly relevant to establishing social order. Hence, at the peak of the Atlantic trade during the eighteenth century, the materiality of European gentility, as represented in clothing, served to differentiate the coastal African elite (all men) from the lower classes, as well as from the elites of the mainland who presided over much older institutions. The appropriation of European clothing by the coastal African elite also served to forge an Atlantic identity that cut across culture, race, and ethnicity.[26] Nevertheless, on both the mainland and the coast, the captains of societies such as Májǒtú, Àdèlé, Onísàrẹ́, and Adémọ́lá—men at different steps of the social ladder—used imported fabrics and accessories to enrich their stock of sartorial splendor, communicate social hierarchies and political power, and highlight their worldly connections.

It was not only the varieties of fabric that increased after 1630. The style of clothing, especially for men, also changed, and the volume of clothing for covering the body of both the living and the dead drastically increased. The more diverse and voluminous the fabrics, the more evident the wealth and high status of the wearer. For men, the one-piece clothing style, usually draped over the shoulder or worn as a wrap during the Classical period, gave way to the long, flowing outer garment during the seventeenth and eighteenth centuries. The Ọ̀yọ́ metropolis was the gateway for the introduction of this sewn garment, which originated in the Sudanic belt, into the Yorùbá world. There were very few changes, if any, in the style of women's attire, but different varieties of new fabric were added to the female sartorial portfolio. Women generally wore a wrap that extended from the chest to the ankle, held in place on the chest by a knotted cloth belt. Women's attire also included *ìborùn*, a piece of cloth draped around the neck and shoulder, and *ìdikù*, a piece wrapped around the head.

It was, however, in men's clothing that new styles were most elaborate, the epitome of which was *gbárìyẹ̀-onígba-awẹ́*, a large, flowing garment made of several panels of fabric (plate 6). The garment could be made of one fabric type or a collage of fabrics, incorporating silk, damask, and velvet with very expensive local weaves of three types—*sányán* (cloth made of native silk created by *anaphe* caterpillars), *àláárì* (a cotton cloth with rich ruby-red dye), and *ẹtù* (a cotton cloth dyed to a dark blue). The Onísàrẹ́ of Ìjànà was possibly wearing a *gbárìyẹ̀-onígba-awẹ́* during the reception he organized in 1825 in honor of Clapperton and his entourage.[27] When he took to the dance floor, the governor was described as "sailing majestically around in [his] damask robe," with a trainbearer behind him to hold the flying sleeves of his voluminous garment.[28] Indeed, the multicolor and voluminous multi-fabric gown was designed for public performance. Rowland Abíọ́dún's metaphysical reading of this garment type is instructive. He notes that the movements of the wearer of *gbárìyẹ̀-onígba-awẹ́* not only are "arresting" but also "redefine the spatial architecture of the performance arena." He continues: "Through the aesthetic impact of *gbárìyẹ̀-onígba-awẹ́*, we witness the transformation and redefinition of self through dress, an essential component of one's *ìwà*. For this reason, the Yorùbá say that 'We greet Aṣọ (Cloth) before we greet its wearer.'"[29]

Aláàfin Májǒtú conveyed this much to Clapperton when he instructed the later that a ruler, noble, chieftain, or prince must dress in conformity with the expectations, "whims[,] and fancies of his people." Such an attire that met public approval would include the most fanciful, choicest, and most expensive clothing items to distinguish the elite from those below him on the social ladder.[30] What may have been lost in translation during the conversation between the king and the explorer is the meaning of *cloth—aṣọ* in Yorùbá language. Etymologically, *aṣọ* translates into a phenomenon (object and experience) that renews, regenerates, and keeps one fresh and presentable.[31] Hence, owning one of the plethora of voluminous Yorùbá gowns (for men)—*agbádá*, *dàńdógó*, and *gbárìyẹ̀-onígba-awẹ́*—made of expensive fabrics, locally made or imported, was an evocation of success and self-realization. Rowland Abíọ́dún sums up the implications of this for Yorùbá metaphysics and theory of power: the ambition to rise on the sociopolitical ladder must begin with owning one of these expensive voluminous garments; they "enhance the image of their wearer, affirming an authoritative and substantial presence that hints at the divinity believed to reside in every Yorùbá person."[32] In this respect, the integrity and character of a person who had realized or was in the process of realizing his or her potential were enhanced by the volume, variety, beauty, and fineness of his or her sartorial presentation. Such clothing transformed the body into "a sublime work of art," a deliberate and meaningful composition of colors, patterns, and fabrics that "transcended the ordinary, the haphazardly fashioned, and the fragmentary."[33] With cloth, the body projected the wholeness and wholesomeness that is the quintessential quality of "a complete and perfect human."[34] Hence, it was through the apparel that a person of status became the subject of aspirational spectacle, admiration, and commentary. Hence, the Yorùbá maxim: "We greet the clothing before we greet its wearer."

To be the subject of public admiration and approval was an important step in the journey toward achieving the potentiality of one's divinity—becoming an ancestor and attaining immortality. Except for the *ọba-aládé*, who became immortal on assuming office, other people can accomplish immortality only after their physical death. As we discussed in chapter 2, death was construed, since the early stages of the Yorùbá community of practice, not as the automatic end of life but as the beginning of the potential of becoming an ancestor, elevating to the status of an *òrìṣà*, and attaining immortality. A person who became an ancestor therefore never died. The person lived on in the multiple worlds of the living, the *òrìṣà*, and the ancestors. But for the new life of the ancestor to be purposeful and meaningful, the deceased and their living descendant must unite at least once a year to renew their commitment to one another. The visiting ancestors (*égúngún*) usually returned in masking outfits (*ẹ̀ku*) at a particular season of the year. This was a festive occasion during which the names and achievements of the deceased in each family would be invoked with prayers, sacrifices, and feasting.

The annual return of the ancestors to the land of the living had taken place for hundreds of years before the seventeenth century.[35] The ethnographic evidence from the Okun and Èkìtì areas indicates that the costumes of *égúngún* were limited to split raffia in the deep-time Yorùbá history, especially in the Archaic and Early Formative periods (chap. 2). It is in the Okun area, the core homeland of the Yorùbá-speaking people, that this ancient practice is most excellently preserved. Even when both cloth and raffia are combined in making the costumes of most *égúngún* among the Okun and some areas of Èkìtì, the raffia component is usually much more in volume than the cotton fabric. And the latter is often limited in variety to the *aṣọ ipó* fabric, a red-and-tan patterned cloth used only in funerary rituals and in masquerade performances to honor and worship the ancestors.[36] The split raffia and *aṣọ ipó* were the fabrics of the earliest Yorùbá ancestors (proto-Yoruboid speakers). While the other Yorùbá areas innovated with a diversity of fabrics in their ancestral veneration ceremonies beginning with the Classical period, the Okun and some parts of Èkìtì have preserved the ancient split raffia and *aṣọ ipó* fabrics till today. During the Atlantic period, the increased scale of locally produced cotton fabric and the influx of imported fabric of wide diversity translated into an increase in the varieties and volumes of clothing in all areas penetrated by the merchant capital revolution, for both the living and their ancestors.

If becoming an ancestor was a process of attaining immortality, ancestral veneration was the means of periodically renewing that immortality. Under the material influence of merchant capital, ostentatious clothing became an integral part of the *égúngún* festival. The voluminous fabric that marked the success of the living also elevated the deification and immortality of the ancestor.[37] These outfits included, in addition to the local fabrics—*àdìrẹ* and the expensive *aṣọ-òkè* among the Ọ̀yọ́ and *aṣọ-ọlọ̀nà* among the Ìjẹ̀bú—the imported velvet, silk, damask, linen, satin, and brocade.[38] Foreign clothing articles such as stockings and gloves were also often incorporated into the garment of the *égúngún* as marks of the ancestor's worldliness, cosmopolitanism, and social distinction. The other objects of the merchant capital that were used to accessorize ancestral garments included cowrie shells, glass beads, and knickknacks such as mirrors and whistles. Captain Clapperton saw the masquerades of several of these ancestral figures in Ọ̀yọ́-Ilé in 1826. He vividly described them as "dressed in large sacks [garments] covering every part of the body; the head most fantastically decorated with strips . . . of damask silk, and cotton, of as many glaring colours as it was possible." They had their faces covered with a veil or mesh of cowries.[39]

As a consequence of the merchant capital revolution, the textiles and other paraphernalia for making *ẹ̀kú* (*égúngún*'s costumes) increasingly originated as commodities. Once these fabrics became part of the ancestral costume, it meant they had been permanently removed from transactional circulation and converted into treasures to be stored and kept as heirlooms. Thus, the fabrics of the *égúngún* were the threads (metaphorical as well as literal) that connected the past to the present and the living to the ancestors. Those annual returns of the ancestors in their voluminous clothing were occasions to celebrate the common ancestry of the members of the *ilé* and to affirm their solidarity and renew the bond of their kinship.[40] Some of the fabric that went into making an *ẹ̀kú* usually came from the clothing the deceased owned and wore during his or her lifetime, so that the costume had the overall effect of projecting an apparition of the individual. Members of the *ilé* usually added strips of new and expensive fabric to the *ẹ̀kú* almost every year. This made the volume and layers of the *égúngún* costume increase over several years. Those who constituted the leadership of the *ilé* were generally responsible for contributing new fabric to the garment of the *ilé's* ancestral masquerades, with each generation always seeking to use expensive fabric that met the fashion and taste of the time. The contribution of fabrics to the *ẹ̀kú* provided the donor with a claim to the past in the negotiations for access to the power, privileges, honor, and other assets of the *ilé*. Participation in the annual dressing-up of the ancestor was therefore a critical site for enhancing "the power of [the] living actors."[41] If the ceremonial cloth of the elite served as an object and a conduit of aspirational self-realization, the masquerade costume articulated the "regenerative power of cloth" for the living.[42]

Taste and Social Difference II: Spirits and Power

Imported fabrics were just one class of the merchant capital that was central to the culture of sociability in the Yorùbá Atlantic age. The imported alcoholic beverages, especially Brazilian aguardientes, a cane-sugar-based liquor, was another. Aguardientes was the second-ranking import by value, next to tobacco, during the eighteenth and early nineteenth centuries. The Portuguese/Brazilian ships, originating mainly from Brazil, were responsible for the import of both commodities. Rum and brandy were also favored alcohol imported from the various European colonies in the Americas. Aguardientes, rum, and brandy were central to the culture of hospitality and entertainment during the Atlantic period. The enslaved

African labor was critical to the production of these three commodities in the Americas. These exotic drinks and an assortment of wines from Europe were staples of merchant capital imported to the Bight of Benin and other parts of Atlantic Africa.

Generous hospitality had been an important aspect of sociability in the Yorùbá world, and, for the elite of the Atlantic Age, imported hard liquor was the favored means of performing it. This was especially the case along the trails of the commercial networks linking the coastal emporia to the mainland's centers of power. The numerous fragments of case gin and wine bottles excavated in Savi and Abomey, dating to the period between 1630 and 1830, are a testament to this.[43] The original contents of these bottles lubricated the spinning wheels of social relationships. The rich merchants and political elite, in particular, used these *powerful drinks* and *drinks of power* to entertain associates and friends, as well as to maintain the loyalty and mobilize the services of followers and dependents. The number of these hangers-on began to multiply on the coast after 1730, especially with the increase in the number of port towns, such as Badagry, Lagos, Àjàṣẹ́ (Porto-Novo), Popo, and Keta, as centers of merchant-capital wealth and the slave trade. The *big* men of these port towns did not go about publicly without the company of attendants and subordinates. These were often joined by the hangers-on, who simply wanted to be part of the spectacle of power and who expected the largesse of food and drink that usually accompanied such outings. The elites usually entertained these hangers-on with hard liquor. Hence, Ọba Àdèlé asked Clapperton to give eight gallons of rum to the mob who accompanied him (Àdèlé) on what turned out to be a casual outing on December 2, 1825.[44]

Direct access to imported drinks was the near-exclusive preserve of merchants and chieftains directly involved in the Atlantic slave trade. These drinks were far more common on the coast than elsewhere, and when they traveled far inland, they followed the exchange networks of the elite and the slave trade. For example, many years of archaeological excavations in the Yorùbá region at several Atlantic-period sites have produced only two contexts of alcoholic beverage containers: a case gin bottle fragment from the compound of Ẹdẹ-Ilé's governor and several liquor bottle fragments from a residence in the palace grounds at Ọ̀yọ́-Ilé. Both contexts dated to ca. 1770–1836. Whereas the assortment of Brazilian aguardientes, rum, and brandy were an exceptional and rare treat in the Yorùbá mainland,[45] these powerful drinks were very accessible on the coast, where high-ranking men and their dependents and staff liberally used alcohol. As a result, alcoholism was already a social and health problem in Badagry and other coastal emporia in the 1820s when the entourages of Hugh Clapperton and Richard Lander passed through the area.

The two political advisers and interpreters serving Àdèlé were, for example, both given to a spirituous life. The Lander brothers described one of them, Hooper, a man of mixed race with an English father, as "the most confirmed drunkard alive, always getting intoxicated before breakfast, and remaining in a soaking state all day long."[46] Yet they noted that Hooper was always alive to his responsibility, especially in matters where his interests were at stake. We get the impression from the travel diaries of Hugh Clapperton, Richard Lander, and John Lander that Badagry, flooded with European and American spirits, was in a permanent state of drunkenness. Likewise, loafers, troublemakers, and miscreants, drawn to an assortment of spirits, abounded in the port town during the early nineteenth century. This situation was in sharp contrast to the conditions in nearby mainland towns. In 1830, the Landers observed that the "gloomy fastnesses and wildnesses of nature" on the coast were less common as they penetrated deeper into the interior. By the time they reached Ìlarò, fifty-five kilometers from the coast, the "importunate beggars" seen in Badagry had "disappeared entirely."[47] This does not mean that imported alcohol was absent in the mainland. It trickled inland through trading and tributary networks to merchants, nobility, and royalty. On December 19, 1825, the governor of Ìjànà provided Clapperton with twenty-five gallons of rum for the entertainment of the crowd who had gathered to celebrate the arrival of Clapperton and his men in the Ọ̀yọ́ colony. The governor reportedly told Clapperton that the Ọ̀yọ́ "people liked rum too much" and that the distribution of rum to the teeming crowd would give the visitors a good reputation.[48] Because it was one of the highly valued merchant capital items, it is not surprising that a demijohn of rum was one of the gift items that Clapperton gave to Aláàfin Májǒtú about a month later in 1826.[49]

Taste and Social Difference III: Addictive Pleasure

The inland penetration of imported alcohol was no doubt inhibited by the high cost of transportation. The opposite was the case for tobacco, especially the molasses-enriched Brazilian *tabacum*, a high-value, low-bulk commodity with relatively little cost of transportation over the long distances between the coast and the deep mainland. Tobacco was the first truly global commodity. Its pleasurable use and addictive consumption began in the sixteenth century and followed the trails of connections that characterized the political, economic, social, and cultural relationships of the early modern world.[50] As "the most widely and rapidly distributed item" in the Columbian Exchange—a process of social, cultural, and biological exchanges between the New and Old Worlds—tobacco usage was central to the consumption culture of Yorùbá Atlantic modernity.[51]

It was primarily through tobacco that most Yorùbá people, orally and olfactorily, tasted the bitterness and sweetness of this modernity. Tobacco snuffing, chewing, and smoking had become a popular aspect of everyday life throughout the Yorùbá world by early eighteenth century. The ship manifest and eyewitness accounts affirm that tobacco accounted for the highest value of imports to the Bight of Benin from ca. 1650 to 1860 (see chap. 6). The telltale sign that tobacco usage was widespread across the Yorùbá region is the ubiquity of tobacco pipes in all archaeological sites dating to the Atlantic period. In Early Òṣogbo, for example, I recovered more than seventy tobacco pipes from a ten-by-eight-meter excavated unit. But these pipes do not tell the whole story about tobacco usage. For every gram of tobacco smoked in a pipe, perhaps twenty grams were chewed or snuffed. These different methods of tobacco usage were status defining and located in the fields of sociability.

Across the Yorùbá world, as elsewhere in the early modern world, the tobacco pipe and the paraphernalia of snuffing were individuality-affirming objects. These implements of addictive taste, pleasure, and luxury also offered multiple ways of communicating status, leisure, class, emulation, aspiration, and gendered identity. As one observer noted: "The pipe represented a leisurely smoke and required a certain amount of paraphernalia; snuff (with its essential accoutrements) demanded the deliberateness of an aristocratic age."[52] Tobacco smoking, in Yorùbá cultural parlance, was a masculine consumption, and its use mostly took place in the leisurely space of homosocial relationships and patricentric authority. The Yorùbá sculptures of the seventeenth through nineteenth centuries are replete with adult male figures smoking tobacco pipes (fig. 7.2). Absent are any pipe-smoking images of pubescent figures or women. The representation of tobacco-smoking figures in Yorùbá wood carvings strictly adhered to the convention of equating smoking with masculinity, but we know from ethnographic and historical sources that women across the Yorùbá world and Atlantic Africa also smoked tobacco.[53] These were usually women of post-menopausal age or of independent authority. These categories of women were socially male in the cultural universe of the Yorùbá and the neighboring cognate groups, especially the Aja-Fon people.[54] Tobacco smoking was, therefore, an act of sociality in which some biological women transgressed ascribed biological gender roles and affirmed their masculine authority and patricentric roles. Unlike the masculine tobacco smoking, the snuffing and chewing of tobacco were androgynous acts in which both Yorùbá men and Yorùbá women widely indulged.[55]

Tobacco also offered an avenue for the Yorùbá to demarcate class boundaries. Hence, in the eighteenth and early nineteenth centuries, many eminent personalities did not go for a public outing without taking with them the paraphernalia of tobacco. Ọba Àdèlé's large entourage

Figure 7.2. Representations of male tobacco pipe smokers in Yorùbá art (*left*, H. 34 cm; *right*, H. 57 cm)

that visited Clapperton in Badagry in 1826 included not only the political chieftains, military captains, and advisers but also the servants who carried his tobacco pipe and spittoon. Aláàfin Májǒtú in Ọ̀yọ́ was also accompanied in his outings by a spittoon bearer. This was a woman "who attends upon him on all occasions bearing a handsome carved gourd, having a small round hole covered with a clean white cloth."[56] The presence of a spittoon bearer in the entourage indicates that the king regularly engaged in tobacco chewing and possibly snuffing. In this acquired taste and addiction of the Atlantic period, the elite were able to put authority and respectability on display through the public parade of tobacco paraphernalia and dependents—spittoon, tobacco pipe, and tobacco pouch bearers. Smoking, snuffing, and chewing may have been personal, but the public performance of this act of leisure and pleasure served a social need—to see and to be seen. As the most versatile commodity of Atlantic modernity, made popular by addictive taste and cerebral pleasure, the use of tobacco was entrenched in the participation of new social hierarchies and discourses of power brought about by the merchant-capital revolution.[57]

Domesticating Atlantic Modernity I: Cowrie and Critics

We noted in the previous chapter that of all the merchant capital of the Atlantic slave trade, the item that circulated and exchanged hands the most among the Yorùbá was the cowrie shell. It was also the most durable. Cowrie was the currency for all transactions; it was used to store wealth, and it served as a conversion unit for the use-value of other commodities, social wants, and social relationships. Since cowries could be used to buy not only people, things, and services but, as we shall see below, also good health, power, prestige, status, and self-realization, these imported commodities became the ultimate merchant capital for seeking aspirational goals. The access of almost everyone in the Yorùbá region to cowrie shells at the height of the Atlantic period also made the cowrie a special object for articulating the "elements of intersubjective experience in everyday life" and a powerful tool of social communication.[58] Hence, the monetization of cowries had as many cultural, social, and contemplative ramifications as the commercial revolution that it birthed. Cowries were the most evocative of the Atlantic experience in the Yorùbá world. They served as the medium and symbol for articulating the revolutionary impact of merchant capital, as well as the thought, practice, and worldview about the changes in the ideas of personhood and self-realization. As a result, the cowrie occupied all three of the spaces, according to J. Daniel Rogers, that constitute signs of culture—indexical, symbolic, and iconic.[59] As an index, it served as the value register of wealth, production, and accumulation. As a symbolic object, it was the value register and representation of ideas, worldly awareness, and social relations that were not directly related to the immediacy of production, consumption, and accumulation and for which the cowrie was only referential and might not necessarily be physically present. And as an iconic object, it was the interface between the materialities and the meanings of social life. All combined, the cowrie was transformed into an elastic sign through which society contemplated what was (before the merchant-capital revolution), what is (the social constitution of the Atlantic age), and what would be (both anxiety and optimism for the uncertain future). For these reasons, the cowrie was at the center of contemplating and generating self-awareness about the world; the evolving social changes; as well as disputations and critical commentaries about the nature of the Atlantic commercial revolution, the place of the individual and community in it, and the inequality that came out of it.

Cowries did not become epistemic objects like *ṣẹ̀gi* and *iyùn*, but they were used as divination instruments for seeking metaphysical knowledge. Moreover, cowries proved to be richer in cultural biography, with a far greater elasticity of meaning and more question-generating characteristics, than *ṣẹ̀gi* and *iyùn*. Whereas these glass beads were identified with royal or chiefly authority and legitimacy, the cowrie was every person's object, with an uncommon capacity to mutate and unfold ideas and meaning almost indefinitely. It was defined, as we shall soon discover, as much by "what it was not" as "what it is" and "what it might be."[60]

As it happened in many societies that adopted a monetized economy, the liquidity associated with the cowrie currency and its use as a means of economic, political, and social payment led to the creation of ideas and concepts of social and material relations that were theoretical and abstract.[61] In other words, cowries came to embody the material-intellectual infrastructures through which the meanings, purposes, anxieties, and aspirations of the Atlantic experience were represented, contemplated, and contested in the Yorùbá world. Likewise, cowries were central to the communicative interactions over the new sensibility of personhood, which merchant capital revolution brought out through the objectification of human bodies and labor in monetary and material terms.[62] For example, while the political elite on the coast presented celebratory narratives about merchant capitalism and cowries, the exploited class admonished the elite for the damages caused by the Atlantic commercial revolution. Here, the royalist oral traditions of Benin Kingdom associated the prosperity brought by cowrie currency with the reign of Ọba Eresoyen (1735–37). According to one version, the boom in the supply of cowries was a product of the peace that the *ọba* made with Olókun, the deity of the ocean and wealth in the Yorùbá community of practice. This reconciliation followed a period of turmoil: "Eresoyen once quarreled with Olókun, the god of the sea, and closed the way so Olókun could not get water. Through the mediation of a palm wine tapper, Eresoyen agreed to release the water. As a reward, Olókun heaped up cowries to the sky for Eresoyen, and they were packed [brought in large quantities] to the palace."[63]

This tradition refers to the regaining of control of the Atlantic trade by Eresoyen after about eighty years (ca. 1608–1690s), during which the Benin monarchy lost political power and control of the coastal commerce to the town chiefs. Following the death of Ọba Ehengbuda (r. ca. 1570–1608), the town chiefs became the effective power wielding authority in Benin, and they represented their interests rather than those of their monarch in the many riverside village ports that mushroomed during the seventeenth century.[64] The reign of Ọba Eresoyen was a major turning point in the history of Benin. His reign is credited in Benin traditions with the full restoration of monarchical authority and influence, return to territorial expansion, reopening of direct trade with the Europeans, introduction of new artistic forms, and reorganization of Benin's pantheon. The reestablishment of the king's control over the various trading routes and ports in the early eighteenth century, and the resurgence of the European demand for Benin products, now including slaves in addition to ivory, camwood, and cotton, are represented in the oral traditions as the product of the peace pact between Eresoyen and Olókun.[65] The story projects the ideology that it was the peaceful coexistence between the divine king of the land (the *ọba* of Benin) and the divine king of the ocean (Olókun) that ensured cosmological balance for the Benin Kingdom. Cowries, as the payment for the exports leaving Benin, were now recontextualized as the symbol of wealth and its other significations—fertility, fecundity, health, and self-realization—bequeathed by Olókun to Benin. Therefore, the ocean, as the supply route of cowries, became central to the discourse of material accumulation and wealth. This narrative is a reworking of the older one that associated glass beads with the Olókun goddess in Ilé-Ifẹ̀ (see chap. 3).[66]

Naivete, as Michel-Rolph Trouillot reminds us, could be a good instrument of mass deception by those who exercise power. But it is often a grave mistake for those on whom that power is exercised to buy into this naivete.[67] Considering that human cargo paid for the cowries brought to the shores of the Bight of Benin by Olókun, it is not surprising that there were other narratives on the origins of these cowries. Thus, there is a tradition in Ọ̀ṣogbo—an important node of commercial traffic in the Yorùbá mainland (chap. 5)—that speaks of cowrie as money fished from the Atlantic Ocean using slave corpses as bait.[68] The Ayizo, one of the coastal peoples in the Bight of Benin, were also direct in their traditions about the origin of cowries:

> In the beginning of the world we had the forge and we forged things, we had weaving-looms and we wove our clothes . . . we had boats from which we caught fish. We had no guns. We had no cowrie-money (*akwa*). If you went to the market, you took beans in order to exchange them for sweet potatoes. You exchanged something for something else [barter]. Then the king brought the cowrie-money. What did the king do in order to bring the cowrie-money? He caught people and broke their legs and their arms. Then he built a hut in a banana plantation, put the people in it, and fed them bananas until they became big and fat. The king killed the people, and he gave orders to his servants to attach strings to their bodies and to throw them into the sea where the cowrie-shells (*akwa*) lived. When the cowrie-shells started to eat the corpses, they pulled them in, collected the shells, and put the live cowries in hot water to kill them. That is how cowrie-money came to exist.[69]

The Ayizo were vassals to the Allada Kingdom, and later to Dahomey between 1600 and 1830. They were raided for captives and forced to include men and women in their annual tributes to their overlords.

Most of these individuals became part of the human cargo loaded for the Middle Passage. The story that this exploited group presents about the advent of cowrie therefore starkly contrasts the royalist narrative in the court of Benin. The Ayizo offered an indictment of the hegemonic and predatory states and brigand-merchants whose wealth depended on the slave-cowrie exchange. Their story frames the advent of cowrie currency, and the wealth it signifies, in zero-sum terms. Here, wealth (represented by cowrie currency) was conceptualized as finite, and its production could only be drawn "from the property . . . and vital energies of someone else."[70] This alternative narrative, from below, calls attention to the convertibility of human life to cowrie and provides a more accurate provenance of merchant capitalism and its wealth, not as a product of some esoteric relationship between a king and a deity but as an outcome of capture, bondage, loss, and death. The conceptualization of wealth in zero-sum terms also rejects the epistemology of Western capitalism, in which wealth is "capable of infinite expansion to the mutual benefit of all participants in an increasingly efficient division of labor."[71] After all, the enslaved Africans who generated the wealth of capitalism between 1630 and 1830 did not share in its benefit. And the Africans who bartered slaves for merchant capital in the Bight of Benin and other parts of Atlantic Africa were only marginal gainers, leaving the majority as losers in the commercial revolution that gave birth to the modern world as we know it.[72]

Beyond the coast, other narratives address the sociality of cowries in everyday life, especially the institutionalization of the cowrie in the market economy of the Yorùbá mainland. One well-cited example is a narrative collected by Jacob Olupona in Oǹdó town in 1988:

> After the first market of the Oǹdó had been established, the people were faced with the problem of which form of exchange to use. It was decided that Olódùmarè [the supreme deity] should be met and the problem be presented to Him for [a] solution. Olódùmarè was met and the matter was discussed. He . . . instructed that a ritual be done with a mother hen, a he-goat and a frog. Thereafter the contingent should meet with Ajé, goddess of trade and wealth. The ritual sacrifice was to protect the contingent from death or any danger on their way to Ajé's house. But then, in spite of the rituals, there were no human volunteers to meet with Ajé. After a lot of persuasion, and several days of waiting, the vulture bird agreed to go. Two women also volunteered. However, only the vulture eventually met with Ajé, the women stood at a distance. On getting to Ajé, the vulture narrated its mission. Ajé knew so much already because she had been informed of the mission by Olódùmarè. She responded to the vulture's request by giving it some cowrie shells which were to be used as [a] medium of exchange. The vulture thanked her, swallowed the cowries to ensure that they were not lost, and traveled back to the waiting human crowd. She vomited the cowries in

> their presence. In appreciation of the role played by the vulture, it was elevated to the level of sacredness. The Oǹdó [people] were forbidden from killing the bird.[73]

The above story, about the origins of formalized, market-based social relations mediated by cowries, is consistent with the history of Oǹdó's early history as a frontier camp for elephant hunters and traders during the late sixteenth and early seventeenth century (chap. 5). The role of the vulture as the mediator between Ajé, the goddess of the market and wealth, on one hand, and women (traders) on the other, is revealing. In the process of building a new economic system and a new regime of value, there was a collaboration between the vulture and women in the sacrifice that they made to Ajé. It was, however, the vulture—the agent of death, greed, and misfortune—that secured the cowries that were needed for exchange, and it was the one who carried these cowries to the market, a sphere of activity dominated by women. The vulture is an opportunistic predator that feeds on the weak and the dead. Yet it heralded the introduction of cowries into Oǹdó. The provenance and circumstances of cowrie monetization and the market economy it birthed are clear in this story. The vulture refers to three categories of people: (1) the European slavers who brought cowries to Atlantic Africa in large amounts; (2) the African slave raiders and traders who exchanged people (the captives) for the cowries on the coast and who were responsible for the flow of these shells into the mainland market; and (3) the local political elite who legitimized the use of cowries as monetary and social currency through the taxes and tolls they collected in the form of cowries. The compromised participants were the women who transacted market affairs with this medium of exchange brought by these agents of death. By so doing, they made cowries relevant in the domestic economy and perpetuated the slave/merchant-capital exchange. The gendered implication of the two primary and interdependent agents responsible for the institutionalization of cowries as a medium of formal market-based transactions is not in doubt. On one side of the spectrum, we have predominantly men who were agents of death and destruction—slavers and bulk importers of cowries. The retail redistributors of the imported cowries in the domestic market space, predominantly women, occupied the other side of the spectrum.

The cultural biography of cowrie seems to know no boundaries in how it permeated every social crevice of Yorùbá intellectual life and its knowledge system. With the infusion of cowries into the local economy, a new category of diviners who specialized in the use of cowries for divination also emerged in the course of the seventeenth and eighteenth centuries. Known as *ẹ́ẹ́rìndínlógún*, this cowrie-based divination technique is modeled after *ifá*'s numerological system, in the sense that it makes use of sixteen cowries for casting (instead of sixteen *ikin* or *ọ̀pẹ̀lẹ̀*). It is also based on the *ifá* literary corpus (chap. 3). However, the textual component of *ẹ̀ẹ́rìndínlógún* is very minimal, not as detailed as that of *ifá*; its practice is open to both men and women (unlike *ifá*, which is generally practiced by men); and it is the preferred divination system used by the priests and priestesses of all the major Yorùbá deities (except Ifá)—especially Ọbàlátá, Ṣàngó, Èṣù, Ọ̀ṣun, Ọya, and Yemọja. Hence, in the course of the Atlantic age, cowrie divination came to enjoy wider practice than *ifá*, but it did not have the same prestige.[74] Making cowries into divination tools enlarged the portfolio of this merchant capital as a sacred object that could be used to seek knowledge, make the invisible become visible, and make the unknown known. This sacralization of the cowrie did not stop with divination. It has been (and continues to be) used as a sacrificial object for cleansing a person of disease, sickness, poverty, and other afflictions—physical, spiritual, and social.[75] Such cowries used for spiritual purification and healing rites were thrown in the bush, crossroads, marketplace, or refuse site. These are all ambiguous spaces, places of in-between, transition, and transformation. Yet for these very reasons, they could be places of danger and confusion, with bad outcomes.[76]

The Yorùbá cultural repertoire is replete with the ways cowries were used in transformative processes, converted as currency into ritual objects, for "propitiatory sacrifices" as "symbols of fertility" and "repositories of magical power," as well as vehicles of coded communication, "emblems of certain gods," and personal adornment.[77] Cowrie also served as the social valuation index for how individuals perceived themselves in relation to others in the world, including the far places beyond the Atlantic horizons where cowries originated. Those who had plenty of cowries in storage or who held enormous assets of wealth—people, land, and authority—used cowries to decorate their residential and religious architecture. This public display of cowrie (currency) accumulation reached a frenzy during the eighteenth century, simultaneous with the peak in its supply to the Bight of Benin. Ọba Eresoyen is remembered in the traditions as the king who "built a house of money" because he "decorated the walls of his palace with cowries."[78] Important and high-ranking chiefs and princes of eighteenth-century Benin followed suit. They also used cowries as floor and wall tiles in their private rooms and public courtyards. In the last quarter of the eighteenth century, Frenchman Capitaine Landolphe described "a large room" in the house of High Chief Ezomo Ekeneza that was elegantly "encrusted with cowry shells."[79] At least four such floors of cowrie tiles survived to the 1960s in Benin.[80] The incorporation of cowries into the architectural design of the elite residences not only pronounced the success and worldliness of these men of power and wealth but also called attention to their intimate spiritual connection with Olókun, the goddess whose house beneath the sea was built with cowrie shells. These successful men were the critical agents in the long-distance trade that connected Benin City, the Yorùbá mainland, and the Bight of Benin with far-flung places. They were a manifestation of Olókun's blessings.

A private incident in October 1827 in Ọ̀yọ́-Ilé also reveals how individuals used cowrie shells to conceptualize themselves in relation to the wider world or to imagine the world that existed beyond their direct knowledge. Ebo, Aláàfin Májǒtú's chamberlain and political adviser, pulled Richard Lander aside and showed him a small room in his palace apartment filled with cowries. Exuding an air of boastfulness, Ebo asked his Cornish guest whether the king of England was as rich as himself. He did not find any other merchant capital as useful as cowrie for comparing his wealth with that of the monarch of the United Kingdom of Great Britain and Ireland. The cowrie fueled his imagination of connectivity, and this was what he used to compare himself with a foreign king across the ocean.[81] As a full-time administrator in the service of the empire who was totally bound to the personality of the *aláàfin*, the powerful eunuch and arguably the most powerful palace official would have acquired this wealth of cowries mainly from tolls and other types of levies connected to the market and tributes. After all, Ebo co-supervised (with the *ẹni-ọjà*, a titled lady in the palace) the Aláàfin market—Akẹ̀sán—from which levies and other forms of taxes were collected and deposited in his official apartment.[82]

Domesticating Atlantic Modernity II: Cowrie and Self-Realization

The investment of cowrie with the qualities of universal convertibility across many registers of value transformed it into an object for seeking, accessing, harnessing, accumulating, and expending social resources and translating experiences from one domain (e.g., economic) to another (e.g., social and intellectual). Therefore, paying close attention to the cultural biography of cowrie shells is necessary to understand how the changing theory of knowledge, stimulated by the merchant-capital revolution, affected the idea of personhood, individuality, and self-realization in the Yorùbá world. I will use my excavation of a grave in Ẹdẹ-Ilé to illustrate this point. The burial was that of an individual who lived during the Atlantic period. On his death, he was buried in a fetal position on his right side, facing north. Five cowries were placed on top of his head. An arrow and a serving bowl, possibly containing food, were placed beneath the head. The arrow also pointed north. A piece of iron slag was buried with him, placed between his thighs (plate 7). The grave was located only two meters from a blacksmithing pit furnace. In fact, blacksmithing and iron smelting were two major crafts practiced in that neighborhood of Ẹdẹ-Ilé where the individual was buried.[83] The individual was certainly a blacksmith. He might have been called Alágbẹ̀dẹ (Blacksmith) by his neighbors and customers on account of his profession.[84] The paraphernalia of slag and an arrowhead associated with his burial meant that his survivors wanted him to be remembered as a blacksmith and to continue with this profession in the afterlife.

Alágbẹ̀dẹ was a man of middling socioeconomic status. His burial goods were modest and would have included the clothes in which his remains were wrapped, but these organic materials and most of his remains did not survive the acidic lateritic soils of Ẹdẹ-Ilé. His skeletal remains and the inorganic mortuary goods, however, were preserved. The presence and arrangement of the serving bowl, iron slag, arrowhead, and cowries in the burial's composition tell us something about the blacksmith's earthly life, the beliefs of his contemporaries about the afterlife, and his survivors' expectations for him in the afterlife and for their households in the aftermath of his demise. The bowl may have contained his favorite food so that he could be continuously nourished in the afterlife; the slag/bloom certainly indicates his profession as a blacksmith and also connotes the expectation that he would have the bloom to carry on forging weapons, tools, and household implements in the land of the ancestors. The placement of iron slag/bloom in between the deceased's thighs is suggestive of fecundity and virility, a prayerful gesture to the new ancestor to ensure the increase and continued purposiveness of the household he left behind, the same way that a bloom is transformed inside the furnace into tools and weaponry. The inclusion of an arrowhead in Alágbẹ̀dẹ's modest mortuary goods is likely an indication that he was also a soldier or a hunter. Or he may have specialized in, or had the notoriety for, making weaponry rather than domestic and other tools.

In this humble burial arrangement, Alágbẹ̀dẹ's survivors coherently highlighted the deceased's communal identity as a blacksmith and as a member of a blacksmithing household. Alágbẹ̀dẹ was buried in the blacksmithing forge where he probably spent most of his life as an adult. If his descendants or survivors continued the craft in that very location, they would have invoked his name and spirit periodically in the course of carrying out the family occupation of forging tools from iron blooms. The five cowries delicately placed on his forehead marked him out as a man of the Atlantic age. He did not simply barter the tools from his forge for other goods. He sold them for money—cowrie shells. Whereas the forge, slag, and arrowhead defined the blacksmith's communal identity, it was through cowrie currency that he expected, and was expected, to attain self-realization. This is because all fortunes and assets were convertible into cowries. It was also believed that liabilities could be paid off with cowries, the same way that sacrifices that involved cowries could change a misfortune into fortune. The five cowries on Alágbẹ̀dẹ́'s forehead therefore offer rich fodder for conjecture. They could be symbolic money that the deceased would pay for his entry into the otherworld, in the bid to fully join the community of ancestors rather than dangerously roam in the abyss. It is also possible that the five cowries were meant to call on his Orí (the deity of individuality, fate, and destiny) to help in the deceased's successful transition into the ancestral world.[85]

Orí had occupied a central place in Yorùbá metaphysics from at least the Classical period, when stylized cone-shaped human heads were molded in clay and placed on ancestral shrines or in the mortuary complex in which the naturalistic sculptures of particular ancestors were also present. Such assemblages, like the one excavated by Peter Garlake at the Ọbalára site, suggest that the destiny of the deceased—represented by the naturalistic figure—was intimately linked to that of the communal House—stylized conical figures—(see plate 3a–e).[86] This linkage was weakened during the seventeenth and eighteenth centuries, when the commercial revolution moved the primary means of accumulation to the market space and made it easier for the individual to pursue trading full-time and therefore to accumulate wealth outside the resources of his or her *ilé* and household. In other words, the merchant capital revolution expanded the opportunities and possibilities for individuals to pursue and achieve self-realization outside the arrangements of labor and land resources within their *ilé*. Of course, such individuals could use their profits as full-time traders to build a new household, and even a new House, for themselves, as Ọsĩnwọ̀ did in the second half of the eighteenth century at Ẹ̀pẹ́ (chap. 6).

As a result of this trend of individualized accumulation, by the early eighteenth century, the iconography of Orí changed from the stylized and naturalistic human terracotta heads of the Classical era (representing communal and individual *orí* respectively) to impersonal, symbolic, and abstract forms. The latter are conical and cylindrical boxes packed with ritually potent materials and elaborately covered with cowries, the symbol of the market, accumulation, and abstraction of value. The shrine was of two parts—*ìbọrí* and *ilé orí* (fig. 7.3). Both were made of the same types of materials. The *ìbọrí* was conical, "in the shape of a crown," often with a protruding ball-like feature at the top. With an exterior covered with forty-one cowries, *ìbọrí* was the symbol of personhood and the individual's spiritual head. It was then placed inside a large container, the *ilé orí* (literally, house of the head). The pyramid-shaped shrine, *ilé orí*, houses the *ìbọrí*. It conceals the inner/spiritual head from the public gaze;

Figure 7.3. Ìbọrí and Ilé Orí (reproduced with the permission of the Fowler Museum, the University of California at Los Angeles)

protects its privacy and preservation; and prevents it (and the owner) from the "evil eyes" of ill-minded people. The whole shrine of Orí "conveys one's commitment to respect oneself and, by extension, all the forces shaping one's journey in life."[87]

The making of a shrine to one's Orí marked the state of full consciousness of one's mission in life, of having reached the milestone of self-realization and crossed the threshold toward achieving one's potentiality as a divine being. Although everyone prayed to his or her deity of individuality (Orí), not every adult had the resources to make and consecrate a shrine for this deity. The making of the shrine was an expensive venture. In the late eighteenth and early nineteenth century, it cost as much as twelve thousand cowries to make a shrine to Orí, and the maker of the piece would also receive the same amount as his wages.[88] The total cost of building the shrine of individuality and destiny could, therefore, exceed twenty-four thousand cowries. Considering the festivities that normally accompanied the debut of a new Orí shrine, the occasion when the individual formally introduced himself or herself to the community as a person who was realizing his or her potential as a divine being, the total cost of this life-course accomplishment could exceed sixty thousand cowries. This was a lot of money, even with the inflationary trends of the early nineteenth century.[89] Hence, the exorbitant price of making and debuting an Orí shrine marked the celebrant as a successful person, an owner and dispenser of valuable social capital and assets—money, people, land, titles, and authority. Alágbẹ̀dẹ, whom we previously encountered, and most people of middling status like him were unlikely to be able to afford a shrine to Orí that publicly announced the realization of their being and becoming, but this did not mean that these people did not invoke Orí as part of their everyday spiritual devotion. This individualized personal deity, according to Samuel Johnson, was "worshipped by both sexes as the god of fate." He continued: "It is believed that good or ill fortune attends one, according to the will or decree of this god; and hence it is propitiated in order that good luck might be the share of its votary."[90] Nineteenth-century observers conveyed the sense that Orí was the most universal and the most portable of all the Yorùbá deities. It was the first deity to be worshipped before any other *òrìṣà*. Hence the saying *Orí l'àbá bọ k'á tó b'Ọ̀ọ̀sà, tí mo bá jí l'òwúrọ̀ ma d'orí mi mú*: "It is one's Orí [deity of destiny] that deserves to be worshipped first before turning to any other deity; when I wake up in the morning I hold on (pray) to my Orí." The primacy of Orí in the Yorùbá pantheon is further illustrated thus:

Orí Oníṣe
Àpèré
Àtètè gbeni ju Òrìṣà
Orí àtètè níran
Orí lokùn
Orí nidẹ
Kò sí Òrìṣà tí dáni gbè lẹ́yìn Orí ẹni
Orí ní ṣeni tá a fí dádé owó
Orí ní ṣeni tá a fí tẹpá ìlẹ̀kẹ̀ wọjà
Orí ní ṣeni tá a fí lo mọ́saàjí aṣọ ọba
Orí gbè mí
Orí là mí
Orí má padà lẹ́yìn mi[91]

Translation:

Orí, the competent Creator
Occupant of the highest throne
The One who is faster than the other Òrìṣà in providing assistance
Orí who instantly remembers "their" devotee
Orí is the precious bead
Orí is brass
No Òrìṣà can favor one without the consent of one's Orí
It is Orí that aids one to attain the crown of money
It is Orí that gives the blessing for one to use a beaded walking stick to the market

It is the blessing of Orí that allows one to use valuable cloths
Orí, please, support me
Orí, please, bless me
Orí, please, never turn against me.

The importance of Orí in Yorùbá metaphysics is well represented in visual arts and performative genres.[92] The similarity in the concepts of personhood, destiny, and fate among most Niger-Congo peoples—including the Bantu-speaking, Igbo, Akan, Edo, Tiv, and Yorùbá, among others—indicates that the metaphysics of Orí has a long history, likely reaching far back to the proto-Benue-Kwa and proto-Yoruboid eras.[93] However, the distinctive Yorùbá forms and mythoi of this pan-Niger-Congo metaphysics were elaborated during the Classical period, when the Yorùbá community of practice was born. According to Yorùbá cosmology, every person randomly chose his or her unique destiny (*orí-inú*) in the house of Ọbàtálá (the divine sculptor of human bodies, among others), before arriving on earth. The fate of each person in life depended first and foremost on the destiny that he or she had selected.[94] Some *orí* may bring a fortune in some aspects of life and misfortune or ill luck in others. For example, a woman might have the fate of becoming wealthy but not of having children. But one's fated misfortunes could be corrected with appropriate sacrifices. This was where Ifá (a.k.a. Ọ̀rúnmìlà), the deity of wisdom and knowledge, came in. In Yorùbá belief, this deity had (and still has) the wherewithal to correct bad fate and less satisfactory destiny. With divination, the deity helped to identify the source of the problem, the appropriate sacrifices, and the acceptable delivery of the rituals and sacrifices prescribed. Hence this praise for Ọ̀rúnmìlà: *Òdùdù tí ndu orí emèrè, atún orí tí kò sunwọ̀n ṣe*: "The one who saves those who are destined to die young, the one who repairs a bad destiny."

There are clues in the orature of Òrìṣà biographies that Orí assumed a new role in the Yorùbá pantheon and cosmology in the context of the social and economic transformations of the early seventeenth through the mid-eighteenth century. Orí is identified in the traditions as a late bloomer in the pantheon of the divinities, long occupying an ordinary and "back-bencher" status in the pantheon. The deity was involved in a protracted feud with the other Òrìṣà over the issue of seniority. Orí eventually won the battle after showing the ability to assign to each of the Òrìṣà the unique functions and essence for which they are known, and the power to transform the destiny, character, and potentialities of all the deities and all other creatures.[95] With Orí's power no longer in doubt, the other Òrìṣà began to give this deity of destiny, fate, and potentiality their unalloyed respect. In the end, they made Orí their leader. This myth-historical narrative of Orí's travails and triumph suggests that the individualistic Orí was secondary to the process of self-realization in the earlier time but that this changed during the Atlantic age as a result of the individual-based accumulation that accompanied the commercial revolution of the seventeenth century.[96] The integration of the mainland economy into the slave/merchant capital exchange restructured the Yorùbá world economically, and this also affected the social organization and the processes of accumulation and self-realization. The ability of the individual to organize labor outside the traditional extended family and therefore to accumulate wealth via the market and nontraditional commodity production made the individual the primary agent of success. Orí, the embodiment of individuality, challenged the communal ethos of the other Òrìṣà and *ilé*. Therefore, as the circulation of cowries, via the market, was changing social relationships at interpersonal, household, interhousehold, community, and state levels, and across different statuses and hierarchies, these processes became codified in the Yorùbá Atlantic age cosmology as the victory of Orí over all the other divinities.[97] This was a celebration of the individualistic ethos over that of communalism. Hence, merchant capital revolution reorganized the theogony and social relationships among the Òrìṣà, the same way that it reconfigured the social relations among their devotees.

Meanwhile, to return to the *ilé-orí* complex, the cowrie-studded shrines of self-realization were discursively represented as entreaties by each individual to Orí so that "the endlessly slippery, circulating medium" of cowrie could stay with the person, not leave him or her for a rival.[98] It is significant to note that these shrines were not expected to outlive the person for whom they were made; neither were they converted into the ancestral altar for the deceased. Instead, on the death of the owner of the shrine, both the *ìbọrí* and *ilé orí* were destroyed, and the cowries were shared by the deceased's survivors who could spend the money as they wished.[99] This process, from the construction of the Orí shrine to its destruction and the return of the cowries to the market space, is a philosophical reflection of what the Atlantic commerce meant in Yorùbá worldview: the wealth derived from merchant capital revolution, especially the flow and value of cowries, was unpredictable and outside the individual's control. Unlike *ṣẹ̀gi*, *iyùn*, and *àkún*, the infrastructures of the old regime of value, which were locally produced, cowries, the material of the new (Atlantic age) regime of value, were externally sourced. Neither the state nor the *ilé* had control over the supply and flow of this currency obtained from the slave/merchant capital exchange. Its accumulation ultimately depended on the individual engaged in market-related practices, and the greatness and respectability that the cowrie bestowed on those who had it in plenty were not guaranteed to their descendants. Hence the popular saying *owó kò ní ran*: "money has no relatives." Cowrie, then, came to embody an ideology of individualism that developed in Atlantic-age

Yorùbáland. This was the period when the traditional process of labor allocation was challenged by the needs of the Atlantic economy and the demands of the hegemonic state, when individual accumulation and self-realization began to compete with the imperatives of the *ilé*'s social and biological reproduction. This was also the period when several young men of both noble and humble birth moved to frontier market towns, colonies, and the coastal region to pursue their commercial interests independent of the labor needs of their *ilé* or household. All of these changes weakened the *ilé* as the focus of production, accumulation, and redistribution. In addition, the expanding scope of domestic slavery between 1630 and 1860 enabled individuals to recruit and accumulate labor outside the traditional familial pool, and this in turn enabled such individuals to generate wealth autonomous of the *ẹbí* (kinship) system in the *ilé*, a point that I will discuss in detail in chapter 8.

With the opportunities for accumulation offered by a monetized economy, virtually all the deities of the Atlantic-age Yorùbá community of practice valorized merchant capital. However, there was one exception among them who sounded a warning of moderation and caution against the atomistic and individualistic pursuit of wealth. This voice of caution came from the ritual field of Ọbàtálá, the father of the Yorùbá pantheon. The Ọbàtálá school spoke against the unbridled pursuit of money and the elevation of individual interest over communal needs. According to the old Òrìṣà, these were vices, the source of death, trouble, self-destruction, and societal collapse. As acute observers of their time and its contradictions, the Yorùbá intellectuals of the Atlantic age invoked the moral authority of Ọbàtálá in *ọ̀bàrà kosùn*, a chapter in the *ọ̀bàrà* book of Ifá, to critique the implications of atomistic self-interest at the expense of the community. The *ọ̀bàrà kosùn* tells the story of how three brothers destroyed one another in the bid by each of them to have Ajé (deity of the market and commercial wealth) all to himself.[100] According to the story, one day Ọbàtálá and three brothers were traveling from Ìrànjé-Ilé to Ìrànjé-Oko.[101] In the course of their journey, they encountered the corpse of a rich woman. Ọbàtálá identified her as Ajé, a daughter of Olókun. A large heap of cowries and other valuables covered her corpse. The three brothers rushed with the intention of scooping up as much of the money (cowries) as they could, but Ọbàtálá sternly warned them not to go near the corpse of Ajé. "Can't you see she is the beginning of all evil, death, and trouble?" he asked them. He implored the men to go forth on their journey and not to look back. The three brothers feigned deference to Ọbàtálá and assured him they would not return. But as soon as Ọbàtálá was gone from sight, they returned to Ajé's corpse. They took as much money and other valuables as they could carry, but then each began to think how wonderful it would be to have all the wealth to himself. The older two brothers connived and sent their youngest to go and buy them food. Their plan was to kill him on his return. The youngest brother had his own plan. He poisoned the food he bought so he could kill his older brothers. As soon as he returned, the older brothers clubbed the younger to death, and as soon as they ate the food, they also died.

Soon after, Ọbàtálá finished his business in Ìrànjé-Oko and was returning to Ìrànjé-Ilé. On his way, he encountered the remains of the three brothers. He saw their lifeless bodies amid the wealth of Ajé. Ọbàtálá lamented the trouble that Ajé had brought to the world: "In the search for money, people's struggles had multiplied; they worked more, accumulated more, but they had no satisfaction. The spirit of brotherly love had gone from their heart; money had dissolved the familial bond and had replaced communal ethos with atomistic selfishness." This critique by Ọbàtálá, the most ascetic of Yorùbá deities and the father of the pantheon, called out the antisocial dimension of merchant capital and contested the idea of merchant capital "as signs of divine benefits and mythic bestowals," according to the royalist ideology of wealth in Benin Kingdom, which is also ingrained in the Atlantic-age Òrìṣà pantheon.[102] The possession of merchant capital and participation in the market economy had become necessary to social life in the course of the seventeenth and eighteenth centuries. Therefore, it can be argued that the intellectuals who composed the *ọ̀bàrà kosùn* narrative as a moral critique of merchant capital were not trying to negate the pursuit of wealth, money, and self-realization. Rather, they were asking for moderation, patience, and satisfaction; avoidance of greed and selfishness; and attentiveness to civic order and community building in the process of self-realization.

Summing Up

The insertion of merchant capital into everyday social lives transformed the Yorùbá community of practice into an "object-centered" and an "object-created emotional" world.[103] The unprecedented increase in the volume and diversity of merchant capital enlarged market-driven productivity since everyone had to produce and offer something in the market so as to acquire any of the commodities of merchant capital. The acquired and addictive taste for tobacco; the entanglement of aguardiente and rum in the performance of hospitality, status, and other aspects of sociality; the transactional, symbolic, and abstract character of cowrie shells as objects of commerce and self-realization; and the communicative qualities of foreign clothing for identity and boundary making characterized how the Yorùbá world became part of the globality of merchant capital during the early modern period. The imported commodities were used to establish connectivity across different spectrums of social relationships. At the particular moment of encounter between Prince Adémọlá and Hugh Clapperton, for example, the sociality of merchant capital between these men of different climes but of the same era was in full display. Textiles, as a category of merchant capital, were used in both the performance and the verbal articulation for self-endorsement, the geographical extension of the self, and the definition of intercultural solidarity and connectivity. This process of inserting the self into the world is also evident in the use of cowries for cultural translations of the Yorùbá Atlantic experience. Cowrie was at once a signifying object that was translated into different signs and meanings and also an object used for seeking and contemplating knowledge in the multiple domains of social life, to paraphrase one of Karin Knorr Cetina's musings about objects of sociality.[104] Embedded in this sociality of cowries and other objects of merchant capital were social differences and social inequality based on labor, class, gender, wealth, and power relations. The intersectionality of these different spheres of social life, and the consequences on cultural forms and practices, will be the focus of the next chapter.

Notes

1. Belasco, *Entrepreneur*, xi.

2. Bernard Belasco's *The Entrepreneur as Culture Hero* is the first detailed treatment of the social and ideological transformations that resulted from the penetration of Atlantic merchant capital into the Yorùbá world. The book emphasizes how new entrepreneurial processes evolved among the Yorùbá as a consequence of their entanglement in merchant capital circulation and how these rearranged the pantheon, redefined the idea of wealth, and restructured gender relations. The book is a seminal culturalist interpretation of Yorùbá Atlantic modernity, and many aspects of Belasco's structural interpretation regarding the social relations of "market-centered beliefs and practices" remain valid. His attempt to write the cultural history of Yorùbá gender and cosmology with reference to Atlantic modernity is, however, sometimes compromised by his penchant for a priori and ahistorical evolutionary Marxist explanations. This penchant led him to organize some of his historical materials in accordance with his model instead of building a model from the historical materials, according to Karin Barber's critique in "Money," 206. Moreover, the 1970s historiography in which he grounded the premise of his structural analysis is now outdated and has been supplanted by new archaeological and historical evidence and interpretations. Nevertheless, his pioneering work has inspired other works. For accounts of the semiotic intensification of cultural production in everyday lives as a result of the unprecedented expansion in the slave/merchant capital exchange and the commercial revolution that accompanied it, see Falola and Adebayo, *Culture, Politics & Money*; Ogundiran, "Of Small Things Remembered"; Ogundiran, "Cowries and Rituals." Also see Kea, *Cultural and Social History of Ghana*, vols. 1 and 2.

3. For more insight on this, see Georg Simmel's conceptualization of commodity and money in *The Philosophy of Money.*

4. Eltis, *Rise of African Slavery*; Law and Strickrodt, *Ports of the Slave Trade*.

5. Knorr Cetina, "Sociality with Objects," 1.

6. Knorr Cetina, 9.

7. Bruce-Lockhart and Lovejoy, *Hugh Clapperton*, 1.

8. Clapperton passed his name down to us as Adamoli, but the correct phonetic spelling of the resident commissioner's name is most likely A-dé-mọ́-lá (The Crown has taken the honor). His name strongly indicates a person of royal pedigree. In fact, the resident commissioner represented himself to Clapperton as "the King's son" (Bruce-Lockhart and Lovejoy, *Hugh Clapperton*, 107).

9. Clapperton, *Journal of a Second Expedition*, 1.

10. A yellow cotton cloth from Nanking, China. See Bruce-Lockhart and Lovejoy, *Hugh Clapperton*, 106fn.

11. Clapperton, *Journal of a Second Expedition*, 3.

12. Law, *Horse in West African History*.

13. Weiner and Schneider, *Cloth*.

14. Sahlins, "Cosmologies of Capitalism," 34.

15. Ìjàǹà was the capital of the Yéwá-Ògùn province in the late eighteenth and early nineteenth century. Its governor, the *Onísàrẹ́*, was usually an *ìlàrí*, one of the high-ranking royal administrators, and was usually of servile background.

16. Clapperton, *Journal of a Second Expedition*, 14.

17. The early nineteenth-century British travelers Hugh Clapperton, Richard Lander, and John Lander called him "Mansolah." This is a transliteration devised to capture the phonetic sound of "Mọ́-sọ-lá," an abbreviation of Ọmọ́-sọlá: "The Child brought honor and social elevation." Ọmọ́sọlá is most likely his proper name, but the king is more popularly referred to in the historiography as Májǒtú (Don't let it collapse). This must have been an appellative name that he acquired during his reign. He was the last king to hold the Ọ̀yọ́ Empire together, if only in name and principle. The empire came to an end soon after his death.

18. Hallett, *Niger Journal*, 84.

19. Hallett, 84–85. This piece indeed appeared on the inventory of gifts that Clapperton presented to Májǒtú in 1826, as a fifty-yard blue/scarlet cloth, and the stockings that Májǒtú was wearing also appear on the inventory. Bruce-Lockhart and Lovejoy, *Hugh Clapperton*, 145.

20. Lloyd, "Osifekunde," 265.

21. For example, in 1826, Aláàfin Májǒtú ornamented his damask robe with coral beads. Lander, *Records*, 2:195.

22. Lander, *Records*, 1:113.

23. Bruce-Lockhart and Lovejoy, *Hugh Clapperton*, 116.

24. There is indirect evidence that Mediterranean and possibly Asian textiles arrived in the Yorùbá region between the twelfth and fourteenth centuries. The representation of guilloche and rosette designs on the terracotta and copper-alloy sculptures of Classical Ifẹ̀ and Ọ̀wọ̀ are likely motifs inspired by the decorations on imported silks from the Mediterranean. For further discussion, see Eyo, "Recent Excavations," 588–89.

25. Bruce-Lockhart and Lovejoy, *Hugh Clapperton*, 96.

26. DuPlessis, *Material Atlantic*.

27. Also known as *girike*, the Hausa word for a large robe, this is "the largest and heaviest" type of gown; it was the most ample and "much

embroidered, reaching . . . as far as the ankles, and extend[ing] beyond the arms." Johnson, *History*, 111.

28. Clapperton, *Journal of a Second Expedition*, 14.
29. Abiodun, *Yoruba Art*, 142.
30. Lander, *Records*, 1:112.
31. Abiodun, *Yoruba Art,* 164.
32. Abiodun, 168.
33. Nylan, "On the Politics of Pleasure," 120.
34. Nylan, 120.
35. Babayemi, *Egúngún*; Kalilu, "Costumes."
36. Famule, "Art and Spirituality," 185–89.
37. Fitzgerald, Drewal, and Okediji, "Transformation through Cloth."
38. Locally woven cotton cloth is the most common fabric for the majority of the people, the predominant colors being white and blue, followed by "yellow, red, crimson, and green, some in solid colors, others multicolored" (Lloyd, "Osifekunde," 263).
39. Clapperton, *Journal of a Second Expedition*, 54. The so-called sacks refer to *ẹ̀kú*, the voluminous, multilayered panels of garments usually worn by the *égúngún.*
40. Drewal, "Pageantry and Power."
41. Schneider and Weiner, "Introduction," 6.
42. Schneider and Weiner, 14.
43. Kelly, "Transformation"; Monroe, "Dynamics of State Formation"; Norman, "Archaeology of West African Atlanticization."
44. Bruce-Lockhart and Lovejoy, *Hugh Clapperton*, 97.
45. Local beers brewed from millet, sorghum, and maize and of mild alcohol content were the usual beverages produced and consumed locally (see Lander, *Records*, 1:133).
46. Hallett, *Niger Journal*, 45.
47. Hallett, 61.
48. Bruce-Lockhart and Lovejoy, *Hugh Clapperton*, 118–19.
49. Demijohns are "large ovoid or globular bottles with capacities from 4 to 20 gallons." Bottle Books, "Big Bottles Big History."
50. Agbe-Davies, *Tobacco*, 293. Also see Baram, "Clay Tobacco Pipes"; Benedict, *Golden-Silk Smoke*; Rafferty and Mann, *Smoking and Culture.*
51. Trubowitz, "Smoking Pipes," 143.
52. Brooks, *Tobacco*, 1:172–73.
53. See Handler, "Aspects of the Atlantic Slave Trade."
54. Bay, *Wives of the Leopard*; Oyěwùmí, *The Invention of Women.*
55. Tobacco was possibly given to the adolescent boys and girls participating in caravans. The use of tobacco would have stimulated the endurance and alertness of the youths while also reducing their appetite and fatigue during the often tedious travel. We know that Native American and English women and school-age children liberally consumed tobacco in seventeenth-century Virginia. See Nassaney, "Men and Women," 130.
56. Clapperton, *Journal of a Second Expedition*, 52.
57. Baram, "Clay Tobacco Pipes," 140.
58. Arno, "Cobo and Tabua," 56.
59. Rogers, "Archaeology," 342.
60. Knorr Cetina, "Sociality with Objects," 12.

61. Also see Green, *Rise of the Trans-Atlantic Slave Trade*, 128.
62. Sharp, "Commodification," 293.
63. Ben-Amos, *Art, Innovation, and Politics*, 103–4.
64. Ryder, *Benin and the Europeans*, 88–89.
65. This process of restoration of the monarchy's power started, though slowly, under Ọba Ozuere (ca. 1710–13) and Akenzua I (ca. 1711–15). See Ben-Amos, *Art, Innovation, and Politics*, 46–52.
66. Although Olókun is often translated as "Lord of the Atlantic Ocean," the deity originally referred to the spirit that resides in any large body of water, such as a river, pond, lake, or ocean. These bodies of water are called *òkun*. Olókun therefore means "the owner of a large body of water." The Olókun Grove in Ilé-Ifẹ̀ is indeed located beside what used to be a large body of water—a lake, to be specific, still called *òkun*. Olókun is named after this lake. The names Òkun and Olókun therefore were variants of the same thing for the coastal and mainland Yorùbá before the sixteenth century. To the people of Ilé-Ifẹ̀, Olókun was the goddess of wealth, represented by the glass beads produced on the banks of Òkun lake. To the coastal people, fishermen and salt makers, who relied on the ocean as the source of their livelihood, Olókun was not only the patron deity of the ocean and of the resources of their livelihood that it harbors but also the ruler of the earth's water mass, and all life, wealth, and prosperity (see Drewal, "Image and Indeterminacy"). With the advent of the Atlantic commerce, the divinity of the ocean was extended to include the rich storehouse of cowries said to lie in the palace of Olókun beneath the ocean (oral interview, Kàsálí Àkàngbé Ògún, Charlotte, NC, February 14, 2013). In the post-sixteenth century, the paraphernalia of Olókun in the Yorùbá world included cowries and imported crockery, especially copper and iron cooking pots and chinaware.
67. Trouillot, *Silencing the Past*, xix.
68. Oral interviews with Olálékan Òrìṣàdáre, Ọ̀sun Grove, Òṣogbo, May 4–5, 2004.
69. This narrative was originally collected and published in the Ayizo language in 1979, and it was later translated into English and published by Christopher A. Gregory, "Cowries and Conquest," 195.
70. Austen, "Slave Trade," 238. For similar idiomatic narratives of the Atlantic slave trade in West and Central Africa, see Bailey, *African Voices*; Harms, *River of Wealth*; Holsey, *Routes of Remembrance*; Shaw, *Memories*.
71. Austen, "Slave Trade," 238.
72. Guyer, *Marginal Gains*.
73. Falola and Adebayo, *Culture, Politics and Money*, 42.
74. *Ẹ́ẹ́rìndínlógún* is also more widely practiced than Ifá outside Africa, wherever diasporic Yorùbá cultural presence is prominent, such as Cuba, Brazil, and the United States (Bascom, *Sixteen Cowries*, 3–5).
75. Oral interview, Chief J. Aje, Ìlàrè-Ìjẹ̀sà, June 21, 1997.
76. For example, a two-by-one-meter unit excavated at a refuse mound in Ẹdẹ-Ilé produced fifteen cowries. These are interpreted as sacrificial objects deliberately thrown into the midden as part of several instances of sacrifice in which cowries were used for spiritual cleansing or the healing of a person's ailment, a quest for attainment of the desired material needs, or the fulfillment of social needs. Ogundiran, "Cowries and Rituals," 83.

77. Belasco, *Entrepreneur*, 136. Also see Eluyemi, "Excavations at Isoya"; Falola and Lawuyi, "Not Just a Currency"; Ogundiran, "Of Small Things Remembered."

78. Ben-Amos, *Art, Innovation, and Politics*, 104.

79. Ryder, *Benin and the Europeans*, 202.

80. Egharevba, *Short History*, 41.

81. Lander, *Records*, 2:203–4. Also see Ogundiran, "End of Prehistory?," 796–97.

82. Johnson, *History*, 59.

83. Ogundiran and Agbaje-Williams, "Oyo Empire," 74.

84. In Yorùbá culture, this is a common practice in which individuals could acquire a new name and identity based on their profession.

85. The anatomical head is also called *orí*.

86. A conical head with naturalistic features and four other cones with stylized human eyes and mouths were found in the mortuary complex at the Ọbalára site in Ilé-Ifẹ̀. The excavator perceptively suggests that these four cones represent crowns of the type worn by a Yorùbá *ọba* today, which usually have human faces around them (Garlake, "Excavations at Obalara's Land," 123, 132, 145). If this was the case, then the assemblage of cones with human features would have denoted the communal symbol of sacred authority, whereas the conical head would indicate a generalized ancestral figure.

87. Drewal and Mason, *Beads, Body, and Soul*, 199.

88. Johnson, *History*, 27.

89. In 1826, according to Hugh Clapperton, sixty thousand cowries would purchase two to three cows or a prime adult male slave in Ọ̀yọ́-Ile (Clapperton, *Journal of a Second Expedition*, 59). To put things in perspective, purchasing a cow was outside the reach of the vast majority of people and households.

90. Johnson, *History*, 27.

91. Fakayode, "Orí."

92. For example, Gbadegesin, "Toward a Theory of Destiny"; Lawal, *Ori*.

93. Edeh, *Towards an Igbo Metaphysics*; Kagame, "Problem of Man"; Idowu, *Olódùmarè*; Wiredu, *Companion*.

94. Omosade Awolalu, "Yorùbá Sacrificial Practice," 84.

95. Abiodun, "Understanding Yoruba Art," 77.

96. Also see Belasco, *Entrepreneur*.

97. It is therefore not surprising that during a Christian evangelism session in Ibadan in 1868, a woman opined that the adoption of Christianity would not make them abandon their loyalty to Orí, "their god and maker" (W. S. Allen, *CMS Journal*, October 25, 1868, CMS, CAO/049).

98. Barber, "Money," 217.

99. Johnson, *History*, 27.

100. Oral interviews with Olálékan Òrìṣàdáre, Àwòrò Ọ̀ṣun-Òṣogbo, Ọ̀ṣun Grove, Òṣogbo, May 4–5, 2004. Also, see Elebuibon, *Adventures*.

101. These are the two homes of Ọbàtálá, one (Ìrànjé-Ilé) in the city of Ilé-Ifẹ̀ and the other, Ìrànjé-Oko, on the outskirts of Ilé-Ifẹ̀.

102. Sahlins, "Cosmologies of Capitalism," 6.

103. Knorr Cetina, "Sociality with Objects," 9.

104. Knorr Cetina, 15.

8

Perennial Inequality

A NEW SYSTEM OF LABOR organization evolved during the seventeenth and eighteenth centuries to support the merchant capital revolution of monetized economy, market-focused production, and object-centered sociality. There are four major parts to this new labor organization. First, there was a dramatic increase in labor recruitment outside the traditional familial social networks. Second, the labor of a significant number of men and women was transferred from the traditional familial pool to wage-based services (e.g., porterage), individual-driven entrepreneurial opportunities, and state bureaucracy. Third, there was an astronomical growth in the ranks of an underclass of servile laborers employed in the market-centered production activities. Fourth, the division of labor along gender lines intensified, in which the female dominated the domestic market-based production activities. The impacts of this labor reorganization on gender and class is the subject of this chapter. The emphasis will be on the expansion of polygyny and other marriage practices; the strengthening of the power of patricentric authorities at the expense of matricentric institutions and female-centered authorities; and the new forms of social stratification that developed during the seventeenth and eighteenth centuries. I will show that these practices of stratification and class hardened the layers of institutionalized inequality at different scales of social organization, within the household, *ilé*, and *ìlú*; across intergenerational relations; and along the cleavages of the metropolis-province divide. The result was a widespread social discontentment in the second half of the eighteenth century with far-reaching consequences during the early nineteenth century.

Gender, Labor, and Production

Paul Lovejoy has convincingly shown that the various phases of the external demand for enslaved African labor increased the incidence of domestic slavery in Africa at different junctures in the history of the continent: trans-Saharan, trans-Indian Ocean, and transatlantic.[1] In the case of the Yorùbá experience, the number of domestic slaves and other forms of servitude rose on the coast and in the mainland as the Bight of Benin became, cumulatively, the second most important region in Atlantic Africa for slave-merchant capital exchange (see table 6.1). Whether obtained through warfare, tribute, or purchase, not all the captives went to the various slave markets on the coast. Many were retained domestically for various economic, social, and political needs, and female slaves were retained locally in greater numbers than males. This was a mirror image of the higher ratios of males to females (approximately 62 percent and 38 percent, respectively) who were forced to depart the shores of the Bight for the New World between 1630 and 1830.[2]

As the households in the middle to upper strata sought to ratchet up production in the increasingly competitive monetized market economy, the use of forced labor (slaves) became a desirable path to achieving that goal.[3] The enslaved people were deployed in four major areas: (1) agricultural (food and cash crops) and other primary production activities (e.g., mining of ores and salt); (2) military and administrative duties; (3) manufacturing (e.g., cotton, iron); and (4) trading. The political and military elite as well as the leaders of middle-class households benefited from the retention of a larger percentage of enslaved and captive women because they were able to recruit wives from the ranks of these women for themselves, their sons, and other male dependents. Hence, those households in the upper echelons of society had far greater access to wives and reproduction opportunities than those in the lower social rank. The former used this advantageous access to wives and sources of labor to increase their household population (through reproduction) and economic production. This development helped to widen social inequality.

Textile-related crafts were the centerpiece of female work in the commercial revolution of the Atlantic age. The long chain of cloth production, from cotton cultivation to finished dyed fabric, relied on the labor of women. Unlike the time before the seventeenth century, when women wove the fabric that clothed their families and most cloth-manufacturing activities were small-scale and domesticized, the Atlantic-age merchant-capital revolution commodified cloth and significantly increased the economic value of an important aspect of female work (see chap. 6).[4] The shift from the domesticity of cotton-cloth manufacture to market-driven production was complete by the mid-seventeenth century. In no other sphere of manufacturing did women have better prospects of achieving socioeconomic autonomy during the age of merchant-capital revolution than in producing cotton thread and weaving, dyeing, and selling cloth products. This was in addition to the fact that women also dominated the market space. The "pivotal place [of women] in the local and state economy—organizing household industries . . . the local market system, and . . . long-distance trade networks" was, therefore, the cornerstone of Yorùbá economic life during the Atlantic period.[5] Women's domination of the general commercial life of the Yorùbá world cumulatively increased their assets, and this gave them a measure of economic autonomy, especially in a society where women could own and dispose of property autonomously of their husbands, brothers, and fathers.[6]

The independently and fabulously wealthy women were an exception, not the rule. The majority were small-scale traders and artisans in the middle range of the social hierarchy. There were also many women in socially circumscribed but sometimes enviable positions as wives and daughters in elite households. These women were by far the most numerous residents of the metropolitan and provincial palaces across the Yorùbá region. In the Ọ̀yọ́ Empire, for example, most of the palace women were referred to as *ayaba*, king's wives. These wives included the regnal ones (those married to the king before and after his accession to the throne), widows of the previous kings (whom the new king was obligated to provide for), and female slaves. These women played important roles in the economy of the palace and the empire.[7] The widows of the previous kings lived in separate quarters reserved for them on the palace grounds and in the nearby royal towns—Bàrá and Kòso. Although royal widows and slaves were collectively referred to as "king's wives," this serves only to indicate their dependency on the person of the king and the state. As residents of the palace, these women enjoyed the protection that the power of their "social husband" (*ọkọ*) guaranteed them. And in turn, they provided services and labor to the king and the state.

The women of servile and tributary origins, as well as widows of the previous kings, formed the bulk of the *aláàfin*'s labor force. For their master and the state, some of the enslaved women worked in the agricultural sector along with the male slaves; performed a myriad of domestic chores, especially food preparation; and engaged in craft production and commercial activities, including itinerant trading. British slaver Robert Norris's observation about the palace women in Dahomey applies to the case of Ọ̀yọ́, given the immense influence that flowed between the two and the similarities in the role of women in the palace administration:[8]

"Besides agriculture, they [the king's 'wives'] were also occupied in spinning cotton, weaving cloths, and brewing pitto, a kind of beer . . . in dressing victuals for sale, and carrying merchandises to the market."[9] Cotton cloth was the most widespread manufactured product in the Ọ̀yọ́ metropolis, and it was also the major commodity produced by women in the palace at Ọ̀yọ́-Ilé. Likewise, textile production was the chief female occupation in the palaces of the provincial governors and resident commissioners, as it was in many households.[10]

The palace women also formed a redistribution network for local and foreign commodities, including some of the goods that flowed into the palace as tributes.[11] The older members of the king's harem were commissioned to trade on behalf of the *aláàfin* across the length and breadth of the empire in commodities of low volume but high value, such as trona, local cloth, and an assortment of beads. Across the Ọ̀yọ́ Empire, these royal "wives" could be found trading for the king, "and, like other women of the common class, carrying large loads on their heads from town to town."[12] The Landers came across about a hundred such royal ladies at Jadoo, about a thirty-day journey from Ọ̀yọ́-Ilé. The women, most of whom had "passed the prime of life," had brought trona and cloth to sell in exchange "for salt, and various articles of European manufacture, particularly beads." They wrapped a particular type of cloth around their wares as a mark of their royal identity. The penalties for imitating this mark were draconian, and they included "perpetual slavery" or death.[13] The king's wives enjoyed many privileges in their commercial activities. First, the governor or chief of the Ọ̀yọ́ colony/province whose territory they were passing through had to provide them and the officials who accompanied them (for administrative and security purposes) with board and lodging. Second, these royal traders were exempted from all turnpike tolls and market levies. Third, they were given the opportunity to sell their wares in the market before other traders. All these privileges afforded the royal wives the opportunity to offer the best prices and therefore garner profits that were not available to others. The profits from these trading missions were "uniformly given to the sovereign."[14] In other words, the work of these royal women was an integral part of the revenue sources for financing the state.

Of all the hegemonic Yorùbá states of the Atlantic age, it was in Ọ̀yọ́ that slave labor was most prevalent. In fact, the economic, military, and political affairs of the empire were run on the backs of slaves from the seventeenth through the early nineteenth century. By recruiting a large, unprecedented amount of slave labor from the Central Sudan (Hausa and Borno) through trade; from the surrounding territories through warfare; and from its provinces through tributes, Ọ̀yọ́ was able to dominate commodity production by volume. It also used its superior military power to control far more trading outlets than any other single state in the region. The need for labor was especially high in the elite Houses. The military responsibilities of the aristocratic and royal families, for example, placed on their shoulders the burden to maintain large stables of horses. These horses represented the power of the empire, and they were also the most expensive property, considering that a healthy horse was worth at least two enslaved prime adults in Ọ̀yọ́-Ilé during the nineteenth century.[15] Horses require an enormous amount of care. Apart from the veterinarians who treated the horses for wounds, dehydration, saddle sores, and a myriad of equine illnesses, and the professional trainers who worked with the horses, there were also handlers who fed and watered these horses two or three times daily. It could take up to four handlers, working full-time, to take care of one horse. The personnel required to deliver this care were mostly the enslaved men originating from the Central Sudan, but the other enslaved populations from different parts of the empire would also have been recruited into the important service of horse handling.

Despite the fact that the cavalry was the backbone of the empire, the Ọ̀yọ́ citizens and the free were generally not employed in the menial tasks associated with horse maintenance—cleaning the horse stable or feeding and washing the horses. These were reserved for the men in bondage. It was a taboo and a mark of indignity for an Ọ̀yọ́ citizen to partake in horse maintenance, even when his or her material conditions ranked below that of the enslaved horse handler.[16] In this instance, there was a direct relationship between a type of labor and citizenship/freedom. Therefore, the labor requirements for maintaining the empire's growing horse stables, owned by the Ọ̀yọ́ elite, accentuated domestic slavery throughout the seventeenth and eighteenth centuries. The implication, then, is that the security of the empire depended on the labor of a large group of people of servile origin. These full-time male horse handlers were fed and clothed by the state, using the proceeds from the work of other enslaved members of the elite households, revenues from state-sponsored commerce, and the various levies imposed on citizens, visitors, and tributary polities, among others. However, the horse-handling service was not a dead-end job for those in the palace bureaucracy. It was from the rank of horse handlers that eunuchs and *ìlàrí* (state messengers) were sometimes recruited and promoted to higher offices within the expansive bureaucracy of the empire.

Initially, access to slave labor was restricted to the elite families and the high-ranking military men who acquired slaves through trade and predatory warfare. The increased availability of the Central Sudanese captives in the slave markets of the Niger valley between 1630 and 1730 and the escalation of Ọ̀yọ́ military activities between the 1730s and 1760s sharply increased the slave population in the metropolis and across the empire (see chap. 6). By the second half of the eighteenth century, an increasing number of middle-class households were able to acquire slaves, whose labor they deployed for market-driven production activities.[17] Ann O'Hear's study of domestic slavery in Ìlọrin, one of the towns in the metropolitan core of the Ọ̀yọ́ Empire, is insightful on how members of the middle class recruited and made use of slaves. Although O'Hear was writing about the second half of the nineteenth century, her historical account is succinctly applicable to the eighteenth and early nineteenth centuries. Her research shows that warfare, brigandage, and purchase offered members of both the chiefly and the middle classes the most reliable path to building the labor force needed for maximized economic production. Òjíbàrà was one of those middle-class individuals with an entrepreneurial disposition. He was a warrior and a large-scale farmer, owning four farms with at least ten slaves working on each. He also used his slaves to dig the clay on his land for sale to potters, an indication that even potters relied on the market-exchange system, powered by slavery, for their raw materials. O'Hear elaborates on the importance of enslaved laborers to various industries in Ìlọrin: "A number of prosperous weavers owned slaves, and used them for farming and . . . weaving. Traders in woven cloth bought slaves and used them as carriers in the long-distance trade. Members of *lantana* beadmaking families . . . employed them in beadmaking and on the farm. Leatherworkers from Ile Alawo were prosperous enough to buy slaves from the baloguns (war chiefs) to help them in their work."[18] However, in most middle-class households, slaves were supplementary, not the primary or sole source of labor. In general, the free members of the household (*ọmọ ilé*) worked alongside the enslaved, and there were opportunities for the favorite slaves to acquire power, wealth, and status that sometimes surpassed those of the *ọmọ ilé*. In fact, the difference between a slave and a freeborn could be blurred and even erased over time.[19]

Irrespective of social status, women were the backbone of the Atlantic-age merchant-capital revolution, both as a source of labor and as a source of biological reproduction of labor. Across the region, they bore the brunt of the increased production in the monetized and specialized economy. Women performed a myriad of tasks, including housekeeping, trading, and manufacturing. Although a mid-nineteenth-century observer noted that cultivation devolved mostly on men,[20] the women in the middle- and lower-class families also participated in farmwork, including gathering and foraging, crop harvesting, and transportation of harvests both to their residence and to the market. Young enslaved women were likely used for extensive farming activities on large plantations owned by Ọ̀yọ́ kings and the aristocratic families. In 1702, the versatility of women in production activities in the Yorùbá community of practice prompted an observer in Benin City to write: "In short they have so much employment, that they [tend] not to sit still; notwithstanding which, they dispatch it all very briskly."[21] More than a century later, Hugh Clapperton noted that the women of Ọ̀yọ́-Ilé generally appeared to bear the "drudgery" of production activities.[22] Women and children were the constant and dominant presence in the several caravan trains that crisscrossed the Yorùbá world during the Atlantic age. The women were described as carrying on their heads gargantuan loads "that would tire a mule," while young children "trudged after them" with loads that the Lander brothers thought could give an adult "brain fever."[23] The choice of melancholic similes by these Cornish brothers notwithstanding, they offered a good approximation of the burden borne by women and children in the production and circulation of goods across the Yorùbá region in the age of merchant capital revolution.

The drudgery of production affected women differently based on social rank. Women of low socioeconomic status, female slaves, and junior wives in large polygynous households provided more demanding labor than women of the upper class, including the senior wives in elite homes. Independently rich women had dependents, like their male counterparts, ranging from the junior co-wives to slaves. This *òríkì* (panegyric) of Ọ̀ṣun—patron deity of female power and femininity, among others—illustrates the diversity of roles that women played in the production and commercial activities:

Hail My Beloved Mother Aládékojú[24] . . .
The descendent of the one who uses the crown made of brass . . .
Ọ̀ṣun surrounds her whole body with *ẹdan* (brass)
With the shining brass as a lantern at night
She very quickly moves round the house . . .
My mother who provides bean cake for the Ẹ̀fọ̀n people
When my mother wakes up, she prepares food for her household
My mother will then proceed to the kolanut stall
As she trades in kolanut,
She is also carrying her corn to the mill to grind
At the same time she is also dyeing clothes [*àdìrẹ*] . . . by the sideway
There is no task my mother cannot do
She even keeps a stable for rearing horses[25]
My mother lives in the deep water[26]
And yet sends errands to the mainland
Aládékojú, my Olódùmarè (supreme Goddess)
Who turns a bad destiny (*orí*) into a good one
Ọ̀ṣun has plenty of brass ornaments in her storage.[27]

This *òríkì* presents the imagery of a rich, hardworking, and entrepreneurial woman devoted to family care and engaged in different manufacturing endeavors and commerce. She may have been born into wealth, but she also created wealth on account of her hard work, acquired skills, and business acumen. According to the *oríkì*, Aládékojú not only had stockpiles of brass but also kept a stable of horses, a manly possession and the ultimate hardware of military power. An intrepid merchant, she linked the mainland to the coast through her itinerant commercial networks. The women of Aládékojú's caliber also acquired slaves, whom they employed in their various industries, including potting, cloth weaving, dyeing, and trading.

Although women of means were not the major purchasers or recruiters of domestic slaves, they were nevertheless involved in the local redistribution of the labor of young male and female captives. For example, Àjàyí (later known as Samuel Àjàyí Crowther) was purchased from his captors by a middle-aged itinerant female trader in August 1821.[28] She was an Ọ̀yọ́ citizen and a Muslim who was living in Ìtokò (an Ẹ̀gbá town) at the time. We don't know her name, but, consistent with the life-course cumulative naming practices among the Yorùbá, her relatives might have called her Màmá Ìtokò.[29] Like Aládékojú, mentioned in the above verse, Màmá Ìtokò was one of those itinerant traders who linked the coast to the deep mainland, but she also engaged in cloth weaving when she was not on the road as part of a caravansary. Her conversations with Àjàyí indicate that she traversed the trade routes between the Àjàṣẹ́ on the coast and the southern reaches of metropolitan Ọ̀yọ́ (Ìbàràpá/Ẹ̀gbá boundary), about 100 and 130 kilometers, respectively, from her Ìtokò base.[30] Young captives such as the twelve-year-old Àjàyí were a desirable source of labor, for augmenting the production capacity of these actively mobile itinerant female traders who also managed cottage industries. Some of these women succeeded in building good fortunes by supplementing their domestic labor pool (children, co-wives, and other dependents) with the labor of enslaved adolescents and women. As a result, they were able to establish medium- to large-scale agricultural and craft-production businesses.[31] The young captives also had a strong exchange value. Young slaves were less likely to run away or attack their captors. They provided an itinerant trader like Màmá Ìtokò the safe means to store and transport wealth and value (merchant capital) from one trading entrepôt to another. At the right market, the captives were exchanged for cash (cowries), local commodities, or other Atlantic merchant capital.

Wifehood, Class, and Social Reproduction

The gendered division of labor was as old as the Yorùbá community of practice. Economic activities were among the sites for performing and articulating gender and sexuality. The gendering of economic activities and an emphasis on the interdependency of male and female work spheres continued during the era of the Atlantic commercial revolution. Nevertheless, the ideology and practices of a gendered division of labor went through transformations as a result of the astronomical rise in polygyny, the impact of the market economy on wife recruitment, and changes in the role of the household as the primary unit of production.

Polygyny had been an integral part of the cultural fabric and socioeconomic organization of the Yorùbá community of practice since at least the Late Formative period. However, the commercial revolution, merchant capital/slave exchange, and hegemonic state formation of the seventeenth and eighteenth centuries significantly enabled the expansion of polygyny in three ways. First, the imperatives of the participation in market economy required an increase in productivity. This in turn put pressures on households to increase the number of their labor force by marrying more wives who would give birth to the next generation of children, as helping hands in farming, crafts, trading, and other professions. Second, the merchant capital/slave exchange facilitated the unprecedented recruitment of captive and enslaved women as wives. And third, political expansion by the militaristic states brought a large number of women into the metropolis and the provinces as wives through the channels of warfare and tributary obligations. Hence, women of servile (captured or bought) and tributary origins provided the political elite and their immediate clients—the male House and household leaders, merchants, and war captains—with the most viable pathway to increase their sources of labor and reproductive power outside the traditional marriage contracts. The latter usually involved more demanding social networks and obligations. The result was that a large number of female captives and victims of tributary payments became wives in mostly elite and middle-class households as workers for the husband and bearers of the husband's children, mirroring on a smaller scale what was happening in the royal palaces. This development favored men of power, who controlled the instruments of military conquest and the levers of political authority. They were the ones who were able to enlarge their households through wives of servile and tributary origins.

This arrangement of bringing slave wives into the households benefited not only the alpha men or patricians. There were also certain classes of women who were beneficiaries. These were the senior wives and older daughters of the household (adult women who lived in their natal compounds—*ilémosú*[32]) who co-ruled the household with the patrician. All the three usually appropriated a large percentage of the slave and junior wives' productivity.[33] While the senior wives could lay claim to most of the produce of their labor, the slave wives and junior wives of indigent background could not. In addition to using their reproductive assets to increase the numbers of the household, the slave wives were also tasked with a myriad of chores needed for provisioning the household, of which food preparation and tending to the economic interests of their husband-master and senior co-wives ranked the highest. The ability of the alpha men to bring wives into the household from outside the traditional marriage arrangements had the effect of weakening the matricentric authority and destabilizing the ethos of patricentric-matricentric interdependency, duality, and balance that were in place before the seventeenth century. Disconnected from their natal home by enslavement or as victims of tributary obligations, most of these women entered the marital relationship in large polygamous households as junior wives. The situation of these women was precarious, for in their new homes they were without social capital for protection from abuse and exploitation. Lacking the natal kin to turn to for support, these wives of servile and foreign origin had no network of matricentric authority (as daughter and sister) they could mobilize in their new (though forced) home. Such women, therefore, had no choice but to safeguard the patricentric authority of their husband on behalf of their children. The implication of the increase in the number of slave wives is that there was also an increase in the number of children who grew up to become adults and citizens but who lacked matrilineal affiliation. Therefore, these children of slave wives had an undivided loyalty and commitment to patrilineal authority. As a result of all of these developments, the patricentric realm was elevated at the expense of the matricentric sphere in many areas of the Yorùbá region where the hegemonic power of the state, militarism, and merchant capital revolution prevailed.

The power, honor, prestige, and wealth attached to the alpha Houses and households made them desirable as families to marry into as part of the strategy of strengthening social and political relationships locally and regionally. This gave the young men from these *ilé*, especially those with political capital, high-ranking military pedigree, or elite/wealthy backgrounds, a head start in marriage compared with their peers from poor or middling-status homes. It was estimated that the sons of elite households generally married five to seven years earlier than the commoners.[34] These new men of the Atlantic age—traders, warriors, and the political elite—and their households, therefore, had greater resources than those in the middle and lower strata to accumulate wives and increase the number of their households in both the short and the long term. Those prosperous households also recruited young men of servile background and from lower-class households as a ready pool of labor in the military, administrative, production (agriculture and manufacturing), and commercial domains. They gave some of their daughters and other female dependents in marriage to the most promising of these young men in a matrilocal residency that ensured that the children of both their daughters and their sons remained in the patricentric household. Hence, elite or upper-class families had the opportunity to increase their number faster than those on the lower rungs of the social ladder. They also had a larger pool of dependents and labor than the middle and lower-class households, and were therefore able to outperform the latter in productivity and accumulation of wealth.

The accumulation of wives by the alpha men in settings where many young male dependents either did not have the resources to marry or had to delay marriage also led to the development of concubinage networks within the expansive households and *ilé*, between those marginalized young men and the alpha male's junior wives. Once such an illicit relationship was discovered, however, both the guilty wife and the young man (possibly an older son, a junior brother, or a client of the household's chieftain) were often permitted to beg for forgiveness and to pay a low-stakes fine. The patrician would then allow the two to continue to have their concubinage relationship, but any children that came out of it belonged to him. This arrangement provided some restricted sexual freedom for the junior wives while also helping retain the services and loyalty of the transgressive male members in the household. As the legal father of the children who resulted from such concubinage relationships, the patrician was able to increase the population of his household (or House) and his labor force. And the tolerated concubinage within the household or House helped minimize the potential friction between the elite men and their younger male dependents while also burnishing the image of the patrician as a kind and considerate elder.[35] Hence, the saying *Àgbà tí kò bínú l'ọmọrẹ̀ ńpọ̀ jọjọ* (Only the elder who has a forgiving spirit will increase the number of his children).

The monetized economy of the merchant-capital revolution also fostered the development and increase of indentured labor as a means of financing credit-debt obligations.[36] Again, this development benefited the owners of merchant capital who were in the position to lend money or advance credit in goods to the poor. The borrower used his or her partial labor or that of his dependent, usually a son or a junior brother, as collateral (and interest) for the debt until full repayment. The formalization of the creditor-debtor relationship not only resulted in the institutionalization of pawnship but also increased the incidence of the forced betrothal of daughters to creditors, a practice that destitute debtors (usually the father) used in exchange for unpaid debts.[37] The creditor was, therefore, able to use access to indentured labor and wife-for-debt exchange to increase production and reproduction respectively. All of these only served to widen the gaps between the rich and the poor, the haves and the have-nots.

Since most households were of middle and lower socioeconomic status, they could only generate labor through biological reproduction rather than through slavery and pawning. Those households confronted two challenges. First, the middle and lower classes had to compete for wives among themselves and with the upper class, but the latter had the advantages of wealth and privilege and could use these to outbid others for wives. Second, the monetized economy transformed the symbolic gift exchanges in marriage contracts to formal, transactional agreements. In this case, the cash payments ("bride price") made by the groom's family to the bride's family officially transferred the claim of both the productive and reproductive labor of a woman from her natal kin to her husband's household. For the common people, the bride price paid for marrying off their daughter (in cash and kind) was an important source of the household's wealth, and this could be used to finance the marriage expenses for a young man in the household. This meant that the families could favor the highest-bidding suitor or force the daughter to marry the suitor least desirable to her.[38] The ever-perceptive Hugh Clapperton was no doubt wading through the muddy pond of socioeconomic and cultural transactions that undergirded the changing dynamics of marriage relations in the age of commercial revolution when he surmised in 1826 that "wives are bought [in Ọ̀yọ́-Ilé] . . . according to the circumstances of the bridegroom."[39] This means that the bride price was assessed based on the social station of the groom and his family in a hyper-monetized context. Therefore, one of the consequences of the market economy was that it monetized marriage contracts and commodified both the labor and the wombs of women of lower classes. Moreover, as children had now become a means of realizing the economic objectives of their fathers (and mothers as well) in a competitive market economy, the economic value placed on women as mothers also increased.

The ability of a few men of power and wealth to garner multiple wives under their roof would have created a scarcity of marriageable women for young men from middling and poor backgrounds. As a result, the common people increasingly resorted to preemptive long-drawn-out marriage arrangements for their prepubescent children. This was a practice whereby two families negotiated marriage partners for their respective underage boys and girls "at a very early age, at about seven or eight," according to Ọsìnfẹ́kundé, an early nineteenth-century eyewitness. The practice often took the form of parents of a boy making "a formal request of the girl's parents for her hand in marriage, (and) stipulating the [future] bride price the young man will bring to his fiancée." The agreement was formalized with an engagement ceremony presided over by a priest. "From then on," Ọsìnfẹ́kundé continued, "the boy's mother often goes to visit his little fiancée carrying gifts, and the two children often play together."[40] This was a proactive approach to social reproduction, enabling families to develop a long-term strategy to save and build relationships toward marriage for their young family members. The strategy reveals how the people from below responded to the market forces and social inequality that were reshaping the institutions of marriage, family, and gender traditions during the Atlantic period.

Despite the monetization of marriage as a social contract, however, female citizens did not lose their rights to divorce, inherit, own property, accumulate capital, or dispose of their property.[41] Divorce, however, required refunding the bride price to the groom's family. This obligation placed a burden on a family whose daughter abandoned a marriage, eloped, or divorced.[42] Wives of servile origin did not, however, have the same leverage. Although a wife who was originally brought into the household as a slave could no longer be sold, exchanged, or bought, she was nevertheless stuck in this relationship until her children came of age. However, the children of the slave wife were not slaves, and they could, in theory, rise to the top status in the *ilé*. These children, once they came of age, usually protected their mothers from abuse and exploitation.

Moreover, women from high-ranking and wealthy families did not have to follow the marriage practices of the middling and lower classes. Those daughters of the elite Houses and households had the freedom to select whom they married or had conjugal liaisons with, except when they were being used to broker diplomatic relations with the other elites or to retain the service of a valuable male dependent.[43] Even when they were married off, many of them continued to maintain at least partial residence in their natal homes after marriage, and they had an easier path to walking away from a marriage than the commoners. A little inconvenience often provided these daughters of elite families with the excuse to return to their natal home, where they became *ilémosú*, a term that can be translated as daughter-husband. The *aláàfin*'s daughters, for example, had the liberty to take in any man without marriage.[44] These daughters of the elite Houses and households were, therefore, social males and advocates of patricentric authority. Their femininity as biological women was practiced through patriarchy, and this gave them the sexual freedom that their peers from the lower and middle classes lacked. The freedom of the daughters of elite Houses to shun or terminate their wifely status demonstrates that their social rank came before their biological sex or gender.[45] Unlike in the general society, where motherhood and wifehood were intimately linked, the women from elite households had the opportunity to separate the two. In their natal homes, they were social males combining motherhood with daughterhood and sisterhood, a position they could not attain in their virilocal homes.

In converse, just as it was possible for biological women to become social males, it was also possible for biological men to become social females. This was prevalent in Ọ̀yọ́ Empire, thanks to the rapid increase of domestic slavery between 1630 and 1790. The numerous male slaves and other bonded men retained by the elite chieftains—civil and military—meant that there was a vast population of men who had no prospect of becoming heads of their own households. Within the palace of Ọ̀yọ́-Ilé especially, a large number of men of foreign origin were forced to become eunuchs, although there were also a few citizens who chose this path in order to realize their aspirations for political status, power, and influence. The eunuchs and slaves had no chance of heading a household or becoming an ancestor. A large majority spent most of their servile career doing menial jobs on the farms, in craft workshops, and in horse stables. Some of the priests and priestesses of Ṣàngó, the empire's administrators (*ìlàrí*), and even soldiers were also recruited from the ranks of the men and women of servile origin. Such appointments elevated their status and provided them with many privileges. Their servile origins notwithstanding, they were citizens within the extra-House system of the palace. These were the true public servants in the administration of the empire because their loyalty was to the palace institution and not to any of the Houses. As dependents of the *aláàfin* and as individuals who did not have their own household or family, the eunuchs were regarded as "wives of the king." Those among them who were inducted into the priesthood of Ṣàngó cross-dressed as women and took on feminine characteristics, including plaiting their hair. All of these served to project their dependent (wifely) social status in relation to the king and his patron deity, Ṣàngó.[46]

Overall, there was a general decline in wifehood status throughout the Atlantic period as a result of the monetized economy and increase in domestic slavery. The former commodified marriage by making bride price increasingly prominent in the social contracts of the marriage relationship. The latter facilitated an influx of women of servile and bonded backgrounds into the elite and some of the middle-class households. The commodification of labor and marriage contracts, as well as the expansion of polygyny outside the traditional social relationships that promoted the ethos of patricentric-matricentric balance and inter-House mutual obligations, significantly weakened wifely status. As a result, the citizen daughters were now competing with women of bondage in wifely spaces. Also, monetized marital contracts gave more authority to the husband household (payer of bride price) over that of the wife's (recipient of bride price). These changes resulted in a new form of gender ideology in which patricentric authority (male) was associated with absolute social power and matricentric authority (female) assumed more of a symbolic and supportive authority with less social power. In this scenario, daughters (irrespective of social status) who were part of the patricentric order in their natal homes were also victims of the general decline of feminine and matricentric authority throughout the Atlantic period. In general, men of high and middling status lived a life of more leisure than women of similar status. In the panegyric composed for the noblemen and other male elite, for example, they were not celebrated for their work and hard labor but for their military prowess, accumulative exploits, political sagacity, generosity, and knowledge.

In contrast, women of high status, including the independently wealthy ones, were celebrated for their motherhood and their never-ending, back-breaking, multitasking work, as illustrated in the praise poem of Alá-dékojú mentioned above. Work and biological reproduction were the two primary means that a chiefly woman could use to define her social value and femininity. And the work that women did, especially in cloth-related production and market activities, was essential to the economic well-being of the state, community, and household. If work was seen as the epitome of womanhood and femininity and served as the path-way for women to achieve autonomy and economic independence, then leisure, generosity, and military exploits defined masculinity and man-hood during the Yorùbá Atlantic age. Hence, the political economy of the seventeenth-century commercial revolution created a system of class stratification, gendered ideology, and marriage practices that devalued wifely status and reduced the influence of matricentric sphere while the influence of the patricentric sphere increased.

The mortuary practices associated with the *aláàfin* and some of his provincial governors during the eighteenth and early nineteenth centu-ries clearly illustrate the degree to which women's status increasingly depended on the honor of their husbands. The senior and sometimes the "favorite" wives of these male officials of the state were expected to commit suicide before sunset on the very same day their husband gave up the ghost. The scale of these mandatory honor suicides by wives and other dependents was greatest in the burial of the *aláàfin*. In addition to about twenty-three individuals who were immolated and buried with the deceased king, fourteen high-ranking palace officials—six men and eight women—were also required to commit suicide in their respective homes, where they were buried with fanfare.[47] Honorific suicides also occurred in smaller scales in Ọ̀yọ́ provinces. At Ìjànà, for example, two of the governor's "favorite wives were required to quit the world on the same day" the governor passed away.[48] These favorite wives included the senior wife, whom the governor co-ruled the household with, and this senior wife bore the responsibility of redistributing his wealth among relatives and friends before she committed suicide.

The three-dimensional art of the Yorùbá Atlantic age also docu-mented this decline in the general status of wifehood as an institution and of the women who predominantly bore this social identity. For the first time in the corpus of Yorùbá art, women were depicted in subordinated and dependent postures, sometimes barely clad, kneeling, and with a baby on their back. These images emphasized the biological reproductive role of women. The serene and dignified portraits of the female ancestors that adorned the temples, house shrines, and public mortuaries of the Late Formative and Classical periods, as evident at Èsìẹ́, Ilé-Ifẹ̀, and Ọ̀wọ̀, were not in vogue among the political elite of the Atlantic period. Neither were these in vogue for men, certainly not for men of servile background. But whereas elite men were generally depicted in military postures on horseback, women were only represented in diminutive status (relative to the enlarged imagery of men). And when women were the sole representation in these sculptures, they were portrayed as the instrument of worship of the male deities, as in the dancing wands (*osé*) of Ṣàngó (patron deity of the Ọ̀yọ́ Empire) and Èṣù (patron deity of the market). These visual images documented the reality of a new experience that hinged on the reduction of wifehood, children, and other dependents (especially slaves and other bonded men and women) to instruments of male honor, power, and wealth (fig. 8.1).

Although the territorial expansion of the hegemonic states and their integration into the market economy resulted in the general decline of wifely status, many of the smaller communities who were also vassals of the dominant powers of the region managed to hold on to the representation of womanhood and female ancestors as the center of their social reproduction, and communal well-being. For the most part, those areas, such as Èkìtì, Upper Ọ̀ṣun, Ẹ̀gbá, Yéwá, Àwórì, Okun, Ìbàràpá, and Ìlàjẹ́, did not have any significant servile population to tap into as a source of labor and wives. Until the 1820s, the commodification of wifely status and decline in the general status of women were not as prevalent and precipitous in those smaller non-hegemonic polities as in the metropolises of the hegemonic states and hotbeds of merchant-capital revolution, including Ọ̀yọ́, Ìjẹ̀bú-Òde, and Iléṣà. This is most evident among the Èkìtì principalities dotting the rugged terrain of the central Yorùbá country and among the various Yorùbá groups of the southern Yéwá-Ògùn frontiers.

The continued recognition of female power as the pillar of Èkìtì society was exemplified in the Ẹpa festival. Although, as discussed in chapter 5, the militaristic ethos of the post-Classical period was incorporated into this ancient tradition, Ẹpa retained its original purpose as a matricentric festival for community regeneration. The Èkìtì area did not escape the general impact of merchant capital and the regional hegemonic powers on the decline in the influence of matricentric power. However, the continued representation of female-authority-centered compositions by Èkìtì sculptors highlighted the persistence of the balance that their ancestors had established since the Formative period between the patricentric and

Figure 8.1. Ṣàngó staff (H. 59 cm)

matricentric spheres of authority.[49] The Gẹ̀lẹ̀dẹ́ festival among the Yéwá, Kétu, Ànàgó, and other Western Yorùbá peoples offers another example of an enduring tradition that recognized and celebrated female power and authority as the center of social reproduction and spiritual life. The Gẹ̀lẹ̀dẹ́ tradition has survived till today. The main purpose of its rituals, festivals, and ceremonies is to honor the Ìyá Ńlá, the Great Mother or the first woman, the primal source of fertility, who also controls the ultimate power of life and death over the community.[50] Since this power is latent in all women, according to the Yorùbá belief, the Gẹ̀lẹ̀dẹ́ masking tradition is a ceremony for placating the mystical power of women without whose benevolence the society cannot reproduce itself. As in the Ẹpa masking tradition, the maskers in Gẹ̀lẹ̀dẹ́ are men, "but they usually masquerade as women."[51] In both Ẹ̀pa and Gẹ̀lẹ̀dẹ́, therefore, we have an ancient female-centered festival that revered the potent power of women in social reproduction and community sustainability.[52]

In addition to the recognition and celebration of the importance of womanhood through Gẹ̀lẹ̀dẹ́, Ẹpa, and other matricentric festivals, titled women continued to be appointed to important executive and religious positions, including the hegemonic ones. In many instances, with the exception of the Ọ̀yọ́ metropolis where most female chieftains served the interest of the *aláàfin*, these titled female offices represented women's interests in the central government. This was a way of acknowledging the important roles of women in the economic life and social reproduction of the polity and upholding the principle of matricentric authority. In Oǹdó, for example, the institution and office of the female king known as the *lọ́bùn* survived through the Atlantic period (and into the present day) as a revered autonomous political office with two primary duties. First, she held and dispensed the power to invest a new male king (the *òṣémàwé*) with the authority to rule. Second, the *lọ́bùn* presided (and still does) over all the Oǹdó markets; served as the chief priestess of Ajé, the deity of wealth and commerce; and performed the rituals for opening new markets. Like the patricentric *òṣémàwé* dynasty, which ruled over Oǹdó kingdom as a whole, the office of *lọ́bùn* was hereditary; she had her own palace, and she presided over a hierarchy of female chiefs called *opójì*. Both oral and ritual traditions indicate that the *lọ́bùn* was the original king of the town before the male *òṣémàwé* (king of Oǹdó) displaced her.[53] The ascendance of this patricentric authority, as previously discussed in chapter 5, took place during the late sixteenth or early seventeenth century as part of the political reshuffling that the Yorùbá region as a whole experienced. The preservation of the *lọ́bùn* institution and its continued vitality in Oǹdó's political system indicates the high status of female-held political offices before the sixteenth century. Although the *lọ́bùn* institution lost significant political power during the Restoration period, this matricentric field nevertheless retained enormous political influence. The advent of the merchant-capital revolution strengthened the economic power of the *lọ́bùn* and members of her all-female administration, but it must be emphasized that the *lọ́bùn* and the *opójì* chieftains exercised their role as social males outside the wifely space.

Gendered Inequality, State, and Critics

Both in the metropolises and in the provinces, as well as in hegemonic and non-hegemonic states throughout the Yorùbá community of practice, the deep-time principles of gender duality and gender complementarity continued to hold sway as the basis for social order.[54] But these principles must not be mistaken for the equality of the material basis of gender relations. Thus, at the very time that the Yorùbá were firmly holding on to the belief in the "hidden powers (*àṣẹ*) of women" as the source of the social and moral order,[55] the patricentric authority was being strengthened over the control of the levers of political power, privilege, and wealth. The Atlantic age was indeed a period of contradictions. The same merchant-capital revolution that led to the general decline in wifely status also created opportunities for some women to accumulate wealth through their participation in the expanding market economy. And, as the dominant figures in the market sphere, women supplied most of the levies and taxes that the state exacted from all commercial transactions. Hence, the womenfolk not only bore the brunt of the work and social reproduction that sustained the merchant-capital revolution but also provided a significant portion of the revenue that supported the state. The glaring imbalance of power between the matricentric and patricentric spheres was even used by the Ọ̀yọ́ metropolis as an ideology to codify the relationship between it and its provinces. In this respect, the metropolis was configured as the husband of the tribute-paying wifely provinces. That is, the conquered and annexed territories under Ọ̀yọ́ were feminized or reduced, metaphorically speaking, to a subordinated wifely status under the husbandly control of the metropolis (chap. 5). The empire was therefore genderized based on the very same logic of power dynamics that were playing out in the domestic space between the husbandly patricians and their wives, at the state level between the *aláàfin* and the dependent palace officials, and in the larger society between the patricentric and matricentric spheres of authority. This articulation of gender inequality unleashed intense dialogue in the society between the Ọ̀yọ́ metropolis and its provinces and between the agents of the patricentric and matricentric spheres everywhere.

The *òrìṣà* pantheon, once again, gives us a great insight into how the agents on both sides of this spectrum of power commented on and reacted to this trend of institutionalized and gendered ideology of social inequality. On the imperial side, Ọ̀yọ́ used the imagery of the axe-wielding, hypermasculine Ṣàngó in its ritual field to articulate the hegemonic epistemology that represents the metropolis and its officials and citizens as the lord of the realm and husband of the feminized provinces (see chap. 5). In response, the priests and priestesses of the female-centered deities who dominated the ritual fields of the provinces mobilized the intellectual fervor of their respective patron deities to critique this overbearing gendered disparity and the exploitation and impoverishment of the provinces (in human and material terms) by the metropolis. Through their mythoi, these provincial deities became critics of the patricentric empire and its hegemonic practices. One of these counter-hegemonic *òrìṣà* critics of the patricentric order was Ọ̀ṣun. Rising from the local ritual field that originally developed in Early Òṣogbo and its immediate environs in the early seventeenth century, Ọ̀ṣun became a formidable pan-regional female-centered deity during the eighteenth century. The Ọ̀ṣun ritual field was, and still is, a woman's religious world in which the authority of the female priesthood ranked above that of the male priests (plate 8). Hers was a sphere of resilient female authority in the face of the increasing masculine authority of the state and *ilé*.

It is therefore not surprising that the school of Ọ̀ṣun was at the center of the gendered dialogue between the patricentric state and the matricentric domestic market, between the masculine metropolis and the feminized provinces, as well as between the male-dominated elite households and their numerically superior but subordinated female residents. Through the mythos of Ọ̀ṣun, the Yorùbá community of practice contested and critiqued the power that the state/political class had over the appropriation of profit and wealth from three sources: (1) the feminized domestic market; (2) women's reproductive and economic labor; and (3) feminized provinces. All of these were not compatible with the age-old principles of gendered duality, interdependency, and complementarity, one of the core pillars of Yorùbá sociology that goes back to the proto-Yoruboid era. The merchant capital revolution and the hegemonic state (e.g., Ọ̀yọ́ Empire) had unleashed a tension between the ways of being (ontology) and their theory of knowledge (epistemology). And this tension could not be masked, contained, or explicated within the existing body of the Ifá literary corpus (the Yorùbá book of knowledge) composed of sixteen books (*odù*). As it always happens in autonomous societies, the theory of knowledge must be revised from within so that it can be aligned with the new ways of being and the value system. Therefore, sometime in the seventeenth or early eighteenth century, the seventeenth book of Ifá was created, as an addendum to the existing corpus, to rationalize, explicate, and critique the widening gulf between the patricentric and matricentric poles. According to the book, Odù Ọ̀ṣẹ̀tura, at the beginning of time, Olódùmarè (the supreme being) created seventeen deities, sixteen men and one woman, and sent them to earth to create and govern human societies. The only woman among them was Ọ̀ṣun. When they arrived on earth, the male deities set about the task. But they did not consult with Ọ̀ṣun in their deliberations, contrary to the instructions of Olódùmarè. However, these sixteen deities soon realized that in spite of their efforts to maintain peace and well-being on earth, there was disorder. Famine, war, and barrenness were common. Nothing was working as they expected. These male deities then returned to Olódùmarè to seek an explanation for their problem.

> Olódùmarè greeted them
> And asked of their seventeenth person.
> Olódùmarè asked them "Why
> Don't you . . . consult with her?"
> They replied, "It was because
> She was only a female among us."
> Olódùmarè said, "No, it should not be so!
> Ọ̀ṣun is a manly woman."[56]

Olódùmarè then commanded them to immediately return to the world and bring Ọ̀ṣun to their fold and take her contributions into consideration. This time, the sixteen male deities complied with the order of Olódùmarè. They apologized to Ọ̀ṣun for their oversight and male chauvinism and promised her a better status and more participation in governance. Before Ọ̀ṣun would accept their apologies and entreaties, she demanded that she must become part of all the initiation rituals they perform for men from which she had been excluded. She also asked them to teach her the knowledge of divination (ways of knowing). Not only that, but she wanted every woman who was powerful like her to be initiated into the various knowledge fields that had been closed to women.[57] All the male *òrìṣà* complied. From then on, solutions were found to the world's problems. Social order prevailed. There were bountiful harvests, prosperity, peace, and fertility. Because of the attentiveness of the male deities to Ọ̀ṣun's interests and needs, she rewarded them with success and bestowed wealth on the society in the form of children (biological reproduction); cloth, beads, brass, and cowries (imported Atlantic merchant capital); and dyestuff and woven cloth (local products and export commodities). The following panegyric celebrates Ọ̀ṣun's manly power, matricentric authority, benevolence, and wealth:

> Most powerful woman who can burn a person
> Ọ̀ṣun don't let the world dance evil on my head
> Curing without fee, she gives the healing, honeyed water to the child
> Rich as she is, she speaks sweetly to the multitude
> She has bought all the secrets of copper.
> Here she comes dancing, making her bracelets tinkle like the forest brook
> She is dancing in the depths of underwater riches
> My mother has hollowed out something in the sand,
>   hollowed out something in the sand.
> Crowned woman is very rare
> Elegant in the way she handles money

Ọ̀ṣun, master of the depths of wealth
Owner of innumerable parrot feathers . . .
Water murmuring over stones is Ọ̀ṣun dancing with her jewels of brass,
dancing with her tinkling rings of brass
Only the children of Ọ̀ṣun have such copper bracelets on their arms.[58]

The above narrative and the verse that follows are the core elements of Odù Ọ̀ṣẹ̀tura. They constitute a counter-discourse to the rising power of the patricentric authority, to emphasize the importance of women in social, political, and economic affairs. The *odù* does not only preach respect and honor for women; it is also a womanist discourse that articulates the transformative agency of women as courageous and willful leaders with the power to make things happen on their own terms. It is an archetype of female power in Yorùbá conception of gendered duality. The Atlantic-age provenance of the above verse and of the Odù Ọ̀ṣẹ̀tura is suggested by the phrase "underwater riches," a reference to the Atlantic Ocean as the source of merchant-capital wealth, and the mention of "money" in the verse denotes cowrie shells. Likewise, the "rings of brass" and "copper bracelets" that Ọ̀ṣun used to decorate her body were part of the Atlantic merchant capital coming to the mainland from the coast.[59] Therefore, the seventeenth *odù* developed in response to the changes in the political economy and the reconfiguration of social order, including the transformations in gender relations.

There is also something insightful about the numerology of Ọ̀ṣun and Odù Ọ̀ṣẹ̀tura. Whereas the *odù* is the seventeenth book of Ifá," Ọ̀sun is the seventeenth principal deity in the Yorùbá pantheon. And both the deity and the *odù* are devoted primarily to female issues, especially the rights and upliftment of women. The number seventeen is more than an addendum to the numerologically significant sixteen in Yorùbá cosmology and knowledge system (see chap. 3). Seventeen is a counter-hegemonic numerological symbol. It is disruptive to the orderliness, wholesomeness, and status quo that sixteen represents in the Yorùbá mythoi. The recognition of Ọ̀ṣun as a principal deity destabilized that social order dominated by men and called for a different way of thinking about women. This was a corrective to the gendered marginalization that state hegemony and merchant capital brought into existence during the seventeenth century. The Odù Ọ̀ṣẹ̀tura was also an intellectual acknowledgment that the economic powers being acquired by women as traders made them a major source of revenue for the hegemonic state at the very same time that the decline in wifely status was cumulatively weakening the matricentric sphere of authority. Yet the matricentric sphere was crucial to the survival and sustenance of the state structures that were established by the male state-builders. The ability of the state, Houses, and households to reproduce themselves as corporate units depended on the labor and reproductive abilities of women.

There are two converging streams of ideas in the mythoi of Odù Ọ̀ṣẹ̀tura. One stream is a womanist agenda for the advancement of women's interests, with a commitment "to the survival and wholeness of an entire people, male and female."[60] The other stream represents Ọ̀ṣun as a "manly woman" and emphasizes that "manly women" (not "wifely women") deserve to know the secrets of divination and enjoy the same privileges as biological men. Here, class and wealth mediated gender in the integration of Ọ̀ṣun into the patricentric social space. This second stream seems to suggest that only women who were co-opted into the hegemonic states of the seventeenth and eighteenth centuries deserved to be listened to and appreciated. These manly women were the senior wives who co-ruled the households with their husbands, not the junior wives from indigent natal homes or those who were slave or captive wives. The manly women also included the daughters of elite and upper-class households, not the commoner households. They were also the independently rich women, not the poor women eking out a living as retail traders on the roadside. Like Ọ̀ṣun, the senior wives, priestesses, daughters of elite households, and independently rich women were the females who became social males while also keeping the privileges of their femininity and motherhood status.[61] These women contested the disadvantages of wifely status. Therefore, Odù Ọ̀ṣẹ̀tura was an intra-class dialogue.

The insertion of Ọ̀ṣun into the knowledge base of *ifá* through the creation of Odù Ọ̀ṣẹ̀tura was an effort to tamp down the growing gendered tension and contain the disruptiveness of merchant capital revolution to the ideology of gendered duality in Yorùbá worldview. The *odù* also provided an intellectual framework to critique the new configurations of patricentric and matricentric inequality created by the political economy of a male-centered merchant capitalism and hegemonic state, a global phenomenon during the seventeenth and eighteenth centuries.[62] By juxtaposing Ọ̀ṣun with an all-male *òrìṣà*, the mythoi of Odù Ọ̀ṣẹ̀tura articulated the resistance of a cross section of manly women to the doggedness of the male-dominated state institutions to appropriate the wealth generated in the matricentric market sphere, domestic production, and household reproduction, as well as in the feminized provinces. The major pan-Yorùbá deities representing these patricentric institutions were Ṣàngó, Ògún, Èṣù, and Ifá.[63] These deities were all agents of the state. However, Èṣù is the one most intimately linked to the appropriation of the profits generated in the female-centered commerce and feminized provinces through taxation, tolls, market levies, and different kinds of tribute extraction.

Èṣù is better known in the Yorùbá religious traditions as the intercessor between all the Òrìṣà and Olódùmarè, as the go-between among the different Òrìṣà, and as the link between them and their devotees.[64] However, he was also an instrument of governance used by the state to collect taxes and tolls from all commercial arenas (e.g., markets) and political spaces (e.g., turnpikes and city gates) in Ọ̀yọ́ Empire. Therefore, he became especially dedicated to Ṣàngó, the royal and patron deity of Ọ̀yọ́.[65] Here, the deity of the crossroads, indeterminacy, and liminal spaces was mobilized to serve as the intermediary between the patricentric statesmen and the matricentric market women, and between the metropolis and the tributary provinces. Therefore, in quotidian life, Èṣù lived in such liminal spaces as the market, town/city gates, toll/customs houses, and crossroads. These were "paradigmatic sites of anonymous and ill-defined interaction among people," where the state machinery was most visible for managing "market-borne riches" and the flow of people.[66] Variously referred to as the "lord of the market" and "father of witchcraft," Èṣù sanctioned the power and authority of the state to exact tolls from arenas of intense wealth-generating activities that women dominated.[67] His leisurely life was embodied by the toll collectors, such as the *ìlàrí* in the Ọ̀yọ́ Empire, who sat around all day at the entrances of city gates and customs houses, waiting for passers-by to harass and collect tolls from. Hence, Èṣù is saluted as:

Láàlú
Ògiri ò kò
Ajímu tábà oògùn.

Laalu
The person who occupies the empty spaces between walls [i.e., the city gates]
He who wakes up and spends the whole day smoking powerful tobacco.[68]

This salutation acknowledges Èṣù and his men as the ones who guarded the city gates, manned the turnpikes, and collected tolls and taxes in the market.

Èṣù is one of the oldest deities in the Yorùbá pantheon, having originated during the Classical period, if not earlier. Representing unambiguous male energy, his cultural biography was revised during the seventeenth and eighteenth centuries to serve the authority of the patricentric state in the female-dominated market space. The masculine whirlwind dancing style of Èṣù, and his energetic, rapid, forceful tempo, is similar to that of Ṣàngó and Ògún—the empire builders—whose interests Èṣù served and supported during the Atlantic period.[69] This contrasts with the slow, graceful, swaying, and shuffling feminine dance of Ọ̀ṣun and Yemọja. Èṣù's liminality is not only evident in the spaces he occupied—the market and crossroads—but also in the officials who manifested his authority as the agents of the state. Just as these officials had no loyalty to familial networks and were devoted only to the state, Èṣù also was not affiliated with any descent group. He was everywhere, and in every home—the first to be seen before all the other *òrìṣà* were seen. This unique character of the deity has prompted Eva Krapf-Askari to submit that Èṣù "symbolize[s] all that is impersonal, superficial, transitory and segmental" and that Èṣù is "the most recognizably 'urban' of all Yorùbá divinities."[70] And, I may add, he is the most transactional of all the deities in the Yorùbá pantheon. The panegyric of Èṣù, "master of the marketplace, one who buys without paying, and who causes nothing to be bought or sold at the market"; his legendary phallic symbol (the punishing club known as *Ọ̀gọ Ẹlẹ́gbàrá*); and his electrifying dance recall the strong, impatient, implacable, and ruthless gatekeepers and other royal messengers who were usually the devotees of Èṣù in the Ọ̀yọ́ Empire. These were usually men of servile background who lacked any filial relationship with any *ilé* and instead belonged to the extra-House of the palace. These men, known as *ìlàrí* in Ọ̀yọ́ Empire, were often incorrigibly mean-spirited. Nineteenth-century sources, reflecting the sentiments of the time, describe them as "worthless characters," of "low social status," and as "ex-convicts."[71] All of these labels demonstrate societal spitefulness toward these male agents of the state who presided over the market, city gates, and crossroads, collecting taxes from traders, tolls from caravansaries, and levies from travelers. Although the face of the toll collector was that of the ruthless, impersonal, low-ranking man, the toll system was, indeed, controlled by the powerful chieftains. They recruited the meanest and toughest officials to staff the city gates, customs houses, and market spaces so they could receive the funds needed to run the state.

In Yorùbá mythoi, Èṣù is the son of Ọ̀ṣun and Ifá, and the very name Ọ̀ṣẹ̀tura, the seventeenth *odù* (book) of *ifá*, is a cognomen of Èṣù. And it was Ọ̀ṣun, the mother, who granted Èṣù the *àṣẹ* (power and legitimacy) to control the market and all the crossroads where he collected taxes and tolls.[72] In other words, Èṣù (agent of the state) derives his power from the market women (Ọ̀ṣun)—the tax- and the toll-paying majority—on whom the state depended for a part of its revenue.[73] By tracing the source of the power and legitimacy of Èṣù to Ọ̀ṣun, the Ọ̀ṣun/Ọ̀ṣẹ̀tura/Èṣù mythos attempted to narrow the widening gulf between the patricentric state and matricentric market and instead emphasized the complementarity of gendered duality. This explains why Èṣù's two-piece dancing wands are of female and male characters (fig. 8.2). Through this iconography, there is the acknowledgement that the patricentric sphere, in which both men and women were present, controlled the levers of power, but the patricentric

Figure 8.2. Èṣù staffs (*left*, H. 35.5 cm; *right*, H. 35 cm)

state depended on the matricentric sphere for labor, biological reproduction, and a significant portion of the state revenue.

Widening Gaps in the Metropolitan-Provincial Divide

The Yorùbá world came under the control of a few hegemonic states during the Atlantic age. These militarized polities increasingly depended on their conquered territories for the workforce, finance, and other resources needed to support their growing administration and opulence in the capital. The biggest of these Yorùbá states, Ọ̀yọ́, used an unprecedented number of full-time personnel to manage its affairs. The empire's bureaucracy was staffed by professionals whose labor was totally withdrawn from direct production, whether in agriculture or in manufacturing.

Numbering in the thousands, the bureaucracy supporting this political juggernaut had to be fed and clothed through the revenues coming in as taxes, levies, and tributes. Sourcing this revenue was a burden for households and *ilé* on the middle and lower rungs of the socioeconomic ladder, both in the metropolis and in the provinces. And by the third quarter of the eighteenth century, it became increasingly harder for the provinces to balance the needs of their members with the unrelenting demands of the metropolis.

In Ọ̀yọ́-Ilé and other capitals throughout the region, those from the low and middle socioeconomic strata faced several levies, such as tolls and market taxes, in contrast to those in the upper echelon of the society. The latter controlled a larger and cheaper labor pool but also had privileged access to the market and were mostly exempted from tolls or levies (since the political and military chieftains controlled the turnpikes). Therefore, those in the upper strata had huge advantages, in terms of lower production costs and higher profits, over the members of the lower and middle classes. Meanwhile, the tributary provinces faced two main types of levies: those paid directly to the local political unit (in the form of tolls and market-based taxes) and the levies contributed by each *ilé* and other social groups to the annual tributes sent to the capital of the hegemonic state. In the case of Ọ̀yọ́, a substantial part of these tributes had to be paid in monetary form, thereby forcing the majority of the population in the provinces to engage in the market economy. However, the transfer of human capital to the metropolis also accounted for a large part of these tributes. Some of the men and women who were sent to the metropolis as tributes were retained there as sources of domestic labor and a myriad other state services, but many were also sent to the coast and traded for merchant capital. As everyday life revolved around the political machinery of the hegemonic state with its never-ending demands for military service, corvée, taxation, tributes, and tolls, not to talk of random extortions by the agents of the state, the ability of the *ilé* and provincial towns and villages to reproduce themselves was drastically curtailed across most of the Yorùbá region.

The demands of the few metropolises on the labor and economic production of their tributary provinces forced the latter to part with some of their material wealth and prime human resources, especially adolescents and young adults. This created tension and conflict within the tributary communities and between them and the metropolis. In Iléṣà, for example, one of its seventeenth-century kings, Olúodò, is said to have built the defensive walls of the city "with the reluctant help" of Èkìtì potentates.[74] The "reluctant help" mentioned here is a euphemism for the tributary relationships between Iléṣà and many of its Èkìtì provinces. And this narrative is an acknowledgment that the Èkìtì rulers had to part with their valuable male population to secure the walls of the hegemonic capital, Iléṣà.[75] The pressure that the hegemonic state's demands exerted on the labor and economic proceeds of the provinces and their households weakened the integrity of the leadership of those tributary towns and villages and their ability to protect their members. Likewise, the emphasis of the market economy on individualized, rather than familial, pathway to material accumulation and self-realization weakened the corporate integrity of the *ilé* as the primary unit of production. These had the effect of breaking the *ilé* or tributary towns/villages apart, especially as young men and women dispersed across the region to escape the draconian exactions of labor and tributes by the metropolises.[76]

In response to these challenges, many of the tributary communities within the Ọ̀yọ́ Empire, especially in the Ẹ̀gbá and Yéwá areas, turned to the Ògbóni institution for protection and as a source of resistance against their exploitation. Despite the enormous strain in the relationships between the patricentric and matricentric poles brought on by the merchant-capital revolution and the hegemonic states, the Ògbóni institution continued to extol the virtues of unity, complementarity, balance, equivalence, and interdependency between the two. The Ògbóni institution had served as an important council of civic leaders in many parts of the Yorùbá community of practice for more than six hundred years before the advent of the Atlantic period (chap. 2).[77] By then, the institution was prevalent in small polities, where it served as an important arm of governance, mediating local political conflicts, deciding the most difficult judicial and criminal cases, and serving as a neutral, autonomous, and apolitical institution.[78] The relevance of the institution was accentuated in the seventeenth century as these small polities were being converted into the tributary provinces of the hegemonic states. This was especially the case in most Upper Ọ̀ṣun, Ìgbómìnà, Yéwá, and Ẹ̀gbá provinces of Ọ̀yọ́.[79]

In those small polities and tributary provinces where the challenges of self-reproduction were most dire and urgent as a result of imperial impositions, the Ògbóni stepped in to play a direct role, rather than an advisory one, in governance. The institution became the rallying point for these provincial towns and villages suffering from the burden of imperial demands for people, money, labor, and other resources, as well as the daily harassment and extortions of imperial agents. Its egalitarian model of membership recruitment and emphasis of communal cooperation between women and men for social sustenance and continuity in the face of Ọ̀yọ́ imperial impositions made the Ògbóni into a moral compass for those provincial communities.[80] As an institution that operated mostly in secrecy (outside the public purview), it became the main underground political bulwark among the tributary Ẹ̀gbá and Yéwá polities against the encroaching hegemonic power of Ọ̀yọ́. That is, the Ògbóni institution served as a pillar of resistance against imperial agents such as Prince Adémọ̀lá in Ìpókía and Onísàrẹ̀ (an *ìlàrí*) in Ìjànà (see chap. 7).

These small communities did not have the war booty, in people or materials, to use for augmenting their reproduction and labor productivity. In fact, they were the ones facing a deficit of people, labor, and materials as a result of the annual demands of the metropolitan areas for tributes. Moreover, the tributary provinces had to contend with living side by side with the outsiders, many of whom were the agents of their exploitation. These agents included the imperial administrators, tribute collectors, and soldiers. Tributary communities on major caravansary routes also attracted traders and other settlers from everywhere. In these frontier environments of immigrant communities, where population diversity and unequal power relations were in open display, the Ògbóni institution promoted the ethos of indigeneity in order to defend the interest of the local population and enhance their ability to self-reproduce. Therefore, the emphasis was on recruiting only the natives—the sons and daughters of the land (*ilẹ̀*)—into the Ògbóni council.

The feminine principle was crucial to achieving the aspirations of these local communities for social reproduction and continuity. Hence, Erelú, the only female among the four most senior titled officials of Ògbóni, has the praise-name "Ìyá Àbíyè," (the mother whose children will live on to old age).[81] This cognomen identifies not only Erelú but also all the female members of Ògbóni as good mothers and midwives who also possessed the spiritual power to multiply the community with healthy children. The members of Ògbóni call themselves *ọmọ ìyá* (children of the same mother) to emphasize the spirit of kinship and indigeneity, social cohesion, primordial unity, and the glue of matricentric ethos that binds them together. Economically and politically weakened by the demands of the empire, the tributary frontiers of Ọ̀yọ́ were reduced to emphasizing the biological reproductive role of women rather than the role of women in the social reproduction of *ilé*. Despite its commitment to the principle of male and female balance and provision of a space for female participation in community governance, however, the Ògbóni institution did not arrest the region-wide decline in matricentric authority. The provinces and small communities on the peripheries of the hegemonic states were not immune to the forces that widened the gaps between the patricentric and matricentric spheres across the region.

Conflation of Power, Wealth, and Class

Social class was intensely negotiated during the Atlantic age because institutional power and inherited status of nobility were in constant competition with individual achievement via commerce and militarism.

Moreover, although the market revolution created opportunities for individualized accumulation, political power and commercial wealth did not exist autonomously. Through the market, the political elite had to compete for the merchant capital needed to sustain their power. However, as we have previously seen, the elite had an advantageous position that guaranteed them success in comparison to those in the middling and lower strata. This put burdens on the merchants and traders who were not associated with power. Those generally sought to conceal their wealth to avoid the rapacious attention of the state. A contemporary observer in Benin City, for example, noted that the merchants "who have no share in government" preferred to keep a low profile and manage "their trade with utmost secrecy, out of fear of being represented as great traders to their governors."[82] Such men of commercial wealth exhibited modesty and civility toward the political class to avoid being dispossessed through heavy taxation and extortion. Power and wealth reinforced one another, and independent wealth that was not backed by power was precarious and unsustainable. Without political power, it was difficult to become wealthy or to maintain that wealth beyond a generation. Of all the Yorùbá polities during the Atlantic period, only in the Ìjẹ̀bú region did the organized merchant class mature enough to become a major autonomous branch of government. Known as the Ìpàm̀pá, this association of leading merchants not only served as the chamber of commerce but also became an integral part of the ruling body in Ìjẹ̀bú-Ode and other commercial towns in the area. With their wealth and direct access to merchant capital, through Badagry and Lagos ports, after 1730, the Ìpàm̀pá presided over all matters dealing with commerce and also served as the patrons and financiers of brigandage and war for the sole purpose of acquiring captives for the European slave ships. The ability that the Ìpàm̀pá had in waging war outside the state apparatus was unprecedented, and soon they would use their wealth and access to firearms and mercenaries to dominate political affairs in Ìjẹ̀bú-Òde and other parts of Ìjẹ̀bú-Rẹ́mọ area. The Ìpàm̀pá, with their laser-focused commitment to individual accumulation rather than communal preservation, would also play a decisive role in the events that unfolded in the Yorùbá world between 1790 and 1840. I will return to this in the next chapter.

Suffice to say that the conflation of institutional power and wealth had far-reaching implications in everyday social life. Most importantly, this conflation helped to institutionalize social inequality through the administration of the law, especially in how penalties were levied and remitted. With the advent of cowrie as the domestic currency and unit of pricing, it became possible to redeem guilt and penalty with a monetary payment for offenses ranging from infringement on the honor of citizens (e.g., adultery and rape) to capital crimes such as dismemberment, manslaughter, and murder. Those who could not afford this luxury of paying judicial penalties with money (cowries) could be killed and sacrificed to the deities, reduced to a state of servitude, banished to exile, or sold into slavery. In the coastal Ìjẹ̀bú region, for example, Adésùlú—a man of wealth, son of a former treasurer of Ẹ̀pẹ́, a great merchant in his own right, and a captain of war and brigandage—committed murder on two separate occasions within about six to eight years. Reputed for his "hot temper and a quick hand," Adésùlú ran into exile on each occasion. In the first incident, sometime between 1798 and 1802, the case against him was settled after he reportedly paid the aggrieved family the huge sum of four million cowries. He was able to return to his hometown in Ẹ̀pẹ́ afterward. However, a few years later, he committed the second capital offense and repeated the cycle of exile and payment of a fine. If he had been of poor or middle-class status, he would have been sacrificed to one of the deities or sold into slavery. Wealth, political network, and social class enabled him to escape the worst penalties on both occasions. He went on to marry at least five more wives after the first capital offence. That is, his wealth and prominence in society rose even higher after 1798.[83]

If the monetized economy helped the rich and the politically connected to avoid the harsh penalties for murderous transgressions, it placed a heavy burden on the common people, and it marked in sharp relief the social inequality in the society. The result was that society developed a new materialized theory of rights and privileges that was based on class. Given the centrality of political power to class identity, independently wealthy men and women sought to use their capital to finance access to power in order to protect their wealth and their most valuable asset—their household. However, while institutional power almost guaranteed access to wealth, it was more difficult to use independent wealth to access institutionalized power because wealth was competing with other poles of individual accomplishment—military service/honor and political clientship.[84] That is, power could not easily be bought with money, but power could more easily be used to accumulate wealth. As a result, the conflation of power, wealth, and social rank not only widened social inequalities but also limited the ability of members of the middle class and the poor to climb the social ladder.

There were also obstacles to the intergenerational transfer of wealth. The death tax imposed on the rich, especially those with weak networks of political power or weak access to the privileges of government, was one way by which the state could take much of the liquid assets of the deceased and therefore deny the survivors of any substantial inheritance.[85] The elaborate funeral ceremonies for the wealthy created another way by which the movable and consumable assets of a household or *ilé* could be exhausted. For example, unlike the simple burial for those in the middle and lower social strata, such as that of Alágbẹ̀dẹ discussed in chapter 7, the elite and the wealthy enjoyed elaborate and expensive burial. As in life, their expired bodies were bedecked with fine and voluminous clothing and jewelry according to their wealth."[86] The corpses of the wealthy might be covered by as many as twenty large pieces of costly cloth, and their graves were lined with large pieces of fine imported cloth as well as "plenty of money" (cowries). Whereas the funeral ceremony of a middle-class individual lasted for about three to four days, those of the elite and the rich could take up to eight days, during which guests were elaborately feasted and enjoyed carnival-like parades accompanied by music and dancing through the town or city.[87] Other than the diversity and range of objects that became part of the grave goods during the Atlantic period, the mortuary culture and its meaning did not change from the Classical period. The ultimate goal of the living remained the quest to become an ancestor. The door of this goal was closed, however, to the increasing number of people in bondage or whose existence depended on the personality of others and who could not head their own household. Included in this group were administrators who entered the state bureaucracy as slaves. These men and women served the state as members of the palace, a complex organization that was based not on blood relations but on class. There were also those who were dispossessed of their *ilé* by the hegemonic state expansion and relocated to capital as war captives or part of the annual tributes. And there were others pushed to the bottom of the stiffening stratification through debt and peonage, a product of the merchant-capital revolution. As the bandwidth of marginalization expanded, it became increasingly difficult and impossible for a very large number of people, in the Ọ̀yọ́ Empire especially, to become ancestors and therefore to achieve immortality and realize their full potential as divine beings. Included in this group were the vast number of eunuchs, slaves, and slave wives across the empire and in other parts of the Yorùbá world.

No doubt, prospects were good for those in the upper social classes to use their inherited status and its associated social networks, as well as factors of production—people/labor, tools/weaponry, and land assets—as resources to accumulate wealth. However, they were also faced with the challenges of intergenerational social mobility. With the tendency to expend potential inheritance in expensive mortuary rituals and postmortem rites, many children of the junior wives in the elite *ilé* were forced to start the process of wealth accumulation from scratch. In large polygynous and alpha households, most of the sons often inherited the social status and fame of their father but did not inherit his material wealth. Such sons, according to an early nineteenth-century observer, were therefore left to their "own sagacity and exertions to procure wealth, which can seldom be obtained without rapine, enslavement, and bloodshed."[88] This obstacle to the intergenerational transfer of wealth expanded the ranks of the deprived citizens and left those born into the Houses of privilege and wealth, and quite a large number of them, with status in name only. They lacked the corresponding material resources to live up to their socioeconomic status, and most such men never built wealth and status comparable to what their fathers had attained.

Summing Up

The expansion in domestic slavery, in direct proportion to the increase in the Atlantic slave exports from the Bight of Benin, gave the political elite and some members of the middle class the advantage to increase their production and material accumulation at the expense of the majority who did not have access to slave labor. The wealth that the upper-class households accumulated was used to finance the procurement of more labor—wives, children, slaves, and other dependents and clients. This had the multiplier effect of greater wealth and power accumulation for the upper class. In contrast, the unrelenting state demands for resources—taxes, tributes, and labor—as well as extortion and unfair trade practices by the political elite and their agents limited the opportunities for the middling and lower classes. Throughout the eighteenth century, the concentration of wealth and power increased in the hands of the few, and new forms of social hierarchy developed. But as those few became wealthier, the number of enslaved men and women also increased in the metropolitan area of Ọ̀yọ́. By 1790, the boundaries of those hierarchies had hardened and become impermeable for the majority of people below. Individual mobility across social ranks became increasingly difficult, and the gulf of the divide, between the metropolis of Ọ̀yọ́ and its provinces, for example, significantly widened. Communication across social boundaries was also becoming almost impossible to achieve.

The ascendance of hegemonic states and the advent of the commercial revolution during the seventeenth and eighteenth centuries combined to significantly increase the value of male-centered authority and create new forms of class stratification. These not only weakened the influence and authority of the matricentric sphere but also destabilized the *ilé* as the primary unit of self-reproduction. The women who powered the engine of Atlantic Yorùbá's economy worked in a juxtaposed space occupied by slave wives, tributary wives, pawned wives, free junior wives, senior wives, and *ilémosú* daughters. These were female groups with different interests. The interactions among them, and between them and the patriarchs of the household, revealed the conflicting and changing notions of women as pillars of social reproduction, in biological, economic, and community terms. The recruitment of an unprecedented number of slaves and captives into wifehood, commodification of marriage, and the state appropriation of the market wealth generated by women, through tolls and taxes, weakened matricentric authority in general. The commodification of products such as manufactured cloth, which women had used for exercising social authority before 1630, weakened kin ties across gender and removed one instrument of interdependency between the patricentric and matricentric spheres. The result is that the representation of the two as opposing and unequal, rather than complementary and coequal, intensified in the seventeenth through the nineteenth centuries.

The Òrìṣà and their cultural biographies simultaneously mask and reveal these social changes and the underlying material relations of production and power. The Yorùbá ritual field that evolved during the seventeenth and eighteenth centuries articulated and reflected this tension between the male-dominated state structures and the female economic and reproductive powers. The cultural biographies of the male deities such as Ṣàngó, Ògún, and Èṣù and those of the female—Ọ̀ṣun and Yemọja, especially—provide us with insights into the impacts of merchant capital and its political economy on changes in gender, labor, and sociopolitical relations. The profits that women generated from their economic endeavors were significant parts of the resources that the political class used to finance the state and its projects of interclass social distinctions. As bearers of the next generation, these women also enabled the social reproduction of households and Houses as corporate entities. With the opportunity to recruit wives through slavery and tributary relationship, wifely status declined and so did matricentric authority. The female-centered cults of Ọ̀ṣun and Yemọja expressed their disaffection of this development and called out the rising gendered inequality, especially the rising profile of patricentric authority at the expense of matricentric power. Their critiques have been well preserved in the Òrìṣà mythoi, both in Atlantic Africa and the African Diaspora. Contemporary scholars have interpreted the round, voluptuous ritual pots of the Yoruba as representations of female power and "wifely resistance." Others see the ubiquitous iconographic birds surmounting the beaded crowns and ritual staffs of Yorùbá monarchs as references to the "mystical powers of women."[89] These interpretations of the Yorùbá visual imageries are spot on, showing the versatility of Yorùbá iconographies and visual metaphors for critical intercommunication. The ritual pots (vessels), the bird imagery, and the female kneeling figures (some with babies on their back) so prevalent in the corpus of Yorùbà art are important representations, but not the substance, of matricentric and the biological female power. The basis of that power during the Atlantic age was the women's domination of the marketplace and the huge remittances women made to the state on account of their economic activities, as well as their role in the biological reproduction of the state and corporate groups. They indeed carried the state and their households on their heads, in their wombs, and on their backs. Cumulatively, the market economy and the state gave women more obligations but with reduced power and influence. In contrast, they gave men more power and influence but with fewer obligations. The perennial social inequality that grew across the region between ca. 1630 and 1840 as a result of the penetration of merchant capitalism and the activities of the hegemonic states was similar in many respects to the situation in other world areas at the same period. There were far-reaching consequences that crystalized in the early nineteenth century, the topic for the next chapter.

Notes

1. Lovejoy, *Transformations in Slavery*. Also see Law, *Slave Coast*; Manning, *Slavery, Colonialism*.
2. Lovejoy, "Impact," 382; Eltis, *Rise of African Slavery*, 85–113.
3. I use the term *middle class* here to refer to the people and households who were free and had the means to own property of any type and pursue the goals of social mobility without any legal inhibition. Below such individuals and households were indigent individuals and families who did not have the means to acquire property beyond subsistence and basic needs, although such people were also involved in market economy. And below them were the enslaved. Above the middle class was the elite who controlled political, military, and economic power.
4. These cloths included not only the fabric made of cotton but also the expensive raffia fiber cloth known as *ọ̀dún*. The use of *ọ̀dún* fabric is now restricted to sacred and ritual performances, especially among the Èkìtì and Okun (Famule, "Art and Spirituality").
5. Denzer, "Yoruba Women," 3.
6. Also, neither husband nor wife could inherit the other's wealth. Instead, the deceased's children and brothers inherited assets and liabilities.
7. In the Ọ̀yọ́ Empire, these "wives" of the king—social and conjugal—numbered in the hundreds for provincial governors and monarchs, and in the thousands for the *aláàfin*. Clapperton, for example, estimated that the king of the provincial city of Saki had as many as two thousand wives in 1826. The same year, Aláàfin Májǒtú admitted that he did not know the number of his wives but speculated that if his wives were to stand shoulder to shoulder they would stretch from Ọ̀yọ́ to Ìjànà, a distance of about 300 km. Clapperton, *Journal of a Second Expedition*, 25, 46.
8. See Akinjogbin, *Dahomey*; Bay, *Wives of the Leopard*; Monroe, *Precolonial State*.
9. Norris, *Memoirs*, 142.
10. Many of the widows at Jadoo, an Ọ̀yọ́ provincial town in the Yéwá-Ògùn frontier, employed "their time and earn their livelihood by 'spinning and weaving'" (Hallett, *Niger Journal*, 71). The spindle whorls recovered from the excavation of the governor's house in Ẹdẹ-Ilé and the residences

associated with the palace in Ọ̀yọ́-Ilé and other parts of the metropolitan area also demonstrate the ubiquity of spinning in the domestic contexts. Ogundiran, "Material Life and Domestic Economy"; Ogundiran, Preliminary Report of the First Season; Ogundiran, Preliminary Report of the Second Season; Ogundiran, Preliminary Report of the Third Season.

11. The work of these "wives" in cloth production and other endeavors complemented the roles that sons and male slaves played in trading for the *aláàfin* in capital-intensive "commodities" such as slaves, horses, and Atlantic merchant capital in Ògòdò, Àjàṣẹ́, Badagry, and Ouidah, among others.

12. Clapperton, *Journal of a Second Expedition*, 21.

13. Hallett, *Niger Journal*, 71.

14. Lander, *Records of Captain Clapperton's Last Expedition*, 2:197.

15. In 1826, Clapperton listed the price of a horse in Ọ̀yọ́-Ilé at 80,000–100,000 cowries, and that of a prime slave at 40,000–60,000. In most cavalry societies with slavery institutions, the exchange value of a fit horse had historically been much higher than that of a prime adult (male or female). In the Senegambia region of West Africa, a small savanna pony could generally be exchanged for one slave, whereas the much bigger and taller Barbary horses from across the Sahara exchanged for as many as ten to fifteen slaves, and sometimes more (Collins and Burns, *History*, 236).

16. Law, *Horse in West African History*, 75.

17. Many of these slaves came from the Central Sudan. At Ìjànà in 1827, Hugh Clapperton saw an enslaved Bornu dwarf, about thirty years old, employed in a household of weavers and dyers (Bruce-Lockhart and Lovejoy, *Hugh Clapperton*, 120). There was also Ali Eisami from the Bornu Empire, born in the late 1780s, captured by Fulani kidnappers in late 1812, sold to Hausa traders, and moved on to Borgu before being brought to the Ọ̀yọ́ metropolitan area ca. 1813, where he was bought and used as a household slave. See Smith, Last, and Gubio, "Ali Eisami."

18. O'Hear, *Power Relations*, 26.

19. O'Hear, 29. See also Oroge, "Institution of Slavery."

20. Clarke, *Travels and Explorations*, 260.

21. Van Nyendael, "Description of Rio Formosa," 463.

22. Clapperton, *Journal of a Second Expedition*, 58.

23. Hallett, *Niger Journal*, 70.

24. A nickname of Ọ̀ṣun.

25. To own a horse stable was the ultimate mark of wealth and political power, but this was a near-exclusive elite male achievement.

26. The Atlantic Ocean.

27. Olupona, "Òrìsà Ọ̀ṣun," 46–47.

28. Kidnapped at the age of twelve in March 1821 by a detachment of brigands, Àjàyí was put on a Brazilian slave ship on the way to Brazil in April 1822. He was rescued by the British antislavery squadron and relocated to Sierra Leone. In July 1864, he was consecrated the first African bishop of the Anglican Church, covering the countries of Western Africa beyond the Queen of England's dominions.

29. This means "the mama who lives in Ìtokò."

30. Ajayi, "Samuel Ajayi Crowther," 306–7.

31. Their nineteenth-century progeny, such as Madam Tinúbú of Abẹ́òkúta and Lagos (1805–87) and Madam Ẹfúnṣetán Aníwúrà of Ìbàdàn

(ca. 1810s–1874), became prominent merchants and political figures in the 1840s, and they attested that they learned the craft of trading from their mothers or grandmothers, who only had very modest means. See Ogunleye, "Male-Centric Modification of History"; Yemitan, *Madame Tinubu*.

32. The *ilémosú* included not only the female divorcées who returned to their natal homes but also women who never married or those who never formalized divorce but chose to return to their natal homes.

33. Ojo, "Beyond Diversity," 361.

34. This is based on the estimates provided for the late nineteenth century by Olatunji Ojo ("Beyond Diversity," 359). The pattern is likely similar in the second half of the long eighteenth century, given the similarities in the political economies of the two centuries. For the continuation of the class divide in the marriage age for men between ca. 1890 and 1910, see Hopkins, "Report on the Yorùbá"; NAI, Èkìtì Div4/4, Civil Record Book, July 14, 1903.

35. Ojo, "Beyond Diversity," 361. For a documented case, see CMS, CA2/098/10, Young journal, June 27, 1875. This concubinage relationship, it must be emphasized, was tolerated only within the household or the House, not with anyone outside the House. For similar scenarios that developed in West Africa and other world areas during the long seventeenth and eighteenth centuries, see Allman, "Adultery and the State"; Hämäläinen, *Comanche Empire* (especially chap. 6).

36. Oroge, "Institution of Slavery."

37. Falola and Lovejoy, *Pawnship in Africa*, 6.

38. My argument here is based on the late nineteenth-century practices, which I would argue applied to the scenario during the eighteenth century. See Byfield, "Women, Marriage, Divorce."

39. Bruce-Lockhart and Lovejoy, *Hugh Clapperton*, 156.

40. Lloyd, "Osifekunde," 258.

41. Lloyd, 284.

42. If the woman remarried, the new husband was required to refund the bride price or pay a penalty to the previous husband.

43. Ellis, *Yoruba-Speaking Peoples*, 187.

44. Bruce-Lockhart and Lovejoy, *Hugh Clapperton*, 153. For comparative insights relating to marriage practices across social classes in eighteenth-century Dahomey, see Edna Bay's *Wives of the Leopard*. Contemporary European observers generally showed a poor understanding of the circumstances of these independent women and mistakenly called them prostitutes because of the autonomy they enjoyed in developing sexual relationship with any consenting man. It is for this category of women that this panegyric was composed in salutation of their sexual freedom and autonomy:

> *Ṣọ̀kí kò dó t'àná*
> *Okó ọjọ́ kejì kíkan ní ǹkan*
> "Ṣọ̀kí (a name) does not keep the same lover every day
> The penis of yesterday always turns sour the day after"

45. Oyèrónkẹ́ Oyěwùmí (*Invention of Women*) has already eloquently argued this case.

46. See Tishken et al., *Sàngó*; Matory, *Sex and the Empire*.

47. These included the crown prince; three princes with hereditary titles, Magàjí Ìyàjìn, Agúnpópó, and Olusami; two eunuchs who were also high-ranking palace officials, Iba Òsì Ẹ̀fà (the king's chamberlain and political adviser, and supervisor of the king's family) and Olókùnẹṣin (the master of the king's horse stables); and the following female palace officials: Ìyá Ọba (the king's "official mother"), Ìyá Nàsó, Iyalagbon (the crown prince's mother), Ìyá Ilé Imọlẹ̀ (high priestess of Ṣàngó), Olorun-ku-mefun, Ìyámọ̀nàrí, Ìyá Ilé Orí, and Ààrẹ Orí Ìtẹ́ (the chief wife in the king's harem). These officials were the ones closest to the king, and just as his life and security depended on them, the requirement that they commit suicide after the king's death ensured that they had the self-interest to cooperate to preserve the life of the king for as long as they could (see Johnson, *History*, 54–57).

48. Hallett, *Niger Journal*, 64.

49. The centrality of the matricentric worldview is echoed in some of the sculptures of Ọlọ́wẹ̀ of Ìsẹ́, an Èkìtì wood-carver during the early twentieth century (Walker, *Ọlọ́wẹ̀ of Ìsẹ̀*). In the non-dynastic Okun area of northeastern Yorùbá, there are instances of historical heroines such as Ìyéyedò of Òrò-Ìffẹ̀ serving as the focus of communal festival, apart from the fact that female deities were predominant in Okun and that some of the most conspicuous hills there were identified as female. Pemberton and Afọlayan, *Yoruba Sacred Kingship*, 45.

50. Washington, *Our Mothers*.

51. Lawal, "New Light on Gelede," 66.

52. For more details on the Gẹ̀lẹ̀dẹ́ festival and its masking traditions as well as its gendered roles in social reproduction, see Drewal and Drewal, *Gẹlẹdẹ*; Lawal, *Gẹ̀lẹ̀dé Spectacle*; Washington, *Our Mothers*.

53. Olupona, *Kingship, Religion, and Rituals*, 37, 65.

54. For example, the practice of cognatic descent that had been prevalent since the foundation of the Yorùbá community of practice continued to hold sway in the face of the general decline in matricentric authority during the Atlantic period. Peter Lloyd, in "Agnatic and Cognatic Descent," suggested that cognatic descent was more noticeable in the southern part of the region than in the Ọ̀yọ́ spheres of influence, but this regional dichotomy may have been more apparent than real. For we know that succession to as high a political office as *aláàfin* could be contested from both the female and male line. Àfọ̀njá, for example, laid claim to the throne of Ọ̀yọ́, although only his maternal line had royal blood. There were many people in the metropolis and core provinces of the empire who sympathized with his ambition. For more details on the ethnography of Yorùbá kinship and descent, see Bascom, *Yoruba*; Schwab, "Kinship and Lineage."

55. Pemberton and Afọlayan, *Yoruba Sacred Kingship*, 45.

56. Ogungbile, "Eerindinlogun," 193.

57. Badejo, *Ọ̀ṣun Seegesi*, 73.

58. Thompson, *Face of the Gods*, 208–9.

59. One such copper-alloy bracelet was excavated in Ọ̀ṣun-Òṣogbo Grove, the birthplace of the deity and her most sacred site. Ogundiran, "Making of an Internal Frontier," 16.

60. Walker, *In Search*, xii.

61. The many avatars of Ọ̀ṣun indicate the complex personality of the deity, showing that she is an empowering and encompassing Yorùbá goddess:

feminine and beautiful, but also a warrior and a savvy businesswoman—fertile, motherly, hardworking, and wealthy. Hence, we have Abalu, the oldest and most matronly Ọ̀ṣun; the coquettish Ọ̀ṣun Jùmu and Ọ̀ṣun Mẹ́rin; the very feminine Ọ̀ṣun Àbòtó; and the youngest and most martial, Ọ̀ṣun Ọpara. There are also the old and quarrelsome Yèyé Ọ̀gà, the extremely feisty Yèyé Kare, and the bellicose Yèyé Òkè and Yèyé Onira. Ọ̀ṣun Ajagùrá, Yèyé Olókè, and Yèyé Ìpọ̀ndá are other warrior manifestations of Ọ̀ṣun (Thompson, *Face of the Gods*, 207).

62. For example, see Costa, *Brazilian Empire*; Hämäläinen, *Comanche Empire*; Mies, *Patriarchy and Accumulation.*

63. There were others, such as Obòkun of Iléṣà, but these were restricted to particular city-states.

64. Falola, *Èsù.*

65. Pemberton, "Eshu-Elegba," 22.

66. Matory, *Sex and the Empire*, 205.

67. Abraham, *Dictionary*, 167.

68. Láàlú is a cognomen of Èṣù. It means the person who traverses multiple spaces, the connector of liminal spaces. Oral interview, Kàsálí Àkàngbé Ògún, Charlotte, NC, February 18, 2013.

69. Westcott, "Sculpture," 344.

70. Krapf-Askari, *Yoruba Towns*, 114.

71. Falola, "Yoruba Toll System," 72.

72. In Yorùba myth-history, Ọ̀ṣẹ̀tura is the son of Ọ̀ṣun and Ifá. Oral interview, Kàsálí Àkàngbé Ògún, Charlotte, NC, February 18, 2013.

73. Pemberton, "Eshu-Elegba," 68.

74. Peel, *Ijeshas and Nigerians*, 24.

75. See Abiọla, Babafẹmi, and Ataiyero, *Iwe Itan Ijẹṣa*, especially chap. 12.

76. Chief Ìbílọlá Omilẹ̀yẹ, Yèyé Ọ̀ṣun of Òṣogbo (June 25, 2003), mentioned that many migrants running away from the "draconian laws" of Ọ̀yọ́-Ilé and Iléṣà came to Òṣogbo (a frontier market town) early in the later's history, in the seventeenth and eighteenth centuries. According to her, most of them were young men and women attracted to Osogbo because of its commercial opportunities and a much more relaxed lifestyle.

77. An exception was the Ọ̀yọ́ metropolitan area, where Ògbóni was neither a significant presence nor a part of governance. See Atanda, "Yoruba Ogboni."

78. Fadipẹ, *Sociology of the Yoruba*, 243–47; Lawal, "À Yà Gbó," 39.

79. The disruption created in the local hierarchies of power by the merchant capital revolution also made the Ògbóni to play major roles in the governance of most Ìjẹ̀bú polities, although none was a province of Ọ̀yọ́. In the case of both the Ẹ̀gbá and Ìjẹ̀bú during the eighteenth century, the Ògbóni institution became the mediator between the merchant class and the political authorities. As a result, in Ìjẹ̀bú-Òde, the Ògbóni (or Òṣúgbó) served as one of the three major pillars of government, mediating between the powerful Ìpàm̀pá (chamber of commerce) on one hand and the civil authority of the king (Awújalẹ̀) and the traditional aristocrats (Ìlámùrẹ̀n) on the other. The Awújalẹ̀, Ìlámùrẹ̀n, and Ìpàm̀pá had representatives in the Ògbóni society. Ayandele, *Ijebu*, 6.

80. Drewal, Pemberton, and Abiodun, *Yoruba*, 130. Lawal, "À Yà Gbó," 38.

81. The three titles held by men were Olúwo, Apènà, and Olúrìn. Drewal, Pemberton, and Abiodun, *Yoruba*, 138.

82. Van Nyendael, "Description of Rio Formosa," 434.

83. Lloyd, "Osifekunde," 285. This is an exaggeration, for such an amount was sufficient to purchase up to 540 captives in the Bight of Benin in 1770 according to Hogendorn and Johnson, *Shell Money*, 111.

84. The most glaring exception to this rule was the Ìjẹ̀bú-Rẹ́mọ area, which had the most direct access to the coastal trade and whose merchants used their wealth to constitute themselves into a branch of government and also became war commanders of their respective states.

85. Ọsìnfẹ́kundé noted that the royal official in charge of taxation was a regular presence at funeral ceremonies among the Ìjẹ̀bú during the late eighteenth century, obviously to collect or finalize the collection of death tax. Lloyd, "Osifekunde," 262.

86. Lloyd, 262.

87. Curtin, "Joseph Wright," 328.

88. Hallett, *Niger Journal*, 66.

89. Matory, *Sex and the Empire*, 141; Drewal and Mason, *Beads, Body, and Soul*, 202. Also see Apter, *Black Critics*.

9

A House Divided

IKÚN Ń JỌ̀GẸ̀DẸ̀ Ó Ń rẹ̀dí, ikún ò mọ̀ pé oun tó dùn ní í pa ni: "The bush rodent exuberantly feeds on (stolen) banana, but it forgets that sweet things can lead to death." Considering the fundamentals of the Atlantic-age commercial revolution, it is not surprising that the slave/merchant-capital exchange that supported this revolution was not a sustainable economic endeavor. The losses and deficits that the Yorùbá and the other peoples of Atlantic Africa were incurring, in social, political, and economic terms, far outweighed the gains.[1] The cataclysmic breakdown of social order that resulted from the two-hundred-year exchange is the subject of this chapter. The breakdown was a long, drawn-out process lasting from 1790 to 1837, with consequences that reverberated until the end of the nineteenth century. There were many related sources and causes of the crisis. The dominant among these were the decline in Ọ̀yọ́'s export market share; inter-elite power struggles in the Ọ̀yọ́ metropolis and political instability in the empire; and rebellion of the underclass in the empire's metropolis and provinces as a result of the institutionalization of social inequality and the narrowed paths for social mobility. The increasing demand for enslaved labor in the Americas also created conflict and instability that eventually culminated in turbulence across the entire Yorùbá region. The reoccurring episodes of drought and famine between ca. 1810 and 1835 caused restlessness and social discontentment, and these added fuel to the raging fire of instability. The tumultuous storm that resulted from the collision of these different but overlapping factors sank the ship of the Ọ̀yọ́ Empire, caused the destruction of several thousands of polities, towns, and villages across the Yorùbá world, and permanently displaced millions of people. About four hundred thousand Yorùbá were shipped to the Americas at the peak of the turbulence, between 1817 and 1850.

Crisis of Power Politics in the Metropolis

I will start this complex story with the Ọ̀yọ́ metropolitan crisis. This was long in the making and had its immediate roots in the mid-eighteenth century. It began with the leadership of the Ọ̀yọ́ Empire, who failed to use the commercial wealth that accrued from its territorial conquests to achieve political stability in the metropolis and in the provinces (chap. 6). While Ọ̀yọ́'s military power continued to extend the boundaries of the empire, the political leadership in the metropolis was imploding under the stress of intra-elite conflict between the two dominant pillars of Ọ̀yọ́ monarchy—the *aláàfin* and the *ọ̀yọ́mèsì*. The two were victims of their own political success. At the core of their conflict was the struggle over the distribution and control of the gains that derived from Ọ̀yọ́'s territorial expansion.[2]

The new conquests in the Yéwá-Ògùn province and new trading opportunities in Badagry between 1736 and 1750 brought significantly more resources and wealth to the metropolis, but this only exacerbated the *aláàfin-ọ̀yọ́mèsì* rivalry for control of the spoils of military expansion. This issue came to a head with the appointment of Gáà as *baṣọ̀run* in the late 1750s. A hero of the Ọ̀yọ́ military expansion in Yéwá-Ògùn, Gáà was already wielding a vast influence over the military, political, and economic affairs of the empire before his appointment as the head of the *ọ̀yọ́mèsì*. Now occupying the position that was second in rank only to that of *aláàfin*, he wasted no time in using his office, fame and influence to take full control and advantage of the contentions between the two pillars of the monarchy. Using divide-and-conquer tactics, he first gained the unwavering support of the *ọ̀yọ́mèsì* and then gradually stripped them of their power and reduced them to his clients.[3] More important, by using various ruses to kill four successive kings within twenty years, he instilled fear in the populace and reduced the office of *aláàfin* to a ceremonial one. For two decades, Gáà effectively usurped the powers of all political institutions, presiding over the empire's domestic affairs, external relations, and political and military matters. The ruthlessness with which Gáà pursued Ọ̀yọ́ imperial expansion in the Yéwá-Ògùn frontier was the same with which he ruled the empire. He subverted the institutional checks and balances, silenced opposition with assassination and exile, and kept the royal House and all the other *ọ̀yọ́mèsì* in submission to his will.

Gáà's success at subverting the institutional checks and balances and the excesses that he perpetrated as a result revealed the fragility of Ọ̀yọ́'s political institutions. But this fragility had preceded Gáà by almost a century. The rivalry between the royal House and the nonroyal noble Houses (especially between the *aláàfin* and *baṣọ̀run*) was already in place during the time of Àjàgbó, one of the most revered early kings of Ọ̀yọ́. Before the great warrior-king and consolidator of Ọ̀yọ́'s expanding territories joined his ancestors, he had the foresight to put in place a mechanism that he hoped would contain this problem: he created the office of *àrẹ-ọ̀nà-kakaǹfò* as the head (commander-general) of all the combined military forces of Ọ̀yọ́. Both the *aláàfin* and each member of the *ọ̀yọ́mèsì* contributed soldiers and weaponry to every war effort, and it was the responsibility of the two institutions to maintain several units of soldiers. Àjàgbó sought to unite these diverse military contingents under the leadership of a professional soldier appointed to the office on the basis of military distinction rather than political pedigree. This ensured that the head of the army would not be beholden to any of the seven members of *ọ̀yọ́mèsì* but would rather answer to the *aláàfin*. For this reason, the *àrẹ-ọ̀nà-kakaǹfò* was to be a career officer appointed to the office by the *aláàfin*, though in consultation with the *ọ̀yọ́mèsì*. The initial preference was to promote a person of servile background but with a distinguished military career to the position. This was a person who would not have any legitimate stake in the metropolitan politics. Therefore, on appointment, the holder of the office of *àrẹ-ọ̀nà-kakaǹfò* was forbidden to live in the capital, a step aimed at shielding him from the internal politics in the metropolis. Àjàgbó's decisive step to professionalize the army and unify all the soldiers (cavalry and infantry) under a career officer was a sound political judgment. But it had the effect of reducing the influence of *baṣọ̀run*, the designated military leader in the constitution that birthed the imperial Ọ̀yọ́ during the first quarter of the seventeenth century. It is possible that this step only further deepened the mistrust between the two pillars of Ọ̀yọ́ monarchy. Whatever may have been the initial success of Àjàgbó's reorganization of the military, the creation of the office of *àrẹ-ọ̀nà-kakaǹfò* as a counterforce to the military duties of *baṣọ̀run* did not seem to have had much long-term effect in curtailing the power and influence of the latter. In fact, this arrangement seems to have broken down with the ascendancy of Baṣọ̀run Gáà.

Gáà would have enjoyed support from the majority, if not all, of the other members of the *ọ̀yọ́mèsì* at the beginning of his career as *baṣọ̀run*. They possibly saw him as one of them, a worthy champion of the interests of the nonroyal Houses against the expanding power of the *aláàfin*/royal House. Gáà's excesses, however, soon alienated the rest of the *ọ̀yọ́mèsì* and the general public. By arrogating the power to appoint and dismiss the *aláàfin*, usurping all the powers that previously had been shared between the *ọ̀yọ́mèsì* and the king, and brutally silencing all voices of dissent, Gáà lost the support of the other members of *ọyọ́mèsì* and the majority of the public. His last appointee to the throne of Ọ̀yọ́—Abíọ́dún Adégórolú—capitalized on those popular resentments and mobilized the Ọ̀yọ́ army under the *àrẹ-ọ̀nà-kakaǹfò*, a number of provincial governors, and the metropolitan chieftains against the formidable private army of Gáà. It was a bitter and bloody civil war. Hundreds died, including Gáà, and most of the *baṣọ̀run*'s extensive households were destroyed. A number of Gáà's family members and supporters fled to exile, taking refuge in the frontiers and outskirts of the empire where the *baṣọ̀run* had sympathetic connections, such as in the Ìbàrìbá and Yéwá-Ògùn areas.[4] The involvement of the third and fourth pillars of the empire—the military and the provincial governors—in the metropolitan power struggle had dire consequences. First, it exposed the weakness of the metropolis and the self-centered power politics of its leaders. Second, the conflict divided the loyalty of the army and the provinces between different factions. Aláàfin Abíọ́dún won the day, but the price of victory, as we shall soon see, was very costly. Nevertheless, the defeat of Gáà and his loyalists restored the honor of the *aláàfin* and re-centered him as the soul and the centripetal force of the empire. In the years that followed, Abíọ́dún took the empire to its highest glory, not so much in terms of adding new territories but by virtue of the stability and peace that he facilitated during most of his nineteen-year reign (1770–89). He also enabled commercial expansion and economic growth.[5]

Imperial Apogee

With Gáà out of the way, the splendor of the *aláàfin* blossomed under Abìọ́dún. His reign marked Ọ̀yọ's golden age. Traders and artists flooded to the capital in search of profits and patrons. Sartorial and gastronomic tastes, music, and architecture were used to flaunt wealth, prestige, and class (chap. 7). The following song captures the spirit of the time:

Láyé Olúgbọ́n mo gé'borùn mẹ́ta
Ẹ o ma kọ̀ yí lórin
Láyé Arẹ̀sà, mo gé'borùn mẹ́fà
Ẹ o ma kọ̀ yí lórin
Láyé Abìọ́dún, èmi ra kókò,
Mo rà'rán, mo ra sányán baba aṣọ,
Àf'ọ̀lẹ ló lè pé'lẹ̀ yí ò'dùn
Àf'ọ̀lẹ.

Translation:

In the time of Olúgbọ́n, I made three shawls,
Join me in this chorus.

In the time of Arẹ̀sà, I made six shawls,
Join me in this chorus.
In the reign of Abìọ̀dún, I bought *kókò,*
I bought velvet and *sányán*, the father of all cloths.
Only a lazy man would say this empire is not pleasant,
Only a lazy man.[6]

The song was composed in the late eighteenth century as a commentary on the wealth, peace, and commercial opportunities that prevailed during the high noon of Ọ̀yọ́'s imperial power. It speaks of the good times during the reign of Olúgbọ̀n, when the singer owned three shawls. Then there was the better time under Arẹ̀sà, when the singer possessed six shawls. The third was the best and most glorious time, under Aláàfin Abìọ̀dún, when the singer owned different kinds of imported fabric—*kókò* and velvet, as well as the expensive local fabric, *sányán*, a cloth of light-brown or beige color, woven from silk locally obtained from the cocoons of *Anaphe* moths.

By the time the king ascended the throne of his fathers, the imperial capital had become the most powerful and wealthiest city in the Yorùbá world. Hence, it became fashionable for the Ọ̀yọ́ to pride themselves as the pacesetters for arts and culture with the saying *ajíṣe bí Ọ̀yọ́ làárí, Ọ̀yọ́ kìí ṣe bí baba ẹnìkọ́ọ̀kan*: "Others emulate the Ọ̀yọ́, the Ọ̀yọ́ do not emulate anyone." This served to affirm the city of Ọ̀yọ́-Ilé as the place of reference for high culture and high taste, the place of originality whose act others copied. This was not an empty boast. At the height of its glory, between 1730 and 1789, the metropolis of Ọ̀yọ́ Empire set the trends for taste, fashion, and beauty and modeled the innovation and grandeur associated with these. It attracted some of the best talents from across and beyond the empire, the same way that its predecessor, Ilé-Ifẹ̀, had achieved fame as the "house of abundance" and center of diversity about five hundred years earlier. Ọ̀yọ́-Ilé was the meeting point for several Yorùbá groups, people from the empire's vast vassal territories, including the Nupe in the northeast and the Ìbàrìbá in the northwest, as well as thousands of slaves and freemen from the Sudanic belt: Songhai, Hausa, and Kanuri. This cosmopolitanism was reflected in all aspects of Ọ̀yọ́ culture. We have already seen how Sudanic and Arab-Mediterranean clothing styles penetrated the Yorùbá world through the Ọ̀yọ́ (chap. 7). The same things applied to music. Here, the Ọ̀yọ́ integrated the musical instruments of the Yorùbá, such as the *gbẹ̀du* drum, with the wind instruments of the savanna. The epitome of this synthesis of cultural diversity was the Ọ̀yọ́ palace orchestra. It consisted of more than two hundred members, with *ọkinkin*, *igbá*, *ekùtù*, *òge*, *tiyako*, and *kàkàkí* among the wind instruments, and *dùndún*, *ṣẹ̀kẹ̀rẹ̀*, *bẹ̀nbẹ́*, *bàtá*, *gbẹ̀du*, *àgídìgbo*, *yangede*, *àyé*, *aro* (cymbal), and *kósó* among the percussion.[7] The splendors of the palace as a fountain of high culture also included an a capella group called *àkùnyùngbà*. This comprised the wives of the *aláàfin*. Numbering in the hundreds, they were instructed in a special room by a teacher. When a new performance was to be learned, the teacher might come to the palace "three times daily for three months or more until the learners are perfect in their studies."[8] An estimated five hundred wives of Aláàfin Ọmọ́sọlá Májŏtú accompanied their lord to pay a condolence visit to Richard Lander in 1827 when the latter returned to Ọ̀yọ́-Ilé after the death of his master, Hugh Clapperton, in Sokoto (April 13, 1827). Each carrying a spear, they sang a dirge in honor of the explorer. "The music of their voices was wild but sweet," recalled Richard Lander, "reverberating from the hills . . . saddening, although by no means [of] a disagreeable effect."[9]

The built landscape in Ọ̀yọ́-Ilé was no less elaborate. The architectural styles of elite houses were accented with elaborate sculptures to project the status of their residents. In this field, Ọ̀yọ́-Ilé attracted some of the most talented wood-carvers from the Ìgbómìnà, Èkìtì, Ìbàrìbá, and Nupe areas. Of these, Làgbàyí, a native of Ọ̀jọwọ̀n (from Ìgbómìnà-Èkìtì area) and the chief sculptor of Aláàfin Abìọ́dún, is the most celebrated in the oral traditions.[10] The elite used the services of these sculptors to adorn their houses and compounds with carved wooden posts and ornately carved doors in bas-relief. The carvings were usually a medium for telling stories about particular events, communicating power and authority, and commemorating an experience in the life of the *ilé* and its chief resident. Some of the motifs were allusions, such as the boa killing an antelope, and hog processions. Others were realistic and highly expressive representations of matching warriors and drummers.[11] The elite adorned their residences with the architectural details that pronounced their power and resources, but they reserved the finest and most detailed architectural artworks and ornamentation for the temples of their deities. The temple of Ṣàngó, the most revered of all the deities in Ọ̀yọ́, illustrates this. To Clapperton, the Ṣàngó temple at Ọ̀yọ́-Ilé was "the largest and most fancifully ornamented of any of a similar kind in the interior of Africa." This perfectly square building was at least twenty yards on each side, with floors and walls that were highly polished and stained a deep red. The size and number of sculptures dedicated to this temple were stupendous, with no parallel in other architectural settings, including that of the palace in Ọ̀yọ́-Ilé. "Directly opposite the entrance" of the temple, Clapperton wrote, "is an immense, beautifully executed wooden figure of a giant bearing a lion on its head." The giant was possibly a representation of Ṣàngó. Clapperton goes into detail describing the other figures outside the temple: "About twenty-six or twenty-seven figures, in bas-relief, are placed on each of the sides of the hut, but all in a kneeling posture, with their faces turned towards the larger figure, to which they are apparently paying their devotions. On the heads of the small figures are wooden images of tigers, hyenas, snakes, crocodiles, etc. exquisitely carved; and painted, or rather stained, with a variety of colours."[12] Smaller versions of Ṣàngó's architectural art were replicated in the provinces. In town after town, there were well-executed "busts of men, as well as figures of tigers, crocodiles, serpents, carved on blocks of wood" adorning temples and elite houses. Many of these sculptures were also commentaries on the novelty of the age. For example, a temple in Ìlarò (Yéwá-Ògùn) was described as "a large square building" supported by round pillars, against which were set sculptures of men, some "armed with sword and shield" and others holding pistols "with both hands in the act of lifting it to fire." Of the finesse of the Yéwá-Ògùn sculptors, Hugh Clapperton approvingly wrote: "the natives of that part of Africa appear to have a genius for the art of sculpture, which is in great repute with them; and some of their productions rival[s], in point of delicacy, any of a similar kind that I have seen in Europe."[13]

The base of this colossal grandeur of culture and art was, however, filthy, as was the case for other edifices of taste throughout the Atlantic world, more so in the Americas and Europe, where the economics of slavery and the high culture of taste were inseparable.[14] Abíọ̀dún's economic policy was not different from that of his predecessors. He financed his administration, as well as his political and cultural projects, with proceeds from the war captive–slave trade continuum in addition to the tributes that poured in from the provinces. As a result, many tributary provinces suffered great losses of human capital because of his insatiable demand for captives for both the Atlantic slave trade and labor in the metropolis. It is therefore not accurate that under Abíọ̀dún's reign "the people to the remotest part of the kingdom were so happy and contented," as written in Samuel Johnson's romanticized description.[15] No doubt Ọ̀yọ́ citizens enjoyed their most extravagant years during his reign. But the peoples in the peripheries of the empire, especially the tributary provinces, groaned under the heavy burden of taxation and abuse of power perpetrated by the imperial agents. Abíọ̀dún also appears to have neglected the military, focusing instead on the promotion of commerce. As a result, cracks in the military might of the empire began to show during his reign. It should be noted that in spite of Gáà's excesses, the Ọ̀yọ́ Empire achieved its greatest territorial extent under his surrogate leadership. Abíọ̀dún brutally defeated Gáà in the metropolitan power struggle, but he could not maintain the territorial gains that Gáà had achieved for the empire. In fact, Ọ̀yọ́'s grip on its northern provinces began to slip in the later years of Abíọ̀dún's reign, when the tributary states of Nupe and Borgu rebelled and defeated Ọ̀yọ́'s army.[16] While the northern extremities of the empire were declaring their independence, Abíọ̀dún tightened his iron fist on the empire's southern regions, especially Màhì, Dahomey, Ẹ̀gbá, and Yewá-Ògùn (chap. 6 and 8).

Cracks in the Imperial Wall

Like most empires, Ọ̀yọ́ was an exploitative economic system, especially from the point of view of its client states and tributary appendages.[17] The empire's military and political institutions were geared toward achieving its economic interests—expansion, taxes, tributes—and creating favorable markets for the empire's products. The major wrinkle in the case of Ọ̀yọ́ was that its wars of expansion were intimately tied to the need to raise human capital (enslaved men and women) for its external trade (for horses and Atlantic merchant capital) and domestic labor.[18] And during the third quarter of the eighteenth century, Ọ̀yọ́ became increasingly reckless in exploiting its tributary provinces and buffer zones for these human resources. Ọ̀yọ́ was no doubt "the rudder for stabilizing the ship of commerce on the turbulent political waters of the Bight of Benin during the eighteenth century," as I stated in chapter 6. For many of its tributary provinces after 1750, however, this cavalry state was an agent of instability and pain.[19] There was a dramatic increase in the number of Yorùbá captives entering the Middle Passage between 1750 and 1775 because of the direct link between Ọ̀yọ́'s expansionist program and its slave-trading machine.

There were many reasons for this inward-looking approach to furnishing supplies to the Middle Passage. First, Ọ̀yọ́ reached the limits of its territorial expansion during the 1750s, and therefore the non-Yorùbá corridors that it could attack and sweep for captives were drastically narrowed. Second, the empire lost a huge market share to the Asante Kingdom, with whom the Hausa and other Central Sudanese merchants created alternative and direct trade in the mid-eighteenth century via the Ìbàrìbá territory and the middle Volta basin.[20] The routes for this commerce bypassed Ọ̀yọ́ and provided the Hausa traders and others with more diversified outlets for their exports, which "were the same as those (originally) shipped to Ọ̀yọ́."[21] The consequence was that these alternative routes reduced Ọ̀yọ́'s access to the Central Sudanese captives being bartered for Atlantic merchant capital. The decline of Ọ̀yọ́'s market share of Central Sudanese exports was compounded by the Abíọ̀dún-Gáà conflict in the metropolis, the outcome of which degraded Ọ̀yọ́'s military throughout the reign of Abíọ̀dún. The empire's diminished military capability and the new trade routes linking the Central Sudan with the Volta region encouraged Borgu to declare its independence from Ọ̀yọ́ in 1783.[22] The Nupe not only followed suit shortly after but also returned to brigandage activities in the northeastern and north-central Yorùbá region, raiding several polities and communities in Ìgbómìnà, Okun, and Àkókó for captives.[23] The captives from those areas fed the Central Sudan-Volta trade, as well as the need for labor in the Sudan, a process that lasted through the nineteenth century. This pattern was similar to what had unfolded in the Yorùbá world during the late fifteenth and early sixteenth centuries. Alas, history was repeating itself.

With all of these changes in the north, Ọ̀yọ́ began to put more pressure on its southwest and central tributaries—the Ẹ̀gbá, Ànàgó, Ọ̀họ̀rì, and Ìbòlò in Yorùbá mainland and the Màhi in the Gbe cultural zone—in order to stay competitive in the Atlantic slave trade. The snake had finally begun to bite its own tail. But rather than the cyclical and renewing action of the *ouroboros*, this was the beginning of self-destruction. In this particular situation, the densely populated northern Ẹ̀gbá forest severely suffered from the burden of Ọ̀yọ́'s exploitation for labor and captives between 1775 and 1830. Most of the Ẹ̀gbá had already been brought under the control of Ọ̀yọ́ by the mid-eighteenth century and were saddled with enormous annual payments of tributes to the capital. However, the burden of insecurity was added on top of this during the last quarter of the century, when Ọ̀yọ́ mercenaries proliferated in the Ẹ̀gbá forest. Disguised as independent agents or brigands, these mercenaries were clandestinely sponsored by the leading chieftains of the metropolis and their provincial agents to carry out surprise attacks and "harvest" captives for the Atlantic trade.[24] These slaving expeditions often coincided with the arrival of European slave ships. To cite one example, the docking of a Portuguese slave brig and a Spanish slave schooner in Badagry in December of 1825 created waves of restlessness in the mainland, as far as sixty kilometers from the coast. In order to furnish these vessels with their desired cargo, the governor of Ìjànà, Ọ̀yọ́'s dominant colony in the Yéwá-Ògùn frontier, sent a slaving party to the territories of the Essa, near the town of Ẹ̀gùà. Infuriated by the unneighborly action of the Ọ̀yọ́ governor, the king of Essa mounted a counteroffensive war against Ìjànà. As a result, the roads linking the two became unsafe. The tension was so high in the area that about a hundred travelers placed themselves under the protection of Clapperton's exploration team when the latter left Ìjànà for Ẹ̀gùà on January 3, 1826, on their journey to Ọ̀yọ́.

In other instances of reckless exploitation and abuse of power, Aláàfin Abíọ́dún and his immediate successor, Aólẹ̀ Arógangan (1789–96), ordered attacks on the provinces whose leaders they accused of insubordination during their princely years. For example, Abíọ́dún claimed that the son of the potentate of Ìjàyè, an Ẹ̀gbá town, insulted him during one of his trading missions there. On ascending the throne, according to Ọ̀yọ́'s palace informants, "he avenged the alleged insult by ordering the destruction" of this prominent trading town.[25] Likewise, Aláàfin Aólẹ̀ ordered military action against Apòmù, a provincial town of Ilé-Ifẹ̀, in order to avenge his humiliation at the hands of the *baálẹ̀* (head) of the town during his princely years as a trader. He also took the misstep of ordering an attack against Ìwéré (Ìbàràpá area), reputed to be the maternal town of Aláàfin Àjàgbó. However, the reasons that these two monarchs offered for the military actions against these provinces were mere pretexts for capturing men and women for enslavement. Such attacks against the tributary towns and provinces of the empire abused the honor of the military, undermined respect for the *aláàfin*'s institution, and did not endear the loyalty of the provinces toward the Ọ̀yọ́ metropolis. The attacks also divided the loyalty of the metropolis's population, some of whom had relatives in those tributary towns. In effect, Abíọ́dún's attack on Ìjàyè hardened the resolve of Ẹ̀gbá provinces for independence, and it galvanized their mobilization for the removal of the yoke of Ọ̀yọ́ imperialism. As a result, full-blown uprisings dogged Ọ̀yọ́'s rule among the Ẹ̀gbá at different periods between 1790 and 1820.[26] Aólẹ̀'s military action against Apòmù also made him and Ọ̀yọ́ unpopular not only in Ilé-Ifẹ̀ but also in other parts of the Yorùbá region, especially in the Ìjẹ̀bú region, for reasons that will soon become obvious.

All of the above instances were acts of desperation. They were the early signs of cracks in the wall of wealth and power that the merchant capital revolution had built for Ọ̀yọ́ Empire. As a Yorùbá proverb puts it, *ilé tí a fi itọ́ mọ, ìrì ní ó wo*: "a house whose building blocks are molded with saliva will be brought down by the dewdrops." For close to two hundred years, the Ọ̀yọ́ Empire had played a major role in integrating a large section of the Yorùbá community of practice into the Atlantic slave trade. They were not alone. Traders and political chieftains of Ìjẹ̀bú-Rẹ́mọ, Ifẹ̀, and some of the southern Ẹ̀gbá kingdoms, as well as the Àwórì, Ànàgó, Màhin, and Lagos chieftains, also contributed in different ways and scales to this integration, which was based on the predatory economy of the Atlantic slavery. The captains of these trading states on the coast and on the mainland by 1770 increasingly depended on the influx of Euro-American merchant capital via Badagry, Apa, and Lagos to finance power and build wealth. This means that the activities associated with slaving and the slave trade increased in their territories. They were building a house of cards.

The factional conflicts among the chieftains of the Ọ̀yọ́ metropolis intensified during the reign of Aólẹ̀, and this caused a tremor that began to shake and break the edifice of the empire. Aólẹ̀ was the unfortunate inheritor of an empire whose military capability had been degraded under the reign of his predecessor. He also came to the throne at a time when the weak economic foundation of the empire was no longer able to support the enormous, towering weight of the structure that Ọbalókun, Àjàgbó, Oníṣílé, Gáà, and others had built. Meanwhile, his inept leadership, vain and haughty personality, and poor diplomatic skills did not help matters. His order to the military to attack Ìwéré, a provincial town that many saw as a loyal ally of the metropolis, was the last straw that broke the back of his wobbly camel. This order was so unpopular that it led to the rebellion of the army, several provinces, and a large section of the metropolis's chieftains against his rule.[27] As a result of his growing unpopularity at home and in the provinces, Aólẹ̀ was forced to commit suicide in 1796. But the damage was done. The passing of Aólẹ̀ and the metropolitan anti-*aláàfin* revolt that led to his death marked the beginning of the end of the Ọ̀yọ́ Empire. It was a long-drawn-out collapse lasting for four decades. During this period, mayhem was unleashed in multiple spots across most of the Yorùbá world. The "age of confusion," what some historians have also called the "revolutionary period," had started.[28]

An interregnum that lasted for about five years followed the demise of Aólẹ̀. The Ọ̀yọ́mèsì could not agree on who would succeed him, another sign of political coma in the capital. The interregnum ended in 1802 with the installation of Aláàfin Májǒtú, but the political instability and rebellion against the capital did not abate.[29] All eyes were now on Májǒtú to see whether he would pull the horse of the empire back from the precipice. Perhaps a solution would have been found to the problem if not for Àfọ̀njá, an influential Ọ̀yọ́ prince (on his maternal side) and commander-general of the army (*àrẹ-ọ̀nà-kakaǹfò*) who became the emblematic figure of anti-*aláàfin* sentiment in the metropolitan area. Àfọ̀njá had aspirations for the throne of Ọ̀yọ́, but the kingmakers bypassed him on three occasions between 1789 and 1802. In fact, Aláàfin Aólẹ̀ made him the commander-general of the Ọ̀yọ́ army sometime in 1789–90 to bribe him out of his ambition, but this had no effect. His hostility toward the metropolis seemed to grow on each occasion that he was bypassed for the throne.[30] Rather than fighting to save the empire from external intrigues as his office required of him, Àfọ̀njá only fanned the embers of internal discord between 1790 and 1824. He elevated his ambition above the survival of the empire. Denied of his aspiration to become the *aláàfin*, he embarked on a quest to carve his own autonomous polity out of the metropolitan area of Ọ̀yọ́. The empire was now divided against itself, but it was about to get worse. From his base in Ìlọrin, only sixty kilometers south of the capital, Àfọ̀njá allegedly issued a call to the entire metropolitan area in 1817, promising freedom to the teeming slaves in the capital and its suburbs who were willing to join his resistance force in the provincial town. This supposed call may have started as a rumor, but it is significant that thousands of people responded to it. This led to the first known slave revolt in Yorùbá history. Thousands of these slaves enthusiastically responded to the promise of freedom. They fought their way out of the capital, causing chaos in their wake. These men, and they were mostly men, were seeking freedom from bondage. They fled to Ìlọrin, where Àfọ̀njá and his supporters had established their oppositional base against the capital. But the slaves were not the only ones who fled the capital. They were joined by many Ọ̀yọ́ citizens and others of the Yorùbá underclass who were seeking better economic and social opportunities.

The revolt of slaves of mostly Central Sudanese origins and the Ọ̀yọ́ underclass was a watershed in the history of the Ọ̀yọ́ Empire. There were unique social, cultural, and economic dimensions to the revolt. It was a multiethnic uprising: the majority were slaves, most of them were of foreign origins, and the majority were identified as Hausa, but there were also Kanuri, Ìbàrìbá, Nupe, Aja, and non-Ọ̀yọ́ Yorùbá among them. Most of these Central Sudanese rebels (Hausa and Kanuri) identified or sympathized with Islam, but not all were Muslim, and not all Central Sudanese slaves in the metropolis joined the uprising. Ọ̀yọ́ citizens were also among the defectors. The majority were of lower-class status, and they were Òrìṣà believers, but a few of them were Muslims, and a tiny fraction were of high and middle social classes. All of these rebels were united by their rejection of the prevailing arbitrary power that had come to define the authority of the monarchy—both *aláàfin* and *ọ̀yọ́mèsì*. However, there is another element to this uprising that has been omitted in the historiography: the food shortages caused by the incessant episodic droughts in the metropolitan area resulted in excruciating hunger in Ọ̀yọ́-Ilé, and this, in turn, exacerbated unrest in the capital where there was a large population of dependents. Àfọ̀njá took advantage of the restlessness and disorder in the capital by encouraging underclass revolt.[31] I will return to the impacts of drought on the crisis later in the chapter.

According to a Yorùbá proverb, *kòkòrò tí ńj'ẹ̀fọ́, ara ẹ̀fọ́ ní ńgbé*: "The bacteria or fungi spoiling the vegetable lives inside the vegetable." It is ironic that the person charged with maintaining social order was the same incalcitrant fomenting trouble within the empire. Àfọ̀njá's alleged call for the revolt and emancipation of the enslaved was not based on his altruistic belief in the equality of humankind. His goal was to weaken the *aláàfin* institution. He knew quite well that the desertion of the capital by the servile population would undermine the empire economically and militarily. Both the slaves and the free underclass who responded to his call were united primarily by their common socioeconomic plight. They were the exploited segment of the empire. They had eaten crumbs at the feet of the elite and their masters and had suffered the humiliation of being spat on.[32] They were also the ones being severely affected by the food shortage that the city and its environs were experiencing at that time because of irregular rainfall and perhaps exhaustion of land productivity.

Any promise of freedom, even if a ruse, was acceptable to them. It was the only prospect for freedom and social mobility they ever had. The initial support that they received from some prominent Ọ̀yọ́ citizens resident in Ìlọrin gave the insurrection some measure of legitimacy. This slave-underclass revolt stripped the empire's cloth. It was a well-known fact that servile and underclass labor was the bulwark of the empire's economic and military strength, the basis of the metropolitan power. With such a huge loss of personnel, the revolt drastically reduced the labor force available to the upper and middle classes. As a result of the 1817 revolt, the bottom of the purse of the capital fell out.

Meanwhile, these deserters did not set out to live a life of peaceful harmony with the land as farmers. Neither did they take to trade or craft. Instead, they turned to banditry and began to wreak mayhem across the greater metropolis of the empire. The contiguous northern Ẹ̀gbá, Ìgbómìnà, and Ìbàràpá areas particularly felt the burn, as "Àfọ̀njá's bandits" incessantly ransacked them. As towns and villages in these areas fell to the brutal hands of the bandits who carted the captives away into slavery, hundreds of thousands of people began to evacuate their homes to avoid the fate of their neighbors. They were moving from the savanna region southward, deeper into the rain forest belt. Some used existing networks of relatives to find new homes. But this massive migration and displacement only plunged the Yorùbá region into more instability. The displaced population became a boon to the warlord-merchants who were entrenched in the southern parts of the region: the war refugees became easy targets for the slavers prowling in the rain forest. The prevailing insecurity and lawlessness generated more captives who were sent to the coast and the slave ship. The difference now was that the misfortune had been reversed. Ọ̀yọ́ citizens and others from the greater metropolitan area of the empire constituted a significant percentage of the Yorùbá boarding the slave ships. These acts of brigandage initiated the largest demographic displacement in Yorùbá history over a period of fifty years. It paled in comparison to what happened during the age of atrophy (see chap. 4).

Growing Appetite of the Atlantic Slavery and the Age of Confusion

Let us walk back a little to gain a good understanding of what happened between 1817 and 1840 and continued through the 1860s. Overall, the number of enslaved Yorùbá entering the Middle Passage was negligible before 1651. According to David Eltis's estimate, the number may not even have constituted more than 10 percent of the total embarkation in the Bight of Benin between 1651 and 1725. However, the Yorùbá proportion of the slave cargo departing the region jumped to about 29 percent in the second quarter of the eighteenth century and more than 50 percent in the third quarter. Following the rebellion of 1817, the Yorùbá accounted for 80–90 percent of those forced aboard the slave ships in the Bight of Benin from 1825 through 1866 (fig. 9.1).[33] To put things in perspective, the Yorùbá-speaking people had been (and still are) the largest cultural group in the Bight of Benin and its mainland both in population and landmass since at least the eleventh century. At the onset of the eighteenth century, they possibly accounted for about 70–75 percent of the population in the region, between River Mono in the Benin Republic and River Osse in present-day Nigeria, and as far north as the River Niger.[34] By 1820, the proportions of the enslaved Yorùbá population entering the Middle Passage via the Bight of Benin ports had exceeded their share of the region's population. There were two reasons for this. The first was the exponential increase in European demand for human cargo in the Bight of Benin and other parts of Atlantic Africa after 1750. The second reason was the opening of several slave trading ports on Yorùbá coastlands, at Àjàṣẹ́ (Porto Novo), Badagry (Apa), Lagos (Èkó/Onim), and Ẹ̀pẹ́ (see fig. 6.2). These slave-trading ports put enormous pressure on the mainland. There were two mainland outlets that delivered captives to the European slave ship, especially between 1750 and 1860. One was the Yéwá-Ògùn frontier, whose suppliers were initially dominated by the agents of the Ọ̀yọ́ Empire but with private merchants becoming increasingly common in the slaving business after 1817. The second outlet stretched about two hundred kilometers from the Badagry-Lagos-Ẹ̀pẹ́ axis to the central Yorùbá region, in the upper reaches of River Ọ̀ṣun on one side, and to the eastern Yorùbá in Ọ̀wẹ̀nà frontier on the other side (see fig. 5.1). Private merchants, specializing in human trafficking, dominated these routes from the beginning. These merchants were financiers of banditry across the region, and some of them were also dreadful warlords. The most successful of these slave merchants originated in the mainland areas adjacent to the coastal slave malls, especially in Ìjẹ̀bú area.

The resuscitation of Lagos as a slave-trading entrepôt in the last quarter of the eighteenth century significantly increased the tempo of disturbances being created by Atlantic slavery in the Yorùbá mainland. The Ìjẹ̀bú traders and warlords served as the dominant carriers of Atlantic trade goods entering the Lagos and Badagry ports into the central Yorùbá region, and they also supplied most of the enslaved who passed through these ports. These traders therefore played the most important role in using merchant capital to finance the process of enslavement in areas between River Ògùn and River Ọ̀nì. This put enormous pressure and strain on the political and social fabric of the area as far north as Upper Ọ̀ṣun, especially between the Ọ̀bà and Ọ̀ṣun Rivers (see fig. 1.1). For the

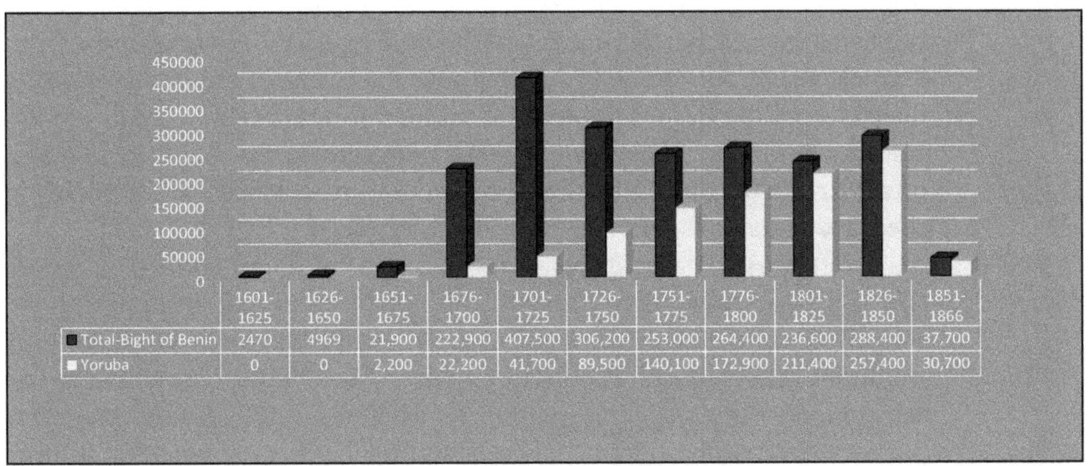

	1601-1625	1626-1650	1651-1675	1676-1700	1701-1725	1726-1750	1751-1775	1776-1800	1801-1825	1826-1850	1851-1866
■ Total-Bight of Benin	2470	4969	21,900	222,900	407,500	306,200	253,000	264,400	236,600	288,400	37,700
■ Yoruba	0	0	2,200	22,200	41,700	89,500	140,100	172,900	211,400	257,400	30,700

Figure 9.1. Estimated quarterly embarkation of captives from the Bight of Benin and Yorùbá region to the Americas, 1601–1866 (source: Eltis, "Diaspora of Yoruba Speakers," 38)

first time, after 1750, this area became a major outlet for commerce in general and the slave trade in particular. There was intense competition between Òwu and Ifẹ̀ kingdoms to control this new commercial opportunity. Ọ̀ṣìnladé Otùtùbíosùn, the king of Ilé-Ifẹ̀, however, had the upper hand. He succeeded in establishing Apòmù as a frontier market town sometime between 1770 and 1780.[35] This mainland commercial entrepôt served not only the Ifẹ̀ and Ìjẹ̀bú traders but also traders from Ọ̀yọ́, Ìjẹ̀ṣà, Ẹ̀gbá, and Òwu.

The establishment of Apòmù directly brought the Atlantic slave trade to the central Yorùbá region. Captives immediately became the most lucrative commodity in Apòmù. With the increasing European demand for human cargo on the coast and the flooding of the mainland with merchant capital, kidnapping activities increased regionally and spread beyond central Yorùbá to the eastern region, as far as the Èkìtì area and the Ọ̀wẹ̀nà frontier. The panic and fear associated with the rising incidents of kidnapping created anguish and uncertainty as well as social and political instability in areas that had been marginal to the Atlantic slave trade before 1770. As a result, an urgent sense of insularity emerged in the late eighteenth century across eastern and southcentral Yorùbá, especially among the Ìjẹ̀bú, Ìjẹ̀ṣà, Àwórì, Oǹdó, Ọ̀wọ̀, and Èkìtì. To save their citizens from pillaging and attacks, many villages, towns, and cities reinforced their perimeter walls with deeper ditches and thorny plants, and their narrow gates were guarded around the clock "to keep out strangers who might be kidnappers." Many kingdoms also created new laws and policies that made them unwelcoming to strangers. For example, according to Adebanji Akintoye: "The Ijebu-Ode authorities turned their great city into a land where strangers who could not give clear accounts of themselves faced the danger of being arrested and sacrificed at the shrines. Ilesa traditions are unambiguous that some of the [human] skulls displayed on the Ilesa walls were of suspicious strangers. And Ado (Ekiti) traditions speak of suspicious strangers dragged to the palace, and made to swear at the Esu-Owakunrugbon shrine, or sacrificed at the shrine if their accounts of themselves proved unsatisfactory."[36]

There was another dimension to this story. The period from 1770 through 1866 saw a sharp rise in the use of arms and ammunition by European slave dealers as payment for the captives they were buying in the Bight of Benin and the Gold Coast.[37] As a result, firearms became the period's "most potent weapon of war," especially in the southern parts of the Yorùbá region.[38] The Ìjẹ̀bú merchant-warlords who dominated the intermediary markets feeding captives into these coastal slave marts controlled most of the imported arms and ammunition. With this advantage, they and their bandit-clients as well as their political elite allies stirred trouble in the region. The incidents of kidnapping and brigandage especially became common phenomena in the central Yorùbá region, and many trading routes in the area became unsafe. Most of the unfortunate captives were sold in Apòmù market. The market town quickly garnered notoriety as the largest mainland mart for captives and as a beehive of criminal behavior and dishonesty. Hence the saying *èké d'áyé, áásà d'Ápòmù*: "Dishonesty entered the world at the same time that tobacco arrived in Apòmù." This is a reference to the role that the market town was playing between 1770 and 1830 in human trafficking in exchange for Atlantic merchant capital, of which tobacco was an important component. Meanwhile, the rising kidnapping activities in the central Yorùbá region as a result of the slave trading activities in Apòmù were becoming unbearable for the whole region because of the negative impacts of insecurity, banditry, and lawlessness on commerce and freedom of movement. As a result, the Ọ̀ọ̀ni (king) of Ifẹ̀ and the Olówu (king) of Òwu, the two dominant powers in the area, reportedly led the effort to regulate slave trading, prevent indiscriminate kidnapping, and ban the importation of guns and ammunition into the area.[39] But these efforts were without success, as the region was flooded with an assortment of merchant capital from the coast. Human trafficking only moved from open market to underground market. Moreover, many Ìjẹ̀bú traders and their Ifẹ̀ allies, armed with the imported guns and ammunition, became war captains, capturing their own supplies for the Atlantic trade rather than waiting for dealers and brokers to bring in the victims. All of these exacerbated disturbances and confusion in the central Yorùbá region throughout the first decade of the nineteenth century.

The Ọ̀yọ́ traders and travelers passing through the region seem to have disproportionately suffered from these kidnapping incidents. Hence, the justification of the military action ordered by Aláàfin Aólẹ̀ against Apòmù in 1793, aside from the personal vendetta he nursed against the chief of the trading town, was to protect Ọ̀yọ́ citizens. But this was not enough and did not end the indiscriminate kidnapping of Ọ̀yọ́ traders and travelers in central Yorùbá region. Hence, the leaders of Ọ̀yọ́ turned to their client state, Òwu, to take care of the situation. This was an order that Òwu could not refuse, apart from the fact that everyone knew that Òwu was nursing the ambition of taking control of the lucrative Apòmù market in order to have access to its tax revenues. Òwu quickly moved against Ilé-Ifẹ̀, under whose jurisdiction the market town fell, and against the Ìjẹ̀bú traders who dominated commercial transactions in the town. Òwu easily won the military skirmishes that followed. It wrested the control of the market from Ilé-Ifẹ̀ and began to establish new rules for commercial engagement and security. This action only united the Ifẹ̀ and Ìjẹ̀bú against the coalition of Òwu and Ọ̀yọ́. Yet the kidnapping of Ọ̀yọ́ traders and travelers did not abate. Pressured by the Ọ̀yọ́ metropolis to do more to protect the empire's southern frontiers, Òwu swung into action and carried out punitive expeditions to several Ifẹ̀ towns and villages. These attacks further bred distrust and heightened hostilities between the Òwu-Ọ̀yọ́ coalition on one hand and the Ìjẹ̀bú-Ifẹ̀ coalition on the other. The tipping point was the killing of an Ìjẹ̀bú trader in Apòmù market in 1817, allegedly by an Òwu man. This singular event was a watershed in Yorùbá history. It rallied the well-armed, well-financed, and well-organized Ìjẹ̀bú merchants and their Ifẹ̀ allies to take their hostilities directly to the walls of Òwu. With thousands of "war boys" from anywhere and everywhere (brigands) that they had managed to bring under their control, the Ìjẹ̀bú-Ifẹ̀ coalition sought a revenge disproportionate to what had happened in Apòmù market. The destruction of the sprawling Òwu kingdom, the most formidable client state of Ọ̀yọ́ in the south central frontiers of the empire, was their goal.

The 1817 incident in Apòmù took place shortly after the slave revolt in Ọ̀yọ́-Ilé. It was a perfect storm. With its own crisis at home, the psychologically battered Ọ̀yọ́ metropolis was not in a position to help its client state. The coalition of Ìjẹ̀bú and Ifẹ̀ militarists was aware of the implication. They determinedly mounted a siege on Òwu-Ìpolé, capital of the Òwu Kingdom, from ca. 1817 through 1822. It was one of the largest cities in the central Yorùbá region, more than three kilometers in diameter.[40] The people of Òwu-Ìpolé gallantly defended their city for five years, and some of their sympathetic neighbors, such as Ẹ̀gbá polities and other Òwu towns, also came to their defense to break the military blockade from the rear. But the latter were unsuccessful. Surrounded by enemies who had cut off supplies of food, weapons, and external help, the well-fortified capital of Òwu Kingdom finally fell in 1822 under the heavy fireballs of imported guns and gunpowder. It was the first large-scale use of such weaponry in Yorùbá wars.[41]

The fall of Òwu Kingdom had a cascading effect on all the provincial towns of the vast kingdom and its Ẹ̀gbá neighbors. The city and its satellite towns and villages were ravaged by the coalition of Ìjẹ̀bú and Ifẹ̀ warlords and the opportunist brigands working for them. Interestingly, the brigands included some of the Ọ̀yọ́ refugees who had been displaced by the trouble in the metropolitan area. The invasion of Òwu and Ẹ̀gbá towns and villages yielded thousands of captives, most of whom were taken to the coast and bartered for more merchant capital and instruments of war. "On a scale never known before," a scholar of Ìjẹ̀bú history wrote, "the Ìjẹ̀bú were able to sell to their Portuguese partners large numbers of slaves."[42] By the time the Apòmù crisis and the siege of Òwu was going on, the rebels from the Ọ̀yọ́ metropolitan area had also spread across the northern Ẹ̀gbá, Igbómìnà, Ìbàràpá, and Upper Ògùn, laying waste to towns and villages and enslaving their residents. The hail of mayhem was now falling hard on the Yorùbá world.

Only a very few victims of the mayhem that defined that period, especially between 1817 and 1830, lived to share their story. The twelve-year-old Àjàyí, whom we first encountered in chapter 6, was one of the tens of thousands whose villages and towns were raided by brigands and warlords in the dry season of 1820–21. In one early morning in March 1821, a multiethnic band of brigands, including Ọ̀yọ́, Hausa, and Fúlàní men, attacked his town, Òṣoògùn. Hundreds were captured, including Àjàyí, his mother, his two sisters, and a cousin. His father was one of those who died defending the town. The bandits immediately led their captives out of the town and brought them to nearby town of Ìsẹ́yìn that evening (see fig. 6.4). In the next three or four weeks, Àjàyí was sold no fewer than five times over a distance of about two hundred kilometers before ending up in the hands of Portuguese slavers in Lagos. The latter set sail with their human cargo on April 7, 1822, on the way to Brazil. They had not traveled far from the shores of West Africa when a unit of the United Kingdom's West African Squadron intercepted the slave ship. The captives, including Àjàyí, were freed and resettled in Sierra Leone.[43] As part of the baptism rituals of conversion into Christianity, to which all captives were subjected, Àjàyí was rechristened Samuel Crowther. Better known later in life as Samuel Àjàyí Crowther, he described his horrid journey from freedom to slavery with chilling detail, noting the horror, death, hardship, and inhumanity that befell him, other captives, and his town. "O pitiful sight!" he exclaimed sixteen years after the incident of his capture and enslavement. "Whose heart would not bleed to have seen this?"[44]

Farther south, the Ìjẹ̀bú and Ifẹ̀ warlords who had destroyed the Òwu Kingdom and scores of its satellite towns and villages between 1817 and 1822 now turned their attention to the neighboring Ẹ̀gbá kingdoms and principalities. The young male refugees, displaced from the greater metropolitan area of Ọ̀yọ́ Empire in the north, swelled the private armies of these warlords. Many Ẹ̀gbá villages and towns were easily overwhelmed by these brigands. Captives were taken in the thousands, and most of them ended up in Lagos barracoons. One of them was Joseph Wright (post-captive name), whose experience was similar to that of Àjàyí. Sometime between 1825 and 1827, the brigands sacked his town, Ọ̀bà, after a seven-month siege. He was also about twelve years old when the siege began. In his words:

> All the time we heard of . . . war in a far distant land, we confidently thought they will not come to us. Alas, in the space of about seven years . . . they came to us unexpectedly. . . . These people that raised up this war . . . are not another nation. We are all one nation speaking one language. . . . The war shut us from all business. . . . In this miserable state we lived for about seven months, destitute of all food. We had nothing to eat in order to have [the] strength to fight our enemies.[45]

In the course of the siege, many people of Ọ̀bà died of starvation. A number of the older people died from the shock of the attack, and others committed suicide. Akálà, the chief priest of Ọ̀bà and a close relative of Wright, was one of those who took their lives rather than waiting to suffer the humility of being captured, sold into slavery, or hacked to death. Some parents, including Wright's, abandoned their children, either to avoid seeing their children starve to death before their eyes or to preserve their own lives. Finally, the town's defense broke one morning in January 1827. The hundreds of captives included Wright and his brothers and sisters. He recalled the gory scene he saw while being led out of the town by his captors in chains: "The enemies satisfied themselves with little children, little girls, young men, and young women . . . they did not care about the aged and the old . . . They killed them without mercy. Father knew not the son, and the son knew not the father. Pity had departed from the face of mothers. Abundant heaps of dead bodies were in the streets, and there were none to bury them. Suckling babies were crying at the point of death . . . a lamentable day!"[46] His captor presented him to the war captain as war booty. After that, he was sold to two other slave traders in the Ìjẹ̀bú area before he arrived in Lagos, where a Portuguese slaver bought him. His journey to Brazil was, like that of Àjàyí, aborted by British abolitionist patrolmen. Wright was resettled in Sierra Leone, where he lived for the rest of his life.

Discontentment of the Underclass and War Culture

One dimension of the age of confusion that the historiography has overlooked was the role that underclass revolt played in changing the direction of the Ọ̀yọ́ metropolitan crisis and in emboldening the Ìjẹ̀bú-Ifẹ̀ warlords of the early nineteenth century. Historians tend to treat the 1817 slave uprising in Ọ̀yọ́-Ilé as a product of the uncompromising intra-elite conflict in the metropolis rather than seeing it as an autonomous event in its own right.[47] We should bear in mind that competitions and intrigues among the political elite, especially between the *aláàfin* and *ọ̀yọ́mèsì,* were part of the social constitution of the Ọ̀yọ́ metropolis throughout the imperial period.[48] So what was different in the early nineteenth century? Building on the discussion in chapter 8, I would argue that the 1817 revolt originated from the simmering soup of social inequality and that the intra-elite power struggle in Ọ̀yọ̀ was only a catalyst, not the primary cause, of the revolt. That is, the cause of the revolt was the widening, self-perpetuating, and arbitrary social inequality. This "perennial inequality," as I termed it, was not limited to class relations in the metropolis. It also manifested in class and power relations in the tributary provinces and independent kingdoms. The slave revolt in the Ọ̀yọ̀ metropolitan area, the abandonment of the empire project by the underclass citizens, and the rebellion of the provinces against the empire, especially among the Ẹ̀gbá, were manifestations of the social discontentment of the various exploited groups against the status quo. The implication of this is that the 1817 uprising in the metropolis was more than a slave revolt. Neither was the revolt organized along ethnic lines. The rebellious group was multiethnic and multireligious. No doubt the enslaved rebels were predominantly Muslims, but their ethnolinguistic affiliations included Hausa, Kanuri, Nupe, and others between the Central Sudan and the Niger-Benue Confluence. Members of the various Yorùbá subgroups were also among this rank of disaffected people. These included those enslaved or transferred to the capital as part of the tributary obligations of the provinces to the metropolis. And there were underclass Ọ̀yọ́ citizens among these anti-empire rebels. The majority of the Yorùbá elements in the uprising were not Muslims; they were believers of the Òrìṣà (Yorùbá) religion.

As discussed in chapter 8, in both the empire and the corridors of merchant capital, a significantly large number of households and communities lost the capacity to reproduce themselves in the last quarter of the eighteenth century. This trend continued in the early nineteenth century. The declining prospects for the social mobility of a vast number of young men from middling and poor backgrounds, and of sons of the junior wives from the elite households, generated a large population of marginalized and exploited young men. They faced mountainous disadvantages in competing for resources but were nevertheless ambitious and aggressive. Lacking any inheritance to fall back on, many of these men joined the orgy of banditry, working side by side with the most marginalized members of the society—self-liberated slaves and the free underclass. Usually operating under the patronage of a *balógun* (warlord), these men looted, captured, enslaved, and shared war booty. Their choice of victims was indifferent to political, ethnic, family, or religious affiliation. Some were fighting for survival in the face of the social displacement caused by wars, instability, and structural inequality. Others took up brigandage to pursue purely personal gains.

Most of the young men who took to brigandage, irrespective of their social background, were primarily concerned with sheer survival. Their options were limited, and most had none. They took the same road that the state and the elite had taken for more than two hundred years to achieve wealth, self-realization, and aggrandizement—raiding, looting, and enslaving. By the beginning of the nineteenth century, these acts of institutionalized violence had become expanded, indiscriminate, diffuse, and open to every man (self-interested warlords) with imported arms and ammunition who was able to recruit "war boys" to do his bidding. Most of these warlords were either stateless or operating outside the political institutions of their state. Their followers were often socially displaced men unrestrained by whatever remained of the moral order of the Ọ̀yọ́ Empire or any other constituted state authority in the region. They lived on rapine and banditry. They were loyal only to themselves and their warlord-patrons (*balógun*), not to any state or even any corporate group. This is evident in the fact that many of the men displaced in the Ọ̀yọ́ metropolitan crisis joined the Ìjẹ̀bú-Ifẹ̀ coalition to attack Òwu, the most formidable and loyal client state of the Ọ̀yọ́ metropolis in the southeast frontier of the empire. Likewise, ethnic or subregional loyalty broke down in the wake of the crisis of 1817. In its place, the principle of "every man for himself" prevailed. As a result, many young men in the Ẹ̀gbá region who had been displaced from their homes as a result of war also turned to banditry and joined the Ìjẹ̀bú-Ifẹ̀-Ọ̀yọ́ militarists to attack other Ẹ̀gbá towns.[49] It is therefore inaccurate to characterize the nineteenth-century crisis of 1790–1840 as intergroup or interethnic warfare. Neither was it a political conflict between kingdoms. At every level of the conflict, this was a house divided against itself.

While social disaffection and displacement no doubt pushed the underclass into brigandage, their sponsors and patrons (warlord-merchants) financed pillaging and slave raiding with the credit facilities being advanced to them by Lagos and Badagry merchants—Europeans and Africans. In 1777, for example, Ọba Ológunkútéré (King of Lagos, 1775–80) wrote to Richard Miles (Governor in Chief of Cape Coast

Castle, 1777–85), requesting an advance of goods, including tobacco, in exchange for a "Good Trade" in slaves.[50] The cache of letters of Ológunkútéré's grandson and king, Ọba Kòsọ́kọ́ (r. 1845–51), shows "how Europeans and Bahians advanced goods to Yorùbá traders" with the agreement that payment would be made in "slaves and other produce."[51] As the networks of credit expanded, so did the pressure to pay off the debt. In this slave/merchant-capital exchange, the meter of violence was elevated. Not a small percentage of more than half a million Yorùbá-speaking people delivered to the slave ships between 1818 and 1866 were snatched away by these tendrils of credit in the form of tobacco, cowries, spirits, arms and ammunition, and a suite of other European imports. With large supplies of arms and ammunition at their disposal, some of the merchants of the 1780s–1860s became warlords in order to cut off the middlemen, get to their supplies more quickly, pay off their debt sooner, and reap larger profits. They used their merchant capital to recruit war captains and brigands from among the socially marginalized young men who realized that the life of farming and craftwork was less secured and not as rewarding as the commerce of brigandage and human trafficking. A number of these merchant-warlords, especially in the Ìjẹ̀bú area, effectively hijacked power from the state authorities, waging war against their neighbors as they saw fit and constituting themselves into the military and civilian authority of the state. For example, although Ọba Fìgbàjoyè Aníkiláyà of Ìjẹ̀bú-Òde opposed the attack on the Ẹ̀gbá in the 1820s, the Ìjẹ̀bú merchant-warlords defied him.[52] With their wealth and military arsenals, they subverted the authority of the monarchy and promoted themselves as the protectors of their communities. With these ruses, they invaded Ẹ̀gbá towns and villages to obtain captives for the Middle Passage.

Specific actions of these roaming brigands suggest that many of them were rebelling against the society that had produced them. Joseph Wright, a young eyewitness to the carnage, recalled that on the day that his Ẹ̀gbá town of Ọ̀bà fell to the siege of the invaders, not only were the living taken captive but the dead were also attacked. These militants dug up the graves of the elite "in order to take the money and fine clothes with which the dead bodies were dressed."[53] The abominable act of digging up the dead and desecrating the graves of the ancestors was a means of humiliating their descendants and taking revenge on the dead elite while also satisfying a reckless material lust. These acts of disturbing the dead also reveal something deep about the state of mind of the perpetrators: they had lost confidence in the society that gave birth to them. With hundreds of towns and villages vanquished and deserted between 1817 and 1827, and thousands sold into slavery, most of these displaced young men partaking in brigandage had lost more than a home. They had also lost their relatives and the past. Ancestral dignity meant nothing to them. The drive to survive the present moment was far more important than the quest for the ideal of ancestral life and immortality, an aspiration that had eluded two generations of the underclass and even many children of the elite households. These men of war were surely in search of a new beginning, but with the rapacious bloodletting going on, they faced an uncertain future. This magnitude of instability that swept across the Yorùbá world between 1796 (the death of Aláàfin Aólẹ̀) and 1837 (the final collapse of the empire and evacuation of the capital) was the first since the atrophy of the 1450s–1560s. The immediate perpetrators of this second and more profound blanket of upheaval were, however, homegrown, not external invaders like the first. Going by the accounts of the survivors of that era who witnessed the carnage firsthand, the men of war and brigandage whose depredations defined the character of 1817–40 had the head of a man but the body of a lion and a steely heart. Their blank gaze was often as pitiless as the harmattan sun. Their victims had no shelter to protect them from the storm tumbling down the rumbling sky of confusion.[54] If Ṣàngó's men, like Àfọ̀njá and Aólẹ̀, thought they could control the wind of trouble they had released on the world, they were mistaken. Unheeding Ọbàtálá's admonition for moderation (chap. 7), they were taken away by the wind of calamitous change. The rushing wind was strengthened by the rebellious underclass in the empire (and elsewhere), the rapacious appetite of warlords for merchant capital goods on the coast, and the insatiable European hunger for human captives and slave labor in the Caribbean and South America.

The Collapse

Aláàfin Májọ̀tú died in 1830 or 1831 without achieving his ambition of rebuilding his father's house—the empire, which the revolts of Àfọ̀njá and the underclass revolt had reduced to rubble and a shell of its old glory.[55] He was one of the longest-reigning kings in Ọ̀yọ́ history, ruling for about twenty-eight years. The events that defined his reign give the impression that he was an ineffective king, but the point should not be lost that he inherited an imploding empire.[56] Surrounded by the intrigues of the metropolitan lords and by infighting among the governors of the empire's frontier provinces; beset by the festering rebellion of Ìlọrin and other eastern provinces; and constrained by sharply reduced revenue, Májọ̀tú did not succeed in stopping the implosion.[57] To the contrary, his reign witnessed several calamitous events. These included the underclass revolt of 1817; the collapse of Òwu in 1822; and the killing of Àfọ̀njá and many of his supporters in 1823. The Hausa-Fúlàní jihadists who had infiltrated Àfọ̀njá-led anti-metropolis rebellion perpetrated the third act with the backing of the Sokoto Caliphate. These newcomers not only took over the reins of power in Ìlọrin afterward but also began their aggressive expansion to other parts of the Yorùbá region, especially in Ìgbómìnà and Upper Ọ̀ṣun. This effectively turned what had been a political conflict in the Ọ̀yọ́ metropolitan area into a religious one—Islamist insurgence against the Yorùbá religion and political institution. The ascendance of the jihadists was alarming and unsettling to the capital and core provinces of the empire. To the provincial governors in particular, it became obvious that the metropolis had lost control over its political affairs. Some of the Yorùbá chieftains in the provinces were coerced to become allies of the jihadists in Ìlọrin, while others joined them voluntarily for self-preservation. What is more, several tributary provinces of the empire, especially in Ìgbómìnà and Gbe territory, including Dahomey, successfully declared their independence from Ọ̀yọ́ between 1823 and 1830.

Overall, the pace of the disintegration of the empire was slow but steady under Májǒtú (fig. 9.2). The fact that he held Àfọ̀njá and the jihadists at bay in their Ìlọrin stronghold, only sixty kilometers from Ọ̀yọ́-Ilé, for about twenty years and prevented the insurgents from invading the capital shows the resilience that characterized the imperial capital during his reign. It is perhaps for this reason that he earned the nickname Májǒtú, "Don't let it collapse," which eventually became his regnal name. He lived up to this name. A steady manager rather than a transformative leader, the old king appears to have applied great shrewdness to holding the western wing of the empire together while the status of the eastern flank of the empire was uncertain. The deaths of Àfọ̀njá and other Yorùbá elements (including Muslims) at the hands of their former allies—Hausa and Fúlàní—rattled the metropolis and its loyal provinces. There was an urgency to act against the festering trouble in Ìlọrin. Therefore, Májǒtú forged an alliance with the Nupe in 1825 to subdue Ìlọrin and expel the jihadists, but the coalition was defeated. That loss further weakened the confidence of the core administrative provinces and colonies of Ọ̀yọ́ in the metropolitan cause (especially those in the eastern and central frontiers, such as Ìkòyí and Ẹdẹ). The metropolis had become a liability rather than an asset, and many of the governors and resident commissioners who had defended the interest of the empire in the frontiers and borderlands for so long began to pursue their autonomous interests of survival. In 1830, Ọ̀yọ́ effectively lost what was remaining of its shaky grip on the Yéwá-Ògùn provinces.

Bí ìyà ńlá bá gbé ni sánlẹ̀, ìyà kékèké á ma gun orí ẹni: "Whenever one is debilitated by a great shame, one also suffers from other little insults." About the time that the Ọ̀yọ́-Nupe coalition laid siege to Ìlọrin in the dry season of 1825, a new round of multiyear droughts was setting in across the savanna, the worst of which Ọ̀yọ́ metropolitan area experienced between 1828 and 1831.[58] Oral traditions, eyewitness accounts,

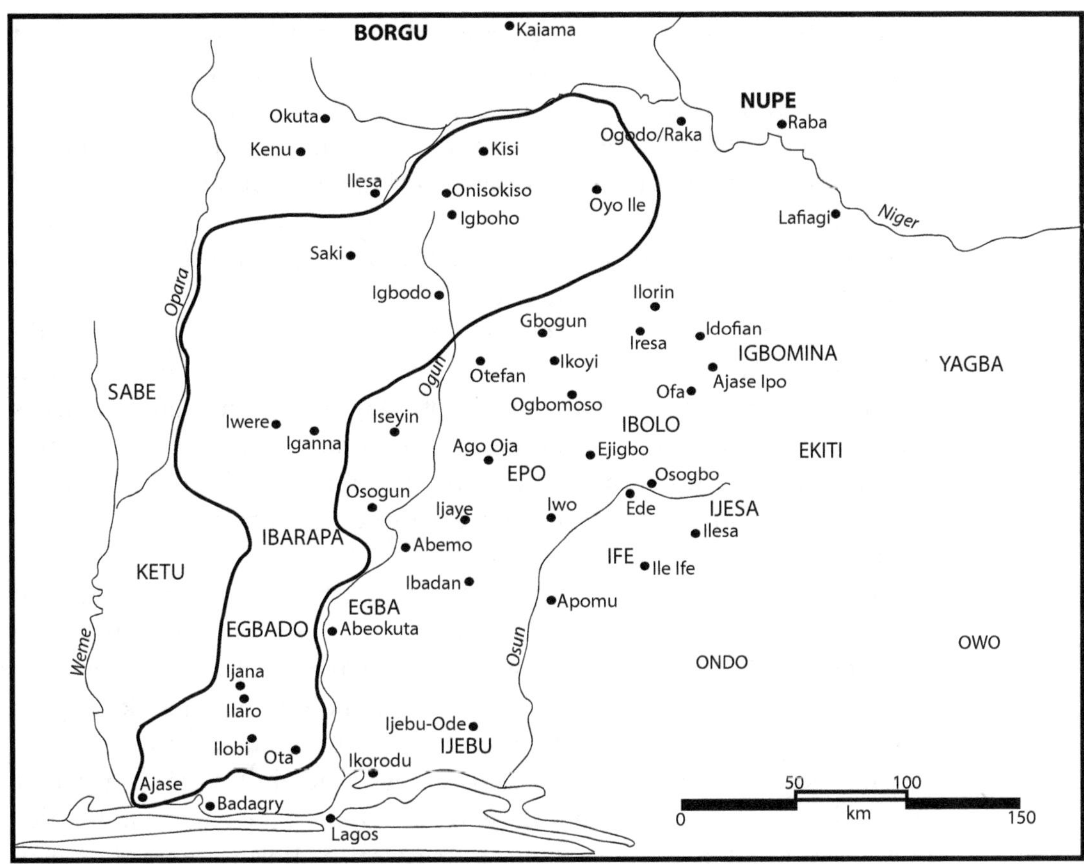

Figure 9.2. Remnant of the Ọ̀yọ́ Empire, ca. 1827

and palynological evidence have converged to show that Ọ̀yọ́-Ilé and the metropolitan area in general witnessed debilitating droughts in the last decades of the empire.[59] With inadequate rainfall, many water sources dried out, and farmlands were untilled. The insecurity in the countryside and political instability had already depressed agricultural efforts and output even in the previous years of minimally adequate rainfall. But now, the severe famine that followed the droughts worsened the crisis. A series of debilitating ailments, one of which was a respiratory infection, was also associated with the drought. Many people died from both hunger and disease. Aláàfin Májǒtú had reached advanced age by this time. He also succumbed to a respiratory infection that ravaged through Ọ̀yọ́ in 1830–31, and joined his ancestors. The accounts of Richard Lander's second visit to Ọ̀yọ́-Ilé in 1827 and his third visit (with his brother, John) in 1830 give us a good sense of how the capital was already exhausted by war, impoverished by drought, weakened by famine, and debilitated by contagious diseases in the last years of Májǒtú's reign. In 1827, Richard Lander observed that many sick people who were suffering from some contagious diseases were being removed to a nearby bush about "half a mile from the town" in order to stem the spread of infection. There, the sick were provided with food and provisions, as demanded by the law. However, food supplies were very low, and most families were so impoverished that many of the isolated sick people actually "die[d] from . . . starvation."[60] The depopulation of the metropolitan area accelerated during those peak years of drought, famine, and disease, between 1827 and 1831.[61] For those who survived and sought relief elsewhere, the direction of movement was southward from the savanna into the rain forest belt, where the effect of drought was minimal, if even noticeable. Therefore, during the last five years of Májǒtú's reign, many refugees from the metropolitan area settled in several new polities, such as Ìjàyè, Abẹ́òkúta, and Ìbàdàn, that were springing up in the very Ẹ̀gbá territory that was once under the Ọ̀yọ́ Empire.[62] Others sought refuge in the old towns, such as Òṣogbo.

With the transition of Májǒtú, the events that led to the collapse of the metropolitan area accelerated. More provinces peeled away from the metropolis. The empire's cloth was being removed layer by layer. The Ìlọrin jihadists seized on this opportunity. Following their killing of Àfọ̀njá, the jihadists (now led by the Fúlàní) installed an emir in Ìlọrin. About two years after Májǒtú's death, they invaded Ọ̀yọ́-Ilé for the first time. They ransacked the capital, reportedly looted the palace of its valuables, and proclaimed the *aláàfin* as a vassal of Ìlọrin's emir. The new *aláàfin* who suffered this indignity was Olúewu, a son of Aólẹ̀. Described as handsome and haughty, like his father, the new king vowed to revenge the humiliation. Destiny, heritage, and an uncertain future became his burden. *Ikú yá j'ẹ̀sín*, "To die is better than living in disgrace," is a popular Yorùbá refrain underpinning the spirit of honor and bravery. He was the descendant of Ọbalókun and Àjàgbó, and son of Aólẹ̀, the monarch might have reminded himself. His fathers did not bow to anyone. Why should he? Rather than holing up in the capital, Olúewu decided to fight for the restoration of the dignity of the institution of *aláàfin* and the survival of the empire. Olúewu proved to be better than his father as a builder of a coalition. As his ancestors had done in the late fifteenth and early sixteenth century when confronted by similar challenges, he appealed to his Ìbàrìbá neighbors for assistance. They, like the Nupe, were also facing the threat of the rising power of the Fúlàní jihadists within their territories. In fact, the Ìbàrìbá were already feeling the brunt of the jihadists, who frequently raided these territories for captives. They feared that should the jihadists establish full suzerainty over Ọ̀yọ́-Ilé, they would be next in line for conquest. Again, as in the calculations that their forebears had made more than three hundred years earlier, many Ìbàrìbá chieftains considered it necessary to ally with Ọ̀yọ́ in order to also save themselves. At least four Ìbàrìbá kingdoms and principalities—Nikki, Bussa, Kaiama, and Wawa—responded to Olúewu's appeal by sending strong military contingents to the war effort. Olúewu also rallied the support of several Ọ̀yọ́ provinces and new Ọ̀yọ́ towns that had emerged in the south—especially Ìbàdàn, Ìjàyè, and Àgọ́-Ọ̀já. In the final effort to remove the thorn of Ìlọrin jihadists already buried deep in their flesh, the combined forces of Ìbàrìbá under Siru Kpera, the king of Nikki, and Ọ̀yọ́, under Olúewu, marched in the dry season of 1837 against Ìlọrin. Revealing the religious character of the war, Ìlọrin was supported by soldiers from the Gwandu Emirate (the patron of Ìlọrin) and fought under the banner of the Sokoto Caliphate.

The Ìbàrìbá proved to be a formidable ally, but Olúewu did not seem to have received the full support he desperately needed from many of the chieftains of the metropolis and provinces. *Aṣọ ò bá Ọmọ́yẹ mọ́, Ọmọ́yẹ ti rin ìhòhò w'ọjà*: "It's too late to clothe Ọmọ́yẹ, she has already walked into the market naked." The proverbial Ọmọ́yẹ is the *aláàfin* institution. The rank and file of the leaders of Ọ̀yọ́ provincial contingents that assembled for the decisive war were rife with deception, disunity, and disloyalty to Olúewu. Many of them were not fully committed to the cause. While the king was fighting to save the empire, some of his provincial governors were either fighting for their own independence from Ọ̀yọ́ or wishing for the king to fail. As a result of a lack of collective will and unity rather than as a result of errors of combat strategy, the Ọ̀yọ́-Ìbàrìbá coalition lost the battle. Thousands were killed, including Olúewu and his son. Siru Kpera, the potentate of Nikki, as well as the potentates of Wawa and Kaiama, also perished in the war. Dubbed the Eléduwẹ War, after the Ọ̀yọ́ stock name for Ìbàrìbá potentates,[63] this was the final and failed attempt to restore the lost glory of the empire. As the news of the fall of Olúewu reached Ọ̀yọ́-Ilé and its environs, the remaining residents quickly packed up and began to evacuate the capital and the surrounding towns and villages.[64]

And so the largest Yorùbá political experience in the early modern era came to an end. Ọ̀yọ́-Ilé and scores of other cities, towns, villages, kingdoms, and principalities in the northwest Yorùbá region have since lain in ruins. The alleys and avenues through which mounted men of chivalry once galloped and the old compounds of the elite and the underclass are now taken over by the thickets and thorns of woodland savanna and other wildlife who now call the place home.[65] Today, the once colorful and boisterous Akẹ̀sán market is in utter silence, with the ageless boulders and some of the baobab trees being the only witnesses of the past transactions. The evacuation of Ọ̀yọ́-Ilé marked the final phase of the Yorùbá demographic shift from the north to the south, savanna to the rain forest belt. Many of the evacuees headed west to the Ṣakí/Kìṣì area, and others moved eastward, even to Ìlọrin. But most traveled farther south. Some went to Àgọ́-Ọ̀já, where the capital of the New Ọ̀yọ́ kingdom was being established by an Ọ̀yọ́ prince, Àtìbà. Yet others moved to the war camps and towns that had emerged in the upper reaches of the rain forest, especially Ìjàyè, Ìlọrà, and Ìbàdàn.

The evacuation of Ọ̀yọ́-Ilé and the collapse of the empire was the end of an era in the history of the Yorùbá world. The detailed story of what followed is outside the scope of this current study. It belongs to a different horizon of time. Understanding and making sense of the post-1840 Yorùbá history requires a different conceptual framework and a treatment as long as this book. Nevertheless, the nineteenth century has enjoyed the most detailed attention in Yorùbá historiography. The historical events and dramatis personae that defined the collapse of the "house of cards" that merchant capital and hegemonic states had built are well known in the literature. The aftermath—wars, political reorganization, the transition to agricultural commodity export, religious change, and the advent of European colonial modernity—has also been well attended to in the historiography.[66] A holistic cultural history of that era, however, is yet to be written. I will provide a summary of the aftermath of 1837 in order to bring this book to a close.

House Breakers and House Savers

With the defeat of Olúewu-led forces, the jihadists of Ìlọrin and their allies were intoxicated by the fermented fruit of victory and were determined to take over the entire Yorùbá region. They, therefore, shifted their focus toward those new Ọ̀yọ́ towns already planted in the upper reaches of the rain forest. Their goal was to "dip the Koran in the sea," a metaphor for subjugating the Yorùbá world to the control of the Sokoto Caliphate via the emirate of Ìlọrin. For what this implied, no existential crisis that enormous had ever confronted the Yorùbá, not even the Nupe crisis of the late fifteenth and early sixteenth centuries. Displaced and demoralized, most of the Yorùbá region, especially in the old territory of the Ọ̀yọ́ Empire, was still licking its wounds. The only Yorùbá polity brave enough to confront the jihadist threat was Ìbàdàn. It was a new kid on the block of regional politics, but it was a rising military power in the aftermath of the fall of Ọ̀yọ́ Empire. While the Ìlọrin army was advancing southward, Olúyọ̀lé, the second ruler of Ìbàdàn and a grandson of Aláàfin Abíọ́dún, rallied to confront the enemy.[67] He presided over the military plans to stop the advancing Ìlọrin army. He mobilized other scattered Ọ̀yọ́ elements to the cause of saving their ancestral land from what he rightfully considered a foreign invasion, although there were high-ranking Yorùbá soldiers in the Ìlọrin contingent. There was nothing in his favor to assure victory, but his foresight, audacity to act, and timely intervention paid off. Under the command and leadership of his war commander Balógun Ọdẹ́rìnlọ, the advance of Ìlọrin's ambition was halted on the outskirts of Òṣogbo in 1840. The Ìlọrin army was thoroughly beaten. The victory put to rest the threat of the jihadist agenda in the Yorùbá world. With this, Olúyọ̀lé achieved what had eluded Olúewu and five other *aláàfin*. This military victory was the most consequential event in Yorùbá history during the nineteenth century. According to the patriarch of Yorùbá historiography, Samuel Johnson, the outcome of the war marked "a turning point in Yorùbá history. It saved the Yorùbá country . . . from total absorption by the Fulanis."[68] If not for Olúyọ̀lé and his military superstars, many beaded-crown kings and potentates of Yorùbá kingdoms would have since been replaced by turban-wearing emirs. Ìbàdàn's victory over Ìlọrin saved the House of Odùduwà (Ilé-Ifẹ̀), the House of Ṣàngó (Ọ̀yọ́), the House of Obòkun (Iléṣà), the House of Ọ̀ràngún (Ìlá), the House of Ọbáǹta (Ìjẹ̀bú-Òde), and others from becoming emirates. The victory was not only over Ìlọrin. It was also a defeat of its patron, the Gwandu emirate, and of the Sokoto Caliphate as a whole.

Olúyọ̀lé must have felt a sense of pride and satisfaction that he had avenged the desecration of his ancestral home by preventing the Ìlọrin jihadists from overrunning the Yorùbá region and dipping the Koran in the ocean. The victory energized Ìbàdàn to embark on an ambitious expansionist program across central and eastern Yorùbá region, a process that kicked off its short-lived empire, 1840–93 (fig. 9.3).[69] Nevertheless, that victory did not lead to peace and stability for the Yorùbá world. It was only the beginning of more than fifty years of wars defined by (1) the competition for supremacy among the newly emerged states; (2) conflict over the control of trade routes, especially the ones leading to the coast; (3) the aggressive expansionist agenda of the Ìbàdàn Empire; and (4) the counteroffensive, revolt, resistance, and liberation movement of the eastern half of the empire against Ìbàdàn, between 1877 and 1893. These topics have received much scholarly attention, and their full treatment is outside the purview of this book.[70] Suffice it here to say that those wars ended with the intervention of the British government, who brokered peace among the exhausted warring parties in 1893 and immediately maneuvered to bring the Yorùbá warlords and their political dominions under the British colonial rule.

Altogether, about three-quarters of the Yorùbá region experienced war, dislocation, and demographic reshuffling during the nineteenth century. The southeast region, comprising the Oǹdó, Ìjẹ̀bú, Ìlàjẹ, and Ọ̀wọ̀, was less affected by the demographic shifts and massive dislocations, but they did not live in the splendid isolation of the turbulence that surrounded them. The Oǹdó, for example, who did not suffer much from

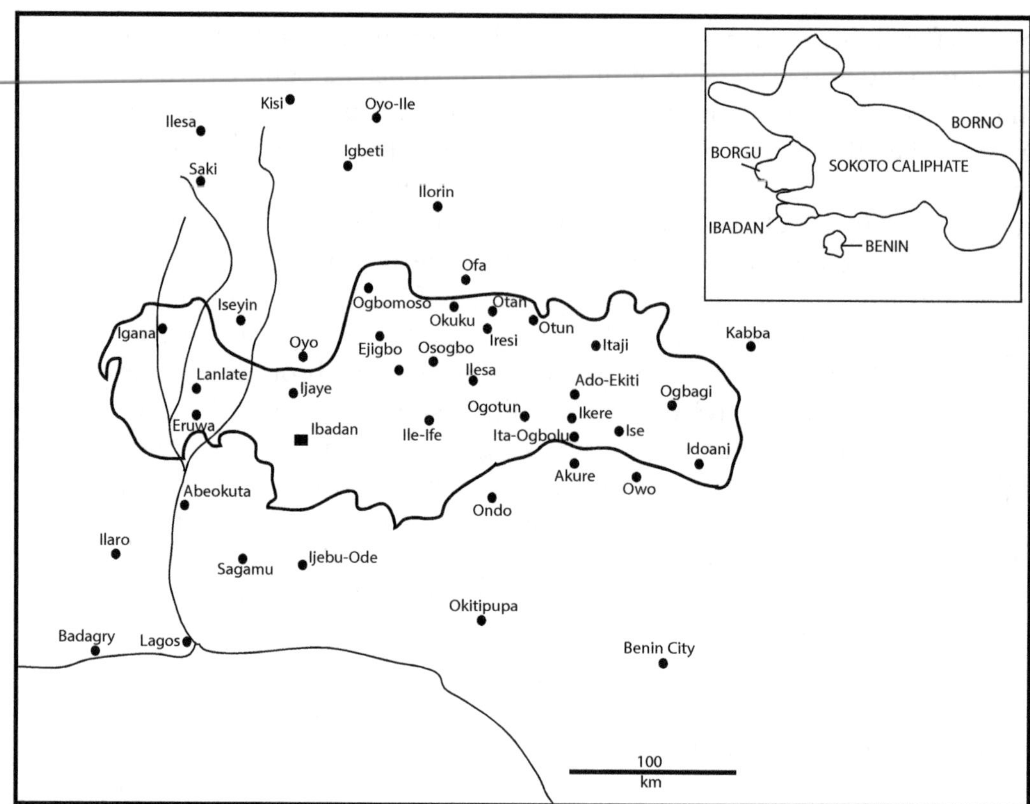

Figure 9.3. Ìbàdàn Empire

external aggression, nevertheless succumbed to "a disastrous civil war that [reportedly] destroyed 127 of their settlements" in 1830.[71] In contrast, most of the Ìjẹ̀bú territory did not suffer from internal displacement despite the fact that the Ìjẹ̀bú merchant-warriors were principal instigators of the regional conflicts of 1817–30 in central and southern Yorùbá. However, they were drawn into the regional conflict that followed the ascendance of Ìbàdàn expansionist power in 1840 and other conflicts associated with the struggle to control the commercial traffic linking the coast to the mainland. Moreover, there were frequent disputes between the traditional civil authorities, especially the king and chieftains of Ìjẹ̀bú-Òde, on one hand, and the merchant-warrior class on the other, over the kingdom's policy on external relations and trade.[72] Nevertheless, because of its impenetrable geography and organizational structure, most people in the Ìjẹ̀bú territory did not suffer displacement, anarchy, and political dismemberment during the sad century.[73] This situation was like that of the Ìjẹ̀bú experience in the fifteenth and sixteenth centuries when their northern neighbors underwent a similar though less excruciating anarchy but the Ìjẹ̀bú were relatively untouched.

Yorùbá in the Diaspora

By the time the dust of wars of aggression and liberation, opportunism and brigandage, self-defense and lawlessness that had begun in the 1790s was settling down in the 1890s, about six hundred thousand Yorùbá had been shipped across the Atlantic in chains (see fig. 9.1). About four hundred thousand more had reached the Americas before 1790. So between 1600 and 1866, approximately one million Yorùbá entered the Middle Passage. During those 250+ years, they disembarked in a geographically wide area stretching from Chesapeake in the United States to Rio de Plata in the South American Cone and from the Caribbean to Peru and Mexico. However, more than two-thirds of their number concentrated in three locations—Saint-Domingue (Haiti), Cuba, and Brazil—especially during the peak years of their arrival, 1775–1850. Their arrival in Saint-Domingue ended soon after the outburst of the Haitian Revolution, 1791–1804, while their numbers in British Windwards and Trinidad, French Windwards, and Barbados grew moderately between 1801 and 1850. The majority of those who arrived in Trinidad were rescued from mostly Portuguese-Brazilian slave ships by the British antislavery squadrons.[74]

Although the Yorùbá were among the African cultural and language groups to arrive in concentrated numbers in the Americas between 1736 and 1850, they were not more numerous than many other major African ethnolinguistic groups. Overall, they accounted for about 8.3 percent of the over twelve million enchained Africans who arrived in the Americas throughout the history of the Atlantic slave trade. Of their three major points of disembarkation, they were not more than 12 percent of Africans carried to Cuba, and they were less than 20 percent of those who disembarked in Saint-Domingue. It was only in Bahia that they constituted a majority, accounting for about 40 percent of the African disembarkments during the nineteenth century.[75] Despite their relatively small numbers overall, no other African tradition or community of practice had as much influence as the Yorùbá in the formation of the New World African diaspora culture during the nineteenth century. In other words, as many previous observers have noted, the overall gargantuan impact of Yorùbá culture and political agency on the New World was out of proportion to their comparatively light demographic weight.[76] Nevertheless, the increasing number of Yorùbá arrivals in the Americas during the nineteenth century breathed new vitality into the lives of African cultures in the Americas. Their presence in large numbers also infused new sociopolitical urgency into the antislavery and anti-empire struggles in the Western hemisphere. The reasons for these Yorùbá historical footprints remain a subject of intense and exciting scholarly debate.[77]

The impacts of the Yorùbá on the cultural landscape of the Americas are most evident in religious practices and social organization, especially in Candomblé (Brazil), Lucumí or Santeria (Cuba), Ṣàngó (Trinidad), Voudon (Haiti), and Òrìṣà (United States). The preservation and adaption of the principle of *ilé* within those religious traditions (e.g., *cabildo* in Cuba and *irmandades* in Brazil) enabled free and enslaved Yorùbá to build new and strong communities in the Americas. Although these *ilé* were Yorùbá-centric and served as the conduits for recreating Yorùbá communities of practice in the New World, they accepted members of other ethnicities and races into their fold.[78] This conformed to the ontology and sociology of *ilé* as a cosmopolitan and diverse institution in the homeland. The *cabildo* or *irmandade* in the diaspora served the same purposes that the *ilé* had served for close to two thousand years in the homeland: "a social league for mutual support and protection."[79] The *cabildo*, *irmandade*, or *ilé* was an institution of social bonding for the creation of new "families" and organizations of people of diverse backgrounds but shared interests; the forging of kinship relationships irrespective of bloodlines; the accumulation and redistribution of resources; and the protection and advocacy of common interests, including spirituality, knowledge, and value.[80] The same way that the *ilé* had been organized around the ancestors and the Òrìṣà in the homeland for hundreds of years, the Yorùbá descendants in the diaspora used the *ilé* institution to reorganize themselves and others into "families," "brotherhoods," and "sisterhoods." These *ilé* were the nerve centers for the experimentation and innovation that enabled the reconstitution of Yorùbá cultures and the rebirth of Yorùbá communities of practice in the New World. For their generative, adaptive, and resilient qualities, some of these *ilé* became powerful spaces for self-help and pathways for self-realization. They also served as conduits for political agitation and the plotting of rebellion against the institutions of plantocracy, oppression, and racism. The organizational structure of the Yorùbá pantheon was so successful in Brazil, for example, that other communities of practice such as the Central African Bantu, West African Gbe, and Native American groups adopted not only the *Ọ̀rìṣà* framework but also the individual deities in the pantheon and their priestly hierarchies. These non-Yorùbá communities of practice thereby replicated the *Ọ̀rìṣà* conventions—the same deities, organizational structure, mode of worship, and ceremonies—but conducted worship in their respective languages and music.[81] Similar patterns occurred in Cuba, where the Òrìṣà institution also emerged as the dominant Afro-Cuban religious experience.

The necessity of using Yorùbá as the liturgical language for the highly structured and institutionalized Òrìṣà worship ensured the preservation of many aspects of Yorùbá language in the Americas, even if these have since been inflected by the official languages of the host colonial and postindependence society, as seen in Trinidad, Cuba, and Brazil.[82] Some of the surviving Yorùbá vocabularies in the New World give us a sense of the nature of Yorùbá lexicon and knowledge system, as well as their regional variations during the nineteenth century. The Yorùbá also left imprints on the African diaspora's economic culture. For example, in the French and British Caribbean, the Yorùbá introduced a credit and lending association system called *èsúsú* (or *súsú*). This is a capital-raising and money-saving mechanism organized by a loose network of individuals who contribute an equal amount of money at "fixed intervals; the total amount contributed by the entire group is assigned to each of the members in rotation" (see chap. 6).[83] The *èsúsú* helped African diaspora entrepreneurs to raise capital in the harsh environment of slavery and post-abolition poverty, and this enabled their members to start a trade, meet social obligations, or buy their freedom. Likewise, in artistic expressions and intellectual traditions—folklore, myths, legends, and philosophy—the indelible marks of Yorùbá culture have permeated both the discursive and nondiscursive aspects of everyday life in the Americas. This has transformed Yorùbá culture into a transatlantic and Black Atlantic civilization. Therefore, the Yorùbá political philosophy, practices of social organization, religious worldviews, and intellectual traditions became the compass used by those uprooted from the ancestral land to navigate the challenges of everyday life in the new environment.

Both the freed and the enslaved Yorùbá were responsible for the experimentations, communicative interactions, and innovations that shaped the adaptiveness, flexibility, and institutionalization of Yorùbá culture in the Americas. Among them were Àyànbí (Ño Juan el Cojo) and Àtàndá (Ño Filomena García), two men who arrived in Cuba in their prime age at different times during the 1820s and 1830s. They are credited with introducing the *bàtá* drum to Havana. According to Cuban oral history and traditions, while Àyànbí was an Ifá priest and herbalist before his enslavement, Àtàndá was a master wood-carver and master drummer. Also, Adéṣínà Ọ̀bàràméjì (a.k.a. Ño Remigio Herrera) arrived in Cuba in 1830 at about the age of nineteen. He was from the Ìjẹ̀ṣà country, and he was already an Ifá priest before his capture and enslavement. On gaining his freedom in 1850, he collaborated with both Àyànbí and Àtàndá to establish the Cabildo de Yemaya (House of Yemọja) in Regla (Havana). As a freeman, Adéṣínà established himself as "a stonemason, a significant . . . property owner, a protector of other Africans, and *padrino* [godfather] to influential Spaniards."[84] With his financial security and social networks, he funded the establishment of the House of Yemọ ja, and after his death in 1905, his daughter succeeded him as the head of the *ilé*. Enslaved and free women of Yorùbá descent, especially from southern Yéwá-Ògùn, also played a major role in establishing religious and mutual-aid Houses in nineteenth-century Cuba. They institutionalized the worship of Yorùbá female deities and standardized the Òrìṣà initiation rituals in Matanzas and Havana. Many of these women are still celebrated in Lucumí traditions. They included Ọbátérò (Oba Tero, or Ma Monserrate González), a priestess of Ṣàngó from Yéwá; her goddaughter, Òòsàbí Tíńbẹlẹ́sẹ̀ Olódùmarè (Ferminita Gómez), a priestess of Yemọja and Olókun, also from Yéwá; Ẹfúnṣe Warikondo (Rosalía Abreú); and Ayají Latuán (Timotea Albear).[85]

These men and women were not only agents of Yorùbá cultural production and builders of the Yorùbá communities of practice in the Americas. In Bahia (Brazil) as well as Havana and Matanzas (Cuba), the Yorùbá also played several roles as "generative actors in the intertwined process of slave emancipation and independence" during the age of revolution.[86] Aroused by the political disturbance in the homeland, and continuing with the restless militarism that had created the condition of their capture, enslavement, and the Middle Passage, the Yorùbá led and participated in some of the largest agitations for freedom from slavery and colonial rule in the Americas. Although most of these agitations stemmed from the basic concern of improving the living conditions of the enslaved and the poor, the ultimate goal of nearly all of them was to gain freedom from slavery by any means necessary. For example, the Yorùbá were the dominant contingent of the January 1835 Malê Uprising in Salvador, Bahia, the largest slave revolt in Brazil's history. The more than six hundred poorly armed rebels were, however, overwhelmed by the state security personnel. Apart from the few leaders who were sentenced to death, imprisonment, or public flogging, the majority of the rebels who survived the insurrection were deported to Lagos in present-day Nigeria. This was the Brazilian government's way of preventing the occurrence of a Haitian Revolution scenario in the newly independent country.[87] The Malê Uprising failed to achieve its immediate goal, but it changed the public discourse about slavery and its abolition in Brazil. However, this was only one of several Yorùbá-led or Yorùbá-populated revolts and uprisings in the Americas between 1835 and 1850. For example, between August and November 1843 in Matanzas, Cuba, two women of Yorùbá origin, Carlota and Fermina, led a revolt against plantocracy, grim working conditions, and slavery. Armed with machetes, these women and their followers launched attacks on sugar, coffee, and cattle estates to free their fellow enslaved men and women. The rebellion failed, and sixty of the rebels were killed, including Carlota. What followed was a repressive government policy toward African religious, cultural, and social institutions, but the event is now considered one of the milestones in Cuba's march toward the abolition of slavery and the colony's liberation from

Spanish rule.[88] In those last decades of slavery institution in the Spanish Caribbean and Lusophone South America, the Yorùbá (the Lucumí in Cuba and Nagô in Brazil) proved to be the fishbone in the throat of those governments seeking to prolong the life of their slave economy. In public and official discourses, the Yorùbá earned the sobriquet of "troublemakers"; they were the favorite subject of criticism and condemnation among the white and some of the other African populations. Some expressed fear and exaggerated sentiment that "these Lucumí rascals are going to finish their masters and everything else."[89]

Hundreds of thousands of enchained Yorùbá left the shores of the Bight of Benin for foreign lands in the nineteenth century, but thousands also returned from those sites of dislocation to their ancestral land between the late 1830s and the 1880s. Some were deported by the colonial state, as was the case in the aftermath of the Malê Uprising. The majority, however, self-repatriated to the homeland after purchasing their freedom from bondage, and others utilized "the limited legal and official avenues open to them at the time to gain liberty."[90] Many Yorùbá who were liberated from Spanish, Brazilian, and Portuguese slave ships by British abolitionists and resettled in Sierra Leone also returned home in large numbers, beginning in the midcentury. Most of these repatriates resettled in Lagos and Abẹ̀òkúta. The century also witnessed the advent of the Christian mission activities, in which Yorùbá missionaries, especially liberated captives from Sierra Leone, were active.[91] These returnees from Sierra Leone, Brazil, and Cuba served as cultural brokers between the Yorùbá communities and the emerging European Enlightenment and colonial project in the Bight of Benin. Those from Sierra Leone in particular became arrowheads for the spread of Christianity by the England-based Church Missionary Society (CMS).[92]

Àjàyí, the boy from Ọ̀ṣoògùn, was the most notable of these returnees. Nineteen years after a British antislavery patrol team rescued and resettled him in Sierra Leone, he returned in 1841 to the Bight of Benin and the Bight of Biafra. Now officially known as Samuel Crowther, he was a member of the British missionary team charged with exploring the Lower Niger River for commercial opportunities, spreading Christianity, and ending the slave trade in the interior. A year later, he was trained and ordained as a minister in London and was sent by the CMS in 1843 to open a mission in Abẹ̀òkúta. In this role, he administered the process of spreading the gospel and gaining souls for the church deep in the mainland. But more important, he was the architect of Yorùbá modernization through his efforts as a linguist to reduce the Yorùbá language to writing, a major revolution in Yorùbá cultural and intellectual history.[93] His accomplishments in this regard included the translation of the Bible into Yorùbá and the development of the first Yorùbá dictionary. He rose through the clergy ranks to become the first African Bishop of the Anglican Church in 1864. A polyglot and culturalist, he sought to Christianize his people but insisted that their culture, language, and history must also be preserved. In fact, the goal of his cultural nationalist project was to domesticate Christianity. By insisting that Àjàyí be used as his middle name, he proudly claimed his Yorùbá identity and his past while also asserting that one can be a good African Christian without losing one's Africanness and history.[94]

With vibrant communities of literate Yorùbá in Lagos, Porto Novo, Badagry, Abẹ́òkúta, Ọ̀yọ́, and Ìbàdàn during the second half of the nineteenth century, the Yorùbá language became a medium for documenting Yorùbá history and indigenous cultural practices. The written language was also used to elaborate on the Yorùbá vigesimal (base-20) numeral system, for mass communication via the print media, and for disseminating the Christian gospel. For example, the first Yorùbá language newspaper was launched in Abẹ́òkúta in 1859. The new intelligentsia—mostly Christian and comprising Sàró (Yorùbá returnees from Sierra Leone) and Amáro (Yorùbá returnees from Brazil and Cuba)—did not write only in Yorùbá. They also wrote about Yorùbá history and culture in English.[95] Hence, by 1897 Samuel Johnson, a Sàró of Ọ̀yọ́ ancestry, had completed his monumental *History of the Yorubas*, a book that has proved indispensable for any understanding of the nineteenth-century Yorùbá history.[96]

The middle of the nineteenth century also saw a rise in the profile of British agents in Yorùbá affairs. By 1851, the British were intervening militarily in the political affairs of Lagos for causes associated with the end of the slave trade and royal succession disputes.[97] Although it was a good twist, it was ironic that the largest slave-exporting and human-trafficking European nation of the seventeenth and eighteenth centuries became the champion of ending the Atlantic slave trade between 1808 and 1860 (table 9.1).[98] By then, the buzzing British steamships of the Industrial Revolution were puffing their way across the oceans, in search of raw materials as well as new consumers and trading outlets. Connecting the Yorùbá to the new industrial cities of England as suppliers of raw materials had become a priority. The British traders, missionaries, and administrators used their abolition-movement efforts and peacemaking missions among the warring Yorùbá states as stepping-stones to achieve that objective. All of these began with the annexation of Lagos as a British crown colony in 1861. By 1893, all the major Yorùbá kingdoms had been made to sign treaties pledging allegiance to the English monarch. Those who were unwilling to sign or abide by the terms of the one-sided conditions of the treaties were bombarded into submission by the British artillery and mercenaries.[99]

Table 9.1. Number of Slave Embarkations per European/American "National" Carrier, 1501–1875

Year Range	Spain / Uruguay	Portugal / Brazil	Great Britain	Netherlands	United States	France	Denmark	Other	Total
1501–1600	7,803	55,323	1,749	1,031	0	523	0	0	66,429
1601–1700	41,764	279,631	291,733	226,174	3,135	33,958	25,920	575	902,890
1701–1800	10,157	1,561,220	2,493,256	361,633	161,545	1,075,192	60,887	0	5,723,890
1801–1875	473,748	1,997,241	274,048	3,044	202,115	200,034	16,071	3,111	3,169,412
Total	**533,472**	**3,893,415**	**3,060,786**	**591,882**	**366,795**	**1,309,707**	**102,878**	**3,686**	**9,862,621**

Source: Slave Voyages, accessed May 4, 2019, https://www.slavevoyages.org/voyage/database.

Summing Up

The power politics and political intrigues in metropolitan Ọyọ́; the increasing demand for human cargo in the waters of the Bight of Benin; and the unsustainability of the merchant capital that underwrote power, wealth, and social inequality pushed the Yorùbá region to reach its sociopolitical breaking point between 1790 and 1837. During that long night of confusion, the underclass revolt in Ọ̀yọ́ and the Ifẹ̀-Ìjẹ̀bú siege of Òwu were particularly momentous. Both events launched the Yorùbá world into its worst region-wide crisis since the second half of the fifteenth century. The aftermath culminated in the collapse of the Ọ̀yọ́ Empire in 1837. The competition to fill the vacuum of hegemony created by Ọ̀yọ́'s fall fueled more wars. Ìbàdàn emerged as the dominant state in the region in 1840 following its defeat of Ìlọrin jihadists. The young state had proved to be the most resilient avenger of Ọ̀yọ́ humiliation during the Eléduwẹ War three years earlier, but its own draconian style of imperialism led to provincial revolts and a sixteen-year war (the Èkìtìparapọ̀ War) that pitted a regional alliance against Ìbàdàn between 1877 and 1893.

Between the death of Aólẹ̀ in 1796 and the British annexation of Lagos in 1861, more than half a million Yorùbá, mostly of the Ọ̀yọ́, Yéwá, Kétu, Ìdáṣà, Ẹ̀gbá, Ìbàràpá, and Ìjẹ̀ṣà subgroups, crossed the Atlantic in chains. Hundreds of thousands died as a result of the wars, displacement, fatigue, famine, and disease that accompanied the instability. Millions more were permanently displaced. Hundreds of thousands were enslaved locally as a source of labor for the bourgeoning export trade in agricultural products, especially palm oil and cotton. A few thousand more, especially from the Okun subgroup, also crossed the River Niger in chains to enter the Sokoto Caliphate. In all, about three-quarters of the Yorùbá region witnessed major demographic displacement. In the aftermath, new political experiments developed among the new and reconstituted polities, ranging from military autocracy to military republicanism and the federation system. The institution of *ọba* remained the apex of social order in most areas, but it remained subject to the militaristic ethos of the time in which warlords often usurped the powers of the *ọba* and the civil authorities. Uniquely, Ìbàdàn (a former war camp) rejected monarchy and adopted military republicanism as the model of its governance. In all of these experiments, the *ilé* continued to serve as the basic unit of organization. Its membership was now far more heterogeneous than ever before because of the massive region-wide demographic breakup and displacement, leading to the aggregation of people of diverse backgrounds into the new *ilé* and *ìlú* that sprouted up throughout the region. There was a silver lining to that century of confusion and suffering. Through the Ìbàdàn-led defense against the advancing Ìlọrin jihadists, the political heritage of the Yorùbá was preserved. And the cultural project of the new Yorùbá intelligentsia on the coast set the tone for Yorùbá modernization in the era of the European Enlightenment. In these two respects, Baṣọ̀run Olúyọ̀lé and Samuel Àjàyí Crowther were the most consequential figures in the nineteenth-century Yorùbá history. According to oral traditions, both were descendants of Aláàfin Abíọ́dún.[100]

Notes

1. Guyer, *Marginal Gains*; Inikori and Engerman, "Introduction."
2. As previously mentioned, in chap. 5, the *aláàfin* and the members of the *ọ̀yọ́mèsì* shared in the responsibilities for military expansion and security of the empire's territories. This involved recruiting and fielding soldiers and equipping them with arms and ammunition. In return, the king and the *ọ̀yọ́mèsì* shared in the proceeds of conquest: war booty, taxes, tributes, and tolls. Law, "Constitutional Troubles," 36.
3. It is likely that the later historians and social commentators exaggerated some of the excesses of Gáà in terms of his abuse of power (see Adébáyọ̀ Fálétí's *Itan Ibanujẹ* and Samuel Johnson's *History*). Nevertheless, Gáà was indeed the de facto ruler of Ọ̀yọ́ by the time Abíọ́dún ascended the throne.
4. Traditions remember Òjó Agùnbambarù as one of Gáà's sons who escaped to the Ìbàrìbá country (Akintoye, *History*, 278).
5. Johnson, *History*, 186–87.
6. This is still a popular song. It is a memory work that conveys a general sense of nostalgia about the apogee of the Ọ̀yọ́ Empire. Apart from Aláàfin Abìọ̀dún, mentioned in the text, Olúgbọ́n and Arẹ̀sà are titles of the governors of two prominent Ọ̀yọ́ provinces. Kókò is a type of imported green cloth, while sányán is a type of textile woven from anaphe wild silk and cotton yarns.
7. The *kàkàkí*, *kósó*, and *bẹ̀ǹbẹ́* were introduced from the Sudan, and the first two were restricted for the use of the *aláàfin* alone. Johnson, *History*, 58, 121.
8. Johnson, *History*, 65.
9. Lander, *Records of Captain Clapperton's Last Expedition*, 2:192.
10. Abimbọla, "Lagbayi"; Kalilu, "Between Tradition and Record."
11. Clapperton, *Journal of a Second Expedition*, 58–59.
12. For this and preceding quotes on sculptures, see Lander, *Records of Captain Clapperton's Last Expedition*, 2:197–98.
13. Lander, 83.
14. Gikandi, *Slavery and the Culture of Taste.*
15. Johnson, *History*, 186.
16. Adekunle, *Politics and Society*, 110.
17. For general comparisons that range from ancient to modern empires, see Alcock, *Empires*, and Sinopoli, "Archaeology of Empires"; and for case studies, see Hämäläinen, *Comanche Empire*, and Hopkins, "Taxes and Trade."
18. Cooper, *Africa in the World*, 38.
19. Following the lead of Samuel Johnson (*History*), many scholars have exaggerated the stabilizing force of Ọ̀yọ́ in the Yorùbá world between 1650

and 1800. For example, Akinjogbin, "Oyo Empire"; Akintoye, *History*; Smith, *Kingdoms*.

20. This trading network was also stimulated by the increasing importance of the Gold Coast in the Atlantic slave trade, dominated by traders whose ships flew the English flag.

21. Lovejoy, "Interregional Monetary Flows," 570.

22. Adekunle, *Politics and Society*, 110.

23. Usman, "Crisis and Catastrophe," 366–68.

24. One of these platoons was headed by Adégbiyì, an Ọ̀yọ́ man and a *balógun* (war commander) who was stationed at Ìjànà sometime in the middle of the eighteenth century (Adewale, "Ijanna").

25. Johnson, *History*, 187.

26. Smith, *Kingdoms*, 69.

27. Johnson, *History*, 191–92.

28. Akintoye, *Revolution*; Peel, *Religious Encounter*.

29. Law, *Oyo Empire*, 55. Two kings, Adébọ̀ and Mâkú, reigned for perhaps one year combined, 1796–97, before the five-year interregnum.

30. Akintoye, *History*, 276–79.

31. Professor Wándé Abímbọ́lá, personal communication, Lagos, April 7, 2018. Also see Abimbọla, "Ruins."

32. Captain Hugh Clapperton, for example, recorded how Prince Adémọ́lá, the resident commissioner of Ìpókíá, removed the cap from the head of one of his attendants, spit "his quid of tobacco into it," and returned the cap to its owner (Bruce-Lockhart and Lovejoy, *Hugh Clapperton*, 108).

33. Eltis, "Diaspora of Yoruba Speakers."

34. The 2016 projections suggest that there are about 55 million people in present-day southwest Nigeria (including the Edo-speaking area) and the Benin Republic. This is the core population center of the Bight of Benin and its hinterland. Of this figure, about 42 million (76%) are Yorùbá (Central Intelligence Agency, "World Factbook"; World Atlas, "Largest Ethnic Groups in Nigeria."

35. Akinjogbin, "The Growth of Ife," 110–11.

36. Akintoye, *History*, 177.

37. Kea, "Firearms and Warfare."

38. Falola and Oguntomisin, *Yoruba Warlords*, 5.

39. Johnson, *History*, 189.

40. This estimation was based on my reconnaissance visit to the site in 2011, courtesy of Dr. Adérẹ̀mí Àjàlá, the late Mr. Philip Gbádégẹsin, and Dr. Bọ́lánlé Túbọ̀sún.

41. Akintoye, *History*, 295–96.

42. Ayandele, *Ijebu*, 3.

43. The West African Squadron was established to patrol the waters of West Africa and enforce the United Kingdom's Slave Trade Act of 1807, which abolished the Atlantic slave trade in the British Empire and encouraged the British government to press other European states to abolish slave trading. To this effect, there was an 1815 treaty between Portugal and Britain making it unlawful "for any of the Subjects of the Crown of *Portugal* to purchase Slaves, or to carry on the Slave Trade, on any Part of the Coast of *Africa* to the Northward of the Equator, upon any Pretext, or in any Manner whatsoever." A convention of 1817 was added to include Brazil in observing the

terms of the 1815 treaty. Not only was Brazil the major colony of Portugal in the Atlantic world, but it was also the primary financier of the slave trade and destination for the captives leaving the Bight of Benin. By prohibiting the slave trade north of the equator, the treaty forbade human trafficking on the waters of the Bight of Benin and the coast of West Africa in general, but it was still permissible between Central Africa and Brazil. Davis, "Treaty between Great Britain and Portugal."

44. Crowther, *Second Narrative*; Crowther, "Letter to the Rev. William Jowett, Secretary of the Church Missionary Society, Detailing the Circumstances Connected with His Being Sold as a Slave. Fourah Bay. Feb. 22, 1837." For more details, see Page, *Samuel Crowther.*

45. Curtin, "Joseph Wright," 323.

46. Curtin, 326–27.

47. For example, Akintoye, *History,* 261–89; Also see Falola and Oguntomisin, *Yoruba Warlords*; Law, *Oyo Empire.*

48. The many episodes of regicide that Ọ̀yọ́'s palace historians recounted to Samuel Johnson, before Gáà's usurpation, should be understood as representation of this persistent conflict and negotiation between the palace and the nonroyal lords of the metropolis (see Johnson, *History*).

49. This was articulated by Joseph Wright of Ọ̀bà in his memoir when he said the people who attacked his town were of the same language and cultural group as he was. Curtin, "Joseph Wright," 323.

50. Hodgkin, *Nigerian Perspectives*, 225–26.

51. Ojo, "Organization," 90. For a detailed discussion and publication of these letters, see Ojo, "Document 2." But the credit-debt relationship was not one-way. The Luso-Portuguese traders, especially Bahians, were also indebted to the Yorùbá slave merchants. For example, when Kòsọ́kọ́ took two hundred bales of tobacco on credit from Silva Pereira of Bahia in 1849, he "also had credit worth 3,553,350 to 10,987,725 réis with Domingo Bello in Bahia" (Ojo, "Organization," 92). This would be between about $700,000 and $2,160,000 in 2016 US dollars, judging by calculations of the milréis-US dollar exchange rate in the 1840s and the value of the 1845 US dollar in 2016. See Manuel, "Inflation Calculator."

52. Okùbọ́tẹ́, *Ìwé Ìtàn Ìjẹ̀bú*, 49.

53. Curtin, "Joseph Wright," 328.

54. This is adapted from William Butler Yeats's "The Second Coming," https://www.poetryfoundation.org/poems-and-poets/poems/detail/43290.

55. During Májǒtú's meeting with Captain Hugh Clapperton on January 24, 1826, the king reportedly asked for the Captain's assistance to defeat his enemies so that he could "build up his fathers [*sic*] houses which war had destroyed." According to Clapperton, the king spoke about rebuilding his father's houses "in such a feeling and energetic manner and repeated [it] . . . 2 or 3 times so that I felt sincerely for him." Bruce-Lockhart and Lovejoy, *Hugh Clapperton*, 146–47.

56. This impression was particularly expressed by the Lander brothers during their 1830 visit (see Hallett, *Niger Journal*, 91) and echoed by Robin Law, *Oyo Empire*, 289.

57. In the Ìbọ̀lọ̀ area, where the metropolis enjoyed some loyalty, competitions between the governors of Ìkòyí, Gbogun, Ògbómọ̀ṣọ́, and Ẹdẹ prevented the development of a united effort to confront the expanding influence of Ìlọrin. Johnson, *History*, 210–11.

58. The fact that the Ọyọ́ and Nupe coalition that besieged Ìlọrin in 1825 was reduced to subsisting on locust fruit (*ìgbá*) suggests that famine was already setting in around the mid-1820s. The famine may have been exacerbated by the inadequate number of people to till the ground because of insecurity in the countryside and preoccupation with war.

59. The record of palynomorphs (plant microfossils) in Mejiro rockshelter shows the prevalence of very dry conditions during the terminal phase of Ọyọ́-Ilé's occupation (Orijemie, "Palaeoenvironmental Research"). For oral traditions about the drought that plagued the last years of the metropolis, see Abimbọla, "Ruins," 17.

60. Lander, *Records of Captain Clapperton's Last Expedition*, 2:219–20. The accounts of 1830 mention the meager presents that Aláàfin Májǒtú gave to the party of Richard and John Lander in May of that year. In fact, the only major gift that the king gave to the visitors, five days after their arrival, was described as "disgraceful in the extreme," a sharp contrast to the lavish presents that the king gave to Captain Clapperton four years earlier. These accounts show that the fortunes of the monarch, and Ọyọ́ in general, had steeply declined over that period. See Lander and Lander, *Journal of an Expedition*, 92.

61. The general tendency in the historiography is to credit brigandage for the massive abandonment of towns and villages in the metropolitan Ọyọ́ area. However, the traditions collected by Professor Wándé Abímbọ́lá attributed the depopulation of many villages, towns, and cities north of Òkè Ògùn to the famine of 1828–1830. "Ruins," 17. Abímbọ́lá also shared some of the stories of the impact of famine on the demographic collapse of Ọyọ́ metropolitan area with me (based on his 1960s fieldwork) on April 7, 2018, in Lagos.

62. For detailed discussion and a sequence of these events, see Johnson, *History*, 197–268. Other accounts largely derived from that of Johnson are Akintoye, *History*, 261–81, and Law, *Oyo Empire*, 245–99.

63. Law, *Oyo Empire*, 292.

64. Abimbọla, "Ruins." For the dramatic and fast-paced events that unraveled the empire between 1831 and 1836, see Johnson, *History*, 217–68. For a retelling of the story from an academic historian's perspective based on Johnson's account, see Akintoye, *History*, 261–89; Law, *Oyo Empire*, 278–99.

65. Ọyọ́-Ilé is now part of the Old Oyo National Park in the Federal Republic of Nigeria, and it has been the focus of my archaeological research since 2017.

66. For a few examples, see Ajayi, *Christian Missions*; Falola and Oguntomisin, *Yoruba Warlords*; Johnson, *History*; Law, *From Slave Trade*; Peel, *Religious Encounter*; Zachernuk, *Colonial subjects*.

67. Olúyọ̀lé was a man of great pedigree. On his father's side, he was a descendant of Başọ̀run Yáḿbà, one of the greatest *başọ̀run* in Ọyọ́ history; and his mother, Àgbọ̀nrín, was a daughter of Aláàfin Abíọ́dún (Johnson, *History*, 174, 281).

68. Johnson, *History*, 288.

69. Awe, "The Ajele system"; Falola, *Ibadan*. It should be noted that before the Òşogbo war, several Èkìtì, Ìjẹ̀sà, and Ìbọ̀lọ̀ areas were already under Ìlọrin's control, most of which Ìbàdàn later wrested from Ìlọrin.

70. Johnson, *History*, 638–50. Also see Ajayi and Akintoye, "Yorubaland"; Falola, *Ibadan*; Falola and Oguntomisin, *Yoruba Warlords*.

71. Ayandele, *Ijebu*, 5.
72. As a result of one of those conflicts, for example, the war chief of Ìjẹ̀bú-Òde, Balógun Ọ̀nàfọwọ́kàn, succeeded in driving several high-ranking civil chiefs, princes, and the king, Ọba Fìdípọ̀tẹ̀, into exile in 1883. Falola and Oguntomisin, *Yoruba Warlords*, 132.
73. Ayandele, *Ijebu*, 3–6.
74. Eltis, "Diaspora of Yoruba Speakers," 32–33; Lovejoy, "Yoruba Factor," 45.
75. Eltis, "Diaspora of Yoruba Speakers," 32.
76. For example, Eltis, *Rise of African Slavery*, 253. For a summary of the multidimensional aspects of these influences, see Falola and Childs, *Yoruba Diaspora.*
77. See Barcia, *West African Warfare*; Eltis, "Diaspora of Yoruba Speakers"; Matory, *Black Atlantic Religion*; Thompson, *Flash of the Spirit.* For an insightful conceptualization of the need to look beyond demographic strength to understand African cultural adaptations and generative powers in the Americas, see Kriger, "Conundrum of Culture," and Ogundiran and Saunders, "On the Materiality."
78. Barcia, *West African Warfare*, 18.
79. Warner-Lewis, *Trinidad Yoruba*, 44.
80. Apter, "Yoruba Ethnogenesis."
81. Bastide, *African Religions of Brazil*, 194–95; For an extended discussion of Bastide's research, observations, and conclusions, see Apter, *Oduduwa's Chain*, 143–47.
82. Agwuele, "'Yorubaisms'"; Lewis, *Yoruba Songs.*
83. Bascom, "Esusu," 63.
84. Brown, *Santería Enthroned*, 64–65.
85. Santeria Church, "Importance of Women in Santeria."
86. Rushing, "Review," 652.
87. Brazil declared its independence from Portugal on September 7, 1822.
88. Araujo, *Shadows*, 198; Gott, *Cuba*, 111–49.
89. Barcia, *West African Warfare*, 154–55; Also see Reis, *Slave Rebellion*, 157–58.
90. Otero, *Afro-Cuban Diasporas*, 37.
91. For details, see Ajayi, *Christian Missions*; Peel, *Religious Encounter.*
92. Originally founded in England in 1799 as the Society for Missions to Africa and the East, the organization was renamed Church Missionary Society in 1812. Stock, *The History of the Church.*
93. Ajayi, "How Yoruba." Not only did Crowther create Yorùbá orthography, write some of the language's earliest texts, and lead efforts to standardize Yorùbá writing, but he also contributed to the development of several other African languages as written texts. For example, he "produced a primer for the Igbo language in 1857, another for Nupe in 1860, and a full grammar and vocabulary of Nupe in 1864" (Àkàngbé, "Crowther").
94. Ajayi, *Patriot.*
95. Zachernuk, *Colonial Subjects.*
96. Falola, *Pioneer, Patriot, and Patriarchy.*
97. Mann, *Slavery.*
98. For example, the vessels flying the flag of Great Britain carried nearly 44% of the 5.7 million enslaved Africans to the Americas during the

eighteenth century. See Slave Voyages, accessed May 4, 2019, https://www.slavevoyages.org/voyage/database.

99. For example, the British attacked Ìjẹ̀bú-Òde and Ọ̀yọ́ in 1892 and 1894, respectively (Johnson, *History*, 619–22; Falola and Heaton, *History of Nigeria*, 95).

100. Whereas Olúyọ̀lé's mother was a daughter of Aláàfin Abíọ́dún, Àjàyí (on his mother's side) was a great-great-grandson of the *aláàfin*. See Ajayi, "Samuel Ajayi Crowther," 293–94; Johnson, *History*, 174, 281.

Part V: Conclusion

10

The Past in the Present

THE DEEP-TIME HISTORY OF THE Yorùbá is a lived history, in that the two thousand years of history (ca. 300 BC–AD 1840) covered in this book are embodied, compressed, flattened, and embellished in contemporary and everyday practices. One of my goals in this study is to disaggregate the multiple layers of this past and the ways in which they inform the present. I hope I have provided, with clarity, the stratigraphy of time and the social relations that constituted the Yorùbá history. Change is a constant theme in this narrative. But what makes it possible for this past to live on in the present is that there is a profound continuity or stability of certain core ideas and practices. These are the historical ontologies—the long-lasting general ways of being and understanding that make it possible for a community of practice "to carry forward historical change" and invent new epistemologies and axiologies for those changes.[1] It is this juxtaposition of continuity and change that help us understand the Yorùbá community of practice as a social and historical being. We recognize this community not simply because of the changes it experienced but, most important, because of the particular types of changes that its ontologies conditioned or mediated. The unique experience of time by any autonomous community of practice owes much to its ontology. But the latter is not immune from transformation, considering that it is the driving force of historical movement. Ontologies can be transformed gradually or abruptly by internal changes in social valuation (axiology) and theories of knowledge (epistemology) or by drastic events of internal or external origin.[2]

We encountered one of these ontologies in chapter 2. By the Late Formative period, if not much earlier, it had become prevalent for the ancestral Yorùbá to seek immortality by aspiring to become an ancestor, a deity of the household or *ilé*. The desire to live forever by becoming a deified ancestor was what made life meaningful. This quest was about the immortality of the soul and memory, not the body. It was a search for timelessness, to live on in the memory of the descendants as a venerated ancestor, from generation to generation, and therefore to become part of living history. A common prayer by contemporary Yorùbá elders that reaffirms the continuity of this belief asks for the "blessing of money and children as well as the blessing of immortality—the epitome of wealth and fortune" (*ire owó, ire ọmọ, àìkú, baálẹ̀ ọrọ̀*). This quest for divinity also gave rise to the Yorùbá divine kingship institution. In the eighth or ninth century AD, some individuals began to claim the status of divinity during their lifetime (as opposed to after physical death). These individuals defined themselves as living gods and used this claim to assert a status that was above that of the House chieftains and mega-House lords. In other words, they claimed to have achieved divinity and immortality while they were still alive. This was the origin of the Yorùbá divine kingship institution. The purveyors of this idea were also the ones championing a new model of governance—the *ìlú*, or the city-state. It was a profoundly revolutionary idea, and in the Èkìtì-Ifẹ̀ axis where this idea possibly originated, some House chieftains initially opposed or contested it. Nevertheless, the idea weathered the storm and became the preferred principle, practice, and philosophy of legitimizing power, authority, governance, and social order. This Yorùbá brand of divine kingship (*ọba aládé*) has lasted for more than a thousand years.

From Ọni Ìtaàkpá in the third or second century BC to Samuel Àjàyí Crowther in the nineteenth century, the stories that I have told in this book are not of gods and goddesses but of a people—their ideas, practices, institutions, and experiences. Like all human stories, these experiences were shaped by odds and challenges, creativity and innovation, ambition and imagination of greatness, weaknesses and strengths, vulnerability and sustainability, tribulation and triumph, as well as atrophy and regeneration. Some scholars have used an aquatic metaphor to describe the relentless currents of Yorùbá history as the river that never rests (chap. 4). But it is also a river whose velocity and volume expanded and contracted several times in the course of the twenty centuries covered in this book. I would add that the metaphor of an undulating landscape of hills and valleys is also appropriate for contemplating Yorùbá history. It was a history characterized by oscillations from efflorescence to stress, to regeneration, and so on. Stress came in different forms, as we have seen in the previous chapters.

Environmental stress has been a dominant factor in Yorùbá history. However, until now, this factor has been ignored in Yorùbá historiography. The climatic stress of the Big Dry stimulated the geographic spread of the proto-Yoruboid peoples between ca. 300 BC and AD 300, a process of adaptive radiation that eventually culminated in the birth of the Yorùbá community of practice early in the second millennium AD. A lesson here is that environmental crisis is not always a predictor of social death or cultural decline. The ecological contractions caused by the Big Dry played a significant role in the proto-Yoruboid and later the proto-Yorùbá social and demographic expansion. The cumulative effects of the reduction in precipitation in the tenth and eleventh centuries also launched the political conflicts and negotiations that gave rise to the classical city of Ilé-Ifẹ̀, the largest and wealthiest city of its time in West Africa, south of River Niger. The city that emerged from the domestic crisis of the tenth or eleventh century was founded on a universalizing epistemology and knowledge capital. Ilé-Ifẹ̀ was the place where the ideas that defined the Yorùbá community of practice were consolidated and given unprecedented clarity. With this, the Classical period began, and Ilé-Ifẹ̀ became the mecca of knowledge, identity making, and economic opportunity for a far-ranging region. Incorporated within its vast sphere of influence were other speech communities, including the Edo to the southeast. Its commercial empire stretched to the River Niger, and its fame reached as far as the Niger Bend in the Mali Empire and beyond.

Hence, about a thousand years after the proto-Yoruboid first began to radiate out from their small villages and hamlets in the southwestern corner of the Niger-Benue Confluence, their Yorùbá descendants had created the largest community of practice south of the River Niger. About this time, they were building cities and kingdoms; mastering material science in glass, iron, and copper-alloy production; and creating some of the most exquisite visual and verbal arts in different media and genres. Ilé-Ifẹ̀ was the arrowhead of this thrust of innovation that marked the Yorùbá Classical age. The locally produced Ifẹ̀ glass beads circulated widely across the West African region and possibly beyond, from Igbo-Ukwu, east of the Niger, to the Sudanic belt north of the Inland Niger Delta (chap. 3). And the Classical Ifẹ̀ sculptors succeeded in casting naturalistic human figures of nearly pure copper (96.8–99.7 percent), "a feat that artists of ancient Greece and Rome, the Italian Renaissance, and Chinese bronze casters never achieved."[3] Not only that, but the intellectuals of the "city of daybreak" also formulated a coherent corpus of religious and philosophical traditions that have been the hallmarks of Yorùbá civilization.

The highly celebrated modalities of Yorùbá urbanism may date back to the ninth century, but the emergent qualities of cosmopolitanism, diversity, intensity, interdependency, and openness that have since characterized

Yorùbá towns and cities are most noticeable from the twelfth century onward. These *ìlú* became the ultimate and ideal units of the Yorùbá sociopolitical order. They were generative, adaptive, and creative strategies for complex organizational management. This mode of urbanism is critical to understanding the sociology and philosophy of Yorùbá culture and its contributions to world history. However, we should not lose sight of the fact that the *ìlú* took on the characteristics of its building blocks, *ilé*, which had existed as a sociological unit for several centuries before the ninth or twelfth century. Conceptually originating as a familial and multigenerational unit of production and reproduction in the Early Formative period, each *ilé* grew to become an associational corporate group with its own Òrìṣà ritual field and institutionalized leadership (e.g., *ọba*). Whereas an *ilé* can exist and thrive on its own, there cannot be an *ìlú* without several *ilé*. Much of the debate about the resilience of the Yorùbá community of practice and its global influence will be resolved when we begin to pay attention to these two fundamental components of Yorùbá culture.[4]

I have situated the regional history of the Yorùbá within the broad subcontinental interactions, thereby establishing links between events, people, and practices in far-flung places. Until now, these subcontinental interactions have largely been ignored, and their consequences mostly undetected in the historiography. The extreme droughts of the 1380s through 1550s in the southern hemisphere (equivalent to the Little Ice Age in the northern hemisphere) led to subcontinental population redistribution, conflicts, and the reconfiguration of the political landscape in different ecological zones of West Africa. Those processes put enormous pressure on the Yorùbá world. The turmoil that accompanied the slow collapse of the Mali Empire, the meteoric rise of the Songhai Empire, and the ascendancy of Hausa city-states in Western and Central Sudan sent waves of terror across the northern Yorùbá and deep into the central part of the region. The recurrent multiyear droughts shriveled the wooded landscape and paved the way for Nupe horsemen to cause mayhem in the Yorùbá world, ca. 1450–1550. In the process, many northern Yorùbá, and some in the central region, were carted away into slavery in Western and Central Sudan, and across the Sahara. Ironically, it was during those tumultuous decades of the fifteenth through mid-sixteenth century that their northern Songhai neighbors coined the name Yorùbá and entered it into Arabic writing. I explained in chapter 4 that this ethnonym was adapted from Yàgbà, the largest of the north central and northwestern Yorùbá subgroups—the Okun. They were the most affected as victims of enslavement by the Nupe brigands. The name Yorùbá and its iterations in Sudanic languages—Yariba, Uraba, Euroba, or Yarbanci—did not originally refer only to the Ọ̀yọ́, as many scholars have proposed.[5] Rather, from its conception, the ethnonym referred to all the members of the Yorùbá community of practice. These included groups and individuals who subscribed to Ifẹ̀-centric practices and beliefs, as well as those speaking the dialects of the Yorùbá language continuum. The Ọ̀yọ́ became the most popular bearers of the name following their ascendancy as the most prominent Yorùbá group during the early seventeenth century. This is not surprising. Of all the Yorùbá subgroups, the Ọ̀yọ́ established the most enduring political, commercial, military, and diplomatic networks with their Central and Western Sudanese neighbors, especially between the early sixteenth and early nineteenth centuries.

The Yorùbá ethnonym gained wider currency during the nineteenth century in anglicized texts written by a new generation of Yorùbá intelligentsia who were mostly Christians and freed captives or descendants of the enslaved in the Atlantic world.[6] Harbingers of the new literate culture that was based on the Roman alphabet, this intelligentsia spearheaded the reduction of Yorùbá to writing and standardized the internal use of the ethnonym to refer to all the Yorùbá-speaking peoples.[7] It is interesting that the name Yorùbá, which was first mentioned in writing in the early seventeenth century in the aftermath of a period of stress and tribulation, became an instrument of regeneration for the Yorùbá community of practice during the mid-nineteenth century, right in the middle of another cycle of stress. The new generation and social group who appropriated the name were cosmopolitan, just like their deep-past forebears. They used this ethnonym to define a new present and envision a new future. In doing so, they were not creating a new community but were renewing the idea of the Yorùbá community of practice with new idioms.[8] These modernist, creolist, and cultural brokers of the nineteenth century were the continuation of, not a break from, what their pre-nineteenth-century forebears—kings, priests, itinerant artisans, migrants, and others—had kept in motion for more than eight hundred years. Those earlier ancestors made conscious efforts through myths, iconographic symbols and signs, religion, commerce, technology, and political patronage to forge regional identities that transcended local and speech communities. Without that rich deep-history knowledge base to work from, the intellectual pursuit of the nineteenth-century Yorùbá modernists and cosmopolitans such as Samuel Àjàyí Crowther and Samuel Johnson (Àǹlá Ògún) would not have been possible.

The kingdom-by-kingdom approach to writing and interrogating Yorùbá history has had a silo effect that makes it difficult to understand the dynamics and impacts of peer-polity interactions and regional relationships at the subcontinental scale. As a result, the broad patterns of historical processes that transcended these kingdoms have tended to be elusive. I have demonstrated in this book the immense capacity of different polities and political actors to think, strategize, and act across political and even language boundaries to solve regional crises and local problems. The mobilization of several areas of the Yorùbá community of practice against the Nupe militarists during the sixteenth century is a good example. While the Ìgbómìnà, Èkìtì, Ifẹ̀, and even Benin worked in concert to defend their ancestral land against the hostile neighbors from across the River Niger, the same objective led the Ọ̀yọ́ to create alliances with Ìbàrìbá and Wasangari soldiers, mercenaries, and horsemen. These coalitions succeeded in degrading and bringing to an end the overbearing power of the Nupe militarists by the third quarter of the sixteenth century. The regional response to the Nupe crisis is exemplary of a determined people who were able to plan and execute in the long term and across multiple generations in the struggle for their autonomy, security, and self-determination. It was an event long omitted from Yorùbá historiography. Those Ìbàrìbá and Wasangari soldiers, and even some of the Nupe subgroups who assisted the Ọ̀yọ́ in their counteroffensive struggle, would go on to become part of the expansionist military program that culminated in the Ọ̀yọ́ Empire by the mid-seventeenth century. These non-Yorùbá-speaking members of Ọ̀yọ́'s victory and their descendants became Ọ̀yọ́ in their political affiliation and cultural identity. As a result, they also became part of the Yorùbá community of practice while simultaneously recognizing and celebrating their Ìbàrìbá, Djerma, Wasangari, and Nupe ancestral roots. In turn, members of these groups left their indelible imprints on what the Yorùbá community of practice became during the seventeenth and eighteenth centuries (chap. 5 and 9). The distinctive identities of several Ìbàrìbá and Nupe families as integral parts of the Yorùbá community of practice are celebrated till today in Yorùbá orature and social memory. All of these exchanges across language boundaries, including music, clothing style, facial marks, and equestrian culture, attest to the emergent and expansive qualities of this megaregional community and upend the tribal model that has been used for so long to configure the Yorùbá, indeed African, historiography.

The generation of victorious war veterans and their immediate successors who ended the Nupe militarist crisis proved to be masterful agents of change who used power politics, diplomacy, and military strategies to reconfigure the regional political landscape. They were sometimes brutal conquerors, but they were also state-builders who forged regional alliances. Notable among them were Abípa, Ọbalókun, and Àjàgbó of Ọ̀yọ́; Ọ̀bàràbarà Olókùnẹ̀ṣin, Ọwálúṣẹ́, and Àtàkúnmọ̀sà of Iléṣà; and Orhogbua and Ehengbuda of Benin. Two hundred years later, when the Yorùbá of the woodland savanna faced the jihadist crisis, the Ọ̀yọ́, the Ìbàrìbá, and a section of the Nupe would again form alliances to repel the menace. Though unsuccessful, those military coalitions of 1825 (Ọ̀yọ́ and Nupe) and 1827 (Ọ̀yọ́ and Ìbàrìbá) again attest to the broad regional networks that political leaders tapped into in order to achieve self-defense and self-preservation. Those alliances were based on the road map of a deep history that was very familiar to the agents who pursued these collaborations. The long-term history that I have discussed in this book encourages us to ask questions about how people at different junctures of time made use of the past and invoked memory in order to find solutions to the predicaments of their time and to imagine a better future.

The transregional approach of this study also shows that the Yorùbá subgroups, often loosely defined on the criteria of dialect differences, were not a timeless creation or a product of one big-bang event. Instead, they were compounding products of several historical processes originating from different junctures of time. Linguistic evidence and orature demonstrate that each dialect group had its historical pathway, but each pathway intersected and converged with others at different times through regional interactions (see fig. 2.2). The adaptive radiation of the proto-Yorùbá led to the development of the majority of contemporary Yorùbá dialect groups between AD 250 and 750. But a few of them, such as the Ìjẹ̀ṣà, developed as recently as the seventeenth century out of the regional interactions and processes of political negotiation that followed the Nupe militarist crisis. The Iléṣà kingdom, which became the center of the Ìjẹ̀ṣà ethnopolitical identity, arose from the rubble of the collapsed Ifẹ̀ Empire during that period of regeneration, 1570–1650. It was also during that period that the Yéwá (formerly Ẹ̀gbádò) identity began to coalesce from the amalgamation of the much older Ẹ̀gbá, Ọ̀yọ́, and Kétu identities, thanks to Ọ̀yọ́'s imperial agenda in the Yéwá-Ògùn frontier.

We have seen that the vast multitudes of Yorùbá polities were products of different experiences of time, not a spontaneous eruption on a timeless landscape or a product of one moment of migration from a single point of origin. One should, therefore, be wary of the sort of static hierarchical relationships that several political dispensations since the early twentieth century have sought to impose on the history of Yorùbá kingdoms and their royal dynasties. The current hierarchies, distinguishing between the so-called primary and secondary Yorùbá kingdoms, are usually treated as sacrosanct in both academic literature and popular imagination. However, these hierarchies are products of the regional political reorganization that followed the collapse of the Ọ̀yọ́ Empire, the instability of the nineteenth century, and the imposition of the British colonial rule. These gazetted and standardized official template of hierarchies among the Yorùbá kings during the early twentieth century was created at the instigation of the colonial officers, who needed this narrative to implement the British policy of indirect rule.[9] And the hierarchies have been revised several times since independence to accommodate the changing political configurations in postcolonial Nigerian politics. The gazetted royal hierarchies and the intense debates they often generate in both academic and public discourses, therefore, have less to do with the deep-time Yorùbá political history and more to do with present-day politics.[10] Ironically, many Yorùbá *ọba* now reference the British colonial-era Chiefs Law, edicts, and advisories as the basis for justifying or contesting their status in the regional hierarchy of *ọba-aládé*, an illustration of the deepening effect of colonial hegemony on the so-called natives. Such citations often involve the invention of imaginative but spurious stories about history and past dynastic relationships that many *ọba* publicly launder in attacks and counterattacks against one another.[11] This degenerating situation prompted a group of concerned historians and stakeholders to publicly scold the affected *ọba* and call for caution. The group, in a communique issued on March 1, 2019, expressed their concern: "It would . . . appear that some Yoruba Oba are not sufficiently versed in the history and traditions of Yorubaland, including their specific areas of prescribed authority in it. This patent ignorance has resulted in blanket statements that border on either plain falsehood or, worse still, half truths, all of them capable of demeaning the cherished traditions of the Yoruba." The group advocated several remedies, mentioning that the study of Yorùbá history "is in dire need of a serious revival and reinvigoration."[12]

I would admit that the invention of the past is part of the necessary process of creating historical knowledge. However, I hope this book will serve as a guide on how to evaluate such inventions in order to get closer to understanding and differentiating between the past that was and the one that never was. No doubt, the concerns with regional political hierarchies are as old as the origins of the Yorùbá community of practice, but such hierarchical claims have always been in flux and subjected to political negotiations and power politics. The emergence of Ilé-Ifẹ̀ as the place of reference and reverence for the Yorùbá community of practice during the Classical period would have made it imperative to create the earliest versions of this hierarchy of pristine/secondary or senior/junior kingdoms to justify conquest and domination and to institutionalize unequal regional power relations. However, most kingdoms of the Classical period did not survive to the present. With a few exceptions, the majority that survived have since lost the grandeur of their power, as evident in the history of Osi-Èkìtì and Ìlàrè-Ìjẹ̀ṣà, among several others.[13] The contemporary postcolonial landscape of Yorùbá kingdoms is just the latest layer of time. The layers beneath are vastly different from the present. There were great kingdoms that preceded the sixteenth century that have since disappeared, leaving only archaeological and oral historical traces; and there are diminutive dynasties of today whose ancestors were giants in the deep past (chap. 3 and 4). The converse is also true. Hence, I have shown how the malleable Ifẹ̀-centric tradition, with its rich corpus of mythoi, has been revised at different junctures of time since the thirteenth century to justify regional power relations (chap. 3 and 5).

History is more than the facticity of what happened, who did what, when, how it happened, and why it happened. It is also about what it meant to those who lived the experience and what it has meant to the generations of descendants. Therefore, to understand the meaning and meaningfulness of the lived experience of the Yorùbá community of practice, and to account for the rationalities of thought, aspiration, and purposefulness that shaped their experience of time, it is imperative that we place indigenous forms of representation at the forefront of historical inquiry. I hope I have made it clear in these pages that there is no other way of achieving this goal outside the Yorùbá mythoi and Òrìṣà corpus, the very substance of ancestral Yorùbá communicative interactions and knowledge building. Although this substance has generally been omitted in the methodology and conceptual frameworks of Yorùbá historiography, I have demonstrated that these mythoi and the Òrìṣà epistemology are indispensable for writing a decolonized history of the Yorùbá. They move us closer to achieving one of the aspirational goals of decolonial studies: that every way of being must be explained by its own theory of knowledge in order to achieve a truly cross-cultural understanding. The ancestral Yorùbá used the Òrìṣà corpus to create and revise their ways of being; articulate their theories of knowledge; define and rationalize their reality; and validate and critique the material relations of power and social inequality, morals of accumulation and social valuation, as well as the processes of self-realization and social reproduction. The Òrìṣà corpus provided the intellectual contexts in which ancestral Yorùbá sought the meanings and meaningfulness of the time in which they lived. By bringing this corpus under the lens of historical analysis, I have demonstrated that the Òrìṣà are part of the processes and products of time rather than the relics of a fossilized past. The historicity of the Òrìṣà pantheon and the Ògbóni, Ẹpa, and Gẹ̀lẹ̀dẹ́ institutions sheds a bright light on the lives of the people who created gods and goddesses in their own image in the quest to make sense of their living world and their temporality. In turn, we come to the understanding of how these gods and goddesses (re)created the men and women whose experiences fill the pages of this book.

My interest in the meanings and purpose that drove the motor of Yorùbá deep history also requires that I create, borrow, and apply terminologies and concepts that are relevant to the substance of our historical inquiry. Hence, the House society (*ilé*), gender duality, the *ìlúlọba-aládé* dyad, knowledge capital, referentiality, merchant capital, materiality, social valuation, sociality of objects, resilience, and regeneration, among others, feature prominently throughout this book. They speak not only to the nature of our data but also to the new questions being asked of these sources, especially the conceptual frameworks, ideas, and practices that have shaped Yorùbá history. My point of emphasis here is fidelity to historical knowledge, which, according to Jan Vansina, "is . . . an interpretation of *traces* of the past, used as evidence relative to the question being investigated."[14] These traces include embodied memory, imagery, orature, and materials of different forms. I have used these to explore the changes in several ideas and practices that were constitutive of the Yorùbá community of practice at different historical periods. Of these ideas and practices, gender relations have received much attention throughout this book. Here, I seek to understand the changing relationships between men and women from the end of the proto-Yoruboid era during the late first millennium BC to the transformations in political institutions and theories of governance at the onset of the Classical period. I have also devoted a lot of space to the effects of the Yorùbá entanglement in the web of the early modern economy on gender relations. My conclusions challenge us to rethink the celebratory historiography on Yorùbá women. The latter is generally oblivious to how the commodification of labor and the institutionalized stratification adversely affected the general status of women during the seventeenth and eighteenth centuries. This historiography has taken its cue from the anthropological and sociological approaches in Yorùbá studies that tend to emphasize a static structural interpretation of the ideals and symbolism of gender relations.[15] These studies are of immense value and represent some of the best scholarship in African studies. However, by not contextualizing those gendered ideals and symbols in the long-term historicity of practice that produced them, they have missed the dynamics of power, regimes of value, and political economy that shaped the everyday social relations between men and women at different registers of time before the nineteenth century.

I have also underscored that gender in Yorùbá deep-time history was more than the relationship between men and women as social and biological categories. It was also about (1) how patricentric and matricentric authorities, ideas, and practices were socially created, contested, maintained, and transformed over time; and (2) how biological males and females were recruited into the feminine and masculine spheres as socially constructed and complementary gendered categories. A person may belong to both gendered categories simultaneously and at different times in a lifetime. That is, the gendered identities of a person may change over the life course. Gender relations, as in class or kinship relations, were about the negotiation of access and denial to opportunities and privileges, as well as the creation of social order. Power over the control of resources and the means of production has always been central to this negotiation. Hence, the regimes of value and political economy that prevailed at different times in the Yorùbá world affected the dynamics of gender relations and the symbols used to communicate them. A critical takeaway, evident in chapter 8, is that the complementarity of the gendered duality between the patricentric and matricentric spheres was weakened during the era of the Atlantic commercial revolution. This was due to the increasing autonomy and power of the patricentric sphere to accumulate people, merchant capital, and other resources (war booty, land, slaves, tributes) independent of the matricentric authority and outside the traditional marriage social networks that had previously structured production and reproduction. As a result, the matricentric sphere increasingly became dependent on patricentric authority. In this arrangement, men and women of servile or tributary origin may become permanently feminized. Freeborn biological males tend to remain within the patricentric space, whether in their paternal or maternal *ilé*. Freeborn biological women had the option of retaining gendered duality, but class and status mediated this option for them. Those of the elite background, especially daughters of alpha and upper-class Houses (and some senior wives), were more likely to be recruited into the patricentric sphere of authority than their fellow women in the lower socioeconomic ranks. As a mother (in both natal and marital *ilé*) and a husband (in the natal *ilé*) simultaneously, a woman of the elite or middle class could take on a socially androgynous identity, especially in her middle age, that enabled her to exercise both patricentric power and matricentric authority.[16] All of this challenges us to avoid an a priori patriarchal model, originating in Western social science, for interpreting the historical Yorùbá gender experience.

I have emphasized throughout this book the effects of the social lives of objects on the processes of cultural production and the practices that developed from those processes. The preceding chapters show that two regimes of value—knowledge capital (1000–1400) and merchant capital (1500–1840)—shaped Yorùbá history between the twelfth and mid-nineteenth centuries. While the former was based on the proprietary knowledge of primary glass production, the latter was based on the importation of cowrie shells and other commodities from across the Indian and Atlantic Oceans. These objects were both the repository and actant of ideas and narratives about personhood, self-realization, and community building. Glass beads and cowries were more than things. Political authority and power rested, in part, on controlling the production and circulation of these two objects. By paying attention to the social valuation of glass beads and cowries, I have been able to explore the close-knit interdependency between political economy and culture in the making of Yorùbá history. Ilé-Ifẹ̀ succeeded in establishing a vast commercial empire based on its proprietary knowledge of glass production. A rare case in the economic history of Africa, Classical Ifẹ̀'s wealth, commercial power, and political economy were grounded in a complex operational chain of glass production and distribution (chap. 3). With its monopoly of glass-making technology devoted exclusively to bead production, Ilé-Ifẹ̀ used its glass beads to transform itself into the reference city for a new political tradition and religious and mythological cosmogony. By transforming glass beads into objects of desire that underwrote political power and spiritual authorities as well as wealth and self-realization, the "city of abundance"—one of Ile-Ife's nicknames—became the largest emporium in the Yorùbá Classical period. Although overproduction of glass beads seems to have contributed to the eventual decline of Ilé-Ifẹ̀'s economy during the late fourteenth century, Classical Ifẹ̀ gives us an unparalleled example of the mass production of desire over a period of four hundred years. The result was a corresponding regional dependency on Ilé-Ifẹ̀ as the source of wealth and all the other good fortune that glass beads represented in Yorùbá cultural history.[17] Glass beads did more than elevate the status of Ilé-Ifẹ̀ as a regional hub of commerce, prestige, and power. Ilé-Ifẹ̀ used this technological know-how to create regional identities and interdependencies that culminated in the Yorùbá community of practice. It also used this technology and its products to sponsor or finance a new knowledge system that restructured the sense of time, belonging, history, wellness, and memory for that community (chap. 3).

The merchant-capital revolution of the Atlantic exchange marked the beginning of a new regime of value and a social valuation that centered on the importation of cowrie shells, the first mass-market currency in West Africa's economic history. It was the first currency that united dozens of communities of practice from Western Sudan to the Bight of Benin. Although the "cowrification" of the Bight of Benin's economy began in the early sixteenth century, it was only a century later that the vast majority of the Yorùbá mainland became entangled in the web of the commercial revolution that sustained the import of cowries. The novelty of this revolution was not only that the region's local currency was imported, but that people were the primary commodity exchanged for it. This placed the Yorùbá region, like all other parts of Atlantic Africa, on the side of economic dependency at the very time that they were becoming part of the early modern world economic system. The early seventeenth century, therefore, marked a new horizon of time for the Yorùbá. It was the beginning of a new society characterized by new negotiations and cultural translations between the local and the global. This process was shaped by experimentations that sought to migrate some of the ideas of knowledge capital (glass beads) to the temporality of merchant capital (cowries).

No object played as significant a role as cowries in the efforts of the Yorùbá to domesticate, rationalize, and make sense of the Atlantic experience (chap. 7).[18] It was from this process of cultural translation of the merchant-capital revolution that new practices, habits, traditions, and culture were born during the seventeenth and eighteenth centuries. The majority of the enslaved Yorùbá who entered the dark vortex of the Middle Passage originated from this new horizon of time, which scholars have referred to as the Atlantic age or Atlantic modernity. I have shown in this book that the Yorùbá were cocreators of Atlantic modernity, not recipients of it. In other words, the Yorùbá modernity evolved as an integral part of the negotiations and interactions that created the Atlantic modernity globally.[19] The debate among the Yorùbá on how to manage their Atlantic experience is most evident in the new ideas of self-realization and the meanings of individuality, as well as new political culture, class identities, and gendered relationships. These were all consequences of the merchant capital revolution. Some of the outcomes of Yorùbá participation in Atlantic modernity had similarities with other parts of the world. For example, the Yorùbá Atlantic age marked the beginning of consumption society, akin to what Grant McCracken called the second stage in the development of English consumer culture. It was characterized by "a heightened propensity to spend" and "an increased frequency of purchases," since most people consumed most of the things they did not produce and produced less than the totality of what they consumed.[20] For the Yorùbá and other peoples of Atlantic Africa, an integral component of the merchant-capital revolution was monetized economy, a transformative phenomenon that facilitated unprecedented mass participation in commerce and economic specialization (chap. 6). But keeping this monetized economy's momentum going depended on the Atlantic slave trade, the source of the merchant capital (currency imports) needed to finance domestic production and consumption. Herein lies the origin of the zero-sum idea of the Yorùbá and other peoples of Atlantic Africa about wealth and capitalism.[21]

However, it was not the affective qualities of cowries or any other European merchandise that played the dominant role in the Yorùbá entanglement in the early modern world economy. It was the pleasure-taste, habit of consumption, and addiction to tobacco that integrated the Yorùbá and other parts of the Bight of Benin's mainland (as far as Central Sudan) into the networks of the Atlantic exchange. Bahia's tobacco was the dominant import that financed the largest-ever human trafficking in the Bight of Benin and its Yorùbá mainland (chap. 6 and 7). The Yorùbá were not alone in the pleasure-taste-addictive effect of the Atlantic-age merchant-capital revolution. It was worldwide: the entire commodity exchange that defined the early modern world was based on the production, distribution, and consumption of soft drugs with no nutritional value—sugar, tobacco, tea, coffee, chocolate—as well as trifling things of no immediate intrinsic value—gold, silver, and beads (including glass, pearl, and cowrie beads).[22] These commodities made capitalism and the modern world possible. They were so successful because they are addictive, social, and affective objects, with considerable impact on the physiology and chemistry of the body as well as the mentality of self-realization.

While the addictive taste for Portuguese/Brazilian tobacco shaped the processes of slaving and the slave trade in the Bight of Benin, it was the addictive taste for Portuguese/Brazilian alcohol (sugar) that dominated the slave trade in Central Africa.[23] There were other examples beyond Africa. The British, for example, flooded the Chinese market with American silver (ca. 1600–1820) and, later, Indian opium (1820–1860), all to satisfy their addictive taste for tea.[24] Mexico and Peru produced about 85 percent of the world's silver from 1500 to 1800, and about 40 percent of that silver ended up in China, mostly as payment for the imports of Chinese tea to Europe, with most of the carriers being British ships from the 1650s through the 1860s. Other Chinese exports included silk and porcelain. Between 1797 and 1820 alone, the British accumulated a nearly £1.7 million trade deficit with China, as a result of their addiction to Chinese tea. It is estimated that the value of the silver bullion that European merchants imported into China between the late sixteenth century and early nineteenth century was worth over 350 million reals (an equivalent of the British £13 million in the eighteenth century).[25] Likewise, the Chinese paid an exorbitant price—material and mental—for Hawaii's sandalwood, which they burned on the altars for the worship of their ancestors.[26] This juxtaposition of Yorùbá Atlantic experience with other parts of the world challenges us to move away from the false dichotomy of Hegelian dialectics, where "Africa represented a negation of and a necessary antithesis to a triumphant [rational] bourgeois West."[27] The social valuation of merchant capital—or any affective commodity, for that matter—was as rational as every community of practice that defined it.

It is not surprising that the regime of value that the merchant-capital revolution created in Atlantic Africa was unsustainable. This, among other factors discussed in chapter 9, contributed to the collapse of the largest Yorùbá political edifice—the Ọ̀yọ́ Empire. It was a behemoth built on the foundation of the merchant-capital revolution. Because it occupied almost two-thirds of the Yorùbá landscape, its slow and protracted decline had a cascading effect on the entire region, unleashing unprecedented waves of pain and dislocation that have been rightly called the "age of confusion." It was also an "age of revolution," but one without transformative visionaries. The same concerns for freedom that brought about the age of revolution in the Western Hemisphere also led to the revolts of the enslaved, the underclass, and tributary provinces in the Ọ̀yọ́ Empire. However, many of the people who rebelled against the injustices of the empire/merchant-capital duality also contributed to the reproduction of those injustices. This was because the alternative to the very acts that created injustice was unthinkable to many. It was also structurally unattainable within the configurations of Atlantic world power relations in which the Yorùbá community of practice was embedded. However, the nineteenth century was also a period of self-redemption, with the determined military force of Ìbàdàn halting the southward advance of Ìlọrin jihadists in 1840, about three years after the Ọ̀yọ́ Empire had effectively come to an end. But this victory did not bring the age of confusion to an end. Rather, it launched another fifty years of war and instability for reasons discussed in the previous chapter.

The events of the 1790s through the 1830s culminated in the final collapse of the "house of cards" that the Ọ̀yọ́ Empire and merchant capital revolution had built. The rock on which the house was built, however, remained intact. The question that faced the generative agents of that era was the kind of new house to build on that bare rock. They did not find an answer to this question until the British, the French, and the Germans appeared on the scene and made the decision for them, bringing an end to about two thousand years of ancestral Yorùbá political, intellectual, and cognitive autonomy. In the course of that age of confusion and revolution, the Òrìṣà epistemologies, ontologies, and axiologies continued to dominate the framework for making sense of the new experiences of time, but some also began to use Christianity and Islam to seek meaning and understanding of the changing time. From the hot black-soot pot was emerging the flavorful *àdàlú*, the Yorùbá porridge made from black-eyed peas and corn. *Àdàlú* is a quintessential Yorùbá food of globality and Atlantic cultural encounters; it also idiomatically embodies what the Yorùbá had become by the end of the nineteenth century.[28] The *àdàlú* metaphor provides a framework to think about how the new theories of being, ways of being, and referentiality of being were domesticated within the old forms to create the new Yorùbá community of practice in the early twentieth century.

Between 1843 and 1861, the intertwined triple forces of Christianity, Western education, and European colonial rule began to make inroads into the region. The Yorùbá encounter with Western colonial and Industrial Revolution modernity began in earnest, and new practices and worldviews, as well as new yardsticks for measuring social order and value, took hold in the consciousness and aspiration of some segments of the population. The pace of Islamic influence also increased and, with Christianity, steadily gained adherents across the land.[29] The Òrìṣà ontology and epistemology maintained its dominant ground for the remainder of the nineteenth century, as the guiding light for the majority and the very cord of memory that linked most of the people to their past. However, by the end of the century, the Òrìṣà ritual field ceased to monopolize or even dominate the organic platform for generating new myths and intellectual reflections about contemporary events and the future. With Western education becoming the passport for and instrument of socialization into colonial modernity, there was a small but resilient new generation who expressed doubts about the Òrìṣà heritage of practice and rejected its intellectual tradition. There are already several definitive books on the late nineteenth and early twentieth century focusing on Christianity and Islam as agents of social and cultural change, but the history of Òrìṣà traditions for the same period has not been written.[30] Nevertheless, we know that the Òrìṣà intellectual traditions influenced the translations of the Bible into Yorùbá language, shaped the domestication of Christianity and Islam, and enabled the conversion of these Abrahamic religions into Yorùbá cosmologies.[31] A history of the Òrìṣà, not its ethnography, promises to be a rewarding endeavor that would showcase how this religious tradition and its exponents mediated the Yorùbá experience, both in the homeland and in the diaspora, during the turbulent nineteenth century.[32]

The Yorùbá community of practice survived the turbulence of the century but temporarily lost its political independence to three European colonial powers—British (Nigeria), French (Benin Republic), and German (Togo)—between 1860 and 1960. Much water has passed under the bridge since then, and a thorough treatment of that period and its aftermath is outside the scope of this book. Suffice it to say that the Yorùbá community of practice is today a thriving entity with over forty million members worldwide. The vast majority live in the ancestral homeland but they also exist in small groups in some parts of Africa (e.g., the Akú of the Gambia and Sierra Leone) and large communities in Europe and throughout the Americas. In the latter, they usually assume different names, such as Lukumí (Lucumí), Santería, Nago, and Candomblé. Since the last decades of the nineteenth century, the different units of the Yorùbá community of practice have not been defined solely by kingdom rule, dialect, or city-state. The modern nation-state, multireligious affiliations and spiritual networks, United States of America's Black Nationalist movement, multiracial identities, and ancestral provenance studies that are based on oral traditions, documentary sources, and commercial genetic tests are some of the sources of their individual and group identification. Even in the ancestral home, they now live under diverse sets of rules, practices, and epistemic orders that form a collage of different experiences of time, including colonial modernity, multiethnic nation-state, and postcolonial globalization, as well as Christian, Islamic, and Òrìṣà traditions. I hope this book offers a deep understanding of how these people got to where they are and provides some of the frameworks for contemplating and studying the Yorùbá deep history in new ways. *Àṣẹ*.

Notes

1. Souvatzi, Baysal, and Baysal, "Is There *Pre*-history?"; Also see Robb and Pauketat, "From Moments to Millennia."

2. In the extreme, hostile agents seeking to destroy or weaken a community may target its ontologies for annihilation. Since historical ontologies define the being and becoming of a community of practice, destroying the ontology of that community is a sure path to destroying its autonomy and resistance. Expansionist and hegemonic empires and states tend to pursue this strategy, as in the case of European colonial power all over the world in the sixteenth through the twentieth centuries.

3. Blier, "Art in Ancient Ife," 80.

4. Also see Apter, "Yoruba Ethnogenesis."

5. For example, Law, "Ethnicity and the Slave Trade," 206.

6. Law and Mann, "West Africa in the Atlantic community"; Zachernuk, *Colonial Subjects*.

7. Ajayi, "How Yoruba Was Reduced to Writing."

8. A number of scholars who have limited their evidential base to the nineteenth-century archival sources have attributed the forging of a pan-Yorùbá identity to the nineteenth-century Christianized Yorùbá intelligentsia and to the Yorùbá diaspora. These studies incorrectly reduce the *authentic* Yorùbá to a Creole identity and impose a tribal model on Yorùbá historical sensibility. See Matory, "English Professors of Brazil"; Peel, *Religious Encounter*. For a contrary position that argues for the African origin of Yorùbá ethnogenesis, see Apter, "Yoruba Ethnogenesis"; Ojo, "'Heepa' (Hail) Òrìṣà."

9. For example, when the British Governor of Lagos colony, William MacGregor, invited the Ọọ̀ni Olúbùṣe Adélẹ̀kàn of Ifẹ̀ to Lagos in 1903, he conducted several interviews with the king, with the intention of compiling a list of Yorùbá kings who had the authority to wear the beaded crown. The goal of the exercise was to establish the hierarchy of kingship in Yorùbáland. This was needed to implement the British policy of indirect rule—a colonial administrative system that governed through indigenous political institutions. In this configuration, those who supposedly received their beaded crowns from Ilé-Ifẹ̀ were considered to be the direct descendants of Odùduwà and the pristine kings in Yorùbáland. Ọọ̀ni Olúbùṣe supplied MacGregor with the names of twenty kings/dynasties (excluding himself) with the rights and privileges to wear the beaded crown. During the same visit to Lagos, MacGregor pulled the Ọọ̀ni into the Ẹlẹ́pẹ̀ of ẹ̀pẹ́ controversy and was asked to make a pronouncement on whether the Ẹlẹ́pẹ̀ had the authority to wear a beaded crown. See *Government Gazette of the Colony of Lagos*, February 20, 1903. At the instigation of British officials, the Ọọ̀ni was also involved in many other controversies over the wearing of the beaded crown. One example was

the case of the Atáọ̀ja of Ọ̀ṣogbo in 1946. Although Ibadan, the overlord of Ọ̀sogbo, countered that the Atáọ̀ja had no right to wear a beaded crown, the Ọ̀ọ̀ni sided with the claim of Atáọ̀ja that he had the right, based on his pedigree as a son of Ajíbógun Obòkun. This would make Atáọ̀ja a grandson of Odùduwà. Oyo Prof 1/1 File 1372: Crown—Possession of. Letter from Senior Resident of Oyo Province to the Senior District Officer of Ife-Ilesha Division, November 7, 1946.

10. For previous treatment of this politicization of *ọba-aládé* hierarchy and genealogy, see Adepegba, "Descent from Oduduwa"; Law, "Heritage of Oduduwa"; Vaughan, *Nigerian Chiefs*. To cite one contemporary example out of many, on August 27, 2017, Governor Ísíákà Ajímọ̀bi of Ọ̀yọ́ State (Nigeria), 2011–19, installed twenty-one new *ọba-aládé* (divine kings) for different communities in Ìbàdàn, the largest metropolitan area in the Yorùbá region. This action eventually led to court litigations initiated by those who opposed the appointment and who questioned the authority of the governor to make such appointments. Nevertheless, most of the people in the affected communities whose traditional rulers were promoted to the rank of *ọba-aládé* (divine kings) approved of the governor's action because it elevated the status of those communities irrespective of the disputed process by which the appointments were made. See Atoyebi, "Ajimobi Installs 21"; Babalola, "Jubilation in Ibadan"; Ogunesan, "Court Nullifies Installation."

11. For competing claims of royal primacy, see Awoyinfa, "I Stand by My Ranking"; Bello, "Ugbo-Ilaje's Place"; Erediauwa, *I Remain, Sir*; Popoola, "Supremacy Battle"; GoldMyneTV, "I am the True Ooni of Ife"; Ricketts, "Awujale, Alake."

12. Communique, May 1, 2019, accessed May 16, 2019, https://groups.google.com/forum/#!topic/yorubaaffairs/gZrSBVmAO5E.

13. Ogundiran, "Factional Competition"; Obayemi, "Political Culture of the Ekiti," 11–12.

14. Vansina, "Knowledge and Perceptions," 28.

15. Oyěwùmí, *Invention of Women*; Sudarkasa, *Where Women Work*. For examples of historical intervention that generally take the nineteenth century as the starting point of inquiry and inadvertently fossilizes the pre-nineteenth-century gender history, see Denzer, "Yoruba Women"; McIntosh, *Yoruba Women*.

16. The king of Ọ̀yọ́ personifies this androgynous identity. His primary salutation is *ikú, bàbá, yèyé, aláṣẹ, èkejì Òrìṣà:* chief priest, father, mother, owner of transformative power, companion of the gods.

17. Drewal and Mason, *Beads, Body, and Soul.*

18. Ogundiran, "Of Small Things Remembered."

19. For a sample of the discussions on the multiple pathways of modernity, see Appadurai and Breckenridge, "Public Modernity"; Ogundiran, "End of Prehistory?"

20. Friese, *Self-Concept and Identity*, 7; McCracken, *Culture and Consumption.*

21. Ogundiran, *Crises of Culture and Consciousness*, 17. For further discussion, see Enwerem, "Money-Magic and Ritual Killing"; Harms, *River of Wealth*; Isichei, *Voices of the Poor.*

22. For example, Curto, *Enslaving Spirits*; Goodman, "Excitantia"; Mintz, *Sweetness and Power.*

23. Curto, *Enslaving Spirits.*
24. See Hodacs, *Silk and Tea*; Moxham, *Tea.*
25. Mancall, *China at the Center*, 100.
26. Sahlins, "Cosmologies of Capitalism," 10–14.
27. Kea, *Cultural and Social History of Ghana*, 1:12.
28. Whereas black-eyed pea is a West African domesticate transported to the New World as part of the Columbian Exchange, corn was introduced from the Americas to West Africa during the same period. For details, Carney and Rosomoff, *In the Shadow of Slavery.*
29. Gbadamosi, *Growth of Islam*; Hinderer, *Seventeen Years*; Peel, *Religious Encounter*; Zachernuk, *Colonial Subjects.*
30. E.g., Ajayi, *Christian Missions*; Gbadamosi, *Growth of Islam*; Peel, *Religious Encounter.*
31. As evident in Ajayi, "How Yoruba Was Reduced to Writing"; Idowu, *Olódùmarè*; Peel, *Religious Encounter.* This process of domestication also manifests in the scholarly works that link the Yorùbá history of origins to Egypt, Mecca, and the Near East in general. See Biobaku, *Origin of the Yorubas*; Johnson, *History*, 3–7; Lucas, *Religion of the Yorubas.*
32. A recent and important step in this direction, treating one dimension of Òrìṣà as a subject of historical inquiry, is the book by J. T. Willis, *Masquerading Politics.* The book focuses on the Égúngún (ancestral masquerade) in the social history of Ọ̀tà, a southern Yorùbá community.

Appendix 1

Comparative Language Data Collection Form for Descendant Dialects of Proto-Yoruboid (credit: Dr. Christopher Ehret)

Instruction: Please provide the translation of the following words in your native language or dialect.

Language:

Dialect:

Name of Informant (optional):

Contact Information:

English Yoruba Dialect (.............................)

1. all..................
2. arm/hand...............
3. ash.........................
4. back.......................
5. bark........................
6. belly......................
7. big..........................
8. bird.........................
9. bite..........................
10. black.......................
11. blood.....................
12. bone........................
13. breast (woman's)....
14. burn (tr.)................
15. cloud......................
16. cold, be....................
17. come.......................
18. die..........................
19. dog.........................
20. drink.......................
21. dry, be...................
22. ear...........................
23. eat..........................

24. earth (soil).............
25. egg.........................
26. eye........................
27. fat (noun).............
28. feather..................
29. fingernail..............
30. fire........................
31. fish.......................
32. fly (verb)..............
33. give......................
34. go........................
35. good.....................
36. grass.....................
37. hair (of head).........
38. head (anatomical)......................
39. hear......................
40. heart......................
41. horn....................
42. hot, be................
43. kill......................
44. knee...................
45. know...................
46. leaf......................
47. leg/foot...............
48. liver....................
49. long....................
50. louse...................
51. man (male adult)..............
52. many.....................
53. meat.......................
54. moon......................
55. mountain..................
56. mouth......................
57. name.......................
58. neck........................
59. new.........................
60. night........................
61. nose.........................
62. other........................
63. path/road................
64. person.....................
65. rain.........................
66. red..........................
67. root........................
68. sand.......................
69. say.........................
70. see.........................
71. seed........................
72. short.......................
73. sing.........................

74. sit..............................
75. skin (of person)................
76. sleep (verb).................
77. small...........................
78. smoke...........................
79. snake...........................
80. stand...........................
81. star...........................
82. stone...........................
83. sun...........................
84. tail...........................
85. that...........................
86. tongue...........................
87. tooth...........................
88. tree...........................
89. water...........................
90. what?...........................
91. white...........................
92. who? ....
93. woman...........................
94. I....................................
95. you (sing.)...........................
96. we...........................
97. you (pl.)...........................
98. one...........................
99. two...........................
100. three...........................

Supplementary Items

101. four..............................
102. lie (down)......................
103. navel............................
104. swim (as of fish).............
105. wet, be...............................

Appendix 2
Radiocarbon Dates in Yoruba-Edo Region: Archaic through Intermediate Periods†

Location/Site	C14 Dates (Lab. #)	2-sigma Calibration (Age range)	Cultural Period
ILÉ-IFẸ̀			
Ọ̀run Ọba Adó: Pit 11	1390±150 BP (BM-265)	AD 360–979[‡]	Early/Late Formative?
Ọ̀run Ọba Adó: Pit 3	1150±120 BP (M-2114)	AD 656–1158[‡]	Late Formative/Classical?
Ọ̀run Ọba Adó: Pit 5	1150±120 BP (M-2115)	AD 656–1158[‡]	Late Formative/Classical?
Ọ̀run Ọba Adó: Pit 6	1010±150 BP (M-2116)	AD 686–1287[‡]	Late Formative/Classical?
Ọ̀run Ọba Adó: Pit 6	960±130 BP (BM-264)	AD 779–1291[‡]	Early Formative/Classical?
Ìta Yemòó I: Underneath pavement	1100±120 BP (M2121)	AD 665–1209[‡]	Late Formative/Classical
Ìta Yemòó I: Bottom of pit, underneath pavement	990±130 BP (BM 261)	AD 734–1283[‡]	Late Formative/Classical
Ìta Yemòó I: sediment on top of pavement/abandonment	800±200 BP (M 2119)	AD 782–1469[‡]	Classical
Ìta Yemòó I: Underneath pavement	790±130 BP (M 259)	AD 997–1413[‡]	Classical
Ìta Yemòó I: Underneath pavement	480±100 BP (M 2117)	AD 1295–1642[‡]	Classical/Intermediate?
Ìta Yemòó II: Unit C, 2cm under pavement	890±30 BP (Beta-423710)	AD 1116–1217 (63%) AD 1041–1107 (37%)	Classical
Ìta Yemòó II: Unit C, 20cm under pavement	800±30 BP (Beta-423711)	AD 1184–1275	Classical
Ìta Yemòó II: Unit C, 50cm under pavement	860±30 BP (Beta-423713)	AD 1150–1256 (88%) AD 1124–1136 (2%) AD 1049–1084 (10%)	Classical
Ìta Yemòó II: Unit C, 60cm under pavement	770±30 BP (Beta-423712)	AD 1217–1281 CE	Classical
Ìta Yemòó II: Unit C, 70cm under pavement[1]	800±30 BP (Beta-423714)	AD 1184–1275 CE	Classical
Láfógido: from the crevices of *in situ* potsherds in Pavement A	850±95 BP (I-4911)	AD 997–1296§	Classical
Woyè Àsírí: Level?	1165±75 AD (N 1688)	AD 1040–1382[‡]	Classical
Woyè Àsírí: Level?	1135±85 AD (N 1687)	AD 1023–1379[‡]	Classical
Woyè Àsírí: Level?	1280±75 AD (N 1685)	AD 1219–1415[‡]	Classical

Woyè Àsírí: Level?	1405±85 AD (N 1689)	AD 1284–1482‡	Classical
Ọbalara: Concentration I	480±95 BP (N-1390)	AD 1292–1638‡	Classical
Ọbalara: Concentration H	760±85 BP (N-1392)	AD 1044–1395‡	Classical
Ọbalara: Concentration F	625±75 BP (N-1393)	AD 1266–1431‡	Classical
Ọbalara: Concentration C	580±60 BP (N-1391)	AD 1287–1435‡	Classical
Odò Ògbè: Pit in lower cultural level	855±95 YBP (I.4670)	AD 998–1299‡	Classical
Odò Ògbè: Upper cultural level	320±95 YBP (I.4669)	AD 1420–1948‡	Intermediate?
Ayélabówó	590±145 BP (I-10604)	AD 1046–1393*	Classical
Ayélabówó	855±145 BP (I-10605)	AD 1057–1644*	Classical
Ayélabówó	855±80 BP (I-10607)	AD 890–1401*	Classical
Ayélabówó	765±75 BP (I-10608)	AD 1027–1276*	Classical
Ayélabówó	600±115 BP (I-10609)	AD 1169–1619*	Classical
Igbó Olókun: Unit IO-B, Level 7, 70cm depth	840±30 BP (Beta 319447)	AD 1059–1264	Classical
Igbó Olókun: Unit IO-C, Level 7, 130cm depth	570±30 BP (Beta 319448)	AD 1304–1423	Classical
Igbó Olókun: Unit OO-A, Level 6, 92cm depth	610±30 BP (Beta 319450)	AD 1295–1404	Classical
Odùduwà Grove: Unit 1, Level 7, 120–140cm depth	680±30 (GX-33841-AMS)	AD 1270–1316 AD 1354–1389§	Classical
Odùduwà Grove: Unit 1, Level 7, 120–140cm depth	630±40 (GX-33841-AMS)	AD 1285–1401§	Classical
BENIN			
Clerks' Quarters: Cutting II: charcoal from among burial	1180±105 AD (N. 377)	AD 1023–1402‡	Classical
Clerks' Quarters: Cutting II: a piece of iroko wood above the burial	1230±105 AD (N. 376)	AD 1041–1420‡	Classical

(continued)

Location/Site	C14 Dates (Lab. #)	2-sigma Calibration (Age range)	Cultural Period
Clerks' Quarters: Cutting II: a piece of iroko wood above the burial	1385±100 AD (I. 3622)	AD 1268–1487‡	Classical
Clerks' Quarters: Cutting II: charcoal from among burial	1310±90 AD (I. 2722)	AD 1219–1438‡	Classical
Clerks' Quarters: Cutting III: charcoal from layer 14	1490±90 AD (I. 2723)	AD 1301–1641‡	Classical/Intermediate?
Usama Site: a cistern	1500±105 AD (N. 380)	AD 1298–1654‡	Classical/Intermediate?
Ogba Site: Unit and Level	1340±105 AD (N. 379)	AD 1219–1455‡	Classical
Ogba Site: Unit and Level	1305±105 AD (N. 378)	AD 1277–1408‡	Classical
ỌYỌ́-ILÉ			
Site 00/1: Layer XI [Earliest Cultural Level]	1185±90 YBP (I. 12343)-	AD 660–1021‡	Late Formative?
Site 00/1: Layer VI [Earliest Cultural Level]	1160±90 YBP (I. 12353)	AD 665–1025‡	Late Formative?
Site 00/1: Layer V [Intermediate Cultural Level]	900±80YBP (I. 12343)	AD 989–1281‡	Classical
Site 00/1: Layer IV [Intermediate Cultural Level]	810±80 YBP (I. 12343)	AD 1027–1379‡	Classical
Site 0075/3A	855±110 YBP (HAR 1890)	AD 982–1384‡	Classical
Site 0074/IGV	655±80 YBP (HAR 1891)	AD 1222–1429‡	Classical
BÀRÀ-BSM6-E1-L4	640±30 BP (Beta-519730)	AD 1300–1410	Classical
SI/SA OO PRJ 02/2 (105 cm depth)	520±50 (CSIR Pta-9339)	AD 1403–1433	Intermediate
BÀRÀ-S4W14-L5	460±30 BP (Beta-519731)	AD 1428–1614	Intermediate
BÀRÀ-S4W14-E1-L6	430±30 BP (Beta-519732)	AD 1442–1623	Intermediate
SI/SA OO PRJ 02/2 (40 cm depth)	300±45 (CSIR Pta-9352)	AD 1513–1593, 1620 (1637) 1651	Atlantic Period
ÌLÀRÈ DISTRICT			
Ìloyì: Unit 1-B, Stratum IV (90cm below surface)	715±145 YBP (GX-24000)	AD 1021–1447‡	Classical
Ìloyì: Unit 1-A, Stratum II (50cm below surface)	730±155 (GX-23998)	AD 998–1448‡	Classical
Ìloyì: Unit 2-A, Stratum V (140cm below surface)	485±65 (GX-23999)	AD 1326–1620‡	Classical/Intermediate?

ỌWỌ̀			
Igbó'Làjà: Concentration 1 (shrine) associated with terracotta sculptures of human and animal figures.	515590 YBP (I-5634)	AD 1291–1625‡	Classical/Early Intermediate Transition?
ÌGBÓMÌNÀ			
Olúpẹfọ̀n: N40W30 (45–60 cm)	510±80 YBP (Beta-88413)	AD 1300–1515, 1585–1625	Classical/ Intermediate?
Èsìẹ́: Mound 2	520±50 BP (Beta-299369)	AD 1320–1450	Classical
Èsìẹ́: Unit KINSE08-PIT1	650±30 BP (Beta-314876)	AD 1280–1320, 1340–1390	Classical
Ìlá-Ìyàrà	375±40 YBP (A-13054)	AD 1442–1531	Intermediate
Ìlá-Ìyàrà	380±60 YBP (Beta-202610)	AD 1430–1650	Intermediate/Restoration?
Ìlá-Ìyàrà	480±50 YBP (Beta-202611)	AD 1400–1490	Intermediate

† Only the radiocarbon dates in public domain are reported in this appendix. Other chronometric dates such as thermoluminescence, and reported/published radiocarbon dates without laboratory number are excluded. Unless otherwise stated, the laboratory that carried out the radiocarbon date estimation also provided the calibrated age, as reported by the author(s) of the original research. The calibrated age is an estimation calculated from the intercepts of the radiocarbon age and standard deviation. It is based on the 2-sigma standard error limits, with 95% probability or above (unless noted otherwise). The following are the sources (articles and original reports) of the radiocarbon dates: Adeduntan, "Early Glass" (Ayélabówó); Agbaje-Williams, "Contribution" (Oyo-Ile, site 00/1); Adekola, "Spatio-Temporal Inferences" (Èsìẹ́); Aleru, *Old Oyo and the Hinterland* (Obagbo); Babalola, "Ancient History of Technology" (Igbó Olókun); Chouin and Ogunfolakan, "Ife–Sungbo Archaeological Project" (Ita Yemoo II); Connah, *Archaeology of Benin* (All Benin sites); Usman, "Ceramic Seriation" (Olúpẹfọ̀n); Eyo, *Recent Excavations* (for Lafogido, Odo Ogbe, and Igbo'Laja); Folorunso et al., "Revisiting Old Oyo" (Oyo-Ile, site SI/SA OO PRJ 02/2); Garlake, "Excavations on the Woye Asiri Family Land" (Woyé Àsírí); Garlake, "Excavations at Obalara's Land" (Ọbalára); Ogundiran, *Archaeology and History* (Ìlàrè); Ogundiran and Ogunfolakan, "Colonial Modernity" (Odùduwà Grove); Soper, "Archaeological Work at Oyo Ile" (sites 0075/3A and 0074/IGV); Usman, *Yoruba Frontier* (Ìla-Ìyàrà); Willett, "Archaeology" (Ìta Yemòó and Ọ̀run Ọba Adó). The dates for Bàrà have not been published. The AMS and calibrated dates of Bàrà were processed by Beta Analytic Testing Laboratory, and reported to the author (Ogundiran) on March 13, 2019.

* Calibration by Babatunde Babalola using OxCal4.2 software (Babalola, "Ancient History of Technology," 506).

‡ Calibration by this author using CALIB 3 software (Ogundiran, "Chronology," 52–55).

§ Calibration by this author using CALIB 7 software.

Note

1. There are also three thermoluminescence dates from Ita Yemòó, one from a pavement tile (AD 1420±150) and two from potsherds associated with the pavement (AD 1420±150 and AD1170±150). See Eyo, "Recent Excavations," 290.

Notes on Orthography and Glossary of Yorùbá Words

Notes on Yorùbá Orthography

Yorùbá is a tonal language with more than thirty-five mutually intelligible dialects. I have used the modern Standard Yorùbá (SY) orthography throughout this book. The language was reduced to writing in the mid-nineteenth century. The process to adopt the modern SY orthography began in Nigeria in 1964 and was completed by the mid-1970s.[1] This orthography has since been the basis of formal speech, writing, and curriculum in Yorùbá language studies. However, I have preserved the language's dialectical variations in the names of historical figures, informants, and places. For example, I use the Ifẹ̀ dialect for Mọ́rèmí, a heroine in Ifẹ̀ history. To do otherwise would have changed the meaning of her name.

Glossary of Yorùbá words

A

Aálẹ̀	a place
Abalu	an avatar of Ọ̀ṣun
Abìọ́dún	a king of Ọ̀yọ́
Abípa	a king of Ọ̀yọ́
adé	crown
Àdèlé Ajósùn	a king of Èkó (Lagos)
Adémọ́lá	a person
Adéṣínà Ọ̀bàràméjì	a person
Adésùlú	a person
Àdìkún	a place
Adó-Èkìtì (Adó)	a place
Àfọ̀n	a place
Àgẹsinwọ̀	a place
àgídìgbo	a type of drum
agbádá	voluminous gown
Àgbèyìn	a polity

Àgbọ̀nrín	a person
Àgọ́-ọ̀já	a place
Agurá	title of a potentate
Aibo	a place
Aíyẹmí	a person
Àjàgbó	a king of Ọ̀yọ́
Àjàlọ́run	title of a potentate
Àjàṣẹ́	a place
Àjàyí	a person
Ajé	a deity
ajẹ́lẹ̀	resident commissioner
Ajíbọ́dẹ	a place
Ajíbógun Obòkun	a person
ajogun	malevolent forces
àko	a sculpture associated with burial ceremony
Akoko	a place
Àkókó	a Yorùbá subgroup
àkòrì	a type of stone bead
àkún	a type of stone bead
akùnyùngbà	an a cappella group associated with the palace in Ọ̀yọ́ Empire
Àkúrẹ́	a place
aláàfin/Aláàfin	title (e.g., *aláàfin*) and generic name (e.g., Aláàfin Abìọ́dún) for the king of Ọ̀yọ́
àláárì	a type of textile
Aládìkún	title of a potentate
Alágbẹ̀dẹ	a person
alápinnì	title of a chieftain
Alépatà	a military and political chieftain
Alomo	name of a military personality
Ànà	a Yorùbá subgroup in Benin Republic and Togo
Aólẹ̀ Arógangan	a king of Ọ̀yọ́
Àpá	a place
Apamimoya	a place
Ará	a place
Arápatẹ́	a military title and name of the title bearer
Arẹ̀sà	name/title of a potentate
aro	a type of percussion
Àrọ̀wá	name of a person
Asé	a place
àṣẹ	vital force
aṣọ-ipó	a type of clothing fabric
aṣọ-òkè	a type of clothing fabric
aṣọ-ọlọ́nà	a type of clothing fabric
Àtàkúnmọ̀sà	a king
Àtàndá	a person
Àtàpamẹ̀	a place

Atikori	a place
Awamaro	a person
Àwo	serving bowl
Aólẹ̀	a king of Ọ̀yọ́
Àwórì	a Yorùbá subgroup
ayaba	king's wife
Àyànbándélé	a place
Àyànbí	a person
Ayají Latuán	a person
àyé	a type of drum

B

bààmú	a type of facial mark
Balógun Ọnàfọwọ́kàn	a chieftain
baṣọ̀run/ Baṣọ̀run	title/name of a chieftain in Ọ̀yọ́
bàtá	a type of drum
bẹ̀nbẹ́	a type of drum
Boni	name of a military personality

D

dùndún	a type of drum

E

Edo	an ethnolinguistic group
Ẹ̀fọ̀n	a place
Égúngún	ancestral masquerade
Egungunojú	a king of Ọ̀yọ́
Èjìgbòmẹkùn	a place
Èkìtì	Yorùbá subgroup
ekùtù	a wind instrument
Eléduwẹ	a stock name for Borgu potentates
Elésùn	title of a potentate
Eranyiba	a place
Erijiyan	a place
Èsìẹ́	a place
Èṣù	a deity

Ẹ

ẹbí	a corporate group defined in kinship terms
ẹdan	brass
Ẹdẹ-Ilé	a place
Ẹ̀fọ̀n	a place
Ẹfúnṣe Warikondo	a person
Ẹ̀gùà	a kingdom in northern Yéwá

Ẹ̀gbá	Yorùbá subgroup
Ẹ̀gbádò	Yorùbá subgroup
ẹkọ	cornmeal
ẹ̀kú	masquerade's clothing
ẹni-ọjà	title
Ẹpa	a type of masquerade
Ẹ̀pẹ́	a place
ẹrinla	a type of bead
Ẹ̀ṣùrẹ́	a place
ẹtù	a type of textile
Ẹwọ	a place
Ẹ̀wọn	a place

F

Fìgbàjoyè Aníkiláyà	a king

G

Gáà	name of a chieftain in Ọ̀yọ́
Gẹ̀lẹ̀dẹ́	a type of masquerade
gọ̀m̀bọ́	a type of facial mark

GB

Gbandan	name of a military personality
gbárìyè-onígba-awẹ́	a voluminous and large garment
gbẹ̀du	a type of drum
Gbogun	a place

I

Ìbàdàn	a place
Ìbàràpá	a Yorùbá region
Ìbàrìbá	an ethnolinguistic group
Ìbòkun	a place
ìborùn	shawl
ìbọrí	mobile shrine of the deity of inner head and destiny
Ìdànrè	a place
Ìdèta	a place
Ìdí Ajágbọn	a place
ìdikù	head wrap
Ìdó	a place
Ìdòfà	a place
Idofoyi	a place
Ìdôkò	a place
Ifá	deity of divination (same as Ọ̀rúnmílà)
ifá	divination corpus
Ifẹ̀	the people, culture, and abbreviation of Ilé-Ifẹ̀

Iffe-Ijumu	a place
Ifọ̀n	a place
Igala	a people and their kingdom
Ìgànná	a place
Ìgàrè	a place
Ìgigun	a place
Igiisubu	name of a military personality
Ìgún	a place
igbá	a wind instrument
Ìgbìrà	ethnolinguistic group
Igbogbe	a place
Ìgbógì	a place
Igbó Ìlowè	a place
Igbó'Làjà	a place
Ìgbómìnà	Yorùbá subgroup
Ihò Olóko	a place
Ìjànà	a place
Ìjárá	a place
Ìjẹ̀bú	Yorùbá subgroup
Ìjerò	a place
Ìjẹ̀ṣà	Yorùbá subgroup
Ìjòfì	a place
Ìjùgbè	a place
Ìkálẹ̀	a place
Ìkèrèkú	a place
Ìkètèwí	a place
Ìkìrun	a place
ìkòkò	earthenware
Ìkọ̀lé	a place
Ìlàjẹ	a place
Ìlálẹ̀	a place
Ìlàrè	a place
ilé	House (corporate familial)
Ilé-Ifẹ̀	a place
ilémosú	married, unmarried or divorced woman living in her natal home
Ìlémùré	a place
ilé orí	shrine for the deity of destiny
Iléṣà	a place
Ìlésùn	a place
ìlẹ̀kẹ̀	bead
Ìlià	a place
Ìlóròmú	a place
Ìloyì	a place
Ìlọ́jà	a place
Ìlọràn	a place
ìlú	town or city
Ìmálà	a place
Ìmẹ̀kọ	a place
Ìmẹ̀sí	a place

Ìmíkàn	a place
Ìmọ̀	a place
Ìmọjùbì	a place
Ìnikùn	a place
Ipa	a place
Ìpàpó	a place
Ìpásẹ̀	a place
Ìpàyà	a place
Ìpèpèjí	a place
Ìpo	a place
Ìpókíá	a place
Iporo	a place
Ìrágbìjí	a place
Ìrànjé-Oko	a place
Ìrànjé-Ilé	a place
Ìráyè	a place
Ìréé	a place
Ìrè-Èkìtì	a place
Ìrẹ̀lẹ̀	a deity
Ìrorò	a place
ìṣaàsùn	cooking bowl
Itsekiri (Ìṣẹ́kìrì)	a Yoruboid subgroup
Ìsọ́rọ̀	a place
Ìtá	a potentate
Itaakpa	a place
Ìta-Asin	a place
Ìta Ìjerò	a place
Ìtajì	a place
Ìta-Ògbólú	a place
Ìtàpá	a festival
Ìwéré	a place
Ìwìnrìn	a place
Iwò Elérú	a place
Iyùn	red glass bead

J

jáńgbadì	a type of facial mark
Japara	a place

K

kàkàkí	a wind instrument
Keta	a place
Kétu	a place
Kòjọmọnù	a range of granitic hills in Ọ̀yọ́-Ilé
kókò	a type of imported green cloth popular in the late eighteenth and early nineteenth century
Kòrì	a king of Ọ̀yọ́

kóṣó	a type of drum
Kòso	a town in the metroplitan ara of Ọ̀yọ́-Ilé

L

Láfogído	a king
Làgbàyí	a sculptor
Lájamìsán	a king
Lájódogun	a king
Lọ́bùn	title of a chieftain
Loko	a military personality
Lúwò Gbágìdá	a king in Ilé-Ifẹ̀

M

máńdè	a type of facial mark
Mèjíró	a place
mọdéwá	a class of palace officials in Ilé-Ifẹ̀, Ìjẹ̀ṣà, and Èkìtì
Mọ́rèmí	a heroine in Ilé-Ifẹ̀

O

Òbóó	a place
Ódárawu	an *aláàfin*
Odin	a place
Odùduwà	a person
Ọ̀dún	a type of fabric made with the bark of a species of tree
Òfinràn	a king of Ọ̀yọ́
Ògbómọ̀ṣọ́	a place
Ògbóni	a fraternal civic organization associated with governance, administration of justice, and protection of indigenous rights
òge	a wind instrument
Ògò	a place
Ògùdù	a place
Ògún	a deity
Ògùn	a river and areas around it
Ogunlọlá	an Ọ̀yọ́ provincial governor
Òjé-Ilé	a place
Òjíbàrà	a person
Òjìgí	a king of Ọ̀yọ́
Òjó Agùnbambarù	a person
Òjòko	a potentate
Ojowo	a place
Òkè-Ago	a place
Òkè Àwo	a place
Okedagba	a place

Òkè-Ẹrì	a place
Òkè-Ojà	a place
Òkè-Ọnà	a polity
Òkèṣà	a place
Òkè-Sopin	a place
Òkò	a polity
Okokòkó	a place
Oko-Odò	a place
Okun	a place
Olódùmarè	supreme being
Ológò	a potentate
Olókù	a potentate
Olókun	a deity
Olósi	a potentate
olú	generic title of a potentate or revered leader
Olúewu	a king of Ọ̀yọ́
Olúfẹ̀	another name for the king of Ifẹ̀
Olúodò	a king of Ọ̀yọ́
Olúorogbo	a hero figure in Ifẹ̀ history, also known as ẹ̀là
Oluwaju	a place
Olúyọ̀lé	a potentate
Ọmọlógun	a place
Òmùò	a place
Oǹdó	a place
Onigbogí	a king of Ọ̀yọ́
Onísàrẹ́	an Ọ̀yọ́ provincial governor
Oníṣílé	a king of Ọ̀yọ́
Oǹkò	a Yorùbá subgroup
Oǹṣílé	a place
Òòsàbí Tíǹbẹ̀lẹ́ṣẹ̀ Olódùmarè	a person
Òòṣàtàlàbí	a deity (another name of Ọbàtálá)
opóji	a class of chiefs
Orelúere	a deity
Orí	a deity
orí	anatomical head
oríkì	panegyric
Òrìṣà	generic name for a deity or deities in Yorùbá pantheon
Òrìṣàtólú	a place
Orókè-Ọ̀tún	a place
Òrónà	a provincial governor
Osi	a place
Òṣilẹ̀	title of a potentate
Òṣogbo	a place
Òṣoògùn	a place
òṣùmàrè	rainbow
Òúkú	a place
Òwè	a Yorùbá subgroup

Òwu	a kingdom and Yorùbá subgroup
Òyè	a place

Ọ

ọba	generic title for a corporate leader, later became the generic title of a king
Ọba	generic royal title used as part of a name (e.g., Ọba Àdèlé)
Ọ̀bà	an ancient kingdom
Ọbà	a river and its deity; the name of a city-state
ọba-aládé	divine king
Ọ̀bà-Ìgbómìnà	a Yorùbá subgroup and a kingdom
Ọbalálẹ̀	a potentate
Obaléjùgbè	a potentate
Ọbalésùn	a potentate
Ọbalókun	a king of Ọ̀yọ́
Ọbalọ́ràn	a potentate
Ọbalùfọ̀n	a king in Ilé-Ifẹ̀
Ọbamakin	a potentate
Ọ̀bàràbarà Olókùnẹṣin	a potentate
Ọbatáàsà	another name of Ọbatálá
Ọbatálá	a deity
Ọbatero	a person
Ọ̀gọ̀tún	a place
Ọ̀gbọ̀rọ̀	a place
ọjà	market
Ọ̀jọwọ̀n	a place
ọkinkin	a wind instrument
Ọláòṣà	a potentate
ọlọ́jà	generic name of a potentate
Ọlọ́pọ̀ndá	a potentate
ọmọ	child/children
Ọmọ́sọlá Májǒtú	a king of Ọ̀yọ́
ọni	person
ọnọja	generic name of a potentate among the Igala people
ọ̀ọ̀ni/Ọ̀ọ̀ni	title and name of the king of Ilé-Ifẹ̀
Ọpara	river
Ọ̀ra	a place
Ọ̀ràǹfẹ̀	a deity
Ọ̀rànmíyàn	a deity and cultural hero
Ọ̀rọ̀m̀pọ̀tọ̀	a king of Ọ̀yọ́
Ọ̀ṣẹ̀tura	a deity and cultural hero
Ọsin	a river
Ọṣìn	a mighty deity
Ọṣìnfẹ́kundé	a person
Ọṣìnladé Otùtùbíosùn	the name of a king of Ifẹ̀
Ọ̀ṣínwọ̀	a person

Ọsọ́ọ̀sì	a deity
Ọ̀ṣun	a river and its deity
Ọ̀ṣun Àbòtó	an avatar of Ọ̀ṣun
Ọ̀ṣun Àjàgùrá	an avatar of Ọ̀ṣun
Ọ̀ṣun Jùmu	an avatar of Ọ̀ṣun
Ọ̀ṣun Mẹ́rin	an avatar of Ọ̀ṣun
Ọ̀ṣun Ọpara	an avatar of Ọ̀ṣun
Ọtun	a place
Ọya	a deity
Ọ̀yọ́	a polity and a Yorùbá subgroup
Ọ̀yọ́-Ilé	a place
Ọ̀yọ́mèsì	council of nonroyal lords in Ọ̀yọ́ Empire
ọwá	generic title for a corporate leader, later became the generic title of a king
Ọwálàrè	title of a potentate
Ọwálúṣẹ́	a king
Ọwá Obòkun	title of the king of Iléṣà
Ọwárì	a potentate
Òwẹnà	a region
Ọ̀wọ̀	a kingdom
Ọya	a deity

P

Parakin	a place
Pee	a place

S

sányán	a type of textile woven from anaphe wild silk and cotton yarn
Sogba	a deity
Sùngbọ́ Erédò	an embankment

Ṣ

Ṣàngó (Jàkuta)	a deity
ṣẹ̀gi	blue glass beads
ṣẹ̀kẹ̀rẹ̀	a type of drum

T

Tibo	a place
tiyako	a wind instrument
túrè	a type of facial mark

U

Ùgbò	an aboriginal people, and now a Yorùbá subgroup
Ùlésùn	a place
Ùlógò	a place

W

Wàlódè	a place
Woyè Àṣírí	a place

Y

Yàgbà	a Yorùbá subgroup
yangede	a type of drum
Yemọja	a deity
Yéwá	a Yorùbá subgroup (formerly known as Ẹ̀gbádò)
Yèyé Kare	an avatar of Ọ̀ṣun
Yèyé Ìpọ̀ndá	an avatar of Ọ̀ṣun
Yèyé Ọ̀gà	an avatar of Ọ̀ṣun
Yèyé Òkè	an avatar of Ọ̀ṣun
Yèyé Olókè	an avatar of Ọ̀ṣun
Yèyé Onira	an avatar of Ọ̀ṣun

Note

1. See Ajayi, "How Yoruba"; Bamgboṣe, *Yoruba Orthography*; Oyèláràn, "On Yorùbá Orthography."

Bibliography

Oral Interviews and Personal Communications

Professor Wándé Abímbọ́lá, Boston, October 1998; Lagos, April 7, 2018.
Adéníran Adébóyè, email correspondences, January 17–25, 2016.
Chief Adéfióyè Adédèjì, Rísàwẹ̀ of Iléṣà, June 6, 1986.
Ọba S. A. Adékólúrẹ̀jọ, the Olówu of Òwu-Epé, Iléṣà, September 9, 1991.
Ọba Ọládìran Agúnbíadé, the Olósi of Osi-Èkìtì, June 6, 2016.
Chief J. A. Ajé, Lóyè of Ìlàrè-Ìjẹ̀ṣà, March 15, 1997; June 21, 1997.
Mr. O. Ajétọ́mọbí, Department of History, Obafemi Awolowo University, Ilé-Ifẹ̀, July 8, 1990.
Ọba Adéyẹmí Samuel Akinmusire, the Olúdòko of Ùdòko, May 28–29, 2016.
Nurudeen Amuda-Arógundádé, Ilé-Ifẹ̀, July 3, 2014.
Chief Àrọ̀wá of Ìrè-Èkìtì, June 7, 2016.
Madam Ọwárìtóókẹ́ Àyọlo, Ìpolé-Ìjẹ̀ṣà, October 10, 1990.
Chief Ọláolú Ọládọ̀tun Ôkánlàwọ́n Dàda, Ọbalésùn and Chief Priest of Ọbàtálá, Ilé-Ifẹ̀, June 22, 2015.
Dr. Christopher Ehret, email correspondence, October 22, 2015.
Chief Edward Fádípẹ̀, the Ṣàjúkú of Ìpolé Ìjẹ̀ṣà, July 5–10, 1990.
Chief Ọ̀dọ́lé Fágbilé, Ìlàrè-Ìjẹ̀ṣà, April 19, 1997.
Chief Samuel Fákúlújọ, Oyèélá of Ìbòkun, April 2, 1986.
Chief Ọlájídé Fárótìmí Fálọ́ba, Ọbadio and Chief Priest of Odùduwà, Odùduwà Grove, Ilé-Ifẹ̀, July 2, 15, 16, 2015.
Ọba J. O. Fásọ̀yìn, the Alọ́wá of Ìlọ́wá, June 6, 1986.
Ọ̀ṣunfúnkẹ́ Lákọ́kàn (priestess of Ọ̀ṣun), Òṣogbo, August 2, 2011.
Adémọ́lá Lawal, Ògúndìran village, Ìgbẹ́tì district, May 26, 2017.
Chief J. O. Lọ́tùn, Rísà Ẹmẹṣẹ̀ of Ilésà, Àdìmúlà Palace, Ilésà, February 9, 1991.
Chief Adéfióyè Adédèjì, Rísàwẹ̀ of Iléṣà, Iléṣà, June 6, 1986.
Olúṣẹ́gun Moyib, Department of Archaeology and Anthropology, University of Ibadan, personal communication, May 30, 2017.
Kàsálí Àkàngbé Ògún, master woodcarver, Charlotte, NC, February 14, 2013; February 18, 2013.
Alhaji Babatúndé Ògúndìran, Ògúndìran village, Ìgbẹ́tì district, May 24, 2017.

Baálẹ̀ Ògúnléké Ògúndípẹ̀, Arárọmí-Ṣẹ̀pẹ̀tẹ̀rí, June 9, 2016.
Chief Ìbílọlá Omilẹ̀yẹ, Yèyé Ọ̀ṣun of Òṣogbo, Ọ̀ṣun Shrine, Òṣogbo Palace. June 25, 2003.
Ọlálékan Òrìṣàdáre, Àwòrò Ọ̀ṣun-Òṣogbo, Ọ̀sun Grove, Òṣogbo, May 4–5, 2004.
Chief Emmanuel Òrìṣàsùnmí, Balóró of Ìbòkun, September 11, 1990; July 12, 1997.
Ọbà Tijani Oyèdòkun, Àgbọ́nrán II, the late Timi of Ẹdẹ, January 21, 2004.
Ọládọjà Ọlátúnbọ̀sún, Ìgbẹ́tì, October 4, 1992.
Ọba Musa Ọlátúnbọ̀sún-Adébáyọ̀, Akínṣílọ II, the Aláwó of Awó, May 6, 2004.
Dr. Olúṣẹ́gun Ọ̀pádèjì, Department of Archaeology and Anthropology, University of Ibadan, June 5, 2016.
Ọba Adéjọrọ̀ Ọ̀tẹ́bọlákù, Ògìdán III, the Ọwálàrè of Ìlàrè, Ìlàrè-Ìjẹ̀ṣà, January 11, 1997.
Ọbà Adélẹ́gàn Pópóọlá, the Ògbóni of Ìpolé-Ìjẹ̀ṣà, July 8, 1990.
Ọba Ọláyinká Gbọ́lágade Tiamiyu II, the Olójo of Òjo, July 22, 2009.

Colonial Primary Documents

National Archives, Ibadan. Oyo Prof 1/1 File 1372. "Crown—Possession of," Letter from Senior Resident of Oyo Province to the Senior District Officer of Ife-Ilesha Division, November 7, 1946. Accessed June 2005.
National Archives, Ibadan. Èkìtì Div4/4, Civil Record Book, July 14, 1903.
Church Missionary Society Archive, Birmingham University Library. CMS, CAO/049. Yoruba Mission. Original Journals, Letters & Papers. David Hinderer, report of his tour to Ilésà, 1957. Obtained from the Adams Matthew microfilm as interlibrary loan from the University of Florida). Microfilm. Accessed May 2006.
Church Missionary Society Archive, Birmingham University Library. CMS, CA2/098/10. Young journal, June 27, 1875. Adams Matthew microfilm, University of Florida.

Research Notes and Papers in Private Collections

Agbaje-Williams, Babatunde. "Field Notes—Oral Traditions and Archaeology of Ijesaland." Ilesa.
Ọmọtọ́ṣọ̀ Elúyẹmí, "Field Notes—Oral Traditions of Ile-Ife." Ilé-Ifẹ̀.
Ọlátúnbọ̀sún-Adébáyọ̀, Musa. "Private Papers of Ọba Musa Ọlátúnbọ̀sún-Adébáyọ̀, Akínṣílọ II, the Aláwó of Awó." Awó.
Pópóọlá, Ọba Adélẹgàn. "The History of Ìpolé-Ìjẹ̀ṣà, Part 1." Iléṣà.

Unpublished Dissertations, Theses, and Long Essays

Adegoke, Ebenezer Olalekan. "A Study of the Role of Women in the Burial Rituals of the Ife of Southwestern Nigeria." PhD diss., University of London, 1995.
Adegbite, Olutunde K. "Afon and Its Neighbours from the Earliest Times to 1960." BA long essay, Department of History, Obafemi Awolowo University, Ilé-Ifẹ̀, Nigeria, 1988.

Adekola, Kolawole, O. "Spatio-Temporal Inferences from the Study of Soapstone Figurines in Esie, Kwara State, Nigeria." PhD diss., University of Ibadan, 2020.
Adewusi, Adebayo O. "Owu Communities in Yorubaland, 1200–1992." MA thesis, Obafemi Awolowo University, 2012.
Adewuyi, Muritala A. "Agba Festival in Oyan: Historical Development and Significance." BA long essay, University of Ife, Ilé-Ifẹ̀, Nigeria, 1975.
Agbaje-Williams, Babatunde. "A Contribution to the Archaeology of Old Oyo." PhD diss., University of Ibadan, 1983.
Akinkugbe, Olufẹmi Odutayọ. "A Comparative Phonology of Yoruba Dialects, Iṣẹkiri and Igala." PhD diss., University of Ibadan, 1978.
Alabi, Raphael A. "An Environmental Archaeological Study of the Coastal Region of Southwestern Nigeria, with Emphasis on Badagry Area." PhD diss., University of Ibadan, 1998.
Aleru, J. O. "An Investigation into Aspects of Historical Archaeology of North Central Igbomina." PhD diss., University of Ibadan, 1998.
Anifowose, M. "An Ethnoarchaeological Study of Pottery in Ilorin." BA long essay, Department of Archaeology, University of Ibadan, 1984.
Aremu, David A. "The Archaeology of North-East Yorubaland, Kwara State with Emphasis on Early Techniques of Metal Working." PhD diss., University of Ibadan, 1990.
Babalola, Abidemi Babatunde. "Archaeological Investigation of Early Glass Production at Igbo Olokun, Ile-Ife (Nigeria)." PhD diss., Rice University, Houston, 2016.
Chouin, Gerard. "Forests of Power and Memory: An Archaeology of Sacred Groves in the Eguafo Polity, Southern Ghana (c. 500–1900 A.D.)." PhD diss., Syracuse University, Syracuse, NY, 2009.
Davison, Claire. "Glass Beads in African Archaeology: Results of Neutron Activation Analysis, Supplemented by Results of X-Ray Fluorescence Analysis." PhD diss., University of California, Berkeley, 1972.
Eyo, Ekpo. "Recent Excavations at Ife and Owo and Their Implications for Ife, Owo and Benin Studies." PhD diss., University of Ibadan, 1974.
Famule, Olawole Francis. "Art and Spirituality: The Ijumu Northeastern-Yoruba Egúngún." PhD diss., University of Arizona, Tucson, 2005.
Goucher, Candice Lee. "The Iron Industry of Bassar, Togo: An Interdisciplinary Investigation of African Technological History." PhD diss., University of California, Los Angeles, 1984.
Hakeem, Ọláwálé. "Ìtúpalẹ̀ Aláwòmọ̀ Lítíreṣọ̀ Oríkì Orílẹ̀ Ìran Olúfọ̀n (A Literary Analysis of Olúfọ̀n's Lineage Descriptive Poetry)." MA thesis, Ọbáfẹ́mi Awolọ́wọ̀ University, Ilé-Ifẹ̀, Nigeria, 2011.
Kelly, Kenneth G. "Transformation and Continuity in Savi, a West African Trade Town: An Archaeological Investigation of Culture Change on the Coast of Bénin during the 17th and 18th Centuries." PhD diss., University of California, Los Angeles, 1995.
Lasisi, Olanrewaju. "Excavations at Sungbo's Eredo." BA long essay, University of Ibadan, Ibadan, 2015.
Lawal, Babatunde. "Yoruba Sango Sculpture in Historical Retrospect." PhD diss., Indiana University, Bloomington, 1976.
Monroe, J. Cameron. "The Dynamics of State Formation: The Archaeology and Ethnohistory of Pre-Colonial Dahomey." PhD diss., University of California, Los Angeles, 2003.

Norman, Neil L. "An Archaeology of West African Atlanticization: Regional Analysis of the Huedan Palace Districts and Countryside (Bénin), 1650–1727." PhD diss., University of Virginia, Charlottesville, 2008.

Odunbaku, J. B. "Aspects of Settlement History of Egba-Keesi, Abeokuta, Southwestern Nigeria." PhD diss., University of Ibadan, 2006.

Ogundiran, Akinwumi. "Archaeological Reconnaissance and Historical Reconstruction of Ipole-Ijesa." MS thesis, University of Ibadan, 1991.

Ogunfolakan, B. A. "Conflict, War, Displacement and Archaeology in Parts of Osun State, Southwestern Nigeria." PhD diss., University of Ibadan, 2012.

Ogungbemi, Emmanuel. "Igbo Baba Ilare in the History of Ilare." BA long essay, University of Ife, Ilé-Ifẹ̀, 1979.

Omokhodion, Idemudian. "Northwest Benin Sites and Socially Determined Artifact Distribution." PhD diss., Michigan State University, Ann Arbor, 1987.

Oroge, E. Adeniyi. "The Institution of Slavery in Yorubaland with Particular Reference to the Nineteenth Century." PhD diss., University of Birmingham, UK, 1971.

Oteyola, G. "The History and Development of Ìpolé from the Earliest Time to the Present Day." National Certificate of Education long essay, Osun State College of Education, Ilesa, Nigeria, 1985.

Oyelade, S. B. "Odun Irele Ni Ilu Ikirun." BA long essay, University of Ife, Ilé-Ifẹ̀, Nigeria, 1976.

Oyelaran, Philip A. "Archaeological and Palaeoenvironmental Investigations in Iffe-Ijumu Area of Kwara State." PhD diss., University of Ibadan, 1991.

Orefejo, Sunday O. "History of Ijebu-Igbo from the Earliest Time to 1892." BA long essay, University of Ife, Ilé-Ifẹ̀, 1973.

Pogoson, Ohioma Ifounu. "Stylistic Possibilities in Esie Stone Carvings." PhD diss., University of Ibadan, 1984.

Silverstein, Raymond Orson. "Igala Historical Phonology." PhD diss., University of California, Los Angeles, 1973.

Taiwo, Olufemi Y. "History of Iragbiji." Nigerian Certificate in Education long essay, Oyo State College of Education, Ilesa, Nigeria, 1985.

Unpublished Academic Presentations

Adewale, T. J. "The Ijanna Episode in Yoruba History." Paper presented at the 3rd International West African Conference, Ibadan, December 12–21, 1949.

Broderick, Lee, and Akinwumi Ogundiran. "Living on the Edge: Climate, Landscape and Resource Use on the Oyo Empire Frontier." Presented at the 11th Annual African Archaeology Research Day (AARD), University of Bristol, 2014.

Ehret, Christopher, and Akinwumi Ogundiran. "Archaeological and Linguistic Overviews of Yoruba History." Presented at the Joint Congress of the 13th Pan-African Archaeological Congress (PAA) and the 20th Society of Africanist Archaeologists (SAFA) Conference, the University of Cheikh Anta Diop, Dakar, Senegal, November 1–7, 2010.

Obayemi, A. M. "The Political Culture of the Ekiti and the Challenge of the Historiography of the Yoruba." Staff and Post-Graduate Seminar 1980–81, Department of History, University of Ilorin, Nigeria, 1981.

Unpublished Archaeology Reports

Chouin, Gerard. "Ife-Sungbo Archaeological Project: Update 2016." October 7, 2016.
Chouin, Gerard, and Adisa Ogunfolakan. "Ife–Sungbo Archaeological Project Preliminary Report on Excavations at Ita Yemoo, Ile-Ife, Osun State and on Rapid Assessment of Earthwork Sites at Eredo and Ilara-Epe, Lagos State June–July 2015." 2015.
Ogundiran, Akinwumi. "Preliminary Report of the First Season of the Oyo Empire Archaeological Research Project: Fieldwork in the Old Oyo National Park, Nigeria, May 21–June 10, 2017." Submitted to the Nigeria National Park Service, Abuja, 2017.
Ogundiran, Akinwumi. "Preliminary Report of the Second Season of the Oyo Empire Archaeological Research Project: Fieldwork in the Old Oyo National Park and Its Environs, Nigeria, February 10–March 18, 2018." Submitted to the Nigeria National Park Service, Abuja, 2018.
Ogundiran, Akinwumi. "Preliminary Report of the Third Season of the Oyo Empire Archaeological Research Project: Fieldwork in Bara, Nigeria, January 11–February 15, 2019." Submitted to the Nigeria National Park Service, Abuja, 2019.
Orijemie, Emuobosa Akpo. "Palaeoenvironmental Research in Mejiro Cave, Old Oyo National Park, Oyo State, Nigeria: A Report." Submitted to Akin Ogundiran, November 6, 2018.

Published Personal Accounts, Diaries, and Primary Reports

Adams, John. *Remarks on the Country Extending from Cape Palmas to the River Congo: Including Observations on the Manners and Customs of the Inhabitants; With an Appendix Containing an Account of the European Trade with the West Coast of Africa*. London: Whittaker, 1823.
Barbot, Jean. *A Description of the Coasts of North and South-Guinea, and of Ethiopia Inferior, Vulgarly Angola: With Appendix*. London, 1732.
Bosman, Willem. *A New and Accurate Description of the Coast of Guinea, Divided into the Gold, the Slave, and the Ivory Coasts*. London: James Knopton and Dan Midwinter, 1705.
British Houses of Parliament Papers. *Report on the Trade of the Bight of Benin for the Year 1856. Accounts and Papers, 1857, Session 2, Vol. 20.* London: Harrison and Sons, 1857.
Bruce-Lockhart, Jamie, and Paul E. Lovejoy, eds. *Hugh Clapperton into the Interior of Africa: Records of the Second Expedition, 1825–1827*. Leiden: Brill, 2005.
Clapperton, Hugh. *Journal of a Second Expedition into the Interior of Africa, from the Bight of Benin to Soccatoo*. London: J. Murray, 1829.
Crone, G. R. *The Voyages of Cadamosto and Other Documents on Western Africa in the Second Half of the Fifteenth Century*. London: Hakluyt Society, 1937.
Crowther, Samuel. *The Gospel on the Banks of the Niger: Journals and Notices of the Native Missionaries Accompanying the Niger Expedition of 1857–1859, with Appendices and Map*. London: Church Missionary House, 1859.

———. *Journal of an Expedition up the Niger and Tshadda Rivers Undertaken by Macgregor Laird in Connection with the British Government in 1854*. London: Church Missionary House, 1855.

———. *A Second Narrative of Samuel Ajayi Crowther's Early Life*. Society for African Church History, 1965.

Dapper, Olfert. *Description de l'Afrique, contenant les noms, la situation & les confins de toutes ses parties, leurs rivières, leurs villes & leurs habitations, leurs plantes & leurs animaux; les mœurs, les coûtumes, la langue, les richesses, la religion & le gouvernement de ses peuples. Avec des cartes des États, des provinces & des villes, & des figures en taille-douce, qui representent les habits & les principales ceremonies des habitans, les plantes & les animaux les moins connus*. Amsterdam: Wolfgang, Waesberge, Boom & van Someren, 1686.

D'Elbée. *Journal du voyage du sieur Delbée aux isles dans la coste de Guinee*. Paris: G. Glouzier, 1671.

Government Gazette of the Colony of Lagos, February 20, 1903.

Hallett, Robin, ed. *The Niger Journal of Richard and John Lander*. New York: Praeger, 1965.

Hair, P. E. H., Adam Jones, Robin Law, and Hakluyt Society. *Barbot on Guinea: The Writings of Jean Barbot on West Africa, 1678–1712*. London: Hakluyt Society, 1992.

Hinderer, Anna. *Seventeen Years in the Yoruba Country: Memorials of Anna Hinderer, Wife of the Rev. David Hinderer, C.M.S. Missionary in Western Africa*. London: Seeley, Jackson and Halliday, 1877.

Jones, Adam. *German Sources for West African History, 1599–1669*. Wiesbaden: Steiner, 1983.

———. *West Africa in the Mid-Seventeenth Century: An Anonymous Dutch Manuscript*. Atlanta, GA: African Studies Association, 1995.

Kimble, George H. T. *Esmeraldo de Situ Orbis*. London: Hakluyt Society, 1937.

Lander, Richard. *Records of Captain Clapperton's Last Expedition to Africa: With the Subsequent Adventures of the Author*. 2 vols. London: Henry Colburn and Richard Bentley, 1830.

Lander, Richard, and John Lander. *Journal of an Expedition to Explore the Course and Termination of the Niger: With a Narrative of a Voyage Down That River to Its Termination*. London: John Murray, 1832.

Landolphe, Jean François, and Jacques Salbigoton Quesné. *Mémoires du Capitaine Landolphe: Contenant l'histoire de ses voyages pendant trente-six ans, aux Côtes d'Afrique et aux deux Amériques 2*. Paris: Bertrand, 1823.

Levtzion, N., and J. F. P. Hopkins. *Corpus of Early Arabic Sources for West African History*. Princeton, NJ: Markus Wiener, 2000.

Norris, Robert. *Memoirs of the Reign of Bossa Ahadee, King of Dahomy, Written in the Year 1773*. London: Frank Cass, 1789.

Oyo State Chieftaincy Declaration of 1976—Justice Ademola Commission. Gazetted in 1977. Oyo State Government Publication, Federal Republic of Nigeria, 1976.

Palmer, H. R. *Sudanese Memoirs: Being Mainly Translations of a Number of Arabic Manuscripts Relating to the Central and Western Sudan*. Lagos: Government Printer, 1928.

Pereira, Duarte Pacheco. *Esmeraldo de Situ Orbis* [Edição critica annotada por A. E. da Silva Dias]. Lisbon, 1905.
Robertson, G. A. *Notes on Africa: Particularly Those Parts Which Are Situated between Cape Verd and the River Congo: Containing Sketches of the Geographical Situations, the Manners and Customs, the Trade, Commerce, and Manufactures, and the Government and Policy of the Various Nations in This Extensive Tract: Also a View of Their Capabilities for the Reception of Civilization, with Hints for the Melioration of the Whole African Population.* London: Sherwood, Neely and Jones, Paternoster Row, 1819.
Van Nyendael, David. "A Description of Rio Formosa, or the River of Benin." In William Bosman, *A Description of the Slave Coast*, 423–68. London: James Knapton, 1705.

Online Publications and Databases

Alencastro, Luiz Felipe de. "Brazil in the South Atlantic: 1550–1850." Marxist Literary Group. 2007. Accessed March 14, 2015. http://www.mediationsjournal.org/articles/brazil-in-the-south-atlantic.
Aworeni, Babalawo. "Opele: Element of Divination." Accessed December 12, 2015. http://orishada.com/wordpress/?tag=ikin.
Bichler, Shimshon, and Jonathan Nitzan. *Capital as Power: Toward a New Cosmology of Capitalism.* December 15, 2009. Accessed January 8, 2015. http://bnarchives.yorku.ca/274/.
Bottle Books. "Big Bottles Big History: Demijohns and Carboys." Accessed December 29, 2016. http://www.bottlebooks.com/demijohn/big_bottles_big_history_demijohn.htm.
Central Intelligence Agency. "The World Factbook: Nigeria." Accessed July 28, 2017. https://www.cia.gov/library/publications/the-world-factbook/geos/ni.html.
"Communique Issued at the End of an Ad Hoc Meeting of Concerned Nigerian Historians and Stakeholders Held to Address the Lingering Feuds among Some Leading Yoruba Obas, at UI Hotels, University of Ibadan, on 1st May 2019." Accessed May 16, 2019. https://groups.google.com/forum/#!topic/yorubaaffairs/gZrSBVmAO5E.
Davis, Peter. "Treaty between Great Britain and Portugal." Accessed July 28, 2018. http://www.pdavis.nl/Treaty_Portugal.htm.
Fakayode, Fagbemijo A. "Orí: The Divine Value of Self in Yorùbá Cosmology." Accessed November 26, 2016. https://oyekuofun.org/what-is-ori/.
GoldMyneTV. "I am the True Ooni of Ife—Olugbo of Ugboland." Accessed March 24, 2020. https://www.youtube.com/watch?v=0DYNOtk3xqg.
Hühn, Peter. "Event and Eventfulness." *The Living Handbook of Narratology.* June 7, 2011 (Revised September 13, 2013). Accessed March 20, 2020. https://www.lhn.uni-hamburg.de/node/39.html.
Manfredi, Victor. "Before Wazobia: Òminigbọn and Polyglot Culture in Medieval 9ja." June 19, 2015. Accessed March 4, 2016. http://people.bu.edu/manfredi/BeforeWazobia.pdf.
Manuel, Dave. "Inflation Calculator." Accessed April 15, 2016. http://www.davemanuel.com/inflation-calculator.php.

MeasuringWorth. "Purchasing Power of British Pounds from 1270 to Present." Accessed May 5, 2016. https://www.measuringworth.com/ppowercuk/.

Nobles, Wade W. "Critical Ideas and Concepts." Accessed July 18, 2017. https://www.drwadenobles.com/sakhu-scholarship.

"Ọ̀gbórí Ẹlẹ́mọ̀ṣọ́." Accessed July 21, 2017. https://www.youtube.com/watch?v=1Q5PPIVvLUg.

"Slave Voyages: The Trans-Atlantic Slave Trade Database." Accessed October 2018–May 2019. https://www.slavevoyages.org/voyage/database.

Santeria Church. "The Importance of Women in Santeria." June 27, 2012. Accessed November 5, 2017. http://santeriachurch.org/the-importance-of-women-in-santeria/.

Wikipedia. "Deaths from Smallpox." Accessed July 13, 2017. https://en.wikipedia.org/wiki/Category:Deaths_from_smallpox.

World Atlas. "Largest Ethnic Groups in Nigeria." Accessed July 28, 2017. http://www.worldatlas.com/articles/largest-ethnic-groups-in-nigeria.html.

Yeats, William B. *The Second Coming.* 1919. Accessed December 27, 2016. https://www.poetryfoundation.org/poems-and-poets/poems/detail/43290.

Newspaper Publications

Adeseri, Leke, Gbenga Olarinoye, and Dapo Akinrefon. "Osun State Traditional Council of Obas: Ooni Ogunwusi's First Litmus Test." *Nigerian Vanguard*, December 11, 2015. Accessed December 11, 2015. http://www.vanguardngr.com/2015/12/osun-state-traditional-council-of-obas-ooni-ogunwusis-first-litmus-test-2/.

Atoyebi, F. "Ajimobi Installs 21 New Ibadan Kings in One Day," *Punch*, August 28, 2017. Accessed May 20, 2019. https://punchng.com/ajimobi-installs-21-new-ibadan-kings-in-one-day/.

Awoyinfa, Samuel. "I Stand by My Ranking of Yoruba Obas—Alake." *Punch*, March 15, 2016. Accessed May 4, 2016. http://punchng.com/i-stand-by-my-ranking-of-yoruba-obas-alake/.

Babalola, Ademola. "Jubilation in Ibadan as Ajimobi Enthrones 20 New Kings, Olubadan, Ladoja Shun Ceremony." *This Day*, August 28, 2017. Accessed April 17, 2018. https://www.thisdaylive.com/index.php/2017/08/28/jubilation-in-ibadan-as-ajimobi-enthrones-20-new-kings-olubadan-ladoja-shun-ceremony/.

Bello, Niyi. "Ùgbò-Ìlàjẹ́'s Place in Yorùbá History, by Ọba Akinruntan." *Guardian Nigeria*, August 13, 2015. Accessed May 13, 2016. https://guardian.ng/issue/ugbo-ilajes-place-in-yoruba-history-by-oba-akinruntan/.

Makinde, F. "Olugbo's Outburst, Royal Rascality, Says Ooni." *Punch*, December 5, 2016. Accessed January 28, 2017. http://punchng.com/olugbos-outburst-royal-rascality-says-ooni/.

Ogunesan, Tunde. "Court Nullifies Installation of 21 Kings Crowned by Ajimobi." *Nigerian Tribune*, January 19, 2018. Accessed May 2, 2018. https://www.tribuneonlineng.com/127817/.

Olufemi, Alfred, "Alaafin of Oyo Writes Fayemi over Sanction of Ekiti Monarchs." *Premium Times*, March 14, 2020. Accessed January 28, 2020.

https://www.premiumtimesng.com/regional/ssouth-west/381761-alaafin-of-oyo-writes-fayemi-over-sanction-of-ekiti-monarchs.html.
Popoola, Debo. "Supremacy Battle: No Oba Is Greater Than Me—Alafin of Oyo Declares." *Capital*, March 23, 2016. Accessed March 24, 2016. http://www.thecapital.ng/?p=6353.
Ricketts, Olushola. "Awujale, Alake in Supremacy Battle," *Punch*, May 19, 2019. Accessed May 20, 2019. https://punchng.com/awujale-alake-in-supremacy-battle/.

Published Secondary Works

Abaka, Edmund Kobina. *"Kola Is God's Gift": Agricultural Production, Export Initiatives & the Kola Industry of Asante & the Gold Coast, c.1820–1950*. Athens: Ohio University Press, 2005.
Abimbola, Kola. *Yoruba Culture: A Philosophical Account*. Birmingham, UK: Iroko Academic, 2006.
Abimbọla, Wande. *Ifá: An Exposition of Ifá Literary Corpus*. Ibadan: Oxford University Press, 1976.
———. *Ifá Divination Poetry*. New York: NOK, 1977.
———. *Ifá Will Mend Our Broken World*. Roxbury, MA: Aim Books, 1997.
———. *Ìjìnlẹ̀ Ohùn Ẹnu Ifá: Apá Kejì*. Ibadan: University Press PLC, 2006.
———. *Ìjìnlẹ̀ Ohùn Ẹnu Ifá: Apá Kìn-ín-ní*. Ibadan: University Press PLC, 2006.
———. "Lagbayi: The Itinerant Woodcarver of Ojowon." In *The Yoruba Artist: New Theoretical Perspectives on African Arts*, edited by Rowland Abiodun, Henry J. Drewal, and John Pemberton III, 137–42. Washington: Smithsonian Institution Press, 1994.
———. "The Ruins of Oyo Division." *African Notes* 2 (1964): 16–19.
———. "The Yoruba Concept of Human Personality." In *La Notion de Personne En Afrique Noire*, edited by O. Dieterlen, 73–89. Paris: Centre National de la Recherche Scientifique, 1973.
Abiodun, Rowland. "The Kingdom of Owo." In *Yoruba: Nine Centuries of African Art and Thought*, edited by H. J. Drewal, J. Pemberton III, and R. Abiodun, 91–115. New York: Center for African Art, 1989.
———. "A Reconsideration of the Function of Àkó, Second Burial Effigy in Òwò." *Africa* 46 (1976): 4–20.
———. "Understanding Yoruba Art and Aesthetics: The Concept of 'Ase.'" *African Arts* 27, no. 3 (1994): 68–103.
———. "Verbal and Visual Metaphors: Mythical Allusions in Yoruba Ritualistic Art of Ori." *Ife: Annals of the Institute of Cultural Studies, University of Ife, Nigeria* 1 (1986): 8–39.
———. *Yoruba Art and Language: Seeking the African in African Art*. Cambridge: Cambridge University Press, 2014.
Abiọla, J. D. E., J. A. Babafẹmi, and S. O. S. Ataiyero. *Iwe Itan Ijẹṣa Obokun Ilẹ Owurọ*. Ileṣa, 1932.
Abraham, Roy Clive. *Dictionary of Modern Yoruba*. London: University of London Press, 1958.
Adamu, M. "The Hausa and Their Neighbours in the Central Sudan." In *UNESCO General History of Africa, IV: Africa from the Twelfth to the Sixteenth Century*, edited by D. T. Niane, 266–300. Berkeley: University of California Press.

Adediran, Biodun. "The Early Beginnings of the Ife State." In *The Cradle of a Race: Ife from the Beginning to 1980*, edited by I. A. Akinjogbin, 77–95. Port Harcourt: Sunray, 1992.

———. *The Frontier States of Western Yorùbáland, circa 1600–1889: State Formation and Political Growth in an Ethnic Frontier Zone*. Ibadan: Institut français de recherche en Afrique (IFRA), 1994.

———. "Yoruba Ethnic Groups or a Yoruba Ethnic Group?: A Review of the Problem of Ethnic Identification." *Africa* 7 (1984): 57–70.

Adeduntan, John. "Early Glass Bead Technology of Ile-Ife." *West African Journal of Archaeology* 15 (1985): 165–71.

Adegbola, T. "Transmission of Scientific Knowledge in Yoruba Oral Literature." In *Yoruba Fiction, Orature, and Culture: Oyekan Owomoyela and African Literature and the Yoruba Experience*, edited by T. Falola and A. Oyebade, 35–50. Trenton, NJ: Africa World Press, 2011.

Adekunle, Julius. *Politics and Society in Nigeria's Middle Belt: Borgu and the Emergence of a Political Identity*. Trenton, NJ: Africa World Press, 2003.

Ademakinwa, J. A. *Ife, Cradle of the Yoruba*. Ibadan: Ademakinwa, 1953.

Adeniji, David A. A. *Isé Irin Wíwa àti Sísun ní ilè Yorùbá, Iron Mining and Smelting in Yorùbáland*. Ibadan: Institute of African Studies, University of Ibadan, 1977.

Adepegba, Cornelius Oyeleke. "Animals in the Art of Ife." *African Notes* 10 (1986): 50–58.

———. "Associated Place-Names and Sacred Icons of Seven Yorùbá Deities." In *Òrìṣà Devotion as World Religion: The Globalization of Yorùbá Religious Culture*, edited by Jacob O. K. Olupona and Terry Rey, 106–27. Madison: University of Wisconsin Press, 2008.

———. "The Descent from Oduduwa: Claims of Superiority among Some Yoruba Traditional Rulers and the Arts of Ancient Ife." *International Journal of African Historical Studies* 19, no. 1 (1986): 77–92.

———. "Ife Art: An Enquiry into the Surface Patterns and the Continuity of the Art Tradition among the Northern Yoruba." *West African Journal of Archaeology* 12 (1982): 95–109.

———. "Osun and Brass: An Insight into Yoruba Religious Symbology." In *Ọṣun across the Waters: A Yoruba Goddess in Africa and the Americas*, edited by Joseph M. Murphy and Mei-Mei Sanford, 102–12. Bloomington: Indiana University Press, 2001.

Adetugbo, Abiodun. "The Yoruba Language in Yoruba History." In *Sources of Yoruba History*, edited by S. O. Biobaku, 176–204. Oxford: Clarendon, 1973.

Adetunji, J. I. "Industrial Mineral Exploitation, Economic and Environmental Implications: A Case Study of Oyo State, Southwest Nigeria." In *Proceedings of the 3rd International Conference on Sustainable Development Indicators in the Mineral Industries (SDIMI 2007): 17–20 June 2007, Milos Islands, Greece*, edited by Zacharias G. Agioutantis, 109–14. Athens, Greece: Heliotopos, 2007.

Adewuyi, Olayinka Babatunde Ogunsina. *Obatala: The Greatest and Oldest Divinity*. Alamosa, CO: River Water Books, 2013.

Adeyemi, M. C., and Nihinlolawa Aluko-Olokun. *Ondo Kingdom: Its History and Culture*. Ibadan: Bounty, 1993.

Adeyemi-Ale, G. A. *Understanding Ife Modakeke Relationships*. Ede, Nigeria: Moyanjuola, 1999.

Afọlayan, Funso S. "Towards a History of Eastern Yorubaland." In *Yoruba Historiography*, edited by Toyin Falọla, 75–87. Madison: African Studies Program, University of Wisconsin, 1991.

Agbaje-Williams, Babatunde. *Archaeological Investigation of Itagunmodi Potsherd Pavement Site, Ijesaland, Osun State, Nigeria, 1991–1992 Season*. Ibadan: Institut français de recherche en Afrique (IFRA), 1995.

———. "Archaeological Reconnaissance of Ipapo Ile, Kwara State, Nigeria: An Interim Report." *West African Journal of Archaeology* 19 (1989): 21–36.

———. "Archaeology and Yoruba Studies." In *Yoruba Historiography*, edited by Toyin Falola, 5–29. Madison: African Studies Program, University of Wisconsin, 1991.

———. "Diogun and Mejiro Wares: Does This Dichotomy Exist in the Archaeology of Old Oyo?" *Odu New Series* 41 (2001): 1–28.

———. "The Discovery of Koso, an Ancient Oyo Settlement." *Nigerian Field* 54 (1989): 123–27.

———. "Estimating the Population of Old Oyo." *Odu* 30 (1986): 3–24.

———. "Oyo Ruins of NW Yorubaland, Nigeria." *Journal of Field Archaeology* 17 (1990): 367–73.

Agbaje-Williams, Babatunde, and Akinwumi Ogundiran. *Cultural Resources in Ijesaland, Western Nigeria*. Ileşa: Ijeşa Cultural Foundation, 1992.

Agbe-Davies, Anna. *Tobacco, Pipes, and Race in Colonial Virginia: Little Tubes of Mighty Power*. London: Routledge, 2016.

Agiri, Babatunde. "Early Oyo History Reconsidered." *History in Africa* 2 (1975): 1–16.

Agwuele, Augustine H. "'Yorubaisms' in African American 'Speech' Patterns." In *Yoruba Diaspora in the Atlantic World*, edited by T. Falola and M. D. Childs, 325–45. Bloomington: Indiana University Press, 2004.

Aisien, Ekhaguosa. *Ewuare: The Oba of Benin*. Benin City: Aisien Publishers, 2012.

Ajayi, Ibi. *The Evolution of Ondo Kingdom, over 500 Years (1510–2010+)*. Ibadan: Spectrum Books, 2013.

Ajayi, J. F. Ade. *Christian Missions in Nigeria 1841–1891: The Making of a New Élite*. London: Longman, 1965.

———. "Colonialism: An Episode in African History." In *Colonialism in Africa, 1870–1960*, edited by L. H. Gann and P. Duignan, 497–509. London: Cambridge University Press, 1969.

———. "The Continuity of African Institutions under Colonialism." In *Emerging Themes of African History*, edited by T. O. Ranger, 189–200. London: Heinemann Educational, 1969.

———. "How Yoruba Was Reduced to Writing." *Odu* 8 (1960): 49–58.

———. *Patriot to the Core: Bishop Ajai Crowther*. Ibadan: Spectrum Books, 2001.

———. "Professional Warriors in Nineteenth-Century Yoruba Politics." *Tarikh* 1 (1965): 72–81.

———. "Samuel Ajayi Crowther of Oyo." In *Africa Remembered: Narratives by West Africans from the Era of the Slave Trade*, edited by Philip D. Curtin, 289–316. Madison: University of Wisconsin Press, 1967.

———. "Towards a More Enduring Sense of History: A Tribute to K. O. Dike, Former President of Historical Society of Nigeria." *Journal of the Historical Society of Nigeria* 12 (1984): 3–4.

Ajayi, J. F. Ade, and S. A. Akintoye. "Yorubaland in the Nineteenth Century." In *Groundwork of Nigerian History*, edited by O. Ikime, 280–302. Ibadan: Heinemann Educational Books, 1980.

Ajayi, J. F. Ade, and E. J. Alagoa. "Black Africa: The Historian's Perspective." *Daedalus: Journal of the American Academy of Arts and Sciences* (1974): 125–34.

Ajayi, J. F. Ade, and Robert Sydney Smith. *Yoruba Warfare in the Nineteenth Century*. Cambridge: Cambridge University Press, 1964.

Ajekigbe, Philip Gbadegesin. "Pottery Making in Ilora and Its Relationship with Old Oyo Pottery Finds." In *Historical Archaeology in Nigeria*, edited by Kit W. Wesler, 99–141. Trenton, NJ: Africa World Press, 1998.

Ajişafẹ, Ajayi Kọlawọle. *History of Abeokuta*. Abeokuta: Fola Bookshops, 1964.

Ajuwon, Bade. *Funeral Dirges of Yoruba Hunters*. New York: NOK International, 1982.

Àkàngbé, Adéníyì. "Crowther, Samuel Àjàyí," In *Encyclopedia of the Yorùbá*, edited by Toyin Falola and Akintunde Akinyemi, 76–77. Bloomington: Indiana University Press, 2016.

Akinade, Olalekan. *An Archaeological Perspective on the Esie Soapstone Phenomenon*. Abuja: Prints Xray, 2011.

Akinjogbin, I. A. *The Cradle of a Race: Ife from the Beginning to 1980*. Port Harcourt: Sunray, 1992.

———. *Dahomey and Its Neighbours, 1708–1818*. Cambridge: Cambridge University Press, 1967.

———. "The Ebi System Reconsidered." Department of History Seminar Papers 1, University of Ife, Ilé-Ifẹ̀, 1978.

———. "The Economic Foundations of the Oyo Empire." In *Topics on Nigerian Economic and Social History*, edited by I. A. Akinjogbin and S. Osoba, 35–54. Ilé-Ifẹ̀: University of Ife Press, 1980.

———. "The Growth of Ife from Oduduwa to 1800." In *The Cradle of a Race: Ife from the Beginning to 1980*, edited by I. A. Akinjogbin, 96–116. Port Harcourt: Sunray, 1992.

———. *Milestones and Concepts in Yoruba History and Culture: A Key to Understanding Yoruba History*. Ibadan: Olu-Akin, 2002.

———. "The Oyo Empire in the Eighteenth Century: A Reassessment." *Journal of the Historical Society of Nigeria* 3 (1966): 449–60.

———. "The Prelude to the Yoruba Civil Wars of the Nineteenth Century." *Odu* 1 (1965): 24–47.

———. "Towards a Political Geography of Yoruba Civilization." In *The Proceedings of the Conference on Yoruba Civilization Held at the University of Ife*, Nigeria, July 26–31, 1976, edited by I. A. Akinjogbin and G. O. Ekemode, 19–33. Ilé-Ifẹ̀: The University of Ife, 1976.

Akinjogbin, I. A., and E. A. Ayandele. "Yorubaland up to 1800." In *Groundwork of Nigerian History*, edited by Obaro Ikime, 121–43. Ibadan: Heinemann Educational Books, 1980.

Akinrinade, Olusola. "Akinjogbin: The Man and His Works." In *Culture and Society in Yorubaland*, edited by Deji Ogunremi and Biodun Adediran, 224–40. Ibadan: Rex Charles, 1998.

Akinrinsola, Fola. "Ogun Festival." *Nigeria Magazine* 85 (1965): 85–95.
Akintoye, S. A. *A History of the Yoruba People*. Dakar: Amalion, 2010.
———. "Ife's Sad Century." *Nigeria Magazine* 104 (1970): 34–39.
———. *Revolution and Power Politics in Yorubaland, 1840–1893: Ibadan Expansion and the Rise of Ekitiparapo*. New York: Humanities, 1971.
Alabi, Raphael A. "Environment and Subsistence of the Early Inhabitants of Coastal Southwestern Nigeria." *African Archaeological Review* 19, no. 4 (2002): 183–201.
———. "Late Stone Age Technologies and Agricultural Beginnings." In *Precolonial Nigeria: Essays in Honor of Toyin Falola*, edited by A. Ogundiran, 87–104. Trenton, NJ: Africa World Press, 2005.
Alagoa, Ebiegberi Joe. *A History of the Niger Delta: An Historical Interpretation of Ijo Oral Tradition*. Ibadan: Ibadan University Press, 1972.
Alcock, Susan E. *Empires: Perspectives from Archaeology and History*. Cambridge: Cambridge University Press, 2001.
Aleru, J. O. *Old Oyo and the Hinterland: History and Culture in Northern Yorubaland, Nigeria*. Ibadan: Textflow, 2006.
Aleru, J. O., and K. Adekola. "Exploring Frontiers of Archaeology and Cultural Resource Management: Untold Stories of the Esie Stone Figurines." *Journal of Environment and Culture* 7, no. 2 (2010): 50–64.
Allison, P. A. "A Terra-Cotta Head in the Ife Style from Ikirun, Western Nigeria." *Man: The Journal of the Royal Anthropological Institute* 63 (1963): 156–57.
Allman, Jean. "Adultery and the State in Asante: Reflections on Gender, Class, and Power from 1800 to 1950." In *The Cloth of Many Colored Silks: Papers on History and Society, Ghanaian and Islamic in Honor of Ivor Wilks*, edited by John Hunwick and Nancy Lawler, 27–65. Evanston, IL: Northwestern University Press, 1996.
Allsworth-Jones, P., P. A. Oyelaran, C. Stringer, and T. Compton. "Itaakpa, a Late Stone Age Site in Southwestern Nigeria." *Journal of Field Archaeology* 37, no. 3 (2012): 163–77.
Allsworth-Jones, P., and Kit W. Wesler. "Salt Boiling on the Egun Coast: Excavation and Experiment in Lagos State." In *Historical Archaeology in Nigeria*, edited by K. W. Wesler, 41–73. Trenton, NJ: Africa World Press, 1998.
Alpern, Stanley B. "What Africans Got for Their Slaves: A Master List of European Trade Goods." *History in Africa* 22 (1995): 5–43.
Amherd, K. Noel. *Reciting Ifa: Difference, Heterogeneity, and Identity*. Trenton, NJ: Africa World Press, 2010.
Andah, Bassey W. "Prologue." In *Cultural Resource Management: An African Dimension*, edited by B. W. Andah, 2–8. Ibadan: Wisdom, 1990.
———. "Studying African Societies in Cultural Context." In *Making Alternative Histories: The Practice of Archaeology and History in Non-Western Settings*, edited by P. Schmidt and Thomas Peterson, 149–81. Santa Fe, NM: School of American Research Press, 1995.
Appadurai, Arjun, and Carol A. Breckenridge. "Public Modernity." In *Consuming Modernity: Public Culture in a South Asian World*, edited by Carol A. Breckenridge, 1–20. Minneapolis: University of Minnesota Press, 1998.
Apter, Andrew H. *Black Critics and Kings: The Hermeneutics of Power in Yoruba Society*. Chicago: University of Chicago Press, 1992.

———. *Oduduwa's Chain: Locations of Culture in the Yoruba-Atlantic.* Chicago: University of Chicago Press, 2018.

———. "Yoruba Ethnogenesis from Within." *Comparative Studies in Society and History* 55, no. 2 (2013): 356–87.

Araujo, Ana Lucia. *Shadows of the Slave Past: Memory, Heritage, and Slavery.* London: Routledge, 2016.

Aremu, David A. "Demonstration of Brass Casting at Obo Aiyegunle, Kwara State, Nigeria." In *Cultural Resource Management: An African Dimension*, edited by Bassey W. Andah, 209–17. Ibadan: Wisdom, 1990.

———. "Early History of Metal Working among Northeast Yoruba in Kwara State." In *Historical Archaeology in Nigeria*, edited by Kit Wesler, 75–98. Trenton, NJ: Africa World Press, 1998.

Aremu, David A., J. Ogiogwa, J. O. Aleru, Bolanle J. Tubosun, B. A. Ogunfolakan, and P. A. Oyelaran. "Sungbo Eredo, Materiality, Ecology, Culture and Society in Prehistoric Southwestern Nigeria." *West African Journal of Archaeology* 43, no. 2 (2013): 1–21.

Aremu, P. S. O., Yemi Ijisakin, and Shehinde Ademuleya, "The Significance of 'Igbarubi-edi' in Edi Festival in Ile-Ife: A Spiritual Concession." *Journal Research in Peace, Gender and Development* 3, no. 7 (2013): 126–32.

Arifalo, S. O. *An Analysis and Comparison of the Legends of Origin of Akure.* The Text of a Lecture Delivered in the Akure Town Hall on November 8, 1991, as part of the Oyemekun Festival 1991 Celebrations. Akure: Bolasola, 1991.

Armstrong, Robert G. "The Etymology of the Word 'Ogun.'" In *Africa's Ogun: Old World and New*, edited by Sandra T. Barnes, 29–38. Bloomington: Indiana University Press, 1989.

———. *The Study of West African Languages.* Ibadan: Ibadan University Press, 1964.

Arno, Andrew. "Cobo and Tabua in Fiji: Two Forms of Cultural Currency in an Economy of Sentiment." *American Ethnologist* 32 (2005): 46–62.

Aronson, Lisa. "Ijebu Yoruba Aso Olona: A Contextual and Historical Overview." *African Arts* 25, no. 3 (1992): 52–63, 101–2.

Atanda, J. A. *A Comprehensive History of the Yoruba People up to 1800.* Ibadan: John Archers, 2007.

———. "The Fall of the Old Oyo Empire: A Reconsideration of Its Cause." *Journal of the Historical Society of Nigeria* 5 (1971): 477–90.

———. "The Yoruba Ogboni Cult: Did It Exist in Old Oyo?" *Journal of the Historical Society of Nigeria* 6 (1973): 365–72.

Atayero, Samuel. *A Short History of Ọba Ọwa of Ijẹsha-Land, and Ọni of Ifẹ.* Lagos: Ijẹsha Royal, 1948.

Atolagbe, D. *Itan Oore, Otun, Ati Moba.* Ibadan, 1981.

Austen, Ralph A. "The Slave Trade as History and Memory: Confrontations of Slaving Voyage Documents and Communal Traditions." *William and Mary Quarterly* 58, no. 1 (2001): 229–44.

Austen, Ralph A., and Woodruff D. Smith. "Private Tooth Decay as Public Economic Virtue: The Slave-Sugar Triangle, Consumerism and European Industrialization." *Social Science History* 14, no. 1 (1990): 95–115.

Austin, Gareth. "Resources, Techniques, and Strategies South of the Sahara: Revising the Factor Endowments Perspective on African Economic Development, 1500–2000." *Economic History Review* 61, no. 3 (2008): 587–624.

Awe, Bolanle. "The Ajele System: A Study of Ibadan Imperialism in the Nineteenth Century." *Journal of the Historical Society of Nigeria* 3 (1964): 47–60.

Ayandele, E. A. *The Ijebu of Yorubaland, 1850–1950: Politics, Economy, and Society.* Ibadan: Heinemann Educational Books, 1992.

———. "Ijebuland 1800–1891: Era of Splendid Isolation." In *Studies in Yoruba History and Culture: Essays in Honour of Professor S.O. Biobaku,* edited by G. O. Olusanya, 88–107. Ibadan: Ibadan University Press, 1983.

Babalola, Abidemi. "Ancient History of Technology in West Africa: The Indigenous Glass/Glass Bead Industry and the Society in Early Ile-Ife, Southwest Nigeria." *Journal of Black Studies* 48, no. 5 (2017): 501–527.

Babalola, A. B., S. K. McIntosh, L. Dussubieux, and T. Rehren. "Ile-Ife and Igbo Olokun in the History of Glass in West Africa." *Antiquity* 91, no. 357 (2017): 732–50.

Babalola, A. B., T. Rehren, A. Ige, and S. McIntosh. "The Glass Making Crucibles from Ile-Ife, SW Nigeria." *Journal of African Archaeology* 16 (2018): 1–29.

Babayemi, S. O. "Bere Festival in Oyo." *Journal of the Historical Society of Nigeria* 7 (1973): 121–24.

———. *Egúngún among the Ọyọ Yoruba.* Ibadan: Ọyọ State Council for Arts and Culture, 1980.

———. "Upper Ogun: An Historical Sketch." *African Notes* 6 (1971): 72–84.

Bada, S. O. *Iwe Itan Ondo.* Ondo, Nigeria: Igbehin Adun, 1940.

Badejo, Diedre. *Osun Seegesi: The Elegant Deity of Wealth, Power, and Femininity.* Trenton, NJ: Africa World Press, 1996.

Bailey, Anne C. *African Voices of the Atlantic Slave Trade: Beyond the Silence and the Shame.* Boston: Beacon, 2007.

Bakinde, Clement O. "Oral Narrations on the Origin and Settlement Patterns of the Okun People of Central Nigeria." *Journal of Tourism and Heritage Studies* 2, no. 2 (2013): 53–63.

Bamgbose, Ayo. *Yoruba Orthography: A Linguistic Appraisal with Suggestions for Reform, Based on a Talk Given to the Ẹgbẹ Ijinlẹ Yoruba at Ibadan on March 5, 1964.* Ibadan: Ibadan University Press, 1965.

Baram, Uzi. "Clay Tobacco Pipes and Coffee Cup Sherds in the Archaeology of the Middle East: Artifacts of Social Tensions from the Ottoman Past." *International Journal of Historical Archaeology* 3, no. 3 (1999): 137–51.

Barber, Karin. *I Could Speak until Tomorrow: Oriki, Women, and the Past in a Yoruba Town.* Washington, DC: Smithsonian Institution Press, 1991.

———. "Money, Self-Realization and the Person in Yorùbá Texts." In *Money Matters: Instability, Values and Social Payments in the Modern History of West African Communities*, edited by Jane I. Guyer, 205–24. Portsmouth, NH: Heinemann, 1995.

Barcia, Manuel. *West African Warfare in Bahia and Cuba.* Oxford: Oxford University Press, 2016.

Barnes, Sandra T., ed. *Africa's Ogun: Old World and New.* Bloomington: Indiana University Press, 1997.

Barnes, Sandra T., and Paula Girshick Ben-Amos. "Ogun, the Empire Builder." In *Africa's Ogun: Old World and New,* edited by Sandra T. Barnes, 39–64. Bloomington: Indiana University Press, 1997.

Bascom, William Russell. *African Folktales in the New World.* Bloomington: Indiana University Press, 1992.

———. "The Esusu: A Credit Institution of the Yoruba." *Journal of the Royal Anthropological Institute of Great Britain and Ireland* 82 (1970): 63–69.

———. *Ifa Divination: Communication between Gods and Men in West Africa.* Bloomington: Indiana University Press, 1969.

———. *Sixteen Cowries: Yoruba Divination from Africa to the New World.* Bloomington: Indiana University Press, 1980.

———. *The Yoruba of Southwestern Nigeria.* New York: Holt, Rinehart and Winston, 1969.

Bastide, R. *The African Religions of Brazil: Toward a Sociology of the Interpenetration of Civilizations.* 1960. Translated by Helen Sebba. Baltimore, MD: Johns Hopkins University Press, 2007.

Bay, Edna G. *Wives of the Leopard: Gender, Politics, and Culture in the Kingdom of Dahomey.* Charlottesville: University of Virginia Press, 1998.

Beck, Robin A. *Chiefdoms, Collapse, and Coalescence in the Early American South.* Cambridge: Cambridge University Press, 2013.

———., ed. *The Durable House: House Society Models in Archaeology.* Carbondale, IL: Center for Archaeological Investigations, Southern Illinois University, 2007.

Beier, Ulli. "Before Oduduwa." *Odu* 3 (1956): 25–32.

———. "The Palace of the Ogogas in Ikerre." *Nigeria Magazine* 44 (1954): 303–14.

———. *Yoruba Beaded Crowns: Sacred Regalia of the Olokuku of Okuku.* London: Ethnographica, in association with the National Museum, Lagos, 1982.

———. *Yoruba Myths.* Cambridge: Cambridge University Press, 1980.

Belasco, Bernard I. *The Entrepreneur as Culture Hero: Preadaptations in Nigerian Economic Development.* New York: Praeger, 1980.

Ben-Amos, Paula. *Art, Innovation, and Politics in Eighteenth-Century Benin.* Bloomington: Indiana University Press, 1999.

———. *The Art of Benin.* Rev. ed. New York: Thames and Hudson, 1995.

Ben-Amos, Paula, and John K. Thornton. "Civil War in the Kingdom of Benin, 1689–1721: Continuity or Political Change?" *Journal of African History* 42 (2001): 353–76.

Benedict, Carol. *Golden-Silk Smoke: A History of Tobacco in China, 1550–2010.* Berkeley: University of California Press, 2011.

Benedictow, Ole Jørgen. *The Black Death, 1346–1353: The Complete History.* Rochester, NY: Boydell, 2004.

Bhabha, Homi K. *The Location of Culture.* New York: Routledge, 1994.

Bhat, R., and A. A. Karim. "Exploring the Nutritional Potential of Wild and Underutilized Legumes." *Comprehensive Reviews in Food Science and Food Safety* 8, no. 4 (2009): 305–31.

Biobaku, Saburi O. *The Egba and Their Neighbours, 1842–1872.* Oxford: Clarendon, 1957.

———. *The Origin of the Yorubas.* Lagos: Federal Information Service, 1955.

Blackmun, Barbara Winston. "The Elephant and Its Ivory in Benin." In *Elephant: The Animal and Its Ivory in African Culture*, edited by Doran H. Ross, 163–83. Los Angeles: Fowler Museum of Cultural History, 1992.

Bledsoe, Caroline H. *Women and Marriage in Kpelle Society*. Stanford: Stanford University Press, 1980.

Blier, Suzanne Preston. *Art and Risk in Ancient Yoruba: Ife History, Power, and Identity, c. 1300*. Cambridge: Cambridge University Press, 2015.

———. "Art in Ancient Ife, Birthplace of the Yoruba." *African Arts* 45, no. 4 (2012): 70–85.

———. "Cosmic References in Ancient Ife." In *African Cosmos: Stellar Arts*, edited by Christine Mullen Kreamer and Randall Bird, 204–15. New York: Monacelli, 2012.

Boston, John. "Ifa Divination in Igala." *Africa* 44, no. 4 (1974): 350–60.

Bowen, T. J. *Central Africa: Adventures and Missionary Labors in Several Countries in the Interior of Africa, from 1849 to 1856*. New York: Negro Universities Press, 1969.

Bradbury, Raymond E. *The Benin Kingdom and the Edo-Speaking Peoples of South-Western Nigeria*. London: International African Institute, 1957.

———. "Chronological Problems in the Study of Benin History." *Journal of the Historical Society of Nigeria* 1 (1959): 263–87.

Brandon, George. "Hierarchy without a Head: Observations on Changes in the Social Organization of Some Afroamerican Religions in the United States, 1959–1999, with Special Reference to Santeria." *Archives de Sciences Sociales des Religions* 117, no. 1 (2002): 151–74.

Breunig, Peter, ed. *Nok: African Sculpture in Archaeological Context*. Frankfurt am Main: Africa Magna, 2014.

Breunig, Peter, and Nicole Rupp. "An Outline of Recent Studies on the Nigerian Nok Culture." *Journal of African Archaeology* 14, no. 3 (2016): 237–55.

Brooks, George E. *Eurafricans in Western Africa: Commerce, Social Status, Gender, and Religious Observance from the Sixteenth to the Eighteenth Century*. Athens: Ohio University Press, 2003.

———. *Landlords and Strangers: Ecology, Society, and Trade in Western Africa, 1000–1630*. Boulder: Westview, 1993.

Brooks, Jerome E. *Tobacco: Its History Illustrated by the Books, Manuscripts and Engravings in the Library of George Arents, Jr.* Vol. 1. New York: Rosenbach, 1937.

Brown, David H. *Santería Enthroned: Art, Ritual, and Innovation in an Afro-Cuban Religion*. Chicago: University of Chicago Press, 2003.

Brumfiel, Elizabeth M., and John W. Fox. *Factional Competition and Political Development in the New World*. New York: Cambridge University Press, 1994.

Burke, Peter. *Varieties of Cultural History*. Ithaca, NY: Cornell University Press, 1997.

Burton, Richard F. *A Mission to Gelele, King of Dahome*. 2nd ed. Vol. 1. London: Tinsley Brothers, 1864.

Butzer, K. W. "Collapse, Environment, and Society." *Proceedings of the National Academy of Sciences of the United States of America* 109, no. 10 (2012): 3632–39.

Byfield, Judith A. *The Bluest Hands: A Social and Economic History of Women Dyers in Abeokuta (Nigeria), 1890–1940*. Portsmouth, NH: Heinemann, 2002.

———. "Dress and Politics in Post–World War II Abeokuta (Western Nigeria)." In *Fashioning Africa: Power and the Politics of Dress*, 31–49. Bloomington: Indiana University Press, 2004.

———. "Women, Marriage, Divorce and the Emerging Colonial State in Abeokuta (Nigeria) 1892–1904." *Canadian Journal of African Studies* 30, no. 1 (1996): 32–51.

Carney, Judith A., and Richard N. Rosomoff. *In the Shadow of Slavery: Africa's Botanical Legacy in the Atlantic World*. Berkeley: University of California Press, 2009.

Carr, Edward R. "Men's Crops and Women's Crops: The Importance of Gender to the Understanding of Agricultural and Development Outcomes in Ghana's Central Region." *World Development* 36, no. 5 (2008): 900–915.

Casey, Joanna. "The Stone to Metal Age." In *The Oxford Handbook of African Archaeology*, edited by Peter Mitchell and Paul Lane, 603–14. Oxford: Oxford University Press, 2013.

Charland, Maurice. "Technological Nationalism." *Canadian Journal of Political and Social Theory* 10, no. 1–2 (1986): 196–220.

Chatzkel, Jay L. *Knowledge Capital: How Knowledge-Based Enterprises Really Get Built*. New York: Oxford University Press, 2003.

Chikwendu, V. Emenike, and A. C. Umeji. "Local Sources of Raw Material for the Nigerian Bronze/Brass Industry with Emphasis on Igbo Ukwu." *West African Journal of Archaeology* 9 (1979): 151–65.

Clarke, John Digby. "Ilorin Stone Bead Making." *Nigeria* 14 (1938): 156–57.

Clarke, William H. *Travels and Explorations in Yorubaland, 1854–1858*. Ibadan: Ibadan University Press, 1972.

Collins, Robert O., and James McDonald Burns. *A History of Sub-Saharan Africa*. Cambridge: Cambridge University Press, 2007.

Connah, Graham. *The Archaeology of Benin: Excavations and Other Researches in and around Benin City, Nigeria*. Oxford: Clarendon, 1975.

———. *Three Thousand Years in Africa: Man and His Environment in the Lake Chad Region of Nigeria*. Cambridge: Cambridge University Press, 1981.

Connerton, Paul. *How Societies Remember*. Cambridge: Cambridge University Press, 1989.

Cooper, Frederick. *Africa in the World: Capitalism, Empire, Nation-State*. Cambridge, MA: Harvard University Press, 2014.

Costa, Emilia Viotti da. *The Brazilian Empire: Myths and Histories*. Chapel Hill: University of North Carolina Press, 2003.

Costin, Cathy L. Craft Economies of Ancient Andean States. In *Archaeological Perspectives on Political Economies,* edited by Gary M. Feinman and Linda M. Nicholas (189–222). Salt Lake City: University of Utah Press, 2004.

Coursey, D. G., and Cecilia K. Coursey. "The New Yam Festivals of West Africa." *Anthropos* 66 (1971): 3–4.

Craddock, P. T., J. Ambers, Duncan R. Hook, Ronald M. Farquhar, V. Emenike Chikwendu, Alphonse C. Umeji, and Thurstan Shaw. "Metal Sources and the Bronzes from Igbo-Ukwu, Nigeria." *Journal of Field Archaeology* 24 (1997): 405–29.

Crass, David Colin, Bruce R. Penner, and Tammy R. Forehand. "Gentility and Material Culture on the Carolina Frontier." *Historical Archaeology* 33, no. 3 (1999): 14–31.
Crosby, Alfred W. *Germs, Seeds and Animals: Studies in Ecological History.* New York: Routledge, 2015.
Crossley, David W. *Post-Medieval Archaeology in Britain.* New York: Leicester University Press, 1990.
Crowther, Samuel. *A Grammar of the Yoruba Language.* London: Seeleys, 1852.
———. *Slave Trade: African Squadron.* London: John Mortimer, 1850.
Curtin, Philip D. "Joseph Wright of the Egba." In *Africa Remembered: Narratives by West Africans from the Era of the Slave Trade*, edited by Philip D. Curtin, 317–34. Madison: University of Wisconsin Press, 1967.
Curto, José C. *Enslaving Spirits: The Portuguese-Brazilian Alcohol Trade at Luanda and its Hinterland, c. 1550–1830.* London: Brill, 2004.
Dalziel, J. M. *The Useful Plants of West Tropical Africa.* London: Secretary of State for the Colonies, 1937.
Darling, P. J. *Archaeology and History in Southern Nigeria: The Ancient Linear Earthworks of Benin and Ishan.* Oxford: British Archaeological Reports, 1984.
———. "Sungbo's Eredo: Africa's Largest Monument." *Nigerian Field* 62, no. 3–4 (1997): 113–29.
———. "Sungbo's Eredo, Southern Nigeria." *Nyame Akuma* 49 (1998): 55–61.
Davison, Claire C., Robert D. Giauque, and J. Desmond Clark. "Two Chemical Groups of Dichroic Glass Beads from West Africa." *Man* 6 (1971): 645–59.
DeCorse, Christopher R. *An Archaeology of Elmina: Africans and Europeans on the Gold Coast, 1400–1900.* Washington, DC: Smithsonian Institution Press, 2001.
De Luna, Kathryn M. *Collecting Food, Cultivating People: Subsistence and Society in Central Africa.* New Haven: Yale University Press, 2017.
De Luna, Kathryn M., Jeffrey B. Fleischer, and Susan Keech McIntosh. "Thinking across the African Past: Interdisciplinarity and Early History." *African Archaeological Review* 29, no. 2–3 (2012): 75–94.
Demsetz, Harold. "Toward a Theory of Property Rights." *American Economic Review* 57, no. 2 (1967): 347–59.
Denzer, LaRay. "Yoruba Women: A Historiographical Study." *International Journal of African Historical Studies* 27, no. 1 (1994): 1–39.
Depelchin, Jacques. *Reclaiming African History.* Chicago: Pambazuka, 2011.
Dibua, J. I. "The Idol, Its Worshippers, and the Crisis of Relevance of Historical Scholarship in Nigeria." *History in Africa: A Journal of Method History in Africa* 24 (1997): 117–37.
Dietler, Michael, and Brian Hayden. *Feasts: Archaeological and Ethnographic Perspectives on Food, Politics, and Power.* Tuscaloosa: University of Alabama Press, 2010.
Doyle, Laura. *Freedom's Empire: Race and the Rise of the Novel in Atlantic Modernity, 1640–1940.* Durham: Duke University Press, 2008.

Drewal, Henry John. "Image and Indeterminacy: Elephants and Ivory among the Yoruba." In *Elephant: The Animal and Its Ivory in African Culture*, edited by Doran H. Ross, 187–207. Los Angeles: Fowler Museum of Cultural History, 1992.

———. "Pageantry and Power in Yoruba Costuming." In *Fabrics of Culture: The Anthropology of Clothing and Adornment*, edited by Justine M. Cordwell and Ronald M. Schwarz, 189–230. Boston: De Gruyter Mouton, 1979.

Drewal, Henry John, and Margaret Thompson Drewal. *Gęlędę: Art and Female Power among the Yoruba*. Bloomington: Indiana University Press, 1983.

Drewal, Henry John, and John Mason. *Beads, Body, and Soul: Art and Light in the Yorùbá Universe*. Los Angeles: UCLA Fowler Museum of Cultural History, 1997.

Drewal, Henry John, John Pemberton, and Rowland Abiodun. *Yoruba: Nine Centuries of African Art and Thought*. New York: Center for African Art in association with H. N. Abrams, 1989.

Drewal, Henry John, and Enid Schildkrout. *Dynasty and Divinity: Ife Art in Ancient Nigeria*. Seattle: University of Washington Press, 2009.

Drewal, Margaret Thompson. *Yoruba Ritual: Performers, Play, Agency*. Bloomington: Indiana University Press, 2000.

Dubois, Félix. *Timbuctoo the Mysterious*. New York: Negro Universities Press, 1969.

Dueppen, Stephen A. "The Archaeology of West Africa, ca. 800 BCE to 1500 CE." *History Compass* 14, no. 6 (2016): 247–63.

Dunn, Ross E. *The Adventures of Ibn Battuta, a Muslim Traveler of the 14th Century*. Berkeley: University of California Press, 1986.

DuPlessis, Robert S. *The Material Atlantic: Clothing, Commerce, and Colonization in the Atlantic World, 1650–1800*. Cambridge: Cambridge University Press, 2016.

Earle, Timothy K. *How Chiefs Come to Power: The Political Economy in Prehistory*. Stanford, CA: Stanford University Press, 1997.

Eason, Louis, D. I. *Ifa: The Yoruba God of Divination in Nigeria and the United States*. Trenton, NJ: Africa World Press, 2008.

Edeh, Emmanuel M. P. *Towards an Igbo Metaphysics*. Chicago: Loyola University Press, 1985.

Edgerton, David E. H. "The Contradictions of Techno-Nationalism and Techno-Globalism: A Historical Perspective." *New Global Studies* 1, no. 1 (2007): 1–32.

Egharevba, Jacob U. *A Short History of Benin*. Ibadan: Ibadan University Press, 1968.

———. *Twelve Works*. Nendeln: Kraus Reprint, 1973.

Ehret, Christopher. *An African Classical Age: Eastern and Southern Africa in World History, 1000 B.C. to A.D. 400*. Charlottesville: University Press of Virginia, 2001.

———. "Agricultural Origins: What Linguistic Evidence Reveals." In *A World with Agriculture, 12,000 BCE–500 CE*, vol. 2 of *The Cambridge World History*, edited by Graeme Barker and Candice Goucher, 55–92. Cambridge: Cambridge University Press, 2017.

———. *The Civilizations of Africa: A History to 1800*. 2nd ed. Charlottesville: University of Virginia Press, 2016.
———. "Linguistic Archaeology." *African Archaeological Review* 29, no. 2–3 (2012): 109–30.
Ekeh, Peter P. "Social Anthropology and Two Contrasting Uses of Tribalism in Africa." *Comparative Studies in Society and History: An International Quarterly* 32 (1990): 660–700.
Elebuibon, Yemi. *The Adventures of Obatala*. Osogbo, Nigeria: A.P.I. Production, 1989.
Ellis, A. B. *The Yoruba-Speaking Peoples of the Slave Coast of West Africa: Their Religion, Manners, Customs, Laws, Language, Etc., with an Appendix Containing a Comparison of the Tshi, Gã, Ewe and Yoruba Languages*. London: Curzon, 1974.
Eltis, David. "The Diaspora of Yoruba Speakers, 1650–1865: Dimensions and Implications." In *Yoruba Diaspora in the Atlantic World*, edited by Toyin Falola and Matt Childs, 17–39. Bloomington: Indiana University Press, 2004.
———. *Economic Growth and the Ending of the Transatlantic Slave Trade*. New York: Oxford University Press, 1987.
———. *The Rise of African Slavery in the Americas*. Cambridge: Cambridge University Press, 2000.
Eltis, David, and Lawrence C. Jennings. "Trade between Western Africa and the Atlantic World in the Pre-Colonial Era." *American Historical Review* 93, no. 4 (1988): 936–59.
Eltis, David, and David Richardson. *Extending the Frontiers: Essays on the New Transatlantic Slave Trade Database*. New Haven, CT: Yale University Press, 2008.
Eluyemi, Omotoso. "Excavations at Isoya near Ile-Ife (Nigeria), in 1972." *West African Journal of Archaeology* 7 (1977): 97–115.
———. "New Terracotta Finds at Oke-Eso, Ife." *African Arts* 9 (1975): 32–35.
———. "The Role of Oral Traditions in the Archaeological Investigation of the History of Ife." In *Yoruba Oral Traditions*, edited by Wande Abimbola, 115–56. Ilé-Ifẹ̀: Department of African Languages and Literature, University of Ife, 1975.
———. "Selecting an Ooni of Ife." *Nigeria Magazine* 53, no. 4 (1985): 17–23.
———. "The Technology of the Ife Glass Beads: Evidence from Igbo-Olokun." *Odu* (New Series) 32 (1987): 197–220.
Enem, Edith. "Nigerian Dances [Parts 1–2]." *Nigeria Magazine* 115–16 (1975): 65–115.
Enwerem, Iheanyi M. "'Money-Magic' and Ritual Killing in Contemporary Nigeria." In Money Struggles and City Life : Devaluation in Ibadan and Other Urban Centers in Southern Nigeria, 1986–1996, edited by Jane I. Guyer, LaRay Denzer, and Adigun Agbaje, 189–205. Portsmouth, NH: Heinemann, 2002.
Erediauwa, King of Benin. *I Remain, Sir, Your Obedient Servant*. Ibadan: Spectrum Books, 2004.
Esan, O. "Correspondence, 'Before Oduduwa.'" *Odu* 8 (1960): 75–76.

Euba, Titiola. "Of Blue and Red: The Role of Ife in the West African Trade in Kori Beads." *Journal of the Historical Society of Nigeria* 11, no. 1–2 (1981): 109–27.

Eyo, Ekpo. "Igbo'Laja, Owo." *West African Journal of Archaeology* 6 (1976): 37–58.

———. "Odo Ogbe Street and Lafogido: Contrasting Archaeological Sites in Ile-Ife, Western Nigeria." *West African Journal of Archaeology* 4 (1974): 99–109.

Fadipẹ, N. A. *The Sociology of the Yoruba*. Ibadan: Ibadan University Press, 1970.

Fage, J. D. "Slavery and the Slave Trade in the Context of West African History." *Journal of African History* 10, no. 3 (1969): 393–404.

———. "Some Remarks on Beads and Trade in Lower Guinea in the 16th and 17th Centuries." *Journal of African History* 3 (1962): 343–47.

Fagg, William Buller. *Nigerian Images: The Splendor of African Sculpture*. New York: Praeger, 1963.

Fairholt, F. W. *Tobacco: Its History and Associations, Including an Account of the Plant and Its Manufacture, with Its Modes of Use in All Ages and Countries*. Detroit: Singing Tree, 1968.

Falade, S. Ade. *The Comprehensive History of Osogbo*. Osogbo, Nigeria, 2000.

Fálétí, Adébáyọ̀. *Itan Ibanujẹ ti Gaa: Basọrun Ilẹ Yoruba ni Aiye Ọba Abiọdun*. Ibadan: Onibonoje, 1972.

Falola, Toyin, ed. *Èṣù: Yoruba God, Power, and the Imaginative Frontiers*. Durham, NC: Carolina Academic Press, 2013.

———. *Ibadan: Foundation, Growth and Change, 1830–1960*. Ibadan: Bookcraft, 2012.

———. *Pioneer, Patriot, and Patriarchy: Samuel Johnson and the Yoruba People*. Madison: African Studies Program, University of Wisconsin–Madison, 1994.

———. *The Political Economy of a Pre-Colonial African State: Ibadan, 1830–1900*. Ilé-Ifẹ̀: University of Ife Press, 1984.

———. *The Power of African Cultures*. Rochester, NY: University of Rochester Press, 2010.

———. "The Yoruba Caravan System of the Nineteenth Century." *International Journal of African Historical Studies* 24 (1991): 111–32.

———. *Yoruba Gurus: Indigenous Production of Knowledge in Africa*. Trenton, NJ: Africa World Press, 1999.

———. "The Yoruba Toll System: Its Operation and Abolition." *Journal of African History* 30 (1989): 69–88.

Falola, Toyin, and A. G. Adebayo. *Culture, Politics and Money among the Yoruba*. New Brunswick, NJ: Transaction, 2000.

Falola, Toyin, and Matt D. Childs. *The Yoruba Diaspora in the Atlantic World*. Bloomington: Indiana University Press, 2004.

Falola, Toyin, and Matthew M. Heaton. *A History of Nigeria*. Cambridge: Cambridge University Press, 2010.

Falola, Toyin, and Christian Jennings, eds. *Sources and Methods in African History: Spoken, Written, Unearthed*. Rochester, NY: University of Rochester Press, 2010.

Falola, Toyin, and Olatunde Bayo Lawuyi. "Not Just a Currency: The Cowrie in Nigerian Culture." In *West African Economic and Social History: Studies in Memory of Marion Johnson*, edited by David Henige and T. C. McCaskie, 29–36. Madison: African Studies Program, University of Wisconsin, 1990.

Falola, Toyin, and Paul E. Lovejoy, eds. *Pawnship in Africa: Debt Bondage in Historical Perspective*. Boulder, CO: Westview, 1994.

Falola, Toyin, and Paul E. Lovejoy. "Pawnship in Historical Perspective." In *Pawnship, Slavery, and Colonialism in Africa*, edited by Toyin Falola and Paul E. Lovejoy, 1–26. Trenton, NJ: Africa World Press, 2003.

Falola, Toyin, and Dare Oguntomisin. *Yoruba Warlords of the Nineteenth Century*. Trenton, NJ: Africa World Press, 2001.

Fatunsin, Antonia K. "Ifetedo: A Late Stone Age Site in the Forest Region of Southwestern Nigeria." *West African Journal of Archaeology* 26 (1996): 71–87.

———. *Yoruba Pottery*. Lagos: National Commission for Museums and Monuments, 1992.

Feinman, Gary M., and Christopher P. Garraty. "Preindustrial Markets and Marketing: Archaeological Perspectives." *Annual Review of Anthropology* 39 (2010): 167–91.

Fenske, James. "Land Abundance and Economic Institutions: Egbaland and Slavery, 1830–1914." *Economic History Review* 65, no. 2 (2012): 527–55.

Fisher, Humphrey J. "'He Swalloweth the Ground with Fierceness and Rage': The Horse in the Central Sudan. I. Its Introduction." *Journal of African History* 13, no. 3 (1972): 367–88.

———. "'He Swalloweth the Ground with Fierceness and Rage': The Horse in the Central Sudan II. Its Use." *Journal of African History* 14, no. 3 (1973): 355–79.

Fitzgerald, Mary Anne, Henry John Drewal, and Moyosore B. Okediji. "Transformation through Cloth: An Egungun Costume of the Yoruba." *African Arts* 28 (1995): 54–57.

Folorunso, C. A., P. A. Oyelaran, Bolanle J. Tubosun, and P. G. Ajekigbe. "Revisiting Old Oyo: Report on an Interdisciplinary Field Study." In *Proceedings of the 18th Biennial Meeting of the Society of Africanist Archaeologists*, Calgary, Canada, 2006. Accessed June 26, 2017. https://www.researchgate.net/publication/238679406_Revisiting_old_Oyo_Report_on_an_interdisciplinary_field_study.

Fontaine, Laurence. *History of Pedlars in Europe*. Durham, NC: Duke University Press, 1996.

Forde, Cyril Daryll. *The Yoruba-Speaking Peoples of South-Western Nigeria*. London: International African Institute, 1951.

Fortes, Meyer. *Religion, Morality, and the Person: Essays on Tallensi Religion*. Cambridge: Cambridge University Press, 1987.

Fourshey, C. C., Rhonda M. Gonzales, and Christine Saidi. *Bantu Africa: 3500 BCE to Present*. Oxford: Oxford University Press, 2017.

Fọlayan, Kọla. "Egbado to 1832: The Birth of a Dilemma." *Journal of the Historical Society of Nigeria* 4 (1967): 15–33.

Frank, Manfred. *What Is Neostructuralism?* Minneapolis: University of Minnesota Press, 1989.

Freedman, Maurice. *Chinese Lineage and Society: Fukien and Kwangtung.* London: Athlone, 1966.

Friese, Susanne. *Self-concept and Identity in a Consumer Society: Aspects of Symbolic Product Meaning.* Marburg: Tectum-Verlag, 2000.

Frobenius, Leo. *The Voice of Africa: Being an Account of the Travels of the German Inner African Exploration Expedition in the Years 1910–1912.* London: Hutchinson, 1913.

Fyle, C. Magbaily. "The Yoruba Diaspora in Sierra Leone's Krio Society." In *Yoruba Diaspora in the Atlantic World*, edited by T. Falola and M. Childs, 366–82. Bloomington: Indiana University Press, 2004.

Gabel, Creighton, and Norman R. Bennett. *Reconstructing African Culture History.* Boston: Boston University Press, 1967.

Gadamer, Hans-Georg. *Philosophical Hermeneutics.* Berkeley: University of California Press, 1976.

Gailey, Christine Ward. *Kinship to Kingship: Gender Hierarchy and State Formation in the Tongan Islands.* Austin: University of Texas Press, 1987.

Garlake, Peter S. "Excavations at Obalara's Land, Ile-Ife." *West African Journal of Archaeology* 4 (1974): 111–48.

———. "Excavations on the Woye Asiri Family Land in Ife, Western Nigeria." *West African Journal of Archaeology* 7 (1977): 57–96.

Gates, Henry Louis. *The Signifying Monkey: A Theory of Afro-American Literary Criticism.* New York: Oxford University Press, 1988.

Gbadamosi, T. G. O. *The Growth of Islam among the Yoruba, 1841–1908.* London: Longman, 1978.

Gbadegesin, Segun. "Toward a Theory of Destiny." In *A Companion to African Philosophy*, edited by K. Wiredu, 313–23. Malden, MA: Blackwell, 2004.

Gehring, Charles T., Jacob Adriaan Schiltkamp, and Peter Stuyvesant. *Curacao Papers, 1640–1665.* Interlaken, NY: Heart of the Lakes, 1987.

Gikandi, Simon. *Slavery and the Culture of Taste.* Princeton, NJ: Princeton University Press, 2011.

Gillespie, Susan D. "Body and Soul among the Maya: Keeping the Spirits in Place." *APAA Archeological Papers of the American Anthropological Association* 11, no. 1 (2002): 67–78.

———. "When Is a House?" In *The Durable House: House Society Models in Archaeology*, edited by Robin Beck, 25–50. Carbondale, IL: Center for Archaeological Investigations, Southern Illinois University, 2007.

Gitlin, Jay, Barbara Berglund, and Adam Arenson. *Frontier Cities: Encounters at the Crossroads of Empire.* Philadelphia: University of Pennsylvania Press, 2013.

Glickman, Lawrence B. *The "Cultural Turn."* Washington, DC: American Historical Association, 2012.

Glubb, John Bagot. *The Fate of Empires and Search for Survival.* Edinburgh: Blackwood, 1978.

Gluckman, Max. *Economy of the Central Barotse Plain.* Livingstone, Northern Rhodesia: Rhodes-Livingstone Institute, 1941.

Goering, D. Timothy. "Concepts, History and the Game of Giving and Asking for Reasons: A Defense of Conceptual History." *Journal of the Philosophy of History* 7, no. 3 (2013): 426–52.

Gonzales, Rhonda M. *Societies, Religion, and History: Central-East Tanzanians and the World They Created, c. 200 BCE to 1800 CE*. New York: Columbia University Press, 2014.
González-Ruibal, Alfredo. "Archaeology and the Time of Modernity." *Historical Archaeology* 50, no. 3 (2016): 144–64.
Goodman, Jordan. "Excitantia: Or, How Enlightenment Europe Took to Soft Drugs." In *Consuming Habits: Drugs in History and Anthropology*, edited by Jordan Goodman, Paul E. Lovejoy, and Andrew Sherratt, 126–47. New York: Routledge, 1995.
Goodman, Jordan, Paul E. Lovejoy, and Andrew Sherratt, eds. *Consuming Habits: Drugs in History and Anthropology*. New York: Routledge, 1995.
Gott, Richard. *Cuba: A New History*. New Haven, CT: Yale University Press, 2005.
Graeber, David. *Debt: The First 5,000 Years*. Brooklyn, NY: Melville House, 2014.
Gramsci, Antonio. *Antonio Gramsci: Selections from Political Writings, 1910–1920: With Additional Texts by Bordiga and Tasca*. New York: International, 1977.
Green, Monica Helen. *Pandemic Disease in the Medieval World: Rethinking the Black Death*. Bradford, UK: Arc Medieval, 2015.
Green, Toby. "Africa and the Price Revolution: Currency Imports and Socioeconomic Change in West and West-Central Africa during the Seventeenth Century." *Journal of African History* 57, no. 1 (2016): 1–24.
———. *The Rise of the Trans-Atlantic Slave Trade in Western Africa, 1300–1589*. New York: Cambridge University Press, 2012.
Greene, Sandra E. *Gender, Ethnicity, and Social Change on the Upper Slave Coast: A History of the Anlo-Ewe*. Portsmouth, NH: Heinemann, 1996.
Gregory, Christopher A. "Cowries and Conquest: Towards a Subalternate Quality Theory of Money." *Comparative Studies in Society and History* 38 (1996): 195–217.
Grossman, James. "Everything Has a History." *Perspectives on History, the Newsmagazine of the American Historical Association*, December 1, 2015. Accessed March 5, 2017. https://www.historians.org/publications-and-directories/perspectives-on-history/december-2015/everything-has-a-history.
Gurstelle, Andrew W., Nestor Labiyi, and Simon Agani. "Settlement History and Chronology in the Savè Area of Central Bénin." *Azania: Archaeological Research in Africa* 50, no. 2 (2015): 227–49.
Guyer, Jane I. *Marginal Gains: Monetary Transactions in Atlantic Africa*. Chicago: University of Chicago Press, 2004.
———. *Money Matters: Instability, Values, and Social Payments in the Modern History of West African Communities*. Portsmouth, NH: Heinemann, 1995.
———. "Wealth in People and Self-Realization in Equatorial Africa." *Man* 28 (1993): 243–65.
———. "Wealth in People, Wealth in Things: Introduction." *Journal of African History* 36, no. 1 (1995): 83–90.
Guyer, Jane I., and Samuel-Martin Eno Belinga. "Wealth in People as Wealth in Knowledge: Accumulation and Composition in Equatorial Africa" *Journal of African History* 36, no. 1 (1995): 91–120.

Haberland, Eike, ed. *Leo Frobenius on African History, Art and Culture: An Anthology*. Princeton, NJ: Markus Wiener, 2007.
Haggerty, Sheryllynne. "Risk and Risk Management in the Liverpool Slave Trade." *Business History* 51, no. 6 (2009): 817–34.
Hämäläinen, Pekka. *The Comanche Empire*. New Haven, CT: Yale University Press, 2008.
Handler, Jerome S. "Aspects of the Atlantic Slave Trade: Smoking Pipes, Tobacco, and the Middle Passage." *African Diaspora Archaeology Newsletter* 12, no. 2 (2009): 1–12.
Haour, A., S. Nixon, D. N'dah, C. Magnavita, and A. Smith. "The Settlement Mound of Birnin Lafiya: New Evidence from the Eastern Arc of the Niger River." *Antiquity* 90, no. 351 (2016): 695–710.
Harms, Robert W. *River of Wealth, River of Sorrow: The Central Zaire Basin in the Era of the Slave and Ivory Trade, 1500–1891*. New Haven, CT: Yale University Press, 2004.
Hassan, Fekri A., and Barbara R. Stucki. "Nile Floods and Climate Change." In *Climate: History, Periodicity and Predictability*, edited by M. R. Rampino, J. E. Sanders, W. S. Newman, and L. K. Konigsson, 37–46. New York: Van Nostrand Reinhold, 1987.
Hatfield, April Lee. *Atlantic Virginia: Intercolonial Relations in the Seventeenth Century*. Philadelphia: University of Pennsylvania Press, 2004.
Heidegger, Martin. *Being and Time*. New York: Harper, 1962.
Herskovits, Melville J. *Dahomey, an Ancient West African Kingdom*. Evanston, IL: Northwestern University Press, 1967.
Heschel, Abraham Joshua. *Who Is Man? The Raymond Fred West Memorial Lectures at Stanford University, 1963*. Stanford, CA: Stanford University Press, 1966.
Higgins, Karen L. *Economic Growth and Sustainability: Systems Thinking for a Complex World*. Amsterdam: Elsevier, 2015.
Hodacs, Hanna. *Silk and Tea in the North: Scandinavian Trade and the Market for Asian Goods in Eighteenth-Century Europe*. London: Palgrave Macmillan, 2016.
Hodgkin, Thomas. *Nigerian Perspectives: An Historical Anthology*. London: Oxford University Press, 1960.
Hogendorn, Jan S. "Slaves as Money in the Sokoto Caliphate." In *Credit, Currencies, and Culture: African Financial Institutions in Historical Perspective*, edited by Endre Stiansen and Jane I. Guyer, 56–71. Uppsala: Nordic Institute of African Studies, 1999.
Hogendorn, Jan S., and Marion Johnson. *The Shell Money of the Slave Trade*. Cambridge: Cambridge University Press, 1986.
Höhn, Alexa, and Katharina Neumann. "The Palaeovegetation of Janruwa (Nigeria) and its Implications for the Decline of the Nok Culture." *Journal of African Archaeology* 14, no. 3 (2016): 331–53.
Holsey, Bayo. *Routes of Remembrance: Refashioning the Slave Trade in Ghana*. Chicago: University of Chicago Press, 2008.
Hopkins, A. G. *An Economic History of West Africa*. New York: Columbia University Press, 1973.
———. "A Report on the Yoruba, 1910." *Journal of the Historical Society of Nigeria* 5 (1969): 67–100.

Hopkins, Donald R. *The Greatest Killer: Smallpox in History, with a New Introduction*. Chicago: University of Chicago Press, 2002.

Hopkins, Keith. "Taxes and Trade in the Roman Empire (200 B.C.–A.D. 400)." *Journal of Roman Studies* 70 (1980): 101–25.

Horton, Robin. "Ancient Ife: A Reassessment." *Journal of the Historical Society of Nigeria* 9, no. 4 (1979): 69–149.

———. "The Economy of Ife, c. A.D. 900–c. A.D. 1700." In *The Cradle of a Race: Ife from the Beginning to 1980*, edited by I. A. Akinjogbin, 122–47. Port Harcourt: Sunray, 1992.

Hoy, David Couzens. *The Time of Our Lives: A Critical History of Temporality*. Cambridge, MA: MIT Press, 2009.

Hruby, Zachary X., Rowan K. Flad, and Gwen Patrice Bennett, eds. *Rethinking Craft Specialization in Complex Societies: Archaeological Analyses of the Social Meaning of Production*. Arlington, VA: American Anthropological Association, 2007.

Hughes, Diane Owen. "Introduction." In *Time: Histories and Ethnologies*, edited by D. O. Hughes and T. R. Trautmann, 1–18. Ann Arbor: University of Michigan Press, 1995.

Hunt, Lynn, ed. *The New Cultural History*. Berkeley: University of California Press, 2010.

Huysecom, Eric, Michel Rasse, Laurent Lespez, Katharina Neumann, A. Fahmy, Aziz Ballouche, Sylvain Ozainne, M. Magetti, Chantal Tribolo, and S. Soriano. "The Emergence of Pottery in Africa during the 10th Millennium CalBC: New Evidence from Ounjougou (Mali)." *Antiquity* 83, no. 322 (2009): 905–17.

Idowu, E. Bọlaji. *Olódùmarè: God in Yorùbá Belief*. Memorial ed. New York: Wazobia, 1994.

Ige, A., and T. Rehren. "Black Sand and Iron Stone: Iron Smelting in Modakeke, Ife, South Western Nigeria." *Institute for Archaeo-Metallurgical Studies* 23 (2003): 15–20.

Ige, O. A. "Ancient Glass Making in Ile-Ife, Southern Nigeria." In *Annales Du 18e Congrès de l'Association Internationale Pour l'Histoire Du Verre*, edited by D. Ignatiadou and A. Anastassios, 486–90. Thessaloniki: AIHV, 2012.

———. "Classification and Preservation of Ancient Glass Beads from Ile-Ife, Southwest Nigeria." In *Proceeding of the Interim Meeting of the ICOM Working Group on Glass and Ceramics Conservation 2010*, edited by H. Roemich, 63–74. New York: Corning, 2010.

Ige, O. A., and Samuel E. Swanson. "Provenance Studies of Esie Sculptural Soapstone from Southwestern Nigeria." *YJASC Journal of Archaeological Science* 35, no. 6 (2008): 1553–65.

Illife, John. *Honour in African History*. Cambridge: Cambridge University Press, 2005.

Inikori, Joseph E. "Africa and the Globalization Process: Western Africa, 1450–1850." *Journal of Global History* 2 (2007): 63–86.

———. *Africans and the Industrial Revolution in England: A Study in International Trade and Economic Development*. New York: Cambridge University Press, 2002.

———., ed. *Forced Migration: The Impact of the Export Slave Trade on African Societies*. London: Hutchinson, 1982.

———. "Review of 'The Rise of African Slavery in the Americas' by David Eltis." *American Historical Review* 106 (2001): 1751–52.

———. "Transatlantic Slavery and Economic Development in the Atlantic World: West Africa, 1450–1850." In *Cambridge World History of Slavery*, edited by David Eltis and Stanley L. Engerman, 650–74. Cambridge: Cambridge University Press, 2011.

Inikori, Joseph E., and Stanley L. Engerman, eds. *The Atlantic Slave Trade: Effects on Economies, Societies, and Peoples in Africa, the Americas, and Europe*. Durham, NC: Duke University Press, 1992.

———. "Introduction: Gainers and Losers in the Atlantic Slave Trade." In *The Atlantic Slave Trade: Effects on Economies, Societies, and Peoples in Africa, the Americas, and Europe*, edited by J. E. Inikori and S. L. Engerman, 1–24. Durham, NC: Duke University Press, 1992.

Insoll, Timothy. *Urbanism, Archaeology and Trade: Further Observations on the Gao Region (Mali): The 1996 Fieldseason Results*. BAR International Series 829. Oxford: Hadrian Books, 2000.

Insoll, Timothy, and Thurstan Shaw. "Gao and Igbo-Ukwu: Beads, Interregional Trade, and Beyond." *African Archaeological Review* 14 (1997): 9–23.

Isichei, Elizabeth. *Voices of the Poor in Africa: Moral Economy and the Popular Imagination*. Rochester, NY: Boydell and Brewer, 2004.

Jeje, L. K. "Ife Division: The Physical Elements of the Environment." In *The Cradle of a Race: Ife from the Beginning to 1980*, edited by I. A. Akinjogbin, 1–38. Port Harcourt: Sunray, 1992.

Jewsiewicki, Bogumil, and David S. Newbury. *African Historiographies: What History for Which Africa?* Ann Arbor: University of Michigan, 1998.

Johnson, Samuel. *The History of the Yorubas: From the Earliest Times to the Beginning of the British Protectorate*. Lagos: CMS Bookshops, 1921.

Jones, Owain, and Paul J. Cloke. *Tree Cultures: The Place of Trees and Trees in Their Place*. Oxford: Berg, 2002.

Joyce, Rosemary A., and Susan D. Gillespie. *Beyond Kinship: Social and Material Reproduction in House Societies*. Philadelphia: University of Pennsylvania Press, 2000.

Kagame, Abbe Alexis. "The Problem of Man in Bantu Philosophy." *African Mind: Journal of Religion and Philosophy in Africa* 1, no. 1 (1989): 35–40.

Kalilu, R. O. "Between Tradition and Record: A Search for the Legendary Woodcarvers of Old Oyo." *Ufahamu* 20 (1992): 49–63.

———. "Costumes and the Origin of Egungun." *African Studies* 52, no. 1 (1993): 55–69.

Kea, Ray A. *A Cultural and Social History of Ghana from the Seventeenth to the Nineteenth Century: The Gold Coast in the Age of Trans-Atlantic Slave Trade*. Book 1. Lewiston, NY: Edwin Mellen, 2012.

———. "Firearms and Warfare on the Gold and Slave coasts from the Sixteenth to the Nineteenth Centuries." *Journal of African History* 12, no. 2 (1971): 185–213.

———. "Review of 'The Rise of African Slavery in the Americas,' by David Eltis." *Americas* 59, no. 2 (2002): 263–65.

———. *Settlements, Trade, and Politics in the Seventeenth-Century Gold Coast*. Baltimore, MD: Johns Hopkins University Press, 1982.

Kelly, Kenneth G. "The Archaeology of African European Interaction: Investigating the Social Roles of Trade, Traders, and the Use of Space in the Seventeenth and Eighteenth Century Hueda Kingdom, Republic of Bénin." *World Archaeology* 28, no. 3 (1997): 351–69.

Klieman, Kairn A. *"The Pygmies Were Our Compass": Bantu and Batwa in the History of West Central Africa, Early Times to c. 1900 C.E.* Portsmouth, NH: Heinemann, 2005.

Knappett, Carl. *Network Analysis in Archaeology: New Approaches to Regional Interaction*. Oxford: Oxford University Press, 2013.

Knorr Cetina, Karin. "Objectual Knowledge." In *The Practice Turn in Contemporary Theory*, edited by Theodore R. Schatzki, Karin Knorr Cetina, and Eike von Savigny, 175–88. New York: Routledge, 2001.

———. "Sociality with Objects: Social Relations in Postsocial Knowledge Societies." *Theory, Culture & Society* 14, no. 4 (1997): 1–30.

Kopytoff, Igor. *The African Frontier: The Reproduction of Traditional African Societies*. Bloomington: Indiana University Press, 1987.

Krapf-Askari, Eva. *Yoruba Towns and Cities: An Enquiry into the Nature of Urban Social Phenomena*. Oxford: Clarendon, 1969.

Kriger, Colleen E. *Cloth in West African History*. Lanham, MD: AltaMira, 2006.

———. "The Conundrum of Culture in Atlantic History." In *Africa and the Americas: Interconnections during the Slave Trade*, edited by José C. Curto and Renée Soulodre-LaFrance, 259–78. Trenton, NJ: Africa World Press, 2005.

Kuba, R., and O. Akinwumi. "Precolonial Borgu: Its History and Culture." In *Precolonial Nigeria: Essays in Honor of Toyin Falola*, edited by Akinwumi Ogundiran, 319–60. Trenton, NJ: Africa World Press, 2005.

Kusimba, Chapurukha M. *The Rise and Fall of Swahili States*. Walnut Creek, CA: AltaMira, 1999.

Kusimba, Chapurukha, S. Barut-Kusimba, and Babatunde Agbaje-Williams. "Precolonial African Cities: Size and Density." In *Urbanism in the Preindustrial World: Cross-Cultural Approaches*, edited by G. Storey, 145–60. Tuscaloosa: University of Alabama Press, 2006.

Ladipo, Duro. *Moremi: A Yoruba Opera*. Ibadan: School of Drama, University of Ibadan, 1973.

Lankton, James W., O. Akin Ige, and Thilo Rehren. "Early Primary Glass Production in Southern Nigeria." *Journal of African Archaeology* 4 (2006): 111–41.

Laoye I, Adetoyese, and Susanne Wenger. *Oriki ati Orilẹ awọn Idile ni ilẹ Yoruba ni Ẹka-Ẹka Wọn*. Oshogbo: Mbari Mbayo, 1963.

Lasisi, Olanrewaju, and David Aremu. "New Lights on the Archaeology of Sungbo's Eredo, South-Western Nigeria." *Dig It* 3 (2016): 54–63.

Lave, Jean, and Etienne Wenger. *Situated Learning: Legitimate Peripheral Participation*. Cambridge: Cambridge University Press, 1991.

Law, Robin. "Book Review of *Dahomey and Its Neighbours, 1708–1818* by I. A. Akinjogbin." *Journal of the Historical Society of Nigeria* 4, no. 2 (1968): 344–47.

———. "The Constitutional Troubles of Oyo in the Eighteenth Century." *Journal of African History* 12, no. 1 (1971): 25–44.

———. "Cowries, Gold, and Dollars: Exchange Rate Instability and Domestic Price Inflation in Dahomey in the Eighteenth and Nineteenth Centuries."

In *Money Matters: Instability, Values and Social Payments in the Modern History of West African Communities*, edited by Jane I. Guyer, 53–73. Portsmouth, NH: Heinemann, 1995.
———. "Early European Sources Relating to the Kingdom of Ijebu (1500–1700): A Critical Survey." *History in Africa* 13 (1986): 245–60.
———. "Ethnicity and the Slave Trade: Lucumi and Nago as Ethnonyms in West Africa." *History in Africa* 24 (1997): 205–19.
———. "Finance and Credit in Pre-Colonial Dahomey." In *Credit, Currencies, and Culture: African Financial Institutions in Historical Perspective*, edited by E. Stiansen and J. Guyer, 15–37. Uppsala: Nordiska Afrikainstitutet, 1999.
———, ed. *From Slave Trade to "Legitimate" Commerce: The Commercial Transition in Nineteenth-Century West Africa*. Cambridge: Cambridge University Press, 2002.
———. "The Heritage of Oduduwa: Traditional History and Political Propaganda among the Yoruba." *Journal of African History* 14 (1973): 207–22.
———. *The Horse in West African History: The Role of the Horse in the Societies of Pre-Colonial West Africa*. Oxford: Published for the International African Institute by Oxford University Press, 1980.
———. "Horses, Firearms, and Political Power in Pre-Colonial West Africa." *Past & Present* 72, no. 1 (1976): 112–32.
———. *Ouidah: The Social History of a West African Slaving "Port," 1727–1892*. Athens: Ohio University Press, 2004.
———. *The Oyo Empire, c. 1600–c. 1836: A West African Imperialism in the Era of the Atlantic Slave Trade*. Oxford: Clarendon, 1977.
———. "Royal Monopoly and Private Enterprise in the Atlantic Trade: The Case of Dahomey." *Journal of African History* 18, no. 4 (1977): 555–77.
———. *The Slave Coast of West Africa, 1550–1750: The Impact of the Atlantic Slave Trade on an African Society*. Oxford: Clarendon, 1991.
———. "Slaves, Trade, and Taxes: The Material Basis of Political Power in Precolonial West Africa." *Research in Economic Anthropology* 1 (1978): 37–52.
———. "Trade and Politics behind the Slave Coast: The Lagoon Traffic and the Rise of Lagos, 1500–1800." *Journal of African History* 24 (1983): 321–48.
Law, Robin, and Kristin Mann. "West Africa in the Atlantic Community: The Case of the Slave Coast." *William and Mary Quarterly* 56, no. 2 (1999): 307–34.
Law, Robin, and Silke Strickrodt, eds. *Ports of the Slave Trade (Bights of Benin and Biafra)*. Stirling, UK: Centre of Commonwealth Studies, University of Stirling, 1999.
Lawal, Babatunde. "Àwòrán: Representing the Self and Its Metaphysical Other in Yoruba Art." *Art Bulletin* 83, no. 3 (2001): 498–526.
———. "À Yà Gbó, à Yà Tó: New Perspectives on Edan Ògbóni." *African Arts* 28 (1995): 36–49.
———. *The Gẹ̀lẹ̀dé Spectacle: Art, Gender, and Social Harmony in an African Culture*. Seattle: University of Washington Press, 1996.
———. "New Light on Gelede." *African Arts* 11 (1978): 65–70.
———. "Ori: The Significance of the Head in Yoruba Sculpture." *Journal of Anthropological Research* 41, no. 1 (1985): 91–103.

———. "Yoruba-Sango Ram Symbolism: From Ancient Sahara or Dynastic Egypt?" In *African Images: Essays in African Iconology*, edited by Daniel F. McCall and Edna Bay, 225–51. New York: Africana, 1975.

Lawuyi, Olatunde Bayo. "The Obatala Factor in Yoruba History." *History in Africa* 19 (1992): 369–75.

———. "Ogun: Diffusion across Boundaries and Identity Constructions." *African Studies Review* 31, no. 2 (1988): 127–39.

Leigh, John A. *History of Ondo*. Ondo: Self-published.

Lévi-Strauss, Claude. *Anthropology and Myth: Lectures, 1951–1982*. New York: Blackwell, 1987.

———. *The Savage Mind*. Chicago: The University of Chicago Press. 1966.

———. *The Way of the Masks*. Seattle: University of Washington Press, 1992.

Lewis, Jerry M. *History and Social Anthropology*. London: Tavistock, 1968.

Lewis, Maureen Warner. *Yoruba Songs of Trinidad* (with translations). London: Kamak House, 1994.

Lijadu, E. M. *Orunmila*. Nottingham, UK, 1908. Reprint, Ado-Ekiti: Omolayo Standard Press of Nigeria, 1972.

Lloyd, P. C. "Agnatic and Cognatic Descent among the Yoruba." *Man* 1, no. 4 (1966): 484–500.

———. "Conflict Theory and Yoruba Kingdoms." In *History and Social Anthropology*, edited by I. M. Lewis, 25–61. London: Tavistock, 1968.

———. "Osifekunde of Ijebu." In *Africa Remembered: Narratives by West Africans from the Era of the Slave Trade*, edited by Philip D. Curtin, 217–316. Madison: University of Wisconsin Press, 1967.

Logan, Amanda L., and Ann B. Stahl. "Genealogies of Practice in and of the Environment in Banda, Ghana." *Journal of Archaeological Method and Theory* 24, no. 4 (2017): 1356–1399.

Lovejoy, Paul E. "Ethnic Designations of the Slave Trade and the Reconstruction of the History of Trans-Atlantic Slavery." In *Trans-Atlantic Dimensions of Ethnicity in the African Diaspora*, edited by P. E. Lovejoy and D. V. Trotman, 9–42. London: Continuum, 2003.

———. "The Impact of the Atlantic Slave Trade on Africa: A Review of the Literature." *Journal of African History* 30, no. 3 (1989): 365–94.

———. "Interregional Monetary Flows in the Precolonial Trade of Nigeria." *Journal of African History* 15, no. 4 (1974): 563–85.

———. "Nigeria: The Ibadan School and Its Critics." In *African Historiographies: What History for Which Africa?*, edited by B. Jewsiewicki and D. Newbury, 197–206. London: Sage, 1986.

———. "The Role of the Wangara in the Economic Transformation of the Central Sudan in the Fifteenth and Sixteenth Centuries." *Journal of African History* 19, no. 2 (1978): 173–93.

———. *Salt of the Desert Sun: A History of Salt Production and Trade in the Central Sudan*. Cambridge: Cambridge University Press, 1986.

———. *Transformations in Slavery: A History of Slavery in Africa*. Cambridge: Cambridge University Press, 2012.

———. "The Yoruba Factor in the Trans-Atlantic Slave Trade." In *The Yoruba Diaspora in the Atlantic World*, edited by Toyin Falola and Matt Childs, 40–55. Bloomington: Indiana University Press, 2004.

Lovejoy, Paul E., and Toyin Falola. *Pawnship, Slavery, and Colonialism in Africa*. Trenton, NJ: Africa World Press, 2003.

Lovejoy, Paul E., and David Richardson. "British Abolition and Its Impact on Slave Prices along the Atlantic Coast of Africa, 1783–1850." *Journal of Economic History* 55, no. 1 (1995): 98–119.

———. "Competing Markets for Male and Female Slaves: Prices in the Interior of West Africa, 1780–1850." *International Journal of African Historical Studies* 28, no. 2 (1995): 261–93.

———. "'This Horrid Hole': Royal Authority, Commerce and Credit at Bonny, 1690–1840." *Journal of African History* 45, no. 3 (2004): 363–92.

———. "Trust, Pawnship, and Atlantic History: The Institutional Foundations of the Old Calabar Slave Trade." *American Historical Review* 104, no. 2 (1999): 332–55.

Lucas, J. Olumide. *The Religion of the Yorubas*. Lagos: C. M. S. Bookshop, 1948.

Lydon, Ghislaine. *On Trans-Saharan Trails: Islamic Law, Trade Networks, and Cross-Cultural Exchange in Nineteenth-Century Western Africa*. Cambridge: Cambridge University Press, 2012.

Mabogunje, Akin Ladipo. "Some Comments on Land Tenure in Egba Division, Western Nigeria." *Africa* 31 (1961): 258–69.

Mabogunje, Akin Ladipo, and John D. Omer-Cooper. *Owu in Yoruba History*. Ibadan: Ibadan University Press, 1971.

Mabogunje, Akin L., and Paul Richards. "Land and People-Models of Spatial and Ecological Processes in West African History." In *History of West Africa,* vol. 1, edited by J. F. A. Ajayi and M. Crowther, 6–12. Ibadan: Longman, 1985.

Magnavita, Sonja. "The Beads of Kissi, Burkina Faso." *Journal of African Archaeology* 1 (2003): 127–38.

Magnavita, S. "Sahelian Crossroads: Some Aspects on the Iron Age Sites of Kissi, Burkina Faso." In *Crossroads/Carrefour Sahel. Cultural and Technological Developments in First Millennium BC/AD West Africa*, edited by S. Magnavita, L. Kote, P. Breunig, and O. A. Ide, 79–104. Journal of African Archaeology Monograph Series 2. Frankfurt: Africa Magna, 2009.

Mali, Joseph. *Mythistory: The Making of a Modern Historiography*. Chicago: University of Chicago Press, 2003.

Mancall, Mark. *China at the Center: 300 Years of Foreign Policy*. New York: Free Press, 1984.

Mann, Kristin. *Slavery and the Birth of an African City: Lagos, 1760–1900*. Bloomington: Indiana University Press, 2010.

Manning, Patrick. "Slavery and Slave Trade in West Africa, 1450–1930." In *Themes in West Africa's History*, edited by Emmanuel K. Akyeampong, 99–117. Athens: Ohio University Press, 2006.

———. *Slavery, Colonialism, and Economic Growth in Dahomey, 1640–1960*. Cambridge: Cambridge University Press, 1982.

Marcus, Joyce. "The Archaeological Evidence for Social Evolution." *Annual Review of Anthropology* 37 (2008): 251–66.

Matory, J. Lorand. *Black Atlantic Religion Tradition, Transnationalism, and Matriarchy in the Afro-Brazilian Candomblé*. Princeton, NJ: Princeton University Press, 2005.

———. "The English Professors of Brazil: On the Diasporic Roots of the Yorùbá Nation." *Comparative Studies in Society and History* 41, no. 1 (1999): 72–103.

———. *Sex and the Empire That Is No More: Gender and the Politics of Metaphor in Oyo Yoruba Religion.* Minneapolis: University of Minnesota Press, 1994.

McAnany, Patricia Ann. *Living with the Ancestors: Kinship and Kingship in Ancient Maya Society.* Austin: University of Texas Press, 1995.

McAnany, Patricia Ann, and Norman Yoffee. *Questioning Collapse: Human Resilience, Ecological Vulnerability, and the Aftermath of Empire.* Cambridge: Cambridge University Press, 2010.

McCall, Daniel F. *Africa in Time-Perspective: A Discussion of Historical Reconstruction from Unwritten Sources.* Boston: Boston University Press, 1964.

———. "Prehistory as a Kind of History." *Journal of Interdisciplinary History* 3, no. 4 (1973): 733–39.

McCracken, Grant. *Culture and Consumption: New Approaches to the Symbolic Character of Consumer Goods and Activities.* Bloomington: Indiana University Press, 1990.

McIntosh, M. K. *Yoruba Women, Work, and Social Change.* Bloomington: Indiana University Press, 2009.

McIntosh, Roderick J. "Social Memory of the Mande." In *The Way the Wind Blows: Climate, History, and Human Action*, edited by R. McIntosh, Joseph A. Tainter, and Susan K. McIntosh, 141–80. New York: Columbia University Press, 2000.

McIntosh, Susan K., and Roderick J. McIntosh. *Prehistoric Investigations in the Region of Jenne, Mali: A Study in the Development of Urbanism in the Sahel.* Cambridge Monographs in African Archaeology 2. Oxford: Archaeopress, 1980.

Miers, Suzanne, and Igor Kopytoff. *Slavery in Africa: Historical and Anthropological Perspectives.* Madison: University of Wisconsin Press, 1977.

Mies, Maria. *Patriarchy and Accumulation on a World Scale: Women in the International Division of Labour.* London: Zed Books, 2014.

Miller, Joseph C. "The Significance of Drought, Disease and Famine in the Agriculturally Marginal Zones of West-Central Africa." *Journal of African History* 23, no. 1 (1982): 17–61.

———. *Way of Death: Merchant Capitalism and the Angolan Slave Trade, 1730–1830.* Madison: University of Wisconsin Press, 1988.

Millhauser, John K. "Debt as a Double-Edged Risk: A Historical Case from Nahua (Aztec) Mexico." *Economic Anthropology* 4, no. 2 (2017): 263–75.

Mintz, Sidney W. *Sweetness and Power: The Place of Sugar in Modern History.* New York: Viking, 1985.

Mizoguchi, Koji. "The Evolution of Prestige Good Systems: An Application of Network Analysis to the Transformation of Communication Systems and Their Media." In *Network Analysis in Archaeology*, edited by Carl Knappett, 151–78. Oxford: Oxford University Press, 2013.

Monroe, J. Cameron. "In the Belly of Dan: Space, History, and Power in Precolonial Dahomey." *Current Anthropology* 52, no. 6 (2011): 769–98.

———. *The Precolonial State in West Africa: Building Power in Dahomey.* Cambridge: Cambridge University Press, 2014.

Monroe, J. Cameron, and Anneke Janzen. "The Dahomean Feast: Royal Women, Private Politics, and Culinary Practices in Atlantic West Africa." *African Archaeological Review* 31, no. 2 (2014): 299–337.

Monroe, J. Cameron, and Akinwumi Ogundiran. *Power and Landscape in Atlantic West Africa: Archaeological Perspectives*. Cambridge: Cambridge University Press, 2012.

Moore, William A. *History of Itsekiri*. London: Frank Cass, 1970.

Morton, Adam David. *Unravelling Gramsci Hegemony and Passive Revolution in the Global Political Economy*. London: Pluto, 2007.

Morton-Williams, Peter. "The Oyo Yoruba and the Atlantic Trade 1670–1830." *Journal of the Historical Society of Nigeria* 3 (1964): 25–45.

Moseley, William G., and Leslie Gray. *Hanging by a Thread: Cotton, Globalization, and Poverty in Africa*. Athens: Ohio University Press, 2008.

Moxham, Roy. *Tea: Addiction, Exploitation, and Empire*. New York: Carroll and Graf, 2003.

Müller, Jan-Werner. "On Conceptual History." In *Rethinking Modern European Intellectual History*, edited by D. M. McMahon and S. Moyn, 74–111. Oxford: Oxford University Press, 2014.

Mullins, Paul R. "The Archaeology of Consumption." *Annual Review of Anthropology* 40 (2011): 133–44.

Nadel, S. F. *A Black Byzantium: The Kingdom of Nupe in Nigeria*. Oxford: Oxford University Press, 1942.

Nassaney, Michael S. "Men and Women, Pipes and Power in Native New England." In *Smoking and Culture: The Archaeology of Tobacco Pipes in Eastern North America*, edited by S. M. Rafferty and Rob Mann, 125–41. Knoxville: University of Tennessee Press, 2004.

Neimark, Philip John. *The Way of the Orisa: Empowering Your Life through the Ancient African Religion of Ifa*. San Francisco: Harper, 1993.

Ngomanda, Alfred, Katharina Neumann, Astrid Schweizer, and Jean Maley. "Seasonality Change and the Third Millennium BP Rainforest Crisis in Southern Cameroon (Central Africa)." *Quaternary Research* 71, no. 3 (2009): 307–18.

Niane, D. T. "Mali and the Second Mandingo Expansion." In *UNESCO General History of Africa IV: Africa from the Twelfth to the Sixteenth Century*, edited by D. T. Niane, 117–71. Berkeley: University of California Press.

Nishiura, Hiroshi, and Tomoko Kashiwagi. "Smallpox and Season: Reanalysis of Historical Data." *Interdisciplinary Perspectives on Infectious Diseases* (2009). Accessed January 19, 2017. doi:10.1155/2009/591935.

Nitzan, Jonathan, and Shimshon Bichler. *Capital as Power: A Study of Order and Creorder*. New York: Routledge, 2009.

Norman, Neil L. "Feasts in Motion: Archaeological Views of Parades, Ancestral Pageants, and Socio-Political Process in the Hueda Kingdom, 1650–1727 AD." *Journal of World Prehistory* 23, no. 4 (2010): 239–54.

———. "Hueda (Whydah) Country and Town: Archaeological Perspectives on the Rise and Collapse of an African Atlantic Kingdom." *International Journal of African Historical Studies* 42, no. 3 (2009): 387–410.

Northrup, David. *Africa's Discovery of Europe*. New York: Oxford University Press, 2013.

Nwaubani, Ebere. "Kenneth Onwuka Dike: Trade and Politics, and the Restoration of the African in History." *History in Africa* 27 (2000): 229–48.

Nwokeji, G. Ugo. *The Slave Trade and Culture in the Bight of Biafra: An African Society in the Atlantic World*. New York: Cambridge University Press, 2010.

Nye, Joseph S. *Soft Power: The Means to Success in World Politics.* New York: Public Affairs, 2009.
Nylan, Michael. "On the Politics of Pleasure." *Asia Major* 14, no. 1 (2001): 73–124.
Obayemi, Ade M. "Ancient Ile-Ife: Another Cultural Historical Reinterpretation." *Journal of the Historical Society of Nigeria* 9, no. 4 (1979): 151–85.
———. "Cultural Evolution of Northern Yoruba, Nupe and Igala. Part II." *Image: Quarterly Journal of the Kwara State Council for Arts and Culture* 2 (1976): 24–37.
———. "The Evolution of the Culture and Institutions of the Northern Yoruba, the Nupe and the Igala before A.D. 1800." *Image: Quarterly Journal of the Kwara State Council for Arts and Culture* 1 (1974): 5–9.
———. "History, Culture, Yoruba and Northern Factors." In *Studies in Yoruba History and Culture*, edited by G. O. Olusanya, 72–87. Ibadan: Ibadan University Press, 1983.
———. "States and Peoples of the Niger-Benue Confluence Area." In *Groundwork of Nigerian History*, edited by O. Ikime, 144–64. Ibadan: Heinemann Educational Books, 1980.
———. "The Yoruba and Edo-Speaking Peoples and Their Neighbours before 1600." In *History of West Africa*, edited by J. F. A. Ajayi and M. Crowther, 255–322. Oxford: Oxford University Press, 1985.
Obidiegwu, Jude Ejikeme, and Emmanuel Matthew Akpabio. "The Geography of Yam Cultivation in Southern Nigeria: Exploring Its Social Meanings and Cultural Functions." *Journal of Ethnic Foods* 4, no. 1 (2017): 28–35.
Oduwobi, Tunde. "Oral Traditions and Political Integration in Ijebu." *History in Africa* 27 (2000): 249–59.
Ogbomo, Onaiwu W. *When Men and Women Mattered: A History of Gender Relations among the Owan of Nigeria.* Rochester, NY: University of Rochester Press, 1997.
Ogumefu, M. I. *The Staff of Oranyan and Other Yoruba Tales.* London: Sheldon, 1930.
Ogunba, Oyin. "Ceremonies." In *Sources of Yoruba History*, edited by S. Biobaku, 87–110. Oxford: Clarendon, 1973.
Ogundeji, Philip Adedotun. "The Image of Sango in Duro Ladipo's Plays." *Research in African Literatures* 29, no. 2 (1998): 57–75.
Ogundiran, Akinwumi. "Archaeological Survey at Ipole-Ijesa, Southwestern Nigeria: A Preliminary Report." *Nyame Akuma* 42 (1994): 7–13.
———. *Archaeology and History in Ìlàrè District (Central Yorubaland, Nigeria), 1200–1900 A.D.* Oxford: Archaeopress, 2002.
———. "Ceramic Spheres and Regional Networks in the Yoruba-Edo Region, Nigeria, 13th–19th Centuries A.C." *Journal of Field Archaeology* 28 (2001): 27–44.
———. "Chronology, Material Culture, and Pathways to the Cultural History of Yoruba-Edo Region, 500 B.C.–A.D. 1800." In *Sources and Methods in African History: Spoken, Written, Unearthed*, edited by Toyin Falola and Christian Jennings, 33–79. Rochester, NY: University of Rochester Press, 2003.
———. "Collapsing Boundaries: A Continental Vision for African Archaeology." In *African Archaeology without Frontiers: Papers from the 2014*

PanAfrican Archaeological Association Congress, edited by Amanda Esterhuysen, Christine Sievers, and Karim Sadr, 37–51. Johannesburg: Wits University Press, 2016.
———. "Cowries and Rituals of Self-Realization in the Yoruba Region, ca. 1600–1860." In *Materialities of Ritual in the Black Atlantic*, edited by A. Ogundiran and P. Saunders, 68–86. Bloomington: Indiana University Press, 2014.
———. *Crises of Culture and Consciousness in the Postcolony: What Is the Future for Nigeria?* Occasional Paper No. 39, Institute of African Studies, University of Ibadan. Ibadan: John Archers, 2012.
———. "The End of Prehistory? An Africanist Comment." *American Historical Review* 118, no. 3 (2013): 788–801.
———. "Factional Competition, Sociopolitical Development, and Settlement Cycling in Ilare District (ca. 1200–1900): Oral Traditions of Historical Experience in a Yoruba Community." *History in Africa* 28 (2001): 203–23.
———. "Filling a Gap in the Ife-Benin Interaction Field (Thirteenth–Sixteenth Centuries AD): Excavations in Iloyi Settlement, Ijesaland." *African Archaeological Review* 19, no. 1 (2002): 27–60.
———. "The Formation of an Oyo Imperial Colony during the Atlantic Age." In *Power and Landscape in Atlantic West Africa: Archaeological Perspectives*, edited by C. Monroe and A. Ogundiran, 222–52. Cambridge: Cambridge University Press, 2012.
———. "Living in the Shadow of the Atlantic World: History and Material Life in a Yoruba-Edo Hinterland, ca. 1600–1750." In *Archaeology of Atlantic Africa and the African Diaspora*, edited by A. Ogundiran and T. Falola, 77–99. Bloomington: Indiana University Press, 2007.
———. "The Making of an Internal Frontier Settlement: Archaeology and Historical Process in Osun Grove (Nigeria), Seventeenth to Eighteenth Centuries." *African Archaeological Review* 31, no. 1 (2014): 1–24.
———. "Material Life and Domestic Economy in a Frontier of the Oyo Empire during the Mid-Atlantic Age." *International Journal of African Historical Studies* 42, no. 3 (2009): 351–86.
———. "A Multiplex Landscape: Explorations of Place and Practice in Osun Grove, Nigeria." In *Cultural Landscape Heritage in Sub-Saharan Africa*, edited by J. Beardsley, 293–322. Washington, DC: Dumbarton Oaks, 2016.
———. "Of Small Things Remembered: Beads, Cowries, and Cultural Translations of the Atlantic Experience in Yorubaland." *International Journal of African Historical Studies* 35, no. 2–3 (2002): 427–57.
———. "Towns and States of the West African Forest Belt." In *Oxford Handbook of African Archaeology*, edited by Peter Mitchell and Paul Lane, 855–69. Oxford: Oxford University Press, 2013.
Ogundiran, Akinwumi, and Babatunde Agbaje-Williams. "Oyo Empire: Archaeological Survey in the Metropolis and its Colony." In *African Archaeology Field Manual.* Edited by A. E. Smith, E. Cornelissen, O. Gosselain, and S. MacEachern, (69–75). Tervuren, Belgium: Royal Museum for Central Africa, 2017.
Ogundiran, Akinwumi, and O. Akinlolu Ige. "'Our Ancestors Were Material Scientists': Archaeological and Geochemical Evidence for Indigenous

Yoruba Glass Technology." *Journal of Black Studies* 46, no. 8 (2015): 751–72.
Ogundiran, Akinwumi, M. Mangut, and O. Moyib. "The Archaeological Landscape of Bara, near Oyo-Ile." *West African Journal of Archaeology* 48 (2019): 15–32.
Ogundiran, Akinwumi, and Adisa Ogunfolakan. "Colonial Modernity, Rituals and Feasting in Odùduwà Grove, Ilé-Ifẹ̀ (Nigeria)." *Journal of African Archaeology* 15, no. 1 (2017): 77–103.
Ogundiran, Akinwumi, and Paula Saunders. "On the Materiality of the Black Atlantic Rituals." In *Materialities of Ritual in the Black Atlantic*, edited by A. Ogundiran and P. Saunders, 1–27. Bloomington: Indiana University Press, 2014.
———. "Potters' Marks and Social Relations of Ceramic Distribution in the Oyo Empire." *Azania: Archaeological Research in Africa* 46, no. 3 (2011): 317–35.
Ogunfolakan, Adisa, B. J. Tubosun, and J. O. Aleru. "Archaeological Survey of Igbo Oje, near Ogbomoso, Oyo State, Nigeria: A Preliminary Report." *Nyame Akuma* 65 (2006): 47–55.
Ogunfolakan, B. A. "Archaeological Survey of North-East Osun State, Nigeria." *West African Journal of Archaeology* 33, no. 2 (2003): 73–94.
Ogunfolakan, B. A., and A. Olayemi. "Preliminary Report of Elephant Remains in an Archaeological Site within Idanre Township, Ondo State, Nigeria." *Nyame Akuma* 69 (2008): 31–40.
Ogungbile, David. "Eerindinlogun: The Seeing Eyes of Sacred Shells and Stones." In *Osun across the Waters*, edited by Joseph M. Murphy and Mei-Mei Sanford, 189–212. Bloomington: Indiana University Press, 2001.
Ogunleye, Foluke. "A Male-Centric Modification of History: Efunsetan Aniwura Revisited." *History in Africa* 31 (2004): 303–18.
Ogunremi, Olaposi. *Moremi Ajasoro: The Legendary Yoruba Heroine*. Ilé-Ifẹ̀: House of Oduduwa Foundation and Institute of Cultural Studies, Obafemi Awolowo University, 2018.
Oguntomisin, Dare. "Internal Trade and Market Systems, 1900–1955." In *Studies in Ijebu History and Culture*, edited by Dare Oguntomisin, 51–66. Ibadan: John Archers, 2002.
Oguntuyi, A. *A Short History of Ado-Ekiti*. Ado-Ekiti: Bamgboye, 1979.
O'Hear, Ann. "Ilorin Lantana Beads." *African Arts* 19, no. 4 (1986): 36–88.
———. *Power Relations in Nigeria: Ilorin Slaves and Their Successors*. Rochester, NY: University of Rochester Press, 1997.
Ojo, J. R. O. "The Symbolism and Significance of Epa-Type Masquerade Headpieces." *Man* 13 (1978): 455–70.
Ojo, Olatunji. "Beyond Diversity: Women, Scarification, and Yoruba Identity." *History in Africa* 35 (2008): 347–74.
———. "Document 2: Letters Found in the House of Kosoko, King of Lagos (1851)." *African Economic History* 40 (2012): 37–126.
———. "'Heepa' (Hail) Òrìṣà: The Òrìṣà Factor in the Birth of Yoruba Identity." *Journal of Religion in Africa* 39, no. 1 (2009): 30–59.
———. "The Organization of the Atlantic Slave Trade in Yorubaland, ca. 1777 to ca. 1856." *International Journal of African Historical Studies* 41, no. 1 (2008): 77–100.
Ojo, Samuel. *Short History of Ilorin*. Oyo: Atoro Print Works, 1957.

Oka, Rahul, and Chapurukha Kusimba. "The Archaeology of Trading Systems, Part 1: Towards a New Trade Synthesis." *Journal of Archaeological Research* 16, no. 4 (2008): 339–95.

Okùbọ̀tẹ̀, Moses Bótù. *Ìwé Ìtàn Ìjẹ̀bú*. Ibadan: Third World Information Services, 2009.

Olaniyan, R. A., and I. A. Akinjogbin. "Sources of the History of Ife." In *The Cradle of a Race: Ife from the Beginning to 1980*, edited by I. A. Akinjogbin, 30–50. Port Harcourt: Sunray Publications, 1992.

Oliver, Roland Anthony, and Anthony Atmore. *Medieval Africa, 1250–1800*. Cambridge: Cambridge University Press, 2003.

Olivova, Lucie. "Tobacco Smoking in Qing China." *Asia Major* 18, no. 1 (2005): 225–60.

Olomola, Isola. "Ife before Oduduwa." In *The Cradle of a Race: Ife from the Beginning to 1980*, edited by I. A. Akinjogbin, 51–61. Port Harcourt: Sunray Publications, 1992.

———. *A Thousands [sic] Year's [sic] of Ado-History-and-Culture*. Ado-Ekiti: Omolayo Standard Press and Bookshops, 1984.

Olugbadehan, J. Oladipo. *Owo Kingdom, Eastern Yorubaland, Southwestern Nigeria: A Study of History, Politics and Society in an African Ethnic Frontier Zone*. Saarbrücken: VDM Verlag Dr. Müller, 2010.

Olunlade, E. A. *Ede: A Short History*. Ibadan: General Publications Section, Ministry of Education, 1961.

Olúnládé, Taiwo. "Divinatory Systems." In *Encyclopedia of the Yoruba*, edited by Toyin Falola and Akintunde Akinyemi, 101–3. Bloomington: Indiana University Press, 2016.

Olupona, Jacob K. *City of 201 Gods: Ilé-Ifè in Time, Space, and the Imagination*. Berkeley: University of California Press, 2011.

———. *Kingship, Religion, and Rituals in a Nigerian Community: A Phenomenological Study of Ondo Yoruba Festivals*. Stockholm: Almqvist and Wiksell International, 1991.

———. "Òrìsà Osun: Yoruba Sacred Kingship and Civil Religion in Osogbo, Nigeria." In *Ọ̀ṣun across the Waters: A Yoruba Goddess in Africa and the Americas*, edited by Joseph M. Murphy and Mei-Mei Sanford, 46–47. Bloomington: Indiana University Press, 2001.

———. "Where a Woman was King: Continuity and Change in Ondo Religion and Culture." In *The Evolution Ondo Kingdom,* edited by S. Ibi Ajayi, 6–35. Ibadan: Spectrum, 2013.

Olupona, Jacob K., and Rowland Abiodun. *Ifa Divination, Knowledge, Power, and Performance*. Bloomington: Indiana University Press, 2016.

Omosade Awolalu, J. "Yoruba Sacrificial Practice." *Journal of Religion in Africa* 5, no. 2 (1973): 81–93.

Onabajo, O., and O. A. Ige. "Mineralogy and Raw Material Characterization of Esie Stone Sculptures." *Ife Journal of Science* 7, no. 1 (2005): 113–18.

Orijemie, Emuobosa Akpo. "Exploitation of Aquatic Resources in Ahanve, Badagry, South-Western Nigeria." *Internet Archaeology* 37 (2014). Accessed October 14, 2015. http://intarch.ac.uk/journal/issue37/orijemie_index.html.

Orisatoyinbo, Olatoye Ilufoye. *The History and Traditions of Ancient Ifon Orolu Kingdom*. Ketu, Nigeria: Adeley Printing, 2000.

Ortner, Sherry B. *The Fate of "Culture": Geertz and Beyond.* Berkeley: University of California Press, 2007.

———. "Theory in Anthropology since the Sixties." *Comparative Studies in Society and History* 26, no. 1 (1984):126–66.

Osagie, J. I., and F. Ikponmwosa. "Craft Guilds and the Sustenance of Pre-Colonial Benin Monarchy." *International Journal of Arts and Humanities* 4, no. 1 (2015): 1–17.

Otero, Solimar. *Afro-Cuban Diasporas in the Atlantic World.* Rochester, NY: University of Rochester Press, 2013.

Oyediran, Oyeleye. "Modakeke in Ife: Historical Background to an Aspect of Contemporary Ife Politics." *Odù: Journal of Yoruba and Related Studies* 10 (1974): 63–78.

Oyèláràn, O. "On Yorùbá Orthography." *Yorùbá: Journal of the Yorùbá Studies Association of Nigeria* 1, no. 1 (1973): 30–61.

Oyelaran, Philip A. "Early Settlement and Archaeological Sequence of Northeast Yorubaland." *African Archaeological Review* 15, no. 1 (1998): 65–79.

Oyeniyi, Bukola A. *Dress in the Making of African Identity: A Social and Cultural History of the Yoruba People.* Amherst: Cambria, 2015.

Oyerinde, N. D. *Iwe Itan Ogbomọṣọ.* Jos: Niger, 1934.

Oyěwùmí, Oyèrónkẹ́. *Gender Epistemologies in Africa: Gendering Traditions, Spaces, Social Institutions, and Identities.* Basingstoke, NY: Palgrave Macmillan, 2011.

———. *The Invention of Women: Making an African Sense of Western Gender Discourses.* Minneapolis: University of Minnesota Press, 1997.

Ozanne, Paul. "A New Archaeological Survey of Ife." *Odu* (New Series) 1 (1969): 28–45.

Ozturk, Hayriye Tugba, and Huseyin Ozcinar. "Learning in Multiple Communities from the Perspective of Knowledge Capital." *International Review of Research in Open & Distance Learning* 14, no. 1 (2013): 204–21.

Page, Jesse. *The Black Bishop, Samuel Adjai Crowther.* London: Hodder and Stoughton, 1979.

———. *Samuel Crowther, the Slave Boy Who Became Bishop of the Niger.* London: S.W. Partridge, 1889.

Parés, Luis Nicolau. *The Formation of Candomblé: Vodun History and Ritual in Brazil.* Chapel Hill: University of North Carolina Press, 2013.

Peek, Philip M. *African Divination Systems: Ways of Knowing.* Bloomington: Indiana University Press, 1991.

Peel, J. D. Y. "A Comparative Analysis of Ogun in Precolonial Yorubaland." In *Africa's Ogun: Old World and New*, edited by Sandra T. Barnes, 2nd ed., 263–89. Bloomington: Indiana University Press, 1997.

———. *Ijeshas and Nigerians: The Incorporation of a Yoruba Kingdom, 1890s-1970s.* Cambridge: Cambridge University Press, 1983.

———. "Kings, Titles, and Quarters: A Conjectural History of Ilesha I: The Traditions Reviewed." *History in Africa* 6 (1979): 109–53.

———. *Religious Encounter and the Making of the Yoruba.* Bloomington: Indiana University Press, 2000.

Pemberton, John. "Descriptive Catalog." In *Yoruba, Sculpture of West Africa*, edited by William B. Fagg, John Pemberton, and Bryce Holcombe, 52–194. New York: Knopf, 1982.

———. “The Dreadful God and the Divine King.” *Africa’s Ogun: Old World and New*, edited by Sandra T. Barnes, 2nd ed., 105–46. Bloomington: Indiana University Press, 1997.

———. “Eshu-Elegba: The Yoruba Trickster God.” *African Arts* 9 (1975): 20–27, 66–70, 90–92.

Pemberton, John, Rowland Abiodun, and Ulli Beier. *Cloth Only Wears to Shreds: Yoruba Textiles and Photographs from the Beier Collection.* Amherst: Mead Art Museum, Amherst College, 2004.

Pemberton, John, and Funso Afọlayan. *Yoruba Sacred Kingship: “A Power Like That of the Gods.”* Washington, DC: Smithsonian Institution Press, 1996.

Philips, John Edward. *Writing African History.* Rochester, NY: University of Rochester Press, 2007.

Phillips, Thomas. *A Journal of a Voyage Made in the Hannibal of London.* Collection of Voyages and Travels, vol. 6. London: Awnsham and John Churchill, 1732.

Pikirayi, Innocent. *The Zimbabwe Culture: Origins and Decline in Southern Zambezian States.* Walnut Creek, CA: AltaMira, 2001.

Posnansky, Merrick. “Aspects of Early West African Trade.” *World Archaeology* 5 (1973): 149–62.

Price, Jacob M. “Credit in the Slave Trade and Plantation Economies.” In *Slavery and the Rise of the Atlantic System*, edited by Barbara L. Solow, 293–339. Cambridge: Cambridge University Press, 1991.

Pym, Anthony. *Exploring Translation Theories.* New York: Routledge, 2010.

Radcliffe-Brown, A. R. *Structure and Function in Primitive Society.* New York: Free Press, 2013.

Rafferty, Sean M., and Rob Mann. *Smoking and Culture: The Archaeology of Tobacco Pipes in Eastern North America.* Knoxville: University of Tennessee Press, 2004.

Rehren, Thilo, and Ian Freestone. “Ancient Glass from Kaleidoscope to Crystal Ball.” *Journal of Archaeological Science* 56 (2015): 233–41.

Reis, João José. *Slave Rebellion in Brazil: Muslim Uprising of 1835 in Bahia.* Baltimore, MD: Johns Hopkins University Press, 1995.

Reis, João José, and Beatriz Gallotti Mamigonian. “Nagô and Mina: The Yoruba Diaspora in Brazil.” *Yoruba Diaspora in the Atlantic World*, edited by T. Falola and M. Childs, 77–110. Bloomington: Indiana University Press, 2004.

Renfrew, Colin. “Alternative Models for Exchange and Spatial Distribution.” In *Exchange Systems in Prehistory*, edited by T. G. Baugh and J. E. Ericson, 71–90. New York: Academic, 1977.

Renne, Elisha P. *Cloth That Does Not Die: The Meaning of Cloth in Bùnú Social Life.* Seattle: University of Washington Press, 1995.

Ribeiro, A. V. “The Transatlantic Slave Trade to Bahia, 1582–1851.” In *Extending the Frontiers: Essays on the New Transatlantic Slave Trade Database*, edited by D. Eltis and D. Richardson, 130–54. New Haven, CT: Yale University Press, 2008.

Rivers, R., C. Knappett, and T. Evans. “What Makes a Site Important? Centrality, Gateways and Gravity.” In *Network Analysis in Archaeology: New Approaches to Regional Interaction*, edited by Carl Knappett, 125–51. Oxford: Oxford University Press, 2013.

Robb, J., and T. R. Pauketat. "From Moments to Millennia: Theorizing Scale and Change in Human History." In *Big Histories, Human Lives Tackling Problems of Scale in Archaeology*, edited by J. Robb and T. R. Pauketat, 3–33. Santa Fe, NM: School for Advanced Research Press, 2013.

Robertshaw, Peter. "Sibling Rivalry?: The Intersection of Archaeology and History." *History in Africa* 27 (2000): 261–86.

Roddick, Andrew P., and Ann Brower Stahl. "Introduction: Knowledge in Motion." In *Knowledge in Motion: Constellations of Learning across Time and Place*, edited by A. P. Roddick and A. B. Stahl, 3–35. Tucson: University of Arizona Press, 2016.

Rodney, Walter. *How Europe Underdeveloped Africa*. London: Bogle-L'Ouverture, 1988.

Rogers, J. Daniel. "Archaeology and the Interpretation of Colonial Encounters." In *The Archaeology of Colonial Encounters: Comparative Perspectives*, edited by G. Stein, 331–54. Santa Fe, NM: School of American Research Press, 2005.

Rowling, Marjorie. *Everyday Life in Medieval Times*. London: Carousel, 1973.

Rushing, Fannie Theresa. "Review of *The 1812 Aponte Rebellion in Cuba and the Struggle against Atlantic Slavery*." *Americas* 64, no. 4 (2008): 651–53.

Ryder, A. F. C. *Benin and the Europeans, 1485–1897*. London: Longmans, Green and Co., 1969.

———. "Dutch Trade on the Nigerian Coast during the Seventeenth Century." *Journal of the Historical Society of Nigeria* 3 (1965): 195–210.

Sahlins, Marshall. "Cosmologies of Capitalism: The Trans-Pacific Sector of 'the World System.'" *Proceedings of the British Academy* 74 (1988): 1–51.

———. *Islands of History*. Chicago: University of Chicago Press, 1985.

Saidi, Christine. *Women's Authority and Society in Early East-Central Africa*. Rochester, NY: University of Rochester Press, 2010.

Sarr, Assan. "Land, Power, and Dependency along the Gambia River, Late Eighteenth to Early Nineteenth Centuries." *African Studies Review* 57, no. 3 (2014): 101–21.

Schatzki, Theodore R., Karin Knorr Cetina, and Eike Von Savigny, eds. *The Practice Turn in Contemporary Theory*. London: Routledge, 2001.

Schmidt, Peter R. *Historical Archaeology: A Structural Approach in an African Culture*. Westport, CT: Greenwood, 1978.

———. *Historical Archaeology in Africa: Representation, Social Memory, and Oral Traditions*. Lanham, MD: AltaMira, 2006.

———. *Iron Technology in East Africa: Symbolism, Science and Archaeology*. Bloomington: Indiana University Press, 1997.

———. "Rhythmed Time and Its Archaeological Implications." In *Aspects of African Archaeology: Papers from the 10th Congress of the PanAfrican Association for Prehistory and Related Studies*, edited by Gilbert Pwiti and Robert Soper, 655–62. Harare: University of Zimbabwe Publications, 1996.

Schmidt, Peter R., and Alice B. Kehoe. *Archaeologies of Listening*. Gainesville: University Press of Florida, 2019.

Schmidt, Peter R., and Thomas C. Patterson. *Making Alternative Histories: The Practice of Archaeology and History in Non-Western Settings*. Santa Fe, NM: School of American Research Press, 1995.

Schneider, Jane, and Annette B. Weiner. "Introduction." In *Cloth and Human Experience*, edited by J. Schneider and A. B. Weiner, 1–29. Washington, DC: Smithsonian Institution Press, 1989.

Schoenbrun, David Lee. *A Green Place, a Good Place: Agrarian Change, Gender, and Social Identity in the Great Lakes Region to the 15th Century*. Portsmouth, NH: Heinemann, 1999.

Schwab, William B. "Kinship and Lineage among the Yoruba." *Africa* 25, no. 4 (1955): 352–74.

Schwartz, Glenn M., and John J. Nichols, eds. *After Collapse: The Regeneration of Complex Societies*. Tucson: University of Arizona Press, 2006.

Schwartz, Stuart B. "Plantations and Peripheries, c. 1580–c. 1750." In *Colonial Brazil*, edited by Leslie Bethell, 67–144. Cambridge: Cambridge University Press, 1987.

———. *Sugar Plantations in the Formation of Brazilian Society: Bahia, 1550–1835*. Cambridge: Cambridge University Press, 1985.

Scott, Joan Wallach. *Gender and the Politics of History*. New York: Columbia University Press, 1999.

Sewell, William, Jr. *Logics of History*. Chicago: University of Chicago Press, 2010.

Shanahan, T. M., J. T. Overpeck, K. J. Anchukaitis, J. W. Beck, J. E. Cole, D. L. Dettman, J. A. Peck et al. "Atlantic Forcing of Persistent Drought in West Africa." *Science* 324, no. 5925 (2009): 377–80.

Sharp, Lesley A. "The Commodification of the Body and Its Parts." *Annual Review of Anthropology* 29 (2000): 287–328.

Shaw, Rosalind. *Memories of the Slave Trade: Ritual and the Historical Imagination in Sierra Leone*. Chicago: University of Chicago Press, 2002.

Shaw, Thurstan, and S. G. H. Daniels. *Excavations at Iwo Eleru, Ondo State, Nigeria*. Ibadan: Claverianum, 1984.

Simmel, Georg. *The Philosophy of Money*. London: Routledge, 2011.

Sinopoli, Carla M. "The Archaeology of Empires." *Annual Review of Anthropology* 23 (1994): 159–80.

Smith, H. F. C., D. M. Last, and Gambo Gubio. "Ali Eisami Gazirmabe of Bornu." In *Africa Remembered: Narratives by West Africans from the Era of the Slave Trade*, edited by Philip D. Curtin, 199–216. Madison: University of Wisconsin Press, 1967.

Smith, Robert. "The Alafin in Exile: A Study of the Igboho Period in Oyo History." *Journal of African History* 6, no. 1 (1965): 57–77.

———. "Yoruba Armament." *Journal of African History* 8, no. 1 (1967): 87–106.

Smith, Robert Sydney. *Kingdoms of the Yoruba*. Madison: University of Wisconsin Press, 1988.

———. *Warfare and Diplomacy in Pre-Colonial West Africa*. London: Methuen, 1976.

Snelgrave, William. *A New Account of Some Parts of Guinea and the Slave Trade*. London: James, John, and Paul Knapton, 1734.

Soja, Edward W. *Thirdspace: Journeys to Los Angeles and Other Real-and-Imagined Places*. Malden, MA: Blackwell, 2014.

Soper, R. C. "Archaeological Work at Oyo Ile 1978 & 1979." *African Notes* 9 (1982): 1–6.

Sorensen-Gilmour, Caroline. "Slave-Trading along the Lagoons of South-West Nigeria: The Case of Badagry." In *Ports of the Slave Trade (Bights of Benin and Biafra)*, edited by Robin Law and Silke Strickrodt, 84–95. Stirling, UK: Centre of Commonwealth Studies, University of Stirling, 1999.

Souvatzi, S., A. Baysal, and E. Baysal. "Is There *Pre*-history?" In *Time and History in Prehistory*, edited by S. Souvatzi, A. Baysal, and E. Baysal, 1–27. New York: Routledge, 2019.

Sowunmi, M. A., C. A. Folorunso, M. Pyykonen, P. A. Oyelaran, David A. Aremu, Bolanle J. Tubosun, P. G. Ajekigbe, and B. Agbaje-Williams. "Revisit to the Urban Site of Old Oyo: A Preliminary Report." In *The African Archaeology Network: Reports and a Review*, edited by F. Chami, G. Pwiti, and C. Radimilahy, 27–39. Studies in the African Past—4. Dar es Salaam: Dar es Salaam University Press, 2004.

Stahl, Ann Brower. "The Archaeology of African History." *International Journal of African Historical Studies* 42, no. 2 (2009): 241–56.

———. *Making History in Banda Anthropological Visions of Africa's Past.* Cambridge: Cambridge University Press, 2001.

Stein, Gil. "Archaeology and the Interpretation of Colonial Encounters." In *The Archaeology of Colonial Encounters: Comparative Perspectives*, edited by Gil Stein, 331–54. Santa Fe: School of American Research Press, 2005.

Stephens, Rhiannon. *A History of African Motherhood: The Case of Uganda, 700–1900.* Cambridge: Cambridge University Press, 2015.

Stephens, Rhiannon, and Axel Fleisch. "Theories and Methods of African Conceptual History." In *Conceptual History in Africa*, edited by A. Fleisch and R. Stephens, 1–16. New York: Berghahn, 2018.

Stevens, Phillips. *The Stone Images of Esię, Nigeria.* Ibadan: Ibadan University Press / Lagos: Nigerian Federal Department of Antiquities, 1978.

Stock, Eugene. *The History of the Church Missionary Society: Its Environment, Its Men and Its Work* (three volumes). London: Church Missionary Society, 1899.

Strickrodt, Silke. *Afro-European Trade in the Atlantic World: The Western Slave Coast, c.1550–c.1885.* Oxford: James Currey, 2015.

Styhre, A. "The Knowledge-Intensive Company and the Economy of Sharing: Rethinking Utility and Knowledge Management." *Knowledge and Process Management* 9, no. 4 (2002): 228–36.

Sudarkasa, Niara. *Where Women Work: A Study of Yoruba Women in the Marketplace and in the Home.* Ann Arbor: University of Michigan, 1973.

Sweet, James H. "Reimagining the African-Atlantic Archive: Method, Concept, Epistemology, Ontology." *Journal of African History* 55, no. 2 (2014): 147–59.

Talbot, Percy Amaury. *The Peoples of Southern Nigeria.* Vol. 2. Oxford: Oxford University Press, 1926.

Taussig, Michael T. *The Devil and Commodity Fetishism in South America.* Chapel Hill: University of North Carolina Press, 1985.

Tejuoso, Oba Adedapo. *Oranmiyan: What Is in a Name?* Abeokuta: Oba Tejuoso Books, 2014.

Temu, Arnold J., and Bonaventure Swai. *Historians and Africanist History: A Critique.* London: Zed Press, 1982.

Thompson, Robert Farris. *Face of the Gods: Art and Altars of Africa and the African Americas*. New York: Museum for African Art, 1993.

———. *Flash of the Spirit: African and Afro-American Art and Philosophy*. New York: Random House, 2002.

———. "The Sign of the Divine King: An Essay on Yoruba Bead-Embroidered Crowns with Veil and Bird Decorations." *African Arts* 3, no. 3 (1970): 8–17, 74–80.

Thornton, John K. *Africa and Africans in the Making of the Atlantic World, 1400–1680*. Cambridge: Cambridge University Press, 1992.

———. *A Cultural History of the Atlantic World, 1250–1820*. Cambridge: Cambridge University Press, 2012.

———. "Traditions, Documents, and the Ife-Benin Relationship." *History in Africa* 15 (1988): 351–62.

Tishken, Joel E., Akíntúndé Akínyemí, and Toyin Falola. *Sàngó in Africa and the African Diaspora*. Bloomington: Indiana University Press, 2009.

Tracy, James D. Introduction to *The Rise of Merchant Empires: Long Distance Trade in the Early Modern World 1350–1750*, 1–13. Edited by James D. Tracy. Cambridge: Cambridge University Press.

Trigger, Bruce G. *Early Civilizations: Ancient Egypt in Context*. Cairo: American University in Cairo Press, 2001.

Trouillot, Michel-Rolph. *Silencing the Past: Power and the Production of History*. Boston: Beacon, 1995.

Trubowitz, Neal L. "Smoking Pipes: An Archaeological Measure of Native American Cultural Stability and Survival in Eastern North America, A.D. 1500–1850." In *Smoking and Culture: The Archaeology of Tobacco Pipes in Eastern North America*, edited by S. M. Rafferty and Rob Mann, 143–64. Knoxville: University of Tennessee Press, 2004.

Turner, Víctor W. *The Ritual Process: Structure and Anti-Structure*. Ithaca, NY: Cornell University Press, 1966.

Ulin, Robert C. *Understanding Cultures: Perspectives in Anthropology and Social Theory*. 2nd ed. Malden, MA: Wiley-Blackwell, 2001.

Usman, Aribidesi A. "Ceramic Seriation, Sites Chronology, and Old Oyo Factor in Northcentral Yorubaland, Nigeria." *African Archaeological Review* 20, no. 3 (2003): 149–69.

———. "Crisis and Catastrophe: Warfare in Precolonial Northern Yoruba." In *Precolonial Nigeria: Essays in Honor of Toyin Falola*, edited by Akinwumi Ogundiran, 361–83. Trenton, NJ: Africa World Press, 2005.

———. "A Report on Newly Discovered Soapstone Figurines from North-Central Yorubaland, Nigeria." *Nyame Akuma* 44 (1995): 44–51.

———. *State-Periphery Relations and Sociopolitical Development in Igbominaland, North-Central Yoruba, Nigeria: Oral-Ethnohistorical and Archaeological Perspectives*. BAR International Series, 993. Oxford: Archaeopress, 2001.

———. "A View from the Periphery: Northern Yoruba Villages during the Old Oyo Empire, Nigeria." *Journal of Field Archaeology* 27 (2000): 43–61.

———. *The Yoruba Frontier: A Regional History of Community Formation, Experience, and Changes in West Africa*. Durham, NC: Carolina Academic Press, 2012.

Usman, Aribidesi A., Jonathan O. Aleru, and Raphael A. Alabi. "Sociopolitical Formation on the Yoruba Northern Frontier: A Report of Recent Work at Ila-Iyara North Central Nigeria." *Journal of African Archaeology* 3 (2005): 139–54.

Usman, Aribidesi, and Toyin Falola. *The Yoruba from Prehistory to the Present*. Cambridge: Cambridge University Press, 2019.

Usman, Aribidesi A., Robert J. Speakman, and Michael D. Glascock. "An Initial Assessment of Prehistoric Ceramic Production and Exchange in Northern Yoruba, North Central Nigeria: Results of Ceramic Compositional Analysis." *African Archaeological Review* 22, no. 3 (2005): 141–68.

Usuanlele, Uyilawa. "Precolonial Benin: A Political Economy Perspective." In *Precolonial Nigeria: Essays in Honor of Toyin Falola*, edited by Akinwumi Ogundiran, 259–80. Trenton, NJ: Africa World Press.

Vansina, Jan. "A Clash of Cultures: African Minds in the Colonial Era." In *African History: From Earliest Times to Independence*, edited by Philip Curtin, Steven Feierman, Leonard Thompson, and Jan Vansina 469–89. London: Longman, 1996.

———. "Historians, Are Archeologists Your Siblings?" *History in Africa* 22 (1995): 369–408.

———. "Knowledge and Perceptions of the African Past." In *African Historiographies*, edited by Bogumil Jewsiewicki and David Newbury, 28–41. Beverly Hills: Sage Publications, 1986.

———. *Oral Tradition as History*. Madison: University of Wisconsin Press, 1985.

———. *Paths in the Rainforest: Toward a History of Political Tradition in Equatorial Africa*. Madison: University of Wisconsin Press, 1990.

Vaughan, Olufemi. *Nigerian Chiefs: Traditional Power in Modern Politics, 1890s–1990s*. Rochester, NY: University of Rochester Press, 2006.

Verger, Pierre. *Bahia and the West African Trade, 1549–1851*. Ibadan: Ibadan University Press, 1964.

———. "Oral Tradition in the Cult of the Orishas and Its Connection with the History of the Yoruba." *Journal of the Historical Society of Nigeria* 1 (1956): 61–63.

Vitale, J., M. Ouattarra, and G. Vognan. "Enhancing Sustainability of Cotton Production Systems in West Africa: A Summary of Empirical Evidence from Burkina Faso." *Sustainability* 3, no. 8 (2011): 1136–69.

Vogel, Susan. "Foreword." In *Yoruba: Nine Centuries of African Art and Thought*, by Henry Drewal, John Pemberton III, and Rowland Abiodun, 10. New York: Center for African Art in association with H. N. Abrams, 1989.

Waldrop, M. Mitchell. *Complexity: The Emerging Science at the Edge of Order and Chaos*. New York: Simon and Schuster, 2008.

Walker, Alice. *In Search of Our Mother's Gardens: Womanist Prose*. London: Phoenix, 2005.

Walker, Roslyn A. *Ọlọ́wẹ̀ of Isẹ̀: A Yoruba Sculptor to Kings*. Washington, DC: National Museum of African Art, Smithsonian Institution, 1998.

Walters, Raymond J. L. *The Power of Gemstones*. Secaucus, NJ: Chartwell Books, 1996.

Warner-Lewis, Maureen. *Trinidad Yoruba: From Mother-Tongue to Memory.* 2nd ed. Tuscaloosa: University of Alabama Press, 2009.

Washington, Teresa N. *Our Mothers, Our Powers, Our Texts: Manifestations of Ajé in Africana Literature.* Bloomington: Indiana University Press, 2005.

Webb, James L. A. *Desert Frontier: Ecological and Economic Change along the Western Sahel, 1600–1850.* Madison: University of Wisconsin Press, 1995.

Weiner, Annette B., and Jane Schneider. *Cloth and Human Experience.* Washington, DC: Smithsonian Institution Press, 1989.

Wenger, Etienne. *Communities of Practice: Learning, Meaning, and Identity.* Cambridge: Cambridge University Press, 1998.

Wenger, Susanne. *The Sacred Groves of Oshogbo.* Wien: Kontrapunkt, Verlag für Wissenswertes, 1990.

Werner, O., and F. Willett. "The Composition of Brasses from Ife and Benin." *Archaeometry* 17 (1975): 141–56.

Westcott, Joan. "The Sculpture and Myths of Eshu-Elegba, the Yoruba Trickster: Definition and Interpretation in Yoruba Iconography." *Africa* 32, no. 4 (1962): 336–53.

Willett, Frank. "Archaeology." In *Sources of Yoruba History*, edited by S. Biobaku, 111–139. Oxford: Clarendon, 1973.

———. *The Art of Ife: A Descriptive Catalogue and Database.* Glasgow: Hunterian Museum and Art Gallery, 2004.

———. *Baubles, Bangles and Beads: Trade Contacts of Mediaeval Ife.* Edinburgh: Centre of African Studies, University of Edinburgh, 1977.

———. "Bronze Figures from Ita Yemoo, Ife, Nigeria." *Man* 59 (1959): 189–93.

———. *Ife in the History of West African Sculpture.* London: Thames and Hudson, 1967.

———. "Investigations at Old Oyo, 1956–57: An Interim Report." *Journal of the Historical Society of Nigeria* 2 (1960): 59–77.

———. *On the Funeral Effigies of Owo and Benin and the Interpretation of the Life-Size Bronze Heads from Ife, Nigeria.* Evanston: Program of African Studies, Northwestern University, 1966.

———. "Radiocarbon dates and cire-perdue casting in Ife and Benin." *Abhandlungen und Berichte des Staatlichen Museums für Völkerkunde, Dresden* 34 (1975): 291–300.

———. "Recent Archaeological Discoveries at Ilesha." *Odu* 8 (1960): 4–20.

———. "A Survey of Recent Results in the Radiocarbon Chronology of Western and Northern Africa." *Journal of African History* 12, no. 3 (1971): 339–70.

Willett, Frank, and Alan Dempster. "Stone Carvings in an Ife Style from Eshure, Ekiti, Western Nigeria." *Man* 62 (1962): 1–5.

Williams, Denis. *Icon and Image: A Study of Sacred and Secular Forms of African Classical Art.* New York: New York University Press, 1974.

Williams, Eric Eustace. *Capitalism & Slavery.* Chapel Hill: University of North Carolina Press, 1994.

Willis, J. T. *Masquerading Politics: Kinship, Gender, and Ethnicity in a Yoruba Town.* Bloomington: Indiana University Press, 2018.

Wiredu, Kwasi. *A Companion to African Philosophy*. Malden, MA: Blackwell Publishing, 2004.
Wolf, Eric R. *Europe and the People without History*. Berkeley: University of California Press, 1982.
Yai, Olabiyi Babalola. "The Path Is Open: The Legacy of Melville and Frances Herskovits in African Oral Narrative Analysis." *Research in African Literatures* 30 (1999): 1–16.
Yemitan, Ọladipọ. *Madame Tinubu: Merchant and King-Maker*. Ibadan: Ibadan University Press, 1987.
Zachernuk, Philip Serge. *Colonial Subjects: An African Intelligentsia and Atlantic Ideas*. Charlottesville: University Press of Virginia, 2000.

Index

Note: Page numbers in *italics* indicate photographs, tables, and charts.

AKINWUMI OGUNDIRAN is Chancellor's Professor and Professor of Africana Studies, Anthropology, and History at the University of North Carolina, Charlotte. He is author, editor, and co-editor of several publications, including *Precolonial Nigeria* and *Materialities of Ritual in the Black Atlantic* (Indiana University Press, 2014), a 2015 *Choice* magazine Outstanding Academic Title.

www.ingramcontent.com/pod-product-compliance
Lightning Source LLC
LaVergne TN
LVHW082002060826
844660LV00006B/274
* 9 7 8 0 2 5 3 0 5 1 4 8 6 *